THE

A Documentary History

RADICAL

of the American Radical Tradition

READER

Edited by Timothy Patrick McCarthy

and John McMillian

Foreword by Eric Foner

THE NEW PRESS

NEW YORK • LONDON

For our students

Published in the United States by The New Press, New York, 2003
Distributed by W. W. Norton & Company, Inc., New York

Pages 685–688 constitute an extension of this copyright page.

LIBRARY OF CONGRESS CATALOGING-IN-PUBLICATION DATA

The radical reader : a documentary history of the American radical tradition /
edited by Timothy Patrick McCarthy and John McMillian.
    p.   cm.
  Includes bibliographical references and index.
  ISBN 1-56584-827-6 (hc.)—ISBN 1-56584-682-6 (pbk.)
    1. Radicalism—United States—History—Sources.   I. McCarthy, Timothy
Patrick.   II. McMillian, John Campbell.
HN90.R3 R355 2002
303.484—dc21

                                                          2002041051

The New Press was established in 1990 as a not-for-profit alternative to the large,
commercial publishing houses currently dominating the book publishing industry. The New Press operates in the public interest rather than for private gain, and
is committed to publishing, in innovative ways, works of educational, cultural,
and community value that are often deemed insufficiently profitable.

The New Press, 38 Greene Street, 4th floor, New York, NY 10013
www.thenewpress.com

Book design by Kathryn Parise
Composition by Westchester Book Composition

Printed in Canada

2   4   6   8   10   9   7   5   3   1

Contents

CHAPTER EIGHT
Modern Feminism
411

CHAPTER NINE
The New Left and Counterculture
461

CHAPTER TEN
Radical Environmentalism
515

CHAPTER ELEVEN

Queer Liberation   561

EPILOGUE

New Directions   607

Contents

Foreword

With *The Radical Reader*, Timothy McCarthy and John McMillian, two energetic and insightful young scholars, have made a major contribution to our understanding of contemporary America and its history. Although numerous books have gathered together the writings of one or another strand of American radicalism—feminists, abolitionists, Populists, and the like—or particular eras of activism from the Revolution to the 1960s, no volume has previously been published that covers our entire national history and the full range of radical movements. Taken together, these documents offer vivid, eloquent testimony to the persistence and significance of the American radical tradition.

Throughout American history, radical movements have challenged Americans to live up to their professed ideals and have developed penetrating critiques of social and economic inequality. As the documents that follow make clear, they have done so in pursuit of different goals, and using a variety of tactics. Some radical movements accept the society's prevailing emphasis on the ideal of the "free individual" and seek to eliminate obstacles to its fulfilment, or extend it to excluded groups. Much of nineteenth-century labor radicalism fits this pattern, as do many many expressions of feminism and black radicalism. Other movements, based on a collectivist outlook, reject individualist values and see private property as an obstacle to genuine freedom. Various socialist and communitarian movements exemplify this type. Some movements take as their task uplifting the condition of a single group of Americans; others envision a sweeping transformation of the entire social order. Occasionally, radicals have resorted to violence, but most radical movements have reflected the democratic ethos of American life—they have been open rather than secretive and have relied on education, example, or "moral suasion," rather than coercion, to achieve their goals. Radicals have been on the receiving end of violence far more often than initiating it.

As the following documents reveal, although often castigated as foreign-inspired enemies of American institutions, radicals have always sprung from American culture and appealed to some of its deepest values—facts that help to explain radicalism's survival even in the face of tenacious opposition. From nineteenth-century radicals who insisted that the inalienable rights enshrined in the the Declaration of Independence were being undermined by slavery, gender discrimination, or the Industrial Revolution, to New Leftists who sought ways to restore "participatory democracy" to a society dominated by a military-industrial complex, radicals have adapted the language of American society to their own ends. In so doing, they have not only extended the benefits of American liberty to previously excluded groups, but have given American values new meanings.

Indeed, many ideas widely taken for granted and assumed to be timeless features of American culture originated with radical movements. The idea of freedom as a universal entitlement arose not from the founding fathers, who spoke of inalienable rights but made their peace with slavery, but from abolitionists, black and white, who invented the idea of equal citizenship irrespective of race. The modern idea of privacy—the extension of individual rights into the most intimate areas of personal life—arose from the efforts of generations of feminists to secure for women control over their own persons. Our modern understanding of free expression stems not simply from the Bill of Rights, but from the struggles of the labor, birth control, and civil rights movements throughout the twentieth century to overturn laws and governmental practices that restricted the dissemination of ideas deemed radical, obscene, or socially dangerous. In many other ways, radical movements have made American society a better place.

The Radical Reader appears as new forms of radicalism are making their appearance in the United States and, indeed, across the globe. The collapse of communist governments, first in Eastern Europe and then the Soviet Union, produced a profound challenge to assumptions widely shared among radicals in the West. Radicals were forced to rethink the idea that history is moving in a predetermined direction in which the inequities of capitalism would be superseded by a more cooperative organization of politics and society. Many conventional ways of analyzing politics and power today seem obsolete. Socialism no longer seems viable as a goal of radicalism, nor does the industrial working class appear to be the leading agent of social change. But the end of the Cold War has also created opportunities for new kinds of radical thought and action. *The Radical Reader* ends with an epilogue sampling some of today's expressions of radicalism, including recent efforts to revitalize the labor and antiwar movements, rethink the struggle for black liberation, reinvigorate student activism, and challenge the consequences of unregulated economic globalization.

By definition, radicals are a minority. They often feel marginalized—rarely so much as today, when the government and media persistently tell Americans that there can be no vision of the world except for globalized corporate enterprise. But as *The Radical Reader* powerfully demonstrates, every generation of Americans since the Revolution has witnessed the emergence of some kind of radical critique. The twenty-first century is likely to be no different. The history of radicalism gathered in this volume offers confirmation of Max Weber's rebuke to those who counsel the unthinking acceptance of prevailing norms and institutions, or who believe critics should call only for incremental change: "What is possible would never have been achieved if, in this world, people had not repeatedly reached for the impossible."

Eric Foner
Columbia University

Acknowledgments

First, we'd like to thank each other for a rare professional and personal friendship. This has been quite a ride!

One of the great joys of collaborative work is the chance, once it's done, to offer thanks for support along the way. We are extremely grateful to the friends and colleagues who intervened on our behalf when this book was just an idea: Nancy Chauvin, Eric Foner, James Green, Maurice Isserman, Harvey Kaye, Jesse Lemisch, Mark Naison, Harvard Sitkoff, and Cornel West. Indeed, we have been blessed over the years with unconditional support from mentors who have inspired in us a desire to change the world through teaching, scholarship, and social action. Herbert Aptheker and Howard Zinn are those rare historians who have both made and written history; we are humbled by their example and grateful for their wisdom and friendship (we were deeply saddened to learn of Aptheker's passing as this book was going into production). Cornel West has showered us with enthusiasm ever since we first met him, and his support, too, has been indispensable. Other colleagues at Harvard—in the Committee on Degrees in History and Literature, in the Department of Afro-American Studies, and at Quincy House—were very good to us while we were working on this book. Likewise, Brian Palmer, Harry Reed, Robert Hanning, Jesse Lemisch, Carolyn Rathjen, John Summers, Liam Day, Drew Willson, Sue Watts, Elizabeth Studley Nathans, Jeremy Varon, Jonathan Fortescue, Mike Ryan, and John Stauffer have also been wonderful friends to us over the years, and we appreciate their steady presence in our lives.

We would especially like to thank Alan Brinkley, Manning Marable, and Eric Foner, our graduate advisors at Columbia. It is probably safe to say that without Manning's generous friendship, as well as his moral and financial support through the Institute for Research in African-American Studies, we both would have dropped out of graduate school. Eric Foner has also been a terrific mentor. In addition to the wonderful foreword he wrote for this book, Eric helped us with the proposal, initiated contact with publishers, expressed an ongoing interest in the project, and has served, like Manning, as a model teacher, scholar, and activist. We are better at what we do because of their influence on our lives.

We are delighted to thank all the people who helped directly with the book's production. The librarians at Harvard and Columbia deserve special thanks for helping us track down elusive documents and documentary collections. Alice Kessler-Harris, Eliza Byard, Martin Duberman, and Leon Fink gave us excellent suggestions for documents on gender, sexuality, and labor. Steven Biel, Jessica Shubow, and Joseph Entin offered valuable feedback on early drafts of the introduction. Andrew King provided important research assistance, as well as a keen perspective on how this book could be useful in teaching American history to high school students. Anne Sandhurst, at Scholastic Inc., helped us with permissions. Tony Kushner and Frog made that process easier and much more fun! At Columbia University Press, James Warren helped us revise our original proposal. We finally found a home at The New Press, where Matt Weiland was instrumental in the early stages of the project. Once we got going, Marc Favreau, Steve Theodore, Maury Botton, and Paula Reedy were our steady and meticulous editors. We thank them for their patience and commitment to the project. We are also very grateful to André Schiffrin, whose faith in us, and in this book, has been unwavering. Thanks for taking a chance.

Finally, we would like to thank two groups of people who have sustained us over the years. We dedicate this book to our students. At Barnard, Columbia, Harvard, Michigan State, and in the Bard College Clemente Course in the Humanities (at the Codman Square Health Center in Dorchester, MA), we have been extremely fortunate to work with some of the finest students in the world. We are so grateful for their impact on our lives. We'd especially like to thank Lizzie Simon, Josh Breitbart, and Eric Yellin (who also served as a research assistant for this book), who were there at the very beginning and have been there ever since. Finally, we want to thank our families, especially Tom and Michelle McCarthy, Malcolm Green, and Harlon and Judy Mc-Millian. We love you from the bottoms of our hearts. Peace,

Timothy Patrick McCarthy
John McMillian
Cambridge, Massachusetts
March 2003

INTRODUCTION

Timothy Patrick McCarthy
and John McMillian

Ernest Hemingway once wrote, "the dignity . . . of an iceberg is due to only one eighth of it being above water," while the rest remains submerged, invisible to the naked eye. Something of the same might be said for radicalism in American history. Although it's true that social conservatives commonly complain that historians take an excessively critical view of the American past, it bears remembering that this is a fairly recent charge. Throughout the nineteenth and for most of the twentieth century, the story of America was almost invariably told with tremendous sympathy for the perspectives of "great men"—political elites, captains of industry, and military heroes—who, admittedly, have done much to shape the world in which we live. The courage and wisdom of American leaders, the steady march of progress they engendered, and the triumph of democratic ideals like freedom, equality, opportunity, and prosperity—these were the predominate themes of American history.

But we have since learned that this was only the picturesque tip of the iceberg. If one delves below the surface for a closer look, a different story of America becomes visible. As the momentous social upheavals of the 1960s and 1970s reordered American life and promoted new modes of intellectual inquiry, revisionist scholars began taking into account the lives of "ordinary people"—slaves and freedmen, indentured servants, housewives, workers, children, Native Americans, immigrants, gays and lesbians, and other Americans who had long been ignored. But these scholars did much more than just uncover a broader range of human experience; they also experimented with new interpretive paradigms. Thirty years ago it was virtually unheard of for historians to showcase a sophisticated awareness of the ways that race, class, gender, and sexuality have shaped the lives of *all* Americans. Today, it is almost commonplace. And as they expanded their field of inquiry and sharpened their intellectual tools, they also began investigating alternative expressions of democracy—the sundry forms of protest and dissent that have

1

challenged the exclusions and inequalities that have always existed. The result? An overdue recognition that many of the most cherished ideals of American history have been hard fought for and hard won by people who otherwise would have been excluded from the democratic promise. Perhaps the crowning achievement of this last generation of scholarship has been the realization that democracy, indeed a wonderful thing, is neither easy nor inevitable.

I.

"I find it hard to imagine that there's a story more wonderful than being driven by the desire to worship freely, to set off across the ocean, to make a home out of this wild and inhospitable land."

—LYNNE CHENEY

Is there any truth to the conservative charge that today's historians are too quick to glorify the oppressed? Not unlike the golfer who tries to correct a heavy right hand by pulling too hard with the left, do contemporary historians focus too much attention on cultural difference, social division, protest, and dissent? Are we so somber, gloomy, and pride-starved that we've lost sight of all that is good about the United States, and all that is promising about American democracy?

We think not. Although it may be the case that Americans are becoming more aware of the contributions of *individual* activists (Susan B. Anthony, Rosa Parks, and Martin Luther King, Jr., come to mind), the traditions of radicalism that gave these men and women a context—a history, as it were— are poorly understood. In celebrating a roster of individual achievement, we have stripped them of their more ordinary frames of reference, and isolated them from the movements that made them. Cultural warriors like Lynne Cheney are certainly within their right to lament the fact that so few high school seniors know when the Mayflower Compact was signed, where the Battle of the Bulge was fought, and who commanded the troops at Yorktown. But if these pundits really want to get worked up over deficiencies in our historical literacy, they might also consider asking students to identify when the abolitionist movement began, who the Populists were, or what the New Left accomplished. Bluntly put, most Americans are unaware of the dramatic ways that radicalism has shaped the history of the republic. More depressing still, whenever the achievements of progressive social movements *are* recognized, as with the civil rights and feminist revolutions, many of the most important gains of these struggles—such as affirmative action and reproductive choice— are often the target of disingenuous assault from those who claim to respect their legacies. Viewed in this light, the need for a greater understanding of American radical traditions seems more pressing than ever.

However, serious obstacles await those who would make American radical history more accessible to the general public. The first is a problem of terminology. "Radical" has always been an elusive adjective—a contested and fluid concept that owes no allegiance to any particular movement, ideology, or period. Radicalism must always be understood, therefore, within specific historical contexts. It is also a painfully subjective concept: One person's radicalism is often another person's reform. In some circles, "radical" is a term of endearment; more often, it is an epithet. Some historical figures have embodied both radical and conservative traits simultaneously. What is considered "radical" at one moment in history may well be judged by later generations as reasonable, obvious, and even just.

Eugene Debs understood this perfectly. In his final statement to the jury that convicted him of sedition during World War I, he noted that Americans are quick to forget that their own founding fathers—George Washington, Samuel Adams, and Thomas Paine—"were the rebels of their day." Likewise, Debs noted that abolitionists and woman's rights activists were maligned as "infidels" and "monsters of depravity" while they were alive, but only a few generations later, the best citizens of his generation had already begun "teaching children to revere their memories."

To cite another example: Today, every state in the Union pays annual tribute to Martin Luther King, Jr. Not a January passes that we are not reminded, in schools, on op-ed pages, and even in television advertisements, that King devoted the best years of his life to nonviolence and civil rights. At this very moment, Dr. King's portrait hangs proudly in the Bush White House. But how much do students know about the popular resistance and government repression that King faced while he was still alive, or the thorny questions he raised about American materialism, militarism, and classism? Who recalls that even as King was doing his good work, federal agents worked behind the scenes to smear him, tapping his phones, sending him threatening mail, and trying to discredit him among journalists, donors, and supporters? Perhaps an even more ironic example of shifting perceptions about radicalism was the 1999 issuing of a U.S. postage stamp commemorating Malcolm X, a man who once demanded "total liberty for black people still in chains or total destruction for white America" (and who probably could not have mailed a letter in his day without FBI surveillance).

Official hostility to radicalism can also complicate the efforts of scholars who write about American social movements. Early woman's rights activists were called "hysterical" and were banned from public speaking when they challenged the structures of patriarchy that governed their lives. Abolitionists faced violent mobs and hostile legislators who interfered with their mail and destroyed their presses. In 1836, legislators even tried to foil their efforts by passing a comprehensive "gag rule" that prohibited any discussions of slavery on the floor of Congress. In the fallout from the Haymarket affair in 1886, workers and union leaders faced frequent raids of their homes and headquarters, answered the spurious charges of law enforcement, and suffered from histrionic newspaper editors who called them anarchist "serpents" and the "offscourings of Europe." Radical opposition to American entry in World War I led to a slew of Espionage and Sedition Acts that criminalized antiwar behavior and inspired waves of extralegal vigilantism, culminating in the notorious Palmer Raids and the mass arrests of thousands of so-called aliens. Likewise, the McCarthy crusade of the Cold War era gave officials carte blanche to traduce the First Amendment and engineer the harassment and destruction of thousands of law-abiding citizens who were deemed "politically undesirable." And even as we are sending this book into production, official intolerance of dissent has raised its ugly head yet again. In the wake of the horrible attacks on September 11, White House Press Secretary Ari Fleischer warned that "all Americans . . . need to watch what they say." Likewise, Attorney General John Ashcroft told the Senate on December 6, 2001, that those who dared to speak out against the erosion of civil liberties that followed the attacks "only aid terrorists" and "give ammunition to America's enemies and pause to America's friends." In other words, Ashcroft believes that his critics are traitors. In this climate, it is a wonder that radicals are ever taught or studied at all.

Historian Alan Brinkley has identified yet another hurdle for those who seek to make radical history available to a wider public. Although recent scholarship has dismantled the "comfortable myths with which some (perhaps most) Americans viewed history," Brinkley notes that in the process, the public has turned "to other, nonacademic writers whose work is less discomfiting to them." Indeed, even though a recent *Journal of American History* poll showed that a majority of scholars and students think that history "should challenge our preconceptions and assumptions," many Americans seem to prefer palliative history that reinforces the triumphant narrative in which they have always wanted to believe. Conservative pundit George Will has recently made exactly this point, citing the runaway success of David McCullough's biography of John Adams as evidence suggesting "there is an unquenchable hunger for the telling of America's story by focusing on great individuals."

Finally, scholars who promote a broader understanding of radicalism must take care not to romanticize their subject matter. The victimized and the oppressed hardly have a monopoly on virtue and character, and we all know that American protest movements have made their share of mistakes. Indeed, the historical enterprise suffers when scholars form an excessive identification with their topic, or when they mimic the shortcomings of traditional scholarship by reducing the field to a pantheon of heroic individuals to be admired or emulated.

II.

The idea for this anthology came out of our experience as graduate teaching assistants for Eric Foner's course, "The American Radical Tradition," at Columbia University during the 1990s. During our weekly discussion sections, we were delighted at how enthusiastically our students responded to the primary source material we passed out. Throughout the semester, we saw history come alive through the speeches and writings of radicals from the American Revolution to the Civil Rights Movement. The more we turned to primary source material in our lesson plans, the more interested and engaged our students became. They started asking tougher questions—of American history, of contemporary society, and ultimately, of us. As a result, they became better students, and we became better teachers. And we'd like to think that we all became better citizens.

At the semester's end, our desks and files were cluttered with photocopied documents that covered the spectrum of American radicalism, and as historians are wont to do, we gathered them together, arranged them in some semblance of order, and stored them away in the event that they might prove useful in the classroom again. At first, we simply thought we were doing a little spring cleaning. Later, we realized that all of the unwieldy material we'd accumulated was the beginning of a book.

Understanding that we could fill a dozen volumes like this one without ever repeating ourselves, we kept in mind several criteria when selecting documents. First, we are interested in chronicling *progressive* traditions of radicalism—that is, radicalism that primarily emphasizes inclusion and redistribution, and that seeks to expand existing definitions of freedom, equality, justice, and opportunity. Certainly, there is sufficient material (and undoubtedly a large market) to warrant a book on conservative, right-wing, or reactionary radicalism. We leave that enterprise to someone else.

Another criterion for inclusion was representativeness in terms of content and form. With varying success, we have tried to include documents that showcase the diversity of progressive radicalism. Moreover, although we have included some "major" texts—very famous works from the likes of Thomas Paine, Frederick Douglass, Henry David Thoreau, and Betty Friedan—we have also reprinted more obscure material, from lesser known authors whose writings might otherwise remain unavailable. Thus we include documents from small magazines, defunct or underground newspapers, out-of-print memoirs, even the Internet. However, regardless of the source of the document, *readability* was also a factor. Admittedly, not all American radicals are graceful prose stylists, and some of these pieces are considerably more eloquent than others. Nevertheless, we hope our readers will find all of them illuminating and accessible.

Lastly, in an effort to provide historical context, we have mostly selected documents that have some connection to larger social movements or major trends—civil rights, feminism, critique of capitalism, concern for land and nature, and so on. However, there are a few pieces, like Ralph Waldo Emerson's "Self Reliance" and Henry David Thoreau's *Walden,* that are not immediately tied to mass mobilizations but are important because they helped inform and inspire future movements. We have also included several traditional documents, such as the Bill of Rights, the Reconstruction Amendments, and Lincoln's Second Inaugural Address, to demonstrate that there have been a number of occasions in American history when mainstream figures and institutions have embodied the very best progressive ideals.

The book's design serves several purposes. First, in order to emphasize the relationship between radicals and the broader movements for change in which they operate, we have organized the documents into eleven sections, arranged in loose chronological order: American Revolution; Utopian Visions; Abolitionism; Suffrage and Feminism; Land and Labor; Anarchism, Socialism, and Communism; "New Negro" to Black Power; Modern Feminism; The New Left and Counterculture; Radical Environmentalism; and Queer Liberation. An epilogue contains several documents that may, we think, represent "new directions" in American radicalism as we begin the twenty-first century. We should note, however, that some of the documents in this collection could fall under multiple chapters, and our decision about where to place them, while certainly not arbitrary, might still provoke minor disagreement. For example, Harriet Jacob's *Incidents in the Life of a Slave Girl* could be included in either Abolitionism or in Suffrage and Feminism (we chose the latter). Likewise, Margaret Sanger's classic essay "Morality and Birth Control" might well be included in Suffrage and Feminism, but we placed it in Radical Environmentalism. The point is simply that various radicalisms sometimes have a great deal in common, and that individuals may associate with multiple radical movements.

Another objective has been to present these voices to the public without tampering too much with the individual documents themselves. Of course, we have had to edit many of the pieces for length, but when this was necessary, we took great care to preserve the integrity of the material. Given that the charge of social historians is to pay close attention to ordinary voices, we want to offer our readers the opportunity to do the same in the hopes that they will learn something about how to critically engage primary source material on its own terms. Our second goal, then, is a purely pedagogical one.

This book is not meant to replace textbooks and monographs, but rather to complement the work of contemporary historians, to prompt thinking about the relationship between primary and secondary sources, and to open up new avenues of inquiry to secondary and college students.

Finally, *The Radical Reader* would be missing something if it did not have an objective that was more expressly political. In the spirit of our radical forebears, we hope that this collection will lead to more charitable perceptions of the role that radicalism has played. The United States has always been a protest nation. From the political unrest that gave rise to the Declaration of Independence to the recent mobilizations against unbridled corporate greed and war, the United States has boasted rich traditions of resistance and dissent. Radicalism, so the saying goes, is as American as apple pie. Imagine, for a moment, what America would be like today, if not for the contributions of abolitionists, feminists, labor organizers, civil rights workers, gay and lesbian activists, and environmentalists who have struggled to make the founding promises of American democracy a reality. So much of what we love about the United States—its stubborn promise of equality, its opportunities for social mobility, its guarantees of freedom of speech and assembly, its multiculturalism and relative tolerance for diversity—has been achieved through the hard work of radicals. Indeed, if more Americans were to realize that radicalism is responsible for so many of the things we take for granted—from the right to vote to reasonable work days—our democracy might be less difficult to sustain. Let's face it: If left to those in power, the march of progress would look more like a traffic jam or a line outside of a sold-out rock concert. The promises of freedom and equality that lie at the very heart of American democracy have rarely been given freely or distributed equally. Most of the time, they have had to be demanded and taken.

CHAPTER

ONE

American Revolution

1. JAMES OTIS

The Rights of the British Colonies
Asserted and Proved
(1764)

JAMES OTIS (1725–1783) was among the first colonists to question the universal authority of the British Parliament to govern its North American colonies. Born in West Barnstable, Massachusetts, and educated at Harvard, Otis was a distinguished scholar of literature and law who served in the Massachusetts House of Representatives from 1761 to 1771. Following the controversial passage of the Sugar and Stamp Acts in 1764 and 1765, respectively, Otis published his famous pamphlet, *The Rights of the British Colonies Asserted and Proved,* which argued that Britain had no right to tax the colonists if they were not actually represented in Parliament. Originally published in Boston but widely read on both sides of the Atlantic, Otis's pamphlet was notable for its attempt to balance respect for the traditional governing authority of Parliament with emerging colonial demands for rights and representation in legislative matters.

SOURCE: Bernard Bailyn, ed. *Pamphlets of the American Revolution, 1750–1776.* Cambridge, MA: Belknap Press of Harvard University Press, 1965.

SELECTED READINGS: Bernard Bailyn, *The Ideological Origins of the American Revolution* (1967). Edmund S. and Helen M. Morgan, *The Stamp Act Crisis: Prologue to Revolution* (1953). P. D. G. Thomas, *British Politics and the Stamp Act Crisis: The First Phase of the American Revolution, 1763–1767* (1975).

In order to form an idea of the natural rights of the colonists, I presume it will be granted that they are men, the common children of the same Creator with their brethren of Great Britain. Nature has placed all such in a state of equality and perfect freedom to act within the bounds of the laws of nature and reason without consulting the will or regarding the humor, the passions, or whims of any other man, unless they are formed into a society or body politic. This it must be confessed is rather an abstract way of considering men than agreeable to the real and general course of nature. The truth is, as has been shown, men come into the world and into society at the same instant. But this hinders not but that the natural and original rights of each individual may be illustrated and explained in this way better than in any other. We see here, by the way, a probability that this abstract consideration of men, which has its use in reasoning on the principles of government, has insensibly led some of the greatest men to imagine some real general state of nature agreeable to this abstract conception, antecedent to and independent of society. This is certainly not the case in general, for most men become members of society from their birth, though separate independent states are really in the condition of perfect freedom and equality with regard to each other, and so are any number of individuals who separate themselves from a society of which they have formerly been members, for ill treatment or other good cause, with express design to found another. If in such case there is a real interval between the separation and the new conjunction, during such interval the individuals are as much detached and under the law of nature only as would be two men who should chance to meet on a desolate island.

The colonists are by the law of nature freeborn, as indeed all men are, white or black. No better reasons can be given for enslaving those of any color than such as Baron Montesquieu has humorously given as the foundation of that cruel slavery exercised over the poor Ethiopians, which threatens one day to reduce both Europe and America to the ignorance and barbarity of the darkest ages. Does it follow that 'tis right to enslave a man because he is black? Will short curled hair like wool instead of Christian hair, as 'tis called by those whose hearts are as hard as the nether millstone, help the argument? Can any logical inference in favor of slavery be drawn from a flat nose, a long or a short face? Nothing better can be said in favor of a trade that is the most shocking violation of the law of nature, has a direct tendency to diminish the idea of the inestimable value of liberty, and makes every dealer in it a tyrant, from the director of an African company to the petty chapman in needles and pins on the unhappy coast. It is a clear truth that those who every day barter away other men's liberty will soon care little for their own. To this cause must be imputed that ferocity, cruelty, and brutal barbarity that has long marked the general character of the sugar islanders. They can in general form no idea of government but that which in person or by an overseer, the joint and several proper representative of a creole* and of the d——l, is exercised over ten thousand of their fellow men, born with the same right to freedom and the sweet enjoyments of liberty and life as their unrelenting taskmasters, the overseers and planters.

Is it to be wondered at if when people of the stamp of a creolean planter get into power they will not stick for a little present gain at making their own posterity, white as well as black, worse slaves if possible than those already mentioned?

There is nothing more evident, says Mr. Locke, than "that creatures of the same species and rank, promiscuously born to all the same advantages of nature and the use of the same faculties, should also be equal one among another without subordination and subjection, unless the master of them all should by any manifest declaration of his will set one above another and confer on him by an evident and clear appointment an undoubted right to dominion and sovereignty." "The natural liberty of man is to be free from any superior power on earth, and not to be under the will or legislative authority of man, but only to have the law of nature for his rule." This is the liberty of independent states; this is the liberty of every man out of society and who has a mind to live so; which liberty is only abridged in certain instances, not lost to those who are born in or voluntarily enter into society; this gift of God cannot be annihilated.

*Those in England who borrow the terms of the Spaniards, as well as their notions of government, apply this term to all Americans of European extract; but the northern colonists apply it only to the islanders and others of such extract, under the Torrid Zone.

2.

Resolutions of the Stamp Act Congress (1765)

In 1765, the British Parliament passed the STAMP ACT, which required American colonists to pay taxes on stamped paper required for a variety of official documents, including legal papers, sales and licenses, and newspapers. Designed to raise money to fund the presence of British troops in North America following the French and Indian (or Seven Years') War (1756–1763), the Stamp Act sparked a wave of protest in the colonies. In October 1765, delegates from nine colonies denounced the Stamp Act, and drafted a set of grievances regarding Parliament's right to tax the colonists without allowing the colonies actual legislative representation. The resolutions of this "Stamp Act Congress" advanced the claim that while Parliament had the right to approve certain legislation, the authority to tax was reserved for colonial assemblies comprised of locally elected representatives. The Stamp Act Congress, which led to the repeal of the Stamp Act the following year, was the first of many examples of colonial cooperation to resist the power of Parliament.

SOURCE: Samuel Eliot Morison, ed. *Sources and Documents Illustrating the American Revolution, 1764–1788.* 2nd edition. London and New York: Oxford University Press, 1965.

SELECTED READINGS: Edmund S. Morgan, *The Birth of the Republic, 1763–89* (1992). Jack P. Greene, *Peripheries and Center: Constitutional Development in the Extended Policies of the British Empire and the United States, 1607–1788* (1986). Pauline Maier, *From Resistance to Revolution: Colonial Radicals and the Development of American Opposition to Britain, 1765–1776* (1974).

The members of this Congress, sincerely devoted with the warmest sentiments of affection and duty to His Majesty's person and Government, inviolably attached to the present happy establishment of the Protestant succession, and

with minds deeply impressed by a sense of the present and impending mis-
fortunes of the British colonies on this continent; having considered as
maturely as time will permit the circumstances of the said colonies, esteem it
our indispensible duty to make the following declarations of our humble opinion respecting the most essential rights and liberties of the colonists, and of
the grievances under which they labour, by reason of several late Acts of
Parliament.

I. That His Majesty's subjects in these colonies owe the same allegiance to
the Crown of Great Britain that is owing from his subjects born within the
realm, and all due subordination to that august body the Parliament of Great
Britain.

II. That His Majesty's liege subjects in these colonies are intitled to all the
inherent rights and liberties of his natural born subjects within the kingdom
of Great Britain.

III. That it is inseparably essential to the freedom of a people, and the
undoubted right of Englishmen, that no taxes be imposed on them but with
their own consent, given personally or by their representatives.

IV. That the people of these colonies are not, and from their local circumstances cannot be, represented in the House of Commons in Great Britain.

V. That the only representatives of the people of these colonies are persons
chosen therein by themselves, and that no taxes ever have been, or can be
constitutionally imposed on them, but by their respective legislatures.

VI. That all supplies to the Crown being free gifts of the people, it is unreasonable and inconsistent with the principles and spirit of the British Constitution, for the people of Great Britain to grant to His Majesty the property
of the colonists.

VII. That trial by jury is the inherent and invaluable right of every British
subject in these colonies.

VIII. That the late Act of Parliament, entitled *An Act for granting and applying
certain stamp duties, and other duties, in the British colonies and plantations in America, etc.*, by imposing taxes on the inhabitants of these colonies; and the said
Act, and several other Acts, by extending the jurisdiction of the courts of
Admiralty beyond its ancient limits, have a manifest tendency to subvert the
rights and liberties of the colonists.

IX. That the duties imposed by several late Acts of Parliament, from the
peculiar circumstances of these colonies, will be extremely burthensome and
grievous; and from the scarcity of specie, the payment of them absolutely
impracticable.

X. That as the profits of the trade of these colonies ultimately center in
Great Britain, to pay for the manufactures which they are obliged to take from
thence, they eventually contribute very largely to all supplies granted there
to the Crown.

XI. That the restrictions imposed by several late Acts of Parliament on the trade of these colonies will render them unable to purchase the manufactures of Great Britain.

XII. That the increase, prosperity, and happiness of these colonies depend on the full and free enjoyments of their rights and liberties, and an intercourse with Great Britain mutually affectionate and advantageous.

XIII. That it is the right of the British subjects in these colonies to petition the King or either House of Parliament.

Lastly, That it is the indispensible duty of these colonies to the best of sovereigns, to the mother country, and to themselves, to endeavour by a loyal and dutiful address to His Majesty, and humble applications to both Houses of Parliament, to procure the repeal of the Act for granting and applying certain stamp duties, of all clauses of any other Acts of Parliament, whereby the jurisdiction of the Admiralty is extended as aforesaid, and of the other late Acts for the restriction of American commerce.

3. JOHN DICKINSON

Letters from a Farmer in Pennsylvania to the Inhabitants of the British Colonies (1768)

JOHN DICKINSON (1732–1808) was actually neither a farmer nor a native of Pennsylvania, but he was still one of the most eloquent spokesmen for colonial rights during the period before the American Revolution. Born in Maryland, and educated in Delaware and London, Dickinson spent most of his adult life as a prominent lawyer and political figure in Philadelphia. Author of the famous resolutions approved by the Stamp Act Congress in 1765, Dickinson had a keen command of history, law, and philosophy. He was by nature more of a conservative than a revolutionary thinker, so much so that in 1776 he refused to sign the Declaration of Independence on the grounds that it, like the Stamp Act, was a violation of British tradition. Still, Dickinson was regarded by some as the "Penman of the Revolution," in large part due to a series of letters he wrote for colonial newspapers in 1767. Addressed to "My Dear Countrymen" and signed "A Farmer," Dickinson's letters, twelve in all, were published in pamphlet form the following year, and distributed widely in America and Europe. Arguably the most influential pamphlet before Thomas Paine's *Common Sense,* Dickinson's *Letters from a Farmer in Pennsylvania* argued that Parliament had overstepped its authority by imposing taxes to raise revenue for the British Empire, thereby generating suspicion among colonists that there was a "conspiracy" in the works against them.

SOURCE: Forrest McDonald, ed. *Empire and Nation.* 2nd edition. Indianapolis: Liberty Fund, 1999.

SELECTED READINGS: Robert Middlekauff, *The Glorious Cause: The American Revolution, 1763–1789* (1982). James Kirby Martin, *Men in Rebellion: Higher Government Leaders and the Coming of the American Revolution* (1974). Bernard Bailyn, *The Ideological Origins of the American Revolution* (1967).

My dear Countrymen,

I am a *Farmer,* settled, after a variety of fortunes, near the banks of the river *Delaware,* in the province of *Pennsylvania.* I received a liberal education, and have been engaged in the busy scenes of life; but am now convinced, that a man may be as happy without bustle, as with it. My farm is small; my servants are few, and good; I have a little money at interest; I wish for no more; my employment in my own affairs is easy; and with a contented grateful mind, undisturbed by worldly hopes or fears, relating to myself, I am completing the number of days allotted to me by divine goodness.

Being generally master of my time, I spend a good deal of it in a library, which I think the most valuable part of my small estate; and being acquainted with two or three gentlemen of abilities and learning, who honor me with their friendship, I have acquired, I believe, a greater knowledge in history, and the laws and constitution of my country, than is generally attained by men of my class, many of them not being so fortunate as I have been in the opportunities of getting information.

From my infancy I was taught to love *humanity* and *liberty.* Enquiry and experience have since confirmed my reverence for the lessons then given me, by convincing me more fully of their truth and excellence. Benevolence toward mankind, excites wishes for their welfare, and such wishes endear the means of fulfilling them. *These* can be found in liberty only, and therefore her sacred cause ought to be espoused by every man on every occasion, to the utmost of his power. As a charitable, but poor person does not withhold his *mite,* because he cannot relieve *all* the distresses of the miserable, so should not any honest man suppress his sentiments concerning freedom, however small their influence is likely to be. Perhaps he "may touch some wheel," that will have an effect greater than he could reasonably expect.

These being my sentiments, I am encouraged to offer to you, my countrymen, my thoughts on some late transactions, that appear to me to be of the utmost importance to you. Conscious of my own defects, I have waited some time, in expectation of seeing the subject treated by persons much better qualified for the task; but being therein disappointed, and apprehensive that longer delays will be injurious, I venture at length to request the attention of the public, praying, that these lines may be *read* with the same zeal for the happiness of *British America,* with which they were *wrote.*

With a good deal of surprise I have observed, that little notice has been taken of an act of parliament, as injurious in its principle to the liberties of these colonies, as the *Stamp Act* was: I mean the act for suspending the legislation of *New York.*

The assembly of that government complied with a former act of parliament, requiring certain provisions to be made for the troops in *America*, in every particular, I think, except the articles of salt, pepper and vinegar. In my opinion they acted imprudently, considering all circumstances, in not complying so far as would have given satisfaction, as several colonies did: But my dislike of their conduct in that instance, has not blinded me so much, that I cannot plainly perceive, that they have been punished in a manner pernicious to *American* freedom, and justly alarming to all the colonies.

If the *British* parliament has legal authority to issue an order, that we shall furnish a single article for the troops here, and to compel obedience to *that* order, they have the same right to issue an order for us to supply those troops with arms, clothes, and every necessary; and to compel obedience to *that* order also; in short, to lay *any burthens* they please upon us. What is this but *taxing* us at a *certain sum*, and leaving to us only the *manner* of raising it? How is this mode more tolerable than the *Stamp Act?* Would that act have appeared more pleasing to *Americans*, if being ordered thereby to raise the sum total of the taxes, the mighty privilege had been left to them, of saying how much should be paid for an instrument of writing on paper, and how much for another on parchment?

An act of parliament, commanding us to do a certain thing, if it has any validity, is a *tax* upon us for the expense that accrues in complying with it; and for this reason, I believe, every colony on the continent, that chose to give a mark of their respect for *Great Britain*, in complying with the act relating to the troops, cautiously avoided the mention of that act, lest their conduct should be attributed to its supposed obligation.

The matter being thus stated, the assembly of *New York* either had, or had not, a right to refuse submission to that act. If they had, and I imagine no *American* will say they had not, then the parliament had *no right* to compel them to execute it. If they had not *this right*, they had *no right* to punish them for not executing it; and therefore *no right* to suspend their legislation, which is a punishment. In fact, if the people of *New York* cannot be legally taxed but by their own representatives, they cannot be legally deprived of the privilege of legislation, only for insisting on that exclusive privilege of taxation. If they may be legally deprived in such a case, of the privilege of legislation, why may they not, with equal reason, be deprived of every other privilege? Or why may not every colony be treated in the same manner, when any of them shall dare to deny their assent to any impositions, that shall be directed? Or what signifies the repeal of the *Stamp Act*, if these colonies are to lose their *other* privileges, by not tamely surrendering *that* of taxation?

There is one consideration arising from this suspension, which is not generally attended to, but shows its importance very clearly. It was not *necessary* that this suspension should be caused by an act of parliament. The crown might have restrained the governor of *New York*, even from calling the assembly together, by its prerogative in the royal governments. This step, I suppose, would have been taken, if the conduct of the assembly of *New York* had been regarded as an act of disobedience *to the crown alone;* but it is regarded as an act of "disobedience to the authority of the BRITISH LEGISLATURE." This gives the suspension a consequence vastly more affecting. It is a parliamentary assertion of the *supreme authority* of the *British* legislature over these colonies, in *the point of taxation,* and is intended to COMPEL *New York* into a submission to that authority. It seems therefore to me as much a violation of the liberties of the people of that province, and consequently of all these colonies, as if the parliament had sent a number of regiments to be quartered upon them till they should comply. For it is evident, that the suspension is meant as a *compulsion;* and the *method* of compelling is totally indifferent. It is indeed probable, that the sight of redcoats, and the hearing of drums, would have been most alarming; because people are generally more influenced by their eyes and ears, than by their reason. But whoever seriously considers the matter, must perceive that a dreadful stroke is aimed at the liberty of these colonies. I say, of these colonies; for the cause of *one* is the cause of *all.* If the parliament may lawfully deprive *New York* of any of *her* rights, it may deprive any, or all the other colonies of *their* rights; and nothing can possibly so much encourage such attempts, as a mutual inattention to the interests of each other. *To divide, and thus to destroy,* is the first political maxim in attacking those, who are powerful by their union. He certainly is not a wise man, who folds his arms, and reposes himself at home, viewing, with unconcern, the flames that have invaded his neighbor's house, without using any endeavors to extinguish them. When Mr. *Hampden's* ship money case, for *Three Shillings* and *Four-pence,* was tried, all the people of *England,* with anxious expectation, interested themselves in the important decision; and when the slightest point, touching the freedom of *one* colony, is agitated, I earnestly wish, that *all the rest* may, with equal ardor, support their sister. Very much may be said on this subject; but I hope, more at present is unnecessary.

With concern I have observed, that *two* assemblies of this province have sat and adjourned, without taking any notice of this act. It may perhaps be asked, what would have been proper for them to do? I am by no means fond of inflammatory measures; I detest them. I should be sorry that anything should be done which might justly displease our sovereign, or our mother country: But a firm, modest exertion of a free spirit, should never be wanting on public occasions. It appears to me, that it would have been sufficient for the assembly to have ordered our agents to represent to the King's ministers their sense of the suspending act, and to pray for its repeal. Thus we should have borne our testimony against it; and might therefore reasonably expect that, on a like occasion, we might receive the same assistance from the other colonies.

Concordia res parvae crescunt.

Small things grow great by concord.

A Farmer

Nov. 5.*

*The day of King William the Third's landing.

4. SAMUEL ADAMS

A State of the Rights
of the Colonists
(1772)

Regarded by many of his contemporaries as the "Father of the American Revolution," **SAMUEL ADAMS (1722–1803)** was one of the most successful political figures of his era. Born into one of Boston's elite families, Adams was educated at Harvard and went on to practice law, serve as a delegate to the Continental Congress, sign the Declaration of Independence and the U.S. Constitution, and serve as Governor of Massachusetts. Though Adams has been portrayed as an impetuous firebrand, his embrace of independence evolved gradually over time. However, following the Boston Massacre and a series of abuses by Massachusetts Governor Thomas Hutchinson, Adams convened a town meeting on November 2, 1772, to discuss the formation of a "committee of correspondence" to draft a statement about the repeated violations of colonial rights. Designed to generate a "union of sentiments" among the colonists, the resulting publication, *A State of the Rights of the Colonists*, was highly effective in arousing public outrage and action. As with his political career generally, Adams's pamphlet was credited with helping to coordinate public opinion and unite otherwise disparate factions in the cause of independence.

SOURCE: Merrill Jensen, ed. *Tracts of the American Revolution, 1763–1776.* Indianapolis and New York: Bobbs-Merrill Company, 1967.

SELECTED READINGS: Pauline Maier, *The Old Revolutionaries: Political Lives in the Age of Sam Adams* (1990). Richard D. Brown, *Revolutionary Politics in Massachusetts: The Boston Committee of Correspondence and the Towns, 1772–1774* (1970). Steward Beach, *Samuel Adams, The Fateful Years, 1764–1776* (1965).

1st. Natural Rights of the Colonists as Men

Among the natural Rights of the Colonists are these: First, a Right to *Life;* Secondly to *Liberty;* thirdly to *Property;* together with the Right to support and defend them in the best manner they can. Those are evident Branches of, rather than deductions from the Duty of Self Preservation, commonly called the first Law of Nature.

All Men have a Right to remain in a State of Nature as long as they please; And in case of intollerable Oppression, Civil or Religious, to leave the Society they belong to, and enter into another.

When Men enter into Society, it is by voluntary consent; and they have a right to demand and insist upon the performance of such conditions, And previous limitations as form an equitable *original compact.*

Every natural Right not expressly given up or from the nature of a Social Compact necessarily ceded remains.

All positive and civil laws, should conform as far as possible, to the Law of natural reason and equity.

As neither reason requires, nor religion permits the contrary, every Man living in or out of a state of civil society, has a right peaceably and quietly to worship God according to the dictates of his conscience.

"Just and true liberty, equal and impartial liberty" in matters spiritual and temporal, is a thing that all Men are clearly entitled to, by the eternal and immutable laws Of God and nature, as well as by the law of Nations, & all well grounded municipal laws, which must have their foundation in the former.

In regard to Religion, mutual tolleration in the different professions thereof, is what all good and candid minds in all ages have ever practiced; and both by precept and example inculcated on mankind. And it is now generally agreed among christians that this spirit of toleration in the fullest extent consistent with the being of civil society "is the chief characteristical mark of the true church" & In so much that Mr. Lock has asserted, and proved beyond the possibility of contradiction on any solid ground, that such toleration ought to be extended to all whose doctrines are not subversive of society. The only Sects which he thinks ought to be, and which by all wise laws are excluded from such toleration, are those who teach Doctrines subversive of the Civil Government under which they live. The Roman Catholicks or Papists are excluded by reason of such Doctrines as these "that Princes excommunicated may be deposed, and those they call *Hereticks* may be destroyed without mercy; besides their recognizing the Pope in so absolute a manner, in subversion of Government, by introducing as far as possible into the states, under whose protection they enjoy life, liberty and property, that solecism in politicks, Imperium in imperio leading directly to the worst anarchy and confusion, civil discord, war and blood shed.

The natural liberty of Men by entring into society is abridg'd or restrained so far only as is necessary for the Great end of Society the best good of the whole. . . .

3rd. The Rights of the Colonists as Subjects

A Common Wealth or state is a body politick or civil society of men, united together to promote their mutual safety and prosperity, by means of their union.

The *absolute Rights* of Englishmen, and all freemen in or out of Civil society, are principally, *personal security, personal liberty and private property.*

All Persons born in the British American Colonies are by the laws of God and nature, and by the Common law of England, *exclusive of all charters from the Crown,* well Entitled, and by Acts of the British Parliament are declared to be entitled to all the natural essential, inherent & inseperable Rights Liberties and Privileges of Subjects born in Great Britain, or within the Realm. Among those Rights are the following; which no men or body of men, consistently with their own rights as men and citizens or members of society, can for themselves give up, or take away from others.

First, "The first fundamental positive law of all Commonwealths or States, is the establishing the legislative power; as the first fundamental *natural* law also, which is to govern even the legislative power itself, is the preservation of the Society."

Secondly, The Legislative has no right to absolute arbitrary power over the lives and fortunes of the people. Nor can mortals assume a prerogative, not only too high for men, but for Angels; and therefore reserved for the exercise of the *Deity* alone.

"The Legislative cannot Justly *assume* to itself a power to rule by extempore arbitrary decrees; but it is bound to see that Justice is dispensed, and that the rights of the subjects be decided, by promulgated, standing and known laws, and authorized *independent Judges;*" that is independent as far as possible of Prince or People. *"There shall be one rule of Justice for rich and poor; for the favorite in Court, and the Countryman at the Plough."*

Thirdly, The supreme power cannot Justly take from any man, any part of his property without his consent, in person or by his Representative.

5.

Slave Petitions for Freedom
(1773)

With its emphasis on independence, liberty, and equality, the American Revolution helped inspire a mounting opposition to the institution of slavery. By 1804, every Northern state had passed some kind of gradual abolition law, resulting in the largest period of emancipation prior to the Civil War. During the 1770s and 1780s especially, slaves gained their freedom through a variety of means, including private manumissions, individual flight, public petitions, and service in the Revolutionary army. Indeed, an estimated five thousand African Americans—slave and free—performed wartime military service. Caught up in the fervor of Revolution, many blacks also petitioned colonial legislatures for their freedom. Mixing Christian religious principles with political reasoning based on the ideals of the Enlightenment, the following slave petitions highlight the hypocrisy of slavery in a free republic, and demand the full extension of the Revolution's promise to black Americans.

SOURCE: Herbert Aptheker, ed. *A Documentary History of the Negro People in the United States, Volume One.* New York: Carol Publishing Group, 1990.

SELECTED READINGS: Joanne Pope Melish, *Disowning Slavery: Gradual Emancipation and "Race" in New England, 1780–1860* (1998). James and Lois Horton, *In Hope of Liberty: Culture, Community, and Protest Among Northern Free Blacks, 1700–1860* (1997). David Waldstreicher, *In the Midst of Perpetual Fetes: The Making of American Nationalism, 1776–1820* (1997).

Province of the Massachusetts Bay To His Excellency Thomas Hutchinson, Esq; Governor; To The Honorable His Majesty's Council, and To the Honorable House of Representatives in General Court assembled at Boston, the 6th Day of *January,* 1773.

The humble PETITION of many Slaves, living in the Town of Boston, and other Towns in the Province is this, namely.

That your Excellency and Honors, and the Honorable the Representatives would be pleased to take their unhappy State and Condition under your wise and just Consideration.

We desire to bless God, who loves Mankind, who sent his Son to die
for their Salvation, and who is no respecter of Persons; that he hath
lately put it into the Hearts of Multitudes on both Sides of the Water,
to bear our Burthens, some of whom are Men of great Note and Influence; who have pleaded our Cause with Arguments which we hope will
have their weight with this Honorable Court.

We presume not to dictate to your Excellency and Honors, being willing to rest our Cause on your Humanity and Justice; yet would beg
Leave to say a Word or two on the Subject.

Although some of the Negroes are vicious, (who doubtless may be
punished and restrained by the same Laws which are in Force against
other of the King's Subjects) there are many others of a quite different
Character, and who, if made free, would soon be able as well as willing
to bear a Part in the Public Charges; many of them of good natural Parts,
are discreet, sober, honest, and industrious; and may it not be said of
many, that they are virtuous and religious, although their Condition is
in itself so unfriendly to Religion, and every moral Virtue except *Patience*.
How many of that Number have there been, and now are in this Province, who have had every Day of their Lives imbittered with this most
intollerable Reflection, That, let their Behaviour be what it will, neither
they, nor their Children to all Generations, shall ever be able to do, or
to possess and enjoy any Thing, no, not even *Life itself*, but in a Manner
as the *Beasts that perish*.

We have no Property! We have no Wives! No Children! We have no
City! No Country! But we have a Father in Heaven, and we are determined, as far as his Grace shall enable us, and as far as our degraded
contemptuous Life will admit, to keep all his Commandments: Especially
will we be obedient to our Masters, so long as God in his sovereign
Providence shall *suffer* us to be holden in Bondage.

It would be impudent, if not presumptuous in us, to suggest to your
Excellency and Honors any Law or Laws proper to be made, in relation
to our unhappy State, which, although our greatest Unhappiness, is not
our *Fault*; and this gives us great Encouragement to pray and hope for
such Relief as is consistent with your Wisdom, Justice, and Goodness.

We think Ourselves very happy, that we may thus address the Great
and General Court of this Province, which great and good Court is to
us, the best Judge, under God, of what is wise, just and good.

We humbly beg Leave to add but this one Thing more: We pray for
such Relief only, which by no Possibility can ever be productive of the

least Wrong or Injury to our Masters; but to us will be as Life from the dead.

Signed,

Felix

Boston, April 20th, 1773

Sir, The efforts made by the legislative of this province in their last sessions to free themselves from slavery, gave us, who are in that deplorable state, a high degree of satisfaction. We expect great things from men who have made such a noble stand against the designs of their *fellow-men* to enslave them. We cannot but wish and hope Sir, that you will have the same grand object, we mean civil and religious liberty, in view in your next session. The divine spirit of *freedom*, seems to fire every humane breast on this continent, except such as are bribed to assist in executing the execrable plan.

We are very sensible that it would be highly detrimental to our present masters, if we were allowed to demand all that of *right* belongs to us for past services; this we disclaim. Even the *Spaniards*, who have not those sublime ideas of freedom that English men have, are conscious that they have no right to all the services of their fellow-men, we mean the *Africans*, whom they have purchased with their money; therefore they allow them one day in a week to work for themselves, to enable them to earn money to purchase the residue of their time, which they have a right to demand in such portions as they are able to pay for (a due appraizement of their services being first made, which always stands at the purchase money.) We do not pretend to dictate to you Sir, or to the Honorable Assembly, of which you are a member. We acknowledge our obligations to you for what you have already done, but as the people of this province seem to be actuated by the principles of equity and justice, we cannot but expect your house will again take our deplorable case into serious consideration, and give us that ample relief which, *as men*, we have a natural right to.

But since the wise and righteous governor of the universe, has permitted our fellow men to make us slaves, we bow in submission to him, and determine to behave in such a manner as that we may have reason to expect the divine approbation of, and assistance in, our peaceable and lawful attempts to gain our freedom.

We are willing to submit to such regulations and laws, as may be made relative to us, until we leave the province, which we determine to do as soon as we can, from our joynt labours procure money to transport ourselves to some part of the Coast of *Africa*, where we propose a settlement. We are very desirous that you should have instructions relative to us, from your town, therefore we pray you to communicate this letter to them, and ask this favor for us.

In behalf of our fellow slaves in this province, and by order of their Committee.

> Peter Bestes,
> Sambo Freeman,
> Felix Holbrook,
> Chester Joie.

For the Representative of the town of Thompson.

6. PATRICK HENRY

Speech at the
Second Virginia Convention
(1775)

By almost all accounts, PATRICK HENRY (1736–1799) was a peerless orator whose golden tongue broadened support for the Revolution among the colonists. Born and raised in Virginia, he was one of the very first colonists to take up the cause of independence, denouncing the Stamp Act and other acts of Parliament, helping establish the Committees of Correspondence, and serving as a delegate to the Continental Congress. His most famous moment, however, came in the speech he delivered at a session of the Virginia Assembly on March 28, 1775, when he denounced King George III and exclaimed, "Give me liberty or give me death!" A declaration of war as well as independence, Henry's impassioned speech certainly did not reflect the opinion of everyone in the colonies, but it did help to tip the balance of public opinion in favor of armed conflict with Britain. During and after the war, Henry remained in public life, later denouncing the Constitution on the grounds that it threatened the liberty of both individual citizens and the states. His outspoken criticism did not prevent its ratification, but it did help to inspire the inclusion of the Bill of Rights in 1791. Indeed, the safeguarding of individual liberty within the national government is perhaps the most important part of Henry's legacy.

SOURCE: James Albert Woodburn, ed. *American Orations: Studies in American Political History.* New York and London: G. P. Putnam's Sons, 1896.

SELECTED READINGS: Henry Mayer, *A Son of Thunder: Patrick Henry and the American Republic* (1986). Richard R. Beeman, *Patrick Henry: A Biography* (1974). Robert D. Meade, *Patrick Henry.* 2 vols. (1957–1969).

MR. PRESIDENT:

No man thinks more highly than I do of the patriotism, as well as abilities, of the very worthy gentlemen who have just addressed the House. But different men often see the same subject in different lights; and, therefore, I hope that it will not be thought disrespectful to those gentlemen, if, entertaining as I do, opinions of a character very opposite to theirs, I shall speak forth my sentiments freely and without reserve. This is no time for ceremony. The question before the House is one of awful moment to this country. For my own part I consider it as nothing less than a question of freedom or slavery; and in proportion to the magnitude of the subject ought to be the freedom of the debate. It is only in this way that we can hope to arrive at truth, and fulfil the great responsibility which we hold to God and our country. Should I keep back my opinions at such a time, through fear of giving offence, I should consider myself as guilty of treason toward my country, and of an act of disloyalty toward the majesty of heaven, which I revere above all earthly kings.

Mr. President, it is natural to man to indulge in the illusions of hope. We are apt to shut our eyes against a painful truth, and listen to the song of that syren, till she transforms us into beasts. Is this the part of wise men, engaged in a great and arduous struggle for liberty? Are we disposed to be of the number of those who, having eyes, see not, and having ears, hear not, the things which so nearly concern their temporal salvation? For my part, whatever anguish of spirit it may cost, I am willing to know the whole truth; to know the worst and to provide for it.

I have but one lamp by which my feet are guided; and that is the lamp of experience. I know of no way of judging of the future but by the past. And judging by the past, I wish to know what there has been in the conduct of the British ministry for the last ten years, to justify those hopes with which gentlemen have been pleased to solace themselves and the House? Is it that insidious smile with which our petition has been lately received? Trust it not, sir; it will prove a snare to your feet. Suffer not yourselves to be betrayed with a kiss. Ask yourselves how this gracious reception of our petition comports with these war-like preparations which cover our waters and darken our land. Are fleets and armies necessary to a work of love and reconciliation? Have we shown ourselves so unwilling to be reconciled, that force must be called in to win back our love? Let us not deceive ourselves, sir. These are the implements of war and subjugation; the last arguments to which kings resort.

I ask gentlemen, sir, what means this martial array, if its purpose be not to force us to submission? Can gentlemen assign any other possible motives for it? Has Great Britain any enemy, in this quarter of the world, to call for all this accumulation of navies and armies? No, sir, she has none. They are meant for us: they can be meant for no other. They are sent over to bind and rivet upon us those chains which the British ministry have been so long forging. And what have we to oppose to them? Shall we try argument? Sir, we have been trying that for the last ten years. Have we any thing new to offer on the subject? Nothing. We have held the subject up in every light of which it is capable; but it has been all in vain. Shall we resort to entreaty and humble supplication? What terms shall we find which have not been already exhausted? Let us not, I beseech you, sir, deceive ourselves longer. Sir, we have done every thing that could be done, to avert the storm which is now coming on. We have petitioned; we have remonstrated; we have supplicated; we have prostrated ourselves before the throne, and have implored its interposition to arrest the tyrannical hands of the ministry and parliament. Our petitions have been slighted; our remonstrances have produced additional violence and insult; our supplications have been disregarded; and we have been spurned, with contempt, from the foot of the throne. In vain, after these things, may we indulge the fond hope of peace and reconciliation. There is no longer any room for hope. If we wish to be free—if we mean to preserve inviolate those inestimable privileges for which we have been so long contending—if we mean not basely to abandon the noble struggle in which we have been so long engaged, and which we have pledged ourselves never to abandon until the glorious object of our contest shall be obtained, we must fight! I repeat it, sir, we must fight! An appeal to arms and to the God of Hosts is all that is left us!

They tell us, sir, that we are weak; unable to cope with so formidable an adversary. But when shall we be stronger? Will it be the next week, or the next year? Will it be when we are totally disarmed, and when a British guard shall be stationed in every house? Shall we gather strength by irresolution and inaction? Shall we acquire the means of effectual resistance, by lying supinely on our backs, and hugging the delusive phantom of hope, until our enemies shall have bound us hand and foot? Sir, we are not weak, if we make a proper use of the means which the God of nature hath placed in our power. Three millions of people, armed in the holy cause of liberty, and in such a country as that which we possess, are invincible by any force which our enemy can send against us. Besides, sir, we shall not fight our battles alone. There is a just God who presides over the destinies of nations: and who will raise up friends to fight our battles for us. The battle, sir, is not to the strong alone; it is to the vigilant, the active, the brave. Besides, sir, we have no election. If we were base enough to desire it, it is now too late to retire from the contest. There is no retreat, but in submission and slavery! Our chains are forged! Their clanking may be heard on the plains of Boston! The war is inevitable—and let it come! I repeat it, sir, let it come!

It is in vain, sir, to extenuate the matter. Gentlemen may cry peace, peace—but there is no peace. The war is actually begun! The next gale that sweeps from the north will bring to our ears the clash of resounding arms! Our brethren are already in the field! Why stand we here idle? What is it that gentlemen wish? What would they have? Is life so dear, or peace so sweet, as to be purchased at the price of chains and slavery? Forbid it, Almighty God! I know not what course others may take: but as for me, give me liberty, or give me death!

7. THOMAS PAINE

Common Sense
(1776)

Born into a working-class Quaker family in Norfolk, England, **THOMAS PAINE** (1737–1809) was the most important pamphleteer of the American Revolution. Before coming to America in 1774, Paine was a failure at almost everything he attempted—from school to work to marriage. Shortly after arriving in Philadelphia in November 1774, Paine began writing for the *Pennsylvania Magazine*, where his essays and poems earned notoriety for their revolutionary sympathies. After the publication of *Common Sense* on January 10, 1776, Paine's fame soared. As with all of his writings, Paine published the pamphlet anonymously, but he was soon identified as the author. An aggressive attack on the "so much boasted Constitution of England," traditions of hereditary rule, and the monarchy itself, *Common Sense* reached an unprecedented readership; Paine himself estimated that as many as 150,000 copies were circulated in the colonies alone. It was aesthetics, in addition to politics, that ensured the widespread influence of *Common Sense*. Written in clear and simple prose—invoking common metaphors of family and geography to illustrate the broken relationship between the colonies and Britain—Paine's remarkable pamphlet conveyed, both in form and content, democratic and egalitarian sensibilities. Though Paine would ultimately die in obscurity, his political writings—which also included *The Rights of Man* (1791) and *The Age of Reason* (1794), written while he was in Europe—were widely credited with ushering in the "Age of Revolution."

SOURCE: Thomas Paine. *Common Sense*. New York: Penguin Books, 1986.

SELECTED READINGS: John Keane, *Tom Paine: A Political Life* (1995). Jack Fruchtman, Jr., *Thomas Paine, Apostle of Freedom* (1994). Eric Foner, *Tom Paine and Revolutionary America* (1976).

Thoughts on the Present State of American Affairs

In the following pages I offer nothing more than simple facts, plain arguments, and common sense; and have no other preliminaries to settle with the reader, than that he will divest himself of prejudice and prepossession, and suffer his reason and his feelings to determine for themselves; that he will put *on,* or rather that he will not put *off,* the true character of a man, and generously enlarge his views beyond the present day.

Volumes have been written on the subject of the struggle between England and America. Men of all ranks have embarked in the controversy, from different motives, and with various designs; but all have been ineffectual, and the period of debate is closed. Arms, as the last resource, decide the contest; the appeal was the choice of the king, and the continent hath accepted the challenge. . . .

The sun never shined on a cause of greater worth. 'Tis not the affair of a city, a country, a province, or a kingdom, but of a continent—of at least one eighth part of the habitable globe. 'Tis not the concern of a day, a year, or an age; posterity are virtually involved in the contest, and will be more or less affected, even to the end of time, by the proceedings now. Now is the seed time of continental union, faith and honor. The least fracture now will be like a name engraved with the point of a pin on the tender rind of a young oak; the wound will enlarge with the tree, and posterity read it in full grown characters.

By referring the matter from argument to arms, a new æra for politics is struck; a new method of thinking hath arisen. All plans, proposals, &c. prior to the nineteenth of April, *i.e.* to the commencement of hostilities, are like the almanacks of the last year; which, though proper then, are superceded and useless now. Whatever was advanced by the advocates on either side of the question then, terminated in one and the same point, viz. a union with Great Britain; the only difference between the parties was the method of effecting it; the one proposing force, the other friendship; but it hath so far happened that the first hath failed, and the second hath withdrawn her influence.

As much hath been said of the advantages of reconciliation, which, like an agreeable dream, hath passed away and left us as we were, it is but right, that we should examine the contrary side of the argument, and inquire into some of the many material injuries which these colonies sustain, and always will sustain, by being connected with, and dependant on Great Britain. To examine that connexion and dependance, on the principles of nature and common sense, to see what we have to trust to, if separated, and what we are to expect, if dependant.

I have heard it asserted by some, that as America hath flourished under her former connexion with Great-Britain, that the same connexion is necessary towards her future happiness, and will always have the same effect. Nothing can be more fallacious than this kind of argument. We may as well assert, that because a child has thrived upon milk, that it is never to have meat; or that the first twenty years of our lives is to become a precedent for the next twenty. But even this is admitting more than is true, for I answer roundly, that America would have flourished as much, and probably much more, had no European power had any thing to do with her. The commerce by which she hath enriched herself are the necessaries of life, and will always have a market while eating is the custom of Europe.

But she has protected us, say some. That she hath engrossed us is true, and defended the continent at our expence as well as her own is admitted, and she would have defended Turkey from the same motive, viz. the sake of trade and dominion.

Alas, we have been long led away by ancient prejudices, and made large sacrifices to superstition. We have boasted the protection of Great-Britain, without considering, that her motive was *interest* not *attachment;* that she did not protect us from *our enemies* on *our account,* but from *her enemies* on *her own account,* from those who had no quarrel with us on any *other account,* and who will always be our enemies on the *same account.* Let Britain wave her pretensions to the continent, or the continent throw off the dependance, and we should be at peace with France and Spain were they at war with Britain. The miseries of Hanover last war ought to warn us against connexions.

It hath lately been asserted in parliament, that the colonies have no relation to each other but through the parent country, *i.e.* that Pensylvania and the Jerseys, and so on for the rest, are sister colonies by the way of England; this is certainly a very round-about way of proving relationship, but it is the nearest and only true way of proving enemyship, if I may so call it. France and Spain never were, nor perhaps ever will be our enemies as *Americans,* but as our being the *subjects of Great Britain.*

But Britain is the parent country, say some. Then the more shame upon her conduct. Even brutes do not devour their young, nor savages make war upon their families; wherefore the assertion, if true, turns to her reproach; but it happens not to be true, or only partly so, and the phrase *parent* or *mother country* hath been jesuitically adopted by the—and his parasites, with a low papistical design of gaining an unfair bias on the credulous weakness of our minds. Europe, and not England, is the parent country of America. This new world hath been the asylum for the persecuted lovers of civil and religious liberty from *every part* of Europe. Hither have they fled, not from the tender embraces of the mother, but from the cruelty of the monster; and it is so far true of England, that the same tyranny which drove the first emigrants from home, pursues their descendants still. . . .

The authority of Great-Britain over this continent, is a form of government, which sooner or later must have an end: And a serious mind can draw no true pleasure by looking forward, under the painful and positive conviction, that what he calls 'the present constitution' is merely temporary. As parents, we can have no joy, knowing that *this government* is not sufficiently lasting to ensure any thing which we may bequeath to posterity: And by a plain method of argument, as we are running the next generation into debt, we ought to do the work of it, otherwise we use them meanly and pitifully. In order to discover the line of our duty rightly, we should take our children in our hand, and fix our station a few years farther into life; that eminence will present a prospect, which a few present fears and prejudices conceal from our sight.

Though I would carefully avoid giving unnecessary offence, yet I am inclined to believe, that all those who espouse the doctrine of reconciliation, may be included within the following descriptions. Interested men, who are not to be trusted; weak men who *cannot* see; prejudiced men who *will not* see; and a certain set of moderate men, who think better of the European world than it deserves; and this last class by an ill-judged deliberation, will be the cause of more calamities to this continent than all the other three.

It is the good fortune of many to live distant from the scene of sorrow; the evil is not sufficiently brought to *their* doors to make *them* feel the precariousness with which all American property is possessed. But let our imaginations transport us for a few moments to Boston, that seat of wretchedness will teach us wisdom, and instruct us for ever to renounce a power in whom we can have no trust. The inhabitants of that unfortunate city, who but a few months ago were in ease and affluence, have now no other alternative than to stay and starve, or turn out to beg. Endangered by the fire of their friends if they continue within the city, and plundered by the soldiery if they leave it. In their present condition they are prisoners without the hope of redemption, and in a general attack for their relief, they would be exposed to the fury of both armies.

Men of passive tempers look somewhat lightly over the offences of Britain, and, still hoping for the best, are apt to call out, *'Come we shall be friends again for all this.'* But examine the passions and feelings of mankind. Bring the doctrine of reconciliation to the touchstone of nature, and then tell me, whether you can hereafter love, honour, and faithfully serve the power that hath carried fire and sword into your land? If you cannot do all these, then are you only deceiving yourselves, and by your delay bringing ruin upon posterity. Your future connection with Britain, whom you can neither love nor honour, will be forced and unnatural, and being formed only on the plan of present convenience, will in a little time fall into a relapse more wretched than the first. But if you say, you can still pass the violations over, then I ask, Hath your house been burnt? Hath your property been destroyed before your face? Are your wife and children destitute of a bed to lie on, or bread to live on? Have you lost a parent or a child by their hands, and yourself the ruined and wretched survivor? If you have not, then are you not a judge of those who have. But if you have, and can still shake hands with the murderers, then are you unworthy the name of husband, father, friend, or lover, and whatever may be your rank or title in life, you have the heart of a coward, and the spirit of a sycophant. . . .

8. PHILLIS WHEATLEY

On Being Brought from
Africa to America (1773)
and To His Excellency
General Washington (1776)

Born in Gambia in western Africa, **PHILLIS WHEATLEY (c. 1753–1784)** became the first African American to publish a work of literature, and only the second woman in America to publish a book of poems. She was taken from Africa as a slave at age seven or eight and was sold to John and Susanna Wheatley of Boston in July 1761. She published her first poem in the *Newport Mercury* in 1767, and thereafter continued to write poetry—mostly elegies of personal acquaintances and prominent individuals. By the early 1770s, Wheatley had mastered eighteenth-century poetic form, but her verse clearly reflects an integration of African, European, and American influences. In 1773, after considerable controversy among Boston's leading men over the authenticity of her manuscript, Wheatley sailed to London to seek support for her first collection of poetry, which was published under the title *Poems on Various Subjects, Religious and Moral.* Shortly thereafter, she earned her freedom and returned to America. Combining religious imagery and political patriotism, the following poems reflect both the drive for American independence and the strong desire among blacks to be free. Widely regarded as the "founding mother" of African-American literature, Wheatley's poetry remains a powerful testament to the possibilities of black literary achievement under slavery.

SOURCE: Henry Louis Gates, Jr., and Nellie McKay et al., eds. *The Norton Anthology of African American Literature.* New York and London: W. W. Norton and Company, 1997.

SELECTED READINGS: Dickson D. Bruce, Jr., *The Origins of African American Literature, 1680–1865* (2001). Henry Louis Gates, Jr., *Figures in Black: Words, Signs, and the "Racial" Self* (1987). William H. Robinson, *Phillis Wheatley and Her Writings* (1984).

On Being Brought from Africa to America

'Twas mercy brought me from my *Pagan* land,
Taught my benighted soul to understand
That there's a God, that there's a *Saviour* too:
Once I redemption neither sought nor knew.
Some view our sable race with scornful eye,
"Their colour is a diabolic die."
Remember, *Christians, Negros,* black as *Cain,*
May be refin'd, and join th' angelic train.

To His Excellency General Washington

Sir,

I have taken the freedom to address your Excellency in the enclosed poem, and entreat your acceptance, though I am not insensible of its inaccuracies. Your being appointed by the Grand Continental Congress to be Generalissimo of the armies of North America, together with the fame of your virtues, excite sensations not easy to suppress. Your generosity, therefore, I presume, will pardon the attempt. Wishing your Excellency all possible success in the great cause you are so generously engaged in. I am, Your Excellency's most obedient humble servant,

Phillis Wheatley
1776

Celestial choir! enthron'd in realms of light,
Columbia's scenes of glorious toils I write.
While freedom's cause her anxious breast alarms,
She flashes dreadful in refulgent arms.
See mother earth her offspring's fate bemoan,
And nations gaze at scenes before unknown!
See the bright beams of heaven's revolving light
Involved in sorrows and veil of night!

The goddess comes, she moves divinely fair,
Olive and laurel bind her golden hair:
Wherever shines this native of the skies,
Unnumber'd charms and recent graces rise.

Muse! bow propitious while my pen relates
How pour her armies through a thousand gates,
As when Eolus heaven's fair face deforms,
Enwrapp'd in tempest and a night of storms;
Astonish'd ocean feels the wild uproar,
The refluent surges beat the sounding shore;
Or thick as leaves in Autumn's golden reign,
Such, and so many, moves the warrior's train.
In bright array they seek the work of war,
Where high unfurl'd the ensign waves in air.
Shall I to Washington their praise recite?
Enough thou know'st them in the fields of fight.
Thee, first in peace and honours,—we demand
The grace and glory of thy martial band.
Fam'd for thy valour, for thy virtues more,
Hear every tongue thy guardian aid implore!

One century scarce perform'd its destined round,
When Gallic powers Columbia's fury found;
And so may you, whoever dares disgrace
The land of freedom's heaven-defended race!
Fix'd are the eyes of nations on the scales,
For in their hopes Columbia's arm prevails.
Anon Britannia droops the pensive head,
While round increase the rising hills of dead.
Ah! cruel blindness to Columbia's state!
Lament thy thirst of boundless power too late.

Proceed, great chief, with virtue on thy side,
Thy ev'ry action let the goddess guide.
A crown, a mansion, and a throne that shine,
With gold unfading, WASHINGTON! be thine.

9. ABIGAIL ADAMS

Letter to John Adams
(1776)

ABIGAIL ADAMS (1744-1818) was one of the most politically influential women of the Revolutionary era. Born and raised in a prominent Congregationalist family in Weymouth, Massachusetts, she received no formal schooling, but made good use of her family's large private library. In 1764, she married John Adams, then a struggling Braintree attorney, and the couple moved to Boston, where they were both influenced by the growing revolutionary spirit there. Starting in 1774 and for most of the Revolution, the couple spent more time apart than together—John serving as a diplomat abroad, and Abigail raising their five children and managing the family farm and finances. Over the years, the Adamses generated an abundant correspondence that displays their remarkable intellect, political passion, and deep affection and respect for one another. Never shy or demure, Abigail was as likely to write about public matters as she was the affairs of the home, frequently challenging her husband on the most pressing issues of the day. Perhaps their most famous interaction came in a series of letters, written on the eve of the Revolution, in which Abigail urges John to "Remember the Ladies" in creating the new republic. Specifically, she advocated the abolition of laws—especially those dealing with education—that enforced the subordination of women to men. As with her life generally, this famous correspondence with John demonstrates Abigail's fierce advocacy for the political and social equality of women.

SOURCE: John Rhodehamel, ed. *The American Revolution: Writings from the War for Independence.* New York: Library of America, 2001.

SELECTED READINGS: Edith B. Gelles, *Portia: The World of Abigail Adams* (1992). Phyllis Levin, *Abigail Adams* (1987). Linda Kerber, *Women of the Republic: Intellect and Ideology in Revolutionary America* (1980).

Braintree March 31 1776

I wish you would ever write me a Letter half as long as I write you; and tell me if you may where your Fleet are gone? What sort of Defence Virginia can make against our common Enemy? Whether it is so situated as to make an able Defence? Are not the Gentery Lords and the common people vassals, are they not like the uncivilized Natives Brittain represents us to be? I hope their Riffel Men who have shewen themselves very savage and even Blood thirsty; are not a specimen of the Generality of the people.

I am willing to allow the Colony great merrit for having produced a Washington but they have been shamefully duped by a Dunmore.

I have sometimes been ready to think that the passion for Liberty cannot be Eaquelly Strong in the Breasts of those who have been accustomed to deprive their fellow Creatures of theirs. Of this I am certain that it is not founded upon that generous and Christian principal of doing to others as we would that others should do unto us.

Do not you want to see Boston; I am fearfull of the small pox, or I should have been in before this time. I got Mr. Crane to go to our House and see what state it was in. I find it has been occupied by one of the Doctors of a Regiment, very dirty, but no other damage has been done to it. The few things which were left in it are all gone. Cranch has the key which he never deliverd up. I have wrote to him for it and am determined to get it cleand as soon as possible and shut it up. I look upon it a new acquisition of property, a property which one month ago I did not value at a single Shilling, and could with pleasure have seen it in flames.

The Town in General is left in a better state than we expected, more oweing to a percipitate flight than any Regard to the inhabitants, tho some individuals discoverd a sense of honour and justice and have left the rent of the Houses in which they were, for the owners and the furniture unhurt, or if damaged sufficent to make it good.

Others have committed abominable Ravages. The Mansion House of your President is safe and the furniture unhurt whilst both the House and Furniture of the Solisiter General have fallen a prey to their own merciless party. Surely the very Fiends feel a Reverential awe for Virtue and patriotism, whilst they Detest the paricide and traitor.

I feel very differently at the approach of spring to what I did a month ago. We knew not then whether we could plant or sow with safety, whether when we had toild we could reap the fruits of our own industery, whether we could rest in our own Cottages, or whether we should not be driven from the sea coasts to seek shelter in the wilderness, but now we feel as if we might sit under our own vine and eat the good of the land.

I feel a gaieti de Coar to which before I was a stranger. I think the Sun looks brighter, the Birds sing more melodiously, and Nature puts on a more chearfull countanance. We feel a temporary peace, and the poor fugitives are returning to their deserted habitations.

Tho we felicitate ourselves, we sympathize with those who are trembling least the Lot of Boston should be theirs. But they cannot be in similar circumstances unless pusilanimity and cowardise should take possession of them. They have time and warning given them to see the Evil and shun it.—I long to hear that you have declared an independancy—and by the way in the new Code of Laws which I suppose it will be necessary for you to make I desire you would Remember the Ladies, and be more generous and favourable to them than your ancestors. Do not put such unlimited power into the hands of the Husbands. Remember all Men would be tyrants if they could. If perticuliar care and attention is not paid to the Laidies we are determined to foment a Rebelion, and will not hold ourselves bound by any Laws in which we have no voice, or Representation.

That your Sex are Naturally Tyrannical is a Truth so thoroughly established as to admit of no dispute, but such of you as wish to be happy willingly give up the harsh title of Master for the more tender and endearing one of Friend. Why then, not put it out of the power of the vicious and the Lawless to use us with cruelty and indignity with impunity. Men of Sense in all Ages abhor those customs which treat us only as the vassals of your Sex. Regard us then as Beings placed by providence under your protection and in immitation of the Supreem Being make use of that power only for our happiness.

10.

Declaration of Independence (1776)

The Declaration of Independence is the founding document of American political culture. Prior to 1776, the colonies were divided on the issue of independence; it wasn't until the publication of Thomas Paine's *Common Sense* that the majority of colonists began to think seriously about cutting ties with Britain. After King George III declared the colonies to be in a state of rebellion in early 1776, delegates from Massachusetts and Virginia, the two largest colonies, strongly advocated independence at the Second Continental Congress in Philadelphia. A committee of state delegates was then formed to draft a declaration to that effect. Known for his literary grace, Thomas Jefferson was charged with drafting the document, after which he submitted it first to John Adams and then to the other members for revisions. On June 28, the committee submitted the draft declaration to Congress, revisions were made, and "The Unanimous Declaration of the 13 States of America" was approved on July 4, 1776 (it was not signed, however, until August 2). In addition to a long list of grievances against the King, the Declaration laid out the fundamental political principles of the new nation. By placing "the King" in opposition to "the people," the Declaration replaced a monarchy based on hereditary rule with a republic based on the precepts of liberty and equality.

SOURCE: Eric Foner and John A. Garraty, eds. *The Reader's Companion to American History.* Boston: Houghton Mifflin, 1991.

SELECTED READINGS: Pauline Maier, *Sacred Scripture: The Declaration of Independence* (1997). Jay Fliegelman, *Declaring Independence: Jefferson, Natural Language, and the Culture of Performance* (1993). Garry Wills, *Inventing America: Jefferson's Declaration of Independence* (1978).

The unanimous declaration of the thirteen United States of America

When, in the course of human events, it becomes necessary for one people to dissolve the political bonds which have connected them with another, and to assume, among the powers of the earth, the separate and equal station to which the laws of nature and of nature's God entitle them, a decent respect to the opinions of mankind requires that they should declare the causes which impel them to the separation.

We hold these truths to be self-evident: That all men are created equal; that they are endowed by their Creator with certain unalienable rights; that among these are life, liberty, and the pursuit of happiness; that, to secure these rights, governments are instituted among men, deriving their just powers from the consent of the governed; that whenever any form of government becomes destructive of these ends, it is the right of the people to alter or to abolish it, and to institute new government, laying its foundation on such principles, and organizing its powers in such form, as to them shall seem most likely to effect their safety and happiness. Prudence, indeed, will dictate that governments long established should not be changed for light and transient causes; and accordingly all experience hath shown that mankind are more disposed to suffer, while evils are sufferable, than to right themselves by abolishing the forms to which they are accustomed. But when a long train of abuses and usurpations, pursuing invariably the same object, evinces a design to reduce them under absolute despotism, it is their right, it is their duty, to throw off such government, and to provide new guards for their future security. Such has been the patient sufferance of these colonies; and such is now the necessity which constrains them to alter their former systems of government. The history of the present King of Great Britain is a history of repeated injuries and usurpations, all having in direct object the establishment of an absolute tyranny over these states. To prove this, let facts be submitted to a candid world.

He has refused his assent to laws, the most wholesome and necessary for the public good.

He has forbidden his governors to pass laws of immediate and pressing importance, unless suspended in their operation till his assent should be obtained; and, when so suspended, he has utterly neglected to attend to them.

He has refused to pass other laws for the accommodation of large districts of people, unless those people would relinquish the right of representation in the legislature, a right inestimable to them, and formidable to tyrants only.

He has called together legislative bodies at places unusual, uncomfortable, and distant from the depository of their public records, for the sole purpose of fatiguing them into compliance with his measures.

He has dissolved representative houses repeatedly, for opposing, with manly firmness, his invasions on the rights of the people.

He has refused for a long time, after such dissolutions, to cause others to be elected; whereby the legislative powers, incapable of annihilation, have returned to the people, at large for their exercise; the state remaining, in the mean time, exposed to all the dangers of invasions from without and convulsions within.

He has endeavored to prevent the population of these states; for that purpose obstructing the laws for naturalization of foreigners; refusing to pass others to encourage their migration hither, and raising the conditions of new appropriations of lands.

He has obstructed the administration of justice, by refusing his assent to laws for establishing judiciary powers.

He has made judges dependent on his will alone, for the tenure of their offices, and the amount and payment of their salaries.

He has erected a multitude of new offices, and sent hither swarms of officers to harass our people and eat out their substance.

He has kept among us, in times of peace, standing armies, without the consent of our legislatures.

He has affected to render the military independent of, and superior to, the civil power.

He has combined with others to subject us to a jurisdiction foreign to our constitution, and unacknowledged by our laws, giving his assent to their acts of pretended legislation:

For quartering large bodies of armed troops among us;

For protecting them, by a mock trial, from punishment for any murders which they should commit on the inhabitants of these states;

For cutting off our trade with all parts of the world;

For imposing taxes on us without our consent;

For depriving us, in many cases, of the benefits of trial by jury;

For transporting us beyond seas, to be tried for pretended offenses;

For abolishing the free system of English laws in a neighboring province, establishing therein an arbitrary government, and enlarging its boundaries, so as to render it at once an example and fit instrument for introducing the same absolute rule into these colonies;

For taking away our charters, abolishing our most valuable laws, and altering fundamentally the forms of our governments;

For suspending our own legislatures, and declaring themselves invested with power to legislate for us in all cases whatsoever.

He has abdicated government here, by declaring us out of his protection and waging war against us.

He has plundered our seas, ravaged our coasts, burned our towns, and destroyed the lives of our people.

He is at this time transporting large armies of foreign mercenaries to complete the works of death, desolation, and tyranny already begun with circumstances of cruelty and perfidy scarcely paralleled in the most barbarous ages, and totally unworthy the head of a civilized nation.

He has constrained our fellow-citizens, taken captive on the high seas, to bear arms against their country, to become the executioners of their friends and brethren, or to fall themselves by their hands.

He has excited domestic insurrection among us, and has endeavored to bring on the inhabitants of our frontiers the merciless Indian savages, whose known rule of warfare is an undistinguished destruction of all ages, sexes, and conditions.

In every stage of these oppressions we have petitioned for redress in the most humble terms; our repeated petitions have been answered only by repeated injury. A prince, whose character is thus marked by every act which may define a tyrant, is unfit to be the ruler of a free people.

Nor have we been wanting in our attentions to our British brethren. We have warned them, from time to time, of attempts by their legislature to extend an unwarrantable jurisdiction over us. We have reminded them of the circumstances of our emigration and settlement here. We have appealed to their native justice and magnanimity; and we have conjured them, by the ties of our common kindred, to disavow these usurpations, which would inevitably interrupt our connections and correspondence. They, too, have been deaf to the voice of justice and of consanguinity. We must, therefore, acquiesce in the necessity which denounces our separation, and hold them, as we hold the rest of mankind, enemies in war, in peace friends.

We, therefore, the representatives of the United States of America, in General Congress assembled, appealing to the Supreme Judge of the world for the rectitude of our intentions, do, in the name and by the authority of the good people of these colonies, solemnly publish and declare, that these United Colonies are, and of right ought to be, FREE AND INDEPENDENT STATES; that they are absolved from all allegiance to the British crown, and that all political connection between them and the state of Great Britain is, and ought to be, totally dissolved; and that, as free and independent states, they have full power to levy war, conclude peace, contract alliances, establish commerce, and do all other acts and things which independent states may of right do. And for the support of this declaration, with a firm reliance on the protection of Divine Providence, we mutually pledge to each other our lives, our fortunes, and our sacred honor.

John Hancock
and fifty-five others

11. THOMAS JEFFERSON

An Act for Establishing
Religious Freedom
(1785)

THOMAS JEFFERSON (1743-1826) was one of the most important political figures in the Age of Revolution. Born and raised in Virginia, the very well educated Jefferson began a successful law practice in 1767 and became active in colonial politics soon thereafter. Convinced that the colonists had a natural right to govern themselves, he was one of the early advocates for independence, helping to author the famous Declaration in 1776. Jefferson's political ascendancy was based, as his political rival and friend John Adams noted, on "a reputation for literature, science, and a happy talent for composition." Throughout the Revolution, Jefferson held a number of posts. He later served as the first secretary of state under George Washington, as vice president under John Adams, and, from 1800–1808, as the third president of the United States. Responding to local agitation for religious tolerance, Jefferson introduced his statute on religious freedom to the Virginia Assembly in 1779, but it was not passed until 1786. It remains one of the strongest defenses of religious pluralism ever written in American history.

SOURCE: Samuel Eliot Morison, ed. *Sources and Documents Illustrating the American Revolution, 1764–1788.* 2nd edition. London and New York: Oxford University Press, 1965.

SELECTED READINGS: Joseph Ellis, *American Sphinx: The Character of Thomas Jefferson* (1997). Peter S. Onuf, ed., *Jeffersonian Legacies* (1993). Noble E. Cunningham, Jr., *In Pursuit of Reason: The Life of Thomas Jefferson* (1987).

I. Whereas Almighty God hath created the mind free; that all attempts to influence it by temporal punishments or burthens, or by civil incapacitations, tend only to beget habits of hypocrisy and meanness, and are a departure from the plan of the Holy author of our religion, who being Lord both of body and mind, yet chose not to propagate it by coercions on either, as was in his Almighty power to do; that the impious presumption of legislators and rulers, civil as well as ecclesiastical, who being themselves but fallible and uninspired men, have assumed dominion over the faith of others, setting up their own opinions and modes of thinking as the only true and infallible, and as such endeavouring to impose them on others, hath established and maintained false religions over the greatest part of the world, and through all time; that to compel a man to furnish contributions of money for the propagation of opinions which he disbelieves, is sinful and tyrannical; that even the forcing him to support this or that teacher of his own religious persuasion, is depriving him of the comfortable liberty of giving his contributions to the particular pastor whose morals he would make his pattern, and whose powers he feels most persuasive to righteousness, and is withdrawing from the ministry those temporary rewards, which proceeding from an approbation of their personal conduct, are an additional incitement to earnest and unremitting labours for the instruction of mankind; that our civil rights have no dependence on our religious opinions, any more than our opinions in physics or geometry; that therefore the proscribing any citizen as unworthy the public confidence by laying upon him an incapacity of being called to offices of trust and emolument, unless he profess or renounce this or that religious opinion, is depriving him injuriously of those privileges and advantages to which in common with his fellow-citizens he has a natural right; that it tends only to corrupt the principles of that religion it is meant to encourage, by bribing with a monopoly of worldly honours and emoluments, those who will externally profess and conform to it; that though indeed these are criminal who do not withstand such temptation, yet neither are those innocent who lay the bait in their way; that to suffer the civil magistrate to intrude his powers into the field of opinion, and to restrain the profession or propagation of principles on supposition of their ill tendency, is a dangerous fallacy, which at once destroys all religious liberty, because he being of course judge of that tendency will make his opinions the rule of judgment, and approve or condemn the sentiments of others only as they shall square with or differ from his own; that it is time enough for the rightful purposes of civil government, for its officers to interfere when principles break out into overt acts against peace and good order; and finally, that truth is great and will prevail if left to herself, that she is the proper and sufficient antagonist to error, and has nothing to fear from the conflict, unless by human interposition disarmed of her natural weapons, free argument and debate, errors ceasing to be dangerous when it is permitted freely to contradict them.

II. Be it enacted by the General Assembly, that no man shall be compelled to frequent or support any religious worship, place or ministry whatsoever, nor shall be enforced, restrained, molested, or burthened in his body or goods, nor shall otherwise suffer on account of his religious opinions or belief; but that all men shall be free to profess, and by argument to maintain their opinion in matters of religion, and that the same shall in no wise diminish, enlarge or affect their civil capacities.

III. And though we well know that this Assembly, elected by the people for the ordinary purposes of legislation only, have no power to restrain the acts of succeeding Assemblies, constituted with powers equal to our own, and that therefore to declare this Act to be irrevocable would be of no effect in law; yet as we are free to declare, and do declare, that the rights hereby asserted are of the natural rights of mankind, and that if any Act shall hereafter be passed to repeal the present, or to narrow its operation, such Act will be an infringement of natural right.

Petition from Shays' Rebellion
(1786)

The American Revolution was not exclusively the work of urban elites. From the very beginning, tensions emerged not only between the colonies and England, but also between "local" and "national" interests, farmers and merchants, rural areas and the eastern port cities. In 1786 and 1787, American farmers from New Hampshire to South Carolina took up arms in protest against state and local enforcement of debt assessment and tax collection. Led by Daniel Shays, a former captain in the Continental Army, the most serious and successful rebellion took place in Massachusetts, where bad harvests and high taxes threatened to destroy local farms. Beginning in the summer of 1786, rebel farmers seized control of the federal arsenal in Springfield, and resisted local merchants and politicians before being suppressed by the state militia the following winter. Shays' Rebellion never seriously threatened the fragile new political order, but it did inspire a great deal of concern among the political establishment, leading to significant debate about rights, property, and debt at the Constitutional Convention. The following petition, submitted by several farmers in the Town of Greenwich to the Massachusetts Assembly, expresses the deep concern about debt and bankruptcy that inspired Shays' Rebellion.

SOURCE: Samuel Eliot Morison, ed. *Sources and Documents Illustrating the American Revolution, 1764–1788.* 2nd edition. London and New York: Oxford University Press, 1965.

SELECTED READINGS: Robert A. Gross, ed., *In Debt to Shays: The Bicentennial of Agrarian Rebellion* (1993). Robert A. Feer, *Shays' Rebellion* (1988). David Szatmary, *Shays' Rebellion: The Making of an Agrarian Insurrection* (1980).

To the Honourable Senate and the House of Representatives in General Court assembled att their next session:

A Petition of the Subscribers humbly sheweth—

That in the time of the late war, being desirous to defend secure and promote the wrights and liberties of the people, we spared no pains but freely granted all that aid and assistance of every kind that our civel fathers required of us.

We are sencable also that a great debt is justly brought upon us by the war and are as willing to pay our shares towards itt as we are to injoy our shares in independancy and constatutional priviledges in the Commonwealth, if itt was in our power. And we beleve that if prudant mesuers ware taken and a moderate quantety of medium to circulate so that our property might sel for the real value we mite in proper time pay said debt.

But with the greatest submittion we beg leave to informe your Honours that unles something takes place more favourable to the people, in a little time att least, one half of our inhabitants in our oppinion will become banckerupt—how can itt be otherwise—the constables are dayly vandering our property both real and personal, our land after itt is prised by the best judges under oath is sold for about one third of the value of itt, our cattle about one half the value, the best inglesh hay thirteen shilings per tone, intervale hay att six shilings per tone, and other things att the same rate. And we beg leave further to informe your honours that sutes att law are very numerous and the atturneys in our oppinion very extravigent and oppressive in their demands. And when we compute the taxes laid upon us the five preceeding years: the state and county, town and class taxes, the amount is equil to what our farms will rent for. Sirs, in this situation what have we to live on—no money to be had; our estates dayly posted and sold, as above described. What can your honours ask of us unles a paper curancy or some other medium be provided so that we may pay our taxes and debts. Suerly your honours are not strangers to the distresses of the people but doe know that many of our good inhabitants are now confined in gole for det and for taxes: maney have fled, others wishing to flee to the State of New York or some other State; and we believe that for two years past four inhabitents have removed from this State to some other State to one that has come from some other State to settle in this State.

Honoured Sirs, are not these imprisonments and fleeing away of our good inhabitents very injurious to the credit or honour of the Commonwealth? will not the people in the neighbouring States say of this State: altho' the Massachusets bost of their fine constatution, their government is such that itt devours their inhabitents? Notwithstanding all these distresses, we hear of no abatement of sallerys, but his Excellency the Governor must be paid eleven hundred a year out of the moneys collected as before mentoned, and other sallerys and grants to other gentlemen, as your honours very well know. Iff these things are honest, just and rite, we sincearly wish to be convinced of itt: but we honestly confess itt is beyond our skill to reconsile these sallerys and grants with the principles of our Constatution (viz.) piaty, justice, moderation, temperance, etc.

We observe in the proclamation lately sent out by his Excellency that the promotion of piaty and virtue is highly recommended. We rejoice att the recommendation, and beg leave to mention that maxim, example is stronger than precipt; and who can be more likely to bring forward a reformation by example than the honourable members of the General Court, by a line of conduct agreeable to Scripture and the precipts of the Constatution. If your honours finde anything above mentioned worthy of notice, we earnestly pray that they may be candedly considered, for we have weighted, hoped and expected that the present General Court would point out sum way whereby the people might be releaved. We therefore most humbly pray your honours to admitt a paper currancy and make itt a tender in all payments whatsoever, or some other way to releave your petitioners as your honours in your grate wisdom shall think most proper. And iff no other can be found out, pray send us such a commitee as your honours can confide in to apprise our estates and take them att your own price. And as in duty bound shall every pray

	Jeremiah Powers.
	Nehemiah Stebbins.
	Zebedee Osborn
January 16th 1786.	[and 57 other signatures].

13.

The Bill of Rights
(1791)

As military fighting during the Revolution ceased, the battleground for the new nation shifted once again to the realm of law and politics. One of the principal disagreements among delegates to the Constitutional Convention in Philadelphia had to do with the balance of power between the federal government, state legislatures, and individual citizens. The debate took place among the Federalists, who favored a strong, centralized authority, and the anti-Federalists, who were concerned with states rights and individual liberties. At the Convention, the former prevailed, but only after promising to amend the Constitution, ratified in 1789, with a "Bill of Rights" that would assuage the concerns of the latter. Inspired by James Madison—the Federalist icon who helped to broker the Convention deal with anti-Federalists—the proposed amendments were submitted to Congress, and accepted, in September 1789. Following much public debate and acrimony, Virginia became the tenth state to ratify them on December 15, 1791, thus making the Bill of Rights an official part of the U.S. Constitution. Comprised of the first ten amendments, the Bill of Rights safeguards a number of important rights—including the right to free speech and assembly (First Amendment), the right to bear arms (Second), the right to due process (Fifth), and the right to counsel and public trial by jury (Sixth). The final act of the Revolution, the Bill of Rights has been the site of fierce debates over constitutional interpretation throughout American history.

SOURCE: Eric Foner and John A. Garraty, eds. *The Reader's Companion to American History.* Boston: Houghton Mifflin, 1991.

SELECTED READINGS: Akhil Reed Amar, *The Bill of Rights: Creation and Reconstruction* (1998). Michael J. Lacy and Knud Haakonssen, eds., *A Culture of Rights:*

The Bill of Rights in Philosophy, Politics, and Law, 1791–1991 (1991). Robert Allen Rutland, *The Birth of the Bill of Rights, 1776–1791* (1991).

Amendment I

Congress shall make no law respecting an establishment of religion, or prohibiting the free exercise thereof; or abridging the freedom of speech, or of the press; or the right of the people peaceably to assemble, and to petition the government for a redress of grievances.

Amendment II

A well-regulated militia being necessary to the security of a free State, the right of the people to keep and bear arms shall not be infringed.

Amendment III

No soldier shall, in time of peace, be quartered in any house without the consent of the owner, nor in time of war, but in a manner to be prescribed by law.

Amendment IV

The right of the people to be secure in their persons, houses, papers, and effects, against unreasonable searches and seizures, shall not be violated, and no warrants shall issue but upon probable cause, supported by oath or affirmation, and particularly describing the place to be searched, and the persons or things to be seized.

Amendment V

No person shall be held to answer for a capital, or otherwise infamous crime, unless on a presentment or indictment of a grand jury, except in cases arising in the land or naval forces, or in the militia, when in actual service in time of war or public danger; nor shall any person be subject for the same offense to be twice put in jeopardy of life or limb; nor shall be compelled in any criminal case to be a witness against himself, nor be deprived of life, liberty, or property, without due process of law; nor shall private property be taken for public use without just compensation.

Amendment VI

In all criminal prosecutions, the accused shall enjoy the right to a speedy and public trial, by an impartial jury of the State and district wherein the crime shall have been committed, which district shall have been previously ascertained by law, and to be informed of the nature and cause of the accusation; to be confronted with the witnesses against him; to have compulsory process for obtaining witnesses in his favor, and to have the assistance of counsel for his defense.

Amendment VII

In suits at common law, where the value in controversy shall exceed twenty dollars, the right of trial by jury shall be preserved, and no fact tried by a jury shall be otherwise reexamined in any court of the United States, than according to the rules of the common law.

Amendment VIII

Excessive bail shall not be required, nor excessive fines imposed, nor cruel and unusual punishments inflicted.

Amendment IX

The enumeration in the Constitution, of certain rights, shall not be construed to deny or disparage others retained by the people.

Amendment X

The powers not delegated to the United States by the Constitution, nor prohibited by it to the States, are reserved to the States respectively, or to the people.

14. PRINCE HALL

A Charge

(1797)

PRINCE HALL (c. 1735–1807) was Boston's most outspoken black activist during the Revolutionary era. Born a slave, Hall gained his freedom in 1770, and thereafter worked as a craftsman and community organizer. In 1775, he and fourteen other free blacks formed a fraternal society devoted to education, community building, and moral uplift. At first informal, Hall's organization would, on May 6, 1787, become African Lodge No. 459, a Masonic order that inspired the formation of similar fraternal societies in other nothern cities. In 1808, the African Grand Lodge renamed the national order the "Prince Hall Masons," in honor of its distinguished founder. Throughout the Revolution and early republic, Hall was among the most vociferous advocates for liberty and equality. From the 1770s to the 1790s, Hall petitioned the Massachusetts legislature to end slavery, requested financial assistance to support African emigration, and opened up a school for black children, the first of its kind in Boston, in his home. A gifted writer, Hall published numerous writings to promote community among blacks and to combat prejudice and inequality. His second "Charge," published in 1797, addressed the plight of black Americans and the need for strong community in the wake of racial hostility. Invoking the example of Haiti—where a successful slave rebellion led to the creation of the first independent black nation—Hall's popular tract was an eloquent example of free black resistance to discrimination in the Age of Revolution.

SOURCE: Richard Newman, Patrick Rael, and Phillip Lapsansky, eds. *Pamphlets of Protest: An Anthology of Early African-American Protest Literature, 1790–1860.* New York and London: Routledge, 2001.

SELECTED READINGS: James and Lois Horton, *In Hope of Liberty: Culture, Community, and Protest Among Northern Free Blacks, 1700–1860* (1997). Charles H.

Wesley, *Prince Hall: Life and Legacy* (1977). Sidney Kaplan, *The Black Presence in the Era of the American Revolution* (1973).

Now my brethren, as we see and experience that all things here are frail and changeable and nothing here to be depended upon: Let us seek those things which are above, which are sure, and stedfast, and unchangeable, and at the same time let us pray to Almighty God, while we remain in the tabernacle, that he would give us the grace of patience and strength to bear up under all our troubles, which at this day God knows we have our share. Patience I say, for were we not possess'd of a great measure of it you could not bear up under the daily insults you meet with in the streets of Boston; much more on public days of recreation, how are you shamefully abus'd, and that at such a degree that you may truly be said to carry your lives in your hands, and the arrows of death are flying about your heads; helpless old women have their clothes torn off their backs, even to the exposing of their nakedness; and by whom are these disgraceful and abusive actions committed, not by the men born and bred in Boston, for they are better bred, but by a mob or horde of shameless, low-lived, envious, spiteful persons, some of them not long since, servants in gentlemen's kitchens, scouring knives, tending horses, and driving chaise. 'Twas said by a gentleman who saw that filthy behaviour in the common, that in all the places he had been in, he never saw so cruel behaviour in all his life, and that a slave in the West-Indies, on Sunday or holidays enjoys himself and friends without any molestation. Not only this man, but many in town who hath seen their behaviour to you, and that without any provocation—twenty or thirty cowards fall upon one man—have wonder'd at the patience of the Blacks: 'tis not for want of courage in you, for they know that they dare not face you man for man, but in a mob, which we despise, and had rather suffer wrong than to do wrong, to the disturbance of the community and the disgrace of our reputation: for every good citizen doth honor to the laws of the State where he resides.

My brethren, let us not be cast down under these and many other abuses we at present labour under: for the darkest is before the break of day. My brethren, let us remember what a dark day it was with our African brethren six years ago, in the French West-Indies. Nothing but the snap of the whip was heard from morning to evening; hanging, broken on the wheel, burning, and all manner of tortures inflicted on those unhappy people for nothing else but to gratify their masters pride, wantonness, and cruelty: but blessed be God, the scene is changed; they now confess that God hath no respect of persons, and therefore receive them as their friends, and treat them as brothers. Thus doth Ethiopia begin to stretch forth her hand, from a sink of slavery to freedom and equality.

CHAPTER

TWO

Utopian Visions

15. LYMAN BEECHER

Six Sermons on Intemperance
(1826)

LYMAN BEECHER (1775–1863) was a gifted theologian, educator, and writer who helped to refashion American Protestantism according to the reform impulse that guided his life. Born in New Haven, Connecticut, Beecher studied theology at Yale College, and was ordained as a Presbyterian minister in 1799. That same year, he married Roxanne Foote, and together they had nine children, several of whom—including Henry Ward, Catharine, and Harriet— would become influential nineteenth-century figures in their own right. Beecher's sometimes controversial reform efforts extended in many directions, and he was principally responsible for popularizing a gospel of free will, immediate repentance, and social benevolence throughout New England, New York, and Ohio. His 1825 sermons against "the fiery waves of intemperance" earned him great fame. First published in 1826, Beecher's *Six Sermons on Intemperance* became one of the leading tracts of the antebellum temperance crusade. His powerful call for total abstinence from alcohol inspired a national movement to ensure the "moral health" of the young republic.

SOURCE: Lyman Beecher. *Six Sermons on the Nature, Occasions, Signs, Evils, and Remedy of Intemperance.* Boston: T. R. Martin, 1827.

SELECTED READINGS: Robert Abzug, *Cosmos Crumbling: American Reform and the Religious Imagination* (1994). Vincent Harding, *A Certain Magnificence: Lyman Beecher and the Transformation of American Protestantism, 1775–1863* (1991). James W. Fraser, *Pedagogue for God's Kingdom: Lyman Beecher and the Second Great Awakening* (1985).

We execrate the cruelties of the slave trade—the husband torn from the bosom of his wife—the son from his father—brothers and sisters separated forever—whole families in a moment ruined! But are there no similar enormities to be witnessed in the United States? None indeed perpetrated by the bayonet—but many, very many, perpetrated by intemperance.

Every year thousands of families are robbed of fathers, brothers, husbands, friends. Every year widows and orphans are multiplied, and grey hairs are brought with sorrow to the grave—no disease makes such inroads upon families, blasts so many hopes, destroys so many lives, and causes so many mourners to go about the streets, because man goeth to his long home.

We have heard of the horrors of the middle passage—the transportation of slaves—the chains—the darkness—the stench—the mortality and living madness of woe—and it is dreadful. But bring together the victims of intemperance, and crowd them into one vast lazar-house, and sights of woe quite as appalling would meet your eyes.

Yes, in this nation there is a middle passage of slavery, and darkness, and chains, and disease, and death. But it is a middle passage, not from Africa to America, but from time to eternity, and not of slaves whom death will release from suffering, but of those whose sufferings at death do but just begin. Could all the sighs of these captives be wafted on one breeze, it would be loud as thunder. Could all their tears be assembled, they would be like the sea.

The health of a nation is a matter of vast importance, and none may directly and avowedly sport with it. The importation and dissemination of fevers for filthy lucre's sake, would not be endured, and he who should import and plant the seed of trees, which, like the fabled Upas, poisoned the atmosphere, and paved the earth around with bones, would meet with universal execration. The construction of morasses and stagnant lakes, sending out poisonous exhalations, and depopulating the country around, would soon be stopped by the interposition of law. And should a foreign army land upon our shores, to levy such a tax upon us as intemperance levies, and to threaten our liberties as intemperance threatens them, and to inflict such enormous sufferings as intemperance inflicts, no mortal power could resist the swelling tide of indignation that would overwhelm it.

It is only in the form of ardent spirits in the way of a lawful trade extended over the entire land, that fevers may be imported and disseminated—that trees of death may be planted—that extensive morasses may be opened, and a moral *miasma* spread over the nation—and that an armed host may land, to levy upon us enormous taxations, to undermine our liberties, bind our hands, and put our feet in fetters. This dreadful work is going on, and yet the nation sleeps. Say not that all these evils result from the abuse of ardent spirits; for as human nature is constituted, the abuse is as certain as any of the laws of nature. The commerce therefore, in ardent spirits, which produces no good, and produces a certain and an immense amount of evil, must be regarded as an unlawful commerce, and ought, upon every principle of humanity, and patriotism, and conscience, and religion, to be abandoned and proscribed.

16. THOMAS SKIDMORE

The Rights of Man to Property
(1829)

THOMAS SKIDMORE (1790–1832) was a self-taught artisan who became one of the most important labor radicals of the Jacksonian period. Born in Newton, Connecticut, Skidmore was a precocious child who spent much of his early life teaching and travelling up and down the eastern seaboard. In 1819, he moved to New York City, started work as a machinist, and began to develop a radical critique of property ownership. In April 1829, following an attempt by local employers to extend the workday, Skidmore and his fellow mechanics founded the Working Men's Party. This new organization—combining older traditions of agrarianism with emerging forms of trade unionism—adopted much of Skidmore's theory of property redistribution, which formed the basis of his pamphlet, *The Rights of Man to Property* (1829). Drawing from the work of Enlightenment philosophers as well as American radicals like Thomas Paine, Skidmore's only published work called for the abolition of private property and the redistribution of wealth. His analysis was the most radical challenge posed to early American capitalism, inspiring a number of nineteenth-century land and labor reforms.

SOURCE: Thomas Skidmore. *The Rights of Man to Property.* New York: Burt Franklin, 1829.

SELECTED READINGS: Sean Wilentz, *Chants Democratic: New York City and the Rise of the American Working Class, 1788–1850* (1984). Edward Pessen, *Most Uncommon Jacksonians: The Radical Leaders of the Early Labor Movement* (1967). Walter Hugins, *Jacksonian Democracy and the Working Class: A Study of the New York Workingmen's Movement, 1829–1837* (1960).

There is no man of the least reflection, who has not observed, that the effect, in all ages and countries, of the possession of great and undue wealth, is, to allow those who possess it, to live on the labor of others. And yet there is no truth more readily, cheerfully, and universally acknowledged, than that the *personal* exertions of each individual of the human race, are exclusively and unalienably his own.

It would seem, then, to be no bad specimen of argument, to say, inasmuch as great wealth is an instrument which is uniformly used to extort from others, their property in their personal qualities and efforts—that it ought to be taken away from its possessor, on the same principle, that a sword or a pistol may be wrested from a robber, who shall undertake to accomplish the same effect, in a different manner.

One thing must be obvious to the plainest understanding; that as long as property is unequal; or rather, as long as it is so enormously unequal, as we see it at present, that those who possess it, *will* live on the labor of others, and themselves perform none, or if any, a very disproportionate share, of that toil which attends them as a condition of their existence, and without the performance of which, they have no *just* right to preserve or retain that existence, even for a single hour.

It is not possible to maintain a doctrine to the contrary of this position, without, at the same time, maintaining an absurdity no longer tolerated in enlightened countries; that a part, and that a very great part, of the human race, are doomed, of right, to the slavery of toil, while others are born, only to enjoy.

I, for one, disavow every such doctrine. Even if it be admitted that the present possessors of property, in any country, are the true and rightful owners of it, beyond any question, still I maintain that they have no just right to use it in such a manner, as to extract from others, the result of their labors, for the purpose of exempting themselves from the necessity of laboring as much as others must labor, for a like amount of enjoyment. The moment that any possessor of property, makes such use of it, I care not how, nor under the sanction of what law, or system of laws, as to live in idleness, partial or total, thus supporting himself, more or less, on the labors of others; that moment he contravenes and invades the rights of others; and has placed himself in the condition which would justify the party injured, in dispossessing the aggressor, of the instrument of his aggression. . . .

. . . We live near to a great epoch, in the history of our own country—the Revolution that separated us from England—we are acquainted with the distinguished men, who performed a prominent part, as well in the separation of the two countries, as in erecting the new governments that succeeded. We are able to know their minds, and to judge for ourselves, how far they were adequate to institute government, on principles of original right; for it was on such principles *as they understood them*, that they supported the Revolution and erected the political edifices that in consequence became necessary.

Of all these, no man, more than Mr. Jefferson, deserves to be considered, as possessing in his own mind, not only "the standard of the man," but the standard of the age. If there was any one capable of ascending to first principles, it was he; and if it was not to be expected of him, how was it to be expected of any one else? Yet Mr. Jefferson speaks of the rights of man, in terms, which when they come to be investigated closely, appear to be very defective and equivocal. I do not mean, that he thought or meant them so; for it is evident that the contrary was the fact. Let us quote him, however; let us weigh his expressions; let us arrive at his intentions in the most legitimate manner: and then see, if I am borne out, in my declaration. If I am, I shall be sustained. If I am not, I shall fail, and deserve to do so. He says:—

"We hold these truths to be self-evident; that all men are created equal; that they are endowed by their Creator with certain unalienable rights; that among these are life, liberty, and the *pursuit of happiness.*" These are his words in the declaration of American Independence.

Whoever looks over the face of the world, and surveys the population of all countries; our own, as well as any and every other; will see it divided into rich and poor; into the hundred who have every thing, and the million who have nothing. If, then, Mr. Jefferson, had made use of the word *property,* instead of *"The pursuit of happiness,"* I should have agreed with him. Then his language would have been clear and intelligible, and strictly conformable to natural right. For I hold, that man's natural right to *life* or *liberty,* is not more sacred or unalienable, than his right to property. But if property is to descend only to particular individuals from the previous generation, and if the many are born, having neither parents nor any one else, to give them property, equal in amount to that which the sons of the rich, receive, from their fathers and other testators, how is it established that they are created equal? In the pursuit of happiness, is property of no consequence? Can any one be as happy without property of any kind, as with it? Is even liberty and life to be preserved without it? Do we not every day, see multitudes, in order to acquire property, in the very pursuit of that happiness which Mr. Jefferson classes among the unalienable rights of man, obliged to sacrifice both liberty and health and often ultimately life, into the bargain? If then property be so essential and indispensable in the pursuit of happiness, as it appears to be, how can it be said, that I am created with an equal right to this happiness—with another, when I must purchase property of him, with labor and suffering—and when he is under no necessity to purchase the like of me at the same costly price? If we are created equal—how has he the right to monopolize all, or even an undue share of the property of the preceding generation? If, then, even the rights of liberty and life, are so insecure and precarious, without property—how very essential to *their* preservation is it, that "the pursuit of happiness"—should be so construed, as to afford title to that, without which, the rights of life and liberty are but an empty name?

17. CHARLES GRANDISON FINNEY

Lectures on the Revivals of Religion
(1835)

CHARLES GRANDISON FINNEY (1792–1875) was the most prominent evangelical preacher in antebellum America. Born into a New England farming family with ties to the Revolution, Finney experienced a religious conversion at the age of twenty-nine and became a Presbyterian minister in 1823. For more than a decade, Finney led a series of evangelical revivals in the so-called burned-over district—the booming urban centers located along the newly completed Erie Canal—in upstate New York. Finney's "western revivals" attracted a great deal of attention, from both converts and critics, for their emotional public testimonies, "promiscuous" (male and female) congregations, and insistence on immediate Christian conversion. Finney's *Lectures on the Revivals of Religion,* a collection of lectures he delivered at New York's Broadway Tabernacle, argued for the importance of ongoing evangelical revivals to the meaningful practice and performance of religion. Published as a book in 1835, these lectures earned him both international acclaim and widespread opposition among more conservative Protestants, prompting Finney's own conversion to Congregationalism and relocation to Ohio, where he would later serve as president of Oberlin College. Finney's notion of "true perfection," which he preached and refined throughout his prolific career, inspired many antebellum radicals—from temperance crusaders to abolitionists—to remake their world in God's holy image.

SOURCE: William G. McLoughlin, ed. *Lectures on Revivals of Religion by Charles Grandison Finney.* Cambridge, MA: The Belknap Press of Harvard University Press, 1960.

SELECTED READINGS: Bonnie C. Harvey, *Charles Finney: Apostle of Revival* (1999). Charles E. Hambrick-Stowe, *Charles G. Finney and the Spirit of American*

Evangelicalism (1996). Paul Johnson, *A Shopkeeper's Millennium: Society and Revivals in Rochester, New York, 1815–1837* (1978).

I Am to Show What a Revival Is

It presupposes that the church is sunk down in a backslidden state, and a revival consists in the return of the church from her backslidings, and in the connversion of sinners.

1. A revival always includes conviction of sin on the part of the church. Backslidden professors cannot wake up and begin right away in the service of God, without deep searchings of heart. The fountains of sin need to be broken up. In a true revival, Christians are always brought under such convictions; they see their sins in such a light, that often they find it impossible to maintain a hope of their acceptance with God. It does not always go to that extent; but there are always, in a genuine revival, deep convictions of sin, and often cases of abandoning all hope.

2. Backslidden Christians will be brought to repentance. A revival is nothing else than a new beginning of obedience to God. Just as in the case of a converted sinner, the first step is a deep repentance, a breaking down of heart, a getting down into the dust before God, with deep humility, and forsaking of sin.

3. Christians will have their faith renewed. While they are in their backslidden state they are blind to the state of sinners. Their hearts are as hard as marble. The truths of the Bible only appear like a dream. They admit it to be all true; their conscience and their judgment assent to it; but their faith does not see it standing out in bold relief, in all the burning realities of eternity. But when they enter into a revival, they no longer see men as trees walking, but they see things in that strong light which will renew the love of God in their hearts. This will lead them to labor zealously to bring others to him. They will feel grieved that others do not love God, when they love him so much. And they will set themselves feelingly to persuade their neighbors to give him their hearts. So their love to men will be renewed. They will be filled with a tender and burning love for souls. They will have a longing desire for the salvation of the whole world. They will be in agony for individuals whom they want to have saved; their friends, relations, enemies. They will not only be urging them to give their hearts to God, but they will carry them to God in the arms of faith, and with strong crying and tears beseech God to have mercy on them, and save their souls from endless burnings.

4. A revival breaks the power of the world and of sin over Christians. It brings them to such vantage ground that they get a fresh impulse towards

heaven. They have a new foretaste of heaven, and new desires after union to God; and the charm of the world is broken, and the power of sin overcome.

5. When the churches are thus awakened and reformed, the reformation and salvation of sinners will follow, going through the same stages of conviction, repentance, and reformation. Their hearts will be broken down and changed. Very often the most abandoned profligates are among the subjects. Harlots, and drunkards, and infidels, and all sorts of abandoned characters, are awakened and converted. The worst part of human society are softened, and reclaimed, and made to appear as lovely specimens of the beauty of holiness. . . .

18. ROBERT OWEN

Manifesto

(1840)

ROBERT OWEN (1771–1858) was a pioneering socialist and critic of industrial capitalism in both Britain and America. Born in Newtown, Wales, Owen left home as a child to live with his older brother in London. By the age of twenty, he had rejected Christianity and was managing a small cotton-spinning factory in Manchester. Increasingly disillusioned by the economic misery brought on by industrial capitalism, Owen broke with prevailing economic wisdom and called for a "new moral world" founded on cooperation rather than competition. In 1813, he published his radical pamphlet, *A New View of Society*, in which he advocated the redistribution of profits to improve the living conditions and education of the working class. Discouraged by the criticism his theories encountered in England, Owen became ever more convinced that the "old society" of Europe was morally bankrupt. In 1825, he purchased land in Indiana and, along with nine hundred of his followers, founded the community of New Harmony. Owen's experiment, which failed after several fractious years, was unique in that it was the first of many in the United States not founded on religious principles. The following "Manifesto" is Owen's critique of private property and individual competition that formed the basis for secular socialist alternatives like New Harmony.

SOURCE: Gregory Claeys, ed. *A New View of Society and Other Writings by Robert Owen*. London and New York: Penguin Books, 1991.

SELECTED READINGS: Ronald G. Walters, *American Reformers, 1815–1860* (1978). John F. C. Harrison, *Quest for the New Moral World: Robert Owen and the Owenites in Britain and America* (1969). Mark Halloway, *Heavens on Earth: Utopian Communities in America, 1680–1880* (1966).

On Competition

By commercial competition, I mean the competition which exists in producing and distributing wealth.

This competition necessarily creates a covered civil warfare between the individuals who are engaged in the same profession or business.

Their interests are made to appear, by the existing arrangements of society, to be directly opposed one to another, and they are in opposition to each other, to so great an extent, that feelings of enmity, producing jealousy, discord, and anger, are but too frequently the natural result of men being placed under circumstances compelling them to injure each other, in the means by which they must maintain themselves and families.

Individual and national competition and contest are the best modes that have been, or perhaps can be devised, under the existing irrational notions of the world, by which wealth can be created and distributed; and the object desired is thereby effected, in some manner, to a certain extent. But it is obtained by creating and calling into full action, the most inferior feelings, the meanest faculties, the worst passions, and the most injurious vices, which can be cultivated in human nature; and the objects sought to be obtained by these measures, destructive as they are to the well-being and happiness of mankind, are yet most imperfectly obtained.

It is the true interest of society to procure a full sufficiency of wealth of intrinsic value, and to distribute it for the benefit of all, in the best manner; that is, with the least labour to all the members of the society, and especially with the least amount of unhealthy and disagreeable employment. Now individual and national contest and competition is a mode of producing wealth which, in connection with the other parts of the miserable system, by which the world has ever yet been governed, requires ten- or twentyfold more waste of labour and unhealthy and disagreeable occupation, than would be necessary under a well-devised system of society.

The competition, now rendered unavoidable, between individuals in producing wealth, compels them to apply much capital and labour in their individual establishments, which would not be required in a superior state of society, and gives a wrong direction to a great part of the labour and capital, by holding out inducements to create many things possessing little or no intrinsic worth of usefulness.

But the waste of capital and labour, by unnecessary establishments, and by the production of useless or unjurious articles, created to tempt society to purchase them, are small evils compared to the extent of the injurious feelings, violent passions, vices, and miseries unavoidably attendant on a system of individual competition, and more especially when that competition is carried to the extent it has now attained in the commercial world, and particularly in Great Britain. . . .

On Private Property

Nor yet will there be any necessity for inequality of rank or condition.

All who have deeply studied human society, and traced its innumerable evils to their source, have lamented the existence of those causes which have continually produced the rich and the poor, the ignorant and the learned, the powerful and the weak, and the tyrant and the slave.

They discovered, that with these distinctions among any people, vice must be permanent in their society, and extended among them in proportion as these differences between the members of the community increased. But no parties understood why these distinctions were a necessary part of the only system of society that had been established among men.

The individuals who, in practice, have excluded the most evil, for the longest period, from amongst them, are the Society of Friends; and this beneficial effect has been the result of adopting all the measures they could devise, under the existing system of the world, to obtain equality of wealth and knowledge among all their members. And it is well known to the most intelligent of the society, that their difficulties, vices, and miseries, have gradually increased as inequality of wealth and knowledge has extended among its members. In the nature of things it could not have been otherwise. Poverty and ignorance existing amidst an excess of wealth and exclusive privileges, will necessarily create envy, jealousy, and a desire to possess, by any means in their power, what their rich neighbours appear to enjoy in superfluity and to waste; and poverty and ignorance are sure to create ignoble and inferior characters in the great majority who are trained under those unfavourable and demoralizing circumstances.

While wealth and exclusive privileges are equally certain, when in contact with poverty and ignorance, to create feelings of contempt for those that are inferior to them in wealth, rank, or learning; and to fill them with pride and an overweening importance of their individual superiority, which inevitably leads them to the adoption of measures to obtain and secure for themselves the political power of the country by unjust and oppressive laws, which become, through time, highly injurious to the whole population, not excluding even themselves and their descendants. All parties who have occupied themselves in studying human nature, have uniformly come to the conclusion, that without equality of condition, there can be no permanent virtue or stability in society; and many have been the devices and attempts to obtain it in practice, and to retain private or individual property; but, as might have been anticipated, without any chance of succeeding to their wishes. The Society of Friends has been the most successful in the early period of their association in approaching somewhat near to it for a short period. Private property, however, by giving large possessions to some, and depriving others in the same proportion of the fruits of their industry, has now removed this singular, sagacious, and, in many respects, superior civil sect, farther than ever from their original object, and they are gradually preparing themselves to fall into the general measures which, ere long, must be adopted to relieve all classes from the unavoidable evils of the extremes of wealth and luxury, and of ignorance and poverty. . . .

There can be nothing deserving the name of virtue, of justice, or of real knowledge in society, as long as private property and inequality in rank and condition shall constitute component parts of it; but the present system of the world cannot be supported without private property and inequality of condition; consequently it is irrational to expect to find real virtue, justice, or knowledge, in the present system, in any part of the world.

All, generally speaking, are now dissatisfied with the existing state of society; but few, if any, know the real cause of their discontent. They are not aware, that to support an inequality of condition, arrangements must exist, numerous, complex and tormenting, to prevent, on the part of a large proportion of society, the due and healthy exercise of their natural propensities, faculties, and qualities, without which exercise it is altogether vain and useless to expect the full enjoyment of happiness, or even any approach to contentment or satisfaction with our condition.

It is for these, and numberless other reasons which might be added, that in the new and superior state of society, to which we now, even in this generation, confidently look forward, there will be no necessity for inequality of rank or condition.

19. RALPH WALDO EMERSON

Self-Reliance
(1841)

Although he was not a radical himself, **RALPH WALDO EMERSON (1803–1882)** was the principal architect of Transcendentalism whose writings had an enormous influence on those seeking to transform the role of the individual in modern society. Born in Concord, Massachusetts, Emerson was educated, on scholarship, at the Boston Latin School, Harvard College, and Harvard Divinity School, which provided the foundation for his extraordinary career as an essayist, poet, and lyceum lecturer. His first book, *Nature* (1836), became a kind of manifesto for the spiritual and literary movement of Transcendentalism. After several more years of lecturing and editing, Emerson published two more volumes, entitled *Essays* (1841, 1844), the first of which contained what would become Emerson's most famous essay, "Self-Reliance." In it, Emerson emphasized independence of mind and individual nonconformity in the face of growing materialism and rapid social change. Emerson's concept of "self-reliance"—which posited that divinity existed within each individual man and woman—was viewed by many as a radical rejection of the church. But Emerson was a cautious man, equally skeptical of ideologies and movements as he was of religion and politics. Still, "Self-Reliance" had enormous influence in antebellum America, an age marked by deep spiritual and secular faith in social progress.

SOURCE: Ralph Waldo Emerson. *Essays: First and Second Series.* New York: Library of America, 1990.

SELECTED READINGS: Len Gougeon, *Virtue's Hero: Emerson, Antislavery, and Reform* (1990). John McAleer, *Ralph Waldo Emerson: Days of Encounter* (1984). Gay Wilson Allen, *Waldo Emerson: A Biography* (1982).

Trust thyself: every heart vibrates to that iron string. Accept the place the divine providence has found for you, the society of your contemporaries, the

connection of events. Great men have always done so, and confided themselves childlike to the genius of their age, betraying their perception that the
absolutely trustworthy was seated at their heart, working through their hands,
predominating in all their being. And we are now men, and must accept in
the highest mind the same transcendent destiny; and not minors and invalids
in a protected corner, not cowards fleeing before a revolution, but guides,
redeemers, and benefactors, obeying the Almighty effort, and advancing on
Chaos and the Dark. . . .

These are the voices which we hear in solitude, but they grow faint and
inaudible as we enter into the world. Society everywhere is in conspiracy
against the manhood of every one of its members. Society is a joint-stock
company, in which the members agree, for the better securing of his bread to
each shareholder, to surrender the liberty and culture of the eater. The virtue
in most request is conformity. Self-reliance is its aversion. It loves not realities
and creators, but names and customs.

Whoso would be a man must be a nonconformist. He who would gather
immortal palms must not be hindered by the name of goodness, but must
explore if it be goodness. Nothing is at last sacred but the integrity of your
own mind. Absolve you to yourself, and you shall have the suffrage of the
world. I remember an answer which when quite young I was prompted to
make to a valued adviser, who was wont to importune me with the dear old
doctrines of the church. On my saying, What have I to do with the sacredness
of traditions, if I live wholly from within? my friend suggested,—"But these
impulses may be from below, not from above." I replied, "They do not seem
to me to be such; but if I am the Devil's child, I will live then from the Devil."
No law can be sacred to me but that of my nature. Good and bad are but
names very readily transferable to that or this; the only right is what is after
my constitution, the only wrong what is against it. A man is to carry himself
in the presence of all opposition, as if every thing were titular and ephemeral
but he. I am ashamed to think how easily we capitulate to badges and names,
to large societies and dead institutions. Every decent and well-spoken individual affects and sways me more than is right. I ought to go upright and vital,
and speak the rude truth in all ways. If malice and vanity wear the coat of
philanthropy, shall that pass? If an angry bigot assumes this bountiful cause
of Abolition, and comes to me with his last news from Barbadoes, why should
I not say to him, 'Go love thy infant; love thy wood-chopper: be good-natured
and modest: have that grace; and never varnish your hard, uncharitable ambition with this incredible tenderness for black folk a thousand miles off. Thy
love afar is spite at home.' Rough and graceless would be such greeting, but
truth is handsomer than the affectation of love. Your goodness must have
some edge to it,—else it is none. The doctrine of hatred must be preached as
the counteraction of the doctrine of love when that pules and whines. I shun

father and mother and wife and brother, when my genius calls me. I would write on the lintels of the door-post, *Whim*. I hope it is somewhat better than whim at last, but we cannot spend the day in explanation. Expect me not to show cause why I seek or why I exclude company. Then, again, do not tell me, as a good man did to-day, of my obligation to put all poor men in good situations. Are they *my* poor? I tell thee, thou foolish philanthropist, that I grudge the dollar, the dime, the cent, I give to such men as do not belong to me and to whom I do not belong. There is a class of persons to whom by all spiritual affinity I am bought and sold; for them I will go to prison, if need be; but your miscellaneous popular charities; the education at college of fools; the building of meeting-houses to the vain end to which many now stand; alms to sots; and the thousandfold Relief Societies;—though I confess with shame I sometimes succumb and give the dollar, it is a wicked dollar which by and by I shall have the manhood to withhold.

Virtues are, in the popular estimate, rather the exception than the rule. There is the man *and* his virtues. Men do what is called a good action, as some piece of courage or charity, much as they would pay a fine in expiation of daily nonappearance on parade. Their works are done as an apology or extenuation of their living in the world,—as invalids and the insane pay a high board. Their virtues are penances. I do not wish to expiate, but to live. My life is for itself and not for a spectacle. I much prefer that it should be of a lower strain, so it be genuine and equal, than that it should be glittering and unsteady. I wish it to be sound and sweet, and not to need diet and bleeding. I ask primary evidence that you are a man, and refuse this appeal from the man to his actions. I know that for myself it makes no difference whether I do or forbear those actions which are reckoned excellent. I cannot consent to pay for a privilege where I have intrinsic right. Few and mean as my gifts may be, I actually am, and do not need for my own assurance or the assurance of my fellows any secondary testimony.

What I must do is all that concerns me, not what the people think. This rule, equally arduous in actual and in intellectual life, may serve for the whole distinction between greatness and meanness. It is the harder, because you will always find those who think they know what is your duty better than you know it. It is easy in the world to live after the world's opinion; it is easy in solitude to live after our own; but the great man is he who in the midst of the crowd keeps with perfect sweetness the independence of solitude.

20.

Slave Spirituals
(c. 1600s–1800s)

Throughout the history of slavery, African Americans invented religious songs to guide their secular and spiritual strivings as they struggled for freedom from bondage. Part of a rich black vernacular tradition, these "sorrow songs," as W. E. B. Du Bois famously referred to them, were often mistaken by masters as evidence that slaves were content with the "peculiar institution." Far from it, they expressed a longing for escape and freedom—in this world and the next. Sung during religious settings as well as times of work, play, and rest, the spirituals combined New Testament images of Jesus and resurrection ("Steal Away to Jesus") with Old Testament themes of prophecy and deliverance ("Go Down, Moses"). Spirituals employed the familiar call-and-response patterns of West and Central Africa, wherein an individual chorus voice would be answered by a group of singers. Full of both sorrow and hope, the spirituals were among the many ways African Americans creatively resisted chattel slavery.

SOURCE: Henry Louis Gates, Jr., and Nellie McKay et al., eds. *The Norton Anthology of African American Literature.* New York: W. W. Norton, 1997.

SELECTED READINGS: Albert J. Raboteau, *Slave Religion: The "Invisible Institution" in the Antebellum South* (1978). John Blassingame, *The Slave Community: Plantation Life in the Antebellum South* (1972). Eugene Genovese, *Roll, Jordan, Roll: The World the Slaves Made* (1972).

Steal Away to Jesus

Steal away, steal away, steal away to Jesus,
Steal away, steal away home,
I ain't got long to stay here.

My Lord, He calls me,
He calls me by the thunder,
The trumpet sounds within-a my soul,
I ain't got long to stay here.

Steal away, steal away, steal away to Jesus,
Steal away, steal away home,
I ain't got long to stay here.

Green trees a-bending,
Po' sinner stands a-trembling,
The trumpet sounds within-a my soul,
I ain't got long to stay here.

Steal away, steal away, steal away to Jesus,
Steal away, steal away home,
I ain't got long to stay here.

Go Down, Moses

Go down, Moses,
Way down in Egyptland
Tell old Pharaoh
To let my people go.

When Israel was in Egyptland
Let my people go
Oppressed so hard they could not stand
Let my people go.

Go down, Moses,
Way down in Egyptland
Tell old Pharaoh
"Let my people go."

"Thus saith the Lord," bold Moses said,
"Let my people go;
If not I'll smite your first-born dead
Let my people go.

"No more shall they in bondage toil,
    Let my people go; ,
Let them come out with Egypt's spoil,
    Let my people go."

The Lord told Moses what to do
    Let my people go;
To lead the children of Israel through,
    Let my people go.

Go down, Moses,
    Way down in Egyptland
Tell old Pharaoh,
    "Let my people go!"

21. HENRY DAVID THOREAU

Resistance to Civil Government
(1849)

HENRY DAVID THOREAU (1817–1862) was a leading literary figure and naturalist whose social protests against slavery inspired the radical doctrine of civil disobedience. Born into a family of modest means in Concord, Massachusetts, Thoreau attended Concord Academy and Harvard College on scholarship. After graduating from Harvard in 1837, Thoreau was drawn to the local Transcendentalist ferment in Concord and was influenced by Ralph Waldo Emerson, who became a friend and mentor. After several years of teaching, editing, and writing, Thoreau made his famous move to Walden Pond on July 4, 1845. While at Walden, Thoreau was jailed for refusing to pay his poll taxes in protest over slavery and the Mexican War. His arrest inspired an increasingly radical politics, leading him to distance himself somewhat from Emerson. In 1848, Thoreau delivered a lyceum lecture, "Resistance to Civil Government," in which he defended his antislavery protest. The revised version, *Civil Disobedience*, was published in 1866, four years after Thoreau's untimely death. Among the most influential essays ever published by an American author, it inspired the nonviolent philosophies of Mahatma Gandhi and Martin Luther King, Jr., as well as the Danish resistance to Nazism, student protests against the Vietnam War, and the struggle against apartheid in South Africa.

SOURCE: Nina Baym et al., eds. *The Norton Anthology of American Literature.* Vol. 1. 5th ed. New York: W. W. Norton, 1998.

SELECTED READINGS: William E. Cain, *A Historical Guide to Henry David Thoreau* (2000). Robert Richardson, *Henry Thoreau: A Life of the Mind* (1986). Walter Harding, *The Days of Henry Thoreau* (1982).

I heartily accept the motto,—"That government is best which governs least;" and I should like to see it acted up to more rapidly and systematically. Carried out, it finally amounts to this, which also I believe,—"That government is best which governs not at all;" and when men are prepared for it, that will be the kind of government which they will have. Government is at best but an expedient; but most governments are usually, and all governments are sometimes, inexpedient. The objections which have been brought against a standing army, and they are many and weighty, and deserve to prevail, may also at last be brought against a standing government. The standing army is only an arm of the standing government. The government itself, which is only the mode which the people have chosen to execute their will, is equally liable to be abused and perverted before the people can act through it. Witness the present Mexican war, the work of comparatively a few individuals using the standing government as their tool; for, in the outset, the people would not have consented to this measure.

This American government,—what is it but a tradition, though a recent one, endeavoring to transmit itself unimpaired to posterity, but each instant losing some of its integrity? It has not the vitality and force of a single living man; for a single man can bend it to his will. It is a sort of wooden gun to the people themselves; and, if ever they should use it in earnest as a real one against each other, it will surely split. But it is not the less necessary for this; for the people must have some complicated machinery or other, and hear its din, to satisfy that idea of government which they have. Governments show thus how successfully men can be imposed on, even impose on themselves, for their own advantage. It is excellent, we must all allow; yet this government never of itself furthered any enterprise, but by the alacrity with which it got out of its way. *It* does not keep the country free. *It* does not settle the West. *It* does not educate. The character inherent in the American people has done all that has been accomplished; and it would have done somewhat more, if the government had not sometimes got in its way. For government is an expedient by which men would fain succeed in letting one another alone; and, as has been said, when it is most expedient, the governed are most let alone by it. Trade and commerce, if they were not made of India rubber, would never manage to bounce over the obstacles which legislators are continually putting in their way; and, if one were to judge these men wholly by the effects of their actions, and not partly by their intentions, they would deserve to be classed and punished with those mischievous persons who put obstructions on the railroads.

But, to speak practically and as a citizen, unlike those who call themselves no-government men, I ask for, not at once no government, but at once a better government. Let every man make known what kind of government would command his respect, and that will be one step toward obtaining it.

After all, the practical reason why, when the power is once in the hands of the people, a majority are permitted, and for a long period continue, to rule, is not because they are most likely to be in the right, nor because this seems fairest to the minority, but because they are physically the strongest. But a government in which the majority rule in all cases cannot be based on justice, even as far as men understand it. Can there not be a government in which majorities do not virtually decide right and wrong, but conscience?— in which majorities decide only those questions to which the rule of expediency is applicable? Must the citizen ever for a moment, or in the least degree, resign his conscience to the legislator? Why has every man a conscience, then? I think that we should be men first, and subjects afterward. It is not desirable to cultivate a respect for the law, so much as for the right. The only obligation which I have a right to assume, is to do at any time what I think right. It is truly enough said, that a corporation has no conscience; but a corporation of conscientious men is a corporation *with* a conscience. Law never made men a whit more just; and, by means of their respect for it, even the well-disposed are daily made the agents of injustice. A common and natural result of an undue respect for law is, that you may see a file of soldiers, colonel, captain, corporal, privates, powder-monkeys and all, marching in admirable order over hill and dale to the wars, against their wills, aye, against their common sense and consciences, which makes it very steep marching indeed, and produces a palpitation of the heart. . . .

Unjust laws exist: shall we be content to obey them, or shall we endeavor to amend them, and obey them until we have succeeded, or shall we transgress them at once? Men generally, under such a government as this, think that they ought to wait until they have persuaded the majority to alter them. They think that, if they should resist, the remedy would be worse than the evil. But it is the fault of the government itself that the remedy is worse the evil, It makes it worse. Why is it not more apt to anticipate and provide for reform? Why does it not cherish its wise minority? Why does it cry and resist before it is hurt? Why does it not encourage its citizens to be on the alert to point out its faults, and do better than it would have them? Why does it always crucify Christ, and excommunicate Copernicus and Luther, and pronounce Washington and Franklin rebels?

One would think, that a deliberate and practical denial of its authority was the only offence never contemplated by government; else, why has it not assigned its definite, its suitable and proportionate penalty? If a man who has no property refuses but once to earn nine shillings for the State, he is put in prison for a period unlimited by any law that I know, and determined only by the discretion of those who placed him there; but if I should steal ninety times nine shillings from the State, he is soon permitted to go at large again.

If the injustice is part of the necessary friction of the machine of government, let it go, let it go: perchance it will wear smooth,—certainly the machine will wear out. If the injustice has a spring, or a pulley, or a rope, or a crank, exclusively for itself, then perhaps you may consider whether the remedy will not be worse than the evil; but if it is of such a nature that it requires you to be the agent of injustice to another, then, I say, break the law. Let your life be a counter friction to stop the machine. What I have to do is to see, at any rate, that I do not lend myself to the wrong which I condemn.

As for adopting the ways which the State has provided for remedying the evil, I know not of such ways. They take too much time, and a man's life will be gone. I have other affairs to attend to. I came into this world, not chiefly to make this a good place to live in, but to live in it, be it good or bad. A man has not every thing to do, but something; and because he cannot do *every thing* it is not necessary that he should do *something* wrong. It is not my business to be petitioning the governor or the legislature any more than it is theirs to petition me: and, if they should not hear my petition, what should I do then? But in this case the State has provided no way: its very Constitution is the evil. This may seem to be harsh and stubborn and unconciliatory; but it is to treat with the utmost kindness and consideration the only spirit that can appreciate or deserves it. So is all change for the better, like birth and death which convulse the body.

I do not hesitate to say, that those who call themselves abolitionists should at once effectually withdraw their support, both in person and property, from the government of Massachusetts, and not wait till they constitute a majority of one, before they suffer the right to prevail through them. I think that it is enough if they have God on their side, without waiting for that other one. Moreover, any man more right than his neighbors, constitutes a majority of one already.

I meet this American government, or its representative the State government, directly, and face to face, once a year, no more, in the person of its tax-gatherer; this is the only mode in which a man situated as I am necessarily meets it; and it then says distinctly, Recognize me; and the simplest, the most effectual, and, in the present posture of affairs, the indispensablest mode of treating with it on this head, of expressing your little satisfaction with and love for it, is to deny it then. My civil neighbor, the tax-gatherer, is the very man I have to deal with,—for it is, after all, with men and not with parchment that I quarrel,—and he has voluntarily chosen to be an agent of the government. How shall he ever know well what he is and does as an officer of the government, or as a man, until he is obliged to consider whether he shall treat me, his neighbor, for whom he has respect, as a neighbor and well-disposed man, or as a maniac and disturber of the peace, and see if he can get over this obstruction to his neighborliness without a ruder and more impetuous thought or speech corresponding with his action? I know this well, that if one thousand, if one hundred, if ten men whom I could name,—if ten *honest* men only,—aye, if one HONEST man, in this State of Massachusetts, *ceasing to hold slaves,* were actually to withdraw from this copartnership, and be locked up in the county jail therefor, it would be the abolition of slavery in America. For it matters not how small the beginning may seem to be: what is once well done is done for ever. But we love better to talk about it: that we say is our mission. Reform keeps many scores of newspapers in its service, but not one man. If my esteemed neighbor, the State's ambassador, who will devote his days to the settlement of the question of human rights in the Council Chamber, instead of being threatened with the prisons of Carolina, were to sit down the prisoner of Massachusetts, that State which is so anxious to foist the sin of slavery upon her sister,—though at present she can discover only an act of inhospitality to be the ground of a quarrel with her,—the Legislature would not wholly waive the subject the following winter.

Under a government which imprisons any unjustly, the true place for a just man is also a prison. The proper place to-day, the only place which Massachusetts has provided for her freer and less desponding spirits, is in her prisons, to be put out and locked out of the State by her own act, as they have already put themselves out by their principles. It is there that the fugitive slave, and the Mexican prisoner on parole, and the Indian come to plead the wrongs of his race, should find them; on that separate, but more free and honorable ground, where the State places those who are not *with* her but *against* her,—the only house in a slave-state in which a free man can abide with honor. If any think that their influence would be lost there, and their voices no longer afflict the ear of the State, that they would not be as an enemy within its walls, they do not know by how much truth is stronger than error, nor how much more eloquently and effectively he can combat injustice who has experienced a little in his own person. Cast your whole vote, not a strip of paper merely, but your whole influence. A minority is powerless while it conforms to the majority; it is not even a minority then; but it is irresistible when it clogs by its whole weight. If the alternative is to keep all just men in prison, or give up war and slavery, the State will not hesitate which to choose. If a thousand men were not to pay their tax-bills this year, that would not be a violent and bloody measure, as it would be to pay them, and enable the State to commit violence and shed innocent blood. This is, in fact, the definition of a peaceable revolution, if any such is possible. If the tax-gatherer, or any other public officer, asks me, as one has done, "But what shall I do?" my answer is, "If you really wish to do any thing, resign your office." When the subject has refused allegiance, and the officer has resigned his office, then the revolution is accomplished. But even suppose blood should flow. Is there not a sort of blood shed when the conscience is wounded? Through this wound a man's real manhood and immortality flow out, and he bleeds to an everlasting death. I see this blood flowing now. . . .

22. WALT WHITMAN

Leaves of Grass
(1855)

One of the most gifted and experimental poets of the nineteenth century, **WALT WHITMAN (1819–1892)** was America's first poet laureate of democracy. Born in 1819 on Long Island to a Quaker mother and a working-class father, Whitman was largely self-educated. Unable to hold a job for very long, he went through a long, brooding period, during which he was transient and persecuted for his alleged homosexuality. On July 4, 1855, at the age of thirty-six, Whitman linked his own declaration of independence with the nation's when he self-published *Leaves of Grass*, a controversial "language experiment" containing twelve untitled poems. The final edition, published in 1891, contained more than 350 poems. Written in a highly unconventional ("free verse") style, the poems in *Leaves* quite literally embodied the unfolding of Whitman's democratic voice and vision. His longest and most remarkable poem, "Song of Myself," excerpted here, shifts the poetic eye to celebrate the poet as the representative of all human experience—the daily strivings, physical interactions, and sexual longings of common men and women (he advocated women's equality, homosexual love, and extramarital sex). For all of these reasons, Whitman was one of the first American writers to wrestle poetry from its elite traditions, an accomplishment that has earned him great respect and admiration among modern poets, activists, and bohemians of every stripe.

SOURCE: Walt Whitman. *Poetry and Prose*. New York: Library of America, 1982.

SELECTED READINGS: Jerome Loving, *Walt Whitman: Song of Himself* (1999). David Reynolds, *Walt Whitman's America: A Cultural Biography* (1995). Martin Klammer, *Whitman, Slavery, and the Emergence of Leaves of Grass* (1995).

What is commonest and cheapest and nearest and easiest is Me,
Me going in for my chances, spending for vast returns,
Adorning myself to bestow myself on the first that will take me,
Not asking the sky to come down to my goodwill,
Scattering it freely forever.
The pure contralto sings in the organloft,
The carpenter dresses his plank. . . . the tongue of his foreplane whistles
    its wild ascending lisp,
The married and unmarried children ride home to their thanksgiving
    dinner,
The pilot seizes the king-pin, he heaves down with a strong arm,
The mate stands braced in the whaleboat, lance and harpoon are ready,
The duck-shooter walks by silent and cautious stretches,
The deacons are ordained with crossed hands at the altar,
The spinning-girl retreats and advances to the hum of the big wheel,
The farmer stops by the bars of a Sunday and looks at the oats and rye,
The lunatic is carried at last to the asylum a confirmed case,
He will never sleep any more as he did in the cot in his mother's
    bedroom;
The jour printer with gray head and gaunt jaws works at his case,
He turns his quid of tobacco, his eyes get blurred with the manuscript;
The malformed limbs are tied to the anatomist's table,
What is removed drops horribly in a pail;
The quadroon girl is sold at the stand. . . . the drunkard nods by the
    barroom stove,
The machinist rolls up his sleeves. . . . the policeman travels his beat. . . .
    the gate-keeper marks who pass,
The young fellow drives the express-wagon. . . . I love him though I do
    not know him;
The half-breed straps on his light boots to compete in the race,
The western turkey-shooting draws old and young. . . . some lean on
    their rifles, some sit on logs,
Out from the crowd steps the marksman and takes his position and levels
    his piece;
The groups of newly-come immigrants cover the wharf or levee,
The woollypates hoe in the sugarfield, the overseer views them from his
    saddle;
The bugle calls in the ballroom, the gentlemen run for their partners, the
    dancers bow to each other;
The youth lies awake in the cedar-roofed garret and harks to the musical
    rain,

The Wolverine sets traps on the creek that helps fill the Huron,

The reformer ascends the platform, he spouts with his mouth and nose,

The company returns from its excursion, the darkey brings up the rear
     and bears the well-riddled target,

The squaw wrapt in her yellow-hemmed cloth is offering moccasins and
     beadbags for sale,

The connoisseur peers along the exhibition-gallery with halfshut eyes
     bent sideways,

The deckhands make fast the steamboat, the plank is thrown for the
     shoregoing passengers,

The young sister holds out the skein, the elder sister winds it off in a ball
     and stops now and then for the knots,

The one-year wife is recovering and happy, a week ago she bore her first
     child,

The cleanhaired Yankee girl works with her sewing-machine or in the
     factory or mill,

The nine months' gone is in the parturition chamber, her faintness and
     pains are advancing;

The pavingman leans on his twohanded rammer—the reporter's lead flies
     swiftly over the notebook—the signpainter is lettering with red and
     gold,

The canal-boy trots on the towpath—the bookkeeper counts at his desk—
     the shoemaker waxes his thread,

The conductor beats time for the band and all the performers follow him,

The child is baptised—the convert is making the first professions,

The regatta is spread on the bay. . . . how the white sails sparkle!

The drover watches his drove, he sings out to them that would stray,

The pedlar sweats with his pack on his back—the purchaser higgles about
     the odd cent,

The camera and plate are prepared, the lady must sit for her
     daguerreotype,

The bride unrumples her white dress, the minutehand of the clock moves
     slowly,

The opium eater reclines with rigid head and just-opened lips,

The prostitute draggles her shawl, her bonnet bobs on her tipsy and
     pimpled neck,

The crowd laugh at her blackguard oaths, the men jeer and wink to each
     other,

(Miserable! I do not laugh at your oaths nor jeer you,)

The President holds a cabinet council, he is surrounded by the great
     secretaries,

On the piazza walk five friendly matrons with twined arms;

The crew of the fish-smack pack repeated layers of halibut in the hold,
The Missourian crosses the plains toting his wares and his cattle,
The fare-collector goes through the train—he gives notice by the jingling
    of loose change,
The floormen are laying the floor—the tinners are tinning the roof—the
    masons are calling for mortar,
In single file each shouldering his hod pass onward the laborers;
Seasons pursuing each other the indescribable crowd is gathered. . . . it is
    the Fourth of July. . . . what salutes of cannon and small arms!
Seasons pursuing each other the plougher ploughs and the mower mows
    and the wintergrain falls in the ground;
Off on the lakes the pikefisher watches and waits by the hole in the
    frozen surface,
The stumps stand thick round the clearing, the squatter strikes deep with
    his axe,
The flatboatmen make fast toward dusk near the cottonwood or
    pekantrees,
The coon-seekers go now through the regions of the Red river, or
    through those drained by the Tennessee, or through those of the
    Arkansas,
The torches shine in the dark that hangs on the Chattahoochee or
    Altamahaw;
Patriarchs sit at supper with sons and grandsons and great grandsons
    around them,
In walls of adobe, in canvass tents, rest hunters and trappers after their
    day's sport.
The city sleeps and the country sleeps,
The living sleep for their time. . . . the dead sleep for their time,
The old husband sleeps by his wife and the young husband sleeps by his
    wife;
And these one and all tend inward to me, and I tend outward to them,
And such as it is to be of these more or less I am.

I am of old and young, of the foolish as much as the wise,
Regardless of others, ever regardful of others,
Maternal as well as paternal, a child as well as a man,
Stuffed with the stuff that is coarse, and stuffed with the stuff that is fine,
One of the great nation, the nation of many nations—the smallest the
    same and the largest the same,
A southerner soon as a northerner, a planter nonchalant and hospitable,
A Yankee bound my own way. . . . ready for trade. . . . my joints the
    limberest joints on earth and the sternest joints on earth,

A Kentuckian walking the vale of the Elkhorn in my deerskin leggings,
A boatman over the lakes or bays or along coasts. . . . a Hoosier, a Badger,
      a Buckeye,
A Louisianian or Georgian, a poke-easy from sandhills and pines,
At home on Canadian snowshoes or up in the bush, or with fishermen
      off Newfoundland,
At home in the fleet of iceboats, sailing with the rest and tacking,
At home on the hills of Vermont or in the woods of Maine or the Texan
      ranch,
Comrade of Californians. . . . comrade of free northwesterners, loving
      their big proportions,
Comrade of raftsmen and coalmen—comrade of all who shake hands and
      welcome to drink and meat;
A learner with the simplest, a teacher of the thoughtfulest,
A novice beginning experient of myriads of seasons,
Of every hue and trade and rank, of every caste and religion,
Not merely of the New World but of Africa Europe or Asia. . . . a
      wandering savage,
A farmer, mechanic, or artist. . . . a gentleman, sailor, lover or quaker,
A prisoner, fancy-man, rowdy, lawyer, physician or priest.

I resist anything better than my own diversity,
And breathe the air and leave plenty after me,
And am not stuck up, and am in my place. . . .

23. ABRAHAM LINCOLN

Second Inaugural Address
(1864)

As the sixteenth president of the United States, **ABRAHAM LINCOLN (1809–1865)** navigated the greatest domestic challenge in American history—the Civil War—by enacting a vision of the nation consistent with its professed ideals of liberty and equality. Born in a Kentucky log cabin, Lincoln was a poor, self-educated, "frontier" lawyer and politician who rose to national prominence as a moderate antislavery candidate in the new Republican Party during his famous 1858 debates with Democrat Stephen A. Douglas. His election to the presidency in 1860 hastened the secession of South Carolina and ignited the Civil War. Adopting a broad view of presidential war powers, Lincoln's first term was marked by a series of controversial executive decisions, including the suspension of the writ of habeas corpus and the 1863 Emancipation Proclamation, which symbolically shifted the principle war aim from the preservation of the Union to the abolition of slavery. Easily reelected despite enormous criticism, Lincoln seized the occasion of his Second Inauguration to reaffirm the nation's loftiest ideals. Anticipating the difficult task of Reconstruction, Lincoln acknowledged that slavery "was, somehow, the cause of the war," while also calling on Americans "to bind up the nation's wounds . . . to do all which may achieve and cherish a just, and a lasting peace, among ourselves, and with all nations." With masterful rhetoric and gifted oration, Lincoln's Second Inaugural, like the Gettysburg Address before it, put forth a humane, redemptive vision of democracy that America had yet to achieve.

SOURCE: Paul Lauter et al., eds. *The Norton Anthology of American Literature.* Vol. 1. New York: W. W. Norton, 1990.

SELECTED READINGS: David Blight, *Race and Reunion: The Civil War in American Memory* (2001). David Herbert Donald, *Lincoln* (1995). James McPherson, *Abraham Lincoln and the Second American Revolution* (1991).

FELLOW-COUNTRYMEN:

At this second appearing to take the oath of the presidential office, there is less occasion for an extended address than there was at the first. Then a statement, somewhat in detail, of a course to be pursued, seemed fitting and proper. Now, at the expiration of four years, during which public declarations have been constantly called forth on every point and phase of the great contest which still absorbs the attention and engrosses the energies of the nation, little that is new could be presented. The progress of our arms, upon which all else chiefly depends, is as well known to the public as to myself; and it is, I trust, reasonably satisfactory and encouraging to all. With high hope for the future, no prediction in regard to it is ventured.

On the occasion corresponding to this four years ago, all thoughts were anxiously directed to an impending civil war. All dreaded it—all sought to avert it. While the inaugural address was being delivered from this place, devoted altogether to saving the Union without war, insurgent agents were in the city seeking to destroy it without war—seeking to dissolve the Union, and divide effects, by negotiation. Both parties deprecated war; but one of them would make war rather than let the nation survive; and the other would accept war rather than let it perish. And the war came.

One-eighth of the whole population were colored slaves, not distributed generally over the Union, but localized in the Southern part of it. These slaves constituted a peculiar and powerful interest. All knew that this interest was, somehow, the cause of the war. To strengthen, perpetuate, and extend this interest was the object for which the insurgents would rend the Union, even by war; while the government claimed no right to do more than to restrict the territorial enlargement of it.

Neither party expected for the war the magnitude or the duration which it has already attained. Neither anticipated that the cause of the conflict might cease with, or even before, the conflict itself should cease. Each looked for an easier triumph, and a result less fundamental and astounding. Both read the same Bible, and pray to the same God; and each invokes his aid against the other. It may seem strange that any men should dare to ask a just God's assistance in wringing their bread from the sweat of other men's faces; but let us judge not, that we be not judged. The prayers of both could not be answered—that of neither has been answered fully.

The Almighty has his own purposes. "Woe unto the world because of offences! for it must needs be that offences come; but woe to that man by whom the offence cometh." If we shall suppose that American slavery is one of those offences which, in the providence of God, must needs come, but which, having continued through His appointed time, He now wills to remove, and that He gives to both North and South this terrible war, as the woe due to those by whom the offence came, shall we discern therein any departure from those divine attributes which the believers in a Living God always ascribe to Him? Fondly do we hope— fervently do we pray—that this mighty scourge of war may speedily pass away. Yet, if God wills that it continue until all the wealth piled by the bondman's two hundred and fifty years of unrequited toil shall be sunk, and until every drop of blood drawn with the lash shall be paid by another drawn with the sword, as we said three thousand years ago, so still it must be said, "The judgments of the Lord are true and righteous altogether."

With malice toward none; with charity for all; with firmness in the right, as God gives us to see the right, let us strive on to finish the work we are in; to bind up the nation's wounds; to care for him who shall have borne the battle, and for his widow, and his orphan—to do all which may achieve and cherish a just and lasting peace, among our- selves, and with all nations.

24. MARK TWAIN

The Adventures of Huckleberry Finn
(1884)

One of America's most beloved writers, **MARK TWAIN (1835–1910)** used humor, irony, and regional idiosyncrasies to sharply critique racism, capitalism, and imperialism. The author (whose pen name, after 1863, was "Mark Twain," a riverboat term meaning "two fathoms") was born Samuel Langhorne Clemens in Florida, Missouri, in 1835. He lived most of his childhood in Hannibal, Missouri, from which he would draw the material for two of his most successful novels, *The Adventures of Tom Sawyer* (1876) and *The Adventures of Huckleberry Finn* (1884). As a young man, Clemens served as a printer's apprentice, a Mississippi riverboat pilot, and then as a journalist, earning for himself a reputation as a brilliant regional humorist with a robust public persona. Following the Civil War, Twain emerged as an outspoken critic of racism and imperialism, as well as corporate greed and political corruption, coining the phrase "Gilded Age" to characterize the era. Twain's most cunning assault on racial prejudice appears in *Huck Finn*, the story about the relationship between a white boy and a black slave on the run from family and slavery, respectively. The friendship that Huck and Jim develop as their raft floats down the Mississippi River is a rare example of interracial friendship in postbellum Southern literature.

SOURCE: *The Family Mark Twain.* New York: Dorset Press, 1988.

SELECTED READINGS: Elaine Mensh and Harry Mensh, *Black, White, and Huckleberry Finn* (2000). Shelley Fisher Fishkin, *Was Huck Black?: Mark Twain and African-American Voices* (1993). Victor Doyno, *Writing Huck Finn: Mark Twain's Creative Process* (1991).

Chapter XV
Fooling Poor Old Jim

We judged that three nights more would fetch us to Cairo, at the bottom of Illinois, where the Ohio River comes in, and that was what we was after. We would sell the raft and get on a steamboat and go way up the Ohio amongst the free states, and then be out of trouble.

Well, the second night a fog begun to come on, and we made for a towhead to tie to, for it wouldn't do to try to run in a fog; but when I paddled ahead in the canoe, with the line to make fast, there warn't anything but little saplings to tie to. I passed the line around one of them right on the edge of the cut bank, but there was a stiff current, and the raft come booming down so lively she tore it out by the roots and away she went. I see the fog closing down, and it made me so sick and scared I couldn't budge for most a half a minute it seemed to me—and then there warn't no raft in sight; you couldn't see twenty yards. I jumped into the canoe and run back to the stern, and grabbed the paddle and set her back a stroke. But she didn't come. I was in such a hurry I hadn't untied her. I got up and tried to untie her, but I was so excited my hands shook so I couldn't hardly do anything with them.

As soon as I got started I took out after the raft, hot and heavy, right down the towhead. That was all right as far as it went, but the towhead warn't sixty yards long, and the minute I flew by the foot of it I shot out into the solid white fog, and hadn't no more idea which way I was going than a dead man.

Thinks I, it won't do to paddle; first I know I'll run into the bank or a towhead or something; I got to set still and float, and yet it's mighty fidgety business to have to hold your hands still at such a time. I whooped and listened. Away down there somewheres I hears a small whoop, and up comes my spirits. I went tearing after it, listening sharp to hear it again. The next time it come I see I warn't heading for it, but heading away to the right of it. And the next time I was heading away to the left of it—and not gaining on it much either, for I was flying around, this way and that and t'other, but it was going straight ahead all the time.

I did wish the fool would think to beat a tin pan, and beat it all the time, but he never did, and it was the still places between the whoops that was making the trouble for me. Well, I fought along, and directly I hears the whoop *behind* me. I was tangled good now. That was somebody else's whoop, or else I was turned around.

I throwed the paddle down. I heard the whoop again; it was behind me yet, but in a different place; it kept coming, and kept changing its place, and I kept answering, till by and by it was in front of me again, and I knowed the current had swung the canoe's head down-stream, and I was all right if that was Jim and not some other raftsman hollering. I couldn't tell nothing about voices in a fog, for nothing don't look natural nor sound natural in a fog.

The whooping went on, and in about a minute I come a-booming down on a cut bank with smoky ghosts of big trees on it, and the current throwed me off to the left and shot by, amongst a lot of snags that fairly roared, the current was tearing by them so swift.

In another second or two it was solid white and still again. I set perfectly still then, listening to my heart thump, and I reckon I didn't draw a breath while it thumped a hundred.

I just give up then. I knowed what the matter was. That cut bank was an island, and Jim had gone down t'other side of it. It warn't no towhead that you could float by in ten minutes. It had the big timber of a regular island; it might be five or six miles long and more than half a mile wide.

I kept quiet, with my ears cocked, about fifteen minutes, I reckon. I was floating along, of course, four or five miles an hour; but you don't ever think of that. No, you *feel* like you are laying dead still on the water; and if a little glimpse of a snag slips by you don't think to yourself how fast *you're* going, but you catch your breath and think, my! how that snag's tearing along. If you think it ain't dismal and lonesome out in a fog that way by yourself in the night, you try it once—you'll see.

Next, for about a half an hour, I whoops now and then; at last I hears the answer a long ways off, and tries to follow it, but I couldn't do it, and directly I judged I'd got into a nest of towheads, for I had little dim glimpses of them on both sides of me—sometimes just a narrow channel between, and some that I couldn't see I knowed was there because I'd hear the wash of the current against the old dead brush and trash that hung over the banks. Well, I warn't long loosing the whoops down amongst the towheads; and I only tried to chase them a little while, anyway, because it was worse than chasing a Jack-o'-lantern. You never knowed a sound dodge around so, and swap places so quick and so much.

I had to claw away from the bank pretty lively four or five times, to keep from knocking the islands out of the river; and so I judged the raft must be butting into the bank every now and then, or else it would get further ahead and clear out of hearing—it was floating a little faster than what I was.

Well, I seemed to be in the open river again by and by, but I couldn't hear no sign of a whoop nowheres. I reckoned Jim had fetched up on a snag, maybe, and it was all up with him. I was good and tired, so I laid down in the canoe and said I wouldn't bother no more. I didn't want to go to sleep, of course; but I was so sleepy I couldn't help it; so I thought I would take jest one little cat-nap.

But I reckon it was more than a cat-nap, for when I waked up the stars was shining bright, the fog was all gone, and I was spinning down a big bend stern first. First I didn't know where I was; I thought I was dreaming; and when things began to come back to me they seemed to come up dim out of last week.

It was a monstrous big river here, with the tallest and the thickest kind of timber on both banks; just a solid wall, as well as I could see by the stars. I looked away down-stream, and seen a black speck on the water. I took after it; but when I got to it it warn't nothing but a couple of saw-logs made fast together. Then I see another speck, and chased that; then another, and this time I was right. It was the raft.

When I got to it Jim was setting there with his head down between his knees, asleep, with his right arm hanging over the steering-oar. The other oar was smashed off, and the raft was littered up with leaves and branches and dirt. So she'd had a rough time.

I made fast and laid down under Jim's nose on the raft, and began to gap, and stretch my fists out against Jim, and says:

"Hello, Jim, have I been asleep? Why didn't you stir me up?"

"Goodness gracious, is dat you, Huck? En you ain' dead—you ain' drownded—you's back ag'in? It's too good for true, honey, it's too good for true. Lemme look at you chile, lemme feel o' you. No, you ain' dead! you's back ag'in, 'live en soun', jis de same ole Huck—de same ole Huck, thanks to goodness!"

"What's the matter with you, Jim? You been a-drinking?"

"Drinkin'? Has I ben a-drinkin'? Has I had a chance to be a-drinkin'?"

"Well, then, what makes you talk so wild?"

"How does I talk wild?"

"*How?* Why, hain't you been talking about my coming back, and all that stuff, as if I'd been gone away?"

"Huck—Huck Finn, you look me in de eye; look me in de eye. *Hain't* you ben gone away?"

"Gone away? Why, what in the nation do you mean? *I* hain't been gone anywheres. Where would I go to?"

"Well, looky here, boss, dey's sumfn wrong, dey is. Is I *me*, or who *is* I? Is I heah, or whah *is* I? Now dat's what I wants to know."

"Well, I think you're here, plain enough, but I think you're a tangle-headed old fool, Jim."

"I is, is I? Well, you answer me dis: Didn't you tote out de line in de canoe fer to make fas' to de towhead?"

"No, I didn't. What towhead? I hain't seen no towhead."

"You hain't seen no towhead? Looky here, didn't de line pull loose en de raf' go a-hummin' down de river, en leave you en de canoe behine in de fog?"

"What fog?"

"Why, *de* fog!—de fog dat's been aroun' all night. En didn't you whoop, en didn't I whoop, tell we got mix' up in de islands en one un us got los' en t'other one was jis as good as los', 'kase he didn' know whah he wuz? En didn't I bust up agin a lot er dem islands en have a turrible time en mos' git drownded? Now ain' dat so, boss—ain't it so? You answer me dat."

"Well, this is too many for me, Jim. I hain't seen no fog, nor no islands, not no troubles, nor nothing. I been setting here talking with you all night till you went to sleep about ten minutes ago, and I reckon I done the same. You couldn't 'a' got drunk in that time, so of course you've been dreaming."

"Dad fetch it, how is I gwyne to dream all dat in ten minutes?"

"Well, hang it all, you did dream it, because there didn't any of it happen."

"But, Huck, it's all jis' as plain to me as—"

"It don't make no difference how plain it is; there ain't nothing in it. I know, because I've been here all the time."

Jim didn't say nothing for about five minutes, but set there studying over it. Then he says:

"Well, den, I reck'n I did dream it, Huck; but dog my cats ef it ain't de powerfulest dream I ever see. En I hain't ever had no dream b'fo' dat's tired me like dis one."

"Oh, well, that's all right, because a dream does tire a body like everything sometimes. But this one was a staving dream; tell me all about it, Jim."

So Jim went to work and told me the whole thing right through, just as it happened, only he painted it up considerable. Then he said he must start in and " 'terpret" it, because it was sent for a warning. He said the first towhead stood for a man that would try to do us some good, but the current was another man that would get us away from him. The whoops was warnings that would come to us every now and then, and if we didn't try hard to make out to understand them they'd just take us into bad luck, 'stead of keeping us out of it. The lot of towheads was troubles we was going to get into with quarrelsome people and all kinds of mean folks, but if we minded our business and didn't talk back and aggravate them, we would pull through and get out of the fog and into the big clear river, which was the free states, and wouldn't have no more trouble.

It had clouded up pretty dark just after I got on to the raft, but it was clearing up again now.

"Oh, well, that's all interpreted well enough as far as it goes, Jim," I says; "but what does *these* things stand for?"

It was the leaves and rubbish on the raft and the smashed oar. You could see them first-rate now.

Jim looked at the trash, and then looked at me, and back at the trash again. He had got the dream fixed so strong in his head that he couldn't seem to shake it loose and get the facts back into its place again right away. But when he did get the thing straightened around he looked at me steady without ever smiling, and says:

"What do dey stan' for? I's gwyne to tell you. When I got all wore out wid work, en wid de callin' for you, en went to sleep, my heart wuz mos' broke bekase you wuz los', en I didn' k'yer no' mo' what become er me en de raf'. En when I wake up en fine you back ag'in, all safe en soun', de tears come, en I could 'a' got down on my knees en kiss yo' foot, I's so thankful. En all you wuz thinkin' 'bout wuz how you could make a fool uv ole Jim wid a lie. Dat truck dah is *trash;* en trash is what people is dat puts dirt on de head er dey fren's en makes 'em ashamed."

Then he got up slow and walked to the wigwam, and went in there without saying anything but that. But that was enough. It made me feel so mean I could almost kissed *his* foot to get him to take it back.

It was fifteen minutes before I could work myself up to go and humble myself to a nigger; but I done it, and I warn't ever sorry for it afterward, neither. I didn't do him no more mean tricks, and I wouldn't done that one if I'd 'a' knowed it would make him feel that way.

25. EDWARD BELLAMY

Looking Backward,
2000–1887
(1888)

A celebrated author and journalist, **EDWARD BELLAMY (1850–1898)** is the best known and most influential utopian socialist in American history. Born in an industrializing village in Chicopee Falls, Massachusetts, Bellamy attended Union College after the Civil War, briefly practicing law before becoming a journalist. A prolific and gifted writer, Bellamy achieved his major break-through as a novelist in 1888 with the publication of his utopian novel, *Looking Backward, 2000–1887.* A response to the increasing economic inequality and violent labor uprisings that came with late-nineteenth-century industrial capitalism, Bellamy's tale offers a radically alternative vision of society born of nonviolent revolution and based on the principle of economic equality. In his fictional 2000, capitalism has been replaced by "Nationalism," a new social order wherein citizens are members of an industrial army who share equally in production and distribution. Bellamy's utopian nationalism attracted the attention of a wide range of radicals—from women's rights advocates and socialists to Populists and labor organizers—inspiring a short-lived movement that included new periodicals, Bellamy Nationalist Clubs, and a second utopian novel, *Equality* (1897). An immediate success, *Looking Backward* sold hundreds of thousands of copies in the first two years alone. It was the second best-selling American novel of the nineteenth century—the first was *Uncle Tom's Cabin*—and remains the most popular work of utopian fiction in American history.

SOURCE: John L. Thomas, ed. *Looking Backward, 2000–1887, by Edward Bellamy.* Cambridge, MA: Belknap Press of Harvard University Press, 1967.

SELECTED READINGS: Daphne Patai, ed., *Looking Backward. 1988–1888: Essays on Edward Bellamy* (1988). Arthur Lipow, *Authoritarian Socialism in America:*

Edward Bellamy and the Nationalist Movement (1982). Daniel Aaron, *Men of Good Hope: A Story of American Progressives* (1951).

It was indeed the nineteenth century to which I had awaked; there could be no kind of doubt about that. Its complete microcosm this summary of the day's news had presented, even to that last unmistakable touch of fatuous self-complacency. Coming after such a damning indictment of the age as that one day's chronicle of world-wide bloodshed, greed, and tyranny, was a bit of cynicism worthy of Mephistopheles, and yet of all whose eyes it had met this morning I was, perhaps, the only one who perceived the cynicism, and but yesterday I should have perceived it no more than the others. That strange dream it was which had made all the difference. For I know not how long, I forgot my surroundings after this, and was again in fancy moving in that vivid dream-world, in that glorious city, with its homes of simple comfort and its gorgeous public palaces. Around me were again faces unmarred by arrogance or servility, by envy or greed, by anxious care or feverish ambition, and stately forms of men and women who had never known fear of a fellow man or depended on his favor, but always, in the words of that sermon which still rang in my ears, had "stood up straight before God."

With a profound sigh and a sense of irreparable loss, not the less poignant that it was a loss of what had never really been, I roused at last from my reverie, and soon after left the house.

A dozen times between my door and Washington Street I had to stop and pull myself together, such power had been in that vision of the Boston of the future to make the real Boston strange. The squalor and malodorousness of the town struck me, from the moment I stood upon the street, as facts I had never before observed. But yesterday, moreover, it had seemed quite a matter of course that some of my fellow-citizens should wear silks, and others rags, that some should look well fed, and others hungry. Now on the contrary the glaring disparities in the dress and condition of the men and women who brushed each other on the sidewalks shocked me at every step, and yet more the entire indifference which the prosperous showed to the plight of the unfortunate. Were these human beings, who could behold the wretchedness of their fellows without so much as a change of countenance? And yet, all the while, I knew well that it was I who had changed, and not my contemporaries. I had dreamed of a city whose people fared all alike as children of one family and were one another's keepers in all things.

Another feature of the real Boston, which assumed the extraordinary effect of strangeness that marks familiar things seen in a new light, was the prevalence of advertising. There had been no personal advertising in the Boston of the twentieth century, because there was no need of any, but here the walls of the buildings, the windows, the broadsides of the newspapers in every hand, the very pavements, everything in fact in sight, save the sky, were covered with the appeals of individuals who sought, under innumerable pretexts, to attract the contributions of others to their support. However the wording might vary, the tenor of all these appeals was the same:—

"Help John Jones. Never mind the rest. They are frauds. I, John Jones, am the right one. Buy of me. Employ me. Visit me. Hear me, John Jones. Look at me. Make no mistake. John Jones is the man and nobody else. Let the rest starve, but for God's sake remember John Jones!"

Whether the pathos or the moral repulsiveness of the spectacle most impressed me, so suddenly become a stranger in my own city, I know not. Wretched men, I was moved to cry, who, because they will not learn to be helpers of one another, are doomed to be beggars of one another from the least to the greatest! This horrible babel of shameless self-assertion and mutual depreciation, this stunning clamor of conflicting boasts, appeals, and abjurations, this stupendous system of brazen beggary, what was it all but the necessity of a society in which the opportunity to serve the world according to his gifts, instead of being secured to every man as the first object of social organization, had to be fought for!

I reached Washington Street at the busiest point, and there I stood and laughed aloud, to the scandal of the passers-by. For my life I could not have helped it, with such a mad humor was I moved at sight of the interminable rows of stores on either side, up and down the street so far as I could see—scores of them, to make the spectacle more utterly preposterous, within a stone's throw devoted to selling the same sort of goods. Stores! stores! stores! miles of stores! ten thousand stores to distribute the goods needed by this one city, which in my dream had been supplied with all things from a single warehouse, as they were ordered through one great store in every quarter, where the buyer, without waste of time or labor, found under one roof the world's assortment in whatever line he desired. There the labor of distribution had been so slight as to add but a scarcely perceptible fraction to the cost of commodities to the user. The cost of production was virtually all he paid. But here the mere distribution of the goods, their handling alone, added a fourth, a third, a half and more, to the cost. All these ten thousand plants must be paid for, their rent, their staffs of superintendence, their platoons of salesmen, their ten thousand sets of accountants, jobbers, and business dependents, with all they spent in advertising themselves and fighting one another, and the consumers must do the paying. What a famous process for beggaring a nation!

Were these serious men I saw about me, or children, who did their business on such a plan? Could they be reasoning beings, who did not see the folly which, when the product is made and ready for use, wastes so much of it in getting it to the user? If people eat with a spoon that leaks half its contents between bowl and lip, are they not likely to go hungry?

I had passed through Washington Street thousands of times before and viewed the ways of those who sold merchandise, but my curiosity concerning them was as if I had never gone by their way before. I took wondering note of the show windows of the stores, filled with goods arranged with a wealth of pains and artistic device to attract the eye. I saw the throngs of ladies looking in, and the proprietors eagerly watching the effect of the bait. I went within and noted the hawk-eyed floor-walker watching for business, over-looking the clerks, keeping them up to their task of inducing the customers to buy, buy, buy, for money if they had it, for credit if they had it not, to buy what they wanted not, more than they wanted, what they could not afford. At times I momentarily lost the clue and was confused by the sight. Why this effort to induce people to buy? Surely that had nothing to do with the legit-imate business of distributing products to those who needed them. Surely it was the sheerest waste to force upon people what they did not want, but what might be useful to another. The nation was so much the poorer for every such achievement. What were these clerks thinking of? Then I would remem-ber that they were not acting as distributors like those in the store I had visited in the dream Boston. They were not serving the public interest, but their immediate personal interest, and it was nothing to them what the ultimate effect of their course on the general prosperity might be, if but they increased their own hoard, for these goods were their own, and the more they sold and the more they got for them, the greater their gain. The more wasteful the people were, the more articles they did not want which they could be induced to buy, the better for these sellers. To encourage prodigality was the express aim of the ten thousand stores of Boston.

Nor were these storekeepers and clerks a whit worse men than any others in Boston. They must earn a living and support their families, and how were they to find a trade to do it by which did not necessitate placing their indi-vidual interests before those of others and that of all? They could not be asked to starve while they waited for an order of things such as I had seen in my dream, in which the interest of each and that of all were identical. But, God in heaven! what wonder, under such a system as this about me—what won-der that the city was so shabby, and the people so meanly dressed, and so many of them ragged and hungry! . . .

The folly of men, not their hard-heartedness, was the great cause of the world's poverty. It was not the crime of man, nor of any class of men, that made the race so miserable, but a hideous, ghastly mistake, a colossal world-darkening blunder. And then I showed them how four fifths of the labor of men was utterly wasted by the mutual warfare, the lack of organization and concert among the workers. Seeking to make the matter very plain, I in-stanced the case of arid lands where the soil yielded the means of life only by careful use of the watercourses for irrigation. I showed how in such countries it was counted the most important function of the government to see that the water was not wasted by the selfishness or ignorance of individuals, since otherwise there would be famine. To this end its use was strictly regulated and systematized, and individuals of their mere caprice were not permitted to dam it or divert it, or in any way to tamper with it.

The labor of men, I explained, was the fertilizing stream which alone rendered earth habitable. It was but a scanty stream at best, and its use required to be regulated by a system which expended every drop to the best advantage, if the world were to be supported in abundance. But how far from any system was the actual practice! Every man wasted the precious fluid as he wished, animated only by the equal motives of saving his own crop and spoiling his neighbor's, that his might sell the better. What with greed and what with spite some fields were flooded while others were parched, and half the water ran wholly to waste. In such a land, though a few by strength or cunning might win the means of luxury, the lot of the great mass must be poverty, and of the weak and ignorant bitter want and perennial famine.

26. CHARLOTTE PERKINS GILMAN

Herland
(1915)

CHARLOTTE PERKINS GILMAN (1860–1935) was a social critic, utopian novelist, and feminist-socialist whose trenchant analysis of the economic basis for women's subordination has had an enormous impact on modern feminism. After a tough childhood of abandonment, poverty, and inconsistent schooling, Gilman married Charles Stetson in 1884, gave birth to her only daughter, suffered a nervous breakdown (which she chronicled in her chilling 1892 short story, "The Yellow Wall-Paper"), and finally divorced her husband in 1894 while she was living in Pasadena, California. A popular lecturer and prolific writer, Gilman earned widespread fame with the publication of *Woman and Economics* (1898), a pioneering work of sociology that examined sexual inequality as a function of women's economic dependence on men. Her most creative writing appeared between 1909 and 1916, when she served as editor of *The Forerunner,* a feminist magazine in which her witty and popular utopian novel, *Herland,* was serialized in 1915. *Herland* is a fictional tour through a futuristic utopian island community populated entirely by women and children, and governed by the principle of "New Motherhood," a cooperative feminist alternative to the male-dominated social-sexual order of late-nineteenth-century America. In the following chapter, "Comparisons Are Odious," the narrator and his male companions are humbled by the women they encounter in Herland. Gilman, however, never witnessed the feminist utopia she envisioned. She was diagnosed with inoperable breast cancer, and took her own life in 1935.

SOURCE: Charlotte Perkins Gilman. *Herland.* New York: Pantheon Books, 1979.

SELECTED READINGS: Joanne B. Karpinski, *Critical Essays on Charlotte Perkins Gilman* (1992). Mary A. Hill, *Charlotte Perkins Gilman: The Making of a Radical*

Feminist, 1860–1896 (1980). Ann J. Lane, *To Herland and Beyond: The Life and Work of Charlotte Perkins Gilman* (1980).

There you have it. You see, they were Mothers, not in our sense of helpless involuntary fecundity, forced to fill and overfill the land, every land, and then see their children suffer, sin, and die, fighting horribly with one another; but in the sense of Conscious Makers of People. Mother-love with them was not a brute passion, a mere "instinct," a wholly personal feeling; it was—a religion.

It included that limitless feeling of sisterhood, that wide unity in service which was so difficult for us to grasp. And it was National, Racial, Human—oh, I don't know how to say it.

We are used to seeing what we call "a mother" completely wrapped up in her own pink bundle of fascinating babyhood, and taking but the faintest theoretic interest in anybody else's bundle, to say nothing of the common needs of *all* the bundles. But these women were working all together at the grandest of tasks—they were Making People—and they made them well.

There followed a period of "negative eugenics" which must have been an appalling sacrifice. We are commonly willing to "lay down our lives" for our country, but they had to forego motherhood for their country—and it was precisely the hardest thing for them to do.

When I got this far in my reading I went to Somel for more light. We were as friendly by that time as I had ever been in my life with any woman. A mighty comfortable soul she was, giving one the nice smooth mother-feeling a man likes in a woman, and yet giving also the clear intelligence and dependableness I used to assume to be masculine qualities. We had talked volumes already.

"See here," said I. "Here was this dreadful period when they got far too thick, and decided to limit the population. We have a lot of talk about that among us, but your position is so different that I'd like to know a little more about it.

"I understand that you make Motherhood the highest social service—a sacrament, really; that it is only undertaken once, by the majority of the population; that those held unfit are not allowed even that; and that to be encouraged to bear more than one child is the very highest reward and honor in the power of the state."

(She interpolated here that the nearest approach to an aristocracy they had was to come of a line of "Over Mothers"—those who had been so honored.)

"But what I do not understand, naturally, is how you prevent it. I gathered that each woman had five. You have no tyrannical husbands to hold in check—and you surely do not destroy the unborn—"

The look of ghastly horror she gave me I shall never forget. She started from her chair, pale, her eyes blazing.

"Destroy the unborn—!" she said in a hard whisper. "Do men do that in your country?"

"Men!" I began to answer, rather hotly, and then saw the gulf before me. None of us wanted these women to think that *our* women, of whom we boasted so proudly, were in any way inferior to them. I am ashamed to say that I equivocated. I told her of certain criminal types of women—perverts, or crazy, who had been known to commit infanticide. I told her, truly enough, that there was much in our land which was open to criticism, but that I hated to dwell on our defects until they understood us and our conditions better.

And, making a wide detour, I scrambled back to my question of how they limited the population.

As for Somel, she seemed sorry, a little ashamed even, of her too clearly expressed amazement. As I look back now, knowing them better, I am more and more and more amazed as I appreciate the exquisite courtesy with which they had received over and over again statements and admissions on our part which must have revolted them to the soul.

She explained to me, with sweet seriousness, that as I had supposed, at first each woman bore five children; and that, in their eager desire to build up a nation, they had gone on in that way for a few centuries, till they were confronted with the absolute need of a limit. This fact was equally plain to all—all were equally interested.

They were now as anxious to check their wonderful power as they had been to develop it; and for some generations gave the matter their most earnest thought and study.

"We were living on rations before we worked it out," she said. "But we did work it out. You see, before a child comes to one of us there is a period of utter exaltation—the whole being is uplifted and filled with a concentrated desire for that child. We learned to look forward to that period with the greatest caution. Often our young women, those to whom motherhood had not yet come, would voluntarily defer it. When that deep inner demand for a child began to be felt she would deliberately engage in the most active work, physical and mental; and even more important, would solace her longing by the direct care and service of the babies we already had."

She paused. Her wise sweet face grew deeply, reverently tender.

"We soon grew to see that mother-love has more than one channel of expression. I think the reason our children are so—so fully loved, by all of us, is that we never—any of us—have enough of our own."

This seemed to me infinitely pathetic, and I said so. "We have much that is bitter and hard in our life at home," I told her, "but this seems to me piteous beyond words—a whole nation of starving mothers!"

But she smiled her deep contented smile, and said I quite misunderstood.

"We each go without a certain range of personal joy," she said, "but remember—we each have a million children to love and serve—*our* children."

It was beyond me. To hear a lot of women talk about "our children"! But I suppose that is the way the ants and bees would talk—do talk, maybe.

That was what they did, anyhow.

When a woman chose to be a mother, she allowed the child-longing to grow within her till it worked its natural miracle. When she did not so choose she put the whole thing out of her mind, and fed her heart with the other babies.

Let me see—with us, children—minors, that is—constitute about three-fifths of the population; with them only about one-third, or less. And precious—! No sole heir to an empire's throne, no solitary millionaire baby, no only child of middle-aged parents, could compare as an idol with these Herland children.

But before I start on that subject I must finish up that little analysis I was trying to make.

They did effectually and permanently limit the population in numbers, so that the country furnished plenty for the fullest, richest life for all of them: plenty of everything, including room, air, solitude even.

And then they set to work to improve that population in quality—since they were restricted in quantity. This they had been at work on, uninterruptedly, for some fifteen hundred years. Do you wonder they were nice people?

Physiology, hygiene, sanitation, physical culture—all that line of work had been perfected long since. Sickness was almost wholly unknown among them, so much so that a previously high development in what we call the "science of medicine" had become practically a lost art. They were a clean-bred, vigorous lot, having the best of care, the most perfect living conditions always.

When it came to psychology—there was no one thing which left us so dumbfounded, so really awed, as the everyday working knowledge—and practice—they had in this line. As we learned more and more of it, we learned to appreciate the exquisite mastery with which we ourselves, strangers of alien race, of unknown opposite sex, had been understood and provided for from the first.

With this wide, deep, thorough knowledge, they had met and solved the problems of education in ways some of which I hope to make clear later. Those nation-loved children of theirs compared with the average in our country as the most perfectly cultivated, richly developed roses compare with—tumbleweeds. Yet they did not *seem* "cultivated" at all—it had all become a natural condition.

And this people, steadily developing in mental capacity, in will power, in social devotion, had been playing with the arts and sciences—as far as they knew them—for a good many centuries now with inevitable success.

Into this quiet lovely land, among these wise, sweet, strong women, we, in our easy assumption of superiority, had suddenly arrived; and now, tamed and trained to a degree they considered safe, we were at last brought out to see the country, to know the people.

CHAPTER

THREE

Abolitionism

27. OPENING EDITORIAL

Freedom's Journal

(1827)

Published weekly in New York City from March 1827 to October 1829, *Freedom's Journal* was the first of twenty-four African-American newspapers to appear in the United States before the Civil War. With its aggressive calls for racial equality and uplift, it was also the first antislavery newspaper to espouse an immediate end to slavery and reject popular plans for African colonization. Coedited by black abolitionists John Brown Russwurm and the Reverend Samuel E. Cornish, *Freedom's Journal* served as a rallying cry for free blacks struggling against pervasive forms of discrimination in the North. The prospectus for *Freedom's Journal*, which appeared in the first issue on March 16, 1827, emphasizes abolition, education, and the need for racial solidarity in its demand for the full rights of citizenship for black Americans.

SOURCE: Herbert Aptheker, ed. *A Documentary History of the Negro People in the United States, Volume One.* New York: Carol Publishing Group, 1990.

SELECTED READINGS: Paul Goodman, *Of One Blood: Abolitionism and the Origins of Racial Equality* (1997). Benjamin Quarles, *Black Abolitionists* (1969). Herbert Aptheker, *The Negro in the Abolitionist Movement* (1941).

TO OUR PATRONS

In presenting our first number to our Patrons, we feel all the diffidence of persons entering upon a new and untried line of business. But a moment's reflection upon the noble objects, which we have in view by the publication of this Journal; the expediency of its appearance at this time, when so many schemes are in action concerning our people— encourage us to come boldly before an enlightened publick. For we believe, that a paper devoted to the dissimation of useful knowledge among our brethren, and to their moral and religious improvement, must meet with the cordial approbation of every friend to humanity.

The peculiarities of this Journal, renders it important that we should advertise to the world our motives by which we are actuated, and the objects which we contemplate.

We wish to plead our own cause. Too long have others spoken for us. Too long has the publick been deceived by misrepresentations, in things which concern us dearly, though in the estimation of some mere trifles; for though there are many in society who exercise towards us benevolent feelings; still (with sorrow we confess it) there are others who make it their business to enlarge upon the least trifle, which tends to the discredit of any person of colour; and pronounce anathemas and denounce our whole body for the misconduct of this guilty one. We are aware that there are many instances of vice among us, but we avow that it is because no one has taught its subjects to be virtuous; many instances of poverty, because no sufficient efforts accommodated to minds contracted by slavery, and deprived of early education have been made, to teach them how to husband their hard earnings, and to secure to themselves comfort. . . .

. . . From the press and the pulpit we have suffered much by being incorrectly represented. Men whom we equally love and admire have not hesitated to represent us disadvantageously, without becoming personally acquainted with the true state of things, nor discerning between virtue and vice among us. The virtuous part of our people feel themselves sorely aggrieved under the existing state of things—they are not appreciated.

Our vices and our degradation are ever arrayed against us, but our virtues are passed by unnoticed. And what is still more lamentable, our friends, to whom we concede all the principles of humanity and religion, from these very causes seem to have fallen into the current of popular feeling and are imperceptibly floating on the stream—actually living in the practice of prejudice, while they abjure it in theory, and feel it not in their hearts. Is it not very desirable that such should know more of our actual condition; and of our efforts and feelings, that in forming or advocating plans for our amelioration, they may do it more understandingly? In the spirit of candor and humility we intend by a simple representation of facts to lay our case before the public, with a view to arrest the progress of prejudice, and to shield ourselves against the consequent evils. We wish to conciliate all and to irritate none, yet we must be firm and unwavering in our principles, and persevering in our efforts.

If ignorance, poverty and degradation have hitherto been our unhappy lot; has the Eternal decree gone forth, that our race alone are to remain in this state, while knowledge and civilization are shedding their enlivening rays over the rest of the human family? The recent travels of Denham and Clapperton* in the interior of Africa, and the interesting narrative which they have published; the establishment of the republic of Hayti after years of sanguinary warfare; its subsequent progress in all the arts of civilization; and the advancement of liberal ideas in South America, where despotism has given place to free governments, and where many of our brethren now fill important civil and military stations, prove the contrary.

The interesting fact that there are FIVE HUNDRED THOUSAND free persons of colour, one half of whom might peruse, and the whole be benefitted by the publication of the Journal; that no publication, as yet, has been devoted exclusively to their improvement—that many selections from approved standard authors, which are within the reach of few, may occasionally be made—and more important still, that this large body of our citizens have no public channel—all serve to prove the real necessity, at present, for the appearance of the FREEDOM'S JOURNAL.

---

*Dixon Denham, *Narratives of travel and discoveries in northern and central Africa* . . . (Boston, 1826); Hugh Clapperton, *Journal of a second expedition into the interior of Africa* . . . (Phila., 1829).

28. DAVID WALKER

An Appeal to the Coloured
Citizens of the World
(1829)

DAVID WALKER's *Appeal to the Coloured Citizens of the World* was the most controversial tract of the early abolitionist period. Invoking the Bible, as well as the Declaration of Independence and U.S. Constitution, Walker's *Appeal* denounced the American Colonization Society, excoriated proslavery Christians, and called upon black Americans to rise up—violently if necessary—to overthrow the systems of slavery and white supremacy that undermined American democracy. Widely denounced when it first appeared in Boston in 1829—especially after copies of the pamphlet were found circulating among slaves in several Southern states—Walker's *Appeal* nevertheless inspired abolitionists like Maria W. Stewart, Henry Highland Garnet, and John Brown. Born and raised in Wilmington, North Carolina, David Walker (c. 1796–1830) spent his adult years in the vibrant free black communities of Charleston and Boston. He is considered one of the founding architects of black nationalism.

SOURCE: Peter P. Hinks, ed. *David Walker's Appeal to the Coloured Citizens of the World*. University Park, PA: Pennsylvania State University Press, 2000.

SELECTED READINGS: Peter P. Hinks, *To Awaken My Afflicted Brethren: David Walker and the Problem of Antebellum Slave Resistance* (1996). Vincent Harding, *There Is a River: The Black Struggle for Freedom in America* (1981). Herbert Aptheker, *"One Continual Cry": David Walker's Appeal to the Colored Citizens of the World (1829–1830)—Its Setting and Its Meaning* (1965).

Preamble

My dearly beloved Brethren and Fellow Citizens.

Having travelled over a considerable portion of these United States, and having, in the course of my travels, taken the most accurate observations of things as they exist—the result of my observations has warranted the full and unshaken conviction, that we, (coloured people of these United States,) are the most degraded, wretched, and abject set of beings that ever lived since the world began; and I pray God that none like us ever may live again until time shall be no more. They tell us of the Israelites in Egypt, the Helots in Sparta, and of the Roman Slaves, which last were made up from almost every nation under heaven, whose sufferings under those ancient and heathen nations, were, in comparison with ours, under this enlightened and Christian nation, no more than a cypher—or, in other words, those heathen nations of antiquity, had but little more among them than the name and form of slavery; while wretchedness and endless miseries were reserved, apparently in a phial, to be poured out upon our fathers, ourselves and our children, by *Christian* Americans!

These positions I shall endeavour, by the help of the Lord, to demonstrate in the course of this *Appeal,* to the satisfaction of the most incredulous mind—and may God Almighty, who is the Father of our Lord Jesus Christ, open your hearts to understand and believe the truth. . . .

[ARTICLE II.]

Beloved brethren—here let me tell you, and believe it, that the Lord our God, as true as he sits on his throne in heaven, and as true as our Saviour died to redeem the world, will give you a Hannibal, and when the Lord shall have raised him up, and given him to you for your possession, O my suffering brethren! remember the divisions and consequent sufferings of *Carthage* and of *Hayti.* Read the history particularly of Hayti, and see how they were butchered by the whites, and do you take warning. The person whom God shall give you, give him your support and let him go his length, and behold in him the salvation of your God. God will indeed, deliver you through him from your deplorable and wretched condition under the Christians of America. I charge you this day before my God to lay no obstacle in his way, but let him go.

The whites want slaves, and want us for their slaves, but some of them will curse the day they ever saw us. As true as the sun ever shone in its meridian splendor, my colour will root some of them out of the very face of the earth. They shall have enough of making slaves of, and butchering, and murdering us in the manner which they have. No doubt some may say that I write with a bad spirit, and that I being a black, wish these things to occur. Whether I write with a bad or a good spirit, I say if these things do not occur in their proper time, it is because the world in which we live does not exist, and we are deceived with regard to its existence.—It is immaterial however to me, who believe, or who death in the road! He may see a husband take his dear wife, not unfrequently in a pregnant state, and perhaps far advanced, and beat her for an unmerciful wretch, until his infant falls a lifeless lump at her feet! Can the Americans escape God Almighty? If they do, can he be to us a God of Justice? God is just, and I know it—for he has convinced me to my satisfaction—I cannot doubt him. . . .

Oh! coloured people of these United States, I ask you, in the name of that God who made us, have we, in consequence of oppression, nearly lost the spirit of man, and, in no very trifling degree, adopted that of brutes? Do you answer, no?—I ask you, then, what set of men can you point me to, in all the world, who are so abjectly employed by their oppressors, as we are by our *natural enemies?* How can, Oh! how can those enemies but say that we and our children are not of the HUMAN FAMILY, but were made by our Creator to be an inheritance to them and theirs for ever? How can the slaveholders but say that they can bribe the best coloured person in the country, to sell his brethren for a trifling sum of money, and take that atrocity to confirm them in their avaricious opinion, that we were made to be slaves to them and their children? How could Mr. Jefferson but say, "I advance it therefore as a suspicion only, that the blacks, whether originally a distinct race, or made distinct by time and circumstances, are *inferior* to the whites in the endowments both of body and mind?"—"It," says he, "is not against experience to suppose, that different species of the same genius, or varieties of the same species, may possess different qualifications." [Here, my brethren, listen to him.]

"Will not a lover of natural history, then, one who views the gradations in all the races of *animals* with the eye of philosophy, excuse an effort to keep those in the department of MAN as *distinct* as nature has formed them?"—I hope you will try to find out the meaning of this verse—its widest sense and all its bearings: whether you do or not, remember the whites do. This very verse, brethren, having emanated from Mr. Jefferson, a much greater philosopher the world never afforded, has in truth injured us more, and has been as great a barrier to our emancipation as any thing that has ever been advanced against us. I hope you will not let it pass unnoticed. He goes on further, and says: "This *unfortunate* difference of colour, and *perhaps* of *faculty,* is a powerful obstacle to the emancipation of these people. Many of their advocates, while they wish to vindicate the liberty of human nature are anxious also to preserve its *dignity* and *beauty*. Some of these, embarrassed by the question, 'What further is to be done with them?' join themselves in opposition with those who are actuated by sordid avarice only." Now I ask you candidly, my suffering brethren in time, who are candidates for the eternal worlds, how could Mr. Jefferson but have given the world these remarks respecting us, when we are so submissive to them, and so much servile deceit prevail among ourselves—when we so *meanly* submit to their murderous lashes, to which neither the Indians nor any other people under Heaven would submit? No, they would die to a man, before they would suffer such things from men who are no better than themselves, and *perhaps not so good*. Yes, how can our friends but be embarrassed, as Mr. Jefferson says, by the question, "What further is to be done with these people?" For while they are working for our eman- cipation, we are, by our treachery, wickedness and deceit, working against ourselves and our children—helping ours, and the enemies of God, to keep us and our dear little children in their infernal chains of slavery!!! Indeed, our friends cannot but relapse and join themselves "with those who are actuated by *sordid avarice* only!!!!" For my own part, I am glad Mr. Jefferson has advanced his positions for your sake; for you will either have to contradict or confirm him by your own actions, and not by what our friends have said or done for us; for those things are other men's labours, and do not satisfy the Americans, who are waiting for us to prove to them ourselves, that we are MEN, before they will be willing to admit the fact; for I pledge you my sacred word of honour, that Mr. Jefferson's remarks respecting us, have sunk deep into the hearts of millions of the whites, and never will be removed this side of eternity.—For how can they, when we are confirming him every day, by our *groveling submissions* and *treachery*? I aver, that when I look over these United States of America, and the world, and see the ignorant deceptions and consequent wretchedness of my brethren, I am brought oftimes solemnly to a stand, and in the midst of my reflections I exclaim to my God, "Lord didst thou make us to be slaves to our brethren, the whites?" But when I reflect that God is just, and that millions of my wretched brethren would meet death with glory—yea, more, would plunge into the very mouths of cannons and be torn into particles as minute as the atoms which compose the elements of the earth, in pref- erence to a mean submission to the lash of tyrants, I am with streaming eyes, compelled to shrink back into nothingness before my Maker, and exclaim again, thy will be done, O Lord God Almighty.

29. OPENING EDITORIAL

The Liberator
(1831)

Published weekly in Boston, *The Liberator* was the most important and longest-running newspaper of the abolitionist movement. The opening editorial, entitled "To the Public," was written by William Lloyd Garrison (1805–1879), who served as the paper's editor for the full run of its publication from January 1, 1831, to December 22, 1865. Promising to be "as harsh as truth, and as uncompromising as justice," Garrison's editorial marked the first time in American history that a white newspaper had publicly denounced African colonization and advocated for full black enfranchisement, a commitment that garnered wide political and financial support among African Americans. As such, *The Liberator* was the main voice of "immediatism," the doctrine espoused by the radical wing of the abolitionist movement.

SOURCE: William E. Cain, ed. *William Lloyd Garrison and the Fight against Slavery: Selections from the Liberator.* Boston and New York: Bedford Books, 1995.

SELECTED READINGS: Henry Mayer, *All On Fire: William Lloyd Garrison and the Abolition of Slavery* (1998). James Brewer Stewart, *William Lloyd Garrison and the Challenge of Emancipation* (1991). Walter Merrill, *Against Wind and Tide: A Biography of William Lloyd Garrison* (1965).

Assenting to the "self-evident truth" maintained in the American Declaration of Independence, "that all men are created equal, and endowed by their Creator with certain inalienable rights—among which are life, liberty and the pursuit of happiness," I shall strenuously contend for the immediate enfranchisement of our slave population. In Park-street Church, on the Fourth of July, 1829, in an address on slavery, I unreflectingly assented to the popular but pernicious doctrine of *gradual* abolition. I seize this opportunity to make a full and unequivocal recantation, and thus publicly to ask pardon of my God, of my country, and of my brethren the poor slaves, for having uttered a sentiment so full of timidity, injustice and absurdity. A similar recantation, from my pen, was published in the Genius of Universal Emancipation at Baltimore, in September, 1829. My conscience is now satisfied.

I am aware, that many object to the severity of my language; but is there not cause for severity? I *will be* as harsh as truth, and as uncompromising as justice. On this subject, I do not wish to think, or speak, or write, with moderation. No! no! Tell a man whose house is on fire, to give a moderate alarm; tell him to moderately rescue his wife from the hands of the ravisher; tell the mother to gradually extricate her babe from the fire into which it has fallen;— but urge me not to use moderation in a cause like the present. I am in earnest—I will not equivocate—I will not excuse—I will not retreat a single inch—AND I WILL BE HEARD. The apathy of the people is enough to make every statue leap from its pedestal, and to hasten the resurrection of the dead.

It is pretended, that I am retarding the cause of emancipation by the coarseness of my invective, and the precipitancy of my measures. *The charge is not true.* On this question my influence,—humble as it is,—is felt at this moment to a considerable extent, and shall be felt in coming years—not perniciously, but beneficially—not as a curse, but as a blessing; and posterity will bear testimony that I was right. I desire to thank God, that he enables me to disregard "the fear of man which bringeth a snare," and to speak his truth in its simplicity and power. And here I close with this fresh dedication:

> Oppression! I have seen thee, face to face,
> And met thy cruel eye and cloudy brow;
> But thy soul-withering glance I fear not now—
> For dread to prouder feelings doth give place
> Of deep abhorrence! Scorning the disgrace
> Of slavish knees that at thy footstool bow,
> I also kneel—but with far other vow
> Do hail thee and thy hord of hirelings base:—
> I swear, while life-blood warms my throbbing veins,
> Still to oppose and thwart, with heart and hand,
> Thy brutalising sway—till Afric's chains
> Are burst, and Freedom rules the rescued land,—
> Trampling Oppression and his iron rod:
> *Such is the vow I take*—SO HELP ME GOD!

> William Lloyd Garrison
> Boston, January 1, 1831

30. NAT TURNER,

Confession
(1831)

In August 1831, in the small farm community of Southampton, Virginia, **NAT TURNER (1800–1831)** led the most notable slave revolt in American history. Turner was a literate slave preacher who, in the 1820s, began to see visions of black angels and white angels fighting in the sky, which he interpreted as a sign that God had chosen him to liberate his people. Following his arrest for murder, Turner recorded his account of the uprising with Thomas C. Gray, a local white man. His "confession," which was widely circulated at antislavery gatherings and later reprinted in abolitionist pamphlets and newspapers, is the only published account of the Southampton revolt from Turner's perspective. While Turner's revolt provided ample evidence that slaves were less than "content" with the institution of slavery, it also inspired white retaliation against innocent blacks, a debate among abolitionists over the use of violence, and harsher slave codes throughout the South.

SOURCE: Eric Foner, ed. *Nat Turner.* Englewood Cliffs, NJ: Prentice-Hall, 1971.

SELECTED READINGS: Eugene D. Genovese, *From Rebellion to Revolution* (1979). Stephen B. Oates, *The Fires of Jubilee: Nat Turner's Fierce Rebellion* (1975). Herbert Aptheker, *American Negro Slave Revolts* (1943).

Ques. Do you not find yourself mistaken now? *Ans.* Was not Christ crucified? And by signs in the heavens that it would make known to me when I should commence the great work—and until the first sign appeared, I should conceal it from the knowledge of men—And on the appearance of the sign, (the eclipse of the sun last February) I should arise and prepare myself, and slay my enemies with their own weapons. And immediately on the sign appearing in the heavens, the seal was removed from my lips, and I communicated the great work laid out for me to do, to four in whom I had the greatest confidence, (Henry, Hark, Nelson, and Sam)—It was intended by us to have begun the work of death on the 4th July last—Many were the plans formed and rejected by us, and it affected my mind to such a degree, that I fell sick, and the time passed without our coming to any determination how to commence—Still forming new schemes and rejecting them, when the sign appeared again, which determined me not to wait longer.

Since the commencement of 1830, I had been living with Mr. Joseph Travis, who was to me a *kind master*, and placed the greatest confidence in me; in fact, I had no cause to complain of his treatment to me. On Saturday evening, the 20th of August, it was agreed between Henry, Hark and myself, to prepare a dinner the next day for the men we expected, and then to concert a plan, as we had not yet determined on any. Hark, on the following morning, brought a pig, and Henry brandy, and being joined by Sam, Nelson, Will and Jack, they prepared in the woods a dinner, where, about three o'clock, I joined them.

Q. Why were you so backward in joining them?

A. The same reason that had caused me not to mix with them for years before.

I saluted them on coming up, and asked Will how came he there, he answered, his life was worth no more than others, and his liberty as dear to him. I asked him if he thought to obtain it? He said he would, or lose his life. This was enough to put him in full confidence. Jack, I knew, was only a tool in the hands of Hark, it was quickly agreed we should commence at home (Mr. J. Travis') on that night, and until we had armed and equipped ourselves, and gathered sufficient force, neither age nor sex was to be spared, (which was invariably adhered to). We remained at the feast, until about two hours in the night, when we went to the house and found Austin; they all went to the cider press and drank, except myself. On returning to the house, Hark went to the door with an axe, for the purpose of breaking it open, as we knew we were strong enough to murder the family, if they were awaked by the noise; but reflecting that it might create an alarm in the neighborhood, we determined to enter the house secretly, and murder them whilst sleeping. Hark got a ladder and set it against the chimney, on which I ascended, and hoisting a window, entered and came down stairs, unbarred the door, and removed the guns from their places. It was then observed that I must spill the first blood. On which, armed with a hatchet, and accompanied by Will, I entered my master's chamber, it being dark, I could not give a death blow, the hatchet glanced from his head, he sprang from the bed and called his wife, it was his last word, Will laid him dead, with a blow of his axe, and Mrs. Travis shared the same fate, as she lay in bed. The murder of this family, five in number, was the work of a moment, not one of them awoke; there was a little infant sleeping in a cradle, that was forgotten, until we had left the house and gone some distance, when Henry and Will returned and killed it; we got here, four guns that would shoot, and several old muskets, with a pound or two of powder. We remained some time at the barn, where we paraded; I formed them in a line as soldiers, and after carrying them through all the manoeuvres I was master of marched them off to Mr. Salathul Francis', about six hundred yards distant. Sam and Will went to the door and knocked. Mr. Francis asked who was there, Sam replied it was him, and he had a letter for him, on which he got up and came to the door; they immediately seized him, and dragging him out a little from the door, he was dispatched by repeated blows on the head; there was no other white person in the family. We started from there for Mrs. Reese's, maintaining the most perfect silence on our march, where finding the door unlocked, we entered, and murdered Mrs. Reese in her bed, while sleeping; her son awoke, but it was only to sleep the sleep of death, he had only time to say who is that, and he was no more. From Mrs. Reese's we went to Mrs. Turner's, a mile distant, which we reached about sunrise, on Monday morning. Henry, Austin, and Sam, went to the still, where, finding Mr. Peebles, Austin shot him, and the rest of us went to the house; as we approached, the family discovered us, and shut the door. Vain hope! Will, with one stroke of his axe, opened it, and we entered and found Mrs. Turner and Mrs. Newsome in the middle of a room, almost frightened to death. Will immediately killed Mrs. Turner, with one blow of his axe. I took Mrs. Newsome by the hand, and with the sword I had when I was apprehended, I struck her several blows over the head, but not being able to kill her, as the sword was dull. Will turning around and discovering it, despatched her also. A general destruction of property and search for money and ammunition, always succeeded the murders. By this time my company amounted to fifteen, and nine men mounted, who started for Mrs. Whitehead's, (the other six were to go through a by way to Mr. Bryant's, and rejoin us at Mrs. Whitehead's,) as we approached the house we discovered Mr. Richard Whitehead standing in the cotton patch, near the lane fence; we called him over into the lane, and Will, the executioner, was near at hand, with his fatal axe, to send him to an untimely grave. As we pushed on to the house, I discovered some one run round the garden, and thinking it was some of the white family, I pursued them, but finding it was a servant girl belonging to the house, I returned to commence the work of death, but they whom I left, had not been idle; all the family were already murdered, but Mrs. Whitehead and her daughter Margaret. As I came round to the door I saw Will pulling Mrs. Whitehead out of the house, and at the step he nearly severed her head from her body, with his broad axe. Miss Margaret, when I discovered her, had concealed herself in the corner, formed by the projection of cellar cap from the house; on my approach she fled, but was soon overtaken, and after repeated blows with a sword, I killed her by a blow on the head, with a fence rail. By this time, the six who had gone by Mr. Bryant's, rejoined us, and informed me they had done the work of death assigned them. We again divided, part going to Mr. Richard Porter's, and from thence to Nathaniel Francis', the others to Mr. Howell Harris', and Mr. T. Doyle's. On my reaching Mr. Porter's, he had escaped with his family. I understood there, that the alarm had already spread, and I immediately returned to bring up those sent to Mr. Doyle's, and Mr. Howell Harris'; the party I left going on to Mr. Francis', having told them I would join them in that neighborhood. I met these sent to Mr. Doyle's and Mr. Harris' returning, having met Mr. Doyle on the road and killed him; and learning from some who joined them, that Mr. Harris was from home, I immediately pursued the course taken by the party gone on before; but knowing they would complete *the work of death and pillage,* at Mr. Francis' before I could get there, I went to Mr. Peter Edwards', expecting to find them there, but they had been here also. I then went to Mr. John T. Barrow's, they had been here and murdered him. I pursued on their track to Capt. Newit Harris', where I found the greater part mounted, and ready to start; the men now amounting to about forty, shouted and hurraed as I rode up, some were in the yard, loading their guns, others drinking. They said Captain Harris and his family had escaped, the property in the house they destroyed, robbing him of money and other valuables. I ordered them to mount and march instantly, this was about nine or ten o'clock, Monday morning. I proceeded to Mr. Levi Waller's, two or three miles distant. I took my station in the rear, and as it was my object to carry terror and devastation wherever we went, I placed fifteen or twenty of the best armed and most relied on, in front, who generally approached the houses as fast as their horses could run; this was for two purposes, to prevent escape and strike terror to the inhabitants—on this account I never got to the houses, after leaving Mrs. Whitehead's, until the murders were committed, except in one case. I sometimes got in sight in time to see the work of death completed, viewed the mangled bodies as they lay, in silent satisfaction, and immediately started in quest of other victims . . .

31. AMERICAN ANTI-SLAVERY SOCIETY

Declaration of Sentiments
(1833)

In December 1833, more than sixty delegates—blacks and whites, men and women—met in Philadelphia to form the **AMERICAN ANTI-SLAVERY SOCIETY.** Inspired by the abolition of slavery in the British Empire in August of that same year, American abolitionists sought to create a national antislavery society committed to immediate abolition and racial equality. The following "Declaration of Sentiments," written primarily by William Lloyd Garrison but with suggestions from Samuel J. May and John Greenleaf Whittier, listed the new organization's goals and sentiments, including the fulfillment of the ideals of the American Revolution and an embrace of nonviolence. The "Declaration" served as the ideological blueprint for auxiliary antislavery societies, more than 1,600 of which were in existence by 1840. With this rapid expansion in membership and activity, antislavery agents were able to canvass the North with pamphlets, lectures, and petitions in a vigorous crusade to plead the abolitionist cause.

SOURCE: William H. and Jane H. Pease, eds. *The Antislavery Argument.* Indianapolis: Bobbs-Merrill, 1965.

SELECTED READINGS: James Brewer Stewart, *Holy Warriors: The Abolitionists and American Slavery* (1976). Ronald G. Walters, *The Antislavery Appeal: American Abolitionism after 1830* (1976). Merton Dillon, *The Abolitionists: Growth of a Dissenting Minority* (1974).

The Convention, assembled in the City of Philadelphia to organize a National Anti-Slavery Society, promptly seize the opportunity to promulgate the following DECLARATION OF SENTIMENTS, as cherished by them in relation to the enslavement of one-sixth portion of the American people.

More than fifty-seven years have elapsed since a band of patriots convened in this place, to devise measures for the deliverance of this country from a foreign yoke. The cornerstone upon which they founded the TEMPLE OF FREE-DOM was broadly this—'that all men are created equal; that they are endowed by their Creator with certain inalienable rights; that among these are life, LIBERTY, and the pursuit of happiness.' At the sound of their trumpet-call, three millions of people rose up as from the sleep of death, and rushed to the strife of blood; deeming it more glorious to die instantly as freemen, than desirable to live one hour as slaves. They were few in number—poor in resources; but the honest conviction that TRUTH, JUSTICE and RIGHT were on their side, made them invincible.

We have met together for the achievement of an enterprise, without which, that of our fathers is incomplete, and which, for its magnitude, solemnity, and probable results upon the destiny of the world, as far transcends theirs, as moral truth does physical force.

In purity of motive, in earnestness of zeal, in decision of purpose, in intrepidity of action, in steadfastness of faith, in sincerity of spirit, we would not be inferior to them. . . .

Hence we maintain—

That in view of the civil and religious privileges of this nation, the guilt of its oppression is unequalled by any other on the face of the earth;—and, therefore,

That it is bound to repent instantly, to undo the heavy burden, to break every yoke, and to let the oppressed go free.

We further maintain—

That no man has a right to enslave or imbrute his brother—to hold or acknowledge him, for one moment, as a piece of merchandise—to keep back his hire by fraud—or to brutalize his mind by denying him the means of intellectual, social and moral improvement.

The right to enjoy liberty is inalienable. To invade it, is to usurp the prerogative of Jehovah. Every man has a right to his own body—to the products of his own labor—to the protection of law—and to the common advantages of society. It is piracy to buy or steal a native African, and subject him to servitude. Surely the sin is as great to enslave an AMERICAN as an AFRICAN.

Therefore we believe and affirm—

That there is no difference, *in principle,* between the African slave trade and American slavery;

That every American citizen, who retains a human being in involuntary bondage, as his property, is [according to Scripture] a MAN-STEALER.

That the slaves ought instantly to be set free, and brought under the protection of law;

That if they had lived from the time of Pharaoh down to the present period, and had been entailed through successive generations, their right to be free could never have been alienated, but their claims would have constantly risen in solemnity;

That all those laws which are now in force, admitting the right of slavery, are therefore before God utterly null and void; being an audacious usurpation of the Divine prerogative, a daring infringement on the law of nature, a base overthrow of the very foundations of the social compact, a complete extinction of all the relations, endearments and obligations of mankind, and a presumptuous transgression of all the holy commandments—and that therefore they ought to be instantly abrogated.

We further believe and affirm—

That all persons of color who possess the qualifications which are demanded of others, ought to be admitted forthwith to the enjoyment of the same privileges, and the exercise of the same prerogatives, as others; and that the paths of preferment, of wealth, and of intelligence, should be opened as widely to them as to persons of a white complexion.

We maintain that no compensation should be given to the planters emancipating their slaves—

Because it would be a surrender of the great fundamental principle, that man cannot hold property in man;

Because SLAVERY IS A CRIME, AND THEREFORE IT IS NOT AN ARTICLE TO BE SOLD;

Because the holders of slaves are not the just proprietors of what they claim;—freeing the slaves is not depriving them of property, but restoring it to the right owner;—it is not wronging the master, but righting the slave—restoring him to himself;

Because immediate and general emancipation would only destroy nominal, not real property: it would not amputate a limb or break a bone of the slaves, but by infusing motives into their breasts, would make them doubly valuable to the masters as free laborers; and

Because if compensation is to be given at all, it should be given to the outraged and guiltless slaves, and not to those who have plundered and abused them.

We regard, as delusive, cruel and dangerous, any scheme of expatriation which pretends to aid, either directly or indirectly, in the emancipation of the slaves, or to be a substitute for the immediate and total abolition of slavery.

We fully and unanimously recognise the sovereignty of each State, to legislate exclusively on the subject of the slavery which is tolerated within its limits. We concede that Congress, *under the present national compact,* has no right to interfere with any of the slave States, in relation to this momentous subject.

But we maintain that Congress has a right, and is solemnly bound, to suppress the domestic slave trade between the several States, and to abolish slavery in those portions of our territory which the Constitution has placed under its exclusive jurisdiction.

We also maintain that there are, at the present time, the highest obligations resting upon the people of the free States to remove slavery by moral and political action, as prescribed in the Constitution of the United States. They are now living under a pledge of their tremendous physical force to fasten the galling fetters of tyranny upon the limbs of millions in the southern States;— they are liable to be called at any moment to suppress a general insurrection of the slaves;—they authorise the slave owner to vote for three-fifths of his slaves as property, and thus enable him to perpetuate his oppression;—they support a standing army at the south for its protection;—and they seize the slave who has escaped into their territories, and send him back to be tortured by an enraged master or a brutal driver.

This relation to slavery is criminal and full of danger: IT MUST BE BROKEN UP.

32. MARIA W. STEWART

Productions

(1835)

In 1833, MARIA W. STEWART (1803–1879) became the first American-born woman to publicly address a "promiscuous" gathering of men and women when she delivered a lecture denouncing colonization at Boston's African Masonic Hall. Mixing sacred and secular themes, Stewart's speeches and writings called upon fellow blacks to struggle individually and collectively to overcome slavery, poverty, and racial prejudice. She advocated separate black social and religious institutions, and challenged black women, especially, to become equal participants in public life. In this, she was one of the first American writers to understand that the struggle for equality involved not only the abolition of slavery and the elimination of racial prejudice, but the dismantling of patriarchal institutions as well. In 1835, shortly after she moved from Boston to New York, Stewart published *Productions of Mrs. Maria W. Stewart,* a collection of her religious meditations, public speeches, and political writings. A longstanding advocate for equal education for blacks and women, Stewart also taught in public and private schools in New York City, Baltimore, and Washington, D.C.

SOURCE: Richard Newman, Patrick Rael, and Phillip Lapsansky, eds. *Pamphlets of Protest: An Anthology of Early African-American Protest Literature, 1790–1860.* New York and London: Routledge, 2001.

SELECTED READINGS: Patricia Hill Collins, *Black Feminist Thought: Knowledge, Consciousness, and the Politics of Empowerment* (1990). Marilyn Richardson, ed., *Maria W. Stewart, America's First Black Woman Political Writer: Essays and Speeches* (1987). Shirley J. Yee, *Black Woman Abolitionists: A Study of Activism, 1828–1860* (1982).

African rights and liberty is a subject that ought to fire the breast of every free man of color in these United States, and excite in his bosom a lively, deep, decided, and heart-felt interest. When I cast my eyes on the long list of illustrious names that are enrolled on the bright annals of fame among the whites, I turn my eyes within, and ask my thoughts, "Where are the names of *our* illustrious ones?" It must certainly have been for the want of energy on the part of the free people of color, that they have been long willing to bear the yoke of oppression. It must have been the want of ambition and force that has given the whites occasion to say that our natural abilities are not as good, and our capacities by nature inferior to theirs. They boldly assert that, did we possess a natural independence of soul, and feel a love for liberty within our breasts, some one of our sable race long before this would have testified it, notwithstanding the disadvantages under which we labor. We have made our-selves appear altogether unqualified to speak in our own defence, and are therefore looked upon as objects of pity and commiseration. We have been imposed upon, insulted and derided on every side; and now, if we complain, it is considered as the height of impertinence. We have suffered ourselves to be considered as dastards, cowards, mean, faint-hearted wretches; and on this account, (not because of our complexion) many despise us, and would gladly spurn us from their presence. . . .

But I forbear. Let our money, instead of being thrown away as heretofore, be appropriated for schools and seminaries of learning for our children and youth. We ought to follow the example of the whites in this respect. Nothing would raise our respectability, add to our peace and happiness, and reflect so much honor upon us, as to be ourselves the promoters of temperance, and the supporters, as far as we are able, of useful and scientific knowledge. The rays of light and knowledge have been hid from our view; we have been taught to consider ourselves as scarce superior to the brute creation; and have performed the most laborious part of American drudgery. Had we as a people received one half the early advantages the whites have received, I would defy the government of these United States to deprive us any longer of our rights. . . .

. . . It is of no use for us to wait any longer for a generation of well educated men to arise. We have slumbered and slept too long already; the day is far spent; the night of death approaches; and you have sound sense and good judgment sufficient to begin with, if you feel disposed to make a right use of it. Let every man of color throughout the United States, who possesses the spirit and principles of a man, sign a petition to Congress, to abolish slavery in the District of Columbia, and grant you the rights and privileges of common free citizens; for if you had had faith as a grain of mustard seed, long before this the mountains of prejudice might have been removed. We are all sensible that the Anti-Slavery Society has taken hold of the arm of our whole population, in order to raise them out of the mire. Now all we have to do is, by a spirit of virtuous ambition to strive to raise ourselves; and I am happy to have it in my power thus publicly to say, that the colored inhabitants of this city, in some respects, are beginning to improve. Had the free people of color in these United States nobly and boldly con-tended for their rights, and showed a natural genius and talent, although not so brilliant as some; had they held up, encouraged and patronized each other, nothing could have hindered us from being a thriving and flourishing people. There has been a fault among us. The reason why our distinguished men have not made themselves more influential is, because they fear that the strong current of op-position through which they must pass, would cause their downfall and prove their overthrow. And what gives rise to this opposition? Envy. And what has it amounted to? Nothing, And who are the cause of it? Our whited sepulchres, who want to be great, and don't know how; who love to be called of men 'Rabbi, Rabbi, who put on false sanctity, and humble themselves to their brethren, for the sake of acquiring the highest place in the synagogue, and the upper-most seats at the feast. You, dearly beloved, who are the genuine followers of our Lord Jesus Christ, the salt of the earth and the light of the world, are not so culpable. As I told you, in the very first of my writing, I tell you again, I am but as a drop in the bucket-as one particle of the small dust of the earth. God will surely raise up those among us who will plead the cause of virtue, and the pure principles of morality, more eloquently than I am able to do.

It appears to me that America has become like the great city of Babylon, for she has boasted in her heart, "I sit a queen, and am no widow, and shall see no sorrow?" She is indeed a seller of slaves and the souls of men; she has made the Africans drunk with the wine of her fornication; she has put them completely beneath her feet, and she means to keep them there; her right hand supports the reins of government, and her left hand the wheel of power, and she is determined not to let go her grasp. But many powerful sons and daughters of Africa will shortly arise, who will put down vice and immorality among us, and declare by Him that sitteth upon the throne, that they will have their rights; and if refused, I am afraid they will spread horror and devastation around. I believe that the oppression of injured Africa has come up before the Majesty of Heaven; and when our cries shall have reached the ears of the Most High, it will be a tremendous day for the people of this land; for strong is the arm of the Lord God Almighty.

33. ANGELINA GRIMKÉ

An Appeal to the Christian Women of the South
(1836)

ANGELINA EMILY GRIMKÉ (1805–1879) was among the first women abolitionists to address "mixed" audiences of blacks and whites in the United States. Born into a wealthy slave-owning family in Charleston, South Carolina, Grimké and her sister, Sarah, developed a profound hatred of slavery, prompting them to move to Philadelphia in 1829, where they converted to Quakerism and emerged as leaders in the first group of female antislavery lecturers. Angelina Grimké's firsthand experiences with slavery formed the basis of her most famous work, *An Appeal to the Christian Women of the South*, published by the American Anti-Slavery Society in 1836. This thirty-six-page pamphlet called upon her "Southern sisters" to help overthrow the institution of slavery through prayer and public action. Using the biblical language of "redemption," Grimké's *Appeal* was an eloquent if controversial critique of Southern slavery that inspired many women to question their subordinate role in society and to become active in the abolitionist movement.

SOURCE: Angelina Emily Grimké. *Appeal to the Christian Women of the South*. New York: Arno Press, 1969.

SELECTED READINGS: Anna M. Speicher, *The Religious World of Antislavery Women: Spirituality in the Lives of Five Abolitionist Lecturers* (2000). Catherine Du Pre Lumpkin, *The Emancipation of Angelina Grimké* (1974). Gerda Lerner, *The Grimké Sisters of South Carolina* (1967).

But perhaps you will be ready to query, why appeal to *women* on this subject? *We* do not make the laws which perpetuate slavery. *No* legislative power is vested in *us; we* can do nothing to overthrow the system, even if we wished to do so. To this I reply, I know you do not make the laws, but I also know that *you are the wives and mothers, the sisters and daughters of those who do;*

and if you really suppose *you* can do nothing to overthrow slavery, you are greatly mistaken. You can do much in every way: four things I will name. 1st. You can read on this subject. 2d. You can pray over this subject. 3d. You can speak on this subject. 4th. You can *act* on this subject. I have not placed reading before praying because I regard it more important, but because, in order to pray aright, we must understand what we are praying for; it is only then we can "pray with the understanding and the spirit also."

1. Read then on the subject of slavery. Search the Scriptures daily, whether the things I have told you are true. Other books and papers might be a great help to you in this investigation, but they are not necessary, and it is hardly probable that your Committees of Vigilance will allow you to have any other. The *Bible* then is the book I want you to read in the spirit of inquiry, and the spirit of prayer. Even the enemies of Abolitionists, acknowledge that their doctrines are drawn from it. In the great mob in Boston, last autumn, when the books and papers of the Anti-Slavery Society, were thrown out of the windows of their office, one individual laid hold of the Bible and was about tossing it out to the ground, when another reminded him that it was the Bible he had in his hand. *"O! 'tis all one,"* he replied, and out went the sacred volume, along with the rest. We thank him for the acknowledgment. Yes, *"it is all one,"* for our books and papers are mostly commentaries on the Bible, and the Declaration. Read the *Bible* then, it contains the words of Jesus, and they are spirit and life. Judge for yourselves whether *he sanctioned* such a system of oppression and crime.

2. Pray over this subject. When you have entered into your closets, and shut to the doors, then pray to your father, who seeth in secret, that he would open your eyes to see whether slavery is *sinful,* and if it is, that he would enable you to bear a faithful, open and unshrinking testimony against it, and to do whatsoever your hands find to do, leaving the consequences entirely to him, who still says to us whenever we try to reason away duty from the fear of consequences, *"What is that to thee, follow thou me."* Pray also for that poor slave, that he may be kept patient and submissive under his hard lot, until God is pleased to open the door of freedom to him without violence or bloodshed. Pray too for the master that his heart may be softened, and he made willing to acknowledge, as Joseph's brethren did, "Verily we are guilty concerning our brother," before he will be compelled to add in consequence of Divine judgment, "therefore is all this evil come upon us." Pray also for all your brethren and sisters who are laboring in the righteous cause of Emancipation in the Northern States, England and the world. There is great encouragement for prayer in these words of our Lord. "Whatsoever ye shall ask the Father *in my name*, he *will* give it to you"—Pray then without ceasing, in the closet and the social circle.

3. Speak on this subject. It is through the tongue, the pen, and the press, that truth is principally propagated. Speak then to your relatives, your friends, your acquaintances on the subject of slavery; be not afraid if you are conscientiously convinced it is *sinful*, to say so openly, but calmly, and to let your sentiments be known. If you are served by the slaves of others, try to ameliorate their condition as much as possible; never aggravate their faults, and thus add fuel to the fire of anger already kindled, in a master and mistress's bosom; remember their extreme ignorance, and consider them as your Heavenly Father does the *less* culpable on this account, even when they do wrong things. Discountenance *all* cruelty to them, all starvation, all corporal chastisement; these may brutalize and *break* their spirits, but will never bend them to willing, cheerful obedience. If possible, see that they are comfortably and *seasonably* fed, whether in the house or the field; it is unreasonable and cruel to expect slaves to wait for their breakfast until eleven o'clock, when they rise at five or six. Do all you can, to induce their owners to clothe them well, and to allow them many little indulgences which would contribute to their comfort. Above all, try to persuade your husband, father, brothers and sons, that *slavery is a crime against God and man*, and that it is a great sin to keep *human beings* in such abject ignorance; to deny them the privilege of learning to read and write. The Catholics are universally condemned, for denying the Bible to the common people, but, *slaveholders must not* blame them, for *they* are doing the *very same thing*, and for the very same reason, neither of these systems can bear the light which bursts from the pages of that Holy Book. And lastly, endeavour to inculcate submission on the part of the slaves, but whilst doing this be faithful in pleading the cause of the oppressed.

> "Will you behold unheeding,
>   Life's holiest feelings crushed,
> Where woman's heart is bleeding,
>   Shall woman's voice be hushed?"

4. Act on this subject. Some of you *own* slaves yourselves. If you believe slavery is *sinful*, set them at liberty, "undo the heavy burdens and let the oppressed go free." If they wish to remain with you, pay them wages, if not let them leave you. Should they remain teach them, and have them taught the common branches of an English education; they have minds and those minds, *ought to be improved*. So precious a talent as intellect, never was given to be wrapt in a napkin and buried in the earth. It is the *duty* of all, as far as they can, to improve their own mental faculties, because we are commanded to love God with *all our*

minds, as well as with all our hearts, and we commit a great sin, if we *forbid or prevent* that cultivation of the mind in others, which would enable them to perform this duty. Teach your servants then to read &c, and encourage them to believe it is their *duty* to learn, if it were only that they might read the Bible. . . .

34. THEODORE DWIGHT WELD

American Weld's book

(1839)

THEODORE DWIGHT WELD's *American Slavery As It Is: Testimony of a Thousand Witnesses* was the most widely distributed and influential publication of the American abolitionist movement. Weld (1803–1895), a revivalist minister and renowned orator who was the leading abolitionist in the West during the 1830s, compiled the volume with his wife, Angelina Grimké, and her sister, Sarah, with the financial support of the American Anti-Slavery Society. *American Slavery As It Is*, published in 1839, was a documentary collection of shocking exposés, taken from Southern newspaper accounts of the treatment of slaves, intended to offer conclusive, factual evidence about the horrors of slavery. Harriet Beecher Stowe, author of the antislavery protest novel *Uncle Tom's Cabin* (1852), later admitted that she slept with Weld's book under her pillow "until its facts crystallized into *Uncle Tom*."

SOURCE: William H. and Jane H. Pease, eds. *The Antislavery Argument.* Indianapolis: Bobbs-Merrill, 1965.

SELECTED READINGS: Robert Abzug, *Passionate Liberator: Theodore Weld and the Dilemma of Reform* (1980). Benjamin P. Thomas, *Theodore Weld: Crusader for Freedom* (1950). Gilbert H. Barnes, *The Antislavery Impulse, 1830–1844* (1933).

Two millions seven hundred thousand persons in these States are in this condition. They were made slaves and are held such by force, and by being put in fear, and this for no crime! Reader, what have you to say of such treatment? Is it right, just, benevolent? Suppose I should seize you, rob you of your liberty, drive you into the field, and make you work without pay as long as you live, would that be justice and kindness, or monstrous injustice and cruelty? Now, every body knows that the slaveholders do these things to the slaves every day, and yet it is stoutly affirmed that they treat them well and kindly, and that their tender regard for their slaves restrains the masters from inflicting cruelties upon them. We shall go into no metaphysics to show the absurdity of this pretence. The man who *robs* you every day, is, forsooth, quite too tenderhearted ever to cuff or kick you! True, he can snatch your money, but he does it gently lest he should hurt you. He can empty your pockets without qualms, but if your *stomach* is empty, it cuts him to the quick. He can make you work a life time without pay, but loves you too well to let you go hungry. He fleeces you of your *rights* with a relish, but is shocked if you work bareheaded in summer, or in winter without warm stockings. He can make you go without your *liberty*, but never without a shirt. He can crush, in you, all hope of bettering your condition, by vowing that you shall die his slave, but though he can coolly torture your feelings, he is too compassionate to lacerate your back—he can break your heart, but he is very tender of your skin. He can strip you of all protection and thus expose you to all outrages, but if you are exposed to the *weather*, half clad and half sheltered, how yearn his tender bowels! What! slaveholders talk of treating men well, and yet not only rob them of all they get, and as fast as they get it, but rob them of *themselves*, also; their very hands and feet, all their muscles, and limbs, and senses, their bodies and minds, their time and liberty and earnings, their free speech and rights of conscience, their right to acquire knowledge, and property, and reputation;—and yet they, who plunder them of all these, would fain make us believe that their soft hearts ooze out so lovingly toward their slaves that they always keep them well housed and well clad, never push them too hard in the field, never make their dear backs smart, nor let their dear stomachs get empty.

But there is no end to these absurdities. Are slaveholders dunces, or do they take all the rest of the world to be, that they think to bandage our eyes with such thin gauzes? Protesting their kind regard for those whom they hourly plunder of all they have and all they get! What! when they have seized their victims, and annihilated all their *rights*, still claim to be the special guardians of their *happiness!* Plunderers of their liberty, yet the careful suppliers of their wants? Robbers of their earnings, yet watchful sentinels round their interests, and kind providers for their comfort? Filching all their time, yet granting generous donations for rest and sleep? Stealing the use of their muscles, yet thoughtful of their ease? Putting them under *drivers*, yet careful that they are not hard-pushed? Too humane forsooth to stint the stomachs of their slaves, yet force their *minds* to starve, and brandish over them pains and penalties, if they dare to reach forth for the smallest crumb of knowledge, even a letter of the alphabet! . . .

They tell us, also, that the slaveholders of the South are proverbially hospitable, kind, and generous, and it is incredible that they can perpetrate such enormities upon human beings; further, that it is absurd to suppose that they would thus injure their own property, that self interest would prompt them to treat their slaves with kindness, as none but fools and madmen wantonly destroy their own property; further, that Northern visitors at the South come back testifying to the kind treatment of the slaves, and that the slaves themselves corroborate such representations. All these pleas, and scores of others, are bruited in every corner of the free States; and who that hath eyes to see, has not sickened at the blindness that saw not, at the palsy of heart that felt not, or at the cowardice and sycophancy that dared not expose such shallow fallacies. We are not to be turned from our purpose by such vapid babblings. In their appropriate places, we propose to consider these objections and various others, and to show their emptiness and folly.

35. HENRY HIGHLAND GARNET

An Address to the Slaves of the United States
(1843)

Born a slave in Maryland, **HENRY HIGHLAND GARNET (1815–1882)** issued his "call to rebellion" in 1843, and immediately stirred up controversy in both white and black abolitionist circles over the use of violence in the antislavery movement. Delivered at the Negro Convention in Buffalo, New York, Garnet argued that slaves should use violence when necessary in their dealings with masters and other white oppressors. Debated vigorously at the convention, Garnet's resolution advocating violence was defeated by a narrow margin after leading delegates including Frederick Douglass opposed it on the grounds that it was too militant. During the 1840s, Garnet was widely heralded as an eloquent if controversial speaker and minister, and in the 1850s he emerged as one of the leading voices for black emigration. In 1848, with the financial assistance of abolitionists John Brown and Gerrit Smith, Garnet published his "Address" together with David Walker's *Appeal* as an abolitionist pamphlet.

SOURCE: *Walker's Appeal in Four Articles and Garnet's Address to the Slaves of the United States of America.* New York: Arno Press, 1969.

SELECTED READINGS: David E. Swift, *Black Prophets of Justice: Activist Clergy before the Civil War* (1989). Joel Schor, *Henry Highland Garnet: A Voice of Black Radicalism in the Nineteenth Century* (1977). Earl Ofari, *"Let Your Motto Be Resistance": The Life and Thought of Henry Highland Garnet* (1972).

SLAVERY! How much misery is comprehended in that single word. What mind is there that does not shrink from its direful effects? Unless the image of God is obliterated from the soul, all men cherish the love of Liberty. The nice discerning political economist does not regard the sacred right, more than the untutored African who roams in the wilds of Congo. Nor has the one more right to the full enjoyment of his freedom than the other. In every man's mind the good seeds of liberty are planted, and he who brings his fellow down so low, as to make him contented with a condition of slavery, commits the highest crime against God and man. Brethren, your oppressors aim to do this. They endeavor to make you as much like brutes as possible. When they have blinded the eyes of your mind—when they have embittered the sweet waters of life—when they have shut out the light which shines from the word of God—then, and not till then has American slavery done its perfect work.

To such degradation it is sinful in the extreme for you to make voluntary submission. The divine commandments, you are in duty bound to reverence, and obey. If you do not obey them you will surely meet with the displeasure of the Almighty He requires you to love him supremely, and your neighbor as yourself—to keep the Sabbath day holy—to search the Scriptures—and bring up your children with respect for his laws, and to worship no other God but him. But slavery sets all these at naught and hurls defiance in the face of Jehovah. The forlorn condition in which you are placed does not destroy your moral obligation to God. You are not certain of Heaven, because you suffer yourselves to remain in a state of slavery, where you cannot obey the commandments of the Sovereign of the universe. If the ignorance of slavery is a passport to heaven, then it is a blessing, and no curse, and you should rather desire its perpetuity than its abolition. God will not receive slavery, nor ignorance, nor any other state of mind, for love, and obedience to him. Your condition does not absolve you from your moral obligation. The diabolical injustice by which your liberties are cloven down, neither God, nor angels, or just men, command you to suffer for a single moment. Therefore it is your solemn and imperative duty to use every means, both moral, intellectual, and physical, that promise success. If a band of heathen men should attempt to enslave a race of Christians, and to place their children under the influence of some false religion, surely, heaven would frown upon the men who would not resist such aggression, even to death. If, on the other hand, a band of Christians should attempt to enslave a race of heathen men and to entail slavery upon them, and to keep them in heathenism in the midst of Christianity, the God of heaven would smile upon every effort which the injured might make to disenthral themselves.

Brethren, it is as wrong for your lordly oppressors to keep you in slavery, as it was for the man thief to steal our ancestors from the coast of Africa. You should therefore now use the same manner of resistance, as would have been just in our ancestors, when the bloody foot prints of the first remorseless soul thief was placed upon the shores of our fatherland. The humblest peasant is as free in the sight of God, as the proudest monarch that ever swayed a sceptre. Liberty is a spirit sent out from God, and like its great Author, is no respector of persons.

Brethren, the time has come when you must act for yourselves. It is an old and true saying, that "if hereditary bondmen would be free, they must themselves strike the blow." You can plead your own cause, and do the work of emancipation better than any others. . . .

. . . Let your motto be RESISTANCE! RESISTANCE! RESISTANCE!—No oppressed people have ever secured their liberty without resistance. What kind of resistance you had better make, you must decide by the circumstances that surround you, and according to the suggestion of expediency. Brethren, adieu. Trust in the living God. Labor for the peace of the human race, and remember that you are three millions.

36. FREDERICK DOUGLASS

Narrative of the Life of Frederick Douglass
(1845)

FREDERICK DOUGLASS (c. 1818–1895) was the most prominent black American intellectual and political leader of the nineteenth century. Born a slave in Tuckahoe, Maryland, Douglass escaped to New York in 1838, after which he garnered international fame as an abolitionist lecturer and newspaper editor. Douglass's *Narrative,* published under the auspices of the American Anti-Slavery Society in 1845, was the most popular slave narrative written before the Civil War, and remains a classic American autobiography. Within five years of its original publication (it was twice revised, in 1855 and again in 1881), Douglass's heroic story of slavery and freedom sold more than 30,000 copies in America and Britain and was translated into French, German, and Dutch. During the 1840s, the slave narrative emerged as an important component of abolitionist propaganda, providing Northern readers with accounts of slavery from the perspective of the slave. In this, antebellum slave narratives embodied a dual purpose—they testified, in written form, to the intellectual equality of the slave, and they provided persuasive evidence of the dehumanizing effects of slavery. Douglass's *Narrative,* an exemplary account of the spirit, determination, and intellect of black Americans in the age of slavery, ranks as one of the most important literary achievements of the abolitionist movement.

SOURCE: Houston A. Baker, Jr., ed. *Narrative of the Life of Frederick Douglass. An American Slave.* New York: Penguin Books, 1986.

SELECTED READINGS: William S. McFeely, *Frederick Douglass* (1991). Waldo E. Martin, *The Mind of Frederick Douglass* (1984). Philip S. Foner, *Frederick Douglass* (1960). Benjamin Quarles, *Frederick Douglass* (1943).

I was now about twelve years old, and the thought of being *a slave for life* began to bear heavily upon my heart. Just about this time, I got hold of a book entitled "The Columbian Orator." Every opportunity I got, I used to read this book. Among much of other interesting matter, I found in it a dialogue between a master and his slave. The slave was represented as having run away from his master three times. The dialogue represented the conversation which took place between them, when the slave was retaken the third time. In this dialogue, the whole argument in behalf of slavery was brought forward by the master, all of which was disposed of by the slave. The slave was made to say some very smart as well as impressive things in reply to his master—things which had the desired though unexpected effect; for the conversation resulted in the voluntary emancipation of the slave on the part of the master.

In the same book, I met with one of Sheridan's mighty speeches on and in behalf of Catholic emancipation. These were choice documents to me. I read them over and over again with unabated interest. They gave tongue to interesting thoughts of my own soul, which had frequently flashed through my mind, and died away for want of utterance. The moral which I gained from the dialogue was the power of truth over the conscience of even a slave-holder. What I got from Sheridan was a bold denunciation of slavery, and a powerful vindication of human rights. The reading of these documents enabled me to utter my thoughts, and to meet the arguments brought forward to sustain slavery; but while they relieved me of one difficulty, they brought on another even more painful than the one of which I was relieved. The more I read, the more I was led to abhor and detest my enslavers. I could regard them in no other light than a band of successful robbers, who had left their homes, and gone to Africa, and stolen us from our homes, and in a strange land reduced us to slavery. I loathed them as being the meanest as well as the most wicked of men. As I read and contemplated the subject, behold! that very discontentment which Master Hugh had predicted would follow my learning to read had already come, to torment and sting my soul to unutter-able anguish. As I writhed under it, I would at times feel that learning to read had been a curse rather than a blessing. It had given me a view of my wretched condition, without the remedy. It opened my eyes to the horrible pit, but to no ladder upon which to get out. In moments of agony, I envied my fellow-slaves for their stupidity. I have often wished myself a beast. I preferred the condition of the meanest reptile to my own. Any thing, no matter what, to get rid of thinking! It was this everlasting thinking of my condition that tormented me. There was no getting rid of it. It was pressed upon me by every object within sight or hearing, animate or inanimate. The silver trump of freedom had roused my soul to eternal wakefulness. Freedom now appeared, to disappear no more forever. It was heard in every sound, and seen in every thing. It was ever present to torment me with a sense of my wretched condition. I saw nothing without seeing it, I heard nothing without hearing it, and felt nothing without feeling it. It looked from every star, it smiled in every calm, breathed in every wind, and moved in every storm.

I often found myself regretting my own existence, and wishing myself dead; and but for the hope of being free, I have no doubt but that I should have killed myself, or done something for which I should have been killed. While in this state of mind, I was eager to hear any one speak of slavery. I was a ready listener. Every little while, I could hear something about the abolitionists. It was some time before I found what the word meant. It was always used in such connections as to make it an interesting word to me. If a slave ran away and succeeded in getting clear, or if a slave killed his master, set fire to a barn, or did any thing very wrong in the mind of a slaveholder, it was spoken of as the fruit of *abolition*. Hearing the word in this connection very often, I set about learning what it meant. The dictionary afforded me little or no help. I found it was "the act of abolishing;" but then I did not know what was to be abolished. Here I was perplexed. I did not dare to ask any one about its meaning, for I was satisfied that it was something they wanted me to know very little about. After a patient waiting, I got one of our city papers, containing an account of the number of petitions from the north, praying for the abolition of slavery in the District of Columbia, and of the slave trade between the States. From this time I understood the words *abolition* and *abolitionist*, and always drew near when that word was spoken, expecting to hear something of importance to myself and fellow-slaves. The light broke in upon me by degrees. I went one day down on the wharf of Mr. Waters; and seeing two Irishmen unloading a scow of stone, I went, unasked, and helped them. When we had finished, one of them came to me and asked me if I were a slave. I told him I was. He asked, "Are ye a slave for life?" I told him that I was. The good Irishman seemed to be deeply affected by the statement. He said to the other that it was a pity so fine a little fellow as myself should be a slave for life. He said it was a shame to hold me. They both advised me to run away to the north; that I should find friends there, and that I should be free. I pretended not to be interested in what they said, and treated them as if I did not understand them; for I feared they might be treacherous. White men have been known to be encourage slaves to escape, and then, to get the reward, catch them and return them to their masters. I was afraid that these seemingly good men might use me so; but I nevertheless remembered their advice, and from that time I resolved to run away. I looked forward to a time at which it would be safe for me to escape. I was too young to think of doing so immediately; besides, I wished to learn how to write, as I might have occasion to write my own pass. I consoled myself with the hope that I should one day find a good chance. Meanwhile, I would learn to write.

The idea as to how I might learn to write was suggested to me by being in

Durgin and Bailey's ship-yard, and frequently seeing the ship carpenters, after hewing, and getting a piece of timber ready for use, write on the timber the name of that part of the ship for which it was intended. When a piece of timber was intended for the larboard side, it would be marked thus—"L." When a piece was for the starboard side, it would be marked thus—"S." A piece for the larboard side forward, would be marked thus—"L.F." When a piece was for starboard side forward, it would be marked thus—"S.F." For larboard aft, it would be marked thus—"L.A." For starboard aft, it would be marked thus—"S.A." I soon learned the names of these letters, and for what they were intended when placed upon a piece of timber in the ship-yard. I immediately commenced copying them, and in a short time was able to make the four letters named. After that, when I met with any boy who I knew could write, I would tell him I could write as well as he. The next word would be, "I don't believe you. Let me see you try it." I would then make the letters which I had been so fortunate as to learn, and ask him to beat that. In this way I got a good many lessons in writing, which it is quite possible I should never have gotten in any other way. During this time, my copy-book was the board fence, brick wall, and pavement; my pen and ink was a lump of chalk. With these, I learned mainly how to write. I then commenced and continued copying the Italics in Webster's Spelling Book, until I could make them all without looking on the book. By this time, my little Master Thomas had gone to school, and learned how to write, and had written over a number of copy-books. These had been brought home, and shown to some of our near neighbors, and then laid aside. My mistress used to go to class meeting at the Wilk Street meetinghouse every Monday afternoon, and leave me to take care of the house. When left thus, I used to spend the time in writing in the spaces left in Master Thomas's copy-book, copying what he had written. I continued to do this until I could write a hand very similar to that of Master Thomas. Thus, after a long, tedious effort for years, I finally succeeded in learning how to write.

37. HARRIET BEECHER STOWE

Uncle Tom's Cabin
(1852)

The most controversial and widely read novel of the nineteenth century, **HARRIET BEECHER STOWE**'s *Uncle Tom's Cabin* was among the first works of sentimental fiction to tackle the issue of slavery. Born in Litchfield, Connecticut, the daughter of the famous antebellum preacher Lyman Beecher, and younger sister of the well-known reformer and writer Catharine Beecher, Stowe (1811–1896) was an extremely popular author whose style combined elements of regionalism, realism, and sentimentalism. Religious in tone and uncompromising in its critique of slavery, Stowe's novel was extremely controversial for its depictions of black characters and for its provisional endorsement of emigration as the only viable alternative for African Americans. Still, its impact on the abolitionist movement was enormous. Published in 1852, shortly after the passage of the Fugitive Slave Law, the novel sold more than 300,000 copies in the first year, and was eventually translated into fifty-five languages. President Abraham Lincoln later credited Stowe with starting the Civil War, thereby suggesting the far-reaching influence and enduring importance of *Uncle Tom's Cabin*.

SOURCE: Ann Douglas, ed. *Uncle Tom's Cabin; or, Life Among the Lowly.* New York: Penguin Books, 1986.

SELECTED READINGS: Joan D. Hedrick, *Harriet Beecher Stowe: A Life* (1994). Jane Tomkins, *Sensational Designs: The Cultural Work of American Fiction, 1790–1860* (1986). Eric J. Sundquist, ed., *New Essays on Uncle Tom's Cabin* (1986). Thomas F. Gossett, *Uncle Tom's Cabin and American Culture* (1985).

"Well, Tom!" said Legree, walking up, and seizing him grimly by the collar of his coat, and speaking through his teeth, in a paroxysm of determined rage, "do you know I've made up my mind to KILL you?"

"It's very likely, Mas'r," said Tom, calmly.

"I *have*," said Legree, with a grim, terrible calmness, "*done—just—that—thing*, Tom, unless you'll tell me what you know about these yer gals!"

Tom stood silent.

"D'ye hear?" said Legree, stamping, with a roar like that of an incensed lion. "Speak!"

"*I han't got nothing to tell, Mas'r,*" said Tom, with a slow, firm, deliberate utterance.

"Do you dare to tell me, ye old black Christian, ye don't *know?*" said Legree.

Tom was silent.

"Speak!" thundered Legree, striking him furiously. "Do you know anything?"

"I know, Mas'r; but I can't tell anything. *I can die!*"

Legree drew in a long breath; and, suppressing his rage, took Tom by the arm, and, approaching his face almost to his, said, in a terrible voice, "Hark 'e, Tom!—ye think, 'cause I've let you off before, I don't mean what I say; but, this time, *I've made up my mind*, and counted the cost. You've always stood it out again' me: now, *I'll conquer ye, or kill ye!*—one or t' other. I'll count every drop of blood there is in you, and take 'em, one by one, till ye give up!"

Tom looked up to his master, and answered, "Mas'r, if you was sick, or in trouble, or dying, and I could save ye, I'd *give* ye my heart's blood; and, if taking every drop of blood in this poor old body would save your precious soul, I'd give 'em freely, as the Lord gave his for me. O, Mas'r! don't bring this great sin on your soul! It will hurt you more than 't will me! Do the worst you can, my troubles'll be over soon; but, if ye don't repent, yours won't *never* end!"

Like a strange snatch of heavenly music, heard in the lull of a tempest, this burst of feeling made a moment's blank pause. Legree stood aghast, and looked at Tom; and there was such a silence, that the tick of the old clock could be heard, measuring, with silent touch, the last moments of mercy and probation to that hardened heart.

It was but a moment. There was one hesitating pause,—one irresolute, relenting thrill,—and the spirit of evil came back, with seven-fold vehemence; and Legree, foaming with rage, smote his victim to the ground.

Scenes of blood and cruelty are shocking to our ear and heart. What man has nerve to do, man has not nerve to hear. What brother-man and brother-Christian must suffer, cannot be told us, even in our secret chamber, it so harrows the soul! And yet, oh my country! these things are done under the shadow of thy laws! O, Christ! thy church sees them, almost in silence!

But, of old, there was One whose suffering changed an instrument of torture, degradation and shame, into a symbol of glory, honor, and immortal life; and, where His spirit is, neither degrading stripes, nor blood, nor insults, can make the Christian's last struggle less than glorious.

Was he alone, that long night, whose brave, loving spirit was bearing up, in that old shed, against buffeting and brutal stripes?

Nay! There stood by him One—seen by him alone,—"like unto the Son of God."

The tempter stood by him, too,—blinded by furious, despotic will,—every moment pressing him to shun that agony by the betrayal of the innocent. But the brave, true heart was firm on the Eternal Rock. Like his Master, he knew that, if he saved others, himself he could not save; nor could utmost extremity wring from him words, save of prayers and holy trust.

"He's most gone, Mas'r," said Sambo, touched, in spite of himself, by the patience of his victim.

"Pay away, till he gives up! Give it to him!—give it to him!" shouted Legree. I'll take every drop of blood he has, unless he confesses!"

Tom opened his eyes, and looked upon his master. "Ye poor miserable critter!" he said, "there ain't no more ye can do! I forgive ye, with all my soul!" and he fainted entirely away.

"I b'lieve, my soul, he's done for, finally," said Legree, stepping forward, to look at him. "Yes, he is! Well, his mouth's shut up, at last,—that's one comfort!"

Yes, Legree; but who shall shut up that voice in thy soul? that soul, past repentance, past prayer, past hope, in whom the fire that never shall be quenched is already burning!

Yet Tom was not quite gone. His wondrous words and pious prayers had struck upon the hearts of the imbruted blacks, who had been the instruments of cruelty upon him; and, the instant Legree withdrew, they took him down, and, in their ignorance, sought to call him back to life,—as if *that* were any favor to him.

"Sartin, we 's been doin' a dreffu wicked thing!" said Sambo; "hopes Mas'r'll have to 'count for it, and not we."

They washed his wounds,—they provided a rude bed, of some refuse cotton, for him to lie down on; and one of them, stealing up to the house, begged a drink of brandy of Legree, pretending that he was tired, and wanted it for himself. He bought it back, and poured it down Tom's throat.

"O, Tom!" said Quimbo, "we's been awful wicked to ye!"

"I forgive ye, with all my heart!" said Tom, faintly.

"O, Tom! do tell us who is *Jesus*, anyhow?" said Sambo;—"Jesus, that's been a standin' by you so, all this night!—Who is he?"

The word roused the failing, fainting spirit. He poured forth a few energetic sentences of that wondrous One,—his life, is death, his everlasting presence, and power to save.

They wept,—both the two savage men.

"Why didn't I never hear this before?" said Sambo; "but I do believe!—I can't help it! Lord Jesus, have mercy on us!"

"Poor critters!" said Tom, "I'd be willing to bar' all I have, if it'll only bring ye to Christ! O, Lord! give me these two more souls, I pray!"

That prayer was answered! . . .

Tom had been lying two days since the fatal night, not suffering, for every nerve of suffering was blunted and destroyed. He lay, for the most part, in a quiet stupor; for the laws of a powerful and well-knit frame would not at once release the imprisoned spirit. By stealth, there had been there, in the darkness of the night, poor desolated creatures, who stole from their scanty hours' rest, that they might repay to him some of those ministrations of love in which he had always been so abundant. Truly, those poor disciples had little to give,—only the cup of cold water; but it was given with full hearts.

Tears had fallen on that honest, insensible face,—tears of late repentance in the poor, ignorant heathen, whom his dying love and patience had awakened to repentance, and bitter prayers, breathed over him to a late-found Saviour, of whom they scarce knew more than the name, but whom the yearning ignorant heart of man never implores in vain.

Cassy, who had glided out of her place of concealment, and, by overhearing, learned the sacrifice that had been made for her and Emmeline, had been there, the night before, defying the danger of detection; and, moved by the last few words which the affectionate soul had yet strength to breathe, the long winter of despair, the ice of years, had given way, and the dark, despairing woman had wept and prayed.

When George entered the shed, he felt his head giddy and his heart sick.

"Is it possible,—is it possible?" said he, kneeling down by him. "Uncle Tom, my poor, poor old friend!"

Something in the voice penetrated to the ear of the dying. He moved his head gently, smiled, and said,

"Jesus can make a dying-bed
Feel soft as down pillows are."

Tears which did honor to his manly heart fell from the young man's eyes, as he bent over his poor friend.

"O, dear Uncle Tom! do wake,—do speak once more! Look up! Here's Mas'r George,—your own little Mas'r George. Don't you know me?"

"Mas'r George!" said Tom, opening his eyes, and speaking in a feeble voice; "Mas'r George!" He looked bewildered.

Slowly the idea seemed to fill his soul; and the vacant eye became fixed and brightened, the whole face lighted up, the hard hands clasped, and tears ran down the cheeks.

"Bless the Lord! it is,—it is,—it's all I wanted! They haven't forgot me. It warms my soul; it does my heart good! Now I shall die content! Bless the Lord, on my soul!"

"You shan't die! you! *mustn't* die, nor think of it! I've come to buy you, and take you home," said George, with impetuous vehemence.

"O, Mas'r George, ye're too late. The Lord's bought me, and is going to take me home,—and I long to go. Heaven is better than Kintuck."

"O, don't die! It'll kill me!—it'll break my heart to think what you've suffered,—and lying in this old shed, here! Poor, poor fellow!"

"Don't call me poor fellow!" said Tom, solemnly, "I *have* been poor fellow; but that's all past and gone, now. I'm right in the door, going into glory! O, Mas'r George! *Heaven has come!* I've got the victory!—the Lord Jesus has given it to me! Glory be to His name!"

George was awe-struck at the force, the vehemence, the power, with which these broken sentences were uttered. He sat gazing in silence.

Tom grasped his hand, and continued,—"Ye mustn't, now, tell Chloe, poor soul! how ye found me;—'t would be so dreful to her. Only tell her ye found me going into glory; and that I couldn't stay for no one. And tell her the Lord's stood by me everywhere and al'ays, and made everything light and easy. And oh, the poor chil'en, and the baby;—my old heart's been most broke for 'em, time and agin! Tell 'em all to follow me—follow me! Give my love to Mas'r, and dear good Missis, and everybody in the place! Ye don't know! 'Pears like I loves 'em all! I loves every creatur', everywhar!—it's nothing *but* love! O, Mas'r George! what a thing 't is to be a Christian!"

At this moment, Legree sauntered up to the door of the shed, looked in, with a dogged air of affected carelessness, and turned away.

"The old satan!" said George, in his indignation. "It's a comfort to think the devil will pay *him* for this, some of these days!"

"O, don't!—oh, ye mustn't!" said Tom, grasping his hand; "he's a poor mis'able critter! it's awful to think on 't! Oh, if he only could repent, the Lord would forgive him now; but I'm 'feared he never will!"

"I hope he won't!" said George; "I never want to see *him* in heaven!"

"Hush, Mas'r George!—it worries me! Don't feel so! He an't done me no real harm,—only opened the gate of the kingdom for me; that's all!"

At this moment, the sudden flush of strength which the joy of meeting his young master had infused into the dying man gave way. A sudden sinking fell upon him; he closed his eyes; and that mysterious and sublime change passed over his face, that told the approach of other worlds.

He began to draw his breath with long, deep inspirations; and his broad chest rose and fell, heavily. The expression of his face was that of a conqueror.

"Who,—who,—who shall separate us from the love of Christ?" he said, in a voice that contended with mortal weakness; and, with a smile, he fell asleep.

George sat fixed with solemn awe. It seemed to him that the place was holy; and, as he closed the lifeless eyes, and rose up from the dead, only one thought possessed him,—that expressed by his simple old friend,—"What a thing it is to be a Christian!" . . .

38. FREDERICK DOUGLASS

What to the Slave is the Fourth of July?
(1852)

Widely regarded as one of the most passionate orators of his time, **FRED-ERICK DOUGLASS (c. 1818–1895)** became increasingly confrontational in style and substance as the nation lurched closer to civil war. Initially a follower of William Lloyd Garrison, Douglass developed his own particular brand of abolitionism—embracing not only politics, but also violence and black self-determination, as necessary means to end slavery—after moving from Boston to Rochester, New York, in 1847. This speech, delivered at a Fourth of July celebration in Rochester in 1852, showcased a more defiant Douglass willing to challenge white Americans on their reluctant commitment to the abolitionist movement. Using this public celebration as his point of departure, Douglass invoked all the symbols of American political culture—the Declaration of Independence, the American Revolution, Thomas Jefferson and George Washington—to expose the hypocrisy of American nationalism, and to advance the claim that black equality was not only consistent with, but also necessary for, the fulfillment of America's most cherished revolutionary ideals.

SOURCE: Henry Louis Gates, Jr., and Nellie McKay et al., eds. *The Norton Anthology of African American Literature.* New York: W. W. Norton and Company, 1997.

SELECTED READINGS: Priscilla Wald, *Constituting Americans: Cultural Anxiety and Narrative Form* (1995). John Blassingame, ed., *The Frederick Douglass Papers: Speeches, Debates, and Interviews*, 5 vols. (1979–1992). William S. Andrews, ed., *Critical Essays on Frederick Douglass* (1991). Philip S. Foner, ed., *Life and Writings of Frederick Douglass*, 4 vols. (1950–1975).

Fellow-citizens, pardon me, allow me to ask, why am I called upon to speak here to-day? What have I, or those I represent, to do with your national independence? Are the great principles of political freedom and of natural justice, embodied in that Declaration of Independence, extended to us? and am I, therefore, called upon to bring our humble offering to the national altar, and to confess the benefits and express devout gratitude for the blessings resulting from your independence to us?

Would to God, both for your sakes and ours, that an affirmative answer could be truthfully returned to these questions! Then would my task be light, and my burden easy and delightful. For *who* is there so cold, that a nation's sympathy could not warm him? Who so obdurate and dead to the claims of gratitude, that would not thankfully acknowledge such priceless benefits? Who so stolid and selfish, that would not give his voice to swell the hallelujahs of a nation's jubilee, when the chains of servitude had been torn from his limbs? I am not that man. In a case like that the dumb might eloquently speak, and the "lame man leap as an hart."

But, such is not the state of the case. I say it with a sad sense of the disparity between us. I am not included within the pale of this glorious anniversary! Your high independence only reveals the immeasurable distance between us. The blessings in which you, this day, rejoice, are not enjoyed in common. The rich inheritance of justice, liberty, prosperity and independence, bequeathed by your fathers, is shared by you, not by me. The sunlight that brought life and healing to you, has brought stripes and death to me. This Fourth [of] July is *yours*, not *mine*. You may rejoice, *I* must mourn. To drag a man in fetters into the grand illuminated temple of liberty, and call upon him to join you in joyous anthems, were inhuman mockery and sacrilegious irony. Do you mean, citizens, to mock me, by asking me to speak to-day? If so, there is a parallel to your conduct. And let me warn you that it is dangerous to copy the example of a nation whose crimes, towering up to heaven, were thrown down by the breath of the Almighty, burying that nation in irrecoverable ruin! I can to-day take up the plaintive lament of a peeled and woe-smitten people! . . .

Fellow-citizens; above your national, tumultuous joy, I hear the mournful wail of millions! whose chains, heavy and grievous yesterday, are, today rendered more intolerable by the jubilee shouts that reach them. If I do forget, if I do not faithfully remember those bleeding children of sorrow this day, "may my right hand forget her cunning, and may my tongue cleave to the roof of my mouth!" To forget them, to pass lightly over their wrongs, and to chime in with the popular theme, would be treason most scandalous and shocking, and would make me a reproach before God and the world. My subject, then fellow-citizens, is AMERICAN SLAVERY. I shall see, this day, and its popular characteristics, from the slave's point of view. Standing, there, identified with the American bondman, making his wrongs mine, I do not hesitate to declare, with all my soul, that the character and conduct of this nation never looked blacker to me than on this 4th of July! Whether we turn to the declarations of the past, or to the professions of the present, the conduct of the nation seems equally hideous and revolting. America is false to the past, false to the present, and solemnly binds herself to be false to the future. Standing with God and the crushed and bleeding slave on this occasion, I will, in the name of humanity which is outraged, in the name of liberty which is fettered, in the name of the constitution and the Bible, which are disregarded and trampled upon, dare to call in question and to denounce, with all the emphasis I can command, everything that serves to perpetuate slavery—the great sin and shame of America! "I will not equivocate; I will not excuse"; I will use the severest language I can command; and yet not one word shall escape me that any man, whose judgement is not blinded by prejudice, or who is not at heart a slaveholder, shall not confess to be right and just. . . .

What, to the American slave, is your 4th of July? I answer: a day that reveals to him, more than all other days in the year, the gross injustice and cruelty to which he is the constant victim. To him, your celebration is a sham; your boasted liberty, an unholy license; your national greatness, swelling vanity; your sounds of rejoicing are empty and heartless; your denunciations of tyrants, brass fronted impudence; your shouts of liberty and equality, hollow mockery; your prayers and hymns, your sermons and thanksgivings, with all your religious parade, and solemnity, are, to him, mere bombast, fraud, deception, impiety, and hypocrisy—a thin veil to cover up crimes which would disgrace a nation of savages. There is not a nation on the earth guilty of practices, more shocking and bloody, than are the people of these United States, at this very hour.

Go where you may, search where you will, roam through all the monarchies and despotisms of the old world, travel through South America, search out every abuse, and when you have found the last, lay your facts by the side of the everyday practices of this nation, and you will say with me, that, for revolting barbarity and shameless hypocrisy, America reigns without a rival.

39. MARTIN DELANY

The Condition, Elevation, Emigration, and Destiny of the Colored People of the United States Politically Considered (1852)

One of the most militant and articulate of black abolitionists, **MARTIN DE-LANY (1812–1885)** is considered the "father of black nationalism." Born free in Charles Town, Virginia (now West Virginia), Delany became an abolitionist lecturer, writer, and newspaper editor. A student at Harvard Medical School before student protests led to his removal, he also practiced medicine, used his knowledge of physiology to debunk racist theories of black inferiority, and recruited African-American troops during the Civil War as the first and highest-ranking black field officer in the Union army. More than most of his fellow abolitionists, Delany advocated black self-determination and the voluntary emigration of African Americans from the United States. Angered by pervasive white prejudice inside and outside the abolitionist movement, Delany published his influential pamphlet in 1852 as a "call to arms" for black economic self-sufficiency and migration to Africa. Coming on the heels of the 1850 Fugitive Slave Law and the renaissance of the Negro Convention Movement, Delany's nationalist tract was warmly received by black abolitionists, despite the fact that economic and other circumstances rendered his plan largely impractical.

SOURCE: Martin Delany. *The Condition, Elevation, Emigration, and Destiny of the Colored People of the United States Politically Considered.* New York: Arno Press, 1968.

SELECTED READINGS: Cyril E. Griffith, *The African Dream: Martin R. Delany and the Emergence of Pan-African Thought* (1975). Dorothy Sterling, *The Making of an Afro-American: Martin R. Delany* (1971). Victor Ullman, *Martin Delany: The Beginnings of Black Nationalism* (1971).

We are slaves in the midst of freedom, waiting patiently, and unconcernedly—indifferently, and stupidly, for masters to come and lay claim to us, trusting to their generosity, whether or not they will own us and carry us into endless bondage.

The slave is more secure than we; he knows who holds the heel upon his bosom—we know not the wretch who may grasp us by the throat. His master may be a man of some conscientious scruples; ours may be unmerciful. Good or bad, mild or harsh, easy or hard, lenient or severe, saint or satan—whenever that master demands any one of us—even our affectionate wives and darling little children, *we must go into slavery*—there is *no alternative*. The *will* of the man who sits in judgment on our liberty, is the law. To him is given *all power* to say, whether or not we have a right to enjoy freedom. This is the power over the slave in the South—this is now extended to the North. The will of the man who sits in judgment over us is the law; because it is explicitly provided that the *decision* of the commissioner shall be final, from which there can be no appeal.

The freed man of the South is even more secure than the freeborn of the North; because such persons usually have their records in the slave states, bringing their "papers" with them; and the slaveholders will be faithful to their own acts. The Northern freeman knows no records; he despises the "papers."

Depend upon no promised protection of citizens in any quarter. Their own property and liberty are jeopardised, and they will not sacrifice them for us. This we may not expect them to do.

Besides, there are no people who ever lived, love their country and obey their laws as the Americans.

Their country is their Heaven—their Laws their Scriptures—and the decrees of their Magistrates obeyed as the fiat of God. It is the most consummate delusion and misdirected confidence to depend upon them for protection; and for a moment suppose even our children safe while walking in the streets among them.

A people capable of originating and sustaining such a law as this, are not the people to whom we are willing to entrust our liberty at discretion.

What can we do?—What shall we do? This is the great and important question:—Shall we submit to be dragged like brutes before heartless men, and sent into degradation and bondage?—Shall we fly, or shall we resist? Ponder well and reflect. . . .

But to return to emigration: Where shall we go? We must not leave this continent; America is our destination and our home.

That the continent of America seems to have been designed by Providence as an asylum for all the various nations of the earth, is very apparent. From the earliest discovery, various nations sent a representation here, either as adventurers and speculators, or employed seamen and soldiers, hired to do the work of their employers. And among the earliest and most numerous class who found their way to the New World, were those of the African race. And it is now ascertained to our mind, beyond a peradventure, that when the continent was discovered, there were found in Central America, a tribe of the black race, of fine looking people, having characteristics of color and hair, identifying them originally of the African race—no doubt being a remnant of the Africans who, with the Carthaginian expedition, were adventitiously cast upon this continent, in their memorable excursion to the "Great Island," after sailing many miles distant to the West of the Pillars of Hercules.

We are not inclined to be superstitious, but say, that we can see the "finger of God" in all this; and if the European race may with propriety, boast and claim, that this continent is better adapted to their development, than their own father-land; surely, it does not necessarily detract from our father-land, to claim the superior advantages to the African race, to be derived from this continent. But be that as it may, the world belongs to mankind—his common Father created it for his common good—his temporal destiny is here; and our present warfare, is not upon European rights, nor for European countries; but for the common rights of man, based upon the great principles of common humanity—taking our chance in the world of rights, and claiming to have originally more right to this continent, than the European race. And had we no other claims than those set forth in a former part of this work, they are sufficient to cause every colored man on the continent, to stand upon the soil unshaken and unmoved. . . .

40. JOHN BROWN

Last Speech to the Jury
(1859)

JOHN BROWN (1800-1859) was the most militant and egalitarian white abolitionist in pre–Civil War America. Born in Torrington, Connecticut, Brown received a rudimentary formal education but developed a millennial vision of racial harmony through his vast knowledge of the Bible, close friendships with black Americans, and deep belief that an "eternal war with slavery" was God's plan to redeem the American republic. Following his violent retaliation against proslavery forces in Kansas in 1855–56, Brown led his famous raid on the federal arsenal at Harpers Ferry in October 1859. Brown's forces— fifteen whites and six blacks—were ultimately defeated in their attempt to liberate the slaves, but subsequent events, including a highly publicized trial and public execution on December 2, 1859, secured Brown's reputation as an abolitionist hero and martyr. On the last day of his famous trial, Brown delivered a short but prophetic sermon to the jury that would sentence him to death for murder and conspiracy. Brown's speech reveals a strong and spiritual man defending his impulses and taking responsibility for his actions. Stirring in its vision and simple conviction, it also predicted that the blood of the nation would be spilled, far more extensively than it was at Harpers Ferry, if slavery was not abolished.

SOURCE: F. B. Sanborn, ed. *The Life and Letters of John Brown, Liberator of Kansas, and Martyr of Virginia*. Reprinted from 1885 edition. New York: Negro Universities Press, 1969.

SELECTED READINGS: John Stauffer, *The Black Hearts of Men: Radical Abolitionists and the Transformation of Race* (2002). Benjamin Quarles, *Allies for Freedom: Blacks and John Brown* (1974). Stephen B. Oates, *To Purge This Land with Blood* (1970). W. E. B. Du Bois, *John Brown* (1910).

I have, may it please the Court, a few words to say.

In the first place, I deny everything but what I have all along admitted,—the design on my part to free the slaves. I intended certainly to have made a clean thing of that matter, as I did last winter, when I went into Missouri and there took slaves without the snapping of a gun on either side, moved them through the country, and finally left them in Canada. I designed to have done the same thing again, on a larger scale. That was all I intended. I never did intend murder, or treason, or the destruction of property, or to excite or incite slaves to rebellion, or to make insurrection.

I have another objection: and that is, it is unjust that I should suffer such a penalty. Had I interfered in the manner which I admit, and which I admit has been fairly proved (for I admire the truthfulness and candor of the greater portion of the witnesses who have testified in this case),—had I so interfered in behalf of the rich, the powerful, the intelligent, the so-called great, or in behalf of any of their friends,—either father, mother, brother, sister, wife, or children, or any of that class,—and suffered and sacrificed what I have in this interference, it would have been all right; and every man in this court would have deemed it an act worthy of reward rather than punishment.

This court acknowledges, as I suppose, the validity of the law of God. I see a book kissed here which I suppose to be the Bible, or at least the New Testament. That teaches me that all things whatsoever I would that men should do to me, I should do even so to them. It teaches me, further, to 'remember them that are in bonds, as bound with them.' I endeavored to act up to that instruction. I say, I am yet too young to understand that God is any respecter of persons. I believe that to have interfered as I have done—as I have always freely admitted I have done—in behalf of His despised poor, was not wrong, but right. Now, if it is deemed necessary that I should forfeit my life for the furtherance of the ends of justice, and mingle my blood further with the blood of my children and with the blood of millions in this slave country whose rights are disregarded by wicked, cruel, and unjust enactments,—I submit; so let it be done!

Let me say one word further.

I feel entirely satisfied with the treatment I have received on my trial. Considering all the circumstances, it has been more generous than I expected. But I feel no consciousness of guilt. I have stated from the first what was my intention, and what was not. I never had any design against the life of any person, nor any disposition to commit treason, or excite slaves to rebel, or make any general insurrection. I never encouraged any man to do so, but always discouraged any idea of that kind.

Let me say, also, a word in regard to the statements made by some of those connected with me. I hear it has been stated by some of them that I have induced them to join me. But the contrary is true. I do not say this to injure them, but as regretting their weakness. There is not one of them but joined me of his own accord, and the greater part of them at their own expense. A number of them I never saw, and never had a word of conversation with, till the day they came to me; and that was for the purpose I have stated.

Now I have done.

41.

Thirteenth (1865), Fourteenth (1868), and Fifteenth (1870) Amendments

The Thirteenth, Fourteenth, and Fifteenth Amendments—which were proposed, debated, and adopted during the period of Radical Reconstruction following the Civil War—are among the most radical revisions ever made to the U.S. Constitution. The Thirteenth Amendment, which forever abolished slavery and involuntary servitude, was passed in 1865. The Fourteenth Amendment, which defined equal protection as a function of national citizenship, was ratified in 1868. The Fifteenth Amendment, which granted suffrage rights to black men, was adopted in 1870. Taken together, they represented the successful culmination of the abolitionist movement and the just legacy of a Civil War fought to resolve the issue of slavery. Since Reconstruction, the Fourteenth and Fifteenth Amendments, especially, have been the battleground for feminists, civil rights and labor activists, and gays and lesbians struggling to achieve a broad, inclusive, and truly democratic definition of equal rights.

SOURCE: Eric Foner and John A. Garraty, eds. *A Reader's Companion to American History.* Boston: Houghton Mifflin, 1991.

SELECTED READINGS: Eric Foner, *Reconstruction: America's Unfinished Revolution, 1863–1877* (1988). Donald G. Nieman, *To Set the Law in Motion: The Freedman's Bureau and the Legal Rights of Blacks, 1865–1868* (1979). James M. McPherson, *The Struggle for Equality: Abolitionists and the Negro in the Civil War and Reconstruction* (1964). W. E. B. Du Bois, *Black Reconstruction in America, 1860–1880* (1935).

Amendment XIII
[Adopted 1865]

Section 1 Neither slavery nor involuntary servitude, except as a punishment for crime whereof the party shall have been duly convicted, shall exist within the United States, or any place subject to their jurisdiction.

Section 2 Congress shall have power to enforce this article by appropriate legislation.

Amendment XIV
[Adopted 1868]

Section 1 All persons born or naturalized in the United States, and subject to the jurisdiction thereof, are citizens of the United States and of the State wherein they reside. No State shall make or enforce any law which shall abridge the privileges or immunities of citizens of the United States; nor shall any State deprive any person of life, liberty, or property, without due process of law; nor deny to any person within its jurisdiction the equal protection of the laws.

Section 2 Representatives shall be apportioned among the several States according to their respective numbers, counting the whole number of persons in each State, excluding Indians not taxed. But when the right to vote at any election for the choice of Electors for President and Vice-President of the United States, Representatives in Congress, the executive and judicial officers of a State, or the members of the legislature thereof, is denied to any of the male inhabitants of such State, being twenty-one years of age and citizens of the United States, or in any way abridged, except for participation in rebellion, or other crime, the basis of representation therein shall be reduced in the proportion which the number of such male citizens shall bear to the whole number of male citizens twenty-one years of age in such State.

Section 3 No person shall be a Senator or Representative in Congress, or Elector of President and Vice-President, or hold any office, civil or military, under the United States, or under any State, who, having previously taken an oath, as a member of Congress, or as an officer of the United States, or as a member of any State legislature, or as an executive or judicial officer of any State, to support the Constitution of the United States, shall have engaged in insurrection or rebellion against the same, or given aid or comfort to the enemies thereof. Congress may, by a vote of two-thirds of each house, remove such disability.

Section 4 The validity of the public debt of the United States, authorized by law, including debts incurred for payment of pensions and bounties for services in suppressing insurrection or rebellion, shall not be questioned. But neither the United States nor any State shall assume or pay any debt or obligation incurred in aid of insurrection or rebellion against the United States, or any claim for the loss of emancipation of any slave; but all such debts, obligations, and claims shall be held illegal and void.

Section 5 The Congress shall have power to enforce, by appropriate legislation, the provisions of this article.

Amendment XV
[Adopted 1870]

Section 1 The right of citizens of the United States to vote shall not be denied or abridged by the United States or by any State on account of race, color, or previous condition of servitude.

Section 2 The Congress shall have power to enforce this article by appropriate legislation.

CHAPTER
FOUR
Suffrage and Feminism

42. SARAH GRIMKÉ

Letters on the Equality of the Sexes
(1838)

SARAH GRIMKÉ (1792–1873) was a pioneering activist whose writings and speeches helped pave the way for the emergence of the woman's rights movement. Born into a wealthy slaveholding family in Charleston, South Carolina, Sarah moved to Philadelphia and converted to Quakerism in 1819. After she was publicly censured by Quaker leaders for her radical antislavery views, she moved to New York City with her younger sister Angelina, where they became the first female agents of the American Anti-Slavery Society. During the 1830s, Sarah began to articulate—both as a pamphleteer and a lecturer—connections between slavery and women's inequality. The most famous expression of her views came in *Letters on the Equality of the Sexes, and the Condition of Woman* (1838), a provocative analysis addressed to Mary Parker, president of the Boston Anti-Slavery Society. In it, Grimké invoked a divinely ordained equality between men and women, and exposed the laws and social norms that prevented its realization. She also connected the plight of female slaves and white women, thereby establishing herself as one of the first women to call for interracial alliances.

SOURCE: Sarah Grimké. *Letters on the Equality of the Sexes and the Condition of Woman.* New York: Lenox Hill, 1970.

SELECTED READINGS: Gerda Lerner, *The Grimké Sisters from South Carolina: Pioneers for Woman's Rights and Abolition* (1998). Elizabeth Ann Bartlett, *Liberty, Equality, Sorority: The Origins and Interpretations of American Feminist Thought* (1994). Catherine Hoffman Birney, *The Grimké Sisters: Sarah and Angelina Grimké: The First American Women Advocates of Abolition and Woman's Rights* (1885).

My Dear Sister,—I have now taken a brief survey of the condition of woman in various parts of the world. I regret that my time has been so much occupied by other things, that I have been unable to bestow that attention upon the subject which it merits, and that my constant change of place has prevented me from having access to books, which might probably have assisted me in this part of my work. I hope that the principles I have asserted will claim the attention of some of my sex, who may be able to bring into view, more thoroughly than I have done, the situation and degradation of woman. I shall now proceed to make a few remarks on the condition of women in my own country.

During the early part of my life, my lot was cast among the butterflies of the *fashionable* world; and of this class of women, I am constrained to say, both from experience and observation, that their education is miserably deficient; that they are taught to regard marriage as the one thing needful, the only avenue to distinction; hence to attract the notice and win the attentions of men, by their external charms, is the chief business of fashionable girls. They seldom think that men will be allured by intellectual acquirements, because they find, that where any mental superiority exists, a woman is generally shunned and regarded as stepping out of her 'appropriate sphere,' which, in their view, is to dress, to dance, to set out to the best possible advantage her person, to read the novels which inundate the press, and which do more to destroy her character as a rational creature, than any thing else. Fashionable women regard themselves, and are regarded by men, as pretty toys or as mere instruments of pleasure; and the vacuity of mind, the heartlessness, the frivolity which is the necessary result of this false and debasing estimate of women, can only be fully understood by those who have mingled in the folly and wickedness of fashionable life; and who have been called from such pursuits by the voice of the Lord Jesus, inviting their weary and heavy laden souls to come unto Him and learn of Him, that they may find something worthy of their immortal spirit, and their intellectual powers; that they may learn the high and holy purposes of their creation, and consecrate themselves unto the service of God; and not, as is now the case, to the pleasure of man.

There is another and much more numerous class in this country, who are withdrawn by education or circumstances from the circle of fashionable amusements, but who are brought up with the dangerous and absurd idea, that *marriage* is a kind of preferment; and that to be able to keep their husband's house, and render his situation comfortable, is the end of her being. Much that she does and says and thinks is done in reference to this situation; and to be married is too often held up to the view of girls as the sine qua non of human happiness and human existence. For this purpose more than for any other I verily believe the majority of girls are trained. This is demonstrated by the imperfect education which is bestowed upon them, and the little pains taken to cultivate their minds, after they leave school, by the little time allowed them for reading, and by the idea being constantly inculcated, that although all household concerns should be attended to with scrupulous punctuality at particular seasons, the improvement of their intellectual capacities is only a secondary consideration, and may serve as an occupation to fill up the odds and ends of time. In most families, it is considered a matter of far more consequence to call a girl off from making a pie, or a pudding, than to interrupt her whilst engaged in her studies. This mode of training necessarily exalts, in their view, the animal above the intellectual and spiritual nature, and teaches women to regard themselves as a kind of machinery, necessary to keep the domestic engine in order, but of little value as the *intelligent* companions of men.

Let no one think, from these remarks, that I regard a knowledge of housewifery as beneath the acquisition of women. Far from it: I believe that a complete knowledge of household affairs is an indispensableuisite in a woman's education,—that by the mistress of a family, whether married or single, doing her duty thoroughly and *understandingly*, the happiness of the family is increased to an incalculable degree, os well as a vast amount of time and money saved. All I complain of is, that our education consists so almost exclusively in culinary and other manual operations. I do long to see the time, when it will no longer be necessary for women to expend so many precious hours in furnishing 'a well spread table,' but that their husbands will forego some of their accustomed indulgences in this way, and encourage their wives to devote some portion of their time to mental cultivation, even at the expense of having to dine sometimes on baked potatoes, or bread and butter. . . .

There is another class of women in this country, to whom I cannot refer, without feelings of the deepest shame and sorrow. I allude to our female slaves. Our southern cities are whelmed beneath a tide of pollution; the virtue of female slaves is wholly at the mercy of irresponsible tyrants, and women are bought and sold in our slave markets, to gratify the brutal lust of those who bear the name of Christians. In our slave States, if amid all her degradation and ignorance, a woman desires to preserve her virtue unsullied, she is either bribed or whipped into compliance, or if she dares resist her seducer, her life by the laws of some of the slave States may be, and has actually been sacrificed to the fury of disappointed passion. Where such laws do not exist, the power which is necessarily vested in the master over his property, leaves the defenceless slave entirely at his mercy, and the sufferings of some females on this account, both physical and mental, are intense. Mr. Gholson, in the House of Delegates of Virginia, in 1832, said, 'He really had been under the impression that he owned his slaves. He had lately purchased four women and ten children, in whom he thought he had obtained a great bargain; for he supposed they were his own property, *as were his brood mares.*' But even if any laws existed in the United States, as in Athens formerly, for the protection of female slaves, they would be null and void, because the evidence of a colored person is not admitted against a white, in any of our Courts of Justice in the slave States. 'In Athens, if a female slave had cause to complain of any want of respect to the laws of modesty, she could seek the protection of the temple, and demand a change of owners; and such appeals were never discountenanced, or neglected by the magistrate.' In Christian America, the slave has no refuge from unbridled cruelty and lust. . . .

Can any American woman look at these scenes of shocking licentiousness and cruelty, and fold her hands in apathy ,and say, 'I have nothing to do with slavery'? *She cannot and be guiltless.*

I cannot close this letter, without saying a few words on the benefits to be derived by men, as well as women, from the opinions I advocate relative to the equality of the sexes. Many women are now supported, in idleness and extravagance, by the industry of their husbands, fathers, or brothers, who are compelled to toil out their existence, at the counting house, or in the printing office, or some other laborious occupation, while the wife and daughters and sisters take no part in the support of the family, and appear to think that their sole business is to spend the hard bought earnings of their male friends. I deeply regret such a state of things, because I believe that if women felt their responsibility, for the support of themselves, or their families it would add strength and dignity to their characters, and teach them more true sympathy for their husbands, than is now generally manifested,—a sympathy which would be exhibited by actions as well as words. Our brethren may reject my doctrine, because it runs counter to common opinions, and because it wounds their pride; but I believe they would be 'partakers of the benefit' resulting from the Equality of the Sexes, and would find that woman, as their equal, was unspeakably more valuable than woman as their inferior, both as a moral and an intellectual being.

> Thine in the bonds of womanhood,
> Sarah M. Grimké.

43. MARGARET FULLER

Woman in the Nineteenth Century
(1845)

MARGARET FULLER (1810–1850) was a major literary critic and social reformer in antebellum America. Born in Cambridgeport, Massachusetts, the young Fuller was the oldest of nine children. Fuller joined the ranks of the emerging Transcendentalist movement after attending Ralph Waldo Emerson's Phi Beta Kappa address at Harvard in 1837. Two years later, Fuller accepted the editorship of *The Dial*, a new scholarly journal designed to promote literary Transcendentalism. Following a successful four-year stint in Boston, *New York Tribune* editor Horace Greeley made Fuller the first female journalist for a major newspaper, offering her a platform with which she quickly garnered international acclaim. Fuller's most important book, *Woman in the Nineteenth Century* (1845), had a major influence on the emerging woman's rights movement. The first comprehensive history of American women, Fuller's study challenged the "tyranny of men" by advocating full sexual equality, calling on women to act collectively to transform the conditions and institutions that oppressed them. Although Fuller died prematurely, *Woman in the Nineteenth Century* ensured her lasting reputation.

SOURCE: Margaret Fuller. *Woman in the Nineteenth Century*. Mineola, New York: Dover, 1999.

SELECTED READINGS: Joan von Mehren, *Minerva and the Muse: A Life of Margaret Fuller* (1994). Bell Gale Chevigny, *The Woman and the Myth: Margaret Fuller's Life and Writings* (1994). Charles Capper, *Margaret Fuller: An American Romantic Life* (1992).

Man is a being of two-fold relations, to nature beneath, and intelligences above him. The earth is his school, if not his birth-place: God his object: life and thought, his means of interpreting nature, and aspiring to God.

Only a fraction of this purpose is accomplished in the life of any one man. Its entire accomplishment is to be hoped only from the sum of the lives of men, or man considered as a whole.

As this whole has one soul and one body, any injury or obstruction to a part, or to the meanest member, affects the whole. Man can never be perfectly happy or virtuous, till all men are so.

To address man wisely, you must not forget that his life is partly animal, subject to the same laws with nature.

But you cannot address him wisely unless you consider him still more as soul, and appreciate the conditions and destiny of soul.

The growth of man is two-fold, masculine and feminine.

As far as these two methods can be distinguished they are so as

Energy and Harmony.

Power and Beauty.

Intellect and Love.

Or by some such rude classification, for we have not language primitive and pure enough to express such ideas with precision.

These two sides are supposed to be expressed in man and woman, that is, as the more and less, for the faculties have not been given pure to either, but only in preponderance. There are also exceptions in great number, such as men of far more beauty than power, and the reverse. But as a general rule, it seems to have been the intention to give a preponderance on the one side, that is called masculine, and on the other, one that is called feminine.

There cannot be a doubt that, if these two developments were in perfect harmony, they would correspond to and fulfil one another, like hemispheres, or the tenor and bass in music.

But there is no perfect harmony in human nature; and the two parts answer one another only now and then, or, if there be a persistent consonance, it can only be traced, at long intervals, instead of discoursing an obvious melody.

What is the cause of this?

Man, in the order of time, was developed first; as energy comes before harmony; power before beauty.

Woman was therefore under his care as an elder. He might have been her guardian and teacher.

But as human nature goes not straight forward, but by excessive action and then reaction in an undulated course, he misunderstood and abused his advantages, and became her temporal master instead of her spiritual sire.

On himself came the punishment. He educated woman more as a servant than a daughter, and found himself a king without a queen.

The children of this unequal union showed unequal natures, and more and more, men seemed sons of the hand-maid, rather than princes.

At last there were so many Ishmaelites that the rest grew frightened and indignant. They laid the blame on Hagar, and drove her forth into the wilderness.

But there were none the fewer Ishmaelites for that.

At last men became a little wiser, and saw that the infant Moses was, in every case, saved by the pure instincts of woman's breast. For, as too much adversity is better for the moral nature than too much prosperity, woman, in this respect, dwindled less than man, though in other respects, still a child in leading strings.

So man did her more and more justice, and grew more and more kind.

But yet, his habits and his will corrupted by the past, he did not clearly see that woman was half himself, that her interests were identical with his, and that, by the law of their common being, he could never reach his true proportions while she remained in any wise shorn of hers.

And so it has gone on to our day; both ideas developing, but more slowly than they would under a clearer recognition of truth and justice, which would have permitted the sexes their due influence on one another, and mutual improvement from more dignified relations.

Wherever there was pure love, the natural influences were, for the time, restored.

Wherever the poet or artist gave free course to his genius, he saw the truth, and expressed it in worthy forms, for these men especially share and need the feminine principle. The divine birds need to be brooded into life and song by mothers.

Wherever religion (I mean the thirst for truth and good, not the love of sect and dogma), had its course, the original design was apprehended in its simplicity, and the dove presaged sweetly from Dodona's oak.

I have aimed to show that no age was left entirely without a witness of the equality of the sexes in function, duty and hope.

Also that, when there was unwillingness or ignorance, which prevented this being acted upon, women had not the less power for their want of light and noble freedom. But it was power which hurt alike them and those against whom they made use of the arms of the servile; cunning, blandishment, and unreasonable emotion.

That now the time has come when a clearer vision and better action are possible. When man and woman may regard one another as brother and sister, the pillars of one porch, the priests of one worship.

I have believed and intimated that this hope would receive an ampler fruition, than ever before, in our own land.

And it will do so if this land carry out the principles from which sprang our national life.

44. SENECA FALLS CONVENTION

Declaration of Sentiments and Resolutions
(1848)

The **"Declaration of Sentiments and Resolution"** was written and approved at the July 1848 Woman's Rights Convention in Seneca Falls, New York. The **SENECA FALLS CONVENTION** was the first public meeting in the world devoted exclusively to issues of women's equality. It was attended by several hundred people, including more than thirty men who were subsequently attacked in print as hermaphrodites and "Aunt Nancy Men" for their participation. The Seneca Falls delegates, many of whom were active in the antislavery movement, were convened by Lucretia Mott and Elizabeth Cady Stanton to identify the various forms of women's inequality, and to organize a movement to combat them. The principle document to come out of the two-day convention was the "Declaration of Sentiments and Resolutions." Modeled after the Declaration of Independence, it enumerated the many ways that men oppressed women through laws and social customs. Nearly every measure was passed unanimously; the important exception was a call for woman's suffrage, which passed by a slim margin after a lengthy and heated debate. While the Seneca Falls Convention inspired a national woman's rights movement by issuing a clarion call for full equality, the suffrage debate foreshadowed future divisions that would serve to undermine solidarity, not only among women themselves, but also between woman's rights advocates and abolitionists.

SOURCE: Philip S. Foner, ed. *We, The Other People: Alternative Declarations of Independence.* Urbana: University of Illinois Press, 1976.

SELECTED READINGS: Ellen Carol DuBois, *Feminism and Suffrage: The Emergence of an Independent Women's Movement in America, 1848–1869* (1978). Blanche G. Hersh, *The Slavery of Sex: Feminist-Abolitionists in America* (1978). Eleanor Flexner, *A Century of Struggle: The Woman's Rights Movement in the United States* (1968).

Declaration of Sentiments

When, in the course of human events, it becomes necessary for one portion of the family of man to assume among the people of the earth a position different from that which they have hitherto occupied, but one to which the laws of nature and of nature's God entitle them, a decent respect to the opinions of mankind requires that they should declare the causes that impel them to such a course.

We hold these truths to be self-evident: that all men and women are created equal; that they are endowed by their Creator with certain inalienable rights; that among these are life, liberty, and the pursuit of happiness; that to secure these rights governments are instituted, deriving their just powers from the consent of the governed. Whenever any form of government becomes destructive of these ends, it is the right of those who suffer from it to refuse allegiance to it, and to insist upon the institution of a new government, laying its foundation on such principles, and organizing its powers in such form, as to them shall seem most likely to effect their safety and happiness. . . .

The history of mankind is a history of repeated injuries and usurpations on the part of man toward woman, having in direct object the establishment of an absolute tyranny over her. To prove this, let facts be submitted to a candid world.

He has never permitted her to exercise her inalienable right to the elective franchise.

He has compelled her to submit to laws, in the formation of which she had no voice.

He has withheld from her rights which are given to the most ignorant and degraded men—both natives and foreigners. . . . thereby leaving her without representation in the halls of legislation, he has oppressed her on all sides.

He has made her, if married, in the eye of the law, civilly dead.

He has taken from her all right in property, even to the wages she earns.

He has made her, morally, an irresponsible being, as she can commit many crimes with impunity, provided they be done in the presence of her husband. In the covenant of marriage, she is compelled to promise obedience to her husband, he becoming, to all intents and purposes, her master—the law giving him power to deprive her of her liberty, and to administer chastisement.

He has so framed the laws of divorce, as to what shall be the proper causes, and in case of separation, to whom the guardianship of the children shall be given, as to be wholly regardless of the happiness of women—the law, in all cases, going upon a false supposition of the supremacy of man, and giving all power into his hands.

After depriving her of all rights as a married woman, if single, and the owner of property, he has taxed her to support a government which recognizes her only when her property can be made profitable to it.

He has monopolized nearly all the profitable employments, and from those she is permitted to follow, she receives but a scanty remuneration. He closes against her all the avenues to wealth and distinction which he considers most honorable to himself. As a teacher of theology, medicine, or law, she is not known.

He has denied her the facilities for obtaining a thorough education, all colleges being closed against her.

He allows her in Church, as well as State, but a subordinate position, claiming Apostolic authority for her exclusion from the ministry, and, with some exceptions, from any public participation in the affairs of the Church.

He has created a false public sentiment by giving to the world a different code of morals for men and women, by which moral delinquencies which exclude women from society, are not only tolerated, but deemed of little account in man.

He has usurped the prerogative of Jehovah himself, claiming it as his right to assign for her a sphere of action, when that belongs to her conscience and to her God.

He has endeavored, in every way that he could, to destroy her confidence in her own powers, to lessen her self-respect, and to make her willing to lead a dependent and abject life.

Now, in view of this entire disfranchisement of one-half the people of this country, their social and religious degradation—in view of the unjust laws above mentioned, and because women do feel themselves aggrieved, oppressed, and fraudulently deprived of their most sacred rights, we insist that they have immediate admission to all the rights and privileges which belong to them as citizens of the United States.

In entering upon the great work before us, we anticipate no small amount of misconception, misrepresentation, and ridicule; but we shall use every instrumentality within our power to effect our object. . . .

Resolutions

Whereas, The great precept of nature is conceded to be, that "man shall pursue his own true and substantial happiness." Blackstone in his Commentaries remarks, that this law of Nature being coeval with mankind, and dictated by God himself, is of course superior in obligation to any other. It is binding over all the globe, in all countries and at all times; no human laws are of any validity if contrary to this, and such of them as are valid, derive all their force, and all their validity, and all their authority, mediately and immediately, from this original; therefore,

Resolved, That such laws as conflict, in any way, with the true and substantial happiness of woman, are contrary to the great precept of nature and of no validity, for this is "superior in obligation to any other."

Resolved, That all laws which prevent woman from occupying such a station in society as her conscience shall dictate, or which place her in a position inferior to that of man, are contrary to the great precept of nature, and therefore of no force or authority.

Resolved, That woman is man's equal—was intended to be so by the Creator, and the highest good of the race demands that she should be recognized as such.

Resolved, That the women of this country ought to be enlightened in regard to the laws under which they live, that they may no longer publish their degradation by declaring themselves satisfied with their present position, nor their ignorance, by asserting that they have all the rights they want.

Resolved, That inasmuch as man, while claiming for himself intellectual superiority, does accord to woman moral superiority, it is pre-eminently his duty to encourage her to speak and teach, as she has an opportunity, in all religious assemblies.

Resolved, That the same amount of virtue, delicacy, and refinement of behavior that is required of a woman in the social state, should also be required of man, and the same transgressions should be visited with equal severity on both man and woman.

Resolved, That the objection of indelicacy and impropriety, which is so often brought against woman when she addresses a public audience, comes with a very ill-grace from those who encourage, by their attendance, her appearance on the stage, in the concert, or in feats of the circus.

Resolved, That woman has too long rested satisfied in the circumscribed limits which corrupt customs and a perverted application of the Scriptures have marked out for her, and that it is time she should move in the enlarged sphere which her great Creator has assigned her.

Resolved, That it is the duty of the women of this country to secure to themselves their sacred right to the elective franchise.

Resolved, That the equality of human rights results necessarily from the fact of the identity of the race in capabilities and responsibilities.

Resolved, therefore, That, being invested by the Creator with the same capabilities, and the same consciousness of responsibilitly for their excercise, it is demonstrably the right and duty of woman, equally with man, to promote every righteous cause by every righteous means; and especially in regard to the great subjects of morals and religion, it is self-evidently her right to participate with her brother in teaching them, both in private and in public, by writing and by speaking, by any instrumentalities proper to be used, and in any assemblies proper to be held; and this being a self-evident truth growing out of the divinely implanted principles of human nature, any custom or authority adverse to it, whether modern or wearing the hoary sanction of antiquity, is to be regarded as a self-evident falsehood, and at war with mankind.

45. FREDERICK DOUGLASS

The Rights of Women
(1848)

In addition to his indispensable antislavery work, **FREDERICK DOUGLASS (c. 1818–1895)** devoted his energies to the emerging cause of woman's rights. In 1847, after an editorial dispute with William Lloyd Garrison, Douglass moved to Rochester, New York—a hotbed of radical activism—to start his own newspaper. The following year, he was among the so-called hermaphrodites (male delegates) to the Woman's Rights Convention in Seneca Falls, after which he spoke out vigorously, and often, on behalf of woman's equality. The following editorial, published in Douglass's *North Star* one week after the Seneca Falls Convention, reflects Douglass's respect for the women who organized the historic meeting, as well as his support for the full political rights of women.

SOURCE: Winston E. Langley and Vivian C. Fox, eds. *Women's Rights in the United States: A Documentary History.* Westport: Greenwood Press, 1994.

SELECTED READINGS: William S. McFeely, *Frederick Douglass* (1991). Waldo E. Martin, *The Mind of Frederick Douglass* (1984). Phillip S. Foner, ed., *Frederick Douglass on Woman's Rights* (1976).

THE RIGHTS OF WOMEN.—One of the most interesting events of the past week, was the holding of what is technically styled a Woman's Rights Convention at Seneca Falls. The speaking, addresses, and resolutions of this extraordinary meeting were almost wholly conducted by women; and although they evidently felt themselves in a novel position, it is but simple justice to say that their whole proceedings were characterized by marked ability and dignity. No one present, we think, however much he might be disposed to differ from the views advanced by the leading speakers on that occasion, will fail to give them credit for brilliant talents and excellent dispositions. In this meeting, as in other deliberative assemblies, there were frequent differences of opinion and animated discussion; but in no case was there the slightest absence of good feeling and decorum. Several interesting documents setting forth the rights as well as grievances of women were read. Among these was a Declaration of Sentiments, to be regarded as the basis of a grand movement for attaining the civil, social, political, and religious rights of women. We should not do justice to our own convictions, or to the excellent persons connected with this infant movement, if we did not in this connection offer a few remarks on the general subject which the Convention met to consider and the objects they seek to attain. In doing so, we are not insensible that the bare mention of this truly important subject in any other than terms of contemptuous ridicule and scornful disfavor, is likely to excite against us the fury of bigotry and the folly of prejudice. A discussion of the rights of animals would be regarded with far more complacency by many of what are called the *wise* and the *good* of our land, than would be a discussion of the rights of women. It is, in their estimation, to be guilty of evil thoughts, to think that woman is entitled to equal rights with man. Many who have at last made the discovery that the negroes have some rights as well as other members of the human family, have yet to be convinced that women are entitled to any. Eight years ago a number of persons of this description actually abandoned the anti-slavery cause, lest by giving their influence in that direction they might possibly be giving countenance to the dangerous heresy that woman, in respect to rights, stands on an equal footing with man. In the judgment of such persons the American slave system, with all its con-comifant horrors, is less to be deplored than this *wicked* idea. It is perhaps needless to say, that we cherish little sympathy for such sentiments or respect for such prejudices. Standing as we do upon the watch-tower of human freedom, we can not be deterred from an expression of our approbation of any movement, however humble, to improve and elevate the character of any members of the human family. While it is impossible for us to go into this subject at length, and dispose of the various objections which are often urged against such a doctrine as that of female equality, we are free to say that in respect to political rights, we hold woman to be justly entitled to all we claim for man. We go farther, and express our conviction that all political rights which it is expedient for man to exercise, it is equally so for woman.

46. SOJOURNER TRUTH

Ar'n't I A Woman?
(1851)

SOJOURNER TRUTH (c. 1799–1883) was a popular, self-educated itinerant preacher whose advocacy of abolitionism and woman's rights helped to establish important links between the struggles of women and black Americans. Truth was born a slave named Isabella in upstate New York. After gaining her freedom under the 1827 New York emancipation law, she began a remarkable public career as a preacher and abolitionist. Renowned for her physical presence—she was close to six feet tall—and her robust voice, she changed her name to "Sojourner Truth" in 1843, and joined the Northampton Association, a radical community of abolitionists and woman's rights supporters based in Massachusetts. After the publication of *The Narrative of Sojourner Truth* (1850), the famous autobiography she dictated (she was illiterate) to Olive Gilbert, Truth became the only female ex-slave to lecture regularly on the antebellum reform circuit. At the 1851 National Woman's Suffrage Convention in Akron, Ohio, Truth delivered what would become her most famous speech—"Ar'n't I A Woman?"—in which she boldly challenged male reformers who had spoken in opposition to woman's rights on the grounds that women were physically and mentally weaker than men. Truth's Akron speech was memorialized in print in 1863 by Ohio feminist Frances Dana Gage, who was the first to coin the title, "Ar'n't I A Woman?"

SOURCE: Henry Louis Gates, Jr., and Nellie McKay et al., eds. *The Norton Anthology of African American Literature.* New York and London: W. W. Norton and Company, 1997.

SELECTED READINGS: Nell Irvin Painter, *Sojourner Truth: A Life, A Symbol* (1996). Carleton Mabee, *Sojourner Truth: Slave, Prophet, Legend* (1993). Hertha Pauli, *Her Name Was Sojourner Truth* (1962).

"Slowly from her seat in the corner rose Sojourner Truth, who, till now, had scarcely lifted her head. 'Don't let her speak!' gasped half a dozen in my ear. She moved slowly and solemnly to the front, laid her old bonnet at her feet, and turned her great, speaking eyes to me. There was a hissing sound of disapprobation above and below. I rose and announced 'Sojourner Truth,' and begged the audience to keep silence for a few moments. The tumult subsided at once, and every eye was fixed on this almost Amazon form, which stood nearly six feet high, head erect, and eye piercing the upper air, like one in a dream. At her first word, there was a profound hush. She spoke in deep tones, which, though not loud, reached every ear in the house, and away through the throng at the doors and windows:—

" 'Well, chilern, whar dar is so much racket dar must be something out o' kilter. I tink dat 'twixt de niggers of de Souf and de women at de Norf all a talkin' 'bout rights, de white men will be in a fix pretty soon. But what's all dis here talkin' 'bout? Dat man ober dar say dat women needs to be helped into carriages, and lifted ober ditches, and to have de best place every whar. Nobody eber help me into carriages, or ober mud puddles, or gives me any best place [and raising herself to her full height and her voice to a pitch like rolling thunder, she asked], and ar'n't I a woman? Look at me! Look at my arm! [And she bared her right arm to the shoulder, showing her tremendous muscular power.] I have plowed, and planted, and gathered into barns, and no man could head me—and ar'n't I a woman? I could work as much and eat as much as a man (when I could get it), and bear de lash as well—and ar'n't I a woman? I have borne thirteen chilern and seen 'em mos' all sold off into slavery, and when I cried out with a mother's grief, none but Jesus heard—and ar'n't I a woman? Den dey talks 'bout dis ting in de head—what dis dey call it?' 'Intellect,' whispered some one near. 'Dat's it honey. What's dat got to do with women's rights or niggers' rights? If my cup won't hold but a pint and yourn holds a quart, would n't ye be mean not to let me have my little half-measure full?' And she pointed her significant finger and sent a keen glance at the minister who had made the argument. The cheering was long and loud.

" 'Den dat little man in black dar, he say women can't have as much rights as man, cause Christ want a woman. Whar did your Christ come from?' Rolling thunder could not have stilled that crowd as did those deep, wonderful tones, as she stood there with outstretched arms and eye of fire. Raising her voice still louder, she repeated, 'Whar did your Christ come from? From God and a woman. Man had nothing to do with him.' Oh! what a rebuke she gave the little man.

"Turning again to another objector, she took up the defense of mother Eve. I cannot follow her through it all. It was pointed, and witty, and solemn,

eliciting at almost every sentence deafening applause; and she ended by asserting that 'if de fust woman God ever made was strong enough to turn the
world upside down, all 'lone, dese togedder [and she glanced her eye over
us], ought to be able to turn it back and get it right side up again, and
now dey is asking to do it, de men better let em.' Long-continued cheering.
'Bleeged to ye for hearin' on me, and now ole Sojourner ha'n't got nothing
more to say.'

"Amid roars of applause, she turned to her corner, leaving more than one
of us with streaming eyes and hearts beating with gratitude. She had taken
us up in her strong arms and carried us safely over the slough of difficulty,
turning the whole tide in our favor. I have never in my life seen anything
like the magical influence that subdued the mobbish spirit of the day and
turned the jibes and sneers of an excited crowd into notes of respect and
admiration. Hundreds rushed up to shake hands, and congratulate the glorious
old mother and bid her God speed on her mission of 'testifying again concerning the wickedness of this 'ere people.' "

47. HARRIET JACOBS

Incidents in the Life of a Slave Girl
(1861)

HARRIET JACOBS (c. 1813–1897) was an abolitionist and woman's rights advocate whose poignant slave narrative, *Incidents in the Life of a Slave Girl*, was the most important autobiography written by an African-American woman before the Civil War. Born a slave in Edenton, North Carolina, Jacobs learned to read at an early age, living with several white families before escaping an abusive master at the age of twenty-one. While a fugitive, Jacobs lived a clandestine existence in her grandmother's attic, before finally escaping to Philadelphia in 1842. After reuniting with her children, Jacobs moved to Rochester, New York, where she found herself in the midst of a vibrant, interracial abolitionist community. During the 1850s, at the encouragement of her white abolitionist-feminist friend Amy Post, Jacobs worked on her autobiography. First published under the pseudonym "Linda," and edited by Lydia Maria Child, *Incidents in the Life of a Slave Girl* (1861) garnered immediate acclaim, prompting favorable comparisons with Frederick Douglass's famous tale of bondage and freedom. Though she would retreat from public life after the Civil War, Jacobs's autobiography is still one of the most harrowing accounts of the horrible combination of sexual and racial violence to which female slaves were subjected. The following excerpt chronicles Jacobs's struggle to resist the sexual advances of her white master, Dr. Flint, and the limited choices available to black women in slavery.

SOURCE: Harriet A. Jacobs. *Incidents in the Life of a Slave Girl.* Ed. Jean Fagan Yellin. Cambridge: Harvard University Press, 1987.

SELECTED READINGS: Deborah M. Garfield and Rafia Zafar, eds., *Harriet Jacobs and Incidents in the Life of a Slave Girl* (1996). Carla L. Peterson, *"Doers of the Word": African-American Women Speakers and Writers in the North, 1830–1880* (1995). Joanne Braxton, *Black Women Writing Autobiography: A Tradition*

Within a Tradition (1989). Mary Helen Washington, *Invented Lives: Narratives of Black Women, 1860–1960* (1987).

After my lover went away, Dr. Flint contrived a new plan. He seemed to have an idea that my fear of my mistress was his greatest obstacle. In the blandest tones, he told me that he was going to build a small house for me, in a secluded place, four miles away from the town. I shuddered; but I was constrained to listen, while he talked of his intention to give me a home of my own, and to make a lady of me. Hitherto, I had escaped my dreaded fate, by being in the midst of people. My grandmother had already had high words with my master about me. She had told him pretty plainly what she thought of his character, and there was considerable gossip in the neighborhood about our affairs, to which the open-mouthed jealousy of Mrs. Flint contributed not a little. When my master said he was going to build a house for me, and that he could do it with little trouble and expense, I was in hopes something would happen to frustrate his scheme; but I soon heard that the house was actually begun. I vowed before my Maker that I would never enter it. I had rather toil on the plantation from dawn till dark; I had rather live and die in jail, than drag on, from day to day, through such a living death. I was determined that the master, whom I so hated and loathed, who had blighted the prospects of my youth, and made my life a desert, should not, after my long struggle with him, succeed at last in trampling his victim under his feet. I would do any thing, every thing, for the sake of defeating him. What *could* I do? I thought and thought, till I became desperate, and made a plunge into the abyss.

And now, reader, I come to a period in my unhappy life, which I would gladly forget if I could. The remembrance fills me with sorrow and shame. It pains me to tell you of it; but I have promised to tell you the truth, and I will do it honestly, let it cost me what it may. I will not try to screen myself behind the plea of compulsion from a master; for it was not so. Neither can I plead ignorance or thoughtlessness. For years, my master had done his utmost to pollute my mind with foul images, and to destroy the pure principles inculcated by my grandmother, and the good mistress of my childhood. The influences of slavery had had the same effect on me that they had on other young girls; they had made me prematurely knowing, concerning the evil ways of the world. I knew what I did, and I did it with deliberate calculation.

But, O, ye happy women, whose purity has been sheltered from childhood, who have been free to choose the objects of your affection, whose homes are protected by law, do not judge the poor desolate slave girl too severely! If slavery had been abolished, I, also, could have married the man of my choice; I could have had a home shielded by the laws; and I should have been spared the painful task of confessing what I am now about to relate; but all my prospects had been blighted by slavery. I wanted to keep myself pure; and, under the most adverse circumstances, I tried hard to preserve my self-respect; but I was struggling alone in the powerful grasp of the demon Slavery; and the monster proved too strong for me. I felt as if I was forsaken by God and man; as if all my efforts must be frustrated; and I became reckless in my despair.

I have told you that Dr. Flint's persecutions and his wife's jealousy had given rise to some gossip in the neighborhood. Among others, it chanced that a white unmarried gentleman had obtained some knowledge of the circumstances in which I was placed. He knew my grandmother, and often spoke to me in the street. He became interested for me, and asked questions about my master, which I answered in part. He expressed a great deal of sympathy, and a wish to aid me. He constantly sought opportunities to see me, and wrote to me frequently. I was a poor slave girl, only fifteen years old.

So much attention from a superior person was, of course, flattering; for human nature is the same in all. I also felt grateful for his sympathy, and encouraged by his kind words. It seemed to me a great thing to have such a friend. By degrees, a more tender feeling crept into my heart. He was an educated and eloquent gentleman; too eloquent, alas, for the poor slave girl who trusted in him. Of course I saw whither all this was tending. I knew the impassable gulf between us; but to be an object of interest to a man who is not married, and who is not her master, is agreeable to the pride and feelings of a slave, if her miserable situation has left her any pride or sentiment. It seems less degrading to give one's self, than to submit to compulsion. There is something akin to freedom in having a lover who has no control over you, except that which he gains by kindness and attachment. A master may treat you as rudely as he pleases, and you dare not speak; moreover, the wrong does not seem so great with an unmarried man, as with one who has a wife to be made unhappy. There may be sophistry in all this; but the condition of a slave confuses all principles of morality, and, in fact, renders the practice of them impossible.

When I found that my master had actually begun to build the lonely cottage, other feelings mixed with those I have described. Revenge, and calculations of interest, were added to flattered vanity and sincere gratitude for kindness. I knew nothing would enrage Dr. Flint so much as to know that I favored another; and it was something to triumph over my tyrant even in that small way. I thought he would revenge himself by selling me, and I was sure my friend, Mr. Sands, would buy me. He was a man of more generosity and feeling than my master, and I thought my freedom could be easily obtained from him. The crisis of my fate now came so near that I was desperate. I shuddered to think of being the mother of children that should be owned by my old tyrant. I knew that as soon as a new fancy took him, his victims were sold far off to get rid of them; especially if they had children. I had seen several women sold, with his babies at the breast. He never allowed his off-spring by slaves to remain long in sight of himself and his wife. Of a man who was not my master I could ask to have my children well supported; and in this case, I felt confident I should obtain the boon. I also felt quite sure that they would be made free. With all these thoughts revolving in my mind, and seeing no other way of escaping the doom I so much dreaded, I made a head-long plunge. Pity me, and pardon me, O virtuous reader! You never knew what it is to be a slave; to be entirely unprotected by law or custom; to have the laws reduce you to the condition of a chattel, entirely subject to the will of another. You never exhausted your ingenuity in avoiding the snares, and eluding the power of a hated tyrant; you never shuddered at the sound of his footsteps, and trembled within hearing of his voice. I know I did wrong. No one can feel it more sensibly than I do. The painful and humiliating memory will haunt me to my dying day. Still, in looking back, calmly, on the events of my life, I feel that the slave woman ought not to be judged by the same standard as others.

The months passed on. I had many unhappy hours. I secretly mourned over the sorrow I was bringing on my grandmother, who had so tried to shield me from harm. I knew that I was the greatest comfort of her old age, and that it was a source of pride to her that I had not degraded myself, like most of the slaves. I wanted to confess to her that I was no longer worthy of her love; but I could not utter the dreaded words.

As for Dr. Flint, I had a feeling of satisfaction and triumph in the thought of telling *him*. From time to time he told me of his intended arrangements, and I was silent. At last, he came and told me the cottage was completed, and ordered me to go to it. I told him I would never enter it. He said, "I have heard enough of such talk as that. You shall go, if you are carried by force; and you shall remain there."

I replied, "I will never go there. In a few months I shall be a mother."

He stood and looked at me in dumb amazement, and left the house without a word. I thought I should be happy in my triumph over him. But now that the truth was out, and my relatives would hear of it, I felt wretched. Humble as were their circumstances, they had pride in my good character. Now, how could I look them in the face? My self-respect was gone! I had resolved that I would be virtuous, though I was a slave. I had said, "Let the storm beat! I will brave it till I die." And now, how humiliated I felt!

48. LUCY STONE

Letter to Abby Kelley Foster
(1867)

LUCY STONE (1818–1893) was a radical abolitionist and suffragist who founded the American Woman Suffrage Association (AWSA) and later helped to bridge the gap between the first and second generation of American feminists. Born in West Brookfield, Massachusetts, Stone broke with her family's Congregationalist faith after church leaders criticized the Grimké sisters for their antislavery lectures. She later graduated from Oberlin College and followed in the footsteps of the Grimkés as a popular abolitionist lecturer. In 1855, she married Cincinnati merchant Henry B. Blackwell, a progressive-minded man who encouraged her independent spirit (prompting the popular slur, "Lucy Stoner," which referred to women activists who kept their names after marriage). A staunch proponent of emancipation and black suffrage, she was a founder of the American Equal Rights Association (AERA), a group of antislavery feminists who advocated the extension of voting rights regardless of race or sex. When Elizabeth Cady Stanton and Susan B. Anthony broke with the AERA to form the National Woman Suffrage Association (NWSA) after the passage of the Fourteenth and Fifteenth Amendments, Stone helped found the American Woman Suffrage Association (AWSA) to advance state-level women's suffrage campaigns while continuing to promote black civil rights. The following letter, written to longtime friend and radical abolitionist Abby Kelley Foster in 1867, directly addresses the debate over suffrage—whether the right to vote would be extended universally or to black men only—that long divided the woman's rights movement.

SOURCE: Leslie Wheeler, ed. *Loving Warriors: Selected Letters of Lucy Stone and Henry B. Blackwell, 1853 to 1893.* New York: Dial Press, 1981.

SELECTED READINGS: Andrew Moore Kerr, *Lucy Stone: Speaking Out for Equality* (1992). Carol Lasser and Marlene Deahl Merrill, eds., *Friends and Sisters: Letters*

Between Lucy Stone and Antoinette Blackwell, 1846–1893 (1987). Ellen Carol DuBois, *Feminism and Suffrage: The Emergence of an Independent Woman's Movement in America, 1848–1869* (1978).

New York Post office box 299 Jan. 24-1867

My dear Mrs. [Abby Kelley] Foster

I sit down to write you, with a feeling of despair which never came to me before where a principle is involved.

We have just returned from Philadelphia, where we went to assist in forming an Equal Suffrage Association. Geo. Thompson was there, and said "he did not think it would make any practical difference whether women voted or not." Edward M. Davis said "he sympathised with the Equal suffrage movement but he would take no position in it, that involved work. All his *work*, should be for the Negro." Eight colored men gathered around us during the recess, and said they thought women were well enough represented by their husbands &c. Robert Purvis alone, of them all, said "he should be ashamed to ask suffrage for himself and not at the same time, ask it for women, and he marveled at the patience of women, who were silent as to their own claims, while the great mass of the Negroes for whom they worked, would give their influence like a dead weight against the equality of women with them." Lucretia Mott, clear eyed as ever gave her voice, and her money, for universal justice.

But you, and Phillips, & Garrison, and the brave workers, who for thirty years, have said "let justice be done, if the heavens fall," now smitten by a strange blindness, believe that the nation's peril can be averted, if it can be induced to accept the poor half loaf, of justice for the Negro, poisoned by its lack of justice for every woman in the land. As if the application of a *universal* principle to a single class, *could* suffice for the necessity of this hour!

The broad principle of universal justice put into the foundation of our Temple of Liberty, is the *only* thing that can save it. They who today, stand saying, "this is the Negroes hour," are just in the position of those mistaken men, who after the war of revolution, said, "dont let us meddle with slavery. It is a bad thing, and will die of itself. But the business of this hour is to get a union." They got the union, and we know the results.

Now, as then, those who hold the life of the nation in their hands, do not see, that the path of justice, is the *only* path of peace and safety. They will not even ask for it, and we shall go on, drifting among breakers with no pilot to guide, where the anointed eye sees the clear channel in which we might ride in safety.

O Abby, it is a terrible mistake you are all making. . . . There is no other name given, by which this country *can* be saved, but that of *woman*. The Nation does not know it, and will not learn, Greeley says, "*dont* stir your question." Oliver Johnson sits in Theodore Tiltons chair, and snubs Mrs. Stanton and every one of us, not even opening our replies to Tayler Lewis. During a whole year, till very lately, has the Anti Slavery Standard thought it necessary to apologize, if it gave an item looking toward justice for woman. The "World" refuses to publish anything, because "its position would be misunderstood." So we get no access to the public ear. Susan Anthony gets no money from the Hovey fund, for her work in N.Y. The Greeks, abroad are remembered, and I hope they, and there "Isles" will be saved, but "the Greeks at our door," are forgotten. But the penalty for that forgetting, is not for Woman alone, or for this country alone, but also, for that great multitude whose longing eyes are trained from all shores to our own, for an example of a government, which derives its just powers from the consent of the governed. They alas will be disappointed, as shall we. But the mills of God grind very slow, and as we sow, so must we reap.

Here is a kiss for the hem of your garment, and all good wishes for you, and yours, but the tears are in my eyes, and a wail goes through my heart akin to that which I should feel, if I saw my little daughter drowning before my eyes with no power to help her.

Very truly
Lucy Stone

49. SUSAN B. ANTHONY

Appeal to the National Democratic Convention
(1868)

Arguably the most eloquent and effective spokesperson for women's equality, **SUSAN B. ANTHONY (1820–1906)** was one of the principal organizers of the suffrage movement during the second half of the nineteenth century. Born in Adams, Massachusetts, Anthony went to work as a teacher after the Panic of 1837 to help support her struggling family in upstate New York. In 1851, Anthony was introduced to Elizabeth Cady Stanton, and the two women soon forged one of the most exceptional friendships and political partnerships in American history. For the next half-century, Anthony and Stanton devoted themselves to both abolition and woman's rights. When fellow feminists and abolitionist allies endorsed a constitutional proposal for universal *male* suffrage, Stanton and Anthony formed the independent National Woman Suffrage Association (NWSA), openly campaigning against the Fifteenth Amendment and aligning themselves precariously with racist Democrats. The following appeal, in which Anthony requests the privilege to address the 1868 Democratic National Convention, reflects the shifting political alliances of the post–Civil War period, when Stanton and Anthony turned away from Republicans and former abolitionists for support in their suffrage crusade.

SOURCE: Elizabeth Cady Stanton, Susan B. Anthony, and Matilda Joslyn Gage, eds. *History of Woman Suffrage, Volume II, 1861–1876.* New York: Arno Press, 1969.

SELECTED READINGS: Ellen Carol DuBois, ed., *Elizabeth Cady Stanton, Susan B. Anthony: Correspondence, Writings, Speeches* (1992). Nancy Hewitt, *Women's Activism and Social Change: Rochester, New York* (1984). Alma Lutz, *Susan B. Anthony: Rebel, Crusader, Humanitarian* (1959).

To the President and Members of the National Democratic Convention:

GENTLEMEN:—I address you by letter to ask the privilege of appearing before you during the sittings of this Convention, to demand the enfranchisement of the women of America, the only class of citizens wholly unrepresented in the Government, the only class (not guilty of crime) taxed without representation, tried without a jury of their peers, governed without their consent. And yet in this class are found many of your most noble, virtuous, law-abiding citizens, who possess all the requisite qualifications of voters. Women have property and education. We are not "idiots, lunatics, paupers, criminals, rebels," nor do we "bet on elections." We lack, according to your constitutions, but one qualification—that of sex—which is insurmountable, and, therefore, equivalent to a deprivation of the suffrage; in other words, the "tyranny of taxation without representation."

We desire to lay before you this violation of the great fundamental principle of our Government for your serious consideration, knowing that minorities can be moved by principles as majorities are only by votes. Hence we look to you for the initiative step in the redress of our grievances.

The party in power have not only failed to heed our innumerable petitions, asking the right of suffrage, poured into Congress and State Legislatures, but they have submitted a proposition to the several States to insert the word "male" in the Federal Constitution, where it has never been, and thereby put up a new barrier against the enfranchisement of woman. This fresh insult to the women of the Republic, who so bravely shared the dangers and sacrifices of the late war, has roused us to more earnest and persistent efforts to secure those rights, privileges, and immunities that belong to every citizen under Government. As you hold the Constitution of the fathers to be a sacred legacy to us and our children forever, we ask you to save it from this desecration, which deprives one-half our citizens of the right of representation in the Government. Over this base proposition the nation has stood silent and indifferent: While the dominant party has with one hand lifted up two million black men and crowned them with the honor and dignity of citizenship, with the other it has dethroned fifteen million white women—their own mothers and sisters, their own wives and daughters—and cast them under the heel of the lowest orders of manhood.

We appeal to you, not only because you, being in a minority, are in a position to consider principles, but because you have been the party heretofore to extend the suffrage. It was the Democratic party that fought most valiantly for the removal of the "property qualification" from all white men, and thereby placed the poorest ditch-digger on a political level with the proudest millionaire. This one act of justice to workingmen has perpetuated your power, with but few interruptions, from that time until the war. And now you have an opportunity to confer a similar boon on the women of the country, and thus possess yourselves of a new talisman that will insure and perpetuate your political power for decades to come.

While the first and highest motive we would urge on you, is the recognition in all your action of the great principles of justice and equality that are the foundation of a republican government, it is not unworthy to remind you that the party that takes this onward step will reap its just reward. It needs but little observation to see that the tide of progress in all countries is setting toward the enfranchisement of woman, and that this advance step in civilization is destined to be taken in our day.

We conjure you, then, to turn from the dead questions of the past to the vital issues of the hour. The brute form of slavery ended with the war. The black man is a soldier and a citizen. He holds the bullet and the ballot in his own right hand. Consider his case settled. Those weapons of defense and self-protection can never be wrenched from him. Yours the responsibility now to see that no new chains be forged by bondholders and monopolists for enslaving the labor of the country.

The late war, seemingly in the interest of slavery, was fought by unseen hands for the larger liberties of the whole people. It was not a war between North and South, for the principle of class and caste knows neither latitude or longitude. It was a war of ideas—of Aristocracy and Democracy—of Capital and Labor—the same that has convulsed the race through the ages, and will continue to convulse future generations, until Justice and Equality shall reign upon the earth.

I desire, therefore, an opportunity to urge on this Convention the wisdom of basing its platform on universal suffrage as well as universal amnesty, from Maine to California, and thus take the first step toward a peaceful and permanent reconstruction.

In behalf of the Woman's Suffrage Association,
Respectfully yours,   Susan B. Anthony.

50. NATIONAL WOMAN SUFFRAGE ASSOCIATION

Declaration of the Rights of Women
(1876)

Co-founded in 1869 by Elizabeth Cady Stanton and Susan B. Anthony, the **NATIONAL WOMAN SUFFRAGE ASSOCIATION (NWSA)** issued its "Declaration of the Rights of Women" on July 4, 1876. During the NWSA convention the preceding May, president Matilda Gage threatened that if neither major political party endorsed woman's suffrage in their election-year platforms, American women would be forced to issue their own declaration of independence at the nation's centennial in Philadelphia. Keeping this dramatic promise, Susan B. Anthony and four other NWSA representatives took the podium at the July 4 celebration, read from the "Declaration," and distributed printed copies to those in attendance. Unlike the "Declaration of Sentiments" from the 1848 Seneca Falls Convention, the 1876 document confined itself to indicting the all-male government, rather than *all men*, for "usurpations of power over women." Invoking the spirit of Abigail Adams—who exhorted her Revolutionary husband to "remember the ladies"—the "Declaration of the Rights of Women" demanded the full representation of women in political life (the right to vote, serve on juries, and hold office) as a long overdue remedy for the continued oppression of women in the United States.

SOURCE: Philip S. Foner, ed. *We, The Other People: Alternative Declarations of Independence.* Urbana: University of Illinois Press, 1976.

SELECTED READINGS: Eleanor Flexner and Ellen Fitzpatrick, *Century of Struggle: The Woman's Rights Movement in the United States* (1996). Dee Brown, *The Year of the Century: 1876* (1966). Elizabeth Cady Stanton, Susan B. Anthony, and Matilda Joslyn Gage, eds., *History of Woman Suffrage* (1881–1886).

The history of our country the past hundred years has been a series of assumptions and usurpations of power over woman, in direct opposition to the principles of just government, acknowledged by the United States as its foundation, which are:

First—The natural rights of each individual.

Second—The equality of these rights.

Third—That rights not delegated are retained by the individual.

Fourth—That no person can exercise the rights of others without delegated authority.

Fifth—That the non-use of rights does not destroy them.

And for the violation of these fundamental principles of our government, we arraign our rulers on this Fourth day of July, 1876,—and these are our articles of impeachment:

Bills of attainder have been passed by the introduction of the word "male" into all the State constitutions, denying to women the right of suffrage, and thereby making sex a crime—an exercise of power clearly forbidden in article I, sections 9, 10, of the United States constitution.

The writ of habeas corpus, the only protection against *lettres de cachet* and all forms of unjust imprisonment, which the constitution declares "shall not be suspended, except when in cases of rebellion or invasion the public safety demands it," is held inoperative in every State of the Union, in case of a married woman against her husband—the marital rights of the husband being in all cases primary, and the rights of the wife secondary.

The right of trial by a jury of one's peers was so jealously guarded that States refused to ratify the original constitution until it was guaranteed by the sixth amendment. And yet the women of this nation have never been allowed a jury of their peers—being tried in all cases by men, native and foreign, educated and ignorant, virtuous and vicious. Young girls have been arraigned in our courts for the crime of infanticide; tried, convicted, hanged—victims, perchance, of judge, jurors, advocates—while no woman's voice could be heard in their defense. And not only are women denied a jury of their peers, but in some cases, jury trial altogether. During the war, a woman was tried and hanged by military law, in defiance of the fifth amendment, which specifically declares: "No person shall be held to answer for a capital or otherwise infamous crime, unless on a presentment or indictment of a grand jury, except in cases . . . of persons in actual service in time of war." During the last presidential campaign, a woman, arrested for voting, was denied the protection of a jury, tried, convicted, and sentenced to a fine and costs of prosecution, by the absolute power of a judge of the Supreme Court of the United States.

Taxation without representation, the immediate cause of the rebellion of the colonies against Great Britain, is one of the grievous wrongs the women of this country have suffered during the century. Deploring war, with all the demoralization that follows in its train, we have been taxed to support standing armies, with their waste of life and wealth. Believing in temperance, we have been taxed to support the vice, crime and pauperism of the liquor traffic. While we suffer its wrongs and abuses infinitely more than man, we have no power to protect our sons against this giant evil. During the temperance crusade, mothers were arrested, fined, imprisoned, for even praying and singing in the streets, while men blockaded the sidewalks with impunity, even on Sunday, with their military parades and political processions. Believing in honesty, we are taxed to support a dangerous army of civilians, buying and selling the offices of government and sacrificing the best interests of the people. And, moreover, we are taxed to support the very legislators and judges who make laws, and render decisions adverse to woman. And for refusing to pay such unjust taxation, the houses, lands, bonds, and stock of women have been seized and sold within the present year, thus proving Lord Coke's assertion, that "The very act of taxing a man's property without his consent is, in effect, disfranchising him of every civil right."

Unequal codes for men and women. Held by law a perpetual minor, deemed incapable of self-protection, even in the industries of the world, woman is denied equality of rights. The fact of sex, not the quantity or quality of work, in most cases, decides the pay and position; and because of this injustice thousands of fatherless girls are compelled to choose between a life of shame and starvation. Laws catering to man's vices have created two codes of morals in which penalties are graded according to the political status of the offender. Under such laws, women are fined and imprisoned if found alone in the streets, or in public places of resort, at certain hours. Under the pretense of regulating public morals, police officers seizing the occupants of disreputable houses, march the women in platoons to prison, while the men, partners in their guilt, go free. While making a show of virtue in forbidding the importation of Chinese women on the Pacific coast for immoral purposes, our rulers, in many States, and even under the shadow of the national capitol, are now proposing to legalize the sale of American womanhood for the same vile purposes.

Special legislation for woman has placed us in a most anomalous position. Women invested with the rights of citizens in one section—voters, jurors, office-holders—crossing an imaginary line, are subjects in the next. In some States, a married woman may hold property and transact business in her own name; in others, her earnings belong to her husband. In some States, a woman may testify against her husband, sue and be sued in the courts; in others, she has no redress in case of damage to person, property, or character. In case of divorce on account of adultery in the husband, the innocent wife is held to possess no right to children or property, unless by special decree of the court. But in no State of the Union has the wife the right to her own person, or to any part of the joint earnings of the co-partnership during the life of her husband. In some States women may enter the law schools and practice in the courts; in others they are forbidden. In some universities girls enjoy equal educational advantages with boys, while many of the proudest institutions in the land deny them admittance, though the sons of China, Japan and Africa are welcomed there. But the privileges already granted in the several States are by no means secure. The right of suffrage once exercised by women in certain States and territories has been denied by subsequent legislation. A bill is now pending in congress to disfranchise the women of Utah, thus interfering to deprive United States citizens of the same rights which the Supreme Court has declared the national government powerless to protect anywhere. Laws passed after years of untiring effort, guaranteeing married women certain rights of property, and mothers the custody of their children, have been repealed in States where we supposed all was safe. Thus have our most sacred rights been made the football of legislative caprice, proving that a power which grants as a privilege what by nature is a right, may withhold the same as a penalty when deeming it necessary for its own perpetuation.

Representation of woman has had no place in the nation's thought. Since the incorporation of the thirteen original States, twenty-four have been admitted to the Union, not one of which has recognized woman's right of self-government. On this birthday of our national liberties, July Fourth, 1876, Colorado, like all her elder sisters, comes into the Union with the invidious word "male" in her constitution.

Universal manhood suffrage, by establishing an aristocracy of sex, imposes upon the women of this nation a more absolute and cruel despotism than monarchy; in that, woman finds a political master in her father, husband, brother, son. The aristocracies of the old world are based upon birth, wealth, refinement, education, nobility, brave deeds of chivalry; in this nation, on sex alone; exalting brute force above moral power, vice above virtue, ignorance above education, and the son above the mother who bore him.

The judiciary above the nation has proved itself but the echo of the party in power, by upholding and enforcing laws that are opposed to the spirit and letter of the constitution. When the slave power was dominant, the Supreme Court decided that a black man was not a citizen, because he had not the right to vote; and when the constitution was so amended as to make all persons citizens, the same high tribunal decided that a woman, though a citizen, had not the right to vote. Such vacillating interpretations of constitutional law unsettle our faith in judicial authority, and undermine the liberties of the whole people.

These articles of impeachment against our rulers we now submit to the impartial judgment of the people. To all these wrongs and oppressions woman has not submitted in silence and resignation. From the beginning of the century, when Abigail Adams, the wife of one president and mother of another, said, "We will not hold ourselves bound to obey laws in which we have no voice or representation," until now, woman's discontent has been steadily increasing, culminating nearly thirty years ago in a simultaneous movement among the women of the nation, demanding the right of suffrage. In making our just demands, a higher motive than the pride of sex inspires us; we feel that national safety and stability depend on the complete recognition of the broad principles of our government. Woman's degraded, helpless position is the weak point in our institutions to-day; a disturbing force everywhere, severing family ties, filling our asylums with the deaf, the dumb, the blind; our prisons with criminals, our cities with drunkenness and prostitution; our homes with disease and death. It was the boast of the founders of the republic, that the rights for which they contended were the rights of human nature. If these rights are ignored in the case of one-half the people, the nation is surely preparing for its downfall. Governments try themselves. The recognition of a governing and a governed class is incompatible with the first principles of freedom. Woman has not been a heedless spectator of the events of this century, nor a dull listener to the grand arguments for the equal rights of humanity. From the earliest history of our country woman has shown equal devotion with man to the cause of freedom, and has stood firmly by his side in its defense. Together, they have made this country what it is. Woman's wealth, thought and labor have cemented the stones of every monument man has reared to liberty.

And now, at the close of a hundred years, as the hour-hand of the great clock that marks the centuries points to 1876, we declare our faith in the principles of self-government; our full equality with man in natural rights; that woman was made first for her own happiness, with the absolute right to herself—to all the opportunities and advantages life affords for her complete development; and we deny that dogma of the centuries, incorporated in the codes of all nations—that woman was made for man—her best interests, in all cases, to be sacrificed to his will. We ask of our rulers, at this hour, no special favors, no special privileges, no special legislation. We ask justice, we ask equality, we ask that all the civil and political rights that belong to citizens of the United States, be guaranteed to us and our daughters forever.

51. ANNA JULIA COOPER

Womanhood A Vital Element
(1886)

ANNA JULIA COOPER (c. 1858–1964) was a pioneering educator and social critic whose life was devoted to improving educational and social opportunities for African Americans. Born a slave in North Carolina, Cooper was educated at St. Augustine's Normal School in North Carolina and graduated from Oberlin College in 1881. Shortly thereafter, she began a long tenure as a teacher, and then principal, of Washington Colored High School, which graduated many prominent African Americans. She continued her education at Columbia University, and, later, at the University of Paris, where she received her Ph.D. in French in 1925. Cooper's distinguished career extended beyond education to writing and politics. During the 1890s, while she was also editing *The Southland* magazine, Cooper helped to organize the Colored Woman's League in Washington, D.C., and attended the first meeting of the National Conference of Colored Women in 1895. Her most famous published work, *A Voice from the South by a Black Woman of the South* (1892), was an appeal to broaden the woman's movement of the 1890s to include black women. The following excerpt, "Womanhood a Vital Element in the Regeneration and Progress of the Race," argues not only for the centrality of black women to national progress, but also for the importance of higher education to the "regeneration of the race." Written during the "nadir" of American race relations, but also addressing the great optimism of the "woman's era," Cooper's sometimes witty prose style speaks to the complicated relationship between race and gender in late-nineteenth-century America.

SOURCE: Henry Louis Gates, Jr., and Nellie McKay et al., eds. *The Norton Anthology of African American Literature.* New York and London: W. W. Norton and Company, 1997.

SELECTED READINGS: Karen A. Johnson, *Uplifting the Woman and the Race: The Lives, Educational Philosophies, and Social Activism of Anna Julia Cooper and Nan-*

nie Helen Burroughs (2000). Charles Lemert and Esme Bhan, eds., *The Voice of Anna Julia Cooper* (1998). Paula Giddings, *When and Where I Enter: The Impact of Women on Race and Sex in America* (1984).

We are the heirs of a past which was not our fathers' moulding. "Every man the arbiter of his own destiny" was not true for the American Negro of the past: and it is no fault of his that he finds himself to-day the inheritor of a manhood and womanhood impoverished and debased by two centuries and more of compression and degradation.

But weaknesses and malformations, which to-day are attributable to a vicious schoolmaster and a pernicious system, will a century hence be rightly regarded as proofs of innate corruptness and radical incurability.

Now the fundamental agency under God in the regeneration, the retraining of the race, as well as the ground work and starting point of its progress upward, must be the *black woman*. . . .

Only the BLACK WOMAN can say "when and where I enter, in the quiet, undisputed dignity of my womanhood, without violence and without suing or special patronage, then and there the whole *Negro race enters with me*." Is it not evident then that as individual workers for this race we must address ourselves with no half-hearted zeal to this feature of our mission. The need is felt and must be recognized by all. There is a call for workers, for missionaries, for men and women with the double consecration of a fundamental love of humanity and a desire for its melioration through the Gospel; but superadded to this we demand an intelligent and sympathetic comprehension of the interests and special needs of the Negro.

I see not why there should not be an organized effort for the protection and elevation of our girls such as the White Cross League in England. English women are strengthened and protected by more than twelve centuries of Christian influences, freedom and civilization; English girls are dispirited and crushed down by no such all-levelling prejudice as that supercilious caste spirit in America which cynically assumes "A Negro woman cannot be a lady." English womanhood is beset by no such snares and traps as betray the unprotected, untrained colored girl of the South, whose only crime and dire destruction often is her unconscious and marvelous beauty. Surely then if English indignation is aroused and English manhood thrilled under the leadership of a Bishop of the English church to build up bulwarks around their wronged sisters, Negro sentiment cannot remain callous and Negro effort nerveless in view of the imminent peril of the mothers of the next generation. "*I am my Sister's keeper!*" should be the hearty response of every man and woman of the race, and this conviction should purify and exalt the narrow, selfish and petty personal aims of life into a noble and sacred purpose.

We need men who can let their interest and gallantry extend outside the circle of their aesthetic appreciation; men who can be a father, a brother, a friend to every weak, struggling unshielded girl. We need women who are so sure of their own social footing that they need not fear leaning to lend a hand to a fallen or falling sister. We need men and women who do not exhaust their genius splitting hairs on aristocratic distinctions and thanking God they are not as others; but earnest, unselfish souls, who can go into the highways and byways, lifting up and leading, advising and encouraging with the truly catholic benevolence of the Gospel of Christ. . . .

As Negroes and churchmen we cannot be indifferent to these questions. They touch us most vitally on both sides. We believe in the Holy Catholic Church. We believe that however gigantic and apparently remote the consummation, the Church will go on conquering and to conquer till the kingdoms of this world, not excepting the black man and the black woman of the South, shall have become the kingdoms of the Lord and of his Christ.

That past work in this direction has been unsatisfactory we must admit. That without a change of policy results in the future will be as meagre, we greatly fear. Our life as a race is at stake. The dearest interests of our hearts are in the scales. We must either break away from dear old landmarks and plunge out in any line and every line that enables us to meet the pressing need of our people, or we must ask the Church to allow and help us, untrammelled by the prejudices and theories of individuals, to work agressively under her direction as we alone can, with God's help, for the salvation of our people.

The time is ripe for action. Self-seeking and ambition must be laid on the altar. The battle is one of sacrifice and hardship, but our duty is plain. We have been recipients of missionary bounty in some sort for twenty-one years. Not even the senseless vegetable is content to be a mere reservoir. Receiving without giving is an anomaly in nature. Nature's cells are all little workshops for manufacturing sunbeams, the product to be *given out* to earth's inhabitants in warmth, energy, thought, action. Inanimate creation always pays back an equivalent.

Now, *How much owest thou my Lord*? Will his account be overdrawn if he call for singleness of purpose and self-sacrificing labor for your brethren? Having passed through your drill school, will you refuse a general's commission even if it entail responsibility, risk and anxiety, with possibly some adverse criticism? Is it too much to ask you to step forward and direct the work for your race along those lines which you know to be of first and vital importance?

52. ELIZABETH CADY STANTON

Solitude of Self

(1892)

Organizer of the 1848 Woman's Rights Convention in Seneca Falls, New York, **ELIZABETH CADY STANTON (1815–1902)** was a pioneering advocate for women's emancipation whose speeches, writings, and public activities formed the foundation of early American feminism. Born in Johnston, New York, Stanton was educated at the prestigious Emma Willard's Academy. In 1847, she and her husband Henry Stanton moved to Seneca Falls, New York, where she began her career as a woman's rights activist while becoming increasingly resentful of her burdensome domestic responsibilities to her seven children. In 1848, Stanton joined with Lucretia Mott to organize the world's first woman's rights convention, where she was the most vociferous advocate of a highly contested suffrage resolution. By the time she met Susan B. Anthony in 1851, Stanton was widely recognized as the main leader of the independent woman's movement. Stanton and Anthony collaborated on many important occasions: supporting abolition and enfranchisement through the AERA; founding the National Women Suffrage Association (NWSA); aligning with Democrats to push for a Sixteenth Amendment guaranteeing woman's suffrage; and co-founding the National American Woman Suffrage Association (NAWSA) in 1890. After more than half a century of woman's rights advocacy, Stanton resigned the presidency of NAWSA in 1892. Weary from decades of struggle, yet still hopeful for the future of women in America, Stanton delivered her most famous address, "Solitude of Self," before the Judiciary Committees of the U.S. Senate and House of Representatives the same year as her NAWSA retirement. Considering it the "best thing I have ever written," Stanton used the opportunity to affirm that women deserved the same rights and privileges as men. Striking a solitary tone, Stanton's moving reflection marks the transition between the nineteenth-century woman's suffrage movement and the birth of modern feminism.

SOURCE: Ellen Carol DuBois, ed. *The Elizabeth Cady Stanton-Susan B. Anthony Reader: Correspondence, Writings, Speeches.* Boston: Northeastern University Press, 1991.

SELECTED READINGS: Lois Banner, *Elizabeth Cady Stanton, A Radical for Woman's Rights* (1980). Elizabeth Cady Stanton, *Eighty Years and More: Reminiscences, 1815–1897* (1898). Elizabeth Cady Stanton, *The Woman's Bible* (1898).

The point I wish plainly to bring before you on this occasion is the individuality of each human soul; our Protestant idea, the right of individual conscience and judgement; our republican idea, individual citizenship. In discussing the rights of woman, we are to consider, first, what belongs to her as an individual, in a world of her own, the arbiter of her own destiny, an imaginary Robinson Crusoe, with her woman, Friday, on a solitary island. Her rights under such circumstances are to use all her faculties for her own safety and happiness.

Secondly, if we consider her as a citizen, as a member of a great nation, she must have the same rights as all others members, according to the fundamental principles of our Government.

Thirdly, viewed as a woman, an equal factor in civilization, her rights and duties are still the same—individual happiness and development.

Fourthly, it is only the incidental relations of life, such as mother, wife, sister, daughter, which may involve some special duties and training. . . .

The strongest reason for giving woman all the opportunities for higher education, for the full development of her faculties, her forces of mind and body; for giving her the most enlarged freedom of thought and action; a complete emancipation from all forms of bondage, of custom, dependence, superstition; from all the crippling influences of fear—is the solitude and personal responsibility of her own individual life. The strongest reason why we ask for woman a voice in the government under which she lives; in the religion she is asked to believe; equality in social life, where she is the chief factor; a place in the trades and professions, where she may earn her bread, is because of her birthright to self-sovereignty; because, as an individual, she must rely on herself. No matter how much women prefer to lean, to be protected and supported, nor how much men desire to have them do so, they must make the voyage of life alone, and for safety in an emergency, they must know something of the laws of navigation. To guide our own craft, we must be captain, pilot, engineer; with chart and compass to stand at the wheel; to watch the winds and waves, and know when to take in the sail, and to read the signs in the firmament over all. It matters not whether the solitary voyager is man or woman; nature, having endowed them equally, leaves them to their own skill and judgment in the hour of danger, and, if not equal to the occasion, alike they perish.

To appreciate the importance of fitting every human soul for independent action, think for a moment of the immeasurable solitude of self. We come into the world alone, unlike all who have gone before us, we leave it alone, under circumstances peculiar to ourselves. No mortal ever has been, no mortal ever will be like the soul just launched on the sea of life. There can never again be just such a combination of prenatal influences; never again just such environments as make up the infancy, youth and manhood of this one. Nature never repeats herself, and the possibilities of one human soul will never be found in another. No one has ever found two blades of ribbon grass alike, and no one will ever find two human beings alike. Seeing, then, what must be the infinite diversity in human character, we can in a measure appreciate the loss to a nation when any large class of the people is uneducated and unrepresented in the government.

We ask for the complete development of every individual, first, for his own benefit and happiness. In fitting out an army, we give each soldier his own knapsack, arms, powder, his blanket, cup, knife, fork and spoon. We provide alike for all their individual necessities; then each man bears his own burden. . . .

So it ever must be in the conflicting scenes of life, in the long, weary march, each one walks alone. We may have many friends, love, kindness, sympathy and charity, to smooth our pathway in everyday life, but in the tragedies and triumphs of human experience, each mortal stands alone.

But when all artificial trammels are removed, and women are recognized as individuals, responsible for their own environments, thoroughly educated for all positions in life they may be called to fill; with all the resources in themselves that liberal thought and broad culture can give; guided by their own conscience and judgment, trained to self-protection, by a healthy development of the muscular system, and skill in the use of weapons and defence; and stimulated to self-support by a knowledge of the business world and the pleasure that pecuniary independence must ever give; when women are trained in this way, they will in a measure be fitted for those hours of solitude that come alike to all, whether prepared or otherwise. As in our extremity we must depend on ourselves, the dictates of wisdom point to complete individual development. . . .

Women are already the equals of men in the whole realm of thought, in art, science, literature and government. . . . The poetry and novels of the century are theirs, and they have touched the keynote of reform, in religion, politics and social life. They fill the editor's and professor's chair, plead at the bar of justice, walk the wards of the hospital, speak from the pulpit and the platform. Such is the type of womanhood that an enlightened public sentiment welcomes to-day, and such the triumph of the facts of life over the false theories of the past.

Is it, then, consistent to hold the developed woman of this day within the same narrow political limits as the dame with the spinning wheel and knitting needle occupied in the past? No, no! Machinery has taken the labors of woman as well as man on its tireless shoulders; the loom and the spinning wheel are but dreams of the past; the pen, the brush, the easel, the chisel, have taken their places, while the hopes and ambitions of women are essentially changed.

We see reason sufficient in the outer conditions of human beings for individual liberty and development, but when we consider the self-dependence of every human soul, we see the need of courage, judgment and the exercise of every faculty of mind and body, strengthened and developed by use, in woman as well as man.

Whatever may be said of man's protecting power in ordinary conditions, amid all the terrible disasters by land and sea, in the supreme moments of danger, alone woman must ever meet the horrors of the situation. The Angel of Death even makes no royal pathway for her. Man's love and sympathy enter only into the sunshine of our lives. In that solemn solitude of self, that links us with the immeasurable and the eternal, each soul lives alone forever. A recent writer says: "I remember once, in crossing the Atlantic, to have gone upon the deck of the ship at midnight, when a dense black cloud enveloped the sky, and the great deep was roaring madly under the lashes of demoniac winds. My feeling was not of danger or fear (which is a base surrender of the immortal soul) but of utter desolation and loneliness; a little speck of life shut in by a tremendous darkness. . . ."

And yet, there is a solitude which each and every one of us has always carried with him, more inaccessible than the ice-cold mountains, more profound than the midnight sea; the solitude of self. Our inner being which we call ourself, no eye nor touch of man or angel has ever pierced. It is more hidden than the caves of the gnome; the sacred adytum of the oracle; the hidden chamber of Eleusinian mystery, for to it only omniscience is permitted to enter.

Such is individual life. Who, I ask you, can take, dare take on himself the rights, the duties, the responsibilities of another human soul?

53. FRANCES E. W. HARPER

A Double Standard

(1895)

A Radical activist and prolific writer, **FRANCES E. W. HARPER (1825–1911)** was one of the most versatile and popular African-American writers before the twentieth century. Born to free parents in Baltimore, Maryland, in 1825, Harper was raised and educated by her politically active and religious uncle. After a period of time working as a domestic and as a teacher, Harper moved to Philadelphia and devoted her considerable talents to the abolitionist movement. After the publication of her poem, "Eliza Harris," inspired by the lead female protagonist in Harriet Beecher Stowe's *Uncle Tom's Cabin*, Harper gained notoriety in the front ranks of antislavery circles. After joining the Maine Anti-Slavery Society as a lecturer in 1854, Harper's career took off; she lectured widely, published her first volume of poetry to great acclaim, and worked tirelessly on behalf of woman's rights and abolition, even raising money for the families of the men who had been jailed in the aftermath of John Brown's raid at Harpers Ferry. Harper's writing tackled a variety of themes (slavery and freedom; race and gender; Christianity and education) and covered a range of genres (she published four novels, several volumes of poetry, and countless stories, essays, and letters), and was widely heralded for her striking versatility, redemptive radicalism, and lyrical humanity. The following poem, "A Double Standard" (1895), addresses the familiar theme of hypocrisy in a racist and sexist society.

SOURCE: Henry Louis Gates, Jr., and Nellie McKay et al., eds. *The Norton Anthology of African American Literature*. New York and London: W. W. Norton and Company, 1997.

SELECTED READINGS: Shirley W. Logan, *We Are Coming: The Persuasive Discourse of Nineteenth Century Black Women* (1999). Melba Joyce Boyd, *Discarded Legacy:*

Politics and Poetics in the Life of Frances E. W. Harper, 1825–1911 (1994). Frances Smith Foster, *Written by Herself: Literary Production by African-American Women, 1746–1892* (1993).

Do you blame me that I loved him?
    If when standing all alone
I cried for bread a careless world
    Pressed to my lips a stone.

Do you blame me that I loved him,
    That my heart beat glad and free,
When he told me in the sweetest tones
    He loved but only me?

Can you blame me that I did not see
    Beneath his burning kiss
The serpent's wiles, nor even hear
    The deadly adder hiss?

Can you blame me that my heart grew cold
    That the tempted, tempter turned;
When he was feted and caressed
    And I was coldly spurned?

Would you blame him, when you draw from me
    Your dainty robes aside,
If he with gilded baits should claim
    Your fairest as his bride?

Would you blame the world if it should press
    On him a civic crown;
And see me struggling in the depth
    Then harshly press me down?

Crime has no sex and yet to-day
    I wear the brand of shame;
Whilst he amid the gay and proud
    Still bears an honored name.

Can you blame me if I've learned to think
   Your hate of vice a sham,
When you so coldly crushed me down
   And then excused the man?

Would you blame me if to-morrow
   The coroner should say,
A wretched girl, outcast, forlorn,
   Has thrown her life away?

Yes, blame me for my downward course,
   But oh! remember well,
Within your homes you press the hand
   That led me down to hell.

I'm glad God's ways are not our ways,
   He does not see as man;
Within His love I know there's room
   For those whom others ban.

I think before His great white throne,
   His throne of spotless light,
That whited sepulchers shall wear
   The hue of endless night.

That I who fell, and he who sinned,
   Shall reap as we have sown;
That each the burden of his loss
   Must bear and bear alone.

No golden weights can turn the scale
   Of justice in His sight;
And what is wrong in woman's life
   In man's cannot be right.

54. IDA B. WELLS-BARNETT

A Red Record

(1895)

IDA B. WELLS-BARNETT (1862–1931) was a fearless investigative journalist whose crusade against lynching exposed the depths of white supremacy and the persistence of racial violence in turn-of-the-century America. Born to slave parents in Mississippi less than a year before emancipation, she was educated at a local freedmen's school and then at Fisk University in Memphis, Tennessee, where she also worked as an editor for several small black newspapers. In 1891, Wells founded the *Memphis Free Speech*, a radical newspaper whose coverage of the lynching crisis provoked a mob of local whites to burn her press in 1893. Indeed, it was Wells's coverage of lynching—from 1889 to 1918 more than three thousand blacks, the vast majority of them men, were killed by white mobs—that generated her international reputation. In 1895, while serving as editor and part-owner of the *New York Age*, Wells published *A Red Record*, her keen statistical analysis of lynching. For the next thirty-five years, Wells worked tirelessly in what often seemed like a one-woman crusade against racial violence. She challenged everyone she met to take a strong stance against lynching, and was especially dismayed by the unwillingness of the National American Woman Suffrage Association and the newly formed NAACP to do so. It was only in 1930, one year before Wells's death, that black women and white women formed an interracial coalition—the Association of Southern Women for the Prevention of Lynching—to confront this crisis. This group took its cue from Wells's longstanding argument, expressed in *A Red Record* and other writings, that the main justification for lynching—that black men were inclined by nature to rape white women—was a morally and intellectually bankrupt excuse for violence among white men hell-bent on preserving economic dominance, white supremacy, and patriarchy.

SOURCE: Henry Louis Gates, Jr. and Nellie McKay et al. eds. *The Norton Anthology of African American Literature*. New York and London: W. W. Norton and Company, 1997.

SELECTED READINGS: Philip Dray, *At the Hands of Persons Unknown: The Lynching of Black America* (2002). Patricia A. Schechter, *Ida B. Wells-Barnett and American Reform, 1880–1930* (2001). Linda O. McMurry, *To Keep the Waters Troubled: The Life of Ida B. Wells* (1998).

The student of American sociology will find the year 1894 marked by a pronounced awakening of the public conscience to a system of anarchy and outlawry which had grown during a series of ten years to be so common, that scenes of unusual brutality failed to have any visible effect upon the humane sentiments of the people of our land.

Beginning with the emancipation of the Negro, the inevitable result of unbridled power exercised for two and a half centuries, by the white man over the Negro, began to show itself in acts of conscienceless outlawry. During the slave regime, the Southern white man owned the Negro body and soul. It was to his interest to dwarf the soul and preserve the body Vested with unlimited power over his slave, to subject him to any and all kinds of physical punishment, the white man was still restrained from such punishment as tended to injure the slave by abating his physical powers and thereby reducing his financial worth. While slaves were scourged mercilessly, and in countless cases inhumanly treated in other respects, still the white owner rarely permitted his anger to go so far as to take a life, which would entail upon him a loss of several hundred dollars. The slave was rarely killed, he was too valuable; it was easier and quite as effective, for discipline or revenge, to sell him "Down South."

But Emancipation came and the vested interests of the white man in the Negro's body were lost. The white man had no right to scourge the emancipated Negro, still less has he a right to kill him. But the Southern white people had been educated so long in that school of practice, in which might makes right, that they disdained to draw strict lines of action in dealing with the Negro. In slave times the Negro was kept subservient and submissive by the frequency and severity of the scourging, but, with freedom, a new system of intimidation came into vogue; the Negro was not only whipped and scourged; he was killed.

Not all nor nearly all of the murders done by white men, during the past thirty years in the South, have come to light, but the statistics as gathered and preserved by white men, and which have not been questioned, show that during these years more than ten thousand Negroes have been killed in cold blood, without the formality of judicial trial and legal execution. And yet, as evidence of the absolute impunity with which the white man dares to kill a Negro, the same record shows that during all these years, and for all these murders only three white men have been tried, convicted, and executed. As no white man has been lynched for the murder of colored people, these three executions are the only instances of the death penalty being visited upon white men for murdering Negroes.

Naturally enough the commission of these crimes began to tell upon the public conscience, and the Southern white man, as a tribute to the nineteenth century civilization, was in a manner compelled to give excuses for his barbarism. His excuses have adapted themselves to the emergency, and are aptly outlined by that greatest of all Negroes, Frederick Douglass, in an article of recent date, in which he shows that there have been three distinct eras of Southern barbarism, to account for which three distinct excuses have been made.

The first excuse given to the civilized world for the murder of unoffending Negroes was the necessity of the white man to repress and stamp out alleged "race riots." For years immediately succeeding the war there was an appalling slaughter of colored people, and the wires usually conveyed to northern people and the world the intelligence, first, that an insurrection was being planned by Negroes, which, a few hours later, would prove to have been vigorously resisted by white men, and controlled with a resulting loss of several killed and wounded. It was always a remarkable feature in these insurrections and riots that only Negroes were killed during the rioting, and that all the white men escaped unharmed.

From 1865 to 1872, hundreds of colored men and women were mercilessly murdered and the almost invariable reason assigned was that they met their death by being alleged participants in an insurrection or riot. But this story at last wore itself out. No insurrection ever materialized; no Negro rioter was ever apprehended and proven guilty, and no dynamite ever recorded the black man's protest against oppression and wrong. It was too much to ask thoughtful people to believe this transparent story, and the southern white people at last made up their minds that some other excuse must be had.

Then came the second excuse, which had its birth during the turbulent times of reconstruction. By an amendment to the Constitution the Negro was given the right of franchise, and, theoretically at least, his ballot became his invaluable emblem of citizenship. In a government "of the people, for the people, and by the people," the Negro's vote became an important factor in all matters of state and national politics. But this did not last long. The southern white man would not consider that the Negro had any right which a white man was bound to respect, and the idea of a republican form of government in the southern states grew into general contempt. It was maintained that "This is a white man's government," and regardless of numbers the white man should rule. "No Negro domination" became the new legend on the sanguinary banner of the sunny South, and under it rode the Ku Klux Klan, the Regulators, and the lawless mobs, which for any cause chose to murder one man or a dozen as suited their purpose best. It was a long, gory campaign; the blood chills and the heart almost loses faith in Christianity when one thinks of Yazoo, Hamburg, Edgefield, Copiah, and the countless massacres of defenseless Negroes, whose only crime was the attempt to exercise their right to vote.

But it was a bootless strife for colored people. The government which had made the Negro a citizen found itself unable to protect him. It gave him the right to vote, but denied him the protection which should have maintained that right. Scourged from his home; hunted through the swamps; hung by midnight raiders, and openly murdered in the light of day, the Negro clung to his right of franchise with a heroism which would have wrung admiration from the hearts of savages. He believed that in that small white ballot there was a subtle something which stood for manhood as well as citizenship, and thousands of brave black men went to their graves, exemplifying the one by dying for the other.

The white man's victory soon became complete by fraud, violence, in timidation and murder. The franchise vouchsafed to the Negro grew to be a "barren ideality," and regardless of numbers, the colored people found themselves voiceless in the councils of those whose duty it was to rule. With no longer the fear of "Negro Domination" before their eyes, the white man's second excuse became valueless. With the Southern governments all subverted and the Negro actually eliminated from all participation in state and national elections, there could be no longer an excuse for killing Negroes to prevent "Negro Domination."

Brutality still continued; Negroes were whipped, scourged, exiled, shot and hung whenever and wherever it pleased the white man so to treat them, and as the civilized world with increasing persistency held the white people of the South to account for its outlawry, the murderers invented the third excuse— that Negroes had to be killed to avenge their assaults upon women. There could be framed no possible excuse more harmful to the Negro and more unanswerable if true in its sufficiency for the white man.

Humanity abhors the assailant of womanhood, and this charge upon the Negro at once placed him beyond the pale of human sympathy. With such unanimity, earnestness and apparent candor was this charge made and reiterated that the world has accepted the story that the Negro is a monster which the Southern white man has painted him. And to-day, the Christian world feels, that while lynching is a crime, and lawlessness and anarchy the certain precursors of a nation's fall, it can not by word or deed, extend sympathy or help to a race of outlaws, who might mistake their plea for justice and deem it an excuse for their continued wrongs.

The Negro has suffered much and is willing to suffer more. He recognizes that the wrongs of two centuries can not be righted in a day, and he tries to bear his burden with patience for to-day and be hopeful for to-morrow. But there comes a time when the veriest worm will turn, and the Negro feels to-day that after all the work he has done, all the sacrifices he has made, and all the suffering he has endured, if he did not, now, defend his name and manhood from this vile accusation, he would be unworthy even of the contempt of mankind. It is to this charge he now feels he must make answer.

55. CARRIE CHAPMAN CATT

National Call for a League of Women Voters
(1919)

CARRIE CHAPMAN CATT (1859–1947) was one of the most prominent and effective leaders in the "first wave" of modern feminism. Born in Ripon, Wisconsin, Catt spent her childhood in Iowa, where she attended college, started a teaching career, and became the superintendent of schools in Mason County in 1883. After joining the Iowa suffrage campaign in the late 1880s, she became a close friend of Susan B. Anthony's, faithfully succeeding her as president of the NAWSA from 1900 to 1904, and again from 1915 to 1920. A superb organizer and inspiring speaker, Catt was the undisputed head of the women's suffrage movement from the turn of the century until the ratification of the Nineteenth Amendment in 1920, supervising over a dozen state suffrage campaigns and mobilizing over one million volunteers. A pacifist as well as a feminist, Catt believed that equal participation of women at every level of politics would help ensure a more just and peaceful world. Once the Nineteenth Amendment was passed in 1919, Catt founded the League of Women Voters to promote public interest over partisan politics, and to "finish the fight" for women's equality by promoting the very best ideals of American democracy.

SOURCE: Mary Jo Buhle and Paul Buhle, eds. *The Concise History Woman Suffrage.* Urbana: University of Illinois Press, 1978.

SELECTED READINGS: Nancy Cott, *The Grounding of Modern Feminism* (1987). Jacqueline Van Voris, *Carrie Chapman Catt: A Public Life* (1987). Robert Booth Fowler, *Carrie Catt: Feminist Politician* (1986).

Every suffragist will hope for a memorial dedicated to the memory of our brave departed leaders, to the sacrifices they made for our cause, to the scores of victories won. . . . I venture to propose one whose benefits will bless our entire nation and bring happiness to the humblest of our citizens—the most natural, the most appropriate and the most patriotic memorial that could be suggested—a League of Women Voters to "finish the fight" and to aid in the reconstruction of the nation. What could be more natural than that women having attained their political independence should desire to give service in token of their gratitude? What could be more appropriate than that such women should do for the coming generation what those of a preceding did for them? What could be more patriotic than that these women should use their new freedom to make the country safer for their children and their children's children?

Let us then raise up a League of Women Voters, the name and form of organization to be determined by the members themselves; a league that shall be non-partisan and non-sectarian and consecrated to three chief aims: 1. To use its influence to obtain the full enfranchisement of the women of every State in our own republic and to reach out across the seas in aid of the woman's struggle for her own in every land. 2. To remove the remaining legal discriminations against women in the codes and constitutions of the several States in order that the feet of coming women may find these stumbling blocks removed. 3. To make our democracy so safe for the nation and so safe for the world that every citizen may feel secure and great men will acknowledge the worthiness of the American republic to lead.

56.

Nineteenth Amendment (1920)

After nearly a century of woman's rights activism, the Nineteenth Amendment was finally ratified in 1920, granting women the right to vote. The crusade for woman's suffrage began during the antebellum era, when female participation in the abolitionist movement and the passage of universal (white) manhood suffrage energized women to demand full political equality for themselves. Following the Civil War, woman's rights advocates were bitterly disappointed when debates about citizenship and voting rights for blacks did not yield the same guarantees of equality for women. Following a difficult period, during which some woman's rights advocates applauded the disfranchisement of blacks and immigrants, the suffrage movement regained its radical momentum during the Progressive era, when a series of highly visible state campaigns, combined with a major shift in the public role of women, revived interest in female enfranchisement. After 1916, when both major political parties endorsed woman's suffrage in their national platforms, Congress once again began debating the possibility of constitutional reform, leading to the passage of the Nineteenth Amendment in 1919.

SOURCE: Eric Foner and John A. Garraty, eds. *The Reader's Companion to American History*. Boston: Houghton Mifflin, 1991.

SELECTED READINGS: Eleanor Flexner and Ellen Fitzpatrick, *Century of Struggle: The Women's Rights Movement in the United States* (1996). Barbara Berg, *The Remembered Gate: Origins of American Feminism* (1978). Anne Firor Scott and Andrew MacKay Scott, *One Half the People: The Fight for Woman Suffrage* (1975).

Amendment XIX
[Adopted 1920]

Section 1 The right of citizens of the United States to vote shall not be denied or abridged by the United States or by any State on account of sex.

Section 2 The Congress shall have power to enforce this article by appropriate legislation.

CHAPTER

FIVE

Land and

Labor

57. WORKING MEN'S PARTY

Declaration of Independence
(1829)

The "Working Men's Declaration of Independence" was written in 1829 by George Henry Evans, an English immigrant who became one of the most visible leaders of the early labor movement. After its initial formation in Philadelphia in 1828, the Working Men's Party was established in New York City as the first political organization devoted primarily to the interests of the working class. Embodying the democratic zeal of the era, its platform called for a host of major reforms, including protections for skilled mechanics competing with contracted prison labor, opposition to any extension of the ten-hour workday, the repeal of debt imprisonment, and, later, a proposal for free, universal public education. The "Declaration" of the Working Men's Party first appeared under the heading "Equal Rights" in the *Working Man's Advocate,* an early labor newspaper edited by Evans. The Working Men's Party quickly expanded its influence, but it was unable to achieve any significant electoral success because of internal divisions and shifting political alliances during the Jacksonian period.

SOURCE: Philip S. Foner, ed. *We, The Other People: Alternative Declarations of Independence.* Urbana: University of Illinois Press, 1976.

SELECTED READINGS: Sean Wilentz, *Chants Democratic: New York City and the Rise of the American Working Class, 1788–1850* (1986). Edward Pessen, *Most Uncommon Jacksonians: The Radical Leaders of the Early Labor Movement* (1967). Walter Hugins, *Jacksonian Democracy and the Working Class: A Study of the New York Workingmen's Movement, 1829–1837* (1960).

"When, in the course of human events, it becomes necessary" for one class of a community to assert their natural and unalienable rights in opposition to other classes of their fellow men, "and to assume among" them a political "station of equality to which the laws of nature and of nature's God," as well as the principles of their political compact, "entitle them; a decent respect to the opinions of mankind," and the more paramount duty they owe to their own fellow citizens, "requires that they should declare the causes which impel them" to adopt so painful, yet so necessary, a measure.

"We hold these truths to be self evident, that all men are *created equal*; that they are endowed by their creator with certain unalienable rights; that among these are *life, liberty*, and the *pursuit of happiness*; that to secure these rights" against the undue influence of other classes of society, prudence, as well as the claims of self defence, dictates the necessity of the organization of a party, who shall, by their representatives, prevent dangerous combinations to subvert these indefeasible and fundamental privileges. "All experience hath shown, that mankind" in general, and *we as a class in particular*, "are more disposed to suffer, while evils are sufferable, than to right themselves," by an opposition which the pride and self interest of unprincipled political aspirants, with more unprincipled zeal or religious bigotry, will wilfully misrepresent. "But when a long train of abuses and usurpations" take place, all invariably tending to the oppression and degradation of one class of society, and to the unnatural and iniquitous exaltation of another by political leaders, "it is their right, it is their duty," to use every constitutional means to *reform* the abuses of such a government, and to provide new guards for their future security. The history of the political *parties* in this state, is a history of political *iniquities*, all tending to the enacting and enforcing oppressive and unequal laws. To prove this, let facts be submitted to the candid and impartial of our fellow citizens of all parties.

1. The laws for levying taxes are all based on erroneous principles, in consequence of their operating most oppressively on one class of society, and being scarcely felt by the other.

2. The laws regarding the duties of jurors, witnesses, and militia trainings, are still more unequal and oppressive.

3. The laws for private incorporations are all partial in their operations; favoring one class of society to the expense of the other, who have no equal participation.

4. The laws incorporating religious societies have a pernicious tendency, by promoting the erection of magnificent places of public worship, by the rich, excluding others, and which others cannot imitate; consequently engendering spiritual pride in the clergy and people, and thereby creating odious distinctions in society, destructive to its social peace and happiness.

5. The laws establishing and patronizing seminaries of learning are unequal, favoring the rich, and perpetuating imparity, which natural causes have produced, and which judicious laws ought, and can, remedy.

6. The laws and municipal ordinances and regulations, generally, besides

those specially enumerated, have heretofore been ordained on such principles, as have deprived nine tenths of the members of the body politic, who are *not* wealthy, of the *equal means* to enjoy *"life, liberty, and the pursuit of happiness,"* which the *rich* enjoy exclusively; but the federative compact intended to secure to all, indiscriminately. The lien law in favor of landlords against tenants, and all other honest creditors, is one illustration among innumerable others which can be adduced to prove the truth of these allegations.

We have trusted to the influence of the justice and good sense of our political leaders, to prevent the continuance of these abuses, which destroy the natural bands of equality so essential to the attainment of moral happiness, "but they have been deaf to the voice of justice and of consanguinity."

Therefore, we, the working class of society, of the city of New York, "appealing to the supreme judge of the world," and to the reason, and consciences of the impartial of all parties, "for the rectitude of our intentions, do, in the spirit, and by the authority," of that political liberty which has been promised to us equally with our fellow men, solemnly publish and declare, and invite all under like pecuniary circumstances, together with every liberal mind, to join us in the declaration, "that we are, & of right ought to be," entitled to EQUAL MEANS to obtain equal moral happiness, and social enjoyment, and that all lawful and constitutional measures ought to be adopted to the attainment of those objects. "And for the support of this declaration, we mutually pledge to each other" our faithful aid to the end of our lives.

58. FRANCES WRIGHT

Address to Young Mechanics
(1830)

A leading utopian thinker, labor leader, and feminist, **FRANCES (or "FANNY") WRIGHT (1795–1852)** was one of the most controversial public figures of her time. Born in Dundee, Scotland, Wright moved to London as a child, where she developed great sympathy for the peasants living in squalor on London's streets. Sailing to the United States in 1818, Wright recorded her impressions of America in *Views of Society and Manners in America* (1821), an extremely influential travel book that catapulted her to fame on both sides of the Atlantic. After some time in England and Paris, Wright once again sailed to America, where she attempted a controversial utopian living experiment with land she purchased in Memphis, Tennessee. Devoted to gradual emancipation through slave education, Wright's "Nashoba" community, already suffering from shaky finances, was assailed by critics for its open practice of interracial free love. After Nashoba's wane, she moved to New York City in 1829 and worked tirelessly on behalf of the Working Men's Party to promote a universal system of free public schools. The following address, delivered to an audience of young mechanics at Wright's Hall of Science on June 13, 1830, illustrates her attempt to link education reform with the emerging political sympathies of New York's working class.

SOURCE: Frances Wright D'Arusment. *Life, Letters, and Lectures, 1834–1844.* New York: Arno Press, 1972.

SELECTED READINGS: Elizabeth Ann Bartlett, *Liberty, Equality, Sorority* (1994). Susan S. Kissel, *In Common Cause: The "Conservative" Frances Trollope and the "Radical" Frances Wright* (1993). Celia Morris Eckhardt, *Fanny Wright: Rebel in America* (1984).

In addressing myself this evening to the young mechanics of our city. I would not be understood as considering their interests distinct from those of other classes of the community.

The interests of the whole human family, in nature and in reason, are ever present to my mind as one and the same. But the ill directed efforts of successive generations have placed us in an artificial state of society. The bond of union originating in the common instincts, wants, and desires of all our species, has been severed instead of strengthened by miscalculating ingenuity or fortuitous circumstances. Occupants of the same earth, citizens of the same country, creatures of the same form and nature, we are partitioned off into classes, and arrayed against each other, in despite even of our own will, by the habits of our youth, and the contrasted and conflicting interests of our after years. In such a state of things, they who are desirous of aiding in the cementing the shattered fractions of society into one whole, have to select first the largest and the soundest fraction—they have to address themselves to the more numerous, as well to the more moral of the classes, which, happily, is also that whose immediate interests are most in unison with those real and natural interests which it is desirable that all should be induced to distinguish and consult.

If therefore I have addressed myself, at all times, more especially to the industrious classes, it has been for two reasons—First; that they comprise the only large mass among the heterogeneous fragments of society; and, secondly, that their interests at the time being are more nearly approached to the great natural interests of man, and incline, therefore, more immediately to wholesome reforms and general union.

While addressing myself however, to this largest and soundest body in the state, it has been my endeavour to excite it to action rather than to opposition; and, if ever my words have provoked a feeling of hostility in man towards man, or in class towards class, I have sinned against my intention, which has been ever, singly and purely, so far as I can read my own heart, to arm men collectively against abuses, and to fraternize their feelings towards each other.

In calling you together at the present time, my young friends, it is not therefore with the view of addressing your peculiar interests as a class, but your interests as citizens, and my only motives for selecting you from your fellow citizens are—that your habits of industry must enlist you on the side of reform, and that your age admits of such cultivation of talent and improvement of feeling as may fit you to become effective reformers.

To the title of WORKING MEN as the distinctive epithet of reformers, I object. All men and all women ought to be *workers*, but, at the present time, when operative and intellectual labour is unhappily separated, the title sounds unfairly exclusive, and, our object being union, exclusion, even in sound, should be avoided. As a man is not necessarily honest because he labours with his hands, so neither is he necessarily *dis*honest because he knows only to labour with his head. In both cases there has been error in education, and there is error in habit, but the fault is in the arrangements of society, not in individuals; and in all our efforts to amend those defective arrangements for the next generation, we should bear in mind that we of the present are all more or less imperfect beings; always *half* trained, and almost always *ill* trained. Indulgence, therefore, on the part of one class towards another, is imperiously called for; every expression calculated to excite jealousy should be carefully shunned, and every watchword of the hour should insinuate union, and breathe of national fellowship, liberality, and harmony.

But while I object to the title of WORKING MEN, as distinctive of reformers, and, yet more, to that of a "working man's *party*," as distinctive of the great national cause of reform. I do look to the industrious classes, generally and especially, though by no means *exclusively*, for the salvation of the country, and expect the youth of those classes to supply to sound reason and sound measures their most ardent, and also their most skilful champions.

Whatever may be the *conceived advantages* of college education, it is but rarely that a bold intellect or a sound judgment issues from the walls of privileged, and but too often useless and superannuated learning; while, on the other hand, what are the *real disadvantages* of the neglected child of labour, he is saved from the conceit of pedantry, and the jargon of sophistry, and thus remains free to profit by whatever lessons experience may bring, and to distinguish simple truth whenever it may meet his ears.

I have made human kind my study, from my youth up; the American community I have considered with most especial attention; and I can truly say that, wherever the same are not absolutely pressed down by labour and want, I have invariably found, not only the best feelings, but the soundest sense among the operative classes of society. I am satisfied, and that by extensive observation, that, with few exceptions, the whole sterling talent of the American community lies (latent indeed, and requiring the stimulus of circumstance for its development,) among that large body who draw their subsistence from the labour of their hands. . . .

59. WILLIAM APESS

An Indian's Looking-Glass for the White Man
(1836)

WILLIAM APESS (1798–1839) was a Native American activist, writer and Methodist minister whose book, *A Son of the Forest* (1829), is the first full-length autobiography written by a North American Indian. A descendent of Metacom ("King Philip" of King Philip's War in 1678), Apess was born in Franklin County, Massachusetts, to a father of mixed Pequot and Anglo heritage and to a mother who was probably an African-American slave or indentured servant. After a difficult childhood as an indentured servant, Apess was drawn at an early age to the egalitarian impulses of the Second Great Awakening, converting to Methodism in 1818. Apess spent the 1820s as an itinerant preacher and laborer, spreading his message that Christ, whom Apess considered a man of color, was the Savior of all people, especially the poor and despised. At the end of the decade, Apess published his moving autobiography, the first of five books he wrote between 1829 and 1836. A devout Christian, Apess used his writings to defend native oral traditions, to challenge Euro-American notions of cultural superiority, to examine the incompatibility of Christianity and racial prejudice, and to provide an alternative historical memory—one that told the story of America from the perspective of native peoples rather than the white immigrants who "settled" their land. The following essay, first published in 1836, exemplifies the way that Apess used Christianity to assert full equality for Native Americans in an age of great racial prejudice and political violence.

SOURCE: William Apess. *A Son of the Forest and Other Writings.* Ed. Barry O'Connell. Amherst: University of Massachusetts Press, 1997.

SELECTED READINGS: Barry O'Connell. ed. *On Our Own Ground: The Complete Writings of William Apess, A Pequot* (1992). David Murray, *Forked Tongues: Speech, Writing, and Representation in North American Indian Texts* (1991).

Arnold Krupat, *For Those Who Come After: A Study of Native American Autobi-ography* (1985).

Having a desire to place a few things before my fellow creatures who are traveling with me to the grave, and to that God who is the maker and pre-server both of the white man and the Indian, whose abilities are the same and who are to be judged by one God, who will show no favor to outward appearances but will judge righteousness. Now I ask if degradation has not been heaped long enough upon the Indians? And if so, can there not be a compromise? Is it right to hold and promote prejudices? If not, why not put them all away? I mean here, among those who are civilized. It may be that many are ignorant of the situation of many of my brethren within the limits of New England. Let me for a few moments turn your attention to the res-ervations in the different states of New England, and, with but few exceptions, we shall find them as follows: the most mean, abject, miserable race of beings in the world—a complete place of prodigality and prostitution.

Let a gentleman and lady of integrity and respectability visit these places, and they would be surprised; as they wandered from one hut to the other they would view, with the females who are left alone, children half-starved and some almost as naked as they came into the world. And it is a fact that I have seen them as much so—while the females are left without protection, and are seduced by white men, and are finally left to be common prostitutes for them and to be destroyed by that burning, fiery curse, that has swept millions, both of red and white men, into the grave with sorrow and dis-grace—rum. One reason why they are left so is because their most sensible and active men are absent at sea. Another reason is because they are made to believe they are minors and have not the abilities given them from God to take care of themselves, without it is to see to a few little articles, such as baskets and brooms. Their land is in common stock, and they have nothing to make them enterprising.

Another reason is because those men who are Agents, many of them are unfaithful and care not whether the Indians live or die; they are much im-posed upon by their neighbors, who have no principle. They would think it no crime to go upon Indian lands and cut and carry off their most valuable timber, or anything else they chose; and I doubt not but they think it clear gain. Another reason is because they have no education to take care of them-selves; if they had, I would risk them to take care of their own property.

Now I will ask if the Indians are not called the most ingenious people among us. And are they not said to be men of talents? And I would ask: Could there be a more efficient way to distress and murder them by inches than the way they have taken? And there is no people in the world but who may be destroyed in the same way. Now, if these people are what they are held up in our view to be, I would take the liberty to ask why they are not brought forward and pains taken to educate them, to give them all a common education, and those of the brightest and first-rate talents put forward and held up to office. Perhaps some unholy, unprincipled men would cry out, "The skin was not good enough"; but stop, friends—I am not talking about the skin but about principles. I would ask if there cannot be as good feelings and principles under a red skin as there can be under a white. And let me ask: Is it not on the account of a bad principle that we who are red children have had to suffer so much as we have? And let me ask: Did not this bad principle proceed from the whites or their forefathers? And I would ask: Is it worthwhile to nourish it any longer? If not, then let us have a change, although some men no doubt will spout their corrupt principles against it, that are in the halls of legislation and elsewhere. But I presume this kind of talk will seem surprising and horrible. I do not see why it should so long as they (the whites) say that they think as much of us as they do of themselves.

This I have heard repeatedly, from the most respectable gentlemen and ladies—and having heard so much precept, I should now wish to see the example. And I would ask who has a better right to look for these things than the naturalist himself—the candid man would say none.

I know that many say that they are willing, perhaps the majority of the people, that we should enjoy our rights and privileges as they do. If so, I would ask, Why are not we protected in our persons and property throughout the Union? Is it not because there reigns in the breast of many who are leaders a most unrighteous, unbecoming, and impure black principle, and as corrupt and unholy as it can be—while these very same unfeeling, self-esteemed characters pretend to take the skin as a pretext to keep us from our unalienable and lawful rights? I would ask you if you would like to be disfranchised from all your rights, merely because your skin is white, and for no other crime. I'll venture to say, these very characters who hold the skin to be such a barrier in the way would be the first to cry out, "Injustice! awful injustice!"

But, reader, I acknowledge that this is a confused world, and I am not seeking for office, but merely placing before you the black inconsistency that you place before me—which is ten times blacker than any skin that you will find in the universe. And now let me exhort you to do away that principle, as it appears ten times worse in the sight of God and candid men than skins of color—more disgraceful than all the skins that Jehovah ever made. If black or red skins or any other skin of color is disgraceful to God, it appears that he has disgraced himself a great deal—for he has made fifteen colored people to one white and placed them here upon this earth.

Now let me ask you, white man, if it is a disgrace for to eat, drink, and sleep with the image of God, or sit, or walk and talk with them. Or have you the folly to think that the white man, being one in fifteen or sixteen, are the only beloved images of God? Assemble all nations together in your imagination, and then let the whites be seated among them, and then let us look for the whites, and I doubt not it would be hard finding them; for to the rest of the nations, they are still but a handful. Now suppose these skins were put together, and each skin had its national crimes written upon it—which skin do you think would have the greatest? I will ask one question more. Can you charge the Indians with robbing a nation almost of their whole continent, and murdering their women and children, and then depriving the remainder of their lawful rights, that nature and God require them to have? And to cap the climax, rob another nation to till their grounds and welter out their days under the lash with hunger and fatigue under the scorching rays of a burning sun? I should look at all the skins, and I know that when I cast my eye upon that white skin, and if I saw those crimes written upon it, I should enter my protest against it immediately and cleave to that which is more honorable. And I can tell you that I am satisfied with the manner of my creation, fully—whether others are or not. . . .

60. GEORGE HENRY EVANS

Vote Yourself A Farm
(1846)

GEORGE HENRY EVANS (1805–1856) was a prominent editor of labor newspapers during the Jacksonian period whose later work on behalf of land reform led to the passage of the 1862 Homestead Act. Born in England, Evans immigrated to the United States in 1820. Trained as a printer's apprentice in upstate New York, Evans was drawn to the radical democrats and freethinkers he met there. In 1829, he moved to New York City to become editor of *The Working Men's Advocate*, the nation's first newspaper "designed solely to protect and advance the interests of the working man." When the Working Men's Party failed as a political organization, Evans turned his attention to Western land as a source of economic growth, social equality, and independence. Inspired by the republican writings of Thomas Paine and Thomas Jefferson, Evans developed his proposal for free public land in the West as an alternative solution to the problems of depressed wages and overcrowded work conditions in the East. The following tract, "Vote Yourself A Farm," was written by Evans and widely distributed as a handbill by the National Reform Association, an independent land-reform group he helped to organize. Its central tenet—that the availability of public land would lead to social equality and economic independence—helped to inspire the popular homestead movement and was later incorporated into the political platforms of the Free Soil and Republican parties.

SOURCE: John R. Commons et al., eds. *A Documentary History of American Industrial Society, Volume VII.* New York: Russell and Russell, 1958.

SELECTED READINGS: Jeffrey J. Pilz, *The Life, Work, and Times of George Henry Evans: Newspaperman, Activist, and Reformer, 1829–1849* (2001). Edward Pessen, *Most Uncommon Jacksonians: The Radical Leaders of the Early Labor Movement*

(1967). Helene S. Zahler, *Eastern Workingmen and National Land Policy, 1829–1862* (1941).

Are you an American citizen? Then you are a joint-owner of the public lands. Why not take enough of your property to provide yourself a home? Why not vote yourself a farm?

Remember poor Richard's saying: "Now I have a sheep and a cow, every one bids me 'good morrow.' " If a man have a house and a home of his own, though it be a thousand miles off, he is well received in other people's houses; while the homeless wretch is turned away. The bare right to a farm, though you should never go near it, would save you from many an insult. Therefore, Vote yourself a farm.

Are you a party follower? Then you have long enough employed your vote to benefit scheming office-seekers; use it for once to benefit yourself—Vote yourself a farm.

Are you tired of slavery—of drudging for others—of poverty and its attendant miseries? Then, Vote yourself a farm.

Are you endowed with reason? Then you must know that your right to life hereby includes the right to a place to live in—the right to a home. Assert this right, so long denied mankind by feudal robbers and their attorneys. Vote yourself a farm.

Are you a believer in the scriptures? Then assert that the land is the Lord's, because He made it. Resist then the blasphemers who exact money for His work, even as you would resist them should they claim to be worshipped for His holiness. Emancipate the poor from the necessity of encouraging such blasphemy—Vote the freedom of the public lands.

Are you a man? Then assert the sacred rights of man—especially your right to stand upon God's earth, and to till it for your own profit. Vote yourself a farm.

Would you free your country, and the sons of toil everywhere, from the heartless, irresponsible mastery of the aristocracy of avarice? Would you disarm this aristocracy of its chief weapon, the fearful power of banishment from God's earth? Then join with your neighbors to form a true American party, having for its guidance the principles of the American revolution, and whose chief measures shall be—I. To limit the quantity of land that any one man may henceforth monopolize or inherit; and 2. To make the public lands free to actual settlers only, each having the right to sell his improvements to any man not possessed of other land. These great measures once carried, wealth would become a changed social element; it would then consist of the accumulated products of human labor, instead of a hoggish monopoly of the products of God's labor; and the antagonism of capital and labor would forever cease. Capital could no longer grasp the largest share of the laborer's earnings, as a reward for not doing him all the injury the laws of the feudal aristocracy authorize, viz: the denial of all stock to work upon and all place to live in. To derive any profit from the laborer, it must first give him work; for it could no longer wax fat by levying a dead tax upon his existence. The hoary iniquities of Norman land pirates would cease to pass current as American law. Capital, with its power for good undiminished, would lose the power to oppress; and a new era would dawn upon the earth, and rejoice the souls of a thousand generations. Therefore forget not to Vote yourself a farm.

61. IRA STEWARD

A Reduction of Hours, An Increase in Wages
(1865)

IRA STEWARD (1831–1883) was an economic theorist and labor activist who is now known as the "father of the eight-hour day." Born in New London, Connecticut, Steward received very little formal education, training instead as an apprentice machinist until he lost his job agitating for a shorter workday. Before the end of the Civil War, Steward became president of the Boston Eight-Hour League, a position that allowed him to organize similar labor organizations throughout the country to put pressure on political candidates as well as state and federal legislatures. Despite political and economic setbacks during the 1870s, the movement for an eight-hour workday—eight hours for work, eight hours for rest, eight hours for "what we will"—became one of the principle features of the modern labor movement. In the following 1865 pamphlet, Steward laid out his economic theory, arguing that a reduction in hours would actually lead to an increase in wages, as well as to a profound shift in tastes and habits as members of the working class moved from poverty and subsistence to their increasingly independent role as consumers.

SOURCE: John R. Commons et al., eds. *A Documentary History of American Industrial Society, Volume IX.* New York: Russell and Russell, 1958.

SELECTED READINGS: David Roediger and Philip S. Foner, *Our Own Time: A History of American Labor and the Working Day* (1989). Roy Rosenzweig, *Eight Hours for What We Will: Workers and Leisure in an Industrial City, 1870–1920* (1985). David Montgomery, *Beyond Equality: Labor and the Radical Republicans, 1862–1874* (1967).

"Well," says a workingman, "I should certainly be very glad to work less hours, but I can scarcely earn enough by working ten to make myself and family comfortable."

Sir, as strange as it may seem to you at first blush, it is a fact that your wages will never be permanently increased until the hours of labor are reduced. Have you never observed that those who work the hardest and longest are paid the least, especially if the employment is very disagreeable, while those whose employment is more agreeable usually receive more, and many who do nothing receive more, than either?

You are receiving your scanty pay precisely because you work so many hours in a day, and my point now is to show why this is true, and why reducing the hours for the masses will eventually increase their wages.

It is but little more than three hundred years since everybody believed that the sun revolved around the earth. But Copernicus finally exploded this mistake and proved that the earth goes around the sun; and many have been the cases in which men have been forced to admit that the truth was exactly the reverse of all their past opinions or experiences.

For the safety of society English law made two hundred crimes punishable with death. Thoughtful men said, "We shall be safer if we reduce these to fifty." Parliament tried the experiment, and its wonderful success suggests a still greater reduction, and to-day Lord John Russell says, "Abolish the death penalty altogether."

Men once believed that the use of railroads would leave little work for horses to do. When Sir Rowland Hill first made the statement that reducing the postage on letters would increase the revenue, it met with the same incredulous reception we shall meet in the proposition that as the hours are reduced wages will increase until every producer shall receive the full value of his services.

The truth is, as a rule, that men who labor excessively are robbed of all ambition to ask for anything more than will satisfy their bodily necessities, while those who labor moderately have time to cultivate tastes and create wants in addition to mere physical comforts. How can men be stimulated to demand higher wages when they have little or no time or strength to use the advantages which higher wages can buy, or procure?

Take an extreme case for illustration of this—that of an average operative or mechanic employed by a corporation fourteen hours a day. His labor commences at half-past four in the morning, and does not cease until half-past seven, p.m. How many newspapers or books can he read? What time has he to visit or receive visits? to take baths? to write letters? to cultivate flowers? to walk with his family? Will he not be quite as likely to vote in opposition to his real interests as in favor? What is his opinion good for? Will any one ask his advice? Which will he most enjoy, works of art, or rum? Will he go to meeting on Sunday? Does society care whether he is happy or miserable? sick or well? dead or alive? How often are his eyes tempted by the works of art? His home means to him his food and his bed. His life is work, with the apparition, however, of some time being without, for his work means bread! "Only that and nothing more." He is debased by excessive toil! He is almost without hope!

Think how monotonous that path leading from house to factory, and from factory to house again—the same sidewalk every day, rain or shine, summer or winter—leading by the same low houses—inhabited by beings walking the same social treadmill as himself. Half-past seven comes at last, and as the wheel stops he catches his coat, and half staggering with fatigue, hurries homeward in the darkness, thinking of nothing but food and rest. What are his motives?

From the fourteen hour system let us turn to that of eight hours for a day's work, and see if the real secret of low and high wages does not lie in the vast difference which the two systems make in the daily habits and ways of living of the masses. In the eight hour system labor commences at seven o'clock a.m., and, as an hour and a half is allowed for dinner, the labor of the day ends at half past four in the afternoon, instead of half-past seven in the evening. Think carefully of the difference between the operative and mechanic leaving his work at half-past seven (after dark, the most of the year), and that of the more leisurely walk home at half-past four p.m., or three hours earlier. Remember also that there is a vast difference in the strength and feelings of those who commence labor at half-past four in the morning, and those who commence two hours and a half later, or at seven o'clock. It is the hard practical necessary differences between the two systems which control the daily habits and thoughts of all who are living under them.

You can hardly dwell too long upon this point, for upon it turns this whole question of social science—poverty and wealth—vice and virtue—ignorance and knowledge. The follies, burdens, and crimes of our later civilization are hanging upon this question, and the temptation to leave the simple, and comparatively unimportant fact that reducing the hours will increase the wages, and launch out upon broader and more sublime results, is almost irresistible. The simple increase of wages is the first step on that long road which ends at last in a more equal distribution of the fruits of toil. For wages will continue to increase until the capitalist and laborer are one. But we must confine ourselves to the first simple fact that a reduction of hours is an increase of wages; and when we are perfectly satisfied of its soundness we can build upon it until the consequences grow to the extent of our comprehension or imagination.

62. NATIONAL LABOR UNION

Declaration of Principles

(1867)

THE NATIONAL LABOR UNION (NLU) was founded in Baltimore in 1866. In-spired by the recent formation of several national trade unions, as well as the vigorous efforts of Ira Steward and local eight-hour leagues, the NLU was formed as an alternative political organization devoted to the interests of skilled artisans and mechanics. William H. Sylvis, head of the iron molders' union, and Richard F. Trevellick, president of the Ship Carpenters and Caulk-ers International, were the principal founders of this new national labor or-ganization. Its major achievement came in 1868, when it finally succeeded in pressuring Congress to pass a law calling for an eight-hour workday for all federal workers. In August of the following year, the NLU admitted black delegates to its annual convention in Baltimore, marking the first time in history that African Americans were admitted to a white labor convention. The NLU was an important bridge between the trade union experiments of the antebellum era and the more extensive (and militant) efforts to organize labor after the Civil War, marking an important step forward in establishing labor as a viable independent force in American public life. The following "Declaration of Principles" draws on the language of the American Revolu-tion to advance the notion that the interests of labor are central to the proper functioning of democracy.

SOURCE: Albert Fried, ed. *Except to Walk Free: Documents and Notes in the History of American Labor.* Garden City, NY: Anchor Books, 1974.

SELECTED READINGS: Jonathan Grossman, *William Sylvis, Pioneer of American Labor: A Study of the Labor Movement during the Era of the Civil War* (1973). David Montgomery, *Beyond Equality: Labor and the Radical Republicans, 1862–1872* (1967). Charlotte Todes, *William H. Sylvis and the National Labor Union* (1942).

We beg further to present the following Declaration of Principles:

We hold these truths to be self evident, that all men are created equal, that they are endowed by their Creator with certain inalienable rights; that among them are life, liberty and the pursuit of happiness; that to secure these rights, governments are instituted among men, deriving their just powers from the consent of the governed.

That there are but two pure forms of government, the autocratic and the democratic; under the former the will of the individual sovereign is the supreme law, under the latter the sovereignty is vested in the whole people, all other forms being a modification of the one or the other of these principles, and that ultimately one or other of these forms must prevail throughout all civilized nations, and it is now for the American people to determine which of these principles shall triumph. . . .

That our monetary, financial and revenue laws are in letter and spirit opposed to the principles of freedom and equality upon which our democratic republican institutions are founded, there is in all their provisions manifestly a studied design to shield non-producing capital from its just proportion of the burdens necessary for the support of the government, imposing them mainly on the industrial wealth-producing classes, thereby condemning them to lives of unremunerated toil, depriving them of the ordinary conveniences and comforts of life; of the time and means necessary for social enjoyment, intellectual culture and moral improvement; and ultimately reducing them to a state of practical servitude.

We further hold that while these unrighteous laws of distribution remain in force, laborers cannot, by any system of combination or co-operation, secure their natural rights. That the first and most important step towards the establishment of the rights of labor, is the institution of a system of true co-operation between non-producing capital and labor. That to effect this most desirable object, money, the medium of distribution to capital and labor, must be instituted upon such a wise and just principle that instead of being a power to centralize the wealth in the hands of a few bankers, usurers, middlemen and non-producers generally, it shall be a power that will distribute products to producers in accordance with the labor or service performed in their production—the servant and not the master of labor. This done the natural rights of labor will be secured, and co-operation in production and in the distribution of products, will follow as a natural consequence. . . . We further hold that it is essential to the prosperity and happiness of the people and the stability of our democratic republican institutions, that the public domain be distributed as widely as possible among the people; a land monopoly being equally as oppressive to the people and dangerous to our institutions, as the present money monopoly. To prevent this the public lands should be sold in reasonable quantities, and to none but actual occupants. . . .

We further hold that intelligence and virtue in the sovereignty are necessary to a wise administration of justice, and that as our institutions are founded upon the theory of sovereignty in the people, in order to their preservation and perpetuity, it is the imperative duty of Congress to make such wise and just regulations as shall afford all the means of acquiring the knowledge requisite to the intelligent exercise of the privileges and duties pertaining to sovereignty, and that Congress should ordain that eight hours labor between the rising and setting of the sun should constitute a day's work in all government works and places where the national government has exclusive jurisdiction, and that it is equally imperative on the several states to make like provision by legal enactment. . . .

63. COLORED NATIONAL LABOR UNION

Statement of Principles
(1869)

Excluded at first from the National Labor Union, African Americans sought to establish their own national organization—as well as state and local chapters—to protect and promote the interests of black laborers. Since emancipation had so radically altered labor relations in the South, the need for a black labor organization was all the more pressing. As such, on December 6, 1869, 214 black delegates, representing eighteen states, gathered together in Union League Hall in Washington, D.C., to establish the **COLORED NATIONAL LABOR UNION (CNLU)**, the nation's first labor union for African Americans. Several whites were admitted to the convention, and NLU President Richard F. Trevellick delivered one of the first addresses calling for unity among workers regardless of race, color, or sex, and urging blacks to abandon the Republican Party. Though black delegates welcomed Trevellick's "call for unity," they refused to withdraw their support from the Republican Party, especially since the NLU did not represent the everyday realities of black workers. Instead, the CNLU drew up its own platform calling for harmony between capital and labor—a major departure from the NLU position—as well as the right to work regardless of race, sex, or nationality, a comprehensive system of apprenticeship, education and temperance, equitable compensation for a day's work, land grants, and federal labor protections for sharecroppers and other freedmen. The following address, written by former abolitionist John Mercer Langston and adopted overwhelmingly at the convention, expresses the magnanimity and inclusiveness of the CNLU's call for interracial solidarity among laboring men and women.

SOURCE: Herbert Aptheker, ed. *A Documentary History of the Negro People in the United States, Volume Two.* New York: Carol Publishing Group, 1990.

SELECTED READINGS: David Roediger, *Towards the Abolition of Whiteness: Essays on Race, Politics, and Working Class History* (1994). Philip S. Foner, *Organized Labor and the Black Worker, 1619–1973* (1974). David Montgomery, *Beyond Equality: Labor and the Radical Republicans, 1862–1872* (1967).

In our organization we make no discrimination as to nationality, sex, or color. Any labor movement based upon such discrimination and embracing a small part of the great working masses of the country, while repelling others because of its partial and sectional character, will prove to be of very little value. Indeed, such a movement, narrow and divisional, will be suicidal, for it arrays against the classes represented by it all other laboring classes which ought to be rather allied in the closest union, and avoid these dissensions and divisions which in the past have given wealth the advantage over labor.

We would have "the poor white man" of the South born to a heritage of poverty and degradation like his black compeer in social life, feel that labor in our organization seeks the elevation of all its sons and daughters; pledges its united strength not to advance the interests of a special class; but in its spirit of reasonableness and generous catholicity would promote the welfare, and happiness of all who "earn their bread in the sweat of their brow."

With us, too, numbers count, and we know the maxim, "in union there is strength," has its significance in the affairs of labor no less than in politics. Hence our industrial movement, emancipating itself from every national and partial sentiment, broadens and deepens its foundations so as to rear thereon a superstructure capacious enough to accommodate at the altar of common interest the Irish, the Negro and the German laborer; to which, so far from being excluded, the "poor white" native of the South, struggling out of moral and pecuniary death into life "real and earnest," the white mechanic and laborer of the North, so long ill taught and advised that his true interest is gained by hatred and abuse of the laborer of African descent, as well as the Chinaman whom designing persons, partially enslaving, would make in the plantation service of the South the rival and competitor of the former slave class of the country, having with us one and the same interest, are all invited, earnestly urged, to join us in our movement, and thus aid in the protection and conservation of their and our interests.

In the cultivation of such spirit of generosity on our part, and the magnanimous conduct which it prompts, we hope, by argument and appeal addressed to the white mechanics, laborers and trades unions of our country, to our legislators and countrymen at large, to overcome the prejudices now existing against us so far as to secure a fair opportunity for the display and remuneration of our industrial capabilities.

We launch our organization, then, in the fullest confidence, knowing that, if wisely and judiciously managed, it must bring to all concerned, strength and advantage, and especially to the colored American as its earliest fruits that power which comes from competence and wealth, education and the ballot, made strong through a union whose fundamental principles are just, impartial and catholic.

64. JOSEPH A. DACUS

The Great Uprising
(1877)

The following account, written and published by **JOSEPH A. DACUS,** editor of the *St. Louis Republican,* is probably the best contemporary account of the Great Railroad Strike of 1877. The strike began on July 17, 1877, in Martinsburg, West Virginia, following a series of wage reductions by the Baltimore and Ohio Railroad Company. From the first, strikers blocked trains from running, demanding that wages be restored to their original level. When state militia units sent to suppress the strike refused to fire on the protesting workers, the governor appealed to President Rutherford B. Hayes to deploy federal troops, marking the first time since the antebellum era that the U.S. government actively attempted to break labor strikes. By the time they arrived, the strike had spread along the railroad in nearly every direction—to Baltimore, Pittsburgh, Chicago, and, most dramatically, St. Louis, where a general strike by workers succeeded in shutting down the city for a full week. Bloody altercations ensued, leading to arrests, injuries, and in some cases, deaths. One of the most significant labor uprisings in American history, the strike lasted several weeks before federal troops finally managed to squelch the protests. Its immediate legacy, however, was mixed—energizing the labor movement to even greater organization and militancy, and also leading to more repressive state and federal initiatives to prevent future strikes. Dacus's account ultimately blamed railroad companies for creating the conditions that inspired the workers to strike for "wages and revenge."

SOURCE: Albert Fried, ed. *Except to Walk Free: Documents and Notes in the History of American Labor.* Garden City, NY: Anchor Books, 1974.

SELECTED READINGS: Philip S. Foner, *The Great Labor Uprising of 1877* (1977). Samuel Yellen, *American Labor Struggles, 1877–1934* (1974). Robert V. Bruce, *1877: Year of Violence* (1959).

It was on the 23d day of July, 1877—just seven days after the commencement of the first strike on the Baltimore and Ohio Railroad, at South Baltimore and Martinsburg. Already momentous events had happened. Baltimore, Pittsburgh, and Cumberland had successively attracted the attention of those who cared to observe the course of the remarkable movement among the working classes. Hornellsville, Harrisburgh, Phillipsburg, and Buffalo had been the scene of actions, startling in their nature. Where would the next center of interest be located? It was not necessary to wait long for an answer to this question. For some days there had been trouble on the Philadelphia and Reading Railroad, and among the miners in that vicinity. Reading was favorably situated to become the central point of the movement in that region. . . .

On account of the unmilitary conduct of some companies of General Reeder's regiment, we are compelled to add another story of slaughter to the bloody records of Baltimore and Pittsburgh. Without one word of warning, these militia fired upon an assembled crowd of citizens, in the very heart of the city of Reading, and killed thirteen people, shot five policemen, and altogether severely wounded twenty-seven persons.

Night had just settled upon the city, and North Seventh street, for two squares, was lined with people, sitting in the enjoyment of the cool air of evening, in front of their homes. The main line of the Philadelphia and Reading Railroad Company's road passes through the city on Seventh street. Penn street is the main thoroughfare, running in an opposite direction from the course of the railroad, and crosses Seventh street at right angles. From Penn street northward for two squares, two lines of track are laid, leading to the new depot. These are laid through a deep cut, with a heavy stone wall, twenty feet high on either side. On this section of track the bloody work was done. At ten minutes after eight o'clock the military marched in toward Penn street, through the cut, from the depot. They were about three hundred and fifty strong, and they marched, to the tap of a few drums that could not be heard a square away. Few people were aware of their arrival in the city, and fewer still knew they were advancing upon the crowd.

Steadily they approached, when suddenly three hundred rifles were discharged in volleys, and five men dropped to the pavements. The report that the troops had shot blank cartridges, of course, was incorrect. When the troops fired their first volleys, they were given broadsides of rocks and stones from the tops of the walls. Quite a number of revolver shots were returned by parties in the crowd. The troops continued their firing, and men, women and children fled in fear. They had assembled on Seventh street to look at the train that had been stopped, and they were recklessly and indiscriminately shot by the militia. The citizens were almost universal in their condemnation of these proceedings. In five minutes the streets were cleared, stores were closed, and hotels and restaurants were locked up. Business had been proceeding as usual, and just before the firing, not a single merchant, or business man was aware of the coming of the military. The streets resembled a small battle field, and the pavements were stained with many pools of blood. It was absolutely dangerous for men to come from the alleyways and from behind the brick walls, to go to the assistance of the dying. The heroic militia stood to their guns, and were valiantly disposed to shoot down any citizen who might cross the line of their vision. Finally the sufferers, groaning and shrieking for water, were carried to the drug stores to have their wounds dressed. . . .

The presence of the military did not curb the spirit of the rioters. On the contrary they grew bolder and more threatening. For some days after the fight open attacks on the trains were made.

The strikers mounted a passing loaded coal train, put on the brakes, stopped the train and pushed back the caboose and several loaded cars, thus virtually blockading the down track. One of the eight-ton cars was dumped on the rails. At ten minutes after four o'clock, July 25th, the down express train came along slowly on the other track. The strikers were led by a large man wearing a dark shirt and dark pants. His hair looked as if it had been recently shaved from his head.

Fully two hundred strikers would rush right up squarely to the front of the approaching locomotive, wave their hands, shake their clenched fists, and by many devices intimidate and threaten the engine driver and train employes. An up freight train was compelled to go back, and the crew made to desert the cars. At one time it was feared they would run the engine into the river below the city. The up passenger and express train came through the city at a fearful speed, with the engine whistling lustily. As she sped through the crowd, Engineer Saracool bent low in his cab and gave the engine full stroke, in order to successfully pass the enraged men.

The freight up from Philadelphia and the market train were compelled to halt and go no further. At this point the passenger train down, was stopped in the cut, where the fighting took place. The crew was compelled to desert and the passengers were obliged to leave. These high handed proceedings continued until about seven o'clock, when nearly all the strikers left the ground for parts unknown. Not one of the rioters was either killed or wounded.

The majority, in fact all the unfortunates, were lawabiding, peaceable citizens, who had assembled at Seventh and Penn streets simply to gratify their curiosity.

A large body of Coal and Iron Police, from the coal regions, were quartered at the Company's mammoth car shops, which works the strikers threatened to burn. A large crowd of the friends of the railroad men procured about fifty muskets for the strikers, and there was imminent danger of a desperate conflict.

The military companies engaged in the fight were the Hamburg Rifles, Slatington Rifles, Allentown Continentals, Company I, infantry, of Catasqua, Easton Greys, and a company from Portland, Northampton county. They arrived at eight o'clock in the evening. A number of the military, after their bloody work was done, threw down their arms, and asked for citizens' clothes.

At a quarter after eleven o'clock, the night of the 25th, the strikers had torn down the watch boxes at the street corners, and proceeded down the road to tear up the tracks. They signalized their departure by a perfect hurricane of yells and cheering, as they proceeded in their onward march of ruin and destruction. The city had become turbulent again, and the outlook indicated desperate work. The cry among the men was, "Wages and revenge." . . .

65. KNIGHTS OF LABOR

Preamble

(1878)

THE KNIGHTS OF LABOR began as a secret society of garment workers in Philadelphia in 1869. It started to grow only after the 1877 railroad strike and other expressions of labor militancy galvanized the national labor movement. After Terrence V. Powderly became the Grand Master Workman of the group in 1879, the Knights of Labor flourished as an increasingly political labor organization, advocating the eight-hour workday, child labor protections, and equal pay for equal work. By 1885, the Knights had more than 110,000 members; one year later, following a wave of successful railroad strikes, membership peaked at 750,000, making it the largest American labor organization in the nineteenth century. Although Powderly himself opposed strikes—he preferred boycotts and arbitration—the Knights of Labor embodied the dramatic rise in working-class militancy during labor's heyday in the 1880s. The group was unique among unions in that it was organized "vertically" to include all workers—men and women—in any given industry regardless of skill or trade. Though it struggled with nativism and racial prejudice, the Knights of Labor aimed to consolidate every member of the "producing classes" into one single union. By the mid-1880s, the Knights suffered from increasingly stark internal divisions caused by strong tactical disagreements, often bitter ideological tensions, and rivalries among the different trades. Following the violent repression that followed Chicago's Haymarket Affair, the influence of the Knights of Labor waned, as trade unions began to reorganize themselves under the banner of the newly established American Federation of Labor. Still, the Knights of Labor represented a dramatic new turn in labor organizing. The "Preamble" to their constitution, adopted at the first General Assembly in 1878, articulates the group's far-reaching mission.

SOURCE: Albert Fried, ed. *Except to Walk Free: Documents and Notes in the History of American Labor.* Garden City, NY: Anchor Books, 1974.

SELECTED READINGS: Robert Weir, *Beyond Labor's Veil: The Culture of the Knights of Labor* (1996). Leon Fink, *Workingmen's Democracy: The Knights of Labor and American Politics* (1983). Alan Trachtenberg, *The Incorporation of American: Culture and Society in the Gilded Age* (1982).

The recent alarming development and aggression of aggregated wealth, which, unless checked, will invariably lead to the pauperization and hopeless degradation of the toiling masses, render it imperative, if we desire to enjoy the blessings of life, that a check should be placed upon its power and upon unjust accumulation, and a system adopted which will secure to the laborer the fruits of his toil; and as this much desired object can only be accomplished by the thorough unification of labor, and the united effort of those who obey the divine injunction that "In the sweat of thy brow shalt thou eat bread," we have formed the * * * * * with a view of securing the organization and direction, by co-operative effort, of the power of the industrial classes; and we submit to the world the object sought to be accomplished by our organization, calling upon all who believe in securing "the greatest good to the greatest number" to aid and assist us:—

I. To bring within the folds of organization every department of productive industry, making knowledge a standpoint for action, and industrial and moral worth, not wealth, the true standard of individual and national greatness.

II. To secure to the toilers a proper share of the wealth that they create; more of the leisure that rightfully belongs to them; more societary advantages; more of the benefits, privileges, and emoluments of the world, all those rights and privileges necessary to make them capable of enjoying, appreciating, defending, and perpetuating the blessings of good government.

III. To arrive at the true condition of the producing masses in their educational, moral, and financial condition, by demanding from the various governments the establishment of bureaus of Labor Statistics.

IV. The establishment of co-operative institutions, productive and distributive.

V. The reserving of the public lands—the heritage of the people—for the actual settler;—not another acre for railroads or settlers.

VI. The abrogation of all laws that do not bear equally upon capital and labor, the removal of unjust technicalities, delays, and discriminations in the administration of justice, and the adopting of measures providing for the health and safety of those engaged in mining, manufacturing, or building pursuits.

VII. The enactment of laws to compel chartered corporations to pay their employes weekly, in full, for labor performed during the preceding week, in the lawful money of the country.

VIII. The enactment of laws giving mechanics and laborers a first lien on their work for their full wages.

IX. The abolishment of the contract system on national, state, and municipal work.

X. The substitution of arbitration for strikes, whenever and wherever employers and employes are willing to meet on equitable grounds.

XI. The prohibition of the employment of children in workshops, mines, and factories before attaining their fourteenth year.

XII. To abolish the system of letting out by contract the labor of convicts in our prisons and reformatory institutions.

XIII. To secure for both sexes equal pay for equal work.

XIV. The reduction of the hours of labor to eight per day, so that the laborers may have more time for social enjoyment and intellectual improvement, and be enabled to reap the advantages conferred by the labor-saving machinery which their brains have created.

XV. To prevail upon governments to establish a purely national circulating medium, based upon the faith and resources of the nation, and issued directly to the people, without the intervention of any system of banking corporations, which money shall be a legal tender in payment of all debts, public or private.

66. HENRY GEORGE

The Crime of Poverty

(1885)

A radical agrarian and prominent economic theorist, **HENRY GEORGE (1839–1897)** delivered one of his most famous speeches, "The Crime of Poverty," to a gathering of the Knights of Labor on April 1, 1885. Born in Philadelphia, he left school at the age of thirteen to support his struggling family. During the 1860s, George experienced poverty and periodic unemployment before landing a job as a newspaper editor in California after the Civil War. It was during this time that he began to record his impressions of the contradictions of capitalism—the paradox of "progress and poverty" that would become the hallmark of his future writing. George expanded his critique of capitalism in his masterful book, *Progress and Poverty,* which was published in 1880, the same year that he moved from California to New York City. Assailing "wage-slavery" and the tyranny of "non-producers" (capital) over "producers" (labor), George advocated far-reaching government reforms that were unimaginable prior to the Civil War. By insisting that high rent and private ownership of land were not only the root causes of poverty and growing economic disparities, but also a "sin" and a violation of the nation's egalitarian principles, George placed his concern with the effects of capitalism within America's democratic and religious traditions. Although he sometimes clashed with socialists and other radical labor leaders, his proposals, particularly his call for a "single tax" on land, garnered enormous popular support at the end of the nineteenth century. The following speech, made during his unsuccessful run in the 1886 New York City mayoral race, addresses the most salient aspects of his economic theory.

SOURCE: Albert Fried, ed. *Except to Walk Free: Documents and Notes in the History of American Labor.* Garden City, NY: Anchor Books, 1974.

SELECTED READINGS: Robert V. Andelson, ed., *Critics of Henry George* (1979). Jacob Oser, *Henry George* (1974). Steven Cord, *Henry George: Dreamer or Realist?* (1965). Edward J. Rose, *Henry George* (1968).

Now why is it that men have to work for such low wages? Because if they were to demand higher wages there are plenty of unemployed men ready to step into their places. It is this mass of unemployed men who compel that fierce competition that drives wages down to the point of bare subsistence. Why is it that there are men who cannot get employment? Did you ever think what a strange thing it is that men cannot find employment? Adam had no difficulty in finding employment; neither had Robinson Crusoe; the finding of employment was the last thing that troubled them.

If men cannot find an employer, why cannot they employ themselves? Simply because they are shut out from the element on which human labour can alone be exerted. Men are compelled to compete with each other for the wages of an employer, because they have been robbed of the natural opportunities of employing themselves; because they cannot find a piece of God's world on which to work without paying some other human creature for the privilege.

I do not mean to say that even after you had set right this fundamental injustice, there would not be many things to do; but this I do mean to say, that our treatment of land lies at the bottom of all social questions. This I do mean to say, that, do what you please, reform as you may, you never can get rid of wide-spread poverty so long as the element on which and from which all men must live is made the private property of some men. It is utterly impossible. Reform government—get taxes down to the minimum—build railroads; institute co-operative stores; divide profits, if you choose, between employers and employed—and what will be the result? The result will be that the land will increase in value—that will be the result—that and nothing else. Experience shows this. Do not all improvements simply increase the value of land—the price that some must pay others for the privilege of living? . . .

It is so all over the United States—the men who improve, the men who turn the prairie into farms and the desert into gardens, the men who beautify your cities, are taxed and fined for having done these things. Now, nothing is clearer than that the people of New York want more houses; and I think that even here in Burlington you could get along with more houses. Why, then, should you fine a man who builds one? Look all over this country— the bulk of the taxation rests upon the improver; the man who puts up a building, or establishes a factory, or cultivates a farm, he is taxed for it; and not merely taxed for it, but I think in nine cases out of ten the land which he uses, the bare land, is taxed more than the adjoining lot or the adjoining

160 acres that some speculator is holding as a mere dog in the manger, not using it himself and not allowing anybody else to use it.

I am talking too long; but let me in a few words point out the way of getting rid of land monopoly, securing the right of all to the elements which are necessary for life. We could not divide the land. In a rude state of society, as among the ancient Hebrews, giving each family its lot and making it inalienable we might secure something like equality. But in a complex civilisation that will not suffice. It is not, however, necessary to divide up the land. All that is necessary is to divide up the income that comes from the land. In that way we can secure absolute equality; nor could the adoption of this principle involve any rude shock or violent change. It can be brought about gradually and easily by abolishing taxes that now rest upon capital, labour and improvements, and raising all our public revenues by the taxation of land values; and the longer you think of it the clearer you will see that in every possible way will it be a benefit.

Now, supposing we should abolish all other taxes direct and indirect, substituting for them a tax upon land values, what would be the effect? In the first place it would be to kill speculative values. It would be to remove from the newer parts of the country the bulk of the taxation and put it on the richer parts. It would be to exempt the pioneer from taxation and make the larger cities pay more of it. It would be to relieve energy and enterprise, capital and labour, from all those burdens that now bear upon them. What a start that would give to production! In the second place we could, from the value of the land, not merely pay all the present expenses of the government, but we could do infinitely more. In the city of San Francisco James Lick left a few blocks of ground to be used for public purposes there, and the rent amounts to so much, that out of it will be built the largest telescope in the world, large public baths and other public buildings, and various costly works. If, instead of these few blocks, the whole value of the land upon which the city is built had accrued to San Francisco what could she not do? . . .

But all such benefits as these, while great, would be incidental. The great thing would be that the reform I propose would tend to open opportunities to labour and enable men to provide employment for themselves. That is the great advantage. We should gain the enormous productive power that is going to waste all over the country, the power of idle hands that would gladly be at work. And that removed, then you would see wages begin to mount. It is not that everyone would turn farmer, or everyone would build himself a house if he had an opportunity for doing so, but so many could and would, as to relieve the pressure on the labour market and provide employment for all others. And as wages mounted to the higher levels, then you would see the productive power increased. The country where wages are high is the country of greatest productive powers. Where wages are highest, there will invention be most active; there will labour be most intelligent; there will be the greatest yield for the expenditure of exertion. The more you think of it the more clearly you will see that what I say is true. I cannot hope to convince you in an hour or two, but I shall be content if I shall put you upon inquiry. Think for yourselves; ask yourselves whether this wide-spread fact of poverty is not a crime, and a crime for which every one of us, man and woman, who does not do what he or she can do to call attention to it and do away with it, is responsible.

67. PEOPLE'S PARTY

Omaha Platform
(1892)

Founded in 1892, the **PEOPLE'S PARTY** (or "Populists") was an outgrowth of the agrarian revolt of the 1880s. As agricultural debt increased in the years following the Civil War, farmers organized two major Farmers' Alliances— one in the West, the other in the South—to demand sweeping government reforms to help them survive economically. The Southern Alliance achieved particular success, increasing solidarity through a "suballiance" network of cooperatives, newspapers, and lecture circuits. Over 250,000 strong by 1888, the Farmers' Alliance also attempted to build coalitions with other labor groups, including the Colored Farmers' Alliance and the Knights of Labor. After repeated appeals to the Republicans and Democrats seemed to fall on deaf ears, members of the Farmers' Alliance formed the People's Party, a third party devoted to farm labor interests and free of corporate influence. At the first convention in Omaha, Nebraska, on July 4, 1892, labor radical Ignatius Donnelly introduced his draft of the People's Party platform, which de-manded government control of transportation and communication; a "sub-treasury" plan to grant credit to local farmers; an eight-hour workday; the direct election of senators; the free coinage of silver; paper currency; and a progressive income tax. The electoral success of the Populists was promising but short-lived. After the 1896 presidential election, when the Populists ac-cepted Democrat William Jennings Bryan as their candidate, much of the distinctive radicalism that characterized the group dissipated. Still, the Pop-ulists issued a strong challenge to the entrenched power of big business and the corrupt politics in the late nineteenth century.

SOURCE: George Brown Tindall, ed. *A Populist Reader: Selections from the Works of American Populist Leaders.* Gloucester, MA: Peter Smith, 1976.

SELECTED READINGS: Michael Kazin, *The Populist Persuasion: An American His-tory* (1995). Robert McMath, *American Populism: A Social History, 1877–1898*

(1993). Lawrence Goodwy^ *Democratic Promise: The Populist Moment in America* (1976).

Platform

We declare, therefore—

First.—That the union of the labor forces of the United States this day consummated shall be permanent and perpetual; may its spirit enter into all hearts for the salvation of the Republic and the uplifting of mankind.

Second.—Wealth belongs to him who creates it, and every dollar taken from industry without an equivalent is robbery. "If any will not work, neither shall he eat." The interests of rural and civic labor are the same; their enemies are identical.

Third.—We believe that the time has come when the railroad corporations will either own the people or the people must own the railroads, and should the government enter upon the work of owning and managing all railroads, we should favor an amendment to the Constitution by which all persons engaged in the government service shall be placed under a civil-service regulation of the most rigid character, so as to prevent the increase of the power of the national administration by the use of such additional government employés.

FINANCE.—We demand a national currency, safe, sound, and flexible, issued by the general government only, a full legal tender for all debts, public and private, and that without the use of banking corporations, a just, equitable, and efficient means of distribution direct to the people, at a tax not to exceed 2 per cent, per annum, to be provided as set forth in the sub-treasury plan of the Farmers' Alliance, or a better system; also by payments in discharge of its obligations for public improvements.

1. We demand free and unlimited coinage of silver and gold at the present legal ratio of 16 to 1.

2. We demand that the amount of circulating medium be speedily increased to not less than $50 per capita.

3. We demand a graduated income tax.

4. We believe that the money of the country should be kept as much as possible in the hands of the people, and hence we demand that all State and national revenues shall be limited to the necessary expenses of the government, economically and honestly administered.

5. We demand that postal savings banks be established by the government for the safe deposit of the earnings of the people and to facilitate exchange.

TRANSPORTATION.—Transportation being a means of exchange and a public necessity, the government should own and operate the railroads in the interest of the people. The telegraph, telephone, like the post-office system, being a necessity for the transmission of news, should be owned and operated by the government in the interest of the people.

LAND.—The land, including all the natural sources of wealth, is the heritage of the people, and should not be monopolized for speculative purposes, and alien ownership of land should be prohibited. All land now held by railroads and other corporations in excess of their actual needs, and all lands now owned by aliens should be reclaimed by the government and held for actual settlers only.

68. CHINESE EQUAL RIGHTS LEAGUE

Appeal
(1892)

THE CHINESE EQUAL RIGHTS LEAGUE was formed in 1892 to oppose the Geary Act, which required all Chinese residents of the United States to subject themselves to intrusive government monitoring. The Geary Act was one of the discriminatory laws passed during Congressional debates over the renewal of the 1882 Chinese Exclusion Act, the first immigration restriction law in American history, which halted Chinese immigration for ten years and made the Chinese ineligible for citizenship. Only in 1943—when another group of Asian immigrants, the Japanese, were being detained in U.S. government internment camps during World War II—did the Chinese finally become eligible for American citizenship. In 1892, the Chinese Equal Rights League was formed in New York City by a group of Chinese merchants who opposed the coupling of immigration restrictions with a denial of citizenship to Chinese Americans already living in the United States. The following resolution, which was subsequently published as a pamphlet, was adopted at a meeting of the Equal Rights League at Cooper Union three weeks after its founding. Though pandering to the nativist sympathies of those who opposed Chinese immigration altogether—including most labor groups at the time—this "Appeal" makes a distinction between Chinese immigrants and Chinese Americans, making the case that the latter deserve the rights of full American citizenship.

SOURCE: Philip S. Foner and Daniel Rosenberg, eds. *Racism, Dissent, and Asian Americans from 1850 to the Present*. Westport, CT: Greenwood Press, 1993.

SELECTED READINGS: Andrew Gyory, *Closing the Gate: Race, Politics, and the Chinese Exclusion Act* (1998). Sucheng Chan, ed., *Entry Denied: Exclusion and the Chinese Community in America, 1882–1943* (1991). Ronald Takaki, *Strangers from a Different Shore: A History of Asian Americans* (1989). Alexander Saxton, *The Indispensable Enemy: Labor and the Anti-Chinese Movement in California* (1971).

To the American People, Friends of Humanity:

We, the members of the Chinese Equal Rights League in the United States, who have adopted this country and its customs in the main, are at this moment engaged in a perilous struggle in which our dearest rights as men and residents are involved. Doubtless the reading public is acquainted with the fact that during the last session of the Fifty-second Congress, a Bill was passed, styled the "Geary Bill" or "Chinese Registration Act," in which the attempt is made to humiliate every Chinaman, regardless of his moral, intellectual and material standing in the community, neither his long residence in the country is considered. By this mean and unjust Act discriminating between foreign residents from different countries has traversed and contraversed the fundamental principles of common law.

As residents of the United States we claim a common manhood with all other nationalities, and believe we should have that manhood recognized according to the principles of common humanity and American freedom. This monstrous and inhuman measure is a blot upon the civilization of the Western World, and is destined to retard the progress already made by the good people of this country in the East in art, science, commerce and religion.

We appeal to the humane, liberty-loving sentiment of the American people, who are lovers of equal rights and even-handed justice, a people from who sprung such illustrious characters as Washington, Jefferson, Clay, Sumner, lastly Lincoln, the citizen of the world, the friend of humanity and the champion of freedom: such illustrious warriors as Sherman, Sheridan, Logan and Grant, whose deeds of valor in the cause of freedom are to be seen in the grand march of American development—a development which merits the emulation of the nations of the earth. Must this growth be retarded simply on account of the doings of a misguided element who have suffered their feelings to control reason, encouraging a prejudice fiendish in its nature and purpose against a class of people who are industrious, law-abiding and honest? Can there be found a more inoffensive class in the body politic? not that we are cowards, but because we believe that mildness and simplicity should be the controling element in the character of a great man as well as in a great race of people. We have and are still paying our portion of government taxation, thereby assisting in supporting the Government, and thereby sharing an equal part in the support of the nation.

We love and admire the Government, and look with joy to her instrumentality in promoting every good and just cause among men, to her unwavering love of human rights, to her glorious efforts for the advancement of human happiness.

We, therefore, appeal for an equal chance in the race of life in this our adopted home—a large number of us have spent almost our entire lives in this country and claim no other but this as ours. Our motto is *"Character and fitness should be the requirement of all who are desirous of becoming citizens of the American Republic."*

We feel keenly the disgrace unjustly and maliciously heaped upon us by a cruel Congress. That for the purpose of prohibiting Chinese immigration more than one hundred thousand honest and respectable Chinese residents should be made to wear the badge of disgrace as ticket-of-leave men in your penitentiaries; that they should be tagged and branded as a whole lot of cattle for the slaughter; that they should be seen upon your streets with tearful eyes and heavy hearts, objects of scorn and public ridicule. No! We do not believe it, that so great a people as the Americans would consent to so small a principle toward a mere handful of defenceless men.

Our interest is here, because our homes, our families and our all are here. America is our home through long residence. Why, then, should we not consider your welfare ours? Chinese immigration, as well as Irish, Italian and other immigration, cannot be stopped by the persecution of our law-abiding citizens in the United States.

Treat us as men, and we will do our duty as men, and will aid you to stop this obnoxious evil that threatens the welfare of this Republic. We do not want any more Chinese here than you do. The scarcer the Chinese here, the better would be our conditions among you.

69. PULLMAN WORKERS

Statement to the American Railway Union
(1894)

The Pullman Strike of 1894 was one of the most contentious labor battles of the nineteenth century, playing a significant role in the rise of American socialism. Following his financial and critical success at the 1893 Chicago's World Fair, and in the wake of widespread economic depression later that year, George Pullman, inventor of the sleeping railway car, fired one-third of his workers, cut remaining wages by 30 percent, and refused to reduce housing and food prices in the company town he built near Chicago. When Pullman refused to negotiate with the Pullman workers, Eugene V. Debs, president of the American Railway Union, initiated what would become a month-long strike. The strike itself spread quickly, with owners of other railway companies backing Pullman, and Debs organizing the industry's rank and file to boycott all trains that used Pullman cars. At Pullman's request, President Grover Cleveland deployed federal troops in July to break the strike, after which Debs and other leaders were arrested for contempt and sentenced to jail time. It was during this six months in prison that Debs experienced his conversion from reform-minded labor leader to radical socialist. The following statement by the Pullman workers to the American Railway Union on June 15, 1894, inspired Debs to call the strike. This moving appeal expresses the dire economic circumstances, and callous response of Pullman and his managers, that touched off one of the last bitter conflicts between labor and capital in nineteenth-century America.

SOURCE: Albert Fried, ed. *Except to Walk Free: Documents and Notes in the History of American Labor*. Garden City, NY: Anchor Books, 1974.

SELECTED READINGS: Nick Salvatore, *Eugene V. Debs: Citizen and Socialist* (1982). William H. Carwardine, *The Pullman Strike* (1973). Almont Lindsey,

The Pullman Strike: The Story of a Unique Experiment and of a Great Labor Up-heaval (1967).

Mr. President and Brothers of the American Railway Union: We struck at Pullman because we were without hope. We joined the American Railway Union because it gave us a glimmer of hope. Twenty thousand souls, men, women, and little ones, have their eyes turned toward this convention today, straining eagerly through dark despondency for a glimmer of the heaven-sent message you alone can give us on this earth.

In stating to this body our grievances it is hard to tell where to begin. You all must know that the proximate cause of our strike was the discharge of two members of our grievance committee the day after George M. Pullman, him-self, and Thomas H. Wickes, his second vice-president, had guaranteed them absolute immunity. The more remote causes are still imminent. Five reduc-tions in wages, in work, and in conditions of employment swept through the shops at Pullman between May and December, 1893. The last was the most severe, amounting to nearly thirty per cent, and our rents had not fallen. We owed Pullman $70,000 when we struck May 11. We owe him twice as much today. He does not evict us for two reasons: One, the force of popular senti-ment and public opinion; the other because he hopes to starve us out, to break through in the back of the American Railway Union, and to deduct from our miserable wages when we are forced to return to him the last dollar we owe him for the occupancy of his houses.

Rents all over the city in every quarter of its vast extent have fallen, in some cases to one-half. Residences, compared with which ours are hovels, can be had a few miles away at the price we have been contributing to make a millionaire a billionaire. What we pay $15 for in Pullman is leased for $8 in Roseland; and remember that just as no man or woman of our 4,000 toilers has ever felt the friendly pressure of George M. Pullman's hand, so no man or woman of us all has ever owned or can ever hope to own one inch of George M. Pullman's land. Why, even the very streets are his. His ground has never been platted of record, and today he may debar any man who has acquiring rights as his tenant from walking in his highways. And those streets; do you know what he has named them? He says after the four great inventors in methods of transportation. And do you know what their names are? Why, Fulton, Stephenson, Watt, and Pullman.

Water which Pullman buys from the city at 8 cents a thousand gallons he retails to us at 500 per cent advance and claims he is losing $400 a month on it. Gas which sells at 75 cents per thousand feet in Hyde Park, just north of us, he sells for $2.25. When we went to tell him our grievances he said we were all his "children."

Pullman, both the man and the town, is an ulcer on the body politic. He owns the houses, the schoolhouses, and churches of God in the town he gave his once humble name. The revenue he derives from these, the wages he pays out with one hand—the Pullman Palace Car Company, he takes back with the other—the Pullman Land Association. He is able by this to bid under any contract car shop in this country. His competitors in business, to meet this, must reduce the wages of their men. This gives him the excuse to reduce ours to conform to the market. His business rivals must in turn scale down; so must he. And thus the merry war—the dance of skeletons bathed in human tears— goes on, and it will go on, brothers, forever, unless you, the American Railway Union, stop it; end it; crush it out.

70. SOCIALIST LABOR PARTY

Declaration of Interdependence
(1895)

Founded in 1877, the **SOCIALIST LABOR PARTY (SLP)** was the first major American political party devoted to socialism. Building on the momentum of the great railroad strike and other expressions of labor unrest, the SLP was an attempt to channel the protest energies of the late nineteenth century in a more radical direction, toward the international socialist revolutions of Europe. As such, the early membership of the SLP—some several thousand strong—was comprised chiefly of working-class European immigrants who had recently come to the United States. The SLP drew its major strength from local roots, in cities such as Philadelphia, Chicago, New York, and St. Louis, where primarily German and Jewish immigrants developed a dynamic culture of socialist newspapers, theaters, and clubs that served as a locus for both ethnic identification and political organizing. Although it began in fits and starts, the SLP was important because it represented an increasingly immigrant, multiethnic, working-class radicalism, and because it served as a bridge between the factions of the nineteenth-century labor movement (the NLU, Knights of Labor, AFL, and Populists) and twentieth-century experiments with socialism and communism (the IWW and CPUSA). One of the major leaders of the SLP was Danial De Leon, whose newspaper, *The People*, emerged as the organ of the SLP during the 1890s. The following "Declaration of Interdependence" was written by De Leon to express the grievances of "free-born men held in wage servitude against natural law and social principles." Published in *The People* on July 4, 1895, it calls his readers to join the "class struggle" led by the Socialist Labor Party.

SOURCE: Philip S. Foner, ed. *We, The Other People: Alternative Declarations of Independence*. Urbana: University of Illinois Press, 1976.

SELECTED READINGS: Seymour Martin Lipset and Gary Marks, *It Didn't Happen Here: Why Socialism Failed in the United States* (2000). Paul Buhle, *Marxism in* *the United States: Remapping the History of the American Left* (1991). Ira Kipnis, *The American Socialist Movement, 1897–1912* (1972). John Laslett, *Labor and the Left: A Study of Socialist and Radical Influences in the American Labor Movement, 1881–1927* (1970).

When, in the course of human progression, the despoiled class of wealth producers becomes fully conscious of its rights and determined to take them, a decent respect to the judgment of posterity requires that it should declare the causes which impel it to change the social order.

More truly can we say of our plutocracy than our forefathers did of the British crown that "its history is one of repeated injuries and usurpations, all having in direct object the establishment of an absolute tyranny over these States." Let the facts speak.

The foundation of the Union was co-eval with the birth of the modern system of production by machinery. No sooner was the Federal Constitution adopted than the spirit of capitalism began to manifest its absorbing tendency and corrupting influence. Every new invention was looked upon, not as a means of promoting the welfare of all, but as an instrument of private profit. Every tract of fertile land belonging to the States was appropriated by individuals, regardless of the rights of future generations. Every public franchise of any value was given away to "enterprising" persons and companies.

Thus was already formed in those early days, a privileged class, whose wealth was derived from the labor of others; this growing monopoly of the means of production and exchange, by placing a steadily increasing number of disinherited workers in its dependence for employment, strengthened its hold upon the public powers, which it used more and more unscrupulously for its own aggrandizement.

Even such a public calamity as war was turned by that selfish and unpatriotic class to its own enrichment. By their labor alone the working people not only provided their own sustenance but supplied the means of supporting armies, recruited from their own ranks. Yet, from the fact that the instruments of production were the private property of individuals, the product itself was also the property of those individuals, who stood between the people and their Government. For that part of the product which was required to carry on the war, the nation, therefore, became indebted to capitalists, who availed themselves of the public needs to exact exorbitant prices, further increased by the depreciation of the currency or of the interest-bearing bonds in which the war supplies were paid for, and which would some day have to be redeemed at par. In other words, during and after a war the capitalist class cost to the country several times as much as the enemy.

So did the promises and purposes of the Revolution immediately prove abortive. While the fundamental law declared that the Union was formed "to establish justice, insure domestic tranquillity, promote the general welfare, and secure the blessings of liberty," free scope was given to an economic system replete with injustice, pregnant with the seeds of domestic strife, destructive of every true element of happiness, and fatally tending to class tyranny.

Under that system men, proclaimed free and equal, were soon made to realize that they were only labor power in human form, to be sold in the market for what it could fetch, and to be consumed in the production of wealth for the exclusive benefit of those who already had wealth.

Under that system the value of a man, and, therefore, his remuneration, were not to be measured by the extent to which his industry and intelligence benefited his fellows. They were to be gauged by the necessities of his competitors on the "labor market"; so that, as the competition increased, the tendency of his wages was constantly downward, until it reached the minimum required to keep alive his flesh and bone machine while it was hired to an employer, who thus became the absolute owner of the net product, or, "surplus value," created by that human machine.

Under that system the toiling masses, hungry and despised, turned the wilderness into a garden, the stones, the clay, the trees into resplendent cities, the ore and the coal into new organs of motion, through which human strength, speed and skill were multiplied a thousandfold, the lightning itself into an obedient messenger; they built factories, ships, docks and warehouses; constructed railroads, bridged rivers and pierced mountains; then descended into their nameless graves, leaving all in the hands of their despoilers, to further oppress and degrade the inheritors of their misery.

Under this system society, so called, became a worse pandemonium than it had ever been. Each looked upon his neighbor as a legitimate prey or a dangerous antagonist. The laborer viewed with dismay the appearance of another laborer, while the employer of both plotted the ruin of a rival employer. And this horrible struggle for life among the weak, for dominion among the powerful, ever more intense as the means of life became greater and as the dominion of Man over Nature grew more extensive, was glorified by sophists as the providential law of human progress!

From this state of anarchy emerged at last the plutocracy of our day. How and at what cost we shall now see.

For a century or more anarchy reigned supreme in all the branches of production. At times, without definite or approximate knowledge of actual conditions, but stimulated by a reckless desire for gain, every "captain of industry" went on "rushing business" to the utmost capacity of his means and credit, until the market was "overstocked"; that is, until he found by the event what he might have learned before by a timely use of common sense, namely:

1. That since, under the wage system the people can only buy back a portion of their product, the profit-making class must depend on it self alone for the consumption of the remainder.

2. That in so far, then, as the overproduction, so called, consists of such necessaries as the wage-earning masses require, it must either be sold at a great sacrifice or remain in store until the workers engaged in the production of things exclusively used by the said profit-making class can gradually absorb it.

3. That in the meantime the production of necessaries must stop and the adventurous "captains" who have incurred obligations beyond their means are necessarily bankrupted.

4. That a large number of the very people who purchase those necessaries from retailers are consequently thrown out of employment, and that the current stock of those traders is thereby converted into an overstock, with the inevitable result of widespread failure, reaching at last the industries affected to the production of capitalist commodities.

And then must the strange spectacle be afforded, of a whole people—with the exception of a few drones for whom the sun of prosperity never sets—reduced to the utmost destitution in the midst of the plenty of their own creation; men, women and children starving, apparently, because there is too much wheat and meat; ragged and shoeless, apparently because there is too much clothing and footwear; idle, and therefore miserable, actually because there stands between them and the idle machine, as also between them and busy Nature, a paper wall of private ownership, stamped "Sacred" by the hand of Imposture.

At such times those social functions only which have escaped individual covetousness—those public services like the postoffice, education, and other departments of national, State and municipal administration which have remained socialized—are entirely free from the general paralysis, in so far at least as their working force is involved. And although tainted with the corruption that capitalism imparts to government, they shine in the night of economic chaos as vivid illustrations of individual security and public benefit in social co-operation. By the contrast of their normal activity with the intermittent palsy of all the capitalized organs of the social body, they plainly show that individual suffering is the natural punishment inflicted upon men for their disregard of the fundamental law of social existence—the law of interdependence—or solidarity.

Every such crisis reduced the number of capitalistic combatants and left the survivors stronger than formerly. It also left the wage-workers weaker in proportion. . . .

But throughout the civilized world the wage workers are asserting their interdependence—the natural dependence of every man upon his fellows, of every nation upon all other nations; and under the banner of International

Socialism millions of them are now marching to the conquest of the public powers.

They recognize that the social body is an organism, and, as such, is subject in its life, health and development to the general law which governs organic nature; that the more highly it is developed, the more interdependent are all its members; that the very extent of this mutual dependence of parts determines the amount of freedom and the degree of perfection with which they respectively perform their natural functions, ever so diverse, yet all tending usefully and harmoniously to the common end.

They realize also that the capitalist is no more a legitimate member of the social organism than a parasite in the human body is a necessary part of the organ upon which it feeds, and upon the proper working of which all the other organs depend for support and vigor. And they are determined to expel him.

The class struggle has reached its climax. With the triumph of the united toilers over their combined despoilers will end class privilege and class rule.

Americans, fall into line! Onward to the Co-operative Commonwealth!

To the industrious the tools of industry; to the laborer the fruits of his labor; to mankind the earth!

71. WILLIAM JENNINGS BRYAN

Cross of Gold Speech
(1896)

WILLIAM JENNINGS BRYAN (1860–1925) was a Democratic Party leader whose advocacy of silver coinage and opposition to U.S. imperialism earned him a strong reputation among radicals and reformers. Born in Salem, Illinois, he was an exceptional student who rose to prominence as a young lawyer and politician after he moved with his wife to Lincoln, Nebraska. Bryan arrived in Nebraska at the same time the Populist Party was emerging. Sympathetic to the agrarian revolt, he went after Populist support—first in 1890 and 1892, during successful runs for Congress, and then again in 1896, when he ran against Republican William McKinley for president. Despite losing to McKinley, Bryan's informal campaign style earned the nickname "the Great Commoner"; he traveled eighteen thousand miles during the campaign, giving more than six hundred speeches calling for sweeping political and economic reforms, including the free coinage of silver to help protect farmers and other small producers from inflation and debt. An astute thinker and organizer, Bryan's political influence was chiefly derived from his skill as an orator. In 1896, he electrified the delegates at the Democratic convention with his "Cross of Gold" speech. Humbly claiming that he "put into words the sentiments of a majority of delegates," Bryan's rousing opposition to the gold standard secured for him the presidential nomination, and suggested just how deeply the Populists had influenced American political culture during an age of great economic uncertainty and transformation.

SOURCE: George Brown Tindall, ed. *A Populist Reader: Selections from the Works of American Populist Leaders.* Gloucester, MA: Peter Smith, 1976.

SELECTED READINGS: Leroy Ashby, *William Jennings Bryan: Champion of Democracy* (1987). Robert W. Cherny, *A Righteous Cause: The Life of William Jennings Bryan* (1985). Louis W. Koening, *Bryan: A Political Biography* (1971).

Mr. Chairman and Gentlemen of the Convention: I would be presumptuous, indeed, to present myself against the distinguished gentlemen to whom you have listened if this were a mere measuring of abilities; but this is not a contest between persons. The humblest citizen in all the land, when clad in the armor of a righteous cause, is stronger than all the hosts of error. I come to speak to you in defense of a cause as holy as the cause of liberty—the cause of humanity.

When this debate is concluded, a motion will be made to lay upon the table the resolution offered in commendation of the administration, and also the resolution offered in condemnation of the administration. We object to bringing this question down to the level of persons. The individual is but an atom; he is born, he acts, he dies; but principles are eternal; and this has been a contest over a principle.

Never before in the history of this country has there been witnessed such a contest as that through which we have just passed. Never before in the history of American politics has a great issue been fought out as this issue has been, by the voters of a great party. On the fourth of March, 1895, a few Democrats, most of them members of Congress, issued an address to the Democrats of the nation, asserting that the money question was the paramount issue of the hour; declaring that a majority of the Democratic party had the right to control the action of the party on this paramount issue; and concluding with the request that the believers in the free coinage of silver in the Democratic party should organize, take charge of, and control the policy of the Democratic party. Three months later, at Memphis, an organization was perfected, and the silver Democrats went forth openly and courageously proclaiming their belief, and declaring that, if successful, they would crystallize into a platform the declaration which they had made. Then began the conflict. With a zeal approaching the zeal which inspired the crusaders who followed Peter the Hermit, our silver Democrats went forth from victory unto victory until they are now assembled, not to discuss, not to debate, but to enter up the judgment already rendered by the plain people of this country. In this contest brother has been arrayed against brother, father against son. The warmest ties of love, acquaintance and association have been disregarded; old leaders have been cast aside when they have refused to give expression to the sentiments of those whom they would lead, and new leaders have sprung up to give direction to this cause of truth. Thus has the contest been waged, and we have assembled here under as binding and solemn instructions as were ever imposed upon representatives of the people. . . .

We say to you that you have made the definition of a business man too limited in its application. The man who is employed for wages is as much a business man as his employer; the attorney in a country town is as much a business man as the corporation counsel in a great metropolis; the merchant at the cross-roads store is as much a business man as the merchant of New York; the farmer who goes forth in the morning and toils all day—who begins in the spring and toils all summer—and who by the application of brain and muscle to the natural resources of the country creates wealth, is as much a business man as the man who goes upon the board of trade and bets upon the price of grain; the miners who go down a thousand feet into the earth, or climb two thousand feet upon the cliffs, and bring forth from their hiding places the precious metals to be poured into the channels of trade are as much business men as the few financial magnates who, in a back room, corner the money of the world. We come to speak for this broader class of business men. . . .

And now, my friends, let me come to the paramount issue. If they ask us why it is that we say more on the money question than we say upon the tariff question, I reply that, if protection has slain its thousands, the gold standard has slain its tens of thousands. If they ask us why we do not embody in our platform all the things that we believe in, we reply that when we have restored the money of the Constitution all other necessary reforms will be possible; but that until this is done there is no other reform that can be accomplished. . . .

We go forth confident that we shall win. Why? Because upon the paramount issue of this campaign there is not a spot of ground upon which the enemy will dare to challenge battle. If they tell us that the gold standard is a good thing, we shall point to their platform and tell them that their platform pledges the party to get rid of the gold standard and substitute bimetallism. If the gold standard is a good thing, why try to get rid of it? I call your attention to the fact that some of the very people who are in this convention today and who tell us that we ought to declare in favor of international bimetallism—thereby declaring that the gold standard is wrong and that the principle of bimetallism is better—these very people four months ago were open and avowed advocates of the gold standard, and were then telling us that we could not legislate two metals together, even with the aid of all the world. If the gold standard is a good thing, we ought to declare in favor of its retention and not in favor of abandoning it; and if the gold standard is a bad thing why should we wait until other nations are willing to help us to let go? Here is the line of battle, and we care not upon which issue they force the fight; we are prepared to meet them on either issue or on both. If they tell us that the gold standard is the standard of civilization, we reply to them that this, the most enlightened of all the nations of the earth, has never declared for a gold standard and that both the great parties this year are declaring against it. If the gold standard is the standard of civilization, why, my friends, should we not have it? If they come to meet us on that issue we can present the history of our nation. More than that; we can tell them that they will search the pages of history in vain to find a single instance where the common people of any land have ever declared themselves in favor of the gold standard. They can find where the holders of fixed investments have declared for a gold standard, but not where the masses have.

Mr. Carlisle said in 1878 that this was a struggle between "the idle holders of idle capital" and "the struggling masses, who produce the wealth and pay the taxes of the country;" and, my friends, the question we are to decide is: Upon which side will the Democratic party fight; upon the side of "the idle holders of idle capital" or upon the side of "the struggling masses?" That is the question which the party must answer first, and then it must be answered by each individual hereafter. The sympathies of the Democratic party, as shown by the platform, are on the side of the struggling masses who have ever been the foundation of the Democratic party. There are two ideas of government. There are those who believe that, if you will only legislate to make the well-to-do prosperous, their prosperity will leak through on those below. The Democratic idea, however, has been that if you legislate to make the masses prosperous, their prosperity will find its way up through every class which rests upon them.

You come to us and tell us that the great cities are in favor of the gold standard; we reply that the great cities rest upon our broad and fertile prairies. Burn down your cities and leave our farms, and your cities will spring up again as if by magic; but destroy our farms and the grass will grow in the streets of every city in the country.

My friends, we declare that this nation is able to legislate for its own people on every question, without waiting for the aid or consent of any other nation on earth; and upon that issue we expect to carry every State in the Union. I shall not slander the inhabitants of the fair State of Massachusetts nor the inhabitants of the State of New York by saying that, when they are confronted with the proposition, they will declare that this nation is not able to attend to its own business. It is the issue of 1776 over again. Our ancestors, when but three millions in number, had the courage to declare their political independence of every other nation; shall we, their descendants, when we have grown to seventy millions, declare that we are less independent than our forefathers? No, my friends, that will never be the verdict of our people. Therefore, we care not upon what lines the battle is fought. If they say bimetallism is good, but that we cannot have it until other nations help us, we reply that, instead of having a gold standard because England has, we will restore bimetallism, and then let England have bimetallism because the United States has it. If they dare to come out in the open field and defend the gold standard as a good thing, we will fight them to the uttermost. Having behind us the producing masses of this nation and the world, supported by the commercial interests, the laboring interests, and the toilers everywhere, we will answer their demand for a gold standard by saying to them: You shall not press down upon the brow of labor this crown of thorns, you shall not crucify mankind upon a cross of gold.

72. BLACK ELK

Black Elk Speaks
(1932)

Published in 1932, *Black Elk Speaks* is the spiritual autobiography of **BLACK ELK (1863–1950)**, the visionary holy man of the Oglala Sioux. Told through his son, Ben Black Elk, to the poet John G. Neihardt, Black Elk's personal narrative is also the story of the triumphs and trials of his people during the final decades of the nineteenth century. Black Elk was born on the Little Powder River (present-day Wyoming) and raised among the Oglala Lakota in the territory west of the Black Hills, just as white settlers began taking over the area in the 1860s. At the age of nine, Black Elk had a great vision of conflict and healing that later earned him the respected role of holy man. After the U.S. government seized their land in 1876, the Oglala moved to the Great Sioux Reservation in present-day South Dakota, shortly after which Black Elk performed his vision in a horse dance. After several years of travelling outside of the reservation and of the United States, Black Elk returned to South Dakota in 1889 to assist the Oglala in the Ghost Dance—their epic struggle against the "Wasichus" (whites) to regain the land and culture they had lost during the "settlement" of the West—which ended tragically at the Battle of Wounded Knee in 1890. In 1930, John G. Neihardt, Nebraska's poet laureate, went to the Pine Ridge Reservation to visit Black Elk, who ultimately entrusted him to record and publish the story of his Great Vision, of the Ghost Dance, and of Wounded Knee. What emerged was a sympathetic portrait of a complex man who led the Oglala Sioux resistance at Wounded Knee, one of the final acts of American genocide against its native peoples.

SOURCE: Black Elk. *Black Elk Speaks: Being the Life Story of a Holy Man of the Oglala Sioux, as told to by John G. Neihardt.* New York: MJF Books, 1972.

SELECTED READINGS: Hilda Neihardt, *Black Elk and Flaming Rainbow* (1995). Clyde Holler, *Black Elk's Religion: The Sun Dance and Lakota Catholicism* (1995). Michael F. Steltenkamp, *Black Elk: Holy Man of the Oglala* (1993).

After the soldiers marched away, Red Crow and I started back toward Pine Ridge together, and I took the little baby that I told you about. Red Crow had one too.

We were going back to Pine Ridge, because we thought there was peace back home; but it was not so. While we were gone, there was a fight around the Agency, and our people had all gone away. They had gone away so fast that they left all the tepees standing.

It was nearly dark when we passed north of Pine Ridge where the hospital is now, and some soldiers shot at us, but did not hit us. We rode into the camp, and it was all empty. We were very hungry because we had not eaten anything since early morning, so we peeped into the tepees until we saw where there was a pot with papa (dried meat) cooked in it. We sat down in there and began to eat. While we were doing this, the soldiers shot at the tepee, and a bullet struck right between Red Crow and me. It threw dust in the soup, but we kept right on eating until we had our fill. Then we took the babies and got on our horses and rode away. If that bullet had only killed me, then I could have died with papa in my mouth.

The people had fled down Clay Creek, and we followed their trail. It was dark now, and late in the night we came to where they were camped without any tepees. They were just sitting by little fires, and the snow was beginning to blow. We rode in among them and I heard my mother's voice. She was singing a death song for me, because she felt sure I had died over there. She was so glad to see me that she cried and cried.

Women who had milk fed the little babies that Red Crow and I brought with us.

I think nobody but the little children slept any that night. The snow blew and we had no tepees.

When it was getting light, a war party went out and I went along; but this time I took a gun with me. When I started out the day before to Wounded Knee, I took only my sacred bow, which was not made to shoot with; because I was a little in doubt about the Wanekia religion at that time, and I did not really want to kill anybody because of it.

But I did not feel like that any more. After what I had seen over there, I wanted revenge; I wanted to kill.

We crossed White Clay Creek and followed it up, keeping on the west side. Soon we could hear many guns going off. So we struck west, following a ridge to where the fight was. It was close to the Mission, and there are many bullets in the Mission yet.

From this ridge we could see that the Lakotas were on both sides of the creek and were shooting at soldiers who were coming down the creek. As we looked down, we saw a little ravine, and across this was a big hill. We crossed and rode up the hillside.

They were fighting right there, and a Lakota cried to me: "Black Elk, this is the kind of a day in which to do something great!" I answered: "How!"

Then I got off my horse and rubbed earth on myself, to show the Powers that I was nothing without their help. Then I took my rifle, got on my horse and galloped up to the top of the hill. Right below me the soldiers were shooting, and my people called out to me not to go down there; that there were some good shots among the soldiers and I should get killed for nothing.

But I remembered my great vision, the part where the geese of the north appeared. I depended upon their power. Stretching out my arms with my gun in the right hand, like a goose soaring when it flies low to turn in a change of weather, I made the sound the geese make—br-r-r-p, br-r-r-p, br-r-r-p; and, doing this, I charged. The soldiers saw, and began shooting fast at me. I kept right on with my buckskin running, shot in their faces when I was near, then swung wide and rode back up the hill.

All this time the bullets were buzzing around me and I was not touched. I was not even afraid. It was like being in a dream about shooting. But just as I had reached the very top of the hill, suddenly it was like waking up, and I was afraid. I dropped my arms and quit making the goose cry. Just as I did this, I felt something strike my belt as though some one had hit me there with the back of an ax. I nearly fell out of my saddle, but I managed to hold on, and rode over the hill.

An old man by the name of Protector was there, and he ran up and held me, for now I was falling off my horse. I will show you where the bullet struck me sidewise across the belly here (showing a long deep scar on the abdomen). My insides were coming out. Protector tore up a blanket in strips and bound it around me so that my insides would stay in. By now I was crazy to kill, and I said to Protector: "Help me on my horse! Let me go over there. It is a good day to die, so I will go over there!" But Protector said: "No, young nephew! You must not die to-day. That would be foolish. Your people need you. There may be a better day to die." He lifted me into my saddle and led my horse away down hill. Then I began to feel very sick.

By now it looked as though the soldiers would be wiped out, and the Lakotas were fighting harder; but I heard that, after I left, the black Wasichu soldiers came, and the Lakotas had to retreat.

There were many of our children in the Mission, and the sisters and priests were taking care of them. I heard there were sisters and priests right in the battle helping wounded people and praying.

There was a man by the name of Little Soldier who took charge of me and brought me to where our people were camped. While we were over at the Mission Fight, they had fled to the O-ona-gazhee and were camped on top of it where the women and children would be safe from soldiers. Old Hollow Horn was there. He was a very powerful bear medicine man, and he came over to heal my wound. In three days I could walk, but I kept a piece of blanket tied around my belly.

It was now nearly the middle of the Moon of Frost in the Tepee (January). We heard that soldiers were on Smoky Earth River and were coming to attack us in the O-ona-gazhee. They were near Black Feather's place. So a party of about sixty of us started on the war-path to find them. My mother tried to keep me at home, because, although I could walk and ride a horse, my wound was not all healed yet. But I would not stay; for, after what I had seen at Wounded Knee, I wanted a chance to kill soldiers.

We rode down Grass Creek to Smoky Earth, and crossed, riding down stream. Soon from the top of a little hill we saw wagons and cavalry guarding them. The soldiers were making a corral of their wagons and getting ready to fight. We got off our horses and went behind some hills to a little knoll, where we crept up to look at the camp. Some soldiers were bringing harnessed horses down to a little creek to water, and I said to the others: "If you will stay here and shoot at the soldiers, I will charge over there and get some good horses." They knew of my power, so they did this, and I charged on my buckskin while the others kept shooting. I got seven of the horses; but when I started back with these, all the soldiers saw me and began shooting. They killed two of my horses, but I brought five back safe and was not hit. When I was out of range, I caught up a fine bald-faced bay and turned my buckskin loose. Then I drove the others back to our party.

By now more cavalry were coming up the river, a big bunch of them, and there was some hard fighting for a while, because there were not enough of us. We were fighting and retreating, and all at once I saw Red Willow on foot running. He called to me: "Cousin, my horse is killed!" So I caught up a soldier's horse that was dragging a rope and brought it to Red Willow while the soldiers were shooting fast at me. Just then, for a little while, I was a wanekia myself. In this fight Long Bear and another man, whose name I have forgotten, were badly wounded; but we saved them and carried them along with us. The soldiers did not follow us far into the Badlands, and when it was night we rode back with our wounded to the O-ona-gazhee.

We wanted a much bigger war-party so that we could meet the soldiers and get revenge. But this was hard, because the people were not all of the same mind, and they were hungry and cold. We had a meeting there, and were all ready to go out with more warriors, when Afraid-of-His-Horses came over from Pine Ridge to make peace with Red Cloud, who was with us there.

Our party wanted to go out and fight anyway, but Red Cloud made a speech to us something like this: "Brothers, this is a very hard winter. The women and children are starving and freezing. If this were summer, I would say to keep on fighting to the end. But we cannot do this. We must think of the women and children and that it is very bad for them. So we must make peace, and I will see that nobody is hurt by the soldiers."

The people agreed to this, for it was true. So we broke camp next day and went down from the O-ona-gazhee to Pine Ridge, and many, many Lakotas were already there. Also, there were many, many soldiers. They stood in two lines with their guns held in front of them as we went through to where we camped.

And so it was all over.

I did not know then how much was ended. When I look back now from this high hill of my old age, I can still see the butchered women and children lying heaped and scattered all along the crooked gulch as plain as when I saw them with eyes still young. And I can see that something else died there in the bloody mud, and was buried in the blizzard. A people's dream died there. It was a beautiful dream.

And I, to whom so great a vision was given in my youth,—you see me now a pitiful old man who has done nothing, for the nation's hoop is broken and scattered. There is no center any longer, and the sacred tree is dead.

CHAPTER SIX

Anarchism, Socialism, and Communism

73. UPTON SINCLAIR

The Jungle
(1905)

Among the most celebrated accomplishment of muckraking journalism in the early twentieth century was **UPTON SINCLAIR**'s *The Jungle*, which began appearing serially in the socialist weekly *Appeal to Reason* in early 1905. Sinclair (1878–1968) attended the College of the City of New York and Columbia University, and spent much of his life gravitating in and out of the American Socialist Party. Over the course of his career, he published more than eighty books, many of which helped to lay the groundwork for social and industrial reforms. Although Sinclair won the 1943 Pulitzer Prize in fiction for the novel *Dragon's Teeth*, he is best known for *The Jungle*, a sociological "novel" that exposed the grotesque conditions in Chicago stockyards and led to the passage of federal food inspection laws. Sinclair, however, was disappointed with the book's reception. Dedicated "To the Workingmen of America," *The Jungle* was intended to be a critique of the new industrial order, and was only secondarily about the unsanitary conditions in Chicago stockyards. Wrote Sinclair, "I aimed at the public's heart, and by accident I hit it in the stomach."

SOURCE: Upton Sinclair. *The Jungle*. New York: Doubleday, 1906.

SELECTED READINGS: Leon Harris, *Upton Sinclair, American Rebel* (1975). Upton Sinclair, *Autobiography* (1962).

Jurgis heard of these things little by little, in the gossip of those who were obliged to perpetrate them. It seemed as if every time you met a person from a new department, you heard of new swindles and new crimes. There was, for instance, a Lithuanian who was a cattle butcher for the plant where Marija had worked, which killed meat for canning only; and to hear this man describe the animals which came to his place would have been worth while for a Dante or a Zola. It seemed that they must have agencies all over the country, to hunt out old and crippled and diseased cattle to be canned. There were cattle which had been fed on "whisky-malt," the refuse of the breweries, and had become what the men called "steerly"—which means covered with boils. It was a nasty job killing these, for when you plunged your knife into them they would burst and splash foul-smelling stuff into your face; and when a man's sleeves were smeared with blood, and his hands steeped in it, how was he ever to wipe his face, or to clear his eyes so that he could see? It was stuff such as this that made the "embalmed beef" that had killed several times as many United States soldiers as all the bullets of the Spaniards; only the army beef, besides, was not fresh canned, it was old stuff that had been lying for years in the cellars.

Then one Sunday evening, Jurgis sat puffing his pipe by the kitchen stove, and talking with an old fellow whom Jonas had introduced, and who worked in the canning rooms at Durham's; and so Jurgis learned a few things about the great and only Durham canned goods, which had become a national institution. They were regular alchemists at Durham's; they advertised a mushroom-catsup, and the men who made it did not know what a mushroom looked like. They advertised "potted chicken,"—and it was like the boardinghouse soup of the comic papers, through which a chicken had walked with rubbers on. Perhaps they had a secret process for making chickens chemically—who knows? said Jurgis' friend; the things that went into the mixture were tripe, and the fat of pork, and beef suet, and hearts of beef, and finally the waste ends of veal, when they had any. They put these up in several grades, and sold them at several prices; but the contents of the cans all came out of the same hopper. And then there was "potted game" and "potted grouse," "potted ham," and "deviled ham"—de-vyled, as the men called it. "De-vyled" ham was made out of the waste ends of smoked beef that were too small to be sliced by the machines; and also tripe, dyed with chemicals so that it would not show white; and trimmings of hams and corned beef; and potatoes, skins and all; and finally the hard cartilaginous gullets of beef, after the tongues had been cut out. All this ingenious mixture was ground up and flavored with spices to make it taste like something. Anybody who could invent a new imitation had been sure of a fortune from old Durham, said Jurgis' informant; but it was hard to think of anything new in a place where so many sharp wits had been at work for so long; where men welcomed tuberculosis in the cattle they were feeding, because it made them fatten more quickly; and where they bought up all the old rancid butter left over in the grocery stores of a continent, and "oxidized" it by a forced-air process, to take away the odor, rechurned it with skim milk, and sold it in bricks in the cities! Up to a year or two ago it had been the custom to kill horses in the yards—ostensibly for fertilizer; but after long agitation the newspapers had been able to make the public realize that the horses were being canned. Now it was against the law to kill horses in Packingtown, and the law was really complied with—for the present, at any rate. Any day, however, one might see sharp-horned and shaggy-haired creatures running with the sheep—and yet what a job you would have to get the public to believe that a good part of what it buys for lamb and mutton is really goat's flesh!

There was another interesting set of statistics that a person might have gathered in Packingtown—those of the various afflictions of the workers. When Jurgis had first inspected the packing plants with Szedvilas, he had marveled while he listened to the tale of all the things that were made out of the carcasses of animals, and of all the lesser industries that were maintained there; now he found that each one of these lesser industries was a separate little inferno, in its way as horrible as the killing beds, the source and fountain of them all. The workers in each of them had their own peculiar diseases. And the wandering visitor might be skeptical about all the swindles, but he could not be skeptical about these, for the worker bore the evidence of them about on his own person—generally he had only to hold out his hand.

There were the men in the pickle rooms, for instance, where old Antanas had gotten his death; scarce a one of these that had not some spot of horror on his person. Let a man so much as scrape his finger pushing a truck in the pickle rooms, and he might have a sore that would put him out of the world; all the joints in his fingers might be eaten by the acid, one by one. Of the butchers and floorsmen, the beef-boners and trimmers, and all those who used knives, you could scarcely find a person who had the use of his thumb; time and time again the base of it had been slashed, till it was a mere lump of flesh against which the man pressed the knife to hold it. The hands of these men would be criss-crossed with cuts, until you could no longer pretend to count them or to trace them. They would have no nails,—they had worn them off pulling hides; their knuckles were swollen so that their fingers spread out like a fan. There were men who worked in the cooking rooms, in the midst of steam and sickening odors, by artificial light; in these rooms the germs of tuberculosis might live for two years, but the supply was renewed every hour. There were the beef-luggers, who carried two-hundred-pound quarters into the refrigerator-cars; a fearful kind of work, that began at four o'clock in the morning, and that wore out the most powerful men in a few years. There were those who worked in the chilling rooms, and whose special disease was rheumatism; the time limit that a man could work in the chilling rooms was said to be five years. There were the wool-pluckers, whose hands went to pieces even sooner than the hands of the pickle men; for the pelts of the sheep had to be painted with acid to loosen the wool, and then the pluckers had to pull out this wool with their bare hands, till the acid had eaten their fingers off. There were those who made the tins for the canned meat; and their hands, too, were a maze of cuts, and each cut represented a chance for blood poisoning. Some worked at the stamping machines, and it was very seldom that one could work long there at the pace that was set, and not give out and forget himself, and have a part of his hand chopped off. There were the "hoisters," as they were called, whose task it was to press the lever which lifted the dead cattle off the floor. They ran along upon a rafter, peering down through the damp and the steam; and as old Durham's architects had not built the killing room for the convenience of the hoisters, at every few feet they would have to stoop under a beam, say four feet above the one they ran on; which got them into the habit of stooping, so that in a few years they would be walking like chimpanzees. Worst of any, however, were the fertilizer men, and those who served in the cooking rooms. These people could not be shown to the visitor,—for the odor of a fertilizer man would scare any ordinary visitor at a hundred yards, and as for the other men, who worked in tank rooms full of steam, and in some of which there were open vats near the level of the floor, their peculiar trouble was that they fell into the vats; and when they were fished out, there was never enough of them left to be worth exhibiting,—sometimes they would be overlooked for days, till all but the bones of them had gone out to the world as Durham's Pure Leaf Lard!

74. THE INDUSTRIAL WORKERS OF THE WORLD

Manifesto and Preamble
(1905 and 1908)

The best statements of the ideology of the **INDUSTRIAL WORKERS OF THE WORLD (IWW)** are to be found in the organization's 1905 Manifesto, and in the preamble to the IWW constitution, as amended in 1908. Founded by socialists and trade unionists in Chicago in 1905, the IWW united skilled and unskilled workers—including immigrants, non-whites and women—in a common struggle against capitalism. "Wobblies," as IWW members were nicknamed, were known for their dramatic language and their revolutionary commitment to total class warfare, which involved such tactics as direct action, propaganda, boycotts, and strikes. Before World War I, the organization was involved in at least 150 strikes. As a result of their labor activities and their antimilitarism during World War I, the IWW faced extreme federal and state suppression, and many of its leaders and members were jailed. The group also lost members to sectarian conflict and the appeal of the Communist Party. Whereas the IWW had some thirty thousand members in 1912, there were only ten thousand in 1930. However, many of their tactics have since become commonplace in the American labor movement.

SOURCES: Joyce L. Kornbluh, ed. *Rebel Voices: An IWW Anthology*. Rev. ed. Chicago: Charles H. Kerr, 1988.

SELECTED READINGS: Howard Kimeldorf, *Battling for American Labor: Wobblies, Craft, Workers, and the Making of the Union Movement* (1999). Melvyn Dubofsky, *We Shall Be All: A History of the Industrial Workers of the World* (1988). Steward Bird, Dan Georgakas, and Deborah Shaffer, comps., *Solidarity Forever: An Oral History of the IWW* (1985).

Manifesto

Social relations and groupings only reflect mechanical and industrial conditions. The *great facts* of present industry are the displacement of human skill by machines and the increase of capitalist power through concentration in the possession of the tools with which wealth is produced and distributed.

Because of these facts trade divisions among laborers and competition among capitalists are alike disappearing. Class divisions grow ever more fixed and class antagonisms more sharp. Trade lines have been swallowed up in a common servitude of all workers to the machines which they tend. New machines, ever replacing less productive ones, wipe out whole trades and plunge new bodies of workers into the ever-growing army of tradeless, hopeless unemployed. As human beings and human skill are displaced by mechanical progress, the capitalists need use the workers only during that brief period when muscles and nerves respond most intensely. The moment the laborer no longer yields the maximum of profits, he is thrown upon the scrap pile, to starve alongside the discarded machine. A *dead line* has been drawn, and an age-limit established, to cross which, in this world of monopolized opportunities, means condemnation to industrial death.

The worker, wholly separated from the land and the tools, with his skill of craftsmenship rendered useless, is sunk in the uniform mass of wage slaves. He sees his power of resistance broken by craft divisions, perpetuated from outgrown industrial stages. His wages constantly grow less as his hours grow longer and monopolized prices grow higher. Shifted hither and thither by the demands of profit-takers the laborer's home no longer exists. In this helpless condition he is forced to accept whatever humiliating conditions his master may impose. He is submitted to a physical and intellectual examination more searching than was the chattel slave when sold from the auction block. Laborers are no longer classified by differences in trade skill, but the employer assigns them according to the machines to which they are attached. These divisions, far from representing differences in skill or interests among the laborers, are imposed by the employers that workers may be pitted against one another and spurred to greater exertion in the shop, and that all resistance to capitalist tyranny may be weakened by artificial distinctions.

While encouraging these outgrown divisions among the workers the capitalists carefully adjust themselves to the new conditions. They wipe out all differences among themselves and present a united front in their war upon labor. Through employers' associations, they seek to crush, with brutal force, by the injunctions of the judiciary, and the use of military power, all efforts at resistance. Or when the other policy seems more profitable, they conceal their daggers beneath the Civic Federation and hoodwink and betray those whom they would rule and exploit. Both methods depend for success upon the blindness and internal dissensions of the working class. The employers' line of battle and methods of warfare correspond to the solidarity of the mechanical and industrial concentration, while laborers still form their fighting organizations on lines of long-gone trade divisions. The battles of the past emphasize this lesson. The *textile* workers of Lowell, Philadelphia and Fall River; the *butchers* of Chicago, weakened by the disintegrating effects of trade divisions; the *machinists* on the Santa Fe, unsupported by their fellow-workers subject to the same masters; the long-struggling *miners* of Colorado, hampered by lack of unity and solidarity upon the industrial battle-field, all bear witness to the helplessness and impotency of labor as at present organized.

This worn-out and corrupt system offers no promise of improvement and adaptation. There is no silver lining to the clouds of darkness and despair settling down upon the world of labor.

This system offers only a perpetual struggle for slight relief within wage slavery. It is blind to the possibility of establishing an industrial democracy, wherein there shall be no wage slavery, but where the workers will own the tools which they operate, and the product of which they alone will enjoy.

It shatters the ranks of the workers into fragments, rendering them helpless and impotent on the industrial battle-field. . . .

A movement to fulfill these conditions must consist of one great industrial union embracing all industries,—providing for craft autonomy locally, industrial autonomy internationally, and working class unity generally.

It must be founded on the class struggle, and its general administration must be conducted in harmony with the recognition of the irrepressible conflict between the capitalist class and the working class.

It should be established as the economic organization of the working class, without affiliation with any political party.

All power should rest in a collective membership.

Preamble of the Industrial Workers of the World

The working class and the employing class have nothing in common. There can be no peace so long as hunger and want are found among millions of working people and the few, who make up the employing class, have all the good things of life.

Between these two classes a struggle must go on until the workers of the world organize as a class, take possession of the earth and the machinery of production, and abolish the wage system.

We find that the centering of management of the industries into fewer and fewer hands makes the trade unions unable to cope with the ever growing power of the employing class. The trade unions foster a state of affairs which allows one set of workers to be pitted against another set of workers in the same industry, thereby helping defeat one another in wage wars. Moreover, the trade unions aid the employing class to mislead the workers into the belief that the working class have interests in common with their employers.

These conditions can be changed and the interest of the working class upheld only by an organization formed in such a way that all its members in any one industry, or in all industries if necessary, cease work whenever a strike or lockout is on in any department thereof, thus making an injury to one an injury to all.

Instead of the conservative motto, "A fair day's wage for a fair day's work," we must inscribe on our banner the revolutionary watchword, "Abolition of the wage system."

It is the historic mission of the working class to do away with capitalism. The army of production must be organized, not only for the every-day struggle with capitalists, but also to carry on production when capitalism shall have been overthrown. By organizing industrially we are forming the structure of the new society within the shell of the old.

75. WILLIAM D. "BIG BILL" HAYWOOD

The General Strike

(1911)

WILLIAM D. HAYWOOD's pamphlet "The General Strike" promoted strikes as a means for workers to gain redress for their economic grievances. Haywood (1869–1928) was born in Salt Lake City, Utah, and rose to become one of the most storied labor leaders in U.S. history. In 1905, Haywood participated in the founding of the Industrial Workers of the World (IWW), and in a famous 1907 trial, he was acquitted of the 1906 bombing murder of former Idaho Governor Steunenberg. A lively orator, it was once remarked that Haywood "could make himself understood by a crowd that did not know a word he said, merely by waving his arms and shouting." After the United States entered World War I, Haywood was arrested and convicted of sedition. While out on bail, he fled to the Soviet Union, and died in Moscow in 1928. His pamphlet "The General Strike" was based on a March 16, 1911, speech he gave in New York City. Haywood argued that a *general strike* involving all of the workers of a particular industry, region, or nation, could be an effective revolutionary weapon capable of ending capitalism.

SOURCE: Joyce L. Kornbluh, ed. *Rebel Voices: An IWW Anthology.* Rev. ed. Chicago: Charles H. Kerr, 1988.

SELECTED READINGS: Melvyn Dubofsky, *"Big Bill" Haywood* (1987). Ralph Chaplin, *The General Strike* (1982). Joseph R. Conlin, *Big Bill Haywood and the Radical Labor Movement* (1969).

I came to-night to speak to you on the general strike. And this night, of all the nights in the year, is a fitting time. Forty years ago to-day there began the greatest general strike known in modern history, the French Commune; a strike that required the political powers of two nations to subdue, namely, that of France and the iron hand of a Bismarck government of Germany. That the workers would have won that strike had it not been for the copartnership of the two nations, there is to my mind no question. They would have overcome the divisions of opinion among themselves. They would have re-established the great national workshops that existed in Paris and throughout France in 1848. The world would have been on the highway toward an industrial democracy, had it not been for the murderous compact between Bismarck and the government of Versailles.

There are vote-getters and politicians who waste their time coming into a community where 90 per cent of the men have no vote, where the women are disfranchised 100 per cent and where the boys and girls under age, of course, are not enfranchised. Still they will speak to these people about the power of the ballot, and they never mention a thing about the power of the general strike. They seem to lack the foresight, the penetration to interpret political power. They seem to lack the understanding that the broadest interpretation of political power comes through the industrial organization; that the industrial organization is capable not only of the general strike, but prevents the capitalists from disfranchising the worker; it gives the vote to women, it reenfranchises the black man and places the ballot in the hands of every boy and girl employed in a shop, makes them eligible to take part in the general strike, makes them eligible to legislate for themselves where they are most interested in changing conditions, namely, in the place where they work.

I am sorry sometimes that I am not a better theorist, but as all theory comes from practice you will have observed, before I proceed very long, that I know something about the general strikes in operation. . . .

There are three phases of a general strike. They are:

A general strike in an industry;

A general strike in a community;

A general national strike.

The conditions for any of the three have never existed. So how any one can take the position that a general strike would not be effective and not be a good thing for the working class is more than I can understand. We know that the capitalist uses the general strike to good advantage. Here is the position that we find the working class and the capitalists in. The capitalists have wealth; they have money. They invest the money in machinery, in the resources of the earth. They operate a factory, a mine, a railroad, a mill. They will keep that factory running just as long as there are profits coming in. When anything happens to disturb the profits, what do the capitalists do? They go on strike, don't they? They withdraw their finances from that particular mill. They close it down because there are no profits to be made there. They don't care what becomes of the working class. But the working class, on the other hand, has always been taught to take care of the capitalist's interest in the property. You don't look after your own interest, your labor power, realizing that without a certain amount of provision you can't reproduce it. You are always looking after the interest of the capitalist, while a general strike would displace his interest and would put you in possession of it.

That is what I want to urge upon the working class; to become so organized on the economic field that they can take and hold the industries in which they are employed. Can you conceive of such a thing? Is it possible? What are the forces that prevent you from doing so? You have all the industries in your own hands at the present time. There is this justification for political action, and that is, to control the forces of the capitalists that they use against us; to be in a position to control the power of government so as to make the work of the army ineffective, so as to abolish totally the secret service and the force of detectives. That is the reason that you want the power of government. That is the reason that you should fully understand the power of the ballot. Now, there isn't any one, Socialist, S. L. P., Industrial Worker or any other workingman or woman, no matter what society you belong to, but what believes in the ballot. There are those—and I am one of them—who refuse to have the ballot interpreted for them. I know, or think I know, the power of it, and I know that the industrial organization, as I stated in the beginning, is its broadest interpretation. I know, too, that when the workers are brought together in a great organization they are not going to cease to vote. That is when the workers will *begin* to vote, to vote for directors to operate the industries in which they are all employed.

So the general strike is a fighting weapon as well as a constructive force. It can be used, and should be used, equally as forcefully by the Socialist as by the Industrial Worker.

The Socialists believe in the general strike. They also believe in the organization of industrial forces after the general strike is successful. So, on this great force of the working class I believe we can agree that we should unite into one great organization—big enough to take in the children that are now working; big enough to take in the black man; the white man; big enough to take in all nationalities—an organization that will be strong enough to obliterate state boundaries, to obliterate national boundaries, and one that will become the great industrial force of the working class of the world. (Applause.)

76. EMMA GOLDMAN

Anarchism: What It Really Stands For
(1911)

EMMA GOLDMAN's 1911 essay, "Anarchism: What It Really Stands For," aimed to correct popular misapprehensions about anarchism. Goldman (1869–1940) was born in Lithuania and emigrated to Rochester, New York, in 1886. In 1889, she became active in the anarchist movement, and her frequent lectures attracted national attention. In 1906, Goldman and Alexander Berkman began publishing *Mother Earth*, an anarchist magazine of art and social criticism. Goldman was also an early advocate of free speech, birth control, women's independence, and the eight-hour workday. In 1917 she was sentenced to two years in prison for obstructing the draft, and she was deported to Russia immediately after her release in 1919. In this lively essay, Goldman promoted an essentially libertarian philosophy of total individual freedom, arguing that centralized governments crushed individualism and stifled humanity.

SOURCE: Emma Goldman. *Anarchism and Other Essays.* New York: Mother Earth Publishing Association, 1911.

SELECTED READINGS: Peter Glassgold, ed., *Anarchy! An Anthology of Emma Goldman's* Mother Earth (2001). Emma Goldman, *Red Emma Speaks* (1996). Martha Solomon, *Emma Goldman* (1987).

Anarchy

Ever reviled, accursed, ne'er understood,
  Thou art the grisly terror of our age.
"Wreck of all order," cry the multitude,
  "Art thou, and war and murder's endless rage."

O, let them cry. To them that ne'er have striven
 The truth that lies behind a word to find,
To them the word's right meaning was not given.
 They shall continue blind among the blind.
But thou, O word, so clear, so strong, so pure,
 Thou sayest all which I for goal have taken.
I give thee to the future! Thine secure
 When each at least unto himself shall waken.
Comes it in sunshine? In the tempest's thrill?
 I cannot tell—but it the earth shall see!
I am an Anarchist! Wherefore I will
 Not rule, and also ruled I will not be!

John Henry Mackay

The history of human growth and development is at the same time the history of the terrible struggle of every new idea heralding the approach of a brighter dawn. In its tenacious hold on tradition, the Old has never hesitated to make use of the foulest and cruelest means to stay the advent of the New, in whatever form or period the latter may have asserted itself. Nor need we retrace our steps into the distant past to realize the enormity of opposition, difficulties, and hardships placed in the path of every progressive idea. The rack, the thumbscrew, and the knout are still with us; so are the convict's garb and the social wrath, all conspiring against the spirit that is serenely marching on.

Anarchism could not hope to escape the fate of all other ideas of innovation. Indeed, as the most revolutionary and uncompromising innovator, Anarchism must needs meet with the combined ignorance and venom of the world it aims to reconstruct.

To deal even remotely with all that is being said and done against Anarchism would necessitate the writing of a whole volume. I shall therefore meet only two of the principal objections. In so doing, I shall attempt to elucidate what Anarchism really stands for.

The strange phenomenon of the opposition to Anarchism is that it brings to light the relation between so-called intelligence and ignorance. And yet this is not so very strange when we consider the relativity of all things. The ignorant mass has in its favor that it makes no pretense of knowledge or tolerance. Acting, as it always does, by mere impulse, its reasons are like those of a child. "Why?" "Because." Yet the opposition of the uneducated to Anarchism deserves the same consideration as that of the intelligent man.

What, then, are the objections? First, Anarchism is impractical, though a beautiful ideal. Second, Anarchism stands for violence and destruction, hence it must be repudiated as vile and dangerous. Both the intelligent man and the ignorant mass judge not from a thorough knowledge of the subject, but either from hearsay or false interpretation.

A practical scheme, says Oscar Wilde, is either one already in existence, or a scheme that could be carried out under the existing conditions; but it is exactly the existing conditions that one objects to, and any scheme that could accept these conditions is wrong and foolish. The true criterion of the practical, therefore, is not whether the latter can keep intact the wrong or foolish; rather is it whether the scheme has vitality enough to leave the stagnant waters of the old, and build, as well as sustain, new life. In the light of this conception, Anarchism is indeed practical. More than any other idea, it is helping to do away with the wrong and foolish; more than any other idea, it is building and sustaining new life.

The emotions of the ignorant man are continuously kept at a pitch by the most blood-curdling stories about Anarchism. Not a thing too outrageous to be employed against this philosophy and its exponents. Therefore Anarchism represents to the unthinking what the proverbial bad man does to the child—a black monster bent on swallowing everything; in short, destruction and violence.

Destruction and violence! How is the ordinary man to know that the most violent element in society is ignorance; that its power of destruction is the very thing Anarchism is combating? Nor is he aware that Anarchism, whose roots, as it were, are part of nature's forces, destroys, not healthful tissue, but parasitic growths that feed on the life's essence of society. It is merely clearing the soil from weeds and sagebrush, that it may eventually bear healthy fruit.

Someone has said that it requires less mental effort to condemn than to think. The widespread mental indolence, so prevalent in society, proves this to be only too true. Rather than to go to the bottom of any given idea, to examine into its origin and meaning, most people will either condemn it altogether, or rely on some superficial or prejudicial definition of non essentials.

Anarchism urges man to think, to investigate, to analyze every proposition; but that the brain capacity of the average reader be not taxed too much, I also shall begin with a definition, and then elaborate on the latter.

ANARCHISM: The philosophy of a new social order based on liberty unrestricted by man-made law; the theory that all forms of government rest on violence, and are therefore wrong and harmful, as well as unnecessary.

The new social order rests, of course, on the materialistic basis of life; but while all Anarchists agree that the main evil today is an economic one, they maintain that the solution of that evil can be brought about only through the consideration of *every phase* of life—individual, as well as the collective; the internal, as well as the external phases.

A thorough perusal of the history of human development will disclose two elements in bitter conflict with each other; elements that are only now beginning to be understood, not as foreign to each other, but as closely related and truly harmonious, if only placed in proper environment: the individual and social instincts. The individual and society have waged a relentless and bloody battle for ages, each striving for supremacy because each was blind to the value and importance of the other. The individual and social instincts—the one a most potent factor for individual endeavor, for growth, aspiration, self-realization; the other an equally potent factor for mutual helpfulness and social well-being.

The explanation of the storm raging within the individual, and between him and his surroundings, is not far to seek. The primitive man, unable to understand his being, much less the unity of all life, felt himself absolutely dependent on blind, hidden forces ever ready to mock and taunt him. Out of that attitude grew the religious concepts of man as a mere speck of dust dependent on superior powers on high, who can only be appeased by complete surrender. All the early sagas rest on that idea, which continues to be the *leitmotiv* of the biblical tales dealing with the relation of man to God, to the State, to society. Again and again the same motif, *man is nothing, the powers are everything.* Thus Jehovah would only endure man on condition of complete surrender. Man can have all the glories of the earth, but he must not become conscious of himself. The State, society, and moral laws all sing the same refrain: Man can have all the glories of the earth, but he must not become conscious of himself.

Anarchism is the only philosophy which brings to man the consciousness of himself; which maintains that God, the State, and society are nonexistent, that their promises are null and void, since they can be fulfilled only through man's subordination. Anarchism is therefore the teacher of the unity of life; not merely in nature, but in man. There is no conflict between the individual and the social instincts, any more than there is between the heart and the lungs: the one the receptacle of a precious life essence, the other the repository of the element that keeps the essence pure and strong. The individual is the heart of society, conserving the essence of social life; society is the lungs which are distributing the element to keep the life essence—that is, the individual— pure and strong.

"The one thing of value in the world," says Emerson, "is the active soul; this every man contains within him. The soul active sees absolute truth and utters truth and creates." In other words, the individual instinct is the thing of value in the world. It is the true soul that sees and creates the truth alive, out of which is to come a still greater truth, the reborn social soul.

Anarchism is the great liberator of man from the phantoms that have held him captive; it is the arbiter and pacifier of the two forces for individual and social harmony. To accomplish that unity, Anarchism has declared war on the pernicious influences which have so far prevented the harmonious blending of individual and social instincts, the individual and society.

Religion, the dominion of the human mind; Property, the dominion of human needs; and Government, the dominion of human conduct, represent the stronghold of man's enslavement and all the horrors it entails. Religion! How it dominates man's mind, how it humiliates and degrades his soul. God is everything, man is nothing, says religion. But out of that nothing God has created a kingdom so despotic, so tyrannical, so cruel, so terribly exacting that naught but gloom and tears and blood have ruled the world since gods began. Anarchism rouses man to rebellion against this black monster. Break your mental fetters, says Anarchism to man, for not until you think and judge for yourself will you get rid of the dominion of darkness, the greatest obstacle to all progress.

Property, the dominion of man's needs, the denial of the right to satisfy his needs. Time was when property claimed a divine right, when it came to man with the same refrain, even as religion, "Sacrifice! Abnegate! Submit!" The spirit of Anarchism has lifted man from his prostrate position. He now stands erect, with his face toward the light. He has learned to see the insatiable, devouring, devastating nature of property, and he is preparing to strike the monster dead.

"Property is robbery," said the great French Anarchist Proudhon. Yes, but without risk and danger to the robber. Monopolizing the accumulated efforts of man, property has robbed him of his birthright, and has turned him loose a pauper and an outcast. Property has not even the time-worn excuse that man does not create enough to satisfy all needs. The A B C student of economics knows that the productivity of labor within the last few decades far exceeds normal demand. But what are normal demands to an abnormal institution? The only demand that property recognizes is its own gluttonous appetite for greater wealth, because wealth means power; the power to subdue, to crush, to exploit, the power to enslave, to outrage, to degrade. America is particularly boastful of her great power, her enormous national wealth. Poor America, of what avail is all her wealth, if the individuals comprising the nation are wretchedly poor? If they live in squalor, in filth, in crime, with hope and joy gone, a homeless, soilless army of human prey.

It is generally conceded that unless the returns of any business venture exceed the cost, bankruptcy is inevitable. But those engaged in the business of producing wealth have not yet learned even this simple lesson. Every year the cost of production in human life is growing larger (50,000 killed, 100,000 wounded in America last year); the returns to the masses, who help to create wealth, are ever getting smaller. Yet America continues to the blind to the inevitable bankruptcy of our business of production. Nor is this the only crime of the latter. Still more fatal is the crime of turning the producer into a mere particle of a machine, with less will and decision than his master of steel and iron. Man is being robbed not merely of the products of his labor, but of the power of free initiative, of originality, and the interest in, or desire for, the things he is making.

Real wealth consists in things of utility and beauty, in things that help to create strong, beautiful bodies and surroundings inspiring to live in. But if man is doomed to wind cotton around a spool, or dig coal, or build roads for thirty years of his life, there can be no talk of wealth. What he gives to the world are only gray and hideous things, reflecting a dull and hideous existence—too weak to live, too cowardly to die. Strange to say, there are people who extol this deadening method of centralized production as the proudest achievement of our age. They fail utterly to realize that if we are to continue in machine subserviency, our slavery is more complete than was our bondage to the King. They do not want to know that centralization is not only the deathknell of liberty, but also of health and beauty, of art and science, all these being impossible in a clocklike, mechanical atmosphere.

Anarchism cannot but repudiate such a method of production: its goal is the freest possible expression of all the latent powers of the individual. Oscar Wilde defines a perfect personality as "one who develops under perfect conditions, who is not wounded, maimed, or in danger." A perfect personality, then, is only possible in a state of society where man is free to choose the mode of work, the conditions of work, and the freedom to work. One to whom the making of a table, the building of a house, or the tilling of the soil, is what the painting is to the artist and the discovery to the scientist—the result of inspiration, of intense longing, and deep interest in work as a creative force. That being the ideal of Anarchism, its economic arrangements must consist of voluntary productive and distributive associations, gradually developing into free communism, as the best means of producing with the least waste of human energy. Anarchism, however, also recognizes the right of the individual, or numbers of individuals, to arrange at all times for other forms of work, in harmony with their tastes and desires.

Such free display of human energy being possible only under complete individual and social freedom, Anarchism directs its forces against the third and greatest foe of all social equality; namely, the State, organized authority, or statutory law—the dominion of human conduct.

Just as religion has fettered the human mind, and as property, or the monopoly of things, has subdued and stifled man's needs, so has the State enslaved his spirit, dictating every phase of conduct. "All government in essence," says Emerson, "is tyranny." It matters not whether it is government by divine right or majority rule. In every instance its aim is the absolute subordination of the individual.

Referring to the American government, the greatest American Anarchist, David Thoreau, said: "Government, what is it but a tradition, though a recent one, endeavoring to transmit itself unimpaired to posterity, but each instance losing its integrity; it has not the vitality and force of a single living man Law never made man a whit more just; and by means of their respect for it, even the well disposed are daily made agents of injustice."

Indeed, the keynote of government is injustice. With the arrogance and self-sufficiency of the King who could do no wrong, governments ordain, judge, condemn, and punish the most insignificant offenses, while maintaining themselves by the greatest of all offenses, the annihilation of individual liberty. Thus Ouida is right when she maintains that "the State only aims at instilling those qualities in its public by which its demands are obeyed, and its exchequer is filled. Its highest attainment is the reduction of mankind to clockwork. In its atmosphere all those finer and more delicate liberties, which require treatment and spacious expansion, inevitably dry up and perish. The State requires a taxpaying machine in which there is no hitch, an exchequer in which there is never a deficit, and a public, monotonous, obedient, colorless, spiritless, moving humbly like a flock of sheep along a straight high road between two walls."

Yet even a flock of sheep would resist the chicanery of the State, if it were not for the corruptive, tyrannical, and oppressive methods it employs to serve its purposes. Therefore Bakunin repudiates the State as synonymous with the surrender of the liberty of the individual or small minorities—the destruction of social relationship, the curtailment, or complete denial even, of life itself, for its own aggrandizement. The State is the altar of political freedom and, like the religious altar, it is maintained for the purpose of human sacrifice. . . .

. . . The political superstition is still holding sway over the hearts and minds of the masses, but the true lovers of liberty will have no more to do with it. Instead, they believe with Stirner that man has as much liberty as he is willing to take. Anarchism therefore stands for direct action, the open defiance of, and resistance to, all laws and restrictions, economic, social, and moral. But defiance and resistance are illegal. Therein lies the salvation of man. Everything illegal necessitates integrity, self-reliance, and courage. In short, it calls for free, independent spirits, for "men who are men, and who have a bone in their backs which you cannot pass your hand through."

Universal suffrage itself owes its existence to direct action. If not for the spirit of rebellion, of the defiance on the part of the American revolutionary fathers, their posterity would still wear the King's coat. If not for the direct action of a John Brown and his comrades, America would still trade in the flesh of the black man. True, the trade in white flesh is still going on; but that, too, will have to be abolished by direct action. Trade-unionism, the economic arena of the modern gladiator, owes its existence to direct action. It is but recently that law and government have attempted to crush the trade-union movement, and condemned the exponents of man's right to organize to prison as conspirators. Had they sought to assert their cause through begging, pleading, and compromise, trade-unionism would today be a negligible quantity. In France, in Spain, in Italy, in Russia, nay even in England (witness the growing rebellion of English labor unions), direct, revolutionary, economic action has become so strong a force in the battle for industrial liberty as to make the world realize the tremendous importance of labor's power. The General Strike, the supreme expression of the economic consciousness of the workers, was ridiculed in America but a short time ago. Today every great strike, in order to win, must realize the importance of the solidaric general protest.

Direct action, having proven effective along economic lines, is equally potent in the environment of the individual. There a hundred forces encroach upon his being, and only persistent resistance to them will finally set him free. Direct action against the authority in the shop, direct action against the authority of the law, direct action against the invasive, meddlesome authority of our moral code, is the logical, consistent method of Anarchism.

Will it not lead to a revolution? Indeed, it will. No real social change has ever come about without a revolution. People are either not familiar with their history, or they have not yet learned that revolution is but thought carried into action.

Anarchism, the great leaven of thought, is today permeating every phase of human endeavor. Science, art, literature, the drama, the effort for economic betterment, in fact every individual and social opposition to the existing disorder of things, is illumined by the spiritual light of Anarchism. It is the philosophy of the sovereignty of the individual. It is the theory of social harmony. It is the great, surging, living truth that is reconstructing the world, and that will usher in the Dawn.

77. MOTHER JONES

Speech to Striking Coal Miners
(1912)

MOTHER JONES's "Speech to Striking Coal Miners," in Charleston, West Virginia, was delivered while she was at the height of her fame and influence. Mary Harris "Mother" Jones (1836–1930) was born in Ireland and moved to the United States at age five. She became active in the labor movement in 1867, following the deaths of her husband and children in the Memphis yellow fever epidemic. A flamboyant speaker, Jones is chiefly known for helping organize coal miners, although she also organized garment and streetcar workers, and crusaded against child labor. She continued to work as a union organizer and agitator into her nineties, and she published her *Autobiography* in 1925. The following speech was transcribed by a court reporter for use in a court injunction against her. Later, Jones was accused of inciting violence in the West Virginia coal fields, and she was convicted of conspiracy to commit murder and was sentenced to twenty years in prison. The sentence was later commuted.

SOURCE: Typewritten copy in West Virginia Collection, "Coal Strikes," West Virginia University, Morgantown, West Virginia; reprinted in Philip S. Foner, *Mother Jones Speaks*. Monad Press: New York, 1983.

SELECTED READINGS: Elliot J. Gorn, *Mother Jones: The Most Dangerous Woman in America* (2001). Mary Harris Jones, *Autobiography of Mother Jones*, ed. Mary Field Parton (1990). Dale Featherling, *Mother Jones: The Miner's Angel* (1974).

This great gathering that is here tonight signals there is a disease in the State that must be wiped out. The people have suffered from that disease patiently; they have borne insults, oppression, outrages; they appealed to their chief executive, they appealed to the courts, they appealed to the attorney general, and in every case they were turned down. They were ignored. The people must not be listened to, the corporations must get a hearing. . . .

. . . Take possession of that State House, that ground is yours. (Someone interrupted, and the speaker said: "Shut your mouth.")

You built that state house, didn't you? You pay the public officials, don't you? You paid for that ground, didn't you? (Cries of: "Yes," "yes.")

Then, who does it belong to? Then did the militia chase you off? You have been hypnotized. The trouble has been that they wanted the slave system to continue. They have had a glass for you and your wives and children to look into. They have you hypnotized. They want the ministers to tell you when you die you will have a bed in heaven. The blamed chambermaids might be on strike and we wouldn't get a chance to get a bed. (Loud applause)

Now, then, I will go to the tents and when those poor women—I have seen those little children—my heart bled for them—and I thought, "Oh, how brutish the corporations must be! God Almighty, go down and look at those conditions! Go see those miners!" They tell you about how much—they have a list of questions up here, "How much do the unions do to train the miners to clean the yards?" Did you ever know of such a damned, silly insulting question? (Loud applause)

I want to ask those fellows that put that down, "How do you suppose, when we have to fight you, we have got any time about yards?" You have got the yards. We clean them for you and you don't thank us for it. Your wife lives in style. Look down at those houses there on the river front. She dresses with the blood of children. She buys a dog and calls it "Dear little poodle, I love you." And you stand for it! And you stand for it! And you are a lot of dirty cowards, I want to tell you the truth about it. You are a lot of cowards, and you haven't got enough marrow in your backbone to grease two black cats' tails. If you were men with a bit of revolutionary blood in you, you wouldn't stand for the Baldwin guards, would you?'

(Cries of: "No." "No." "No.") . . .

I have been under martial law before, I have been in states where martial law was, but it was never carried to that extreme. We were at least allowed to go and visit our people. Here in West Virginia you can't go. You can't hold a meeting. I want to say to you that the right of free speech will be carried on if they hire all the militia in the state to murder us. We won't surrender that right. We will hold meetings. We will hold peaceful, law-abiding meetings. We will hold them all along. I have here a book, if I had the light to read it, one of the most damnable documents that those mine owners are sending out for the miners to sign.

I have got letters here from the slaves on the Norfolk and Western, "For God's sake, 'Mother', come up and do something for us." I have got letters from the Fairmont region, "Oh, 'Mother', for God's sake, come and do something for us." I have them from New River, "For God's sake, come and do something for us, and help us."

Isn't there something wrong? Say, boys, stop it. For ages and ages they have kept the lash on you. I could see it the day I went to Kaymoor. The poor devils were scared to death. I had to tell them to come with me. They were afraid of the blood-hounds. And while I talked the blood-hounds sat there. They made me wade the creek.

Now, every citizen will admit that when you rent a house the landlord has a right to give you a passageway to go to that house. You have a right to invite who you please to your table, haven't you? The blood-hounds came along and you have got to get out.

Now, then, is that something that the State must boast of? Is that something that you citizens will endorse?

(Cries of: "No," "No.")

Very good, then. They will come to you on election day. I will tell you when you can carry a bayonet and they can't meddle with you. You can carry a bayonet on November 5th, and you can go to the ballot box and put a bayonet in there and *stick it to their very heart*. (Loud applause) . . .

Now, I want to say, my friends, I have only one journey to go through this life; you have only one journey to go through this life; let us all do the best we can for humanity, for mankind while we are here.

That is my mission, to do what I can to raise mankind to break his chains. The miners are close to me. The steel workers are. I go among them all. One time when I took up the Mexican question, I went to Congress to save some lives; I had never seen them in my life, but they appealed to me and said, "It is up to you, 'Mother,' to save our lives." I went up to carry the matter to Congress. I came up before the big committee. They were Dalzell, Congressmen, representing the Steel Trust—he was chairman of that big committee; Smith, representing the Southern Pacific Railroad, was a member of that committee; Champ Clark also was a member of that committee. Dalzell said to me, "Mother Jones, where do you live?" I said, "In the United States, Sir." "What part of the United States?" said he. I said, "Wherever the Workers are fighting the robbers, there am I." (Loud applause) "Sometimes I am in Arizona fighting the Southern Pacific blood-sucking pirates and thieves," said I. "Sometimes, I am up on the Steel Range, fighting those murderers and plunderers, sometimes I am in Pennsylvania fighting the robbers and murderers and blood-suckers there, and by the Eternal God we will clean you up and put you out of business."

Now, my brothers, don't violate the law. Let them see that you are law-abiding. . . .

. . . Now, my brothers, I want you all to return home, peacefully, law-abiding. Go home. I don't mind you taking a drink, I know you need it. I don't belong to the temperance brigade at all. As long as liquor is manufactured it is going to be sold for profit. When you take the profit out of it, just as you have out of the postage stamps, then you don't need any temperance howlers. It will be made pure, and we will drink it pure. So the temperance brigade will keep in the background. If we want a drink we will take it, and we are not going to offer any apology for it.

Be good, "Mother" is going to stay with you. I am going to Colorado. There was a sheriff in the county, and the mine owners asked for the troops, and the sheriff said, "You can send no troops, no militia into the county I have charge of. The men elected me." He was the sheriff, and he did not allow the Governor to send the troops in there. There was no tyranny in that county. Once and awhile we licked a scab, we wanted to put brains in him, he had none. That sheriff is going to run for Secretary of State, and I am going out to sweep the state with him. I will put him into office, if it is the last thing I do. I want to put in all the officers, and we have got to put out the fellows who stand with the robbing class, and we have got to put them out of business, we have got to make an honest nation. You can't be honest today. A girl goes to school to church and prays to Jesus. One Monday she acts like the devil when she sells to you. The whole machinery of capitalism is rotten to the core. This meeting tonight indicates a milestone of progress of the miners and workers of the State of West Virginia. I will be with you, and the Baldwin guards will go. You will not be serfs, you will march, march, march on from milestone to milestone of human freedom, you will rise like men in the new day and slavery will get its death blow. It has got to die. Good night. (Applause)

78. MARY HEATON VORSE

The Trouble at Lawrence
(1912)

MARY HEATON VORSE's essay "The Trouble at Lawrence" appeared in *Harper's Weekly* in 1912, and marked the beginning of her career as a leading labor reporter. Vorse (1874–1966) was raised in Massachusetts but educated in Europe. Unlike many labor reporters, Vorse lobbied for the inclusion of women in the labor movement. She traveled in prominent intellectual circles in Greenwich Village before World War I, and she served as a delegate to the 1915 women's peace conference at The Hague. Although she grew skeptical of communism, Vorse refused to abet the vicious McCarthyism of the 1950s, and she was under FBI surveillance until at least 1956. Her essay on the famous Lawrence Textile Strike of 1912, which was successfully led by the Industrial Workers of the World (IWW), embarrassed mill owners and may have led to a settlement that brought wage increases to 245,000 exploited workers.

SOURCE: Mary Heaton Vorse. "The Trouble at Lawrence." *Harper's Weekly*, March 16, 1912.

SELECTED READINGS: Dee Garrison, *Mary Heaton Vorse: The Life of an American Insurgent* (1989). Mary Heaton Vorse, *Rebel Pen: The Writings of Mary Heaton Vorse*, ed. Dee Garrison (1985).

It is an eloquent little commentary on the wage scale of Lawrence that the passing of the beneficent fifty-four-hour bill should have been the indirect cause of the strike. This bill limited the work of women and children in Massachusetts to that number of hours a week, and the mills of Lawrence could not run fifty-six hours for their men alone. Therefore they cut the hours to fifty-four as the laws demanded, and at the same time, cut the pay by 3.57 percent. It is also claimed that the mills speeded up the work. January 13th was the last payday before the strike, and a few days later the mills were no longer making cloth.

In the present-day labor situation, as every one knows, strikes are prearranged, and, on a certain given day, the people walk out; but the strike of the textile workers in Lawrence was the spontaneous expression of discontent of a people whose scant wages, averaging between $5 and $6 a week, were cut below the living point. They went out, over 25,000 of them, of all crafts, without organization and without strike demands. They had no leaders and they themselves were composed of all the peoples of the earth, and were of warring nations and warring creeds. In this extraordinary fashion did the strike begin.

At the same time the mill hands went out, the American Federation of Labor (AFL) had a membership, according to John P. Golden, president of the Textile Union of New England, of approximately 250, and the Industrial Workers of the World (IWW) a membership of about 280. The American Federation of Labor has not recognized the strike. Apparently this organization was annoyed that the strikers had not played according to the rules of Hoyle laid down by their organization. It was not their strike, neither was it the strike of the Industrial Workers of the World. The strike was merely the indignant expression of people who considered that their wages had been cut below the living point.

The IWW took immediate steps to bring some order out of the chaos in which the workers were plunged. William D. Haywood, Ettor, and Giovanitti began to organize all of the textile workers into one great industrial union. They enrolled the majority of the 25,000 strikers, men, women, and children, in the IWW. They formulated demands for a flat increase in wages of 15 percent, a fifty-four-hour week, double time for overtime, the abolition of the premium or speeding-up system, and no discrimination against those who were on strike. Arrayed against the strikers, along with the mill owners, the militia, and the police, were the officials of the Textile Union of New England and the Central Labor Union of Lawrence. The American Federation of Labor at Washington was also hostile, seeing in the ideal of labor solidarity that was being preached at Lawrence an attack on craft unionism. But it was a message which appealed strongly to the diverse mass of men and women who made up the strikers, and it held them. After Ettor's arrest the task of welding the alien groups into one fell upon the shoulders of Haywood, and the release of Ettor and Giovanitti was added to the demands.

As a contrast to the action against Ettor, it is interesting to cite this incident. John Ramay, a young Syrian of nineteen, went out on the morning of the 29th of January at six o'clock. He joined a crowd of strikers which the militia moved along. He was at the back of the crowd. At fifteen minutes past six he was brought into his mother's house with a bayonet wound in the back and he died at seven that night. The name of the militiaman who killed Ramay is unknown, nor has any action been taken against him. He was not held for murder nor complicity of murder as it was decided that he was within his rights.

Lawrence is in atmosphere a New England city. It has about 88,000 inhabitants, of which 60,000 are mill workers and their families. Thirty thousand of these people work in the mills, and it is said that over thirty-three dialects are spoken in this New England town and that of full American stock there are not more than 8,000 while 45,000 alone are of English-speaking nations.

The town sits in a basin surrounded by hills. Along one side of it runs the Merrimack River, wide and shining. If you approach Lawrence from South Lawrence you must pass through acre after acre of mill buildings and mill yards until you reach the wide waterway whose sides are factory-bordered, whose surface mirrors the monotonous pale-red brick of factory wall and factory chimney.

If you walk down Essex Street, the principal business street, and glance to your right and then to your left, you will receive an impression of always seeing at the end of the street on the one hand a little church steeple spring upward and on the other an imposing mill chimney. The ever-recurring little church steeples of Lawrence give one the impression of the children of a dying race; the big smokestacks are the young giants of a new, red-blooded generation.

From one end to the other of Lawrence run the mills, most of them situated on a piece of made land between the Merrimack and the canal. The mills *are* Lawrence; you cannot escape them; the smoke of them fills the sky. The great mills of Lawrence make the Lawrence skyline, they dominate and dwarf the churches. From Union Street to Broadway along the canal the mills stretch, a solid wall of brick and wide-paned glass, imposing by their vastness and almost beautiful, as anything is that without pretense is adapted absolutely to its own end. The mills seem like some strange fortress of industry, connected as they are by a series of bridges and separated by a canal from the town. . . .

. . . This is the town, so New England in setting and surroundings, so mixed in its nationalities—this town whose great mills are the latest expression of our tremendous industrial development—a development which has created a situation which no one as yet fully understands in all its complexity, with which our state government cannot cope, and which has caught in its tangled web the people who are the very creators of the situation itself.

The strike of Lawrence involves the questions of emigration and of the tariff, of the ability of a state with a fifty-four-hour law to compete with a state whose workers have two extra working hours: the effect on the country at large of a working community which habitually lives under conditions which do not make for healthy children.

Lawrence is a small town: there are 20,000 people there who, whatever else happens, can never again have the race hatreds and creed prejudices that they did before they had learned what working together may mean. They have learned, too, the value of organization and their one executive ability has been developed, for they have had to feed a great company of people and administer the use of the strike funds. Young girls have had executive positions. Men and women who have known nothing but work in the home and mill have developed a larger social consciousness. A strike like this makes people think. Almost every day for weeks people of every one of these nations have gone to their crowded meetings and listened to the speakers and have discussed these questions afterward, and in the morning the women have resumed their duty on the picket lines and the working together for what they believed was a common good.

79. JOHN REED

War in Paterson
(1913)

JOHN REED's initiation into radical politics began when he was arrested while covering the Paterson, New Jersey, silk workers strike of 1913. A child of wealth and privilege, Reed (1887–1920) graduated from Harvard University in 1910. Soon thereafter, he moved to Manhattan and began publishing in *The Masses,* a bohemian magazine of left-wing politics and avant-garde art. He later reported from Mexico about Pancho Villa, and was in Petrograd (now St. Petersburg) when the Bolsheviks seized power in October 1917. His eyewitness account of the revolution, *Ten Days That Shook the World,* has since been translated into more than thirty languages. He later returned to the USSR, where he worked in the Soviet bureau of propaganda and briefly served as Soviet consul to New York. Reed died of typhus in 1920. His essay "War in Paterson" described the repression of industrialists, police, and city officials during the Paterson textile strike of 1913, which lasted for six months, involved twenty-five thousand workers, and brought together a broad coalition of laborers, intellectuals, socialists, reformers, and unionists. Said one writer, "[Reed] approached the strike as though it were a lark, but his deepest sympathies were aroused when he saw the terror practiced by the police."

SOURCE: John Reed. *The Education of John Reed.* Ed. John Stuart. New York: International Publishers, 1955.

SELECTED READINGS: Leslie Fishbein, *Rebels in Bohemia: The Radicals of* The Masses, *1910–1917* (1982). Robert A. Rosenstone, *Romantic Revolutionary: A Biography of John Reed* (1975).

There's war in Paterson, New Jersey. But it's a curious kind of war. All the violence is the work of one side—the mill owners. Their servants, the police, club unresisting men and women and ride down law-abiding crowds on

horseback. Their paid mercenaries, the armed detectives, shoot and kill innocent people. Their newspapers, the Paterson *Press* and the Paterson *Call*,
publish incendiary and crime-inciting appeals to mob violence against the
strike leaders. Their tool, Recorder Carroll, deals out heavy sentences to peaceful pickets that the police net gathers up. They control absolutely the police,
the press, the courts.

Opposing them are about twenty-five thousand striking silk workers, of
whom perhaps ten thousand are active, and their weapon is the picketline.
Let me tell you what I saw in Paterson and then you will say which side of
this struggle is "anarchistic" and "contrary to American ideals."

At six o'clock in the morning a light rain was falling. Slate-gray and cold,
the streets of Paterson were deserted. But soon came the cops—twenty of
them—strolling along with their nightsticks under their arms. We went ahead
of them toward the mill district. Now we began to see workmen going in the
same direction, coat collars turned up, hands in their pockets. We came into
a long street, one side of which was lined with silk mills, the other side with
the wooden tenement houses. In every doorway, at every window of the
houses clustered men and women, laughing and chatting as if after breakfast
on a holiday. There seemed no sense of expectancy, no strain or feeling of
fear. The sidewalks were almost empty, only over in front of the mills a few
couples—there couldn't have been more than fifty—marched slowly up and
down, dripping with the rain. Some were men, with here and there a man
and woman together, or two young boys. As the warmer light of full day
came the people drifted out of their houses and began to pace back and forth,
gathering in little knots on the corners. They were quick with gesticulating
hands, and low-voiced conversation. They looked often toward the corners of
side streets.

Suddenly appeared a policeman, swinging his club. "Ah-h-h!" said the
crowd softly.

Six men had taken shelter from the rain under the canopy of a saloon.
"Come on! Get out of that!" yelled the policeman, advancing. The men quietly
obeyed. "Get off this street! Go on home, now! Don't be standing here!" They
gave way before him in silence, drifting back again when he turned away.
Other policemen materialized, hustling, cursing, brutal, ineffectual. No one
answered back. Nervous, bleary-eyed, unshaven, these officers were worn out
with nine weeks incessant strike duty.

On the mill side of the street the picket-line had grown to about four hundred. Several policemen shouldered roughly among them, looking for trouble.
A workman appeared, with a tin pail, escorted by two detectives. "Boo! Boo!"
shouted a few scattered voices. Two Italian boys leaned against the mill fence
and shouted a merry Irish threat, "Scab! Come outa here I knock your head
off!" A policeman grabbed the boys roughly by the shoulder. "Get to hell out

of here!" he cried, jerking and pushing them violently to the corner, where he kicked them. Not a voice, not a movement from the crowd.

A little further along the street we saw a young woman with an umbrella, who had been picketing, suddenly confronted by a big policeman.

"What the hell are *you* doing here?" he roared. "God damn you, you go home!" and he jammed his club against her mouth. "I *no* go home!" she shrilled passionately, with blazing eyes. "You big stiff!"

Silently, steadfastly, solidly the picket-line grew. In groups or in couples the strikers patrolled the sidewalk. There was no more laughing. They looked on with eyes full of hate. These were fiery Italians, and the police were the same brutal thugs that had beaten them and insulted them for nine weeks. I wondered how long they could stand it.

It began to rain heavily. I asked a man's permission to stand on the porch of his house. There was a policeman standing in front of it. His name, I afterwards discovered, was McCormack. I had to walk around him to mount the steps.

Suddenly he turned round, and shot at the owner: "Do all them fellows live in that house?" The man indicated the three other strikers and himself, and shook his head at me.

"Then you get to hell off of there!" said the cop, pointing his club at me.

"I have the permission of this gentleman to stand here," I said. "He owns this house."

"Never mind! Do what I tell you! Come off of there, and come off damn quick!"

"I'll do nothing of the sort."

With that he leaped up the steps, seized my arm, and violently jerked me to the sidewalk. Another cop took my arm and they gave me a shove.

"Now you get to hell off this street!" said Officer McCormack.

"I won't get off this street or any other street. If I'm breaking any law, you arrest me!"

Officer McCormack was dreadfully troubled by my request. He didn't want to arrest me, and said so with a great deal of profanity.

"I've *got* your number," said I sweetly. "Now will you tell me your name?"

"Yes," he bellowed, "an' I got *your* number! I'll arrest you." He took me by the arm and marched me up the street. . . .

And so it was that I went up to the county jail. In the outer office I was questioned again, searched for concealed weapons, and my money and valuables taken away. Then the great barred door swung open and I went down some steps into a vast room lined with three tiers of cells. About eighty prisoners strolled around, talked, smoked, and ate the food sent in to them by those outside. Of this eighty almost half were strikers. They were in their street clothes, held in prison under $500 bail to await the action of the Grand Jury.

Surrounded by a dense crowd of short, dark-faced men, Big Bill Haywood towered in the center of the room. His big hand made simple gestures as he explained something to them. His massive, rugged face, seamed and scarred like a mountain, and as calm, radiated strength. These strikers, one of many desperate little armies in the vanguard of the battle-line of labor, quickened and strengthened by Bill Haywood's face and voice, looked up at him lovingly, eloquently. Faces deadened and dulled with grinding routine in the sunless mills glowed with hope and understanding. Faces scarred and bruised from policemen's clubs grinned eagerly at the thought of going back on the picket line. And there were other faces, too—lined and sunken with the slow starvation of a nine weeks' poverty—shadowed with the sight of so much suffering, or the hopeless brutality of the police. But not one showed discouragement; not one a sign of faltering or of fear. As one little Italian said to me, with blazing eyes: "We all one big Union. I.W.W.—the word is pierced in the heart of the people!"

"Yes! Yes! right! I.W.W.! One big Union"—they murmured with soft, eager voices, crowding around.

I shook hands with Haywood.

"Boys," said Haywood, indicating me, "this man wants to *know* things. You tell him everything—"

They crowded around me, shaking my hand, smiling, welcoming me. "Too bad you get in jail," they said, sympathetically. "We tell you everything. You ask. We tell you. Yes. Yes. Yes. You good feller."

And they did. Most of them were still weak and exhausted from their terrible night before in the lockup. Some had been lined up against a wall, as they marched to and fro in front of the mills, and herded to jail on the charge of "unlawful assemblage"! Others had been clubbed into the patrol-wagon on the charge of "rioting," as they stood at the track, on their way home from picketing, waiting for a train to pass! They were being held for the Grand Jury that indicted Haywood and Gurley Flynn. *Four of these jurymen were silk manufacturers, another the head of the local Edison company—which Haywood tried to organize for a strike—and not one a workingman!*

"We not take bail," said another, shaking his head. "We stay here. Fill up the damn jail. Pretty soon no more room. Pretty soon can't arrest no more pickets!"

It was visitors' day. I went to the door to speak with a friend. Outside the reception room was full of women and children, carrying packages, and pasteboard boxes, and pails full of dainties and little comforts lovingly prepared, which meant hungry and ragged wives and babies, so that the men might be comfortable in jail. The place was full of the sound of moaning; tears ran down their work-roughened faces; the children looked up at their fathers' unshaven faces through the bars and tried to reach them with their hands. . . .

The keeper ordered me to the "convicted room," where I was pushed into a bath and compelled to put on regulation prison clothes. I shan't attempt to describe the horrors I saw in that room. Suffice it to say that forty-odd men lounged about a long corridor lined on one side with cells; that the only ventilation and light came from one small skylight up a funnel-shaped air-shaft; that one man had syphilitic sores on his legs and was treated by the prison doctor with sugar-pills for "nervousness"; that a seventeen-year-old boy *who had never been sentenced* had remained in that corridor without ever seeing the sun for over *nine months;* that a cocaine-fiend was getting his "dope" regularly from the inside, and that the background of this and much more was the monotonous and terrible shouting of a man who had lost his mind in that hell-hole and who walked among us.

There were about fourteen strikers in the "convicted" room—Italians, Lithuanians, Poles, Jews, one Frenchman and one "free-born" Englishman! That Englishman was a peach. He was the only Anglo-Saxon striker in prison except the leaders—and perhaps the only one who *had been* there for picketing. He had been sentenced for insulting a mill-owner who came out of his mill and ordered him off the sidewalk. "Wait till I get out" he said to me. "If them damned English-speaking workers don't go on picket *I'll* put the curse o' Cromwell on 'em!"

Then there was a Pole—an aristocratic, sensitive chap, a member of the local strike committee, a born fighter. He was reading Bob Ingersoll's lectures, translating them to the others. Patting the book, he said with a slow smile: "Now I don't care if I stay in here one year . . ."

With laughter, the strikers told me how the combined clergy of the city of Paterson had attempted from their pulpits to persuade them back to work—back to wage-slavery and the tender mercies of the mill-owners on grounds of religion! They told me of that disgraceful and ridiculous conference between the clergy and the strike committee, with the clergy in the part of Judas. It was hard to believe that until I saw in the paper the sermon delivered the previous day at the Presbyterian Church by the Reverend William A. Littell. He had the impudence to flay the strike leaders and advise workmen to be respectful and obedient to their employers—to tell them that the saloons were the cause of their unhappiness—to proclaim the horrible depravity of Sabbath-breaking workmen and more rot of the same sort. And this while living men were fighting for their very existence and singing gloriously of the Brotherhood of Man! . . .

Then there was the strike-breaker. He was a fat man, with sunken, flabby cheeks, jailed by some mistake of the Recorder. So completely did the strikers ostracize him—rising and moving away when he sat by them, refusing to speak to him, absolutely ignoring his presence—that he was in a pitiable condition of loneliness.

"I've learned my lesson," he moaned. "I ain't never goin' to scab on workingmen no more!"

One young Italian came up to me with a newspaper and pointed to three
items in turn. One was "American Federation of Labor hopes to break the
strike next week," another, "Victor Berger says 'I am a member of the A. F.
of L., and I have no love for the I.W.W. in Paterson,'" and the third, "Newark
Socialists refuse to help the Paterson strikers."

"I no understand," he told me, looking up at me appealingly. "You tell me.
I Socialist—I belong union—I strike with I.W.W. Socialist, he say, 'Workmen
of the world, unite!' A. F. of L., he say, 'All workmen join together.' Both
these organizations, he say, 'I am for the working class.' All right, I say, I am
the working class. I unite, I strike. Then he say, 'No! You *cannot* strike.' What
that? I no understand. You explain me."

But I could not explain. All I could say was that a good share of the Socialist
Party and the American Federation of Labor have forgotten all about the class
struggle, and seem to be playing a little game with capitalistic rules, called
"Button, button, who's got the vote!"

When it came time for me to go out I said good-by to all those gentle, alert,
brave men, ennobled by something greater than themselves. *They* were the
strike—not Bill Haywood, not Gurley Flynn, not any other individual. And if
they should lose all their leaders other leaders would arise from the ranks,
even as *they* rose, and the strike would go on! Think of it! Twelve years they
have been losing strikes—twelve solid years of disappointments and incalculable suffering. They must not lose again! They cannot lose!

And as I passed out through the front room they crowded around me again,
patting my sleeve and my hand, friendly, warm-hearted, trusting, eloquent.
Haywood had gone out on bail.

"You go out," they said softly. "That's nice. Glad you go out. Pretty soon
we go out. Then we go back on picket line."

80. EUGENE DEBS

Address to the Jury
(1918)

EUGENE DEBS's "Address to the Jury" was at once an indictment against government repression, a defense of free speech, and a celebration of the American radical tradition. Debs (1855–1926) was born in Terre Haute, Indiana, and he immersed himself in labor activity as a teen. In 1884 he was elected to the Indiana State Legislature as a Democrat. In that year he also participated in the famous Pullman Strike, which involved nearly one hundred thousand workers and briefly shut down the Western railroads; it ended in bloodshed after President Cleveland dispatched federal troops to Chicago. In 1898, Debs helped found the Socialist Democratic Party (renamed the Socialist Party in 1901), and he was a four-time presidential candidate. During World War I, Debs—a leading pacifist—made an antiwar speech in Canton, Ohio, in which he discouraged enlistment in the armed forces and encouraged insubordination in the military. This led to his indictment under the Espionage Act of 1917. Concluding his trial, Debs addressed the jury in his own defense. He was convicted and sentenced to a ten-year prison term. While still incarcerated in 1920, he gained nearly a million votes as the Socialist party presidential candidate. Released in 1921 by President Harding, Debs continued to promote American socialism until his death in 1926.

SOURCE: Jean Y. Tussey, ed. *Eugene V. Debs Speaks.* New York: Pathfinder Press, 1970.

SELECTED READINGS: Eugene V. Debs, *Walls and Bars* (1927). Ray Ginger, *The Bending Cross: A Biography of Eugene Victor Debs* (1949). Nick Salvatore, *Eugene V. Debs: Citizen and Socialist* (1982).

May it please the court, and gentlemen of the jury:

When great changes occur in history, when great principles are involved, as a rule the majority are wrong. The minority are usually right. In every age there have been a few heroic souls who have been in advance of their time, who have been misunderstood, maligned, persecuted, sometimes put to death. Long after their martyrdom monuments were erected to them and garlands woven for their graves.

This has been the tragic history of the race. In the ancient world Socrates sought to teach some new truths to the people, and they made him drink the fatal hemlock. This has been true all along the track of the ages. The men and women who have been in advance, who have had new ideas, new ideals, who have had the courage to attack the established order of things, have all had to pay the same penalty.

A century and a half ago when the American colonists were still foreign subjects; when there were a few men who had faith in the common people and their destiny, and believed that they could rule themselves without a king; in that day to question the divine right of the king to rule was treason. If you will read Bancroft or any other American historian, you will find that a great majority of the colonists were loyal to the king and actually believed that he had a divine right to rule over them . . . But there were a few men in that day who said, "We don't need a king; we can govern ourselves." And they began an agitation that has immortalized them in history.

Washington, Jefferson, Franklin, Paine and their compeers were the rebels of their day. When they began to chafe under the rule of a foreign king and to sow the seed of resistance among the colonists they were opposed by the people and denounced by the press. . . . But they had the moral courage to be true to their convictions, to stand erect and defy all the forces of reaction and detraction; and that is why their names shine in history, and why the great respectable majority of their day sleep in forgotten graves.

At a later time there began another mighty agitation in this country. It was directed against an institution that was deemed eminently respectable in its time—the age-old, cruel and infamous institution of chattel slavery. . . . All the organized forces of society and all the powers of government upheld and defended chattel slavery in that day. And again the few advanced thinkers, crusaders and martyrs appeared. One of the first was Elijah Lovejoy who was murdered in cold blood at Alton, Illinois, in 1837 because he was opposed to chattel slavery—just as I am opposed to wage slavery. Today as you go up or down the Mississippi River and look up at the green hills at Alton, you see a magnificent white shaft erected there in memory of the man who was true to himself and his convictions of right and duty even unto death.

It was my good fortune to personally know Wendell Phillips. I heard the story of his cruel and cowardly persecution from his own eloquent lips just a little while before they were silenced in death.

William Lloyd Garrison, Wendell Phillips, Elizabeth Cady Stanton, Susan

B. Anthony, Gerrit Smith, Thaddeus Stevens and other leaders of the abolition movement who were regarded as public enemies and treated accordingly, were true to their faith and stood their ground. They are all in history. You are now teaching your children to revere their memories, while all of their detractors are in oblivion.

Chattel slavery has disappeared. But we are not yet free. We are engaged today in another mighty agitation. It is as wide as the world. It means the rise of the toiling masses who are gradually becoming conscious of their interests, their power, and their mission as a class; who are organizing industrially and politically and who are slowly but surely developing the economic and political power that is to set them free. These awakening workers are still in a minority, but they have learned how to work together to achieve their freedom, and how to be patient and abide their time.

From the beginning of the war to this day I have never by word or act been guilty of the charges embraced in this indictment. If I have criticized, if I have condemned, it is because I believed it to be my duty, and that it was my right to do so under the laws of the land. I have had ample precedents for my attitude. This country has been engaged in a number of wars and every one of them has been condemned by some of the people, among them some of the most eminent men of their time. The war of the American Revolution was violently opposed. The Tory press representing the "upper classes" denounced its leaders as criminals and outlaws.

The war of 1812 was opposed and condemned by some of the most influential citizens; the Mexican war was vehemently opposed and bitterly denounced, even after the war had been declared and was in progress, by Abraham Lincoln, Charles Sumner, Daniel Webster, Henry Clay and many other well-known and influential citizens. These men denounced the President, they condemned his administration while the war was being waged, and they charged in substance that the war was a crime against humanity. They were not indicted; they were not charged with treason nor tried for crime. They are honored today by all of their countrymen.

The Civil War between the states met with violent resistance and passionate condemnation. In the year 1864 the Democratic Party met in national convention at Chicago and passed a resolution condemning the war as a failure. What would you say if the Socialist Party were to meet in convention today and condemn the present war as a failure? You charge us with being disloyalists and traitors. Were the Democrats of 1864 disloyalists and traitors because they condemned the war as a failure?

And if so, why were they not indicted and prosecuted accordingly? I believe in the Constitution. Isn't it strange that we Socialists stand almost alone today in upholding and defending the Constitution of the United States? The revolutionary fathers who had been oppressed under king rule understood that free speech, a free press and the right of free assemblage by the people were fundamental principles in democratic government. The very first amendment to the Constitution reads:

"Congress shall make no law respecting an establishment of religion, or prohibiting the free exercise thereof; or abridging the freedom of speech, or of the press; or the right of the people peaceably to assemble, and to petition the government for a redress of grievances."

That is perfectly plain English. It can be understood by a child. I believe the revolutionary fathers meant just what is here stated—that Congress shall make no law abridging the freedom of speech or of the press, or of the right of the people to peaceably assemble, and to petition the government for a redress of their grievances.

That is the right I exercised at Canton on the sixteenth day of last June; and for the exercise of that right, I now have to answer to this indictment. I believe in the right of free speech, in war as well as in peace. I would not, under any circumstances suppress free speech. It is far more dangerous to attempt to gag the people than to allow them to speak freely what is in their hearts.

I have told you that I am no lawyer, but it seems to me that I know enough to know that if Congress enacts any law that conflicts with this provision in the Constitution, that law is void. If the Espionage Law finally stands, then the Constitution of the United States is dead. If that law is not the negation of every fundamental principle established by the Constitution, then certainly I am unable to read or to understand the English language. . . .

Now, gentlemen of the jury, I am not going to detain you too long. . . . I cannot take back a word I have said. I cannot repudiate a sentence I have uttered. I stand before you guilty of having made this speech. . . . I do not know, I cannot tell, what your verdict may be; nor does it matter much, so far as I am concerned.

Gentlemen, I am the smallest part of this trial. I have lived long enough to realize my own personal insignificance in relation to a great issue that involves the welfare of the whole people. What you may choose to do to me will be of small consequence after all. I am not on trial here. There is an infinitely greater issue that is being tried today in this court, though you may not be conscious of it. American institutions are on trial here before a court of American citizens. The future will render the final verdict.

And now, your honor, permit me to return my thanks for your patient consideration. And to you, gentlemen of the jury, for the kindness with which you have listened to me.

I am prepared for your verdict.

81. NORMAN THOMAS

Why I Am a Socialist
(1928)

NORMAN THOMAS's "Why I Am a Socialist" explained how he became a leader of the American Socialist Party. Thomas (1884–1968) did his undergraduate work at Princeton University, and in 1911 he was ordained at Union Theological Seminary. Soon thereafter, he became pastor of the East Harlem Presbyterian Church in New York City, embracing socialism, pacifism, and Social Gospel Christianity. Following Eugene Debs's death in 1926, Thomas emerged as the premier leader of the U.S. socialist movement. Between 1928 and 1948 he ran for president six times, and in his best showing in 1932, he polled for nearly 1 million votes. He also wrote more than twenty books and championed a number of left-wing causes that came to fruition, including unemployment insurance, a minimum wage, an end to child labor, and a shorter work week. One of Thomas's greatest admirers was Martin Luther King, Jr., who once told him in a taped message, "I can think of no man who has done more than you to inspire the vision of a society free of injustice and exploitation . . . all that we hear of the Great Society seems only an echo of your prophetic eloquence."

SOURCE: Norman Thomas. "Why I Am a Socialist." *Princeton Alumni Weekly*, April 6, 1928.

SELECTED READINGS: Bernard K. Johnpoll, *Pacifist's Progress: Norman Thomas and the Decline of American Socialism* (1970). W. A. Swanberg, *Norman Thomas: The Last Idealist* (1976). Harry Fleischman, *Norman Thomas: A Biography, 1884– 1968* (1969).

Let us begin by examining the situation in which we find ourself. However much we may differ on many things we shall probably agree that only today, or yesterday at the earliest, after the long millenniums of man's life on this planet, has he acquired the technical skill, the command over the forces of nature, the physical power to produce enough and to spare for all his children upon the face of the earth. From the first dawn of human life poverty has been principally due to man's imperfect knowledge of natural forces. For un-numbered generations he wrestled for a living with a capricious and often unfriendly Nature, armed only with the power of his own hands and the muscles of the few animals he had been able to domesticate, aided by a very imperfect utilization of the weight of falling water on primitive mill wheels and of the winds of heaven to sail his boats and turn his mills. That was all. Today it has been estimated that each of us Americans has the equivalent of the labor of more than thirty slaves in the energy of steam, electricity and internal combustion engines. The energy thus available for the work of men is increasing by leaps and bounds. It is applied to machinery of marvellous in-genuity. The long age of Markham's "Man With the Hoe" is gone forever. It is possible that the pressure of population upon food supply may bring about a new age of poverty. That pressure does not exist today if the world is taken as a unit, and the decline of the birth rate and the increasing knowledge of scientific birth control give some hope that this ultimate danger may be avoided.

In other words, the old excuse of the classical philosophers for human slavery no longer exists. The bitter toil of the many is not the necessary basis for the culture of the few. In the words of Professor Simon Patten we have passed from a necessary "pain economy" to a possible "pleasure economy" as a basis for civilization. Yet how far we are even in "prosperous" America from the abolition of poverty. With all our machinery and with all the natural energy at our disposal we do not produce enough really to banish poverty even were we to distribute what we produce by a system more equitable than that under which 1 per cent of the receivers of income obtain 20 per cent of the national income; 10 per cent receive 40 per cent of the total income, while the poorest 25 per cent receive only 3½ per cent.

For this state of affairs there are today only two possible explanations. One blames our fate on human nature; the other upon the inadequacy of human ideals and institutions. The first is popular because it gives men an excuse for enjoying whatsoever advantages they may have. In a day when to read the *American Mercury* is the mark of membership in the modern intelligentsia it is no longer fashionable to affirm that this is the *best* of possible worlds. But one may without any strain on the intellect or any demand upon energy or will declare that it is the best of *possible* worlds and go about his own business or pleasure with a sense of intellectual superiority. Here I have space only to remark that this dogma of the incapacity of men to control for social advantage the machinery they have had the wit to create is as unscientific and as yet unproved as the optimistic faith of early radicals in the "infinite perfectability" of human nature. At the very least we should not adopt it without further examination into social institutions and ideals. The madness of our civilization may arise less from our unalterable biological inheritance than from the system—political and economic—under which we live, a system which lags dangerously behind the demands of our interdependent society.

I am aware that to speak of a capitalist or any other system is to invite the scorn of those who insist that in the changing process of our economic life there is no rigorous system. There is truth in the argument. Certainly Ricardo or Adam Smith would not recognize the child of their economic dogmas. Men are still trying to justify economic practices by an almost religious faith in, let us say, the "automatic working" of those markets with which they themselves spend many of their working hours successfully interfering by high tariffs, trade agreements, etc. Nevertheless we can describe the capitalist system as characterized by an emphasis upon private ownership of property for power and the operation of that ownership for the profit of the owners. This is a system which has played its part in human history—a part nowhere more sincerely eulogized than in the famous Communist Manifesto itself. But whatever the historic necessity for capitalism, it is not today giving men the bread, the security, the peace, the freedom, the brotherhood which they have a right to expect.

What Capitalism Does Not Give

Those of you who have had the patience to follow me thus far will not demand of me that I take much space to prove how much tragic poverty still persists among us. Mr. Hoover's estimate of an average annual wage for American workers of $1,280 is not only insufficient on the average to maintain the minimum budgets of health and decency which have been set forth by various authorities, but implies a tragic amount of suffering for the large group below this average.

Even worse than the suffering caused by routine conditions of poverty is the misery of insecurity due to unemployment and old age. In the best of times there is a reserve of one million unemployed in the United States. We are so callous, so indifferent to our social responsibilities, that we do not have adequate figures whereby we can check up unemployment in dull times like the present. To recurring cycles of unemployment due primarily to underconsumption (or, if you like, to the Foster-Catchings "dilemma of thrift") we have the present unemployment due to the great increase in the productive efficiency of machinery. Now, as from the very beginning of the machine age, the under-dog pays the bitter cost of these improvements in machinery which in the long run benefit society. Society compensates him with meager and contemptuous charity. As for old age, the estimate that one-third of the population sixty-five years old and upwards is dependent upon some form of charity in prosperous America suggests that for the workers the evening of life has a terror past any eloquence of a Cicero or a Browning to assuage. Even the charity of children is no adequate substitute for independence for the man with, perhaps, some years of vigor before him, but no job and no pension. It is one of the worst reproaches on our American civilization that neither for unemployment nor old age have we applied such alleviation as the present system would permit. Our failure is part of the ethical and humanitarian price exacted by our individualistic capitalism.

A still more dreadful indictment of our existing institutions is the constant menace of war inherent in that union of capitalism and nationalism which brings forth imperialism and out of imperialistic rivalry war itself. Lack of space must again excuse dogmatic assertion. The new attitude of the United States toward foreign problems, the shifting emphasis on the relative importance of "liberty" and "law and order" in the territories of our neighbors, our repeated military intervention in the Carribean countries, in short, our general imperialism, is due to the fact that we are today a creditor nation busily engaged in the quest of markets for goods, sources of supply for raw material and, above all, markets for the investment capital which piles up in the hands of relatively few people at a time when the many cannot buy enough to maintain a proper standard of comfort. The religion of nationalism makes it easy to persuade the exploited themselves to fight the battles of the investors whose adventurous dollars have got in trouble abroad. I do not mean that any considerable class of men deliberately wills war, at least not large scale war. They do desire that imperialism out of which war arises.

It is scarcely necessary to elaborate the statement that men under our present system do not enjoy freedom and brotherhood. I know that it is customary to attack Socialism as the foe of individual liberty. It is quite true that the problem of the relation of the individual to society will not be automatically solved by Socialism. But it is not the champions of the present order who have a right to pose as the defenders of liberty in a society where property is so much better defended than life, and where freedom is too generally the possession of the man who is strong enough to take it for himself. The regimentation of ideas through a property-controlled press and the economic fear under which most workers live, whether they wear overalls or white collars, makes real freedom an almost non-existent commodity. Diogenes might find an honest man with a lantern. He would have to look for a free man with a searchlight in our modern age. As for brotherhood in other than a sentimental Y.M.C.A. sense, that is denied by the very nature of a system based on

> The good old rule, the ancient plan
> That he should take who has the power,
> And he should keep who can.

Kindness there is among us and charity. Yes, and a capacity for brotherhood but not the reality of that "fellowship which is life."

These failures of our civilization in spite of its tremendous mechanical competence are, I repeat, the natural consequence of the economic princi ples and their corresponding ethical ideas on which we operate. They are inherent in the system and not excrescences on it. Take, for example, Stuart Chase's brilliant study of "The Tragedy of Waste." No one has yet shown how we can eliminate the waste of idle men, the waste of the production of "illth" rather than wealth, the waste of uncoordinated industry, the waste of the ruthless destruction of natural resources, without a profound modification of our system of private ownership of basic resources and their operation for private profit.

The Socialist Proposal

What do the Socialists propose to do about this situation? In Socialism as in every great historic movement there are divergencies of opinion and ideas. There is the sharp and bitter division between Socialists and Communists, principally on the important question of method and tactics. In general, however, Socialists propose to bring about as rapidly as possible the social ownership of land, natural resources and the principle means of production, thereby abolishing the possibility of the existence of any class on an income derived not from work but from ownership. This does not necessarily mean that no man will have a home that he can call his own. His right will rest on use and not on a title deed. The rental value of land belongs to society and not to the individual. Socialism would end the monstrous and absurd injustice under which generations of men and women can live in luxury, without useful labor of any sort because they were wise enough to pick an ancestor who in his day had been clever enough to pick, let us say, a farm in New York City on or near which some six million people now have to live. This is a criticism not of individuals but of the social system which hertofore we have collectively tolerated. Socialists unlike single taxers object not merely to economic dynasties founded on ownership of land and natural resources but to similar dynasties founded on the ownership of stocks and bonds passed from generation to generation by inheritance. They do not expect to abolish them with the stroke of the pen or of the sword. . . .

The means by which Socialists hope to make progress include the organization of labor industrially through labor unions, of the power of consumers through consumers cooperatives and of citizens through a labor party. The reliance of Socialism is upon the working class, not because of peculiar virtues possessed by the working class but because it is peculiarly in its interest to end exploitation and waste. The class struggle may not be as simple or clear-cut as some Socialist agitators have supposed. It is, nevertheless, a fact of history. But it is also a fact of history that very valuable sympathy and leadership have been given to the exploited classes down through the ages by men of more favored groups to whom justice and the ultimate good of society are dearer than any immediate class interest of their own. The hope of peaceful and intelligent progress depends in large degree upon increasing the number of these men and women who thus transcend class lines.

82. WILLIAM Z. FOSTER

Acceptance Speech at the National Nominating Convention of the Workers (Communist) Party of America (1928)

Accepting the Workers Party of America's U.S. presidential nomination in 1928, **WILLIAM Z. FOSTER (1881–1961)** illustrated the revolutionary zeal of American communism before the Popular Front. Foster was raised an Irish Catholic in the Philadelphia slums, and throughout his life he was immersed in both radical working-class struggles in America as well as the international communist movement. In 1920, Foster created the Trade Union Educational League (TUEL), a coalition of militant trade unionists who opposed the conservative leadership of the American Federation of Labor (AFL). Foster was also the party's presidential candidate in 1924, 1928, and 1932, and he served as the party's chairperson from 1932 to 1957, witnessing both its zenith and its decline. He died in Moscow in 1961. Wrote Theodore Draper: "[Foster] personified the American proletariat as few radical leaders have ever done." His 1928 speech emphasized the Workers (Communist) Party's relentless and uncompromising struggle against capitalism.

SOURCE: William Z. Foster. "Acceptance Speech." New York: Workers Library Publishers, 1928.

SELECTED READINGS: James R. Barret, *American Bolshevik: William Z. Foster and American Labor Radicalism* (1994). Edward P. Johanningsmeier, *Forging American Communism: The Life of William Z. Foster* (1994). Theodore Draper, *American Communism and Soviet Russia* (1960).

Party Plays Leading Role

Since 1924 our Party has had much mass experience. We have played a leading role in all the important struggles of the American working class, in the

320

mining, shoe, needle, textile, and other industries. Every effort of the workers in the direction of a labor party has found us in the forefront. We have led the fight against imperialism. During these struggles, we have created around our Party a large body of sympathizers, and in the coming election period one of our principal tasks must be to mobilize these workers politically in favor of our platform, and behind our candidates. It is not enough that these workers follow us in strikes, and general wage movements. We must also teach them to actively accept the leadership of the Workers (Communist) Party in its broad political struggles. We must draw these workers into this general political campaign, and induce them to vote for our candidates. We must draw them into membership in the Workers (Communist) Party. These are among the basic tasks confronting us in the present election campaign.

Our Revolutionary Purpose

We are not going into the national election campaign solely for the purpose of getting votes. It is of course important that we register the extent of our Party's support in the working class by mobilizing the maximum number to vote for our candidates. It is also important, should the possibility present itself in any of the state or local elections, to elect Communist candidates, so that they can utilize the legislative bodies as a forum wherefrom to acquaint the workers with the iniquities of capitalism and the necessity of the Communist program. But we also have other, bigger objectives in the national election campaign. Our aim must be to arouse the class-consciousness of the masses in a political sense and to mobilize them for struggle on all fronts. Vote-getting is only one aspect of this general mobilization of the workers.

Our Party, different from the Socialist Party, creates no illusions amongst the workers that they can vote their way to emancipation, that they can capture the ready-made machinery of the state and utilize it for the emancipation of the working class. On the contrary, we must utilize this campaign to carry on a widespread and energetic propaganda to teach the workers that the capitalist class would never allow the working class peacefully to take control of the state. That is their strong right arm and they will fight violently to the end to retain it. The working class must shatter the capitalist state. It must build a new state, a new government, a workers' and farmers' government, the Soviet Government of the United States. (Applause.)

No Communist, no matter how many votes he should secure in a national election, could, even if he would, become president of the present government. When a Communist heads a government in the United States—and that day will come just as surely as the sun rises (Applause)—that government will not be a capitalistic government but a Soviet government, and behind this government will stand the Red Army to enforce the Dictatorship of the Proletariat. (Applause.)

As to Immediate Demands

Our convention has just adopted an election platform. This platform outlines a whole series of immediate measures, advocated by us to relieve unemployment, low wages, long hours, discrimination against the foreign-born, women, youth, Negroes, etc. I shall not, in the brief time at my disposal, review these demands. What I wish to say about them now is that we must lay great stress on these demands during the campaign. It is not enough that we simply put forward our revolutionary slogans. We must also organize and lead the workers in their everyday struggles against the most acute evils under capitalism. Our platform demands point the way to do this.

But on the other hand, we must not put forth our immediate demands in the sense that they of themselves make for the emancipation of the working class. In all our agitation around these demands we must emphasize the absolute necessity for the proletarian revolution. Our strategy is to utilize these immediate demands to educate and organize the masses in preparation for the final revolutionary struggle, which will abolish capitalism altogether. Reliance upon immediate demands would lead us merely to reformism. Our Party is a revolutionary Party. It aims not simply to ease conditions a bit under capitalism for the workers but to abolish capitalism altogether. (Applause.)

Permanent improvement in the conditions of the workers under capitalism is impossible. The inevitable crises, born of the contradictions in the capitalist system of production and distribution, deepening and sharpening as world capitalism goes into its period of decline, and marked by chronic unemployment and organized attacks on the workers' living standards by the employers and the state, sweep away like chaff such reforms as may have been secured by the workers during the periods of capitalism's upward swing. The only way the workers can permanently better their conditions is by wiping out capitalism altogether and by laying the basis of a socialist system in which the capitalist principle of the exploitation of the great masses of producers for the benefit of a relatively few owners of the industries shall be unknown and where the workers will receive the full social value of what they produce. All this, and the whys and wherefores of it we must tell the workers in our election campaign.

Reformism Futile

The working class of the world has had a vast experience with reformism and it all goes to show the utter futility of such reformism. All the conquests, all the little improvements in wages, hours, and working conditions that were secured by the reformist policies and organizations in Germany, England, France, etc., during the upward period of development of capitalism in these countries, in the pre-war days, were swept away with one great sweep in the breakdown and decline of European capitalism in the post-war period. About all that is left now of that period is a reactionary leadership, which after betraying the workers in the world war and defeating their revolutionary efforts just following the war, remains fastened upon the organizations of the workers and which now stands as one of the principal obstacles in the way of the emancipation of the working class. Although we advocate actively our immediate demands, we must always do it in this sense: that the workers should fight and struggle for these demands in the present period but that they must educate and organize themselves to put into effect eventually the full Communist program—the abolishment of the capitalist system itself and the establishment of a Workers' and Farmers' Government.

On the other hand—if limiting ourselves simply to a program of immediate demands would lose us in the swamp of reformism, failure to put forward such demands would condemn us to sectarianism. It would cut us off from the masses. It would make it impossible for us to participate in the actual everyday struggles of the workers and thus to educate, organize and lead them. The Workers (Communist) Party is a Leninist, Marxist Party. It knows how to participate in the daily struggles of the workers, even for the smallest demands, and it knows how to utilize all these struggles to develop class-consciousness, organization and revolutionary leadership among the masses and thus to begin their mobilization for the eventual overthrow of capitalism.

83. HUEY LONG

Share Our Wealth
(1935)

One of the most controversial figures in modern American political history, **HUEY LONG**'s response to the Great Depression was the Share Our Wealth movement. Born on a farm near Winnfield, Louisiana, Long (1893–1935) worked as a traveling salesman before attending (and dropping out of) Tulane Law School. Nevertheless, he passed the state bar exam in 1915 at age twenty-one. A man of great energy and ambition, Long was elected governor of Louisiana in 1928. Although he put thousands to work on public projects, paved thousands of miles of roads, and distributed free textbooks to schoolchildren, Long was also a ruthless and corrupt politician who sometimes resorted to demagoguery. He became a U.S. senator in 1930, where he frequently drew the ire of business interests as well as the Roosevelt Administration, which was threatened by his popularity. Long believed that concentrated wealth was one of the greatest dangers facing society, and he claimed that as many as 7.5 million citizens joined the Share Our Wealth clubs that he helped form in 1934. Long planned to run for president but was assassinated in 1935; Robert Penn Warren's fictionalized account of Long's life, *All the King's Men* won the Pulitzer Prize in 1946.

SOURCE: Huey Long, "To Members and Well-Wishers of the Share Our Wealth Society," *Congressional Record,* 74th U.S. Congress, 1st Session, Vol. 79. Washington, D.C.: U.S. Government Printing Office, 1935; reprinted in Henry C. Dethloff, ed., *Huey P. Long: Southern Demagogue or American Democrat?* Lafayette, LA: University of Southwestern Louisiana Press, 1976.

SELECTED READINGS: Alan Brinkley, *Voices of Protest: Huey Long, Father Coughlin, and the Great Depression* (1982). Robert Penn Warren, *All the King's Men* (1960). T. Harry Williams, *Huey Long* (1981).

To Members and Well-Wishers of the Share Our Wealth Society: For twenty years I have been in the battle to provide that, so long as America has, or can produce, an abundance of the things which make life comfortable and happy, that none should own so much of the things which he does not need and cannot use, as to deprive the balance of the people of a reasonable proportion of the necessities and conveniences of life. The whole line of my political thought has always been that America must face the time when the whole country would shoulder the obligation which it owes to every child born on earth,—that is, a fair chance to life, liberty, and happiness. . . .

Here is the whole sum and substance of the Share Our Wealth movement:

1. Every family to be furnished by the government a homestead allowance, free of debt, of not less than one-third the average family wealth of the country, which means, at the lowest, that every family shall have the reasonable comforts of life up to a value of from $5,000 to $6,000: No person to have a fortune of more than 100 to 300 times the average family fortune, which means that the limit to fortune is between $1,500,000 and $5,000,000, with annual capital levy taxes imposed on all above $1,000,000.

2. The yearly income of every family shall be not less than one-third of the average family income, which means that, according to the estimates of the statisticians of the U.S. Government and Wall Street, no family's annual income would be less than from $2,000 to $2,500: No yearly income shall be allowed to any person larger than from 100 to 300 times the size of the average family income, which means that no person would be allowed to earn in any year more than from $600,000 to $1,800,000, all to be subject to present income tax laws.

3. To limit or regulate the hours of work to such an extent as to prevent over-production; the most modern and efficient machinery would be encouraged so that as much would be produced as possible so as to satisfy all demands of the people, but to also allow the maximum time to the workers for recreation, convenience, education, and luxuries of life.

4. An old age pension to the persons over 60.

5. To balance agricultural production with what can be consumed according to the laws of God, which includes the preserving and storing of surplus commodities to be paid for and held by the Government for the emergencies when such are needed. Please bear in mind, however, that when the people of America have had money to buy things they needed, we have never had a surplus of any commodity. This plan of God does not call for destroying any of the things raised to eat or wear, nor does it countenance whole destruction of hogs, cattle or milk.

6. To pay the veterans of our wars what we owe them and to care for their disabled.

7. Education and training for all children to be equal in opportunity in all schools, colleges, universities and other institutions for training in the professions and vocations of life; to be regulated on the capacity of children to learn, and not on the ability of parents to pay the costs. Training for life's work to be as much universal and thorough for all walks in life as has been the training in the arts of killing.

8. The raising of revenue and taxes for the support of this program to come from the reduction of swollen fortunes from the top, as well as for the support of public works to give employment whenever there may be any slackening necessary in private enterprise.

I now ask those who read this circular to help us at once in this work of giving life and happiness to our people,—not a starvation dole upon which someone may live in misery from week to week. Before this miserable system of wreckage has destroyed the life germ of respect and culture in our American people, let us save what was here, merely by having none too poor and none too rich. The theory of the Share Our Wealth Society is to have enough for all, but not to have one with so much that less than enough remains for the balance of the people.

Please, therefore, let me ask you who read this document,—please help this work before it is too late for us to be of help to our people. We ask you now, (1) help to get your neighbor into the work of this Society, and (2) help get other Share Our Wealth societies started in your county and in adjoining counties and get them to go out to organize other societies.

To print and mail out this circular costs about 60c per hundred, or $6.00 per thousand. Anyone who reads this who wants more circulars of this kind to use in the work, can get them for that price by sending the money to me, and I will pay the printer for him. Better still, if you can have this circular reprinted in your own town or city.

Let everyone who feels he wishes to help in our work start right out and go ahead. One man or woman is as important as any other. Take up the fight! Do not wait for someone else to tell you what to do. There are no high lights in this effort. We have no state managers and no city managers. Everyone can take up the work and as many societies can be organized as there are people to organize them. One is the same as another. The reward and compensation is the salvation of humanity. Fear no opposition. "He who falls in this fight falls in the radiance of the future!"

> *Yours sincerely,*
> Huey P. Long,
> *United States Senator,*
> *Washington, D. C.*

CHAPTER

SEVEN

"New Negro"
To Black Power

84. HUBERT H. HARRISON

Two Negro Radicalisms

(1919)

HUBERT HARRISON's "Two Negro Radicalisms" is among the most important of his editorials, written during his tenure as editor of *New Negro* magazine. Harrison (1883–1927), who is one of the most overlooked figures in early-twentieth-century radicalism, was born in the Danish West Indies and arrived in New York in 1900. Largely self-educated, Harrison helped found and nurture the New Negro movement, introducing black nationalist Marcus Garvey to New York crowds and establishing, in 1917, the Liberty League, a radical alternative to the National Association for the Advancement of Colored People (NAACP). Harrison was also a leading editor and educator, and a legendary street orator. "Two Negro Radicalisms" was Harrison's call for a race-conscious radicalism as opposed to the class-based politics of black socialists.

SOURCE: Hubert Harrison. "Two Negro Radicalisms." *New Negro,* October, 1919.

SELECTED READINGS: Hubert H. Harrison, *A Hubert Harrison Reader*, Jeffrey S. Perry, ed. (2001). Winston James, *"Holding Aloft the Banner of Ethiopia": Caribbean Radicalism in Early Twentieth-Century America* (1988). John G. Jackson, *Hubert Henry Harrison: The Black Socrates* (1987).

Twenty years ago all Negroes known to the white publicists of America could be classed as conservatives on all the great questions on which thinkers differ. In matters of industry, commerce, politics, religion, they could be trusted to take the backward view. Only on the question of the Negro's "rights" could a small handful be found bold enough to be tagged as "radicals"—and they were howled down by both the white and colored adherents of the conservative point of view. Today Negroes differ on all those great questions on which

white thinkers differ, and there are Negro radicals of every imaginable stripe—
agnostics, atheists, I.W.W.'s., Socialists, Single Taxers, and even Bolshevists.

In the good old days white people derived their knowledge of what Negroes
were doing from those Negroes who were nearest to them, generally their
own selected exponents of Negro activity or of their white point of view. A
classic illustration of this kind of knowledge was afforded by the Republican
Party; but the Episcopal Church, the Urban League, or the U.S. Government
would serve as well. To-day the white world is vaguely, but disquietingly,
aware that Negroes are awake, different and perplexingly uncertain. Yet the
white world by which they are surrounded retains its traditional method of
interpreting the mass by the Negro nearest to themselves in affiliation or contact. The Socialist party thinks that the "unrest" now apparent in the Negro
masses is due to the propaganda which its adherents support, and believes
that it will function largely along the lines of socialist political thought. The
great dailies, concerned mainly with their chosen task of being the mental
bellwethers of the mob, scream "Bolshevist propaganda" and flatter themselves that they have found the true cause; while the government's unreliable
agents envisage it as "disloyalty." The truth, as usual, is to be found in the
depths: but they are all prevented from going by mental laziness and that
traditional off-handed, easy contempt with which white men in America, from
scholars like Lester Ward to scavengers like [Archibald E.] Stevenson, deign
to consider the colored population of 12 millions.

In the first place the cause of the "radicalism" among American Negroes is
international. But it is necessary to cause clear distinctions at the outset. The
function of the Christian church is international. So is art, war, the family,
rum and exploitation of labor. But none of these is entitled to extend the
mantle of its own peculiar "internationalism" to cover the present case of the
Negro discontent—although this has been attempted. The international Fact
to which Negroes in America are now reacting is not the exploitation of laborers by capitalists; but the social, political and economic subjection of colored peoples by white. It is not the Class Line, but the Color Line, which is
the incorrect but accepted expression for the Dead Line of racial inferiority.
This fact is a fact of Negro consciousness as well as a fact of externals. The
international Color Line is the practice and theory of that doctrine which holds
that the best stocks of Africa, China, Egypt and the West Indies are inferior
to the worst stocks of Belgium, England, and Italy, and must hold their lives,
lands and liberties upon such terms and conditions as the white races may
choose to grant them.

On the part of the whites, the motive was originally economic; but it is no
longer purely so. All the available facts go to prove that, whether in the United
States or in Africa or China, the economic subjection is without exception
keener and more brutal when the exploited are black, brown and yellow, than

when they are white. And the fact that black, brown, and yellow also exploit each other brutally whenever Capitalism has created the economic classes of plutocrat and proletarian should suffice to put purely economic subjection out of court as the prime cause of racial unrest. For the similarity of suffering has produced in all lands where whites rule colored races a certain similarity of sentiment, viz.: a racial revulsion of racial feeling. The peoples of those lands begin to feel and realize that they are so subjected because they are members of races condemned as "inferior" by their Caucasian overlords. The fact presented to their minds is one of race, and in terms of race do they react to it. Put the case to any Negro by way of test and the answer will make this clear.

The great World War, by virtue of its great advertising campaign for democracy and the promises which were held out to subject peoples, fertilized the Race Consciousness of the Negro people into the stage of conflict with the dominant white idea of the Color Line. They took democracy at its face value—which is—Equality. So did the Hindus, Egyptians, and West Indians. This is what the hypocritical advertisers of democracy had not bargained for. The American Negroes, like the other darker peoples, are presenting their checques and trying to "cash in," and delays in that process, however unavoidable to the paying tellers, are bound to beget a plentiful lack of belief in either their intention or in their ability to pay. Hence the run on Democracy's bank—"the Negro unrest" of the newspaper paragraphers.

This Race Consciousness takes many forms, some negative, others positive. On the one hand we balk at Jim Crow, object to educational starvation, refuse to accept goodwill for good deeds, and scornfully reject our conservative leaders. On the other hand, we are seeking racial independence in business and reaching out into new fields of endeavor. One of the most taking enterprises at present is the Black Star Line, a steamship enterprise being floated by Mr. Marcus Garvey of New York. Garvey's project (whatever may be its ultimate fate) has attracted tens of thousands of Negroes. Where Negro "radicals" of the type known to white radicals can scarce get a handful of people, Garvey fills the largest halls and the Negro people rain money on him. This is not to be explained by the argument of "superior brains," for this man's education and intelligence are markedly inferior to those of the brilliant "radicals" whose "internationalism" is drawn from other than racial sources. But this man holds up to the Negro masses those things which bloom in their hearts—racialism, race-consciousness, racial solidarity—things taught first in 1917 by THE VOICE and The Liberty League. That is the secret of his success so far.

All over this land and in the West Indies Negroes are responding to the call of battle against the white man's Color Line. And, so long as this remains, the international dogma of the white race, so long will the new Negro war against it. This is the very Ethiopianism which England has been combatting from Cairo to the Cape.

Undoubtedly some of these newly-awakened Negroes will take to Socialism and Bolshevism. But here again the reason is racial. Since they suffer racially from the world as at present organized by the white race, some of their ablest hold that it is "good play" to encourage and give aid to every subversive movement within that white world which makes for its destruction "as it is." For by its subversion they have much to gain and nothing to lose. But they build on their own foundations. Parallel with the dogma of Class-Consciousness they run the dogma of Race-Consciousness. And they dig deeper. For the roots of Class-consciousness inhere in a temporary economic order; whereas the roots of Race-Consciousness must of necessity survive any and all changes in the economic order. Accepting biology as a fact, their view is the more fundamental. At any rate, it is that view with which the white world will have to deal.

85. W. A. DOMINGO

The New Negro—What Is He?
(1920)

With the following essay, W. A. DOMINGO helped define the self-assertive and racially conscious mood of the "New Negro." Although born in Jamaica, Domingo (1889–1968) was intensely involved in Harlem radicalism during the 1920s. Domingo was briefly affiliated with Marcus Garvey's newspaper, *Negro World,* but his socialism clashed with Garvey's "Race First" nationalism. Later, he was active in the Socialist Party and in Cyril Brigg's African Blood Brotherhood (ABB). In "The New Negro—What Is He?" Domingo sought to clarify some confusion about how to best define the "New Negro," arguing that "he" should best be understood as an assertive, politically sophisticated socialist, dedicated to the radical transformation of the American social and economic order.

SOURCE: W. A. Domingo. "The New Negro—What Is He?" *The Messenger,* vol. 2. August, 1920.

SELECTED READINGS: Sondra Kathryn Wilson, *The Messenger Reader: Stories, Poetry, and Essays from* The Messenger *Magazine* (2000). Winston James, *"Holding Aloft the Banner of Ethiopia": Caribbean Radicalism in Early Twentieth-Century America* (1988). Philip S. Foner, *American Socialism and Black Americans* (1977).

Now, what are the aims of the New Negro? The answer to this question will fail under three general heads, namely, political, economic, and social.

In politics, the New Negro, unlike the Old Negro, cannot be lulled into a false sense of security with political spoils and patronage. A job is not the price of his vote. He will not continue to accept political promissory notes from a political debtor, who has already had the power, but who has refused to satisfy his political obligations. The New Negro demands political equality. He recognizes the necessity of selective as well as elective representation. He realizes that so long as the Negro votes for the Republican or Democratic party, he

will have only the right and privilege to elect but not to select his representatives. And he who selects the representatives controls the representative.
The New Negro stands for universal suffrage.

A word about the economic aims of the New Negro. Here, as a worker, he
demands the full product of his toil. His immediate aim is more wages, shorter
hours and better working conditions. As a consumer, he seeks to buy in the
market, commodities at the lowest possible price.

The social aims of the New Negro are decidedly different from those of the
Old Negro. Here he stands for absolute and unequivocal *"social equality."* He
realizes that there cannot be any qualified equality. He insists that a society
which is based upon justice can only be a society composed of *social equals.*
He insists upon identity of social treatment. With respect to intermarriage, he
maintains that it is the only logical, sound and correct aim for the Negro to
entertain. He realizes that the acceptance of laws against intermarriage is tantamount to the acceptance of the stigma of inferiority. Besides, laws against
intermarriage expose Negro women to sexual exploitation, and deprive their
offspring, by white men, of the right to inherit the property of their father.
Statistics show that there are nearly four million mulattoes in America as a
result of miscegenation.

So much then for the aims of the New Negro. A word now about his
methods. It is with respect to methods that the essential difference between
the New Negro and the Old Negro relates.

First, the methods by which the New Negro expects to realize his political
aims are radical. He would repudiate and discard both of the old parties—
Republican and Democratic. His knowledge of political science enables him to
see that a political organization must have an economic foundation. A party
whose money comes from working people, must and will represent working
people. Now, everybody concedes that the Negro is essentially a worker. There
are no big capitalists among them. There are a few petit bourgeoisie, but the
process of money concentration is destined to weed them out and drop them
down into the ranks of the working class. In fact, the interests of all Negroes
are tied up with the workers. Therefore, the Negro should support a working
class political party. He is a fool or insane, who opposes his best interests by
supporting his enemy. As workers, Negroes have nothing in common with
their employers. The Negro wants high wages; the employer wants to pay low
wages. The Negro wants to work short hours; the employer wants to work
him long hours. Since this is true, it follows as a logical corollary that the
Negro should not support the party of the employing class. Now, it is a question of fact that the Republican and Democratic Parties are parties of the employing or capitalist class.

On the economic field, the New Negro advocates that the Negro join the
labor unions. Wherever white unions discriminate against the Negro worker,

then the only sensible thing to do is to form independent unions to fight both the white capitalists for more wages and shorter hours, on the one hand, and white labor unions for justice, on the other. It is folly for the Negro to fight labor organization because some white unions ignorantly ignore or oppose him. It is about as logical and wise as to repudiate and condemn writing on the ground that it is used by some crooks for forgery. As a consumer, he would organize cooperative societies to reduce the high cost of living.

The social methods are: education and physical action in self defense. That education must constitute the basis of all action, is beyond the realm of question. And to fight back in self defense, should be accepted as a matter of course. No one who will not fight to protect his life is fit to live. Self defense is recognized as a legitimate weapon in all civilized countries. Yet the Old Crowd Negroes have counseled the doctrine of non-resistance.

As to current movements, the Negro would accept, praise and support that which his enemies reject, condemn and oppose. He is tolerant. He would restore free speech, a free press and freedom of assemblage. He would release Debs. He would recognize the right of Russia to self determination. He is opposed to the Treaty and the League of Nations. Yet, he rejects Lodge's reservations. He knows that neither will help the people. As to Negro leaders, his object is to destroy them all and build up new ones.

Finally, the New Negro arrived upon the scene at the time of all other forward, progressive groups and movements—after the great world war. He is the product of the same world-wide forces that have brought into being the great liberal and radical movements that are now seizing the reins of political, economic and social power in all of the civilized countries of the world.

His presence is inevitable in these times of economic chaos, political upheaval and social distress. Yes, there is a New Negro. And it is he who will pilot the Negro through this terrible hour of storm and stress.

86. MARCUS GARVEY

Africa for the Africans
(1923)

In "**Africa** for the Africans," **MARCUS GARVEY** championed the twin goals of race pride and race solidarity. Garvey (1887–1940) was born in Jamaica, and in 1914 he founded the Universal Negro Improvement Association (UNIA) for the "general uplift of the Negro peoples of the world." Garvey arrived in Harlem in 1916, and by the early 1920s the UNIA had become the largest black activist organization in American history. However, Garvey clashed with other African-American leaders (most notoriously, with W. E. B. Du Bois), and the UNIA weakened in the face of government repression as well as Garvey's own mismanagement. In 1925, Garvey was convicted of mail fraud and he spent three years in prison before being deported to Jamaica in 1927. "Africa for the Africans" promoted Garvey's vision of a great black empire in Africa.

SOURCE: Marcus Garvey. *Philosophy and Opinions of Marcus Garvey.* Amy Jacques-Garvey, ed. New York: Atheneum, 1925.

SELECTED READINGS: Tony Martin, *Race First: The Ideological and Organizational Struggles of Marcus Garvey and the Universal Negro Improvement Association* (1976). Theodore G. Vincent, *Black Power and the Garvey Movement* (1971). Edmund David Cronon, *Black Moses: The Story of Marcus Garvey and the Universal Negro Improvement Association* (1955).

For five years the Universal Negro Improvement Association has been advocating the cause of Africa for the Africans—that is, that the Negro peoples of the world should concentrate upon the object of building up for themselves a great nation in Africa.

When we started our propaganda toward this end several of the so-called intellectual Negroes who have been bamboozling the race for over half a century said that we were crazy, that the Negro peoples of the western world were not interested in Africa and could not live in Africa. One editor and leader went so far as to say at his so-called Pan-African Congress that American Negroes could not live in Africa, because the climate was too hot. All kinds of arguments have been adduced by these Negro intellectuals against the colonization of Africa by the black race. Some said that the black man would ultimately work out his existence alongside of the white man in countries founded and established by the latter. Therefore, it was not necessary for Negroes to seek an independent nationality of their own. The old time stories of "African fever," "African bad climate," "African mosquitos," "African savages," have been repeated by these "brainless intellectuals" of ours as a scare against our people in America and the West Indies taking a kindly interest in the new program of building a racial empire of our own in our Motherland. Now that years have rolled by and the Universal Negro Improvement Association has made the circuit of the world with its propaganda, we find eminent statesmen and leaders of the white race coming out boldly advocating the cause of colonizing Africa with the Negroes of the western world. A year ago Senator MacCullum of the Mississippi Legislature introduced a resolution in the House for the purpose of petitioning the Congress of the United States of America and the President to use their good influence in securing from the Allies sufficient territory in Africa in liquidation of the war debt, which territory should be used for the establishing of an independent nation for American Negroes. About the same time Senator France of Maryland gave expression to a similar desire in the Senate of the United States. During a speech on the "Soldiers' Bonus." He said: "We owe a big debt to Africa and one which we have too long ignored. I need not enlarge upon our peculiar interest in the obligation to the people of Africa. Thousands of Americans have for years been contributing to the missionary work which has been carried out by the noble men and women who have been sent out in that field by the churches of America."

The Dream of a Negro Empire

It is only a question of a few more years when Africa will be completely colonized by Negroes, as Europe is by the white race. What we want is an independent African nationality, and if America is to help the Negro peoples of the world establish such a nationality, then we welcome the assistance.

It is hoped that when the time comes for American and West Indian Negroes to settle in Africa, they will realize their responsibility and their duty. It will not be to go to Africa for the purpose of exercising an over-lordship over the natives, but it shall be the purpose of the Universal Negro Improvement

Association to have established in Africa that brotherly co-operation which will make the interests of the African native and the American and West Indian Negro one and the same, that is to say, we shall enter into a common partnership to build up Africa in the interests of our race.

Oneness of Interests

Everybody knows that there is absolutely no difference between the native African and the American and West Indian Negroes, in that we are descendants from one common family stock. It is only a matter of accident that we have been divided and kept apart for over three hundred years, but it is felt that when the time has come for us to get back together, we shall do so in the spirit of brotherly love, and any Negro who expects that he will be assisted here, there or anywhere by the Universal Negro Improvement Association to exercise a haughty superiority over the fellows of his own race, makes a tremenduous mistake. Such men had better remain where they are and not attempt to become in any way interested in the higher development of Africa.

The Negro has had enough of the vaunted practice of race superiority as inflicted upon him by others, therefore he is not prepared to tolerate a similar assumption on the part of his own people. In America and the West Indies, we have Negroes who believe themselves so much above their fellows as to cause them to think that any readjustment in the affairs of the race should be placed in their hands for them to exercise a kind of an autocratic and despotic control as others have done to us for centuries. Again I say, it would be advisable for such Negroes to take their hands and minds off the now popular idea of colonizing Africa in the interest of the Negro race, because their being identified with this new program will not in any way help us because of the existing feeling among Negroes everywhere not to tolerate the infliction of race or class superiority upon them, as is the desire of the self-appointed and self-created race leadership that we have been having for the last fifty years.

The Basis of an African Aristocracy

The masses of Negroes in America, the West Indies, South and Central America are in sympathetic accord with the aspirations of the native Africans. We desire to help them build up Africa as a Negro Empire, where every black man, whether he was born in Africa or in the Western world, will have the opportunity to develop on his own lines under the protection of the most favorable democratic institutions.

It will be useless, as before stated, for bombastic Negroes to leave America and the West Indies to go to Africa, thinking that they will have privileged positions to inflict upon the race that bastard aristocracy that they have tried to maintain in this Western world at the expense of the masses. Africa shall develop an aristocracy of its own, but it shall be based upon service and loyalty to race. Let all Negroes work toward that end. I feel that it is only a question of a few more years before our program will be accepted not only by the few statesmen of America who are now interested in it, but by the strong statesmen of the world, as the only solution to the great race problem. There is no other way to avoid the threatening war of the races that is bound to engulf all mankind, which has been prophesied by the world's greatest thinkers; there is no better method than by apportioning every race to its own habitat.

The time has really come for the Asiatics to govern themselves in Asia, as the Europeans are in Europe and the Western world, so also is it wise for the Africans to govern themselves at home, and thereby bring peace and satisfaction to the entire human family.

87. LANGSTON HUGHES

The Negro Artist and the Racial Mountain
(1926)

LANGSTON HUGHES's classic essay "The Negro Artist and the Racial Mountain," is one of the most important aesthetic statements to come out of the Harlem Renaissance. Hughes (1902–1967) traveled widely before settling in Harlem in 1921, where he briefly studied at Columbia University. Sometimes called "The Shakespeare of Harlem," Hughes soon emerged as a leading light of the Harlem Renaissance. At the beginning of his career, Hughes made great use of black dialect and jazz rhythms in his poetry, which typically centered upon the urban African-American experience. Later, his work became more overtly political, and he gravitated toward socialism. "The Negro Artist and the Racial Mountain" was Hughes's intervention into a contentious debate about the proper role of the black artist. Whereas some intellectuals urged black writers to uplift the race through propaganda, Hughes encouraged black artists to be true to themselves, and to disregard the artificial standards set by white readers or black activists.

SOURCE: Langston Hughes. "The Negro Artist and the Racial Mountain." *The Nation* 122, June 23, 1926.

SELECTED READINGS: Henry Louis Gates and K. A. Appiah, eds., *Langston Hughes: Critical Perspectives Past and Present* (1998). Langston Hughes, *The Big Sea: An Autobiography* (1993). David L. Lewis, *When Harlem Was in Vogue* (1981).

"An artist must be free to do what he does . . . but he must also never be afraid to do what he might choose."

One of the most promising of young negro poets said to me once, "I want to be a poet—not a Negro poet," meaning, I believe, "I want to write like a white poet"; meaning subconsciously, "I would like to be a white poet"; meaning behind that, "I would like to be white." And I was sorry the young man said that, for no great poet has ever been afraid of being himself. And I doubted then that, with his desire to run away spiritually from his race, this boy would ever be a great poet. But this is the mountain standing in the way of any true Negro art in America—this urge within the race toward whiteness, the desire to pour racial individuality into the mold of American standardization, and to be as little Negro and as much American as possible.

But let us look at the immediate background of this young poet. His family is of what I suppose one would call the Negro middle class: people who are by no means rich yet never uncomfortable nor hungry—smug, contented, respectable folk, members of the Baptist church. The father goes to work every morning. He is a chief steward at a large white club. The mother sometimes does fancy sewing or supervised parties for the rich families of the town. The children go to a mixed school. In the home they read white papers and magazines. And the mother often says "Don't be like niggers" when the children are bad. A frequent phrase from the father is, "Look how well a white man does things." And so the word white comes to be unconsciously a symbol of all the virtues. It holds for the children beauty, morality, and money. The whisper "I want to be white" runs silently through their minds. This young poet's home is, I believe, a fairly typical home of the colored middle class. One sees immediately how difficult it would be for an artist born in such a home to interest himself in interpreting the beauty of his own people. He is never taught to see that beauty. He is taught rather not to see it, or if he does to be ashamed of it when it is not according to Caucasian patterns.

For racial culture that home of a self-styled "high-class" Negro has nothing better to offer. Instead there will perhaps be more aping of things white than in a less cultured or less wealthy home. The father is perhaps a doctor, lawyer, landowner, or politician. The mother may be a social worker, or a teacher, or she may do nothing and have a maid. Father is often dark but he has usually married the lightest woman he could find. The family attend a fashionable church where few really colored faces are to be found. And they themselves draw a color line. In the North they go to white theaters and white movies. And in the South they have at least two cars and a house "like white folks." Nordic manners, Nordic faces, Nordic hair, Nordic art (if any), and an Episcopal heaven. A very high mountain indeed for the would-be racial artist to climb in order to discover himself and his people.

But then there are the low-down folks, the so-called common element, and they are the majority—may the Lord be praised? The people who have their nip of gin on Saturday nights and are not too important to themselves or the community, or too well read, or too learned to watch the lazy world go round. They live on Seventh Street in Washington or State Street in Chicago and they do not particularly care whether they are like white folks or anybody else. Their joy runs, bang! into ecstasy. Their religion soars to a shout. Work maybe a little today, rest a little tomorrow. Play awhile. Sing awhile. O, let's dance! These common people are not afraid of spirituals, as for a long time their more intellectual brethren were, and jazz is their child. They furnish a wealth of colorful, distinctive material for any artist because they still hold their own individuality in the face of American standardizations. And perhaps these common people will give to the world its truly great Negro artist, the one who is not afraid to be himself. Whereas the betterclass Negro would tell the artist what to do, the people at least let him alone when he does appear. And they are not ashamed of him—if they know he exists at all. And they accept what beauty is their own without question.

Certainly there is, for the American Negro artist who can escape the restrictions the more advanced among his own group would put upon him, a great field of unused material ready for his art. Without going outside his race, and even among the better classes with their "white" culture and conscious American manners, but still Negro enough to be different, there is sufficient matter to furnish a black artist with a lifetime of creative work. And when he chooses to touch on the relations between Negroes and whites in this country with their innumerable overtones and undertones, surely, and especially for literature and drama, there is an inexhaustible supply of themes at hand. To these the Negro artist can give his racial individuality, his heritage of rhythm and warmth, and his incongruous humor that so often, as in the Blues, becomes ironic laughter mixed with tears. But let us look again at the mountain. . . .

Most of my own poems are racial in theme and treatment, derived from the life I know. In many of them I try to grasp and hold some of the meanings and rhythms of jazz. I am sincere as I know how to be in these poems and yet after every reading I answer questions like these from my own people: Do you think Negroes should always write about Negroes? I wish you wouldn't read some of your poems to white folks. How do you find anything interesting in a place like a cabaret? Why do you write about black people? You aren't black. What makes you do so many jazz poems?

But jazz to me is one of the inherent expressions of Negro life in America: the eternal tom-tom beating in the Negro soul—the tom-tom of revolt against weariness in a white world, a world of subway trains, and work, work, work; the tom-tom of joy and laughter, and pain swallowed in a smile. Yet the Philadelphia clubwoman is ashamed to say that her race created it and she does not like me to write about it. The old subconscious "white is best" runs through her mind. Years of study under white teachers, a lifetime of white books, pictures, and papers, and white manners, morals, and Puritan standards made her dislike the spirituals. And now she turns up her nose at jazz and all its manifestations—likewise almost everything else distinctly racial. She doesn't care for the Winold Reiss portraits of Negroes because they are "too Negro." She does not want a true picture of herself from anybody. She wants the artist to flatter her, to make the white world believe that all Negroes are as smug and as near white in soul as she wants to be. But, to my mind, it is the duty of the younger Negro artist, if he accepts any duties at all from outsiders, to change through the force of his art that old whispering "I want to be white," hidden in the aspirations of his people, to "Why should I want to be white? I am a Negro—and beautiful."

So I am ashamed for the black poet who says, "I want to be a poet, not a Negro poet," as though his own racial world were not as interesting as any other world. I am ashamed, too, for the colored artist who runs from the painting of Negro faces to the painting of sunsets after the manner of the academicians because he fears the strange unwhiteness of his own features. An artist must be free to choose what he does, certainly, but he must also never be afraid to do what he might choose.

Let the blare of Negro jazz bands and the bellowing voice of Bessie Smith singing Blues penetrate the closed ears of the colored near-intellectuals until they listen and perhaps understand. Let Paul Robeson singing "Water Boy," and Rudolph Fisher writing about the streets of Harlem, and Jean Toomer holding the heart of Georgia in his hands, and Aaron Douglas drawing strange black fantasies cause the smug Negro middle class to turn from their white, respectable, ordinary books and papers to catch a glimmer of their own beauty. We young Negro artists who create now intend to express our individual dark-skinned selves without fear or shame. If white people are pleased we are glad. If they are not, it doesn't matter. We know we are beautiful. And ugly too. The tom-tom cries and the tom-tom laughs. If colored people are pleased we are glad. If they are not, their displeasure doesn't matter either. We build our temples for tomorrow, strong as we know how, and we stand on top of the mountain, free within ourselves.

88. ANGELO HERNDON

You Cannot Kill the Working Class
(1937)

ANGELO HERNDON's "You Cannot Kill the Working Class," helped educate Northerners about the injustices in the Southern legal system. Herndon (1913–) was born into a mining family and as a teenager he joined the Communist Party. In 1932 he was arrested after he helped organize a peaceful, interracial march in Atlanta, Georgia. He was tried before an all-white jury for violating an obscure Georgia insurrection law, and sentenced to eighteen to twenty years on a chain gang. The unjust sentence turned Herndon's case into a cause célèbre. Although primarily supported by the International Labor Defense (ILD), a radical legal-action group that often defended minorities, immigrants, and activists, Herndon's case drew national attention and widespread support from civil rights organizations, labor unions, and religious groups. Herndon was finally freed in 1937 after his case was brought before the United States Supreme Court and the law that he was convicted under was found to be unconstitutional.

SOURCE: Angelo Herndon. *You Cannot Kill the Working Class.* New York: International Labor Defense and League of Struggle for Negro Rights, 1937.

SELECTED READINGS: Mark Solomon, *The Cry Was Unity: Communists and African-Americans, 1917–1936* (1999). Charles H. Martin, *The Angelo Herndon Case and Southern Justice* (1976). Elizabeth Lawson, *Twenty Years on the Chain Gang? Angelo Herndon Must Go Free* (1935).

We lived in the company town. It was pretty bad. The houses were just shacks on unpaved streets. We seldom had anything to eat that was right. We had to buy everything from the company store, or we'd have lost our jobs. They kept our pay low and paid only every two weeks, so we had to have credit

344

between times. We got advances in the form of clackers, which could be used only in the company store. Their prices were very high. I remember paying 30 cents a pound for pork-chops in the company store and then noticing that the butcher in town was selling them for 20 cents. The company store prices were just robbery without a pistol.

The safety conditions in the mine were rotten. The escapeways were far from where we worked, and there was never enough timbering to keep the rocks from falling. There were some bad accidents while I was there. I took all the skin off my right hand pushing a car up into the facing. The cars didn't have enough grease and there were no cross-ties just behind me to brace my feet against. That was a bit of the company's economy. The car slipped, the track turned over, and the next thing I knew I had lost all the skin and a lot of the flesh off my right hand. The scars are there to this day.

This DeBardeleben mine in Lexington was where the Jim-Crow system first hit me. The Negroes and whites very seldom came in contact with each other. Of course there were separate company patches for living quarters. But even in the mine the Negroes and the whites worked in different places. The Negroes worked on the North side of the mine and the whites on the South.

The Negroes never got a look-in on most of the better-paying jobs. They couldn't be section foremen, or electricians, or surveyors, or head bank boss, or checkweighman, or steel sharpeners, or engineers. They could only load the coal, run the motors, be mule-boys, pick the coal, muck the rock. In other words, they were only allowed to do the muscle work.

Besides that, the Negro miners got the worst places to work. We worked in the low coal, only 3 or 4 feet high. We had to wear knee pads, and work stretched flat on our bellies most of the time.

One day the company put up a notice that due to large overhead expenses, they would have to cut our pay from 42 to 31 cents a ton. We were sore as hell. But there wasn't any union in the mine, and practically none of us had had any experience at organization, and though we grumbled plenty we didn't take any action. We were disgusted, and some of us quit. Whites and Negroes both.

I was one of those who quit. My contact with unions, and with organization, and the Communist Party, and unity between black and white miners— all that was still in the future. The pay-cut and the rotten conditions got my goat, and I walked off, because as yet I didn't know of anything else to do. . . .

I wish I could remember the exact date when I first attended a meeting of the Unemployment Council, and met up with a couple of members of the Communist Party. That date means a lot more to me than my birthday, or any other day in my life.

The workers in the South, mostly deprived of reading-matter, have developed a wonderful grapevine system for transmitting news. It was over this grapevine that we first heard that there were "reds" in town.

The foremen—when they talked about it—and the newspapers, and the big-shot Negroes in Birmingham, said that the "reds" were foreigners, and Yankees, and believed in killing people, and would get us in a lot of trouble. But out of all the talk I got a few ideas clear about the Reds. They believed in organizing and sticking together. They believed that we didn't have to have bosses on our backs. They believed that Negroes ought to have equal rights with whites. It all sounded O.K. to me. But I didn't meet any of the Reds for a long time.

One day in June, 1930, walking home from work, I came across some handbills put out by the Unemployment Council in Birmingham. They said: "Would you rather fight—or starve?" They called on the workers to come to a mass meeting at 3 o'clock.

Somehow I never thought of missing that meeting. I said to myself over and over: "It's war! It's war! And I might as well get into it right, now!" I got to the meeting while a white fellow was speaking. I didn't get everything he said, but this much hit me and stuck with me: that the worker could only get things by fighting for them, and that the Negro and white workers had to stick together to get results. The speaker described the conditions of the Negroes in Birmingham, and I kept saying to myself: "That's it." Then a Negro spoke from the same platform, and somehow I knew that this was what I'd been looking for all my life.

At the end of the meeting I went up and gave my name. From that day to this, every minute of my life has been tied up with the workers' movement.

I joined the Unemployment Council, and some weeks later the Communist Party. I read all the literature of the movement that I could get my hands on, and began to see my way more clearly. . . .

We organized a number of block committees of the Unemployment Councils, and got rent and relief fer a large number of families. We agitated endlessly for unemployment insurance.

In the middle of June, 1932, the state closed down all the relief stations. A drive was organized to send all the jobless to the farms.

We gave out leaflets calling for a mass demonstration at the courthouse to demand that the relief be continued. About 1000 workers came, 600 of them white. We told the commissioners we didn't intend to starve. We reminded them that $800,000 had been collected in the Community Chest drive. The commissioners said there wasn't a cent to be had.

But the very next day the commission voted $6,000 for relief to the jobless!

On the night of July 11, I went to the Post Office to get my mail. I felt myself grabbed from behind and turned to see a police officer.

I was placed in a cell, and was shown a large electric chair, and told to spill everything I knew about the movement. I refused to talk, and was held incommunicado for eleven days. Finally I smuggled out a letter through another prisoner, and the International Labor Defense got on the job.

Assistant Solicitor John Hudson rigged up the charge against me. It was the charge of "inciting to insurrection." It was based on an old statute passed in 1861, when the Negro people were still chattel slaves, and the white masters needed a law to crush slave insurrection and kill those found giving aid to the slaves. The statute read:

"If any person be in any manner instrumental in bringing, introducing or circulating within the state any printed or written paper, pamphlet, or circular for the purpose of exciting insurrection, revolt, conspiracy or resistance on the part of slaves, Negroes or free persons of color in this state he shall be guilty of high misdemeanor which is punishable by death."

Since the days of the Civil War that law had lain, unused and almost forgotten. Now the slaves of the new order—the white and black slaves of capitalism—were organizing. In the eyes of the Georgia masters, it was a crime punishable by death.

The trial was set for January 16, 1933. The state of Georgia displayed the literature that had been taken from my room, and read passages of it to the jury. They questioned me in great detail. Did I believe that the bosses and government ought to pay insurance to unemployed workers? That Negroes should have complete equality with white people? Did I believe in the demand for the self-determination of the Black Belt—that the Negro people should be allowed to rule the Black Belt territory, kicking out the white landlords and government officials? Did I feel that the working-class could run the mills and mines and government? That it wasn't necessary to have bosses at all?

I told them I believed all of that—and more.

The courtroom was packed to suffocation. The I.L.D. attorneys, Benjamin J. Davis, Jr., and John H. Geer, two young Negroes—and I myself—fought every step of the way. We were not really talking to that judge, nor to those prosecutors, whose questions we were answering. Over their heads we talked to the white and Negro workers who sat on the benches, watching, listening, learning. And beyond them we talked to the thousands and millions of workers all over the world to whom this case was a challenge.

We demanded that Negroes be placed on jury rolls. We demanded that the insulting terms, "nigger" and "darky," be dropped in that court. We asserted the right of the workers to organize, to strike, to make their demands, to nominate candidate of their choice. We asserted the right of the Negro people to have complete equality in every field.

The state held that my membership in the Communist Party, my possession of Communist literature, was enough to send me to the electric chair. They said to the jury: "Stamp this damnable thing out now with a conviction that will automatically carry with it a penalty of electrocution."

And the hand-picked lily-white jury responded:

"We, the jury, find the defendant guilty as charged, but recommend that mercy be shown and fix his sentence at from 18 to 20 years."

I had organized starving workers to demand bread, and I was sentenced to live out my years on the chain-gang for it. But I knew that the movement itself would not stop. I spoke to the court and said:

"They can hold this Angelo Herndon and hundred of others, but it will never stop these demonstrations on the part of Negro and white workers who demand a decent place to live in and proper food for their kids to eat."

I said: "You may do what you will with Angelo Herndon. You may indict him. You may put him in jail. But there will come thousands of Angelo Herndons. If you really want to do anything about the case, you must go out and indict the social system. But this you will not do, for your role is to defend the system under which the toiling masses are robbed and oppressed.

"You may succeed in killing one, two, even a score of working-class organizers. But you cannot kill the working class. . . ."

89. A. PHILIP RANDOLPH

Why Should We March?
(1942)

A. PHILIP RANDOLPH's "Why Should We March?" promoted his March on Washington movement against job discrimination. Randolph (1889–1979) was born into an impoverished family in Florida and attended the City College of New York, where he built his reputation as an activist. He helped found *The Messenger,* a black socialist magazine, and he organized the Brotherhood of Sleeping Car Porters in 1925. He also served as vice president of the AFL-CIO, and was director of the March on Washington for Jobs and Freedom in 1963. In "Why Should We March?" Randolph threatened to lead a massive demonstration in Washington, D.C., to show that "Negroes are . . . all out for their full rights." Although the march never occurred, it is credited with bringing about President Truman's Executive Order 9981, ending discrimination in the military.

SOURCE: A. Philip Randolph. "Why Should We March?" *Survey Graphic* 31. November, 1942.

SELECTED READINGS: Paula Pfeffer, *A. Philip Randolph: Pioneer of the Civil Rights Movement* (1990). Jervis Anderson, *A. Philip Randolph: A Biographical Portrait* (1973). William Harris, *Keeping the Faith: A Philip Randolph, Milton P. Webster, and the Brotherhood of Sleeping Car Porters, 1925–1937* (1937).

Though I have found no Negroes who want to see the United Nations lose this war, I have found many who, before the war ends, want to see the stuffing knocked out of white supremacy and of empire over subject peoples. American Negroes, involved as we are in the general issues of the conflict, are confronted not with a choice but with the challenge both to win democracy for ourselves at home and to help win the war for democracy the world over.

There is no escape from the horns of this dilemma. There ought not to be escape. For if the war for democracy is not won abroad, the fight for democracy cannot be won at home. If this war cannot be won for the white peoples, it will not be won for the darker races.

Conversely, if freedom and equality are not vouchsafed the peoples of color, the war for democracy will not be won. Unless this double-barreled thesis is accepted and applied, the darker races will never wholeheartedly fight for the victory of the United Nations. That is why those familiar with the thinking of the American Negro have sensed his lack of enthusiasm, whether among the educated or uneducated, rich or poor, professional or non-professional, religious or secular, rural or urban, north, south, east or west.

That is why questions are being raised by Negroes in church, labor union and fraternal society; in poolroom, barbershop, schoolroom, hospital, hair-dressing parlor; on college campus, railroad, and bus. One can hear such questions asked as these: What have Negroes to fight for? What's the difference between Hitler and that "cracker" Talmadge of Georgia? Why has a man got to be Jim-Crowed to die for democracy? If you haven't got democracy yourself, how can you carry it to somebody else?

What are the reasons for this state of mind? The answer is: discrimination, segregation, Jim Crow. Witness the navy, the army, the air corps; and also government services at Washington. In many parts of the South, Negroes in Uncle Sam's uniform are being put upon, mobbed, sometimes even shot down by civilian and military police, and on occasion lynched. Vested political interests in race prejudice are so deeply entrenched that to them winning the war against Hitler is secondary to preventing Negroes from winning democracy for themselves. This is worth many divisions to Hitler and Hirohito. While labor, business, and farm are subjected to ceilings and floors and not allowed to carry on as usual, these interests trade in the dangerous business of race hate as usual.

When the defense program began and billions of the taxpayers' money were appropriated for guns, ships, tanks and bombs, Negroes presented themselves for work only to be given the cold shoulder. North as well as South, and despite their qualifications. Negroes were denied skilled employment. Not until their wrath and indignation took the form of a proposed protest march on Washington, scheduled for July 1, 1941, did things begin to move in the form of defense jobs for Negroes. The march was postponed by the timely issuance (June 25, 1941) of the famous Executive Order No. 8802 by President Roosevelt. But this order and the President's Committee on Fair Employment Practice, established thereunder, have as yet only scratched the surface by way of eliminating discriminations on account of race or color in war industry. Both management and labor unions in too many places and in too many ways are still drawing the color line.

It is to meet this situation squarely with direct action that the March on Washington Movement launched its present program of protest mass meetings. Twenty thousand were in attendance at Madison Square Garden, June 16; sixteen thousand in the Coliseum in Chicago, June 26; nine thousand in the City Auditorium of St. Louis, August 14. Meetings of such magnitude were unprecedented among Negroes. The vast throngs were drawn from all walks and levels of Negro life—businessmen, teachers, laundry workers, Pullman porters, waiters, and red caps; preachers, crapshooters, and social workers, jitterbugs and Ph.D.'s. They came and sat in silence, thinking, applauding only when they considered the truth was told, when they felt strongly that something was going to be done about it.

The March on Washington Movement is essentially a movement of the people. It is all Negro and pro-Negro, but not for that reason anti-white or anti-Semitic, or anti-Catholic, or anti-foreign, or anti-labor. Its major weapon is the nonviolent demonstration of Negro mass power. Negro leadership has united back of its drive for jobs and justice. "Whether Negroes should march on Washington, and if so, when?" will be the focus of a forthcoming national conference. For the plan of a protest march has not been abandoned. Its purpose would be to demonstrate that American Negroes are in deadly earnest, and all out for their full rights. No power on earth can cause them today to abandon their fight to wipe out every vestige of second-class citizenship and the dual standards that plague them.

A community is democratic only when the humblest and weakest person can enjoy the highest civil, economic, and social rights that the biggest and most powerful possess. To trample on these rights of both Negroes and poor whites is such a commonplace in the South that it takes readily to anti-social, anti-labor, anti-Semitic and anti-Catholic propaganda. It was because of laxness in enforcing the Weimar constitution in republican Germany that Nazism made headway. Oppression of the Negroes in the United States, like suppression of the Jews in Germany, may open the way for a fascist dictatorship.

By fighting for their rights now, American Negroes are helping to make America a moral and spiritual arsenal of democracy. Their fight against the poll tax, against lynch law, segregation, and Jim Crow, their fight for economic, political, and social equality, thus becomes part of the global war for freedom.

90. JO ANN ROBINSON

The Montgomery Bus Boycott and the Women Who Made It
(1955)

JO ANN ROBINSON's account of the Montgomery Bus Boycott of 1955–1956 draws attention to the wide-ranging, grassroots nature of that protest. Robinson (1912–1992) was a professor at Alabama State College and president of the Women's Political Council (WPC) of Montgomery Alabama, when Rosa Parks broke a segregation ordinance by famously refusing to give up her seat on a local bus. In response, Robinson and other members of the WPC helped organize and sustain a yearlong boycott of Montgomery's city buses. By the time the boycott was over, local buses were desegregated, Martin Luther King, Jr., had emerged as a national leader, and the modern civil rights movement was underway.

SOURCE: Jo Ann Robinson. *The Montgomery Bus Boycott and the Women Who Made It: The Memoir of Jo Ann Gibson Robinson.* Edited with a foreword by David J. Garrow. Knoxville: University of Tennessee Press, 1987.

SELECTED READINGS: Brian Ward and Tony Badger, *The Making of Martin Luther King and the Civil Rights Movement* (1996). Vicki I. Crawford, Jacqueline Anne Rouse, and Burton Woods, *Women in the Civil Rights Movement, 1941–1965* (1990). Martin Luther King, Jr., *Stride Toward Freedom: The Montgomery Story* (1958).

In October 1955, Mary Louise Smith, an eighteen-year-old black girl, was arrested and fined for refusing to move to the rear of the bus. Her case was unpublicized and no one knew about it until after her arrest and conviction. She, too, was found guilty; she paid her fine and kept on riding the bus.

In the afternoon of Thursday, December I, a prominent black woman named Mrs. Rosa Parks was arrested for refusing to vacate her seat for a white man. Mrs. Parks was a medium-sized, cultured mulatto woman; a civic and religious worker; quiet, unassuming, and pleasant in manner and appearance; dignified and reserved; of high morals and a strong character. She was—and still is, for she lives to tell the story—respected in all black circles. By trade she was a seamstress, adept and competent in her work.

Tired from work, Mrs. Parks boarded a bus. The "reserved seats" were partially filled, but the seats just behind the reserved section were vacant, and Mrs. Parks sat down in one. It was during the busy evening rush hour. More black and white passengers boarded the bus, and soon all the reserved seats were occupied. The driver demanded that Mrs. Parks get up and surrender her seat to a white man, but she was tired from her work. Besides, she was a woman, and the person waiting was a man. She remained seated. In a few minutes, police summoned by the driver appeared, placed Mrs. Parks under arrest, and took her to jail.

It was the first time the soft-spoken, middle-aged woman had been arrested. She maintained decorum and poise, and the word of her arrest spread. Mr. E. D. Nixon, a longtime stalwart of our NAACP branch, along with liberal white attorney Clifford Durr and his wife Virginia, went to jail and obtained Mrs. Parks's release on bond. Her trial was scheduled for Monday, December 5, 1955.

The news traveled like wildfire into every black home. Telephones jangled; people congregated on street corners and in homes and talked. But nothing was done. A numbing helplessness seemed to paralyze everyone. Very few stayed off the buses the rest of that day or the next. There was fear, discontent, and uncertainty. Everyone seemed to wait for someone to *do* something, but nobody made a move. For that day and a half, black Americans rode the buses as before, as if nothing had happened. They were sullen and uncommunicative, but they rode the buses. There was a silent, tension-filled waiting. For blacks were not talking loudly in public places—they were quiet, sullen, waiting. Just waiting! Thursday evening came and went.

Thursday night was far spent, when, at about 11:30 P.M., I sat alone in my peaceful single-family dwelling on a quiet street. I was thinking about the situation. Lost in thought, I was startled by the telephone's ring. Black attorney Fred Gray, who had been out of town all day, had just gotten back and was returning the phone message I had left for him about Mrs. Parks's arrest. Attorney Gray, though a very young man, had been one of my most active colleagues in our previous meetings with bus company officials and Commissioner Birmingham. A Montgomery native who had attended Alabama State and been one of my students, Fred Gray had gone on to law school in Ohio before returning to his home town to open a practice with the only other black lawyer in Montgomery, Charles Langford.

Fred Gray and his wife Bernice were good friends of mine, and we talked often. In addition to being a lawyer, Gray was a trained, ordained minister of the gospel, actively serving as assistant pastor of Holt Street Church of Christ.

Tonight his voice on the phone was very short and to the point. Fred was shocked by the news of Mrs. Parks's arrest. I informed him that I already was thinking that the WPC should distribute thousands of notices calling for all bus riders to stay off the buses on Monday, the day of Mrs. Parks's trial. "Are you ready?" he asked. Without hesitation, I assured him that we were. With that he hung up, and I went to work.

I made some notes on the back of an envelope: "The Women's Political Council will not wait for Mrs. Parks's consent to call for a boycott of city buses. On Friday, December 2, 1955, the women of Montgomery will call for a boycott to take place on Monday, December 5."

Some of the WPC officers previously had discussed plans for distributing thousands of notices announcing a bus boycott. Now the time had come for me to write just such a notice. I sat down and quickly drafted a message and then called a good friend and colleague, John Cannon, chairman of the business department at the college, who had access to the college's mimeograph equipment. When I told him that the WPC was staging a boycott and needed to run off the notices, he told me that he too had suffered embarrassment on the city buses. Like myself, he had been hurt and angry. He said that he would happily assist me. Along with two of my most trusted senior students, we quickly agreed to meet almost immediately, in the middle of the night, at the college's duplicating room. We were able to get three messages to a page, greatly reducing the number of pages that had to be mimeographed in order to produce the tens of thousands of leaflets we knew would be needed. By 4 A.M. Friday, the sheets had been duplicated, cut in thirds, and bundled. Each leaflet read:

Another Negro woman has been arrested and thrown in jail because she refused to get up out of her seat on the bus for a white person to sit down. It is the second time since the Claudette Colvin case that a Negro woman has been arrested for the same thing. This has to be stopped. Negroes have rights, too, for if Negroes did not ride the buses, they could not operate. Three-fourths of the riders are Negroes, yet we are arrested, or have to stand over empty seats. If we do not do something to stop these arrests, they will continue. The next time it may be you, or your daughter, or mother. This woman's case will come up on Monday. We are, therefore, asking every Negro to stay off the buses Monday in protest of the arrest and trial. Don't ride the buses to work, to town, to school, or anywhere on Monday. You can afford to stay out of school for one day if you have no other way to go except by bus. You can also afford to stay out of town for one day. If you work, take a cab, or walk. But please, children and grownups, don't ride the bus at all on Monday. Please stay off of all buses Monday. . . .

When the question was posed as to whether the people would end the one-day bus boycott, thousands of voices shouted the same word, "No! No!" One lone voice cried out in clear tones, "This is just the beginning!" Thunderous applause was the response.

91. ROBERT F. WILLIAMS

We Must Fight Back
(1959)

ROBERT F. WILLIAMS's "We Must Fight Back" argued against the nonviolent tactics of the civil rights movement. Williams (1925–1996) was born in Monroe, North Carolina. After working in Detroit and serving in the U.S. Marines, he returned to Monroe in 1955, and in 1956 he became president of the local branch of the National Association for the Advancement of Colored People (NAACP). He was later suspended for proclaiming that African Americans must be willing "to meet violence with violence." In 1961 he relocated to Cuba in exile, where he produced *Radio Free Dixie*, a radio program that broadcast across the U.S. South and mixed blues and jazz music with news and political commentary. From Cuba, Williams also published the *Crusader*, a newsletter he founded in 1959. Williams returned to the United States in 1969, where he continued to work as an activist until his death in 1996. His editorial "We Must Fight Back" championed armed self-defense for African Americans who could not count on protection from local law enforcement or the federal government. The article first appeared in *Liberation* magazine in September 1959, and it was met with a rejoinder from Martin Luther King, Jr., the following month.

SOURCE: Robert F. Williams. "Is Violence Necessary to Combat Injustice? For the Positive: Williams Says, 'We Must Fight Back.' " *Liberation,* September, 1959.

SELECTED READINGS: Timothy B. Tyson, *Radio Free Dixie: Robert F. Williams and the Roots of Black Power* (1999). Robert F. Williams, *Negroes With Guns,* ed. Marc Schleifer (1962).

In 1954, I was an enlisted man in the United States Marine Corps. I shall never forget the evening we heard the historic Supreme Court decision that segregation in the public schools is unconstitutional.

At last I felt that I was a part of America and that I belonged. That was what I had always wanted, even as a child.

I returned to civilian life in 1955 and the hope I had for Negro liberation faltered. Acts of violence and words and deeds of hate and spite rose from every quarter. There is open defiance to law and order throughout the South today. I have become disillusioned.

Laws serve to deter crime and protect the weak from the strong in civilized society. Where there is a breakdown of law, where is the force of deterrent? Only highly civilized and moral individuals respect the rights of others. The Southern brute respects only force. Nonviolence is a very potent weapon when the opponent is civilized, but nonviolence is no repellent for a sadist.

I have great respect for the pacifist, that is for the pure pacifist. I am not a pacifist and I am sure I may safely say most of my people are not. Passive resistance is a powerful weapon in gaining concessions from oppressors, but I venture to say that if Mack Parker [a black man lynched in 1959] had had an automatic shotgun at his disposal, he could have served as a great deterrent against lynching.

In 1957 the Klan moved into Monroe and Union County (N.C.). Their numbers steadily increased to the point wherein the local press reported 7500 at one rally. They became so brazen that mile-long motorcades started invading the Negro community.

These hooded thugs fired pistols from car windows. On one occasion they caught a Negro woman on the street and tried to force her to dance for them at gun point. Drivers of cars tried to run Negroes down. Lawlessness was rampant. Instead of cowing, we organized an armed guard. On one occasion, we had to exchange gunfire with the Klan.

Each time the Klan came on a raid they were led by police cars. We appealed to the President of the United States to have the Justice Department investigate the police. We appealed to Governor Luther Hodges. All our appeals to constituted law were in vain.

A group of nonviolent ministers met the City Board of Aldermen and pleaded with them to restrict the Klan from the colored community. The city fathers advised these cringing, begging Negro ministers that the Klan had constitutional rights to meet and organize the same way as the NAACP.

Not having been infected by turn-the-other-cheekism, a group of Negroes who showed a willingness to fight caused the city officials to deprive the Klan of its constitutional rights after local papers told of dangerous incidents between Klansmen and armed Negroes. Klan motorcades have been legally banned from the City of Monroe.

On May 5, 1959, while president of the Union County branch of the NAACP, I made a statement to the United Press International after a trial wherein a white man was supposed to have been tried for kicking a Negro maid down a flight of stairs in a local white hotel. In spite of the fact that there was an eyewitness, the defendant failed to show up for his trial, and was completely exonerated.

Another case in the same court involved a white man who had come to a pregnant Negro mother's home and attempted to rape her. In recorder's court the only defense offered for the defendant was that "he's not guilty. He was just drunk and having a little fun." A white woman neighbor testified that the woman had come to her house excited, her clothes torn, her feet bare and begging her for assistance; the court was unmoved.

This great miscarriage of justice left me sick inside, and I said then what I say now. I believe Negroes must be willing to defend themselves, their women, their children and their homes. They must be willing to die and to kill in repelling their assailants. Negroes *must* protect themselves, it is obvious that the federal government will not put an end to lynching; therefore it becomes necessary for us to stop lynching with violence.

Some Negroes leaders have cautioned me that if Negroes fight back, the racist will have cause to exterminate the race.

This government is in no position to allow mass violence to erupt, let alone allow twenty million Negroes to be exterminated.

It is instilled at an early age that men who violently and swiftly rise to oppose tyranny are virtuous examples to emulate. I have been taught by my government to fight. Nowhere in the annals of history does the record show a people delivered from bondage by patience alone.

92. JOHN LEWIS

Wake Up America!
(1963)

The following document is the original text of a speech to be delivered by
JOHN LEWIS before the August 1963 March on Washington. Lewis (1940–)
was born in Troy, Alabama, and received a B.A. from Fisk University in 1963.
While a student in Nashville, Lewis distinguished himself as a leader and
activist, rigidly following the doctrines of nonviolent civil disobedience. He
served as Chairman of the Student Nonviolent Coordinating Committee
(SNCC) from 1963 to 1966, and in 1986 he was elected to the U.S. House of
Representatives, where he is one of the most influential politicians in Congress. At the 1963 March on Washington, some of Lewis's colleagues in the
civil rights movement insisted that he tone down some of the strongest statements in his speech at the Lincoln Memorial. (To cite one example, the sentence "In good conscience, we cannot support the administration's civil rights
bill, for it is too little, too late" was amended to read, "True, we support the
administration's civil rights bill, but this bill will not protect young children
and old women from police dogs and fire hoses.")

SOURCE: John Lewis, "Original text of speech to be delivered at the March
on Washington, August 28, 1963." Courtesy of John Lewis.

SELECTED READINGS: David Halberstam, *The Children* (1998). John Lewis,
Walking With the Wind: A Memoir of the Movement (1998). Clayborne Carson,
In Struggle: SNCC and the Black Awakening of the 1960s (1981).

We march today for jobs and freedom, but we have nothing to be proud of,
for hundreds and thousands of our brothers are not here—for they have no
money for their transportation, for they are receiving starvation wages . . . or
no wages at all.

In good conscience, we cannot support the administration's civil-rights bill, for it is too little, and too late. There's not one thing in the bill that will protect our people from police brutality.

The voting section of this bill will not help the thousands of citizens who want to vote; will not help the citizens of Mississippi, of Alabama and Georgia who are qualified to vote, who are without a sixth-grade education. "One Man, One Vote," is the African cry. It is ours, too.

People have been forced to move for they have exercised their right to register to vote. What is in the bill that will protect the homeless and starving people of this nation? What is there in this bill to insure the equality of a maid who earns five dollars a week in the home of a family whose income is a hundred thousand dollars a year?

This bill will not protect young children and old women from police dogs and fire hoses for engaging in peaceful demonstrations. This bill will not protect the citizens in Danville, Virginia, who must live in constant fear in a police state. This bill will not protect the hundreds of people who have been arrested on trumped-up charges, like those in Americus, Georgia, where four young men are in jail, facing a death penalty, for engaging in peaceful protest.

For the first time in a hundred years this nation is being awakened to the fact that segregation is evil and it must be destroyed in all forms. Our presence today proves that we have been aroused to the point of action.

We are now involved in a serious revolution. This nation is still a place of cheap political leaders allying themselves with open forms of political, economic and social exploitation.

In some parts of the South we have worked in the fields from sun-up to sundown for twelve dollars a week. In Albany, Georgia, we have seen our people indicted by the federal government for peaceful protest, while the Deputy Sheriff beat Attorney C. B. King and left him half-dead; while local police officials kicked and assaulted the pregnant wife of Slater King, and she lost her baby.

It seems to me that the Albany indictment is part of a conspiracy on the part of the federal government and local politicians for political expediency.

I want to know, Which side is the federal government on?

The revolution is at hand, and we must free ourselves of the chains of political and economic slavery. The nonviolent revolution is saying, "We will not wait for the courts to act, for we have been waiting hundreds of years. We will not wait for the President, nor the Justice Department, nor Congress, but we will take matters into our own hands, and create a great source of power, outside of any national structure that could and would assure us victory." For those who have said, "Be patient and wait!" we must say, "Patience is a dirty and nasty word." We cannot be patient, we do not want to be free gradually, we want our freedom, and we want it now. We cannot depend on any political party, for both the Democrats and the Republicans have betrayed the basic principles of the Declaration of Independence.

We all recognize the fact that if any radical social, political and economic changes are to take place in our society, the people, the masses must bring them about. In the struggle we must seek more than mere civil rights; we must work for the community of love, peace and true brotherhood. Our minds, souls and hearts cannot rest until freedom and justice exist for *all the people*.

The revolution is a serious one. Mr. Kennedy is trying to take the revolution out of the streets and put it in the courts. Listen, Mr. Kennedy, listen, Mr. Congressman, listen, fellow citizens—the black masses are on the march for jobs and freedom, and we must say to the politicians that there won't be a "cooling-off period."

We won't stop now. All of the forces of Eastland, Barnett and Wallace won't stop this revolution. The next time we march, we won't march on Washington, but we will march through the South, through the Heart of Dixie, the way Sherman did. We will make the action of the past few months look petty. And I say to you, *Wake up America!!*

All of us must get in the revolution—get in and stay in the streets of every city, village and hamlet of this nation, until true freedom comes, until the revolution is complete. The black masses in the Delta of Mississippi, in Southwest Georgia, Alabama, Harlem, Chicago, Philadelphia and all over this nation are on the march.

93. MARTIN LUTHER KING, JR.

Letter from Birmingham Jail
(1963)

MARTIN LUTHER KING's "Letter from Birmingham Jail" is a classic of American protest literature. King (1929–1968) was born in Atlanta, Georgia. After earning his Ph.D. in theology at Boston University, King became minister of Dexter Avenue Baptist Church in Montgomery, Alabama, where he rose to regional prominence as the leader of a boycott of Montgomery's segregated city buses. Later, he organized the Southern Christian Leadership Conference (SCLC) and emerged as a national leader for civil rights. In 1963 he gave his famous "I Have A Dream" speech at the March on Washington, and in 1964 he was awarded the Nobel Peace Prize. In the last years of his life, he began to move leftward politically, focusing greater attention on poverty and speaking out against the Vietnam War. He was assassinated in Memphis, Tennessee, on April 4, 1968. In "Letter from Birmingham Jail," King argued that segregation betrayed America's democratic faith and violated basic Christian principles. The essay had a great impact, boosting support for civil rights across the country.

SOURCE: Martin Luther King Jr. *Why We Can't Wait*. New York: Harper & Row, 1963.

SELECTED READINGS: Jonathan S. Bass, *Blessed Are the Peacemakers: Martin Luther King, Jr., Eight White Religious Leaders, and the "Letter From Birmingham Jail"* (2001). Taylor Branch, *Parting the Waters: America in the King Years, 1954–1963* (1988). Diane McWhorter, *Carry Me Home: Birmingham, Alabama: The Climactic Battle of the Civil Rights Revolution* (2001).

April 16, 1963

My Dear Fellow Clergymen:

While confined here in the Birmingham city jail, I came across your recent statement calling my present activities "unwise and untimely."

Seldom do I pause to answer criticism of my work and ideas. If I sought to answer all the criticisms that cross my desk, my secretaries would have little time for anything other than such correspondence in the course of the day, and I would have no time for constructive work. But since I feel that you are men of genuine good will and that your criticisms are sincerely set forth, I want to try to answer your statement in what I hope will be patient and reasonable terms.

I think I should indicate why I am here in Birmingham, since you have been influenced by the view which argues against "outsiders coming in." I have the honor of serving as president of the Southern Christian Leadership Conference, an organization operating in every southern state, with headquarters in Atlanta, Georgia. We have some eighty-five affiliated organizations across the South, and one of them is the Alabama Christian Movement for Human Rights. Frequently we share staff, educational and financial resources with our affiliates. Several months ago the affiliate here in Birmingham asked us to be on call to engage in a nonviolent direct-action program if such were deemed necessary. We readily consented, and when the hour came we lived up to our promise. So I, along with several members of my staff, am here because I was invited here. I am here because I have organizational ties here.

But more basically, I am in Birmingham because injustice is here. Just as the prophets of the eighth century B.C. left their villages and carried their "thus saith the Lord" far beyond the boundaries of their home towns, and just as the Apostle Paul left his village of Tarsus and carried the gospel of Jesus Christ to the far corners of the Greco-Roman world, so am I compelled to carry the gospel of freedom beyond my own home town. Like Paul, I must constantly respond to the Macedonian call for aid.

Moreover, I am cognizant of the interrelatedness of all communities and states. I cannot sit idly by in Atlanta and not be concerned about what happens in Birmingham. Injustice anywhere is a threat to justice everywhere. We are caught in an inescapable network of mutuality, tied in a single garment of destiny. Whatever affects one directly, affects all indirectly. Never again can we afford to live with the narrow, provincial "outside agitator" idea. Anyone who lives inside the United States can never be considered an outsider anywhere within its bounds.

You deplore the demonstrations taking place in Birmingham. But your statement, I am sorry to say, fails to express a similar concern for the conditions that brought about the demonstrations. I am sure that none of you would want to rest content with the superficial kind of social analysis that deals merely with effects and does not grapple with underlying causes. It is unfortunate that demonstrations are taking place in Birmingham, but it is even more unfortunate that the city's white power structure left the Negro community with no alternative.

In any nonviolent campaign there are four basic steps: collection of the facts to determine whether injustices exist; negotiation; self-purification; and direct action. We have gone through all these steps in Birmingham. There can be no gainsaying the fact that racial injustice engulfs this community. Birmingham is probably the most thoroughly segregated city in the United States. Its ugly record of brutality is widely known. Negroes have experienced grossly unjust treatment in the courts. There have been more unsolved bombings of Negro homes and churches in Birmingham than in any other city in the nation. These are the hard, brutal facts of the case. On the basis of these conditions, Negro leaders sought to negotiate with the city fathers. But the latter consistently refused to engage in good-faith negotiation.

Then, last September, came the opportunity to talk with leaders of Birmingham's economic community. In the course of the negotiations, certain promises were made by the merchants—for example, to remove the stores' humiliating racial signs. On the basis of these promises, the Reverend Fred Shuttlesworth and the leaders of the Alabama Christian Movement for Human Rights agreed to a moratorium on all demonstrations. As the weeks and months went by, we realized that we were the victims of a broken promise. A few signs, briefly removed, returned; the others remained.

As in so many past experiences, our hopes had been blasted, and the shadow of deep disappointment settled upon us. We had no alternative except to prepare for direct action, whereby we would present our very bodies as a means of laying our case before the conscience of the local and the national community. Mindful of the difficulties involved, we decided to undertake a process of self-purification. We began a series of workshops on nonviolence, and we repeatedly asked ourselves: "Are you able to accept blows without retaliating?" "Are you able to endure the ordeal of jail?" We decided to schedule out direct-action program for the Easter season, realizing that except for Christmas, this is the main shopping period of the year. Knowing that a strong economic-withdrawal program would be the by-product of direct action, we felt that this would be the best time to bring pressure to bear on the merchants for the needed change.

Then it occurred to us that Birmingham's mayoralty election was coming up in March, and we speedily decided to postpone action until after election day. When we discovered that the Commissioner of Public Safety, Eugene "Bull" Connor, had piled up enough votes to be in the run-off, we decided again to postpone action until the day after the run-off so that the demonstrations could not be used to cloud the issues. Like many others, we waited to see Mr. Connor defeated, and to this end we endured postponement after postponement. Having aided in this community need, we felt that our direct-action program could be delayed no longer.

You may well ask: "Why direct action? Why sit-ins, marches and so forth? Isn't negotiation a better path?" You are quite right in calling for negotiation. Indeed, this is the very purpose of direct action. Nonviolent direct action seeks to create such a crisis and foster such a tension that a community which has constantly refused to negotiate is forced to confront the issue. It seeks so to dramatize the issue that it can no longer be ignored. My citing the creation of tension as part of the work of the nonviolent-resister may sound rather shocking. But I must confess that I am not afraid of the word "tension." I have earnestly opposed violent tension, but there is a type of constructive, nonviolent tension which is necessary for growth. Just as Socrates felt that it was necessary to create a tension in the mind so that individuals could rise from the bondage of myths and half-truths to the unfettered realm of creative analysis and objective appraisal, so must we see the need for nonviolent gadflies to create the kind of tension in society that will help men rise from the dark depths of prejudice and racism to the majestic heights of understnd-ing and brotherhood.

The purpose of our direct-action program is to create a situation so crisis-packed that it will inevitably open the door to negotiation. I therefore concur with you in your call for negotiation. Too long has our beloved Southland been bogged down in a tragic effort to live in monologue rather than dialogue.

One of the basic points in your statement is that the action that I and my associates have taken in Birmingham is untimely. Some have asked: "Why didn't you give the new city administration time to act?" The only answer that I can give to this query is that the new Birmingham administration must be prodded about as much as the outgoing one, before it will act. We are sadly mistaken if we feel that the election of Albert Boutwell as mayor will bring the millennium to Birmingham. While Mr. Boutwell is a much more gentle person than Mr. Connor, they are both segregationists, dedicated to maintenance of the status quo. I have hope that Mr. Boutwell will be reasonable enough to see the futility of massive resistance to desegregation. But he will not see this without pressure from devotees of civil rights. My friends, I must say to you that we have not made a single gain in civil rights without determined legal and non-violent pressure. Lamentably, it is an historical fact that privileged groups seldom give up their privileges voluntarily. Individuals may see the moral light and voluntarily give up their unjust posture; but, as Reinhold Niebuhr has reminded us, groups tend to be more immoral than individuals.

We know through painful experience that freedom is never voluntarily given by the oppressor; it must be demanded by the oppressed. Frankly, I have yet to engage in a direct-action campaign that was "well timed" in the view of those who have not suffered unduly from the disease of segregation. For years now I have heard the word "Wait!" It rings in the ear of every Negro with piercing familiarity. This "Wait" has almost always meant "Never." We must come to see, with one of our distinguished jurists, that "justice too long delayed is justice denied."

We have waited for more than 340 years for our constitutional and God-given rights. The nations of Asia and Africa are moving with jetlike speed toward gaining political independence, but we still creep at horse-and-buggy pace toward gaining a cup of coffee at a lunch counter. Perhaps it is easy for those who have never felt the stinging darts of segregation to say, "Wait." But when you have seen vicious mobs lynch your mothers and fathers at will and drown your sisters and brothers at whim; when you have seen hate-filled policemen curse, kick and even kill your black brothers and sisters; when you see the vast majority of your twenty million Negro brothers smothering in an airtight cage of poverty in the midst of an affluent society; when you suddenly find your tongue twisted and your speech stammering as you seek to explain to your six-year-old daughter why she can't go to the public amusement park that has just been advertised on television, and see tears welling up in her eyes when she is told that Funtown is closed to colored children, and see ominous clouds of inferiority beginning to form in her little mental sky, and see her beginning to distort her personality by developing an unconscious bitterness toward white people; when you have to concoct an answer for a five-year-old son who is asking: "Daddy, why do white people treat colored people so mean?" When you take a cross-country drive and find it necessary to sleep night after night in the uncomfortable corners of your automobile because no motel will accept you; when you are humiliated day in and day out by nagging signs reading "white" and "colored"; when your first name becomes "nigger," your middle name becomes "boy" (however old you are) and your last name becomes "John," and your wife and mother are never given the respected title "Mrs."; when you are harried by day and haunted by night by the fact that you are a Negro, living constantly at tiptoe stance, never quite knowing what to expect next, and are plagued with inner fears and outer resentments; when you are forever fighting a degenerating sense of "nobodiness"—then you will understand why we find it difficult to wait. There comes a time when the cup of endurance runs over, and men are no longer willing to be plunged into the abyss of despair. I hope, sirs, you can understand our legitimate and unavoidable impatience.

You express a great deal of anxiety over our willingness to break laws. This is certainly a legitimate concern. Since we so diligently urge people to obey the Supreme Court's decision of 1954 outlawing segregation in the public schools, at first glance it may seem rather paradoxical for us consciously to break laws. One may well ask: "How can you advocate breaking some laws and obeying others?" The answer lies in the fact that there are two types of laws: just and unjust. I would be the first to advocate obeying just laws. One has not only a legal but a moral responsibility to obey just laws. Conversely, one has a moral responsibility to disobey unjust laws. I would agree with St. Augustine that "an unjust law is no law at all."

Now, what is the difference between the two? How does one determine whether a law is just or unjust? A just law is a man-made code that squares with the moral law or the law of God. An unjust law is a code that is out of harmony with the moral law. To put it in the terms of St. Thomas Aquinas: An unjust law is a human law that is not rooted in eternal law and natural law. Any law that uplifts human personality is just. Any law that degrades human personality is unjust. All segregation statutes are unjust because segregation distorts the soul and damages the personality. It gives the segregator a false sense of superiority and the segregated a false sense of inferiority. Segregation, to use the terminology of the Jewish philosopher Martin Buber, substitutes an "I—it" relationship for an "I—thou" relationship and ends up relegating persons to the status of things. Hence segregation is not only politically, economically and sociologically unsound, it is morally wrong and sinful. Paul Tillich has said that sin is separation. Is not segregation an existential expression of man's tragic separation, his awful estrangement, his terrible sinfulness? Thus it is that I can urge men to obey the 1954 decision of the Supreme Court, for it is morally right; and I can urge them to disobey segregation ordinances, for they are morally wrong.

Let us consider a more concrete example of just and unjust laws. An unjust law is a code that a numerical or power majority group compels a minority group to obey but does not make binding on itself. This is *difference* made legal. By the same token, a just law is a code that a majority compels a minority to follow and that it is willing to follow itself. This is *sameness* made legal.

Let me give another explanation. A law is unjust if it is inflicted on a minority that, as a result of being denied the right to vote, had no part in enacting or devising the law. Who can say that the legislature of Alabama which set up that state's segregation laws was democratically elected? Throughout Alabama all sorts of devious methods are used to prevent Negroes from becoming registered voters, and there are some counties in which, even though Negroes constitute a majority of the population, not a single Negro is registered. Can any law enacted under such circumstances be considered democratically structured?

Sometimes a law is just on its face and unjust in its application. For instance, I have been arrested on a charge of parading without a permit. Now, there is nothing wrong in having an ordinance which requires a permit for a parade. But such an ordinance becomes unjust when it is used to maintain segregation and to deny citizens the First-Amendment privilege of peaceful assembly and protest.

I hope you are able to see the distinction I am trying to point out. In no sense do I advocate evading or defying the law, as would the rabid segregationist. That would lead to anarchy. One who breaks an unjust law must do so openly, lovingly, and with a willingness to accept the penalty. I submit that an individual who breaks a law that conscience tells him is unjust, and who willingly accepts the penalty of imprisonment in order to arouse the conscience of the community over its injustice, is in reality expressing the highest respect for law.

Of course, there is nothing new about this kind of civil disobedience. It was evidenced sublimely in the refusal of Shadrach, Meshach and Abednego to obey the laws of Nebuchadnezzar, on the ground that a higher moral law was at stake. It was practiced superbly by the early Christians, who were willing to face hungry lions and the excruciating pain of chopping blocks rather than submit to certain unjust laws of the Roman Empire. To a degree, academic freedom is a reality today because Socrates practiced civil disobedience. In our own nation, the Boston Tea Party represented a massive act of civil disobedience.

We should never forget that everything Adolf Hitler did in Germany was "legal" and everything the Hungarian freedom fighters did in Hungary was "illegal." It was "illegal" to aid and comfort a Jew in Hitler's Germany. Even so, I am sure that, had I lived in Germany at the time, I would have aided and comforted my Jewish brothers. If today I lived in a Communist country where certain principles dear to the Christian faith are suppressed, I would openly advocate disobeying that country's antireligious laws.

I must make two honest confessions to you, my Christian and Jewish brothers. First, I must confess that over the past few years I have been gravely disappointed with the white moderate. I have almost reached the regrettable conclusion that the Negro's great stumbling block in his stride toward freedom is not the White Citizen's Counciler or the Ku Klux Klanner, but the white moderate, who is more devoted to "order" than to justice; who prefers a negative peace which is the absence of tension to a positive peace which is the presence of justice; who constantly says: "I agree with you in the goal you seek, but I cannot agree with your methods of direct action"; who paternalistically believes he can set the timetable for another man's freedom; who lives by a mythical concept of time and who constantly advises the Negro to wait for a "more convenient season." Shallow understanding from people of good will is more frustrating than absolute misunderstanding from people of ill will. Lukewarm acceptance is much more bewildering than outright rejection.

I had hoped that the white moderate would understand that law and order exist for the purpose of establishing justice and that when they fail in this purpose they become the dangerously structured dams that block the flow of social progress. I had hoped that the white moderate would understand that the present tension in the South is a necessary phase of the transition from an obnoxious negative peace, in which the Negro passively accepted his unjust plight, to a substantive and positive peace, in which all men will respect the dignity and worth of human personality. Actually, we who engage in nonviolent direct action are not the creators of tension. We merely bring to the surface the hidden tension that is already alive. We bring it out in the open, where it can be seen and dealt with. Like a boil that can never be cured so long as it is covered up but must be opened with all its ugliness to the natural medicines of air and light, injustice must be exposed, with all the tension its exposure creates, to the light of human conscience and the air of national opinion before it can be cured.

In your statement you assert that our actions, even though peaceful, must be condemned because they precipitate violence. But is this a logical assertion? Isn't this like condemning a robbed man because his possession of money precipitated the evil act of robbery? Isn't this like condemning Socrates because his unswerving commitment to truth and his philosophical inquiries precipitated the act by the misguided populace in which they made him drink hemlock? Isn't this like condemning Jesus because his unique God-consciousness and never-ceasing devotion to God's will precipitated the evil act of crucifixion? We must come to see that, as the federal courts have consistently affirmed, it is wrong to urge an individual to cease his efforts to gain his basic constitutional rights because the quest may precipitate violence. Society must protect the robbed and punish the robber.

I had also hoped that the white moderate would reject the myth concerning time in relation to the struggle for freedom. I have just received a letter from a white brother in Texas. He writes: "All Christians know that the colored people will receive equal rights eventually, but it is possible that you are in too great a religious hurry. It has taken Christianity almost two thousand years to accomplish what it has. The teachings of Christ take time to come to earth." Such an attitude stems from a tragic misconception of time, from the strangely irrational notion that there is something in the very flow of time that will inevitably cure all ills. Actually, time itself is neutral; it can be used either destructively or constructively. More and more I feel that the people of ill will have used time much more effectively than have the people of good will. We will have to repent in this generation not merely for the hateful words and actions of the bad people but for the appalling silence of the good people. Human progress never rolls in on wheels of inevitability; it comes through the tireless efforts of men willing to be co-workers with God, and without this hard work, time itself becomes an ally of the forces of social stagnation. We must use time creatively, in the knowledge that the time is always ripe to do right. Now is the time to make real the promise of democracy and transform our pending national elegy into a creative psalm of brotherhood. Now is the time to lift our national policy from the quicksand of racial injustice to the solid rock of human dignity.

You speak of our activity in Birmingham as extreme. At first I was rather disappointed that fellow clergymen would see my nonviolent efforts as those of an extremist. I began thinking about the fact that I stand in the middle of two opposing forces in the Negro community. One is a force of complacency, made up in part of Negroes who, as a result of long years of oppression, are so drained of self-respect and a sense of "somebodiness" that they have adjusted to segregation; and in part of a few middle-class Negroes who, because of a degree of academic and economic security and because in some ways they profit by segregation, have become insensitive to the problems of the masses. The other force is one of bitterness and hatred, and it comes perilously close to advocating violence. It is expressed in the various black nationalist groups that are springing up across the nation, the largest and best-known being Elijah Muhammad's Muslim movement. Nourished by the Negro's frustration over the continued existence of racial discrimination, this movement is made up of people who have lost faith in America, who have absolutely repudiated Christianity, and who have concluded that the white man is an incorrigible "devil."

I have tried to stand between these two forces, saying that we need emulate neither the "do-nothingism" of the complacent nor the hatred and despair of the black nationalist. For there is the more excellent way of love and nonviolent protest. I am grateful to God that, through the influence of the Negro church, the way of nonviolence became an integral part of our struggle.

If this philosophy had not emerged, by now many streets of the South would, I am convinced, be flowing with blood. And I am further convinced that if our white brothers dismiss as "rabble-rousers" and "outside agitators" those of us who employ nonviolent direct action, and if they refuse to support our nonviolent efforts, millions of Negroes will, out of frustration and despair, seek solace and security in black-nationalist ideologies—a development that would inevitably lead to a frightening racial nightmare.

Oppressed people cannot remain oppressed forever. The yearning for freedom eventually manifests itself, and that is what has happened to the American Negro. Something within has reminded him of his birthright of freedom, and something without has reminded him that it can be gained. Consciously or unconsciously, he has been caught up by the *Zeitgeist,* and with his black brothers of Africa and his brown and yellow brothers of Asia, South America and the Caribbean, the United States Negro is moving with a sense of great urgency toward the promised land of racial justice. If one recognizes this vital urge that has engulfed the Negro community, one should readily understand why public demonstrations are taking place. The Negro has many pent-up resentments and latent frustrations, and he must release them. So let him march; let him make prayer pilgrimages to the city hall; let him go on freedom rides— and try to understand why he must do so. If his repressed emotions are not released in nonviolent ways, they will seek expression through violence; this is not a threat but a fact of history. So I have not said to my people: "Get rid of your discontent." Rather, I have tried to say that this normal and healthy discontent can be channeled into the creative outlet of nonviolent direct action. And now this approach is being termed extremist.

But though I was initially disappointed at being categorized as an extremist, as I continued to think about the matter I gradually gained a measure of satisfaction from the label. Was not Jesus an extremist for love: "Love your enemies, bless them that curse you, do good to them that hate you, and pray for them which despitefully use you, and persecute you." Was not Amos an extremist for justice: "Let justice roll down like waters and righteousness like an ever-flowing stream." Was not Paul an extremist for the Christian gospel: "I bear in my body the marks of the Lord Jesus." Was not Martin Luther an extremist: "Here I stand; I cannot do otherwise, so help me God." And John Bunyan: "I will stay in jail to the end of my days before I make a butchery of my conscience." And Abraham Lincoln: "This nation cannot survive half slave and half free." And Thomas Jefferson: "We hold these truths to be self-evident, that all men are created equal . . ." So the question is not whether we will be extremists, but what kind of extremists we will be. Will we be extremists for hate or for love? Will we be extremists for the preservation of injustice or for the extension of justice? In that dramatic scene on Calvary's hill three men were crucified. We must never forget that all three were crucified for the same crime—the crime of extremism. Two were extremists for immorality, and thus fell below their environment. The other, Jesus Christ, was an extremist for love, truth and goodness, and thereby rose above his environment. Perhaps the South, the nation and the world are in dire need of creative extremists.

I had hoped that the white moderate would see this need. Perhaps I was too optimistic; perhaps I expected too much. I suppose I should have realized that few members of the oppressor race can understand the deep groans and passionate yearnings of the oppressed race, and still fewer have the vision to see that injustice must be rooted out by strong, persistent and determined action. I am thankful, however, that some of our white brothers in the South have grasped the meaning of this social revolution and committed themselves to it. They are still all too few in quantity, but they are big in quality. Some—such as Ralph McGill, Lillian Smith, Harry Golden, James McBride Dabbs, Ann Braden and Sarah Patton Boyle—have written about our struggle in eloquent and prophetic terms. Others have marched with us down nameless streets of the South. They have languished in filthy, roach-infested jails, suffering the abuse and brutality of policemen who view them as "dirty nigger-lovers." Unlike so many of their moderate brothers and sisters, they have recognized the urgency of the moment and sensed the need for powerful "action" antidotes to combat the disease of segregation.

Let me take note of my other major disappointment. I have been so greatly disappointed with the white church and its leadership. Of course, there are some notable exceptions. I am not unmindful of the fact that each of you has taken some significant stands on this issue. I commend you, Reverend Stallings, for your Christian stand on this past Sunday, in welcoming Negroes to your worship service on a nonsegregated basis. I commend the Catholic leaders of this state for integrating Spring Hill College several years ago.

But despite these notable exceptions, I must honestly reiterate that I have been disappointed with the church. I do not say this as one of those negative critics who can always find something wrong with the church. I say this as a minister of the gospel, who loves the church; who was nurtured in its bosom; who has been sustained by its spiritual blessings and who will remain true to it as long as the cord of life shall lengthen.

When I was suddenly catapulted into the leadership of the bus protest in Montgomery, Alabama, a few years ago, I felt we would be supported by the white church. I felt that the white ministers, priests and rabbis of the South would be among our strongest allies. Instead, some have been outright opponents, refusing to understand the freedom movement and misrepresenting its leaders; all too many others have been more cautious than courageous and have remained silent behind the anesthetizing security of stained-glass windows.

In spite of my shattered dreams, I came to Birmingham with the hope that the white religious leadership of this community would see the justice of our cause and, with deep moral concern, would serve as the channel through which our just grievances could reach the power structure. I had hoped that each of you would understand. But again I have been disappointed.

I have heard numerous southern religious leaders admonish their worshipers to comply with a desegregation decision because it is the law, but I have longed to hear white ministers declare: "Follow this decree because integration is morally right and because the Negro is your brother." In the midst of blatant injustices inflicted upon the Negro, I have watched white churchmen stand on the sideline and mouth pious irrelevancies and sanctimonious trivialities. In the midst of a mighty struggle to rid our nation of racial and economic injustice, I have heard many ministers say: "Those are social issues, with which the gospel has no real concern." And I have watched many churches commit themselves to a completely other-worldly religion which makes a strange, un-Biblical distinction between body and soul, between the sacred and the secular.

I have traveled the length and breadth of Alabama, Mississippi and all the other southern states. On sweltering summer days and crisp autumn mornings I have looked at the South's beautiful churches with their lofty spires pointing heavenward. I have beheld the impressive outlines of her massive religious-education buildings. Over and over I have found myself asking: "What kind of people worship here? Who is their God? Where were their voices when the lips of Governor Barnett dripped with words of interposition and nullification? Where were they when Governor Wallace gave a clarion call for defiance and hatred? Where were their voices of support when bruised and weary Negro men and women decided to rise from the dark dungeons of complacency to the bright hills of creative protest?"

Yes, these questions are still in my mind. In deep disappointment I have wept over the laxity of the church. But be assured that my tears have been tears of love. There can be no deep disappointment where there is not deep love. Yes, I love the church. How could I do otherwise? I am in the rather unique position of being the son, the grandson and the great-grandson of preachers. Yes, I see the church as the body of Chirst. But, oh! How we have blemished and scarred that body through social neglect and through fear of being nonconformists.

There was a time when the church was very powerful—in the time when the early Christians rejoiced at being deemed worthy to suffer for what they believed. In those days the church was not merely a thermometer that recorded the ideas and principles of popular opinion; it was a thermostat that transformed the mores of society. Whenever the early Christians entered a town, the people in power became disturbed and immediately sought to convict the Christians for being "disturbers of the peace" and "outside agitators." But the Christians pressed on, in the conviction that they were "a colony of heaven," called to obey God rather than man. Small in number, they were big in commitment. They were too God-intoxicated to be "astronomically intimidated." By their effort and example they brought an end to such ancient evils as infanticide and gladiatorial contests.

Things are different now. So often the contemporary church is a weak, ineffectual voice with an uncertain sound. So often it is an archdefender of the status quo. Far from being disturbed by the presence of the church, the power structure of the average community is consoled by the church's silent—and often even vocal—sanction of things as they are.

But the judgment of God is upon the church as never before. If today's church does not recapture the sacrificial spirit of the early church, it will lose its authenticity, forfeit the loyalty of millions, and be dismissed as an irrelevant social club with no meaning for the twentieth century. Every day I meet young people whose disappointment with the church has turned into outright disgust.

Perhaps I have once again been too optimistic. Is organized religion too inextricably bound to the status quo to save our nation and the world? Perhaps I must turn my faith to the inner spiritual church, the church within the church, as the true *ekklesia* and the hope of the world. But again I am thankful to God that some noble souls from the ranks of organized religion have broken loose from the paralyzing chains of conformity and joined us as active partners in the struggle for freedom. They have left their secure congregations and walked the streets of Albany, Georgia, with us. They have gone down the highways of the South on tortuous rides for freedom. Yes, they have gone to jail with us. Some have been dismissed from their churches, have lost the support of their bishops and fellow ministers. But they have acted in the faith that right defeated is stronger than evil triumphant. Their witness has been the spiritual salt that has preserved the true meaning of the gospel in these troubled times. They have carved a tunnel of hope through the dark mountain of disappointment.

I hope the church as a whole will meet the challenge of this decisive hour. But even if the church does not come to the aid of justice, I have no despair about the future. I have no fear about the outcome of our struggle in Birmingham, even if our motives are at present misunderstood. We will reach the goal of freedom in Birmingham and all over the nation, because the goal of America is freedom. Abused and scorned though we may be, our destiny is tied up with America's destiny. Before the pilgrims landed at Plymouth, we were here. Before the pen of Jefferson etched the majestic words of the Declaration of Independence across the pages of history, we were here. For more than two centuries our forebears labored in this country without wages; they made cotton king; they built the homes of their masters while suffering gross injustice and shameful humiliation—and yet out of a bottomless vitality they continued to thrive and develop. If the inexpressible cruelties of slavery could not stop us, the opposition we now face will surely fail. We will win our freedom because the sacred heritage of our nation and the eternal will of God are embodied in our echoing demands.

Before closing I feel impelled to mention one other point in your statement that has troubled me profoundly. You warmly commended the Birmingham police force for keeping "order" and "preventing violence." I doubt that you would have so warmly commended the police force if you had seen its dogs sinking their teeth into unarmed, nonviolent Negroes. I doubt that you would so quickly commend the policemen if you were to observe their ugly and inhumane treatment of Negroes here in the city jail; if you were to watch them push and curse old Negro women and young Negro girls; if you were to see them slap and kick old Negro men and young boys; if you were to observe them, as they did on two occasions, refuse to give us food because we wanted to sing our grace together. I cannot join you in your praise of the Birmingham police department.

It is true that the police have exercised a degree of discipline in handling the demonstrators. In this sense they have conducted themselves rather "nonviolently" in public. But for what purpose? To preserve the evil system of segregation. Over the past few years I have consistently preached that nonviolence demands that the means we use must be as pure as the ends we seek. I have tried to make clear that it is wrong to use immoral means to attain moral ends. But now I must affirm that it is just as wrong, or perhaps even more so, to use moral means to preserve immoral ends. Perhaps Mr. Connor and his policemen have been rather nonviolent in public, as was Chief Pritchett in Albany, Georgia, but they have used the moral means of nonviolence to maintain the immoral end of racial injustice. As T. S. Eliot has said: "The last temptation is the greatest treason: To do the right deed for the wrong reason."

I wish you had commended the Negro sit-inners and demonstrators of Birmingham for their sublime courage, their willingness to suffer and their amazing discipline in the midst of great provocation. One day the South will recognize its real heroes. They will be the James Merediths, with the noble sense of purpose that enables them to face jeering and hostile mobs, and with the agonizing loneliness that characterizes the life of the pioneer. They will be old, oppressed, battered Negro women, symbolized in a seventy-two-year-old woman in Montgomery, Alabama, who rose up with a sense of dignity and with her people decided not to ride segregated buses, and who responded with ungrammatical profundity to one who inquired about her weariness: "My feets is tired, but my soul is at rest." They will be the young high school and college students, the young ministers of the gospel and a host of their elders, courageously and nonviolently sitting in at lunch counters and willingly going to jail for conscience' sake. One day the South will know that when these disinherited children of God sat down at lunch counters, they were in reality standing up for what is best in the American dream and for the most sacred values in our Judaeo-Christian heritage, thereby bringing our nation back to those great wells of democracy which were dug deep by the founding fathers in their formulation of the Constitution and the Declaration of Independence.

Never before have I written so long a letter. I'm afraid it is much too long to take your precious time. I can assure you that it would have been much shorter if I had been writing from a comfortable desk, but what else can one do when he is alone in a narrow jail cell, other than write long letters, think long thoughts and pray long prayers?

If I have said anything in this letter that overstates the truth and indicates an unreasonable impatience, I beg you to forgive me. If I have said anything that understates the truth and indicates my having a patience that allows me to settle for anything less than brotherhood, I beg God to forgive me.

I hope this letter finds you strong in the faith. I also hope that circumstances will soon make it possible for me to meet each of you, not as an integrationist or a civil-rights leader but as a fellow clergyman and

a Christian brother. Let us all hope that the dark clouds of racial prejudice will soon pass away and the deep fog of misunderstanding will be
lifted from our fear-drenched communities, and in some not too distant
tomorrow the radiant stars of love and brotherhood will shine over our
great nation with all their scintillating beauty.

Yours for the cause of Peace and Brotherhood,
Martin Luther King, Jr.

94. JAMES BALDWIN

My Dungeon Shook
(1963)

JAMES BALDWIN's "My Dungeon Shook"—an open letter to his nephew—displayed the eloquence and brutal honesty that made him one of the most acclaimed writers of the twentieth century. Baldwin (1924–1987) was born into a poor family in Harlem and was a Pentecostal preacher as a teen. His first novels, *Go Tell It on the Mountain* (1953) and *Giovanni's Room* (1956), were written while he lived in Paris. In 1957, Baldwin returned to the United States, where he earned his reputation as one of the most trenchant thinkers on the topic of American race relations. His 1963 work, *The Fire Next Time,* from which "My Dungeon Shook" is excerpted, was prophetic for its warning of widespread turmoil and violence in American cities during the 1960s.

SOURCE: James Baldwin. *The Fire Next Time*. New York: Dial Press, 1963.

SELECTED READINGS: D. Quentin Miller, *Re-Viewing James Baldwin: Things Not Seen* (2000). David Leeming, *James Baldwin: A Biography* (1994). James Baldwin, *The Price of the Ticket: Collected Essays, 1948–1985* (1985).

Dear James:

I have begun this letter five times and torn it up five times. I keep seeing your face, which is also the face of your father and my brother. Like him, you are tough, dark, vulnerable, moody—with a very definite tendency to sound truculent because you want no one to think you are soft. You may be like your grandfather in this, I don't know, but certainly both you and your father resemble him very much physically. Well, he is dead, he never saw you, and he had a terrible life; he was defeated long before he died because, at the bottom of his heart, *he really believed what white* people said about him. This is one of the reasons that he became so holy. I am sure that your father has told you something about all that. Neither you nor your father exhibit any tendency towards holiness: you really *are* of another era, part of what happened when the Negro left the land and came into what the late E. Franklin Frazier called "the cities of destruction." You can only be destroyed by believing that you really are what the white world calls a *nigger*. I tell you this because I love you, and please don't you ever forget it.

I have known both of you all your lives, have carried your Daddy in my arms and on my shoulders, kissed and spanked him and watched him learn to walk. I don't know if you've known anybody from that far back; if you've loved anybody that long, first as an infant, then as a child, then as a man, you gain a strange perspective on time and human pain and effort. Other people cannot see what I see whenever I look into your father's face, for behind your father's face as it is today are all those other faces which were his. Let him laugh and I see a cellar your father does not remember and a house he does not remember and I hear in his present laughter his laughter as a child. Let him curse and I remember him falling down the cellar steps, and howling, and I remember, with pain, his tears, which my hand or your grandmother's so easily wiped away. But no one's hand can wipe away those tears he sheds invisibly today, which one hears in his laughter and in his speech and in his songs. I know what the world has done to my brother and how narrowly he has survived it. And I know, which is much worse, and this is the crime of which I accuse my country and my countrymen, and for which neither I nor time nor history will ever forgive them, that they have destroyed and are destroying hundreds of thousands of lives and do not know it and do not want to know it. One can be, indeed one must strive to become, tough and philosophical concerning destruction and death, for this is what most of mankind has been best at since we have heard of man. (But remember *most* of mankind is not *all* of mankind.) But it is not permissible that the authors of devastation should also be innocent. It is the innocence which constitutes the crime.

Now, my dear namesake, these innocent and well-meaning people, your countrymen, have caused you to be born under conditions not very far removed from those described for us by Charles Dickens in the London of more than a hundred years ago. (I hear the chorus of the innocents screaming, "No! This is not true! How *bitter* you are!"—but I am writing this letter to *you*, to try to tell you something about how to handle *them*, for most of them do not yet really know that you exist. I *know* the conditions under which you were born, for I was there. Your countrymen were *not* there, and haven't made it yet. Your grandmother was also there, and no one has ever accused her of being *bitter*. I suggest that the innocents check with her. She isn't hard to find. Your countrymen don't know that *she* exists, either, though she has been working for them all their lives.)

Well, you were born, here you came, something like fifteen years ago; and though your father and mother and grandmother, looking about the streets through which they were carrying you, staring at the walls into which they brought you, had every reason to be heavy-hearted, yet they were not. For here you were, Big James, named for me—you were a big baby, I was not—here you were: to be loved. To be loved, baby, hard, at once, and forever, to strengthen you against the loveless world. Remember that: I know how black it looks today, for you. It looked bad that day, too, yes, we were trembling. We have not stopped trembling yet, but if we had not loved each other none of us would have survived. And now you must survive because we love you, and for the sake of your children and your children's children.

This innocent country set you down in a ghetto in which, in fact, it intended that you should perish. Let me spell out precisely what I mean by that, for the heart of the matter is here, and the root of my dispute with my country. You were born where you were born and faced the future that you faced because you were black and *for no other reason.* The limits of your ambition were, thus, expected to be set forever. You were born into a society which spelled out with brutal clarity, and in as many ways as possible, that you were a worthless human being. You were not expected to aspire to excellence: you were expected to make peace with mediocrity. Wherever you have turned, James, in your short time on this earth, you have been told where you could go and what you could do (and *how* you could do it) and where you could live and whom you could marry. I know your countrymen do not agree with me about this, and I hear them saying, "You exaggerate." They do not know Harlem, and I do. So do you. Take no one's word for anything, including mine—but trust your experience. Know whence you came. If you know whence you came, there is really no limit to where you can go. The details and symbols of your life have been deliberately constructed to make you believe what white people say about you. Please try to re-member that what they believe, as well as what they do and cause you to endure, does not testify to your inferiority but to their inhumanity and fear. Please try to be clear, dear James, through the storm which rages about your youthful head today, about the reality which lies be-hind the words *acceptance* and *integration.* There is no reason for you to try to become like white people and there is no basis whatever for their impertinent assumption that *they* must accept *you.* The really terrible thing, old buddy, is that *you* must accept *them.* And I mean that very seriously. You must accept them and accept them with love. For these innocent people have no other hope. They are, in effect, still trapped in a history which they do not understand; and until they understand it, they cannot be released from it. They have had to believe for many years, and for innumerable reasons, that black men are inferior to white men. Many of them, indeed, know better, but, as you will discover, people find it very difficult to act on what they know. To act is to be committed, and to be committed is to be in danger. In this case, the danger, in the minds of most white Americans, is the loss of their identity. Try to imagine how you would feel if you woke up one morning to find the sun shining and all the stars aflame. You would be frightened because it is out of the order of nature. Any upheaval in the universe is terrifying because it so profoundly attacks one's sense of one's own reality. Well, the black man has functioned in the white man's world as a fixed star, as an immovable pillar: and as he moves out of his place, heaven and earth are shaken to their foundations. You, don't be afraid. I said that it was intended that you should perish in the ghetto, perish by never being allowed to go behind the white man's definitions, by never being allowed to spell your proper name. You have, and many of us have, defeated this intention; and by a terrible law, a terrible paradox, those innocents who believed that your imprisonment made them safe are losing their grasp of reality. But these men are your brothers—your lost, younger brothers. And if the word *integration* means anything, this is what it means: that we, with love, shall force our brothers to see themselves as they are, to cease fleeing from reality and begin to change it. For this is your home, my friend, do not be driven from it; great men have done great things here, and will again, and we can make America what America must become. It will be hard, James, but you come from sturdy, peasant stock, men who picked cotton and dammed rivers and built railroads, and, in the teeth of the most terrifying odds, achieved an unassailable and monumental dignity. You come from a long line of great poets, some of the greatest poets since Homer. One of them said, *The very time I thought I was lost, My dungeon shook and my chains fell off.*

You know, and I know, that the country is celebrating one hundred years of freedom one hundred years too soon. We cannot be free until they are free. God bless you, James, and Godspeed.

Your uncle,
James

95. MALCOLM X

The Ballot or the Bullet

(1964)

MALCOLM X's "The Ballot or the Bullet" is recognized as one of the most powerful speeches in American history. Born Malcolm Little, Malcolm X (1925–1965) grew up in Michigan and was a hustler and a con artist in Boston before he was arrested for robbery in 1946. While in prison, Malcolm converted to the Nation of Islam (NOI) and changed his name to Malcolm X. Following his release, he quickly became the NOI's most prominent minister. However, he was suspended from the NOI for a controversial remark he made after the assassination of President John F. Kennedy. In 1964, Malcolm left the NOI, traveled to Mecca, and established the Organization of Afro-American Unity. In his last year, Malcolm retreated somewhat from his previously held belief that whites were "devils," and he began to embrace an internationalist socialist philosophy of black liberation. He was assassinated in the Audubon Ballroom in Harlem, New York, in 1965. "The Ballot or the Bullet" was delivered in Cleveland, Ohio, on April 3, 1964. By refusing to repudiate nonviolence, Malcolm recognized that he made Martin Luther King's stance seem more moderate and palatable than it would otherwise have appeared.

SOURCE: George Breitman, ed. *Malcolm X Speaks: Selected Speeches and Statements.* New York: Merit Publishers, 1965.

SELECTED READINGS: Michael Eric Dyson, *The Myth and Meaning of Malcolm X* (1995). James Cone, *Martin and Malcolm: A Dream or a Nightmare?* (1991). George Breitman, *The Last Year of Malcolm X* (1967).

Mr. Moderator, brothers and sisters, friends and enemies: I just can't believe everyone in here is a friend and I don't want to leave anybody out. The question tonight, as I understand it, is "The Negro Revolt, and Where Do We

Go from Here?" or "What Next?" In my little humble way of understanding it, it points toward either the ballot or the bullet. . . .

Before we try and explain what is meant by the ballot or the bullet, I would like to clarify something concerning myself. I'm still a Muslim, my religion is still Islam. That's my personal belief. Just as Adam Clayton Powell is a Christian minister who heads the Abyssinian Baptist Church in New York, but at the same time takes part in the political struggles to try and bring about rights to the black people in this country; and Dr. Martin Luther King is a Christian minister down in Atlanta, Georgia, who heads another organization fighting for the civil rights of black people in this country; and Reverend Galamison—I guess you've heard of him—is another Christian minister in New York who has been deeply involved in the school boycotts to eliminate segregated education; well, I myself am a minister, not a Christian minister, but a Muslim minister; and I believe in action on all fronts by whatever means necessary.

Although I'm still a Muslim, I'm not here tonight to discuss my religion. I'm not here to try and change your religion. I'm not here to argue or discuss anything that we differ about, because it's time for us to submerge our differences and realize that it is best for us to first see that we have the same problem, a common problem—a problem that will make you catch hell whether you're a Baptist, or a Methodist, or a Muslim, or a nationalist. Whether you're educated or illiterate, whether you live on the boulevard or in the alley, you're going to catch hell just like I am. We're all in the same boat and we all are going to catch the same hell from the same man. He just happens to be a white man. All of us have suffered here, in this country, political oppression at the hands of the white man, economic exploitation at at the hands of the white man, and social degradation at the hands of the white man.

Now in speaking like this, it doesn't mean that we're anti-white, but it does mean we're anti-exploitation, we're antidegradation, we're antioppression. And if the white man doesn't want us to be anti-*him*, let him stop oppressing and exploiting and degrading us. Whether we are Christians or Muslims or nationalists or agnostics or atheists, we must first learn to forget our differences. If we have differences, let us differ in the closet; when we come out in front, let us not have anything to argue about until we get finished arguing with the man. If the late President Kennedy could get together with Khrushchev and exchange some wheat, we certainly have more in common with each other than Kennedy and Khrushchev had with each other.

If we don't do something real soon, I think you'll have to agree that we're going to be forced either to use the ballot or the bullet. It's one or the other in 1964. It isn't that time is running out—time has run out! Nineteen sixty-four threatens to be the most explosive year America has ever witnessed. The most explosive year. Why? It's also a political year. It's the year when all of the white politicians will be back in the so-called Negro community jiving you and me for some votes. The year when all of the white political crooks will be right back in your and my community with their false promises, building up our hopes for a letdown, with their trickery and their treachery, with their false promises which they don't intend to keep. As they nourish these dissatisfactions, it can only lead to one thing, an explosion; and now we have the type of black man on the scene in America today—I'm sorry, Brother Lomax—who just doesn't intend to turn the other cheek any longer.

Don't let anybody tell you anything about the odds are against you. If they draft you, they send you to Korea and make you face 800 million Chinese. If you can be brave over there, you can be brave right here. These odds aren't as great as those odds. And if you fight here, you will at least know what you're fighting for.

I'm not a politician, not even a student of politics; in fact, I'm not a student of much of anything. I'm not a Democrat, I'm not a Republican, and I don't even consider myself an American. If you and I were Americans, there'd be no problem. Those Hunkies that just got off the boat, they're already Americans; Polacks are already Americans; the Italian refugees are already Americans. Everything that came out of Europe, every blue-eyed thing, is already an American. And as long as you and I have been over here, we aren't Americans yet.

Well, I am one who doesn't believe in deluding myself. I'm not going to sit at your table and watch you eat, with nothing on my plate, and call myself a diner. Sitting at the table doesn't make you a diner, unless you eat some of what's on that plate. Being here in America doesn't make you an American. Being born here in America doesn't make you an American. Why, if birth made you American, you wouldn't need any legislation, you wouldn't need any amendments to the Constitution, you wouldn't be faced with civil-rights filibustering in Washington, D.C., right now. They don't have to pass civil-rights legislation to make a Polack an American.

No, I'm not an American. I'm one of the twenty-two million black people who are the victims of democracy, nothing but disguised hypocrisy. So, I'm not standing here speaking to you as an American, or a patriot, or a flag-saluter, or a flag-waver—no, not I. I'm speaking as a victim of this American system. And I see America through the eyes of the victim. I don't see any American dream; I see an American nightmare.

These twenty-two million victims are waking up. Their eyes are coming open. They're beginning to see what they used to only look at. They're becoming politically mature. They are realizing that there are new political trends from coast to coast. . . .

So it's time in 1964 to wake up. And when you see them coming up with that kind of conspiracy, let them know your eyes are open. And let them know you got something else that's wide open too. It's got to be the ballot or the bullet. The ballot or the bullet. If you're afraid to use an expression like that, you should get on out of the country, you should get back in the cotton patch, you should get back in the alley. They get all the Negro vote, and after they get it, the Negro gets nothing in return. All they did when they got to Washington was give a few big Negroes big jobs. Those big Negroes didn't need big jobs, they already had jobs. That's camouflage, that's trickery, that's treachery, window-dressing. I'm not trying to knock out the Democrats for the Republicans, we'll get to them in a minute. But it is true—you put the Democrats first and the Democrats put you last. *what votes?*

Look at it the way it is. What alibis do they use, since they control Congress and the Senate? What alibi do they use when you and I ask, "Well, when are you going to keep your promise?" They blame the Dixiecrats. What is a Dixiecrat? A Democrat. A Dixiecrat is nothing but a Democrat in disguise. The titular head of the Democrats is also the head of the Dixiecrats, because the Dixiecrats are a party of the Democratic Party. The Democrats have never kicked the Dixiecrats out of the party. The Dixiecrats bolted themselves once, but the Democrats didn't put them out. Imagine, these low-down Southern segregationists put the Northern Democrats down. But the Northern Democrats have never put the Dixiecrats down. No, look at that thing the way it is. They have got a con game going on, a political con game, and you and I are in the middle. It's time for you and me to wake up and start looking at it like it is, and trying to understand it like it is; and then we can deal with it like it is. . . .

So, what I'm trying to impress upon you, in essence, is this: You and I in America are faced not with a segregationist conspiracy, we're faced with a government conspiracy. Everyone who's filibustering is a Senator—that's the government. Everyone who's finagling in Washington, D.C., is a Congressman—that's the government. You don't have anybody putting blocks in your path but people who are a part of the government. The same government that you go abroad to fight for and die for is the government that is in a conspiracy to deprive you of your voting rights, deprive you of your economic opportunities, deprive you of decent housing, deprive you of decent education. You don't need to go to the employer alone, it is the government itself, the government of America, that is responsible for the oppression and exploitation and degradation of black people in this country. And you should drop it in their lap. This government has failed the Negro. This so-called democracy has failed the Negro. And all these white liberals have definitely failed the Negro.

So, where do we go from here? First, we need some friends. We need some new allies. The entire civil-rights struggle needs a new interpretation, a broader interpretation. We need to look at this civil-rights thing from another angle—from the inside as well as from the outside. To those of us whose philosophy is black nationalism, the only way you can get involved in the civil-rights struggle is to give it a new interpretation. That old interpretation excluded us. It kept us out. So, we're giving a new interpretation to the civil-rights struggle, an interpretation that will enable us to come into it, take part in it. And these handkerchief-heads who have been dillydallying and pussy-footing and compromising—we don't intend to let them pussyfoot and dilly-dally and compromise any longer.

How can you thank a man for giving you what's already yours? How then can you thank him for giving you only part of what's already yours? You haven't even made progress, if what's being given to you, you should have had already. That's not progress. And I love my Brother Lomax, the way he pointed out we're right back where we were in 1954. We're not even as far up as we were in 1954. We're behind where we were in 1954. There's more segregation now than there was in 1954. There's more racial animosity, more racial hatred, more racial violence today in 1964, than there was in 1954. Where is the progress?

And now you're facing a situation where the young Negro's coming up. They don't want to hear that "turn-the-other-cheek" stuff, no. In Jacksonville, those were teenagers, they were throwing Molotov cocktails. Negroes have never done that before. But it shows you there's a new deal coming in. There's new thinking coming in. There's new strategy coming in. It'll be Molotov cocktails this month, hand grenades next month, and something else next month. It'll be ballots, or it'll be bullets. It'll be liberty, or it will be death. The only difference about this kind of death—it'll be reciprocal. You know what is meant by "reciprocal"? That's one of Brother Lomax's words, I stole it from him. I don't usually deal with those big words because I don't usually deal with big people. I deal with small people. I find you can get a whole lot of small people and whip hell out of a whole lot of big people. They haven't got anything to lose, and they've got everything to gain. And they'll let you know in a minute: "It takes two to tango; when I go, you go."

The black nationalists, those whose philosophy is black nationalism, in bringing about this new interpretation of the entire meaning of civil rights, look upon it as meaning, as Brother Lomax has pointed out, equality of opportunity. Well, we're justified in seeking civil rights, if it means equality of opportunity, because all we're doing there is trying to collect for our investment. Our mothers and fathers invested sweat and blood. Three hundred and ten years we worked in this country without a dime in return—I mean without a *dime* in return. You let the white man walk around here talking about how rich this country is, but you never stop to think how it got rich so quick. It got rich because you made it rich.

You take the people who are in this audience right now. They're poor,

we're all poor as individuals. Our weekly salary individually amounts to hardly anything. But if you take the salary of everyone in here collectively it'll fill
up a whole lot of baskets. It's a lot of wealth. If you can collect the wages of
just these people right here for a year, you'll be rich—richer than rich. When
you look at it like that, think how rich Uncle Sam had to become, not with
this handful, but millions of black people. Your and my mother and father,
who didn't work an eight-hour shift, but worked from "can't see" in the
morning until "can't see" at night, and worked for nothing, making the white
man rich, making Uncle Sam rich. . . .

By ballot I only mean freedom. Don't you know—I disagree with Lomax
on this issue—that the ballot is more important than the dollar? Can I prove
it? Yes. Look in the U.N. There are poor nations in the U.N.; yet those poor
nations can get together with their voting power and keep the rich nations
from making a move. They have one nation, one vote—everyone has an equal
vote. And when those brothers from Asia, and Africa and the darker parts of
this earth get together, their voting power is sufficient to hold Sam in check.
Or Russia in check. Or some other section of the earth in check. So, the ballot
is most important.

Right now, in this country, if you and I, twenty-two million African-
Americans—that's what we are—Africans who are in America. In fact, you'd
get farther calling yourself African instead of Negro. Africans don't catch hell.
You're the only one catching hell. They don't have to pass civil-rights bills for
Africans. An African can go anywhere he wants right now. All you've got to
do is tie your head up. That's right, go anywhere you want. Just stop being
a Negro. Change your name to Hoogagagooba. That'll show you how silly the
white man is. You're dealing with a silly man. A friend of mine who's very
dark put a turban on his head and went into a restaurant in Atlanta before
they called themselves desegregated. He went into a white restaurant, he sat
down, they served him, and he said, "What would happen if a Negro came
in here?" And there he's sitting, black as night, but because he had his head
wrapped up the waitress looked back at him and says, "Why, there wouldn't
no nigger dare come in here."

So, you're dealing with a man whose bias and prejudice are making him
lose his mind, his intelligence, every day. He's frightened. He looks around
and sees what's taking place on this earth, and he sees that the pendulum of
time is swinging in your direction. The dark people are waking up. They're
losing their fear of the white man. No place where he's fighting right now is
he winning. Everywhere he's fighting, he's fighting someone your and my
complexion. And they're beating him. He can't win any more. He's won his
last battle. He failed to win the Korean War. He couldn't win it. He had to
sign a truce. That's a loss. Any time Uncle Sam, with all his machinery for
warfare, is held to a draw by some rice-eaters, he's lost the battle. He had to

sign a truce. America's not supposed to sign a truce. She's supposed to be bad. But she's not bad any more. She's bad as long as she can use her hydrogen bomb, but she can't use hers for fear Russia might use hers. Russia can't use hers, for fear that Sam might use his. So, both of them are weaponless. They can't use the weapon, because each's weapon nullifies the other's. So the only place where action can take place is on the ground. And the white man can't win another war fighting on the ground. Those days are over. The black man knows it, the brown man knows it, the red man knows it, and the yellow man knows it. So they engage him in guerrilla warfare. That's not his style. You've got to have heart to be a guerrilla warrior, and he hasn't got any heart. I'm telling you now. . . .

It's time for you and me to stop sitting in this country, letting some cracker Senators, Northern crackers and Southern crackers, sit there in Washington, D.C., and come to a conclusion in their mind that you and I are supposed to have civil rights. There's no white man going to tell me anything about *my* rights. Brothers and sisters, always remember, if it doesn't take Senators and Congressmen and Presidential proclamations to give freedom to the white man, it is not necessary for legislation or proclamation or Supreme Court decisions to give freedom to the black man. You let that white man know, if this is a country of freedom, let it be a country of freedom; and if it's not a country of freedom, change it. . . .

Last but not least, I must say this concerning the great controversy over rifles and shotguns. The only thing that I've ever said is that in areas where the government has proven itself either unwilling or unable to defend the lives and the property of Negroes, it's time for Negroes to defend themselves. Article number two of the Constitutional amendments provides you and me the right to own a rifle or a shotgun. It is constitutionally legal to own a shotgun or a rifle. This doesn't mean you're going to get a rifle and form battalions and go out looking for white folks, although you'd be within your rights—I mean, you'd be justified; but that would be illegal and we don't do anything illegal. If the white man doesn't want the black man buying rifles and shotguns, then let the government do its job. That's all. And don't let the white man come to you and ask you what you think about what Malcolm says—why, you old Uncle Tom. He would never ask you if he thought you were going to say, "Oh, man!" No, he is making a Tom out of you.

So, this doesn't mean forming rifle clubs and going out looking for people, but it is time, in 1964, if you are a man, to let that man know. If he's not going to do his job in running the government and providing you and me with the protection that our taxes are supposed to be for, since he spends all those billions for his defense budget, he certainly can't begrudge you and me spending $12 or $15 for a single-shot, or double-action. I hope you under-stand. Don't go out shooting people, but any time, brothers and sisters, and especially the men in this audience—some of you wearing Congressional Medals of Honor, with shoulders this wide, chests this big, muscles that big— any time you and I sit around and read where they bomb a church and mur- der in cold blood, not some grownups, but four little girls while they were praying . . . if you never see me another time in your life, if I die in the morn- ing, I'll die saying one thing: the ballot or the bullet, the ballot or the bullet.

If a Negro in 1964 has to sit around and wait for some cracker Senator to filibuster when it comes to the rights of black people, why, you and I should hang our heads in shame. You talk about a march on Washington in 1963, you haven't seen anything. There's some more going down in '64. And this time they're not going like they went last year. They're not going singing "We Shall Overcome." They're not going with white friends. They're not going with placards already painted for them. They're not going with round-trip tickets. They're going with one-way tickets.

And if they don't want that non-nonviolent army going down there, tell them to bring the filibuster to a halt. The black nationalists aren't going to wait. Lyndon B. Johnson is the head of the Democratic party. If he's for civil rights, let him go into the Senate next week and declare himself. Let him go in there right now and declare himself. Let him go in there and denounce the Southern branch of his party. Let him go in there right now and take a moral stand—right now, not later. Tell him, don't wait until election time. If he waits too long, brothers and sisters, he will be responsible for letting a condition develop in this country which will create a climate that will bring seeds up out of the ground with vegetation on the end of them looking like something these people never dreamed of. In 1964, it's the ballot or the bullet. Thank you.

96. STOKELY CARMICHAEL

What We Want

(1966)

STOKELY CARMICHAEL's "What We Want," originally published in *The New York Review of Books,* helped explain the Black Power movement to white America. Carmichael (1941–1998) was born in Trinidad, but he moved to New York City in 1952 and graduated from Howard University in 1964. He was active in the early civil rights movement, and in 1966 he replaced John Lewis as chair of the Student Nonviolent Coordinating Committee (SNCC). Carmichael set off a storm of controversy by promoting the volatile slogan "Black Power," and by supporting the expulsion of whites from SNCC. Although Carmichael's increasingly separatist politics won him many admirers, this also fueled a "white backlash" against the civil rights movement. Carmichael moved to Ghana in 1969, where he changed his name to Kwame Ture. He died in 1998. The following essay explained the historical context from which the "Black Power" philosophy emerged, and argued that integration, by itself, was not an adequate solution to the problems of African Americans.

SOURCE: Stokely Carmichael. "What We Want." *The New York Review of Books,* Vol. 7, No. 4. September 22, 1966.

SELECTED READINGS: William Van DeBurg, *New Day in Babylon: The Black Power Movement and American Culture, 1965–1975* (1992). Clayborne Carson, *In Struggle: SNCC and the Black Awakening of the 1960s* (1981). Stokely Carmichael and Charles Hamilton, *Black Power: The Politics of Liberation in America* (1967).

One of the tragedies of the struggle against racism is that up to now there has been no national organization which could speak to the growing militancy of young black people in the urban ghetto. There has been only a civil rights movement, whose tone of voice was adapted to an audience of liberal whites.

It served as a sort of buffer zone between them and angry young blacks. None of its so-called leaders could go into a rioting community and be listened to. In a sense, I blame ourselves—together with the mass media—for what has happened in Watts, Harlem, Chicago, Cleveland, Omaha. Each time the people in those cities saw Martin Luther King get slapped, they became angry; when they saw four little black girls bombed to death, they were angrier; and when nothing happened, they were steaming. We had nothing to offer that they could see, except to go out and be beaten again. We helped to build their frustration.

For too many years, black Americans marched and had their heads broken and got shot. They were saying to the country, "Look, you guys are supposed to be nice guys and we are only going to do what we are supposed to do— why do you beat us up, why don't you give us what we ask, why don't you straighten yourselves out?" After years of this, we are at almost the same point—because we demonstrated from a position of weakness. We cannot be expected any longer to march and have our heads broken in order to say to whites: come on, you're nice guys. For you are not nice guys. We have found you out.

An organization which claims to speak for the needs of a community—as does the Student Nonviolent Coordinating Committee—must speak in the tone of that community, not as somebody else's buffer zone. This is the significance of black power as a slogan. For once, black people are going to use the words they want to use—not just the words whites want to hear. And they will do this no matter how often the press tries to stop the use of the slogan by equating it with racism or separatism.

An organization which claims to be working for the needs of a community—as SNCC does—must work to provide that community with a position of strength from which to make its voice heard. This is the significance of black power beyond the slogan.

Black power can be clearly defined for those who do not attach the fears of white America to their questions about it. We should begin with the basic fact that black Americans have two problems: they are poor and they are black. All other problems arise from this two-sided reality: lack of education, the so-called apathy of black men. Any program to end racism must address itself to that double reality.

Almost from its beginning, SNCC sought to address itself to both conditions with a program aimed at winning political power for impoverished Southern blacks. We had to begin with politics because black Americans are a propertyless people in a country where property is valued above all. We had to work for power, because this country does not function by morality, love, and nonviolence, but by power. Thus we determined to win political power, with the idea of moving on from there into activity that would have economic effects.

With power, the masses could *make or participate in making* the decisions which govern their destinies, and thus create basic change in their day-to-day lives.

But if political power seemed to be the key to self-determination, it was also obvious that the key had been thrown down a deep well many years earlier. Disenfranchisement, maintained by racist terror, makes it impossible to talk about organizing for political power in 1960. The right to vote had to be won, and SNCC workers devoted their energies to this from 1961 to 1965. They set up voter registration drives in the Deep South. They created pressure for the vote by holding mock elections in Mississippi in 1963 and by helping to establish the Mississippi Freedom Democratic Party (MFDP) in 1964. That struggle was eased, though not won, with the passage of the 1965 Voting Rights Act. SNCC workers could then address themselves to the question: "Who can we vote for, to have our needs met—how do we make our vote meaningful?"

SNCC had already gone to Atlantic City for recognition of the Mississippi Freedom Democratic Party by the Democratic convention and been rejected; it had gone with the MFDP to Washington for recognition by Congress and been rejected. In Arkansas, SNCC helped thirty Negroes to run for School Board elections; all but one were defeated, and there was evidence of fraud and intimidation sufficient to cause their defeat. In Atlanta, Julian Bond ran for the state legislature and was elected—twice—and unseated—twice. In several states, black farmers ran in elections for agricultural committees which make crucial decisions concerning land use, loans, etc. Although they won places on a number of committees, they never gained the majorities needed to control them.

All of the efforts were attempts to win black power. Then, in Alabama, the opportunity came to see how blacks could be organized on an independent party basis. An unusual Alabama law provides that any group of citizens can nominate candidates for county office and, if they win 20 percent of the vote, may be recognized as a county political party. The same then applies on a state level. SNCC went to organize in several counties such as Lowndes, where black people—who form 80 per cent of the population and have an average annual income of $943—felt they could accomplish nothing within the framework of the Alabama Democratic Party because of its racism and because the qualifying fee for this year's elections was raised from $50 to $500 in order to prevent most Negroes from becoming candidates. On May 3, five new county "freedom organizations" convened and nominated candidates for the offices of sheriff, tax assessor, members of the school boards. These men and women are up for election in November—if they live until then. Their ballot symbol is the black panther: a bold, beautiful animal, representing the strength and dignity of black demands today. A man needs a black panther on his side when he and his family must endure—as hundreds of Alabamians have endured—loss of job, eviction, starvation, and sometimes death, for political activity. He may also need a gun and SNCC reaffirms the right of black men everywhere to defend themselves when threatened or attacked. As for initiating the use of violence, we hope that such programs as ours will make that unnecessary; but it is not for us to tell black communities whether they can or cannot use any particular form of action to resolve their problems. Responsibility for the use of violence by black men, whether in self-defense or initiated by them, lies with the white community.

This is the specific historical experience from which SNCC's call for "black power" emerged on the Mississippi march last July. But the concept of "black power" is not a recent or isolated phenomenon: It has grown out of the ferment of agitation and activity by different people and organizations in many black communities over the years. Our last year of work in Alabama added a new concrete possibility. In Lowndes County, for example, black power will mean that if a Negro is elected sheriff, he can end police brutality. If a black man is elected tax assessor, he can collect and channel funds for the building of better roads and schools serving black people—thus advancing the move from political power into the economic arena. In such areas as Lowndes, where black men have a majority, they will attempt to use it to exercise control. This is what they seek: control. Where Negroes lack a majority, black power means proper representation and sharing of control. It means the creation of power bases from which black people can work to change statewide or nationwide patterns of oppression through pressure from strength—instead of weakness. Politically, black power means what it has always meant to SNCC: the coming-together of black people to elect representatives and *to force those representatives to speak to their needs*. It does not mean merely putting black faces into office. A man or woman who is black and from the slums cannot be automatically expected to speak to the needs of black people. Most of the black politicians we see around the country today are not what SNCC means by black power. The power must be that of a community, and emanate from there.

SNCC today is working in both North and South on programs of voter registration and independent political organizing. In some places, such as Alabama, Los Angeles, New York, Philadelphia, and New Jersey, independent organizing under the black panther symbol is in progress. The creation of a national "black panther party" must come about: it will take time to build, and it is much too early to predict its success. We have no infallible master plan and we make no claim to exclusive knowledge of how to end racism; different groups will work in their own different ways. SNCC cannot spell out the full logistics of self-determination but it can address itself to the problem by helping black communities define their needs, realize their strength, and go into action along a variety of lines which they must choose for themselves.

Without knowing all the answers, it can address itself to the basic problem of poverty: to the fact that in Lowndes County, 86 white families own 90 percent of the land. What are black people in that county going to do for jobs, where are they going to get money? There must be reallocation of land and money.

Ultimately, the economic foundations of this country must be shared if black people are to control their lives. The colonies of the United States—and this includes the black ghettoes within its borders, north and south—must be liberated. For a century, this nation has been like an octopus of exploitation, its tentacles stretching from Mississippi and Harlem to South America, the Middle East, southern Africa, and Vietnam; the form of exploitation varies from area to area but the essential result has been the same—a powerful few have been maintained and enriched at the expense of the poor and voiceless colored masses. This pattern must be broken. As its grip loosens here and there around the world, the hopes of black Americans become more realistic. For racism to die, a totally different America must be born.

This is what the white society does not wish to face; this is why that society prefers to talk about integration. But integration speaks not at all to the problem of poverty, only to the problem of blackness. Integration today means the man who "makes it," leaving his black brothers behind in the ghetto as fast as his new sports car will take him. It has no relevance to the Harlem wino or to the cottonpicker making three dollars a day. As a lady I know in Alabama once said, "the food that Ralph Bunche eats doesn't fill my stomach."

Integration, moreover, speaks to the problem of blackness in a despicable way. As a goal, it has been based on complete acceptance of the fact that *in order to have* a decent house or education, blacks must move into a white neighborhood or send their children to a white school. This reinforces, among both black and white, the idea that "white" is automatically better and "black" is by definition inferior. This is why integration is a subterfuge for the maintenance of white supremacy. It allows the nation to focus on a handful of Southern children who get into white schools, at great price, and to ignore the 94 percent who are left behind in unimproved all-black schools. Such situations will not change until black people have power—to control their own school boards, in this case. Then Negroes become equal in a way that means something, and integration ceases to be a one-way street. Then integration doesn't mean draining skills and energies from the ghetto into white neighborhoods; then it can mean white people moving from Beverly Hills into Watts, white people joining the Lowndes County Freedom Organization. Then integration becomes relevant. . . .

To most whites, black power seems to mean that the Mau Mau are coming to the suburbs at night. The Mau Mau are coming, and whites must stop them. Articles appear about plots to "get Whitey," creating an atmosphere in which "law and order must be maintained." Once again, responsibility is shifted from the oppressor to the oppressed. Other whites chide, "Don't forget—you're only 10 percent of the population; if you get too smart, we'll wipe you out." If they are liberals, they complain, "what about me?—don't you want my help any more?" These are people supposedly concerned about black Americans, but today they think first of themselves, of their feelings of rejection. Or they admonish, "you can't get anywhere without coalitions," without considering the problems of coalition with whom?; on what terms (coalescing from weakness can mean absorption, betrayal)?; when? Or they accuse us of "polarizing the races" by our calls for black unity, when the true responsibility for polarization lies with whites who will not accept their responsibility as the majority power for making the democratic process work. . . .

Whites will not see that I, for example, as a person oppressed because of my blackness, have common cause with other blacks who are oppressed because of blackness. This is not to say that there are no white people who see things as I do, but that it is black people I must speak to first. It must be the oppressed to whom SNCC addresses itself primarily, not to friends from the oppressing group.

From birth, black people are told a set of lies about themselves. We are told that we are lazy—yet I drive through the Delta area of Mississippi and watch black people picking cotton in the hot sun for fourteen hours. We are told, "If you work hard, you'll succeed"—but if that were true, black people would own this country. We are oppressed because we are black—not because we are ignorant, not because we are lazy, not because we're stupid (and got good rhythm), but because we're black. . . .

The need for psychological equality is the reason why SNCC today believes that blacks must organize in the black community. Only black people can convey the revolutionary idea that black people are able to do things themselves. Only they can help create in the community an aroused and continuing black consciousness that will provide the basis for political strength. In the past, white allies have furthered white supremacy without the whites involved realizing it—or wanting it, I think. Black people must do things for themselves; they must get poverty money they will control and spend themselves, they must conduct tutorial programs themselves so that black children can identify with black people. This is one reason Africa has such importance: The reality of black men ruling their own nations gives blacks elsewhere a sense of possibility, of power, which they do not now have. . . .

Black people do not want to "take over" this country. They don't want to "get whitey"; they just want to get him off their backs, as the saying goes. It was for example the exploitation by Jewish landlords and merchants which first created black resentment toward Jews—not Judaism. The white man is irrelevant to blacks, except as an oppressive force. Blacks want to be in his place, yes, but not in order to terrorize and lynch and starve him. They want to be in his place because that is where a decent life can be had. . . .

As for white America, perhaps it can stop crying out against "black supremacy," "black nationalism," "racism in reverse," and begin facing reality. The reality is that this nation, from top to bottom, is racist; that racism is not primarily a problem of "human relations" but of an exploitation maintained—either actively or through silence—by the society as a whole. Camus and Sartre have asked, can a man condemn himself? Can whites, particularly liberal whites, condemn themselves? Can they stop blaming us, and blame their own system? Are they capable of the shame which might become a revolutionary emotion?

We have found that they usually cannot condemn themselves, and so we have done it. But the rebuilding of this society, if at all possible, is basically the responsibility of whites—not blacks. We won't fight to save the present society, in Vietnam or anywhere else. We are just going to work, in the way we see fit, and on goals we define, not for civil rights but for all our human rights.

97. THE BLACK PANTHER PARTY

What We Want, What We Believe
(1966)

The "Black Panther Party Platform" outlined what cofounder Huey P. Newton called "the essential points for the survival of Black and oppressed people in the United States." The Black Panther Party for Self-Defense was formed in October 1966 in Oakland, California, by Newton and Bobby Seale, and it soon became the most storied black militant organization of the late 1960s. The Panthers called for African Americans to arm themselves in self-defense, and in their early days they followed police cars that patrolled black neighborhoods to see that police didn't violate anyone's civil rights. Accordingly, they were the target of severe harassment and infiltration from law enforcement agencies, and they were involved in several violent confrontations with police. During the early 1970s the group's influence waned under the pressures of government repression, legal difficulties, and internal schisms.

SOURCE: Reprinted in Deirdre Mullane, *Crossing the Danger Water: Three Hundred Years of African-American Writing.* New York: Doubleday, 1993.

SELECTED READINGS: Charles E. Jones, ed., *The Black Panther Party (Reconsidered)* (1998). Hugh Pearson, *The Shadow of the Panther: Huey Newton and the Price of Black Power in America* (1994). Huey P. Newton, *Revolutionary Suicide* (1973).

1. *We want freedom. We want power to determine the destiny of our Black Community.*

We believe that black people will not be free until we are able to determine our destiny.

2. *We want full employment for our people.*

We believe that the federal government is responsible and obligated to give every man employment or a guaranteed income. We believe that if the white

American businessmen will not give full employment, then the means of production should be taken from the businessmen and placed in the community
so that the people of the community can organize and employ all of its people
and give a high standard of living.

3. *We want an end to the robbery by the white man of our Black Community.*

We believe that this racist government has robbed us and now we are
demanding the overdue debt of forty acres and two mules. Forty acres and
two mules was promised 100 years ago as restitution for slave labor and mass
murder of black people. We will accept the payment in currency which will
be distributed to our many communities. The Germans are now aiding the
Jews in Israel for the genocide of the Jewish people. The Germans murdered
six million Jews. The American racist has taken part in the slaughter of over
fifty million black people; therefore, we feel that this is a modest demand that
we make.

4. *We want decent housing, fit for shelter of human beings.*

We believe that if the white landlords will not give decent housing to our
black community, then the housing and the land should be made into cooperatives so that our community, with government aid, can build and make
decent housing for its people.

5. *We want education for our people that exposes the true nature of this decadent
American society. We want education that teaches us our true history and our role in
the present-day society.*

We believe in an education system that will give to our people a knowledge
of self. If a man does not have knowledge of himself and his position in society
and the world, then he has little chance to relate to anything else.

6. *We want all black men to be exempt from military service.*

We believe that black people should not be forced to fight in the military
service to defend a racist government that does not protect us. We will not
fight and kill other people of color in the world who, like the black people,
are being victimized by the white racist government of America. We will protect ourselves from the force and violence of the racist police and the racist
military, by whatever means necessary.

7. *We want an immediate end to POLICE BRUTALITY and MURDER of black
people.*

We believe we can end police brutality in our black community by organizing black self-defense groups that are dedicated to defending our black community from racist police oppression and brutality. The Second Amendment
to the Constitution of the United States gives us a right to bear arms. We
therefore believe that all black people should arm themselves for self-defense.

8. *We want freedom for all black men held in federal, state, county and city prisons
and jails.*

We believe that all black people should be released from the many jails and prisons because they have not received a fair and impartial trial.

9. *We want all black people when brought to trial to be tried in court by a jury of their peer group or people from their black communities, as defined by the Constitution of the United States.*

We believe that the courts should follow the United States Constitution so that black people will receive fair trials. The 14th Amendment of the U.S. Constitution gives a man a right to be tried by his peer group. A peer is a person from a similar economic, social, religious, geographical, environmental, historical and racial background. To do this the court will be forced to select a jury from the black community from which the black defendant came. We have been, and are being tried by all-white juries that have no understanding of the "average reasoning man" of the black community.

10. *We want land, bread, housing, education, clothing, justice and peace. And as our major political objective, a United Nations—supervised plebiscite to be held throughout the black colony in which only black colonial subjects will be allowed to participate, for the purpose of determining the will of black people as to their national destiny.*

When, in the course of human events, it becomes necessary for one people to dissolve the political bands which have connected them with another, and to assume, among the powers of the earth, the separate and equal station to which the laws of nature and nature's God entitle them, a decent respect to the opinions of mankind requires that they should declare the causes which impel them to the separation.

We hold these truths to be self-evident, that all men are created equal; that they are endowed by their Creator with certain unalienable rights; that among these are life, liberty, and the pursuit of happiness. *That, to secure these rights, governments are instituted among men, deriving their just powers from the consent of the governed; that, whenever any form of government becomes destructive of these ends, it is the right of the people to alter or to abolish it, and to institute a new government, laying its foundation on such principles, and organizing its powers in such form, as to them shall seem most likely to effect their safety and happiness.* Prudence, indeed, will dictate that governments long established should not be changed for light and transient causes; and accordingly, all experience hath shown, that mankind are more disposed to suffer, while evils are sufferable, than to right themselves by abolishing the forms to which they are accustomed. *But, when a long train of abuses and usurpations pursuing invariably the same object, evinces a design to reduce them under absolute despotism, it is their right, it is their duty, to throw off such-government, and to provide new guards for their future security.*

98. ANGELA Y. DAVIS

Political Prisoners, Prisons, and Black Liberation
(1971)

ANGELA DAVIS's "Political Prisoners, Prisons, and Black Liberation" called for a unified struggle against the onset of racism and fascism in the United States. Because of her affiliation with the Communist Party, U.S.A., Davis (1944–) was dismissed from her teaching position at the University of California, Los Angeles in 1969. In 1970 she was charged with kidnapping, conspiracy, and murder for her role in connection with a courtroom shootout that resulted from an attempt to free Black Panther George Jackson. Her trial was a cause célèbre, and she was acquitted of all charges. She has continued to champion numerous progressive causes and is currently a professor in the History of Consciousness program at the University of Santa Cruz. As the essay below suggests, Davis has been particularly outspoken against the prison-industrial complex, and she has been a staunch advocate for political prisoners in the United States.

SOURCE: Angela Y. Davis, ed. *If They Come in the Morning: Voices of Resistance.* New York: Third Press, 1971.

SELECTED READINGS: *The Angela Y. Davis Reader,* ed. Joy James (1998). Angela Y. Davis, *Angela Davis: An Autobiography* (1988). Bettina Aptheker, *The Morning Breaks: The Trial of Angela Davis* (1975).

Despite a long history of exalted appeals to man's inherent right of resistance, there has seldom been agreement on how to relate in *practice* to unjust, immoral laws and the oppressive social order from which they emanate.* The conservative, who does not dispute the validity of revolutions deeply buried

---

*Author's note, 1998: I have opted to leave masculinist formulations in this and other early essays, which I hope will be considered in the context of the historical period in which they were produced.

in history, invokes visions of impending anarchy in order to legitimize his demand for absolute obedience. Law and order, with the major emphasis on order, is his watchword. The liberal articulates his sensitivity to certain of society's intolerable details, but will almost never prescribe methods of resistance that exceed the limits of legality—redress through electoral channels is the liberal's panacea.

In the heat of our pursuit of fundamental human rights, black people have been continually cautioned to be patient. We are advised that as long as we remain faithful to the *existing* democratic order, the glorious moment will eventually arrive when we will come into our own as full-fledged human beings.

But having been taught by bitter experience, we know that there is a glaring incongruity between democracy and the capitalist economy which is the source of our ills. Regardless of all rhetoric to the contrary, the people are not the ultimate matrix of the laws and the system which govern them—certainly not black people and other nationally oppressed people, but not even the mass of whites. The people do not exercise decisive control over the determining factors of their lives.

Official assertions that meaningful dissent is always welcome, provided it falls within the boundaries of legality, are frequently a smokescreen obscuring the invitation to acquiesce in oppression, Slavery may have been unrighteous, the constitutional provision for the enslavement of blacks may have been unjust, but conditions were not to be considered so unbearable (especially since they were profitable to a small circle) as to justify escape and other acts proscribed by law. This was the import of the fugitive slave laws.

Needless to say, the history of the United States has been marred from its inception by an enormous quantity of unjust laws, far too many expressly bolstering the oppression of black people. Particularized reflections of existing social inequities, these laws have repeatedly borne witness to the exploitative and racist core of the society itself. For blacks, Chicanos, for all nationally oppressed people, the problem of opposing unjust laws and the social conditions which nourish their growth, has always had immediate practical implications. Our very survival has frequently been a direct function of our skill in forging effective channels of resistance. In resisting we have sometimes been compelled to openly violate those laws which directly or indirectly buttress our oppression. But even when containing our resistance within the orbit of legality, we have been labeled criminals and have been methodically persecuted by a racist legal apparatus. . . .

The prison is a key component of the state's coercive apparatus, the overriding function of which is to ensure social control. The etymology of the term "penitentiary" furnishes a clue to the controlling idea behind the "prison system" at its inception. The penitentiary was projected as the locale for doing penitence for an offense against society, the physical and spiritual purging of proclivities to challenge rules and regulations which command total obedience. While cloaking itself with the bourgeois aura of universality—imprisonment was supposed to cut across all class lines, as crimes were to be defined by the act, not the perpetrator—the prison has actually operated as an instrument of class domination, a means of prohibiting the have-nots from encroaching upon the haves.

The occurrence of crime is inevitable in a society in which wealth is unequally distributed, as one of the constant reminders that society's productive forces are being channeled in the wrong direction. The majority of criminal offenses bear a direct relationship to property. Contained in the very concept of property, crimes are profound but suppressed social needs which express themselves in anti-social modes of action. Spontaneously produced by a capitalist organization of society, this type of crime is at once a protest against society and a desire to partake of its exploitative content. It challenges the symptoms of capitalism, but not its essence. . . .

Especially today when so many black, Chicano, and Puerto Rican men and women are jobless as a consequence of the internal dynamic of the capitalist system, the role of the unemployed, which includes the lumpenproletariat in revolutionary struggle, must be given serious thought. Increased unemployment, particularly for the nationally oppressed, will continue to be an inevitable by-product of technological development. At least 30 percent of black youth are presently without jobs. [In 1997, over 30 percent of young black men were in prison, on probation or on parole.] In the context of class exploitation and national oppression it should be clear that numerous individuals are compelled to resort to criminal acts, not as a result of conscious choice—implying other alternatives—but because society has objectively reduced their possibilities of subsistence and survival to this level. This recognition should signal the urgent need to organize the unemployed and lumpenproletariat, as indeed the Black Panther Party as well as activists in prison have already begun to do.

In evaluating the susceptibility of the black and brown unemployed to organizing efforts, the peculiar historical features of the US, specifically racism and national oppression, must be taken into account. There already exists in the black and brown communities, the lumpenproletariat included, a long tradition of collective resistance to national oppression.

Moreover, in assessing the revolutionary potential of prisoners in America as a group, it should be borne in mind that not all prisoners have actually committed crimes. The built-in racism of the judicial system expresses itself, as Du Bois has suggested, in the railroading of countless innocent blacks and other national minorities into the country's coercive institutions.

One must also appreciate the effects of disproportionally long prison terms on black and brown inmates. The typical criminal mentality sees imprisonment as a calculated risk for a particular criminal act. One's prison term is more or less rationally predictable. The function of racism in the judicial-penal complex is to shatter that predictability. The black burglar, anticipating a two- to four-year term, may end up doing ten to fifteen years, while the white burglar leaves after two years.

Within the contained, coercive universe of the prison, the captive is confronted with the realities of racism, not simply as individual acts dictated by attitudinal bias; rather he is compelled to come to grips with racism as an institutional phenomenon collectively experienced by the victims. The disproportionate representation of the black and brown communities, the manifest racism of parole boards, the intense brutality inherent in the relationship between prison guards and black and brown inmates—all this and more causes the prisoner to be confronted daily, hourly, with the concentrated, systematic existence of racism.

For the innocent prisoner, the process of radicalization should come easy; for the "guilty" victim, the insight into the nature of racism as it manifests itself in the judicial-penal complex can lead to a questioning of his own past criminal activity and a re-evaluation of the methods he has used to survive in a racist and exploitative society. Needless to say, this process is not automatic, it does not occur spontaneously. The persistent educational work carried out by the prison's political activists plays a key role in developing the political potential of captive men and women.

Prisoners—especially blacks, Chicanos, and Puerto Ricans—are increasingly advancing the proposition that they are *political* prisoners. They contend that they are political prisoners in the sense that they are largely the victims of an oppressive politico-economic order, swiftly becoming conscious of the causes underlying their victimization. . . .

Racist oppression invades the lives of black people on an infinite variety of levels. Blacks are imprisoned in a world where our labor and toil hardly allow us to eke out a decent existence, if we are able to find jobs at all. When the economy begins to falter, we are forever the first victims, always the most deeply wounded. When the economy is on its feet, we continue to live in a depressed state. Unemployment is generally twice as high in the ghettos as it is in the country as a whole and even higher among black women and youth. The unemployment rate among black youth has presently skyrocketed to 30 percent. If one-third of America's white youths were without a means of livelihood, we would either be in the thick of revolution or else under the iron rule of fascism. Substandard schools, medical care hardly fit for animals, overpriced, dilapidated housing, a welfare system based on a policy of skimpy concessions, designed to degrade and divide (and even this may soon be canceled)—this is only the beginning of the list of props in the overall scenery of oppression which, for the mass of blacks, is the universe.

In black communities, wherever they are located, there exists an ever-present reminder that our universe must remain stable in its drabness, its poverty, its brutality. From Birmingham to Harlem to Watts, black ghettos are occupied, patrolled and often attacked by massive deployments of police. The police, domestic caretakers of violence, are the oppressor's emissaries, charged with the task of containing us within the boundaries of our oppression. . . .

It goes without saying that the police would be unable to set into motion their racist machinery were they not sanctioned and supported by the judicial system. The courts not only consistently abstain from prosecuting criminal behavior on the part of the police, but they convict, on the basis of biased police testimony, countless black men and women. Court-appointed attorneys, acting in the twisted interests of overcrowded courts, convince 85 percent of the defendants to plead guilty. Even the manifestly innocent are advised to cop a plea so that the lengthy and expensive process of jury trials is avoided. This is the structure of the apparatus which summarily railroads black people into jails and prisons. (During my imprisonment in the New York Women's House of Detention, I encountered numerous cases involving innocent black women who had been advised to plead guilty. One sister had entered her white landlord's apartment for the purpose of paying rent. He attempted to rape her and in the course of the ensuing struggle, a lit candle toppled over, burning a tablecloth. The landlord ordered her arrested for arson. Following the advice of her court-appointed attorney, she entered a guilty plea, having been deceived by the attorney's insistence that the court would be more lenient. The sister was sentenced to three years.)

The vicious circle linking poverty, police courts, and prison is an integral element of ghetto existence. Unlike the mass of whites, the path which leads to jails and prisons is deeply rooted in the imposed patterns of black existence. For this very reason, an almost instinctive affinity binds the mass of black people to the political prisoners. The vast majority of blacks harbor a deep hatred of the police and are not deluded by official proclamations of justice through the courts. . . .

Black people are rushing full speed ahead towards an understanding of the circumstances that give rise to exaggerated forms of political repression and thus an overabundance of political prisoners. This understanding is being forged out of the raw material of their own immediate experiences with racism. Hence, the black masses are growing conscious of their responsibility to defend those who are being persecuted for attempting to bring about the alleviation of the most injurious immediate problems facing black communities and ultimately to bring about total liberation through armed revolution, if it must come to this.

The black liberation movement is presently at a critical juncture. Fascist methods of repression threaten to physically decapitate and obliterate the movement. More subtle, yet no less dangerous ideological tendencies from within threaten to isolate the black movement and diminish its revolutionary impact. Both menaces must be counteracted in order to ensure our survival. Revolutionary blacks must spearhead and provide leadership for a broad anti-fascist movement.

Fascism is a process, its growth and development are cancerous in nature. While today, the threat of fascism may be primarily restricted to the use of the law-enforcement—judicial-penal apparatus to arrest the overt and latent revolutionary trends among nationally oppressed people, tomorrow it may attack the working class *en masse* and eventually even moderate democrats. Even in this period, however, the cancer has already commenced to spread. In addition to the prison army of thousands and thousands of nameless Third World victims of political revenge, there are increasing numbers of white po-litical prisoners—draft resisters, anti-war activists such as the Harrisburg Eight, men and women who have involved themselves on all levels of revolutionary activity.

Among the further symptoms of the fascist threat are official efforts to cur-tail the power of organized labor, such as the attack on the manifestly con-servative construction workers and the trends towards reduced welfare aid. . . .

One of the fundamental historical lessons to be learned from past failures to prevent the rise of fascism is the decisive and indispensable character of the fight against fascism in its incipient phases. Once allowed to conquer ground, its growth is facilitated in geometric proportion. Although the most unbridled expressions of the fascist menace are still tied to the racist domi-nation of blacks, Chicanos, Puerto Ricans, Indians, it lurks under the surface wherever there is potential resistance to the power of monopoly capital, the parasitic interests which control this society. Potentially it can profoundly worsen the conditions of existence for the average American citizen. Conse-quently, the masses of people in this country have a real, direct, and material stake in the struggle to free political prisoners, the struggle to abolish the prison system in its present form, the struggle against all dimensions of racism.

No one should fail to take heed of Georgi Dimitrov's warning: "Whoever does not fight the growth of fascism at these preparatory stages is not in a position to prevent the victory of fascism, but, on the contrary, facilitates that victory" (Report to the VIIth Congress of the Communist International, 1935). The only effective guarantee against the victory of fascism is an indivisible mass movement which refuses to conduct business as usual as long as repression rages on. It is only natural that blacks and other Third World peoples must lead this movement, for we are the first and most deeply injured victims of fascism. But it must embrace all potential victims and most important, all working-class people, for the key to the triumph of fascism is its ideological victory over the entire working class. Given the eruption of a severe economic crisis, the door to such an ideological victory can be opened by the active approval or passive toleration of racism. It is essential that white workers become conscious that historically through their acquiescence in the capitalist-inspired oppression of blacks they have only rendered themselves more vulnerable to attack.

The pivotal struggle which must be waged in the ranks of the working class is consequently the open, unreserved battle against entrenched racism. The white worker must become conscious of the threads which bind him to a James Johnson, a black auto worker, member of UAW, and a political prisoner presently facing charges for the killings of two foremen and a job setter. The merciless proliferation of the power of monopoly capital may ultimately push him inexorably down the very same path of desperation. No potential victim [of the fascist terror] should be without the knowledge that the greatest menace to racism and fascism is unity!

MARIN COUNTY JAIL
May, 1971

99. THE NATIONAL BLACK POLITICAL CONVENTION

The Gary Declaration
(1972)

The "Gary Declaration" of the NATIONAL BLACK POLITICAL CONVENTION tried to unite various Black Power activists into a national political force. The convention was held in March 1972 in Gary, Indiana, and it drew nearly three thousand delegates and some four thousand observers, leading one historian to call it "the zenith of the Black Power movement." Although the National Black Political Convention failed to translate many of its programmatic objectives into reality, "The Gary Declaration" remains an important articulation of the Black Power movement's political agenda.

SOURCE: *The National Black Political Agenda*. Washington, D.C.: National Black Political Convention, 1972.

SELECTED READINGS: Manning Marable, *Race, Reform, and Rebellion: The Second Reconstruction in Black America, 1945–1990* (1991). Komozi Woodard, *A Nation Within a Nation: Amiri Baraka (LeRoi Jones) and Black Power Politics* (1999).

What Time Is It?

We come to Gary in an hour of great crisis and tremendous promise for Black America. While the white nation hovers on the brink of chaos, while its politicians offer no hope of real change, we stand on the edge of history and are faced with an amazing and frightening choice: We may choose in 1972 to slip back into the decadent white politics of American life, or we may press forward, moving relentlessly from Gary to the creation of our own Black life. The choice is large, but the time is very short.

Let there be no mistake. We come to Gary in a time of unrelieved crisis

407

for our people. From every rural community in Alabama to the high-rise com-
pounds of Chicago, we bring to this Convention the agonies of the masses of
our people. From the sprawling Black cities of Watts and Nairobi in the West
to the decay of Harlem and Roxbury in the East, the testimony we bear is the
same. We are the witnesses to social disaster.

Our cities are crime-haunted dying grounds. Huge sectors of our youth—
and countless others—face permanent unemployment. Those of us who work
find our paychecks able to purchase less and less. Neither the courts nor the
prisons contribute to anything resembling justice or reformation. The schools
are unable—or unwilling—to educate our children for the real world of our
struggles. Meanwhile, the officially approved epidemic of drugs threatens to
wipe out the minds and strength of our best young warriors.

Economic, cultural, and spiritual depression stalk Black America, and the
price for survival often appears to be more than we are able to pay. On every
side, in every area of our lives, the American institutions in which we have
placed our trust are unable to cope with the crises they have created by their
single-minded dedication to profits for some and white supremacy above all.

White Realities, Black Choice

A Black political convention, indeed all truly Black politics must begin from
this truth: *The American system does not work for the masses of our people, and it
cannot be made to work without radical fundamental change.* (Indeed, this system
does not really work in favor of the humanity of anyone in America.)

In light of such realities, we come to Gary and are confronted with a choice.
Will we believe the truth that history presses into our face—or will we, too,
try to hide? Will the small favors some of us have received blind us to the
larger sufferings of our people, or open our eyes to the testimony of our
history in America?

For more than a century we have followed the path of political dependence
on white men and their systems. From the Liberty Party in the decades before
the Civil War to the Republican Party of Abraham Lincoln, we trusted in white
men and white politics as our deliverers. Sixty years ago, W. E. B. Du Bois
said he would give the Democrats their "last chance" to prove their sincere
commitment to equality for Black people—and he was given white riots and
official segregation in peace and in war.

Nevertheless, some twenty years later we became Democrats in the name
of Franklin Roosevelt, then supported his successor Harry Truman, and even
tried a "non-partisan" Republican General of the Army named Eisenhower.
We were wooed like many others by the superficial liberalism of John F.

Kennedy and the make-believe populism of Lyndon Johnson. Let there be no more of that.

Both Parties Have Betrayed Us

Here at Gary, let us never forget that while the times and the names and the parties have continually changed, one truth has faced us insistently, never changing: Both parties have betrayed us whenever their interests conflicted with ours (which was most of the time), and whenever our forces were un-organized and dependent, quiescent and compliant. Nor should this be sur-prising, for by now we must know that the American political system, like all other white institutions in America, was designed to operate for the benefit of the white race: It was never meant to do anything else.

That is the truth that we must face at Gary. If white "liberalism" could have solved our problems, then Lincoln and Roosevelt and Kennedy would have done so. But they did not solve ours nor the rest of the nation's. If America's problems could have been solved by forceful, politically skilled and aggressive individuals, then Lyndon Johnson would have retained the presidency. If the true "American Way" of unbridled monopoly capitalism, combined with a ruthless military imperialism could do it, then Nixon would not be running around the world, or making speeches comparing his nation's decadence to that of Greece and Rome.

If we have never faced it before, let us face it at Gary: The profound crisis of Black people and the disaster of America are not simply caused by men nor will they be solved by men alone. These crises are the crises of basically flawed economics and politics, and of cultural degradation. None of the Dem-ocratic candidates and none of the Republican candidates—regardless of their vague promises to us or to their white constituencies—can solve our problems or the problems of this country without radically changing the systems by which it operates.

The Politics of Social Transformation

So we come to Gary confronted with a choice. But it is not the old convention question of which candidate shall we support, the pointless question of who is to preside over a decaying and unsalvageable system. No, if we come to Gary out of the realities of the Black communities of this land, then the only real choice for us is whether or not we will live by the truth we know, whether we will move to organize independently, move to struggle for fundamental transformation, for the creation of new directions, towards a concern for the life and the meaning of Man. Social transformation or social destruction, those are our only real choices.

If we have come to Gary on behalf of our people in America, in the rest of this hemisphere, and in the Homeland—if we have come for our own best ambitions—then a new Black Politics must come to birth. If we are serious, the Black Politics of Gary must accept major responsibility for creating both the atmosphere and the program for fundamental, far-ranging change in America. Such responsibility is ours because it is our people who are most deeply hurt and ravaged by the present systems of society. That responsibility for leading the change is ours because we live in a society where few other men really believe in the responsibility of a truly humane society for anyone anywhere.

Towards a Black Agenda

So when we turn to a Black Agenda for the seventies, we move in the truth of history, in the reality of the moment. We move recognizing that no one else is going to represent our interests but ourselves. *The society we seek cannot come unless Black people organize to advance its coming.* We lift up a Black Agenda recognizing that white America moves towards the abyss created by its own racist arrogance, misplaced priorities, rampant materialism, and ethical bankruptcy. Therefore, we are certain that the Agenda we now press for in Gary is not only for the future of Black humanity, but is probably the only way the rest of America can save itself from the harvest of its criminal past.

So, Brothers and Sisters of our developing Black nation, we now stand at Gary as people whose time has come. From every corner of Black America, from all liberation movements of the Third World, from the graves of our fathers and the coming world of our children, we are faced with a challenge and a call: Though the moment is perilous we must not despair. We must seize the time, for the time is ours.

We begin here and now in Gary. We begin with an independent Black political movement, an independent Black Political Agenda, an independent Black spirit. Nothing less will do. We must build for our people. We must build for our world. We stand on the edge of history. We cannot turn back.

CHAPTER EIGHT

Modern Feminism

100. BETTY FRIEDAN

The Feminine Mystique
(1963)

BETTY FRIEDAN's 1963 book, *The Feminine Mystique,* is often credited with re-viving organized modern feminism. Friedan (1921–) was educated at Smith College and the University of California at Berkeley. In 1966 she founded the National Organization for Women (NOW), and she served as president of that organization until 1970. She also helped found the National Women's Political Caucus in 1971. In *The Feminine Mystique,* Friedan argued against the widely held belief that women could find fulfillment only through child-bearing, mothering, and homemaking. Beneath the 1950s image of the "happy suburban housewife," Friedan found a great deal of discontentment. *The Feminine Mystique* was enormously well-received by millions of quietly desperate housewives, and as a result, Friedan has been called the "Susan B. Anthony of a newly revitalized women's movement."

SOURCE: Betty Friedan. *The Feminine Mystique.* New York: W. W. Norton & Co., 1963.

SELECTED READINGS: Betty Friedan, *Life So Far* (2000). Judith Adler Hennes-see, *Betty Friedan: Her Life* (1999). Daniel Horowitz, *Betty Friedan and the Mak-ing of the Feminine Mystique: The American Left, the Cold War, and Modern Feminism* (1989).

Chapter 1
"The Problem That Has No Name"

Gradually, I came to realize that something is wrong with the way American women are trying to live their lives today. I sensed it first, as a question mark in my own life, as a wife and mother of three small children, half-guiltily and half-heartedly, using my abilities and education that took me away from home. It was this personal question mark that led me in 1957 to my college classmates, fifteen years after our graduation from Smith. The problems and satisfaction of their lives and mine did not fit the image of the modern American woman written about in magazines [and] studied in classrooms and clinics. There was a discrepancy between the reality of our lives and the image to which we were trying to conform, the image I call the feminine mystique. I wondered if other women faced this schizophrenic split. And so I began to hunt down the origins of the feminine mystique, and its effect on women who lived by it, or grew up under it.

The problem lay buried, unspoken, for many years in the minds of American women. It was a sense of dissatisfaction, a yearning. Each suburban housewife struggled with it alone as she made beds, shopped for groceries, matched slipcover material, ate peanut butter sandwiches with her children, chauffeured Cub Scouts and Brownies, lay beside her husband at night—she was afraid to ask the silent question—"Is this all?"

For fifteen years [following World War II] in books and articles by experts, women heard that they could desire no greater destiny than to glory in their own femininity. Experts told them how to catch a man and keep him, how to breastfeed children and handle their toilet training, how to buy a dishwasher, bake bread, cook gourmet snails; how to dress, look, and act more feminine and make marriage more exciting. They were taught to pity the neurotic, unfeminine, unhappy women who wanted to be poets or physicists or presidents. They learned that feminine women did not want careers, higher education, political rights—the independence and opportunities that the old-fashioned feminists fought for.

The suburban housewife—she was the dream of young American women and the envy of women all over the world. She was healthy, beautiful, educated, concerned only about her husband, her children, her home. She had found true feminine fulfillment, free to choose automobiles, clothes, appliances, supermarkets; she had everything that women everywhere dreamed of.

Millions lived the image of the suburban housewife, kissing their husbands goodbye, depositing children at school, smiling as they ran the new waxer over the spotless kitchen floor. They baked bread, sewed their and their children's clothes, kept new washing machines and dryers running all day. They changed the sheets on the bed twice a week, took the rug-hooking class, and pitied their poor frustrated mothers who had dreamed of having a career. Their only dream was to be perfect wives and mothers; their highest ambition to have five children and a beautiful house, their only fight to get and keep their husbands.

If a woman had a problem in the 1950s and 1960s, she knew that something must be wrong with her marriage, or with herself. Other women were satisfied with their lives. What kind of woman was she if she did not feel this mysterious fulfillment waxing the kitchen floor? She was so ashamed to admit her dissatisfaction that she never knew how many other women shared it. Women found it harder to talk about this problem than about sex.

But on an April morning in 1959, I heard a mother of four, having coffee with four other mothers in a suburban development, say in a tone of quiet desperation, "the problem." And the others knew without words that she was not talking about a problem with her husband or her children, or her home. Suddenly they realized that they all shared the same problem, the problem that has no name. They began to talk about it.

Just what was this problem that has no name? Sometimes a woman would say "I feel empty." Or she would say, "I feel as if I don't exist." Sometimes she blotted out the feeling with a tranquilizer. Sometimes she thought the problem was with her husband or her children or that what she needed was to redecorate her house, move to a better neighborhood, have an affair, or another baby.

In 1960, the problem that has no name burst like a boil through the image of the happy housewife from the *New York Times* and *Newsweek* to *Good Housekeeping*. Some said the problem [was] education which naturally made [women] unhappy in their role as housewives. "The road from Freud to Frigidaire, from Sophocles to Spock has turned out to be a bumpy one," reported the *New York Times* (June 28, 1960).

Home economists suggested more realistic preparation for housewives, such as high school workshops on home appliances. College educators suggested more discussion groups on home management and the family to prepare women for the adjustment to domestic life.

A number of educators suggested that women no longer be admitted to colleges and universities [that] the education girls could not use as housewives was needed by boys to do the work of the atomic age.

The problem was dismissed by telling the housewife she doesn't realize how lucky she is—her own boss, no time clock, no junior executive gunning for her job. What if she isn't happy—does she think men are happy? Does she still want to be a man?

The problem was dismissed by shrugging that there are no solutions: this is what being a woman means, and what is wrong with American women that they can't accept their role gracefully?

It is no longer possible to ignore that voice, to dismiss the desperation of so many women. This is not what being a woman means, no matter what the experts say.

It is no longer possible to blame the problem on loss of femininity: to say that education and independence and equality with men have made American women unfeminine.

The problem that has no name is not a matter of loss of femininity, or too much education. It is far more important than anyone recognizes. It may be the key to our future as a nation and a culture. We can no longer ignore that voice within women that says: "I want something more than my husband and my children, and my home."

101. CASEY HAYDEN AND MARY KING

Sex and Caste: A Kind of Memo
(1965)

CASEY HAYDEN and MARY KING's "Sex and Caste: A Kind of Memo," drew attention to gender discrimination in the civil rights movement, and contributed to the development of modern feminism. Hayden (1937–) and King (1940–) were among a group of about one thousand northern activists who volunteered to work for SNCC's Freedom Summer Project, which increased voter registration in Mississippi, and helped African Americans gain a basic education. While in Waveland, Mississippi, they helped generate an internal educational document that noted that the egalitarian ideals of the civil rights movement were not extended to women in SNCC. (This paper later elicited SNCC-leader Stokely Carmichael's now infamous retort that "the only position for women in SNCC is prone.") "Sex and Caste: A Kind of Memo" was written in 1965 and it raised a similar set of concerns. And according to one historian, this document "represented a flowering of women's consciousness" that was generated "by the new strength and self-worth the [civil rights] movement had allowed [women] to develop."

SOURCE: Alexander Bloom and Winn Breines. *"Takin' It To the Streets": A Sixties Reader*. New York: Oxford University Press, 1995.

SELECTED READINGS: Constance Curry et al., *Deep In Our Hearts: Nine White Women in the Freedom Movement* (2000). Mary King, *Freedom Song: A Personal Story of the 1960s Civil Rights Movement* (1987). Sara Evans, *Personal Politics: The Roots of Women's Liberation in the Civil Rights Movement and the New Left* (1979).

We've talked a lot, to each other and to some of you, about our own and other women's problems in trying to live in our personal lives and in our work as independent and creative people. In these conversations we've found what seems to be recurrent ideas or themes. Maybe we can look at these things many of us perceive, often as a result of insights learned from the movement:

Sex and Caste

There seem to be many parallels that can be drawn between treatment of Negroes and treatment of women in our society as a whole. But in particular, women we've talked to who work in the movement seem to be caught up in a common-law caste system that operates, sometimes subtly, forcing them to work around or outside hierarchical structures of power which may exclude them. Women seem to be placed in the same position of assumed subordination in personal situations too. It is a caste system which, at its worst, uses and exploits worsen.

This is complicated by several facts, among them: (1) The caste system is not institutionalized by law (women have the right to vote, to sue for divorce, etc.); (2) Women can't withdraw from the situation (a la nationalism) or overthrow it; (3) There are biological differences (even though those biological differences are usually discussed or accepted without taking present and future technology into account so we probably can't be sure what these differences mean). Many people who are very hip to the implications of the racial caste system, even people in the movement, don't seem to be able to see the sexual caste system and if the question is raised they respond with: "That's the way it's supposed to be. There are biological differences." Or with other statements which recall a white segregationist confronted with integration.

Women and Problems of Work

The caste system perspective dictates the roles assigned to women in the movement, and certainly even more to women outside the movement. Within the movement, questions arise in situations ranging from relationships of women organizers to men in the community, to who cleans the freedom house, to who holds leadership positions, to who does secretarial work, and who acts as a spokesman for groups. Other problems arise between women with varying degrees of awareness of themselves as being as capable as men but held back from full participation, or between women who see themselves as needing more control of their work than other women demand. And there are problems with relationships between white women and black women.

Women and Personal Relations with Men

Having learned from the movement to think radically about the personal worth and abilities of people whose role in society had gone unchallenged before, a lot of women in the movement have begun trying to apply those lessons to their own relations with men. Each of us probably has her own story of the various results, and of the internal struggle occasioned by trying to break out of very deeply learned fears, needs, and self-perceptions, and of what happens when we try to replace them with concepts of people and freedom learned from the movement and organizing. . . .

Lack of Community for Discussion

Nobody is writing, or organizing or talking publicly about women, in any way that reflects the problems that various women in the movement come across and which we've tried to touch above. Consider this quote from an article in the centennial issue of *The Nation*:

> However equally we consider men and women, the work plans for husbands and wives cannot be given equal weight. A woman should not aim for "a second-level career" because she is a *woman*; from girlhood on she should recognize that, if she is also going to be a wife and mother, she will not be able to give as much to her work as she would if single. That is, she should not feel that she cannot aspire to directing the laboratory simply because she is a woman, but rather because she is also a wife and mother; as such, her work as a lab technician (or the equivalent in another field) should bring both satisfaction and the knowledge that, through it, she is fulfilling an additional role, making an additional contribution.

And that's about as deep as the analysis goes publicly, which is not nearly so deep as we've heard many of you go in chance conversations.

The reason we want to try to open up dialogue is mostly subjective. Working in the movement often intensifies personal problems, especially if we start trying to apply things we're learning there to our personal lives. Perhaps we can start to talk with each other more openly than in the past and create a community of support for each other so we can deal with ourselves and others with integrity and can therefore keep working.

Objectively, the chances seem nil that we could start a movement based on anything as distant to general American thought as a sex-caste system. Therefore, most of us will probably want to work full time on problems such as war, poverty, race. The very fact that the country can't face, much less deal with, the questions we're raising means that the movement is one place to look for some relief. Real efforts at dialogue within the movement and with whatever liberal groups, community women, or students might listen are justified. That is, all the problems between men and women and all the problems of women functioning in society as equal human beings are among the most basic that people face. We've talked in the movement about trying to build a society which would see basic human problems (which are now seen as private troubles) as public problems and would try to shape institutions to meet human needs rather than shaping people to meet the needs of those with power. To raise questions like those above illustrates very directly that society hasn't dealt with some of its deepest problems and opens discussion of why that is so. (In one sense, it is a radicalizing question that can take people beyond legalistic solutions into areas of personal and institutional change.) The second objective reason we'd like to see discussion begin is that we've learned a great deal in the movement and perhaps this is one area where a determined attempt to apply ideas we've learned there can produce some new alternatives.

102. NATIONAL ORGANIZATION FOR WOMEN (NOW)

Statement of Purpose

(1966)

The NATIONAL ORGANIZATION FOR WOMEN's "Statement of Purpose" was adopted at its First National Conference in Washington, D.C., on October 29, 1966. Today, NOW is the leading feminist organization in the United States, with over 550 chapters and an estimated 250,000 members. NOW relies on legislative lobbying, litigation, grassroots organizing, and public demonstrations to promote its feminist agenda, which resists sex discrimination in all spheres of life, and supports child care, access to abortion, reproductive rights, maternity leave, and an end to violence against women. In the late 1970s and early 1980s, NOW vigorously promoted an Equal Rights Amendment (ERA) to the U.S. Constitution, which was defeated in 1982. NOW has also been criticized by some feminists for its white, middle-class orientation. NOW's 1966 Statement of Purpose spelled out the central premises behind NOW's formation, and highlighted its strategy of implementing social change through strategic politics, but it does not reflect the organization's current language or priorities.

SOURCE: Mary Beth Norton, ed. *Major Problems in American Women's History.* Lexington, MA: D.C. Heath and Company, 1989.

SELECTED READINGS: Blanche Linden-Ward and Carol Hurd Green, *American Women in the 1960s: Changing the Future* (1993). Ginny Foat, *Never Guilty, Never Free* (1985). Betty Friedan, *It Changed My Life* (1976).

We, men and women who hereby constitute ourselves as the National Organization for Women, believe that the time has come for a new movement toward true equality for all women in America, and toward a fully equal partnership of the sexes, as part of the world-wide revolution of human rights now taking place within and beyond our national borders.

The purpose of NOW is to take action to bring women into full participation in the mainstream of American society now, exercising all the privileges and responsibilities thereof in truly equal partnership with men.

We believe the time has come to move beyond the abstract argument, discussion and symposia over the status and special nature of women which has raged in America in recent years; the time has come to confront, with concrete action, the conditions that now prevent women from enjoying the equality of opportunity and freedom of choice which is their right as individual Americans, and as human beings.

NOW is dedicated to the proposition that women first and foremost are human beings, who, like all other people in our society, must have the chance to develop their fullest human potential. We believe that women can achieve such equality only by accepting to the full the challenges and responsibilities they share with all other people in our society, as part of the decision-making mainstream of American political, economic and social life.

We organize to initiate or support action, nationally or in any part of this nation, by individuals or organizations, to break through the silken curtain of prejudice and discrimination against women in government, industry, the professions, the churches, the political parties, the judiciary, the labor unions, in education, science, medicine, law, religion and every other field of importance in American society. . . .

There is no civil rights movement to speak for women, as there has been for Negroes and other victims of discrimination. The National Organization for Women must therefore begin to speak.

WE BELIEVE that the power of American law, and the protection guaranteed by the U.S. Constitution to the civil rights of all individuals, must be effectively applied and enforced to isolate and remove patterns of sex discrimination, to ensure equality of opportunity in employment and education, and equality of civil and political rights and responsibilities on behalf of women, as well as for Negroes and other deprived groups.

We realize that women's problems are linked to many broader questions of social justice; their solution will require concerted action by many groups. Therefore, convinced that human rights for all are indivisible, we expect to give active support to the common cause of equal rights for all those who suffer discrimination and deprivation, and we call upon other organizations committed to such goals to support our efforts toward equality for women.

WE DO NOT ACCEPT the token appointment of a few women to high-level positions in government and industry as a substitute for a serious continuing effort to recruit and advance women according to their individual abilities. To this end, we urge American government and industry to mobilize the same resources of ingenuity and command with which they have solved problems of far greater difficulty than those now impeding the progress of women.

WE BELIEVE that this nation has a capacity at least as great as other nations, to innovate new social institutions which will enable women to enjoy true equality of opportunity and responsibility in society, without conflict with their responsibilities as mothers and homemakers. In such innovations, America does not lead the Western world, but lags by decades behind many European countries. We do not accept the traditional assumption that a woman has to choose between marriage and motherhood, on the one hand, and serious participation in industry or the professions on the other. We question the present expectation that all normal women will retire from job or profession for ten or fifteen years, to devote their full time to raising children, only to reenter the job market at a relatively minor level. This in itself is a deterrent to the aspirations of women, to their acceptance into management or professional training courses, and to the very possibility of equality of opportunity or real choice, for all but a few women. Above all, we reject the assumption that these problems are the unique responsibility of each individual woman, rather than a basic social dilemma which society must solve. True equality of opportunity and freedom of choice for women requires such practical and possible innovations as a nationwide network of child-care centers, which will make it unnecessary for women to retire completely from society until their children are grown, and national programs to provide retraining for women who have chosen to care for their own children full time.

WE BELIEVE that it is as essential for every girl to be educated to her full potential of human ability as it is for every boy—with the knowledge that such education is the key to effective participation in today's economy and that, for a girl as for a boy, education can only be serious where there is expectation that it will be used in society. We believe that American educators are capable of devising means of imparting such expectations to girl students. Moreover, we consider the decline in the proportion of women receiving higher and professional education to be evidence of discrimination. This discrimination may take the form of quotas against the admission of women to colleges and professional schools; lack of encouragement by parents, counselors and educators; denial of loans or fellowships; or the traditional or arbitrary procedures in graduate and professional training geared in terms of men, which inadvertently discriminate against women. We believe that the same serious attention must be given to high school dropouts who are girls as to boys.

WE REJECT the current assumptions that a man must carry the sole burden of supporting himself, his wife, and family, and that a woman is automatically entitled to lifelong support by a man upon her marriage, or that marriage, home and family are primarily woman's world and responsibility—hers, to dominate, his to support. We believe that a true partnership between the sexes demands a different concept of marriage, an equitable sharing of the responsibilities of home and children and of the economic burdens of their support. We believe that proper recognition should be given to the economic and social value of homemaking and child care. To these ends, we will seek to open a reexamination of laws and mores governing marriage and divorce, for we believe that the current state of "half-equality" between the sexes discriminates against both men and women, and is the cause of much unnecessary hostility between the sexes.

WE BELIEVE that women must now exercise their political rights and responsibilities as American citizens. They must refuse to be segregated on the basis of sex into separate-and-not-equal ladies' auxiliaries in the political parties, and they must demand representation according to their numbers in the regularly constituted party committees—at local, state, and national levels—and in the informal power structure, participating fully in the selection of candidates and political decision-making, and running for office themselves.

IN THE INTERESTS OF THE HUMAN DIGNITY OF WOMEN, we will protest and endeavor to change the false image of women now prevalent in the mass media, and in the texts, ceremonies, laws, and practices of our major social institutions. Such images perpetuate contempt for women by society and by women for themselves. We are similarly opposed to all policies and practices—in church, state, college, factory, or office—which, in the guise of protectiveness, not only deny opportunities but also foster in women self-denigration, dependence, and evasion of responsibility, undermine their confidence in their own abilities and foster contempt for women.

NOW WILL HOLD ITSELF INDEPENDENT OF ANY POLITICAL PARTY in order to mobilize the political power of all women and men intent on our goals. We will strive to ensure that no party, candidate, President, senator, governor, congressman, or any public official who betrays or ignores the principle of full equality between the sexes is elected or appointed to office. If it is necessary to mobilize the votes of men and women who believe in our cause, in order to win for women the final right to be fully free and equal human beings, we so commit ourselves.

WE BELIEVE THAT women will do most to create a new image of women by *acting* now, and by speaking out in behalf of their own equality, freedom, and human dignity—not in pleas for special privilege, nor in enmity toward men, who are also victims of the current half-equality between the sexes—but in an active, self-respecting partnership with men. By so doing, women will develop confidence in their own ability to determine actively, in partnership with men, the conditions of their life, their choices, their future and their society.

103. ROBIN MORGAN

No More Miss America!
(1968)

September 7, 1968, brought "women's lib" to national attention as approximately one hundred radical feminists protested that year's Miss America pageant in Atlantic City, New Jersey. The protest was largely organized by feminist icon **ROBIN MORGAN (1941–)**, who was the primary author of the document reprinted below, and New York Radical Women (NYRW), the first women's liberation group in New York City. Morgan was born in Florida and grew up in New York, and she has been active in the international feminist movement since the 1960s. In 1970 she edited the pioneering feminist anthology, *Sisterhood Is Powerful*. At the 1968 Miss America Pageant, demonstrators argued that beauty pageants were degrading to women. In addition to picketing, they engaged in creative guerrilla theater, throwing various "instruments of torture to women" into a trash can (these included high-heeled shoes, bras, and copies of *Playboy* magazine) and bestowing a Miss America crown upon a sheep in an effort to raise women's consciousness. Later that night, several women disrupted the nationally televised pageant, unfurling a banner and shouting feminist slogans.

SOURCE: Robin Morgan. *Sisterhood Is Powerful: An Anthology of Writings from the Women's Liberation Movement.* New York: Vintage Books, 1970.

SELECTED READINGS: Kathleen C. Berkeley, *The Women's Liberation Movement in America* (1999). Alice Echols, *Daring to Be Bad: Radical Feminism in America, 1967–1975* (1989). Robin Morgan, *Going Too Far: The Personal Chronicle of a Feminist* (1977).

The Ten Points We Protest:

1. *The Degrading Mindless-Boob-Girlie Symbol.* The Pageant contestants epitomize the roles we are all forced to play as women. The parade down the

runway blares the metaphor of the 4-H Club county fair, where the nervous animals are judged for teeth, fleece, etc., and where the best "specimen" gets the blue ribbon. So are women in our society forced daily to compete for male approval, enslaved by ludicrous "beauty" standards we ourselves are conditioned to take seriously.

2. *Racism with Roses.* Since its inception in 1921, the Pageant has not had one Black finalist, and this has not been for a lack of test-case contestants. There has never been a Puerto Rican, Alaskan, Hawaiian, or Mexican-American winner. Nor has there ever been a *true* Miss America—an American Indian.

3. *Miss America as Military Death Mascot.* The highlight of her reign each year is a cheerleader-tour of American troops abroad—last year she went to Vietnam to pep-talk our husbands, fathers, sons and boyfriends into dying and killing with a better spirit. She personifies the "unstained patriotic American womanhood our boys are fighting for." The Living Bra and the Dead Soldier. We refuse to be used as Mascots for Murder.

4. *The Consumer Con-Game.* Miss America is a walking commercial for the Pageant's sponsors. Wind her up and she plugs your product on promotion tours and TV—all in an "honest, objective" endorsement. What a shill.

5. *Competition Rigged and Unrigged.* We deplore the encouragement of an American myth that oppresses men as well as women: the win-or-you're-worthless competive disease. The "beauty contest" creates only one winner to be "used" and forty-nine losers who are "useless."

6. *The Woman as Pop Culture Obsolescent Theme.* Spindle, mutilate, and then discard tomorrow. What is so ignored as last year's Miss America? This only reflects the gospel of our society, according to Saint Male: women must be young, juicy, malleable—hence age discrimination and the cult of youth. And we women are brainwashed into believing this ourselves!

7. *The Unbeatable Madonna-Whore Combination.* Miss America and Playboy's centerfold are sisters over the skin. To win approval, we must be both sexy and wholesome, delicate but able to cope, demure yet titillatingly bitchy. Deviation of any sort brings, we are told, disaster: "You won't get a man!!"

8. *The Irrelevant Crown on the Throne of Mediocrity.* Miss America represents what women are supposed to be: unoffensive, bland, apolitical. If you are tall, short, over or under what weight The Man prescribes you should be, forget it. Personality, articulateness, intelligence, commitment—unwise. Conformity is the key to the crown—and, by extension, to success in our society.

9. *Miss America as Dream Equivalent To*—? In this reputedly democratic society, where every little boy supposedly can grow up to be President, what can every little girl hope to grow to be? Miss America. That's where it's at. Real power to control our own lives is restricted to men, while women get

patronizing pseudo-power, an ermine clock and a bunch of flowers; men are judged by their actions, women by their appearance.

10. *Miss America as Big Sister Watching You.* The Pageant exercises Thought Control, attempts to sear the Image onto our minds, to further make women oppressed and men oppressors; to enslave us all the more in high-heeled, low-status roles; to inculcate false values in young girls; to use women as beasts of buying; to seduce us to prostitute ourselves before our own oppression.

NO MORE MISS AMERICA

104. ANNE KOEDT

The Myth of the Vaginal Orgasm
(1968)

ANNE KOEDT's "The Myth of the Vaginal Orgasm" was a flagship document for the women's revolution. Koedt (1939–) is an influential feminist theorist who was active in Students for a Democratic Society (SDS) and New York Radical Women (the first women's liberationist group in New York City). The first version of "The Myth of the Vaginal Orgasm" was distributed at a November 1968 national conference to commemorate the 120th anniversary of the first women's rights convention at Seneca Falls. According to one historian, "the most memorable of all the workshops" at the conference was the one on sexuality that Koedt co-organized. In "The Myth of the Vaginal Orgasm," Koedt put a feminist slant on the recent findings of sex researchers Masters and Johnson, noting that intercourse was not required for female sexual satisfaction, and that women should "discard the 'normal' concepts of sex and create new guidelines which take into account mutual sexual enjoyment."

SOURCE: Shulamith Firestone and Anne Koedt. *Notes from the Second Year.* New York: Radical Feminism, 1970.

SELECTED READINGS: Susan Brownmiller, *In Our Time: Memoir of a Revolution* (1999). Alice Echols, *Daring to Be Bad: Radical Feminism in America, 1967–1975* (1989). Anne Koedt, Ellen Levine, and Anita Rapone, eds., *Radical Feminism* (1973).

Whenever female orgasm and frigidity is discussed, a false distinction is made between the vaginal and clitoral orgasm. Frigidity has generally been defined by men as the failure of women to have vaginal orgasms. Actually the vagina is not a highly sensitive area and is not constructed to achieve orgasm. It is the clitoris which is the center of sexual sensitivity and which is the female equivalent of the penis.

I think this explains a great many things: First of all, the fact that the so-called frigidity rate among women is phenomenally high. Rather than tracing female frigidity to the false assumptions about female anatomy, our "experts" have declared frigidity a psychological problem of women. Those women who complained about it were recommended psychiatrists, so that they might discover their "problem"—diagnosed generally as a failure to adjust to their role as women.

The facts of female anatomy and sexual response tell a different story. There is only one area for sexual climax, although there are many areas for sexual arousal; that area is the clitoris. All orgasms are extensions of sensation from this area. Since the clitoris is not necessarily stimulated sufficiently in the conventional sexual positions, we are left "frigid."

Aside from physical stimulation, which is the common cause of orgasm for most people, there is also stimulation through primarily mental processes. Some women, for example, may achieve orgasm through sexual fantasies, or through fetishes. However, while the stimulation may be psychological, the orgasm manifests itself physically. Thus, while the cause is psychological, the *effect* is still physical, and the orgasm necessarily takes place in the sexual organ equipped for sexual climax—the clitoris. The orgasm experience may also differ in degree of intensity—some more localized, and some more diffuse and sensitive. But they are all clitoral orgasms.

All this leads to some interesting questions about conventional sex and our role in it. Men achieve orgasms essentially by friction with the vagina, not the clitoral area, which is external and not able to cause friction the way penetration does. Women have thus been defined sexually in terms of what pleases men; our own biology has not been properly analyzed. Instead, we are fed the myth of the liberated woman and her vaginal orgasm—an orgasm which in fact does not exist.

What we must do is redefine our sexuality. We must discard the "normal" concepts of sex and create new guidelines which take into account mutual sexual enjoyment. While the idea of mutual enjoyment is liberally applauded in marriage manuals, it is not followed to its logical conclusion. We must begin to demand that if certain sexual positions now defined as "standard" are not mutually conducive to orgasm, they no longer be defined as standard. New techniques must be used or devised which transform this particular aspect of our current sexual exploitation.

[handwritten margin note: this is kind of wrong now w more research but I support the point]

Anatomical Evidence

Rather than starting with what women *ought* to feel, it would seem logical to start out with the anatomical facts regarding the clitoris and vagina.

The *Clitoris* is a small equivalent of the penis, except for the fact that the urethra does not go through it as in the man's penis. Its erection is similar to the male erection, and the head of the clitoris has the same type of structure and function as the head of the penis. G. Lombard Kelly, in *Sexual Feeling in Married Men and Women*, says:

> The head of the clitoris is also composed of erectile tissue, and it possesses a very sensitive epithelium or surface covering, supplied with special nerve endings called genital corpuscles, which are peculiarly adapted for sensory stimulation that under proper mental conditions terminates in the sexual orgasm. No other part of the female generative tract has such corpuscles. (Pocketbooks; p. 35)

The clitoris has no other function than that of sexual pleasure.

The Vagina—Its functions are related to the reproductive function. Principally, (1) menstruation, (2) receive penis, (3) hold semen, and (4) birth passage. The interior of the vagina, which according to the defenders of the vaginally caused orgasm is the center and producer of the orgasm, is:

> like nearly all other internal body structures, poorly supplied with end organs of touch. The internal entodermal origin of the lining of the vagina makes it similar in this respect to the rectum and other parts of the digestive tract. (Kinsey, *Sexual Behavior in the Human Female*, p. 580)

The degree of insensitivity inside the vagina is so high that "Among the women who were tested in our gynecologic sample, less than 14% were at all conscious that they had been touched" (Kinsey, p. 580).

Even the importance of the vagina as an *erotic* center (as opposed to an orgasmic center) has been found to be minor.

Other Areas—Labia minora and the vestibule of the vagina. These two sensitive areas may trigger off a clitoral orgasm. Because they can be effectively stimulated during "normal" coitus, though infrequent, this kind of stimulation is incorrectly thought to be vaginal orgasm. However, it is important to distinguish between areas which can stimulate the clitoris, incapable of producing the orgasm themselves, and the clitoris:

> Regardless of what means of excitation is used to bring the individual to the state of sexual climax, the sensation is perceived by the genital corpus-

cles and is localized where they are stimulated: in the head of the clitoris
or penis. (Kelly, p. 49)

Psychologically Stimulated Orgasm—Aside from the above mentioned direct
and indirect stimulations of the clitoris, there is a third way an orgasm may
be triggered. This is through mental (cortical) stimulation, where the imagination stimulates the brain, which in turn stimulates the genital corpuscles of
the glans to set off an orgasm.

Why Men Maintain the Myth

1. *Sexual Penetration is Preferred*—The best stimulant for the penis is the
woman's vagina. It supplies the necessary friction and lubrication. From a
strictly technical point of view this position offers the best physical conditions,
even though the man may try other positions for variation.

2. *The Invisible Woman*—One of the elements of male chauvinism is the
refusal or inability to see women as total, separate human beings. Rather, men
have chosen to define women only in terms of how they benefited men's
lives. Sexually, a woman was not seen as an individual wanting to share
equally in the sexual act, any more than she was seen as a person with independent desires when she did anything else in society. Thus, it was easy to
make up what was convenient about women; for on top of that, society has
been a function of male interests, and women were not organized to form
even a vocal opposition to the male experts.

3. *The Penis as Epitome of Masculinity*—Men define their lives greatly in
terms of masculinity. It is a *universal*, as opposed to racial, ego boosting, which
is localized by the geography of racial mixtures.

The essence of male chauvinism is not the practical, economic services
women supply. It is the psychological superiority. This kind of negative definition of self, rather than positive definition based upon one's own achievements and development, has of course chained the victim and the oppressor
both. But by far the most brutalized of the two is the victim.

An analogy is racism, where the white racist compensates his feelings of
unworthiness by creating an image of the black man (it is primarily a male
struggle) as biologically inferior to him. Because of his power in a white male
power structure, the white man can socially enforce this mythical division.

To the extent that men try to rationalize and justify male superiority
through physical differentiation, masculinity may be symbolized by being the
most muscular, the most hairy, the deepest voice, and the biggest penis.
Women, on the other hand, are approved of (i.e., called feminine) if they are
weak, petite, shave their legs, have high soft voice, and no penis.

Since the clitoris is almost identical to the penis, one finds a great deal of evidence of men in various societies trying to either ignore the clitoris and emphasize the vagina (as did Freud), or, as in some places in the Mideast, actually performing clitoridectomy. Freud saw this ancient and still practiced custom as a way of further "feminizing" the female by removing this cardinal vestige of her masculinity. It should be noted also that a big clitoris is considered ugly and masculine. Some cultures engage in the practice of pouring a chemical on the clitoris to make it shrivel up into proper size.

It seems clear to me that men in fact fear the clitoris as a threat to their masculinity.

4. *Sexually Expendable Male*—Men fear that they will become sexually expendable if the clitoris is substituted for the vagina as the center of pleasure for women. Actually this has a great deal of validity if one considers *only* the anatomy. The position of the penis inside the vagina, while perfect for reproduction, does not necessarily stimulate an orgasm in women because the clitoris is located externally and higher up. Women must rely upon indirect stimulation in the "normal" position.

Lesbian sexuality could make an excellent case, based upon anatomical data, for the extinction of the male organ. Albert Ellis says something to the effect that a man without a penis can make a woman an excellent lover.

Considering that the vagina is very desirable from a man's point of view, purely on physical grounds, one begins to see the dilemma for men. And it forces us as well to discard any "physical" arguments explaining why women go to bed with men. What is left, it seems to me, are primarily psychological reasons why women select men at the exclusion of women as sexual partners.

5. *Control of Women*—One reason given to explain the Mideastern practice of clitoridectomy is that it will keep the women from straying. By removing the sexual organ capable of orgasm, it must be assumed that her sexual drive will diminish. Considering how men look upon their women as property, particularly in very backward nations, we should begin to consider a great deal more why it is not in the men's interest to have women totally free sexually. The double standard, as practiced for example in Latin America, is set up to keep the woman as total property of the husband, while he is free to have affairs as he wishes.

6. *Lesbianism and Bisexuality*—Aside form the strictly anatomical reasons why women might equally seek other women as lovers, there is a fear on men's part that women will seek the company of other women on a full, human basis. The establishment of clitoral orgasm as fact would threaten the heterosexual *institution*. For it would indicate that sexual pleasure was obtainable from either men or women, thus making heterosexuality not an absolute, but an option. It would thus open up the whole question of *human* sexual relationships beyond the confines of the present male-female role system.

105. KATE MILLETT

Sexual Politics: A Manifesto for Revolution
(1970)

KATE MILLETT's "Sexual Politics: A Manifesto for Revolution" succinctly described the rationale and the goals of the women's liberation movement.
Millett (1937–) was born in St. Paul, Minnesota, and she earned her Ph.D.
from Columbia University in 1970. Her dissertation, published in book form
as *Sexual Politics,* became a national best-seller and quickly made Millett a
prominent figure in the women's liberation movement. She has also written
several memoirs and books on various social ills. "Sexual Politics: A Manifesto
for Revolution" posited a social movement that would promote sexual freedom and allow for women to attain "full human status after millennia of
deprivation and oppression."

SOURCE: Shulamith Firestone and Anne Koedt. *Notes from the Second Year.*
New York: Radical Feminism, 1970.

SELECT BIBLIOGRAPHY: Jeanne Martha Perreault, *Writing Selves: Contemporary
Feminist Autobiography* (1995). Kate Millett, *Flying* (1974). Kate Millett, *Sexual
Politics* (1970).

When one group rules another, the relationship between the two is political. When such an arrangement is carried out over a long period of time it
develops an ideology (feudalism, racism, etc.). All historical civilizations are
patriarchies: their ideology is male supremacy.
 Oppressed groups are denied education, economic independence, the
power of office, representation, an image of dignity and self-respect, equality
of status, and recognition as human beings. Throughout history women have
been consistently denied all of these, and their denial today, while attenuated
and partial, is nevertheless consistent. The education allowed them is deliberately designed to be inferior, and they are systematically programmed out

of and excluded from the knowledge where power lies today—e.g., in science and technology. They are confined to conditions of economic dependence based on the sale of their sexuality in marriage, or a variety of prostitutions. Work on a basis of economic independence allows them only a subsistence level of life—often not even that. They do not hold office, are represented in no positions of power, and authority is forbidden them. The image of women fostered by cultural media, high and low, then and now, is a marginal and demeaning existence, and one outside the human condition—which is defined as the prerogative of man, the male.

Government is upheld by power, which is supported through consent (social opinion), or imposed by violence. Conditioning to an ideology amounts to the former. But there may be a resort to the latter at any moment when consent is withdrawn—rape, attack, sequestration, beatings, murder. Sexual politics obtains consent through the "socialization" of both sexes to patriarchal policies. They consist of the following:

1) the formation of human personality along stereotyped lines of sexual category, based on the needs and values of the master class and dictated by what he would cherish in himself and find convenient in an underclass: aggression, intellectuality, force and efficiency for the male; passivity, ignorance, docility, "virtue," and ineffectuality for the female.

2) the concept of sex role, which assigns domestic service and attendance upon infants to all females and the rest of human interest, achievement and ambition to the male; the charge of leader at all times and places to the male, and the duty of follower, with equal uniformity, to the female.

3) the imposition of male rule through institutions: patriarchal religion, the proprietary family, marriage, "The Home," masculine oriented culture, and a pervasive doctrine of male superiority.

A Sexual Revolution would bring about the following conditions, desirable upon rational, moral and humanistic grounds:

1) the end of sexual repression—freedom of expression and of sexual mores (sexual freedom has been partially attained, but it is now being subverted beyond freedom into exploitative license for patriarchal and reactionary ends).

2) Unisex, or the end of separatist character-structure, temperament and behavior, so that each individual may develop an entire—rather than a partial, limited, and conformist—personality.

3) re-examination of traits categorized into "masculine" and "feminine," with a total reassessment as to their human usefulness and advisability in both sexes. Thus if "masculine" violence is undesirable, it is so for both sexes; "feminine" dumb-cow passivity likewise. If "masculine" intelligence or efficiency is valuable, it is so for both sexes equally, and the same must be true for "feminine" tenderness or consideration.

4) the end of sex role and sex status, the patriarchy and the male suprem-

acist ethic, attitude and ideology—in all areas of endeavor, experience, and behavior.

5) the end of the ancient oppression of the young under the patriarchal proprietary family, their chattel status, the attainment of the human rights presently denied them, the professionalization and therefore improvement of their care, and the guarantee that when they enter the world, they are desired, planned for, and provided with equal opportunities.

6) Bisex, or the end of enforced perverse heterosexuality, so that the sex act ceases to be arbitrarily polarized into male and female, to the exclusion of sexual expression between members of the same sex.

7) the end of sexuality in the forms in which it has existed historically—brutality, violence, capitalism, exploitation, and warfare—that it may cease to be hatred and become love.

8) the attainment of the female sex to freedom and full human status after millennia of deprivation and oppression, and of both sexes to a viable humanity.

106. SUSAN BROWNMILLER

The Enemy Within
(1970)

In "The Enemy Within," feminist pioneer SUSAN BROWNMILLER (1935–) analyzed the tendency of some women to internalize feelings of inferiority in relation to men. Brownmiller was born in Brooklyn, New York, and in 1968 she helped found New York Radical Feminists. Her 1975 book, *Against Our Will: Men, Women, and Rape*, was a best-seller, and she was featured on the cover of *Time* magazine as one of twelve "Women of the Year." Brownmiller also published a memoir of the women's liberation movement, *In Our Time*, in 1999. Although "The Enemy Within" was clearly an indictment of the cultural forces that caused women to lower their expectations and show deference to men, Brownmiller remained critical of women who capitulated too easily to these forces.

SOURCE: Sookie Stambler, comp. *Women's Liberation: A Blueprint for the Future.* New York: Ace Books, A Division of Charter Communications, 1970.

SELECTED READINGS: Susan Brownmiller, *Femininity* (1984). Alison Edwards, *Rape, Racism, and the White Women's Movement: An Answer to Susan Brownmiller* (1980).

When I was 11 years old and talking in the schoolyard one day with a bunch of girlfriends from class, the discussion came around, as it did in those days, to "What are you going to be when you grow up?" At least three of us wanted to be actresses or models. Two had their sights already set on marriage, motherhood, and a house in the country. But one girl said *she* was going to go to medical school and be a doctor. This announcement was greeted with respectful silence (all those additional years of school!) until Martha, fat, bright, and at the head of the class, said solemnly, "I'd never go to a woman doctor. I just wouldn't have *confidence* in a woman doctor."

"Not even to deliver your baby?" I remember inquiring.

"Nope," Martha replied. "Especially not to deliver my baby. That's too important. Men doctors are better than women doctors."

It has been many years since that schoolyard discussion and I can't even recall the name or the face of the girl who had the ambitions, but I hope she wasn't sidetracked somewhere along the line. But I remember Martha. Calm, the best student, everybody's friend, more advanced physically than the rest of us—she had breasts, we didn't—and utterly positive at that tender age that men did things better than women. I will never forgive her for being the first person of my sex whom I ever heard put down women. I considered it traitorous then in the schoolyard, and I consider it traitorous now. Since that time, I have done a lot of observing of that strange phenomenon, have been guilty of it myself, I think, and have come to the conclusion that woman is often her own worst enemy—the enemy within.

One of the hardest things for a woman with aspirations to do in our society is to admit, first to herself and then to others, that she has ambitions that go beyond the routine—a good marriage, clever children. Early on, we learn that men don't take kindly to the notion of a woman entering the competitive lists. It is in the nature of power and position that those who have it do not relinquish it graciously, as all colonial peoples and all minority groups discover at a certain stage in their development. Well, O.K., so be it. But infinitely more damaging to our psyche is the realization that our ambitions are met with equal hostility—poohpoohed, sniffed at, scoffed at, ignored, or worse, not taken seriously—by mothers, sisters, cousins, aunts and friends, who won't believe that we have set our sights on a different sort of goal than *they* have envisioned, preferring instead to believe that our ambition is merely a "passing phase"—which, unfortunately, it often is because of lack of encouragement. . . .

I have seen women who *admit* to small hankerings of personal ambition (usually expressed by a modest "I'd like to do more at work") throw up unbelievable psychological barriers to their own success. Two conversations I once had in the space of two days with a couple of young ladies who work in television will illustrate what I mean. Both women had neatly resolved their stymied careers with the oddest excuses I have ever heard. One thought she never could rise to a producer because she found the temperature in the film-editing rooms "too cold." The other said she never felt comfortable "near machines." To the first I answered, "Get a sweater." The second rendered me speechless. Of course, what these women were really saying was that their *femininity*—not the fact that they were female—somehow made them unfit for the tough world of television production.

The risk of losing that intangible called femininity weighs heavily on many women who are afraid to compete with men for better jobs. This sad state of affairs has come about because of arbitrary and rigid definitions of what is masculine and what is feminine that our culture has relied on for a variety of complex reasons. We can thank the hippie revolution for knocking down some of the old criteria, particularly external ones like the length of hair and form of dress. But as long as such qualities as self-assertion, decision making, and leadership are considered masculine—and conversely, unfeminine—a woman who worries about her femininity will never make a go of it in terms of career.

It was men who made the arbitrary rules of masculine/feminine that we suffer under, but it is women who continue to buy the stereotypes. At the early women's-liberation meetings that I attended, I was struck with how all of us were unwilling to assume leadership roles, and how often a sensible comment or brilliant new insight was couched between giggles and stutters or surrounded by self-disparaging phrases and gestures. Clearly, we were women who were unused to speaking forthrightly—without the frills and fur belows of "feminine" roundabout logic designed to make a point as gently as possible for fear of offending. Since we had nobody to offend but ourselves, this namby-pambying ceased to some extent with the passage of time.

But a women's-liberation meeting is a very special crucible. In the world outside, the stereotype of the aggressive, castrating bitch is still posted as a warning to us. If a woman believes in the existence of this mythical creature—and believes in her own potential transmogrification—her ease is hopeless. It astounds me that so many women remain convinced that a woman who functions in high gear in business, politics, or in the professions loses something intrinsic that is worth preserving. Personally, I have always felt that true femininity was rather indestructible. One look at the Irish revolutionary Bernadette Devlin should settle the matter once and for all. I suspect that this "castrating bitch" propaganda, a big lie, really, is perpetuated not only by insecure men but also by do-nothing women, the magpies who busy themselves with nothing more than nest-building. There is no getting around the uncomfortable truth that the militant stay-at-homes, the clinging vines, dislike and distrust their liberated sisters. I know exactly what I lost when I gave up pretending that passivity was a virtue and entered the competitive arena—some personality distortions which made me pirouette in concentric circles when I could have simply walked a straight line. And I know what I gained—self-esteem and a stretching of creative muscles and an exercising of a mind which had grown flaccid from disuse since the halcyon days of college.

A major tragedy of the female sex is that friendship and respect between women has never been highly regarded. During the dating years, girls are notoriously quick to ditch an appointment with a girlfriend at the sound of a male voice on the telephone. With marriage and family comes the suspicion that all other women are potentially "the other woman." In an early episode of *The Forsythe Saga* on TV, Irene the adulteress tells Young Jolyon's daughter, "Don't you know that women don't have friends? They have a lover, and they have people that they meet." How pathetic, but how historically accurate.

There is nothing in women's chemical or biological makeup that should preclude deep loyalty to those of the same sex. The sensitivity is certainly there, as is the capacity for warmth and love and fidelity. But until women cease to see themselves strictly in terms of men's eyes and to value men more highly than women, friendship with other women will remain a sometime thing, an expedient among competitors of inferior station that can be lightly discarded. I, for one, would much rather compete with men than for them. This affliction of competition between women for the attention of men—the only kind of women's competition that is encouraged by society—also affects the liberated women who managed to secure an equal footing with men in this man's world. Watch a couple of strong women in the same room and notice the sparks fly. Many women who reject the "woman is inferior" psychology for themselves apply it unsparingly to others of the same sex. An ambitious woman frequently thinks of herself as the only hen in the barnyard, to reverse a common metaphor. *She* is the exception, she believes. Women must recognize that they must make common cause with *all* women. When women get around to really liking—and respecting—other women, why then, we will have begun.

107. FRANCES M. BEAL

Double Jeopardy: To Be Black and Female
(1971)

FRANCES M. BEAL's widely anthologized essay "Double Jeopardy: To Be Black and Female" was an early effort to reconcile feminism and Marxism. Beal (1940–) was educated at the University of Wisconsin and the University of Paris, and she has played leadership roles in many activist organizations, including the Student Nonviolent Coordination Committee (SNCC), the Third World Women's Alliance, and the Black Radical Congress (BRC). Beal attempted to link the women's liberation movement to a larger anticapitalist struggle, contending "If the white [women's] groups do not realize that they are in fact fighting capitalism and racism, we do not have common bonds." Beal also illustrated the links between racism and male dominance, and bravely challenged the machismo that was pervasive in certain segments of the Black Power movement.

SOURCE: Deborah Babcox and Madeline Belkin, eds. *Liberation Now! Writings from the Women's Liberation Movement.* New York: Dell Publishing, 1971.

SELECTED READINGS: Angela Y. Davis, *Women, Race & Class* (1983). bell hooks, *Talking Back: Thinking Feminist, Thinking Black* (1989).

In attempting to analyze the situation of the black woman in America, one crashes abruptly into a solid wall of grave misconceptions, outright distortions of fact and defensive attitudes on the part of many. The system of capitalism (and its afterbirth—racism) under which we all live has attempted by many devious ways and means to destroy the humanity of all people, and particularly the humanity of black people. This has meant an outrageous assault on every black man, woman and child who resides in the United States.

In keeping with its goal of destroying the black race's will to resist its subjugation, capitalism found it necessary to create a situation where it was impossible for the black man to find meaningful or productive employment. More often than not, he couldn't find work of any kind. The black woman likewise was manipulated by the system, economically exploited and physically assaulted. She could often find work in the white man's kitchen, however, and sometimes became the sole breadwinner of the family. This predicament has led to many psychological problems on the part of both man and woman and has contributed to the turmoil found in the black family structure.

Unfortunately, neither the black man nor the black woman understood the true nature of the forces working upon them. Many black women accepted the capitalist evaluation of manhood and womanhood and believed, in fact, that black men were shiftless and lazy, that otherwise they would get a job and support their families as they ought to. Personal relationships between black men and women were torn asunder, and one result has been the separation of husband from wife, mother from child, etc.

America has defined the roles to which each individual should subscribe. It has defined "manhood" in terms of its own interests and "femininity" likewise. An individual who has a good job, makes a lot of money and drives a Cadillac is a real "man," and conversely, an individual who is lacking in these "qualities" is less of a man. The advertising media in this country continuously inform the American male of his need for indispensable signs of his virility—the brand of cigarettes that cowboys prefer, the whiskey that has a masculine tang or the label of the jock strap that athletes wear.

The ideal model that is projected for a woman is to be surrounded by hypocritical homage and estranged from all real work, spending idle hours primping and preening, obsessed with conspicuous consumption, and limited in function to simply a sex role. We unqualitatively reject these models. A woman who stays at home caring for children and the house often leads an extremely sterile existence. She must lead her entire life as a satellite to her mate. He goes out into society and brings back a little piece of the world for her. His interests and his understanding of the world become her own and she cannot develop herself as an individual, having been reduced to a biological function. This kind of woman leads a parasitic existence that can aptly be described as "legalized prostitution."

Furthermore, it is idle dreaming to think of black women simply caring for their homes and children like the middle-class white model. Most black women have to work to help house, feed and clothe their families. Black women make up a substantial percentage of the black working force from the poorest black family to the so-called "middle-class" family.

Black women were never afforded such phony luxuries. Though we have been browbeaten with this white image, the reality of the degrading and de-humanizing jobs that were relegated to us quickly dissipated this mirage of womanhood. . . .

Unfortunately, there seems to be some confusion in the Movement today as to who has been oppressing whom. Since the advent of black power, the black male has exerted a more prominent leadership role in our struggle for justice in this country. He sees the system for what it really is for the most part, but where he rejects its values and mores on many issues, when it comes to women, he seems to take his guidelines from the pages of the *Ladies' Home Journal.* Certain black men are maintaining that they have been castrated by society but that black women somehow escaped this persecution and even contributed to this emasculation.

The black woman in America can justly be described as a "slave of a slave." Since the black man in America was reduced to such abject oppression, the black woman had no protector and was used, and is still being used in some cases, as the scapegoat for the evils that this horrendous system has perpe-trated on black men. Her physical image has been maliciously maligned; she has been sexually molested and abused by the white colonizer; she has suf-fered the worst kind of economic exploitation, having been forced to serve as the white woman's maid and as wet nurse for white offspring while her own children were, more often than not, starving and neglected. It is the depth of degradation to be socially manipulated, physically raped, used to undermine your own household, and to be powerless to reverse this situation.

It is true that our husbands, fathers, brothers and sons have been emas-culated, lynched and brutalized. They have suffered from the cruelest assault on mankind that the world has ever known. However, it is a gross distortion of fact to state that black women have oppressed black men. The capitalist system found it expedient to enslave and oppress them and proceeded to do so without consultation or the signing of any agreements with black women.

It must also be pointed out at this time that black women are not resentful of the rise to power of black men. We welcome it. We see in it the eventual liberation of all black people from this corrupt system of capitalism. However, it is fallacious to think that in order for the black man to be strong, the black woman must be weak.

Those who are exerting their "manhood" by telling black women to step back into a domestic, submissive role are assuming a counterrevolutionary position. Black women, likewise, have been abused by the system, and we must begin talking about the elimination of all kinds of oppression. If we are talking about building a strong nation, capable of throwing off the yoke of capitalist oppression, then we are talking about the total involvement of every man, woman, and child, each with a highly developed political consciousness. We need our whole army out there dealing with the enemy, not half an army.

There are also some black women who feel that there is no more productive role in life than having and raising children. This attitude often reflects the conditioning of the society in which we live and is adopted from a bourgeois white model. Some young sisters who have never had to maintain a household or to accept the confinement which this entails tend to romanticize (along with the help of a few brothers) the role of housewife and mother. Black women who have had to endure this function are less apt to have such utopian visions.

Those who portray in an intellectual manner how great and rewarding this role will be, and who feel that the most important thing that they can contribute to the black nation is children, are doing themselves a great injustice. This reasoning completely negates the contributions that black women such as Sojourner Truth, Harriet Tubman, Mary McLeod Bethune, and Fannie Lou Hamer have historically made to our struggle for liberation.

We live in a highly industrialized society, and every member of the black nation must be as academically and technologically developed as possible. To wage a revolution, we need competent teachers, doctors, nurses, electronics experts, chemists, biologists, physicists, political scientists, and so on. Black women sitting at home reading bedtime stories to their children are just not going to make it.

The New World

The black community and black women especially must begin raising questions about the kind of society we wish to see established. We must note the ways in which capitalism oppresses us and then move to create institutions that will eliminate these destructive influences.

The new world that we are attempting to create must destroy oppression of every type. The value of this new system will be determined by the status of the person who was lowest on the totem pole. Unless women in any enslaved nation are completely liberated, the change cannot really be called a revolution. If the black woman has to retreat to the position she occupied before the armed struggle, the whole movement and the whole struggle will have retreated in terms of truly freeing the colonized population.

A people's revolution that engages the participation of every member of the community, including man, woman, and child, brings about a certain transformation in the participants as a result of this participation. Once we have caught a glimpse of freedom or experienced a bit of self-determination, we can't go back to old routines that were established under a racist, capitalist regime. We must begin to understand that a revolution entails not only the willingness to lay our lives on the firing line and get killed. In some ways, this is an easy commitment to make. To die for the revolution is a one-shot deal; to live for the revolution means taking on the more difficult commitment of changing our day-to-day life patterns.

This will mean changing the traditional routines that we have established as a result of living in a totally corrupting society. It means changing how one relates to one's wife, husband, parents and co-workers. If we are going to liberate ourselves as a people, it must be recognized that black women have very specific problems that have to be spoken to. We must be liberated along with the rest of the population. We cannot wait to start working on those problems until that great day in the future when the revolution somehow, miraculously, is accomplished.

To assign women the role of housekeeper and mother while men go forth into battle is a highly questionable doctrine for a revolutionary to maintain. Each individual must develop a high political consciousness in order to understand how this system enslaves us all and what actions we must take to bring about its total destruction. Those who consider themselves to be revolutionary must begin to deal with other revolutionaries as equals. So far as I know, revolutionaries are not determined by sex.

Old people, young people, men and women must take part in the struggle. To relegate women to purely supportive roles or to purely cultural considerations is dangerous. Unless black men who are preparing themselves for armed struggle understand that the society which we are trying to create is one in which the oppression of *all members* of that society is eliminated, then the revolution will have failed in its avowed purpose.

Given the mutual commitment of black men and black women alike to the liberation of our people and other oppressed peoples around the world, the total involvement of each individual is necessary. A revolutionary has the responsibility not only to topple those who are now in a position of power, but to create new institutions that will eliminate all forms of oppression. We must begin to rewrite our understanding of traditional personal relationships between man and woman. All the resources that the black community can muster must be channeled into the struggle. Black women must take an active part in bringing about the kind of society where our children, our loved ones, and each citizen can grow up and live as decent human beings, free from the pressures of racism and capitalist exploitation.

108. BOSTON WOMEN'S HEALTH BOOK COLLECTIVE

Our Bodies, Ourselves

(1973)

The influential and popular book *Our Bodies, Ourselves* illustrates the women's liberation movement's concern for women's health and sexuality. The **BOSTON WOMEN'S HEALTH BOOK COLLECTIVE** was formed in 1969 in an effort "to empower women with knowledge of their bodies, health, and sexuality." Today the group continues to bring a feminist perspective to debates on women's health care. *Our Bodies, Ourselves* was first published by a nonprofit press in 1970, but it has since been published by Simon & Schuster and has seen several new editions, selling more than 3.5 million copies internationally. According to one historian, the book "has gained almost legendary status because it has revolutionized the way a generation of women think about their bodies." The following excerpt briefly relays the history and mission of the Boston Women's Health Book Collective, and suggests some of the reasons for the success of the women's health movement in the 1970s.

SOURCE: The Boston Women's Health Book Collective. Preface to *The New Our Bodies, Ourselves: A Book By and For Women*. New York: Simon & Schuster, 1984.

SELECTED READINGS: Nancy Worcester and Marianne H. Whatley, *Women's Health: Readings of Social, Economic and Political Issues* (1994). Barbara Ehrenreich and Deirdre English, *For Her Own Good: One Hundred Fifty Years of Experts' Advice to Women* (1989). Sheryl Ruzek, *Women's Health Movement: Feminist Alternatives to Medical Control* (1978).

We are offering a book that can be used in many different ways—individually, in a group, for a course. Our book contains real material about our bodies and ourselves that isn't available elsewhere, and we have tried to present it in a new way—an honest, humane and powerful way of thinking about ourselves and our lives. We want to share the knowledge and power that come with this way of thinking, and we want to share the feelings we have for each other—supportive and loving feelings that show we can indeed help one another grow.

From the very beginning of working together, first on the course that led to this book and then on the book itself, we have felt exhilarated and energized by our new knowledge. Finding out about our bodies and our bodies' needs, starting to take control over that area of our lives, has released for us an energy that has overflowed into our work, our friendships, our relationships with men and women, and for some of us, our marriages and our parenthood. In trying to figure out why this has had such a life-changing effect on us, we have come up with several important ways in which this kind of body education has been liberating for us and may be a starting point for the liberation of many other women.

First, we learned what we learned equally from professional sources—textbooks, medical journals, doctors, nurses—and from our own experiences. The facts were important, and we did careful research to get the information we had not had in the past. As we brought the facts to one another we learned a good deal, but in sharing our personal experiences relating to those facts we learned still more. Once we had learned what the "experts" had to tell us, we found we still had a lot to teach and to learn from one another. For instance, many of us had "learned" about the menstrual cycle in science or biology classes—we had perhaps even memorized the names of the menstrual hormones and what they did. But most of us did not remember much of what we had learned. This time when we read in a text that the onset of menstruation is a normal and universal occurrence in young girls from ages ten to eighteen, we started to talk about our first menstrual periods. We found that, for many of us, beginning to menstruate had not felt normal at all, but scary, embarrassing, mysterious. We realized that what we had been told about menstruation and what we had not been told—even the tone of voice it had been told in—had all had an effect on our feelings about being female. Similarly, the information from enlightened texts describing masturbation as a normal, common sexual activity did not really become our own until we began to pull up from inside ourselves and share what we had never before expressed—the confusion and shame we had been made to feel, and often still felt, about touching our bodies in a sexual way.

Learning about our bodies in this way is an exciting kind of learning, where information and feelings are allowed to interact. It makes the difference between rote memorization and relevant learning, between fragmented pieces of a puzzle and the integrated picture, between abstractions and real knowledge. We discovered that people don't learn very much when they are just passive recipients of information. We found that each individual's response to information was valid and useful, and that by sharing our responses we could develop a base on which to be critical of what the experts tell us. Whatever we need to learn now, in whatever area of our lives, we know more how to go about it.

A second important result of this kind of learning is that we are better prepared to evaluate the institutions that are supposed to meet our health needs—the hospitals, clinics, doctors, medical schools, nursing schools, public health departments, Medicaid bureaucracies and so on. For some of us it was the first time we had looked critically, and with strength, at the existing institutions serving us. The experience of learning just how little control we had over our lives and bodies, the coming together out of isolation to learn from each other in order to define what we needed, and the experience of supporting one another in demanding the changes that grew out of our developing critique—all were crucial and formative political experiences for us. We have felt our potential power as a force for political and social change.

The learning we have done while working on *Our Bodies, Ourselves* has been a good basis for growth in other areas of life for still another reason. For women throughout the centuries, ignorance about our bodies has had one major consequence—pregnancy. Until very recently pregnancies were all but inevitable, biology *was* our destiny—that is, because our bodies are designed to get pregnant and give birth and lactate, that is what all or most of us did. The courageous and dedicated work of people like Margaret Sanger started in the early twentieth century to spread and make available birth control methods that women could use, thereby freeing us from the traditional lifetime of pregnancies. But the societal expectation that a woman above all else will have babies does not die easily. When we first started talking to each other about this, we found that that old expectation had nudged most of us into a fairly rigid role of wife-and-motherhood from the moment we were born female. Even in 1969, when we first started the work that led to this book, we found that many of us were still getting pregnant when we didn't want to. It was not until we researched carefully and learned more about birth-control methods and abortion, about laws governing birth control and abortion, and not until we put all this information together with what it meant to us to be female, that we began to feel we could truly set out to control whether and when we would have babies.

This knowledge has freed us to a certain extent from the constant, energy-draining anxiety about becoming pregnant. It has made our pregnancies better because they no longer happen to us, but we actively choose them and enthusiastically participate in them. It has made our parenthood better because it is our choice rather than our destiny. This knowledge has freed us from playing the role of mother if it is not a role that fits us. It has given us a sense of a larger life space to work in, an invigorating and challenging sense of time and room to discover the energies and talents that are in us, to do the work we want to do. And one of the things we most want to do is to help make this freedom of choice, this life span, available to every woman. This is why people in the women's movement have been so active in fighting against the inhumane legal restrictions, the imperfections of available contraceptives, the poor sex education, the highly priced and poorly administered health care that keep too many women from having this crucial control over their bodies.

There is a fourth reason why knowledge about our bodies has generated so much new energy. For us, body education is core education. Our bodies are the physical bases from which we move out into the world; ignorance, uncertainty—even, at worst, shame—about our physical selves create in us an alienation from ourselves that keeps us from being the whole people that we could be. Picture a woman trying to do work and to enter into equal and satisfying relationships with other people—when she feels physically weak because she has never tried to be strong; when she drains her energy trying to change her face, her figure, her hair, her smells, to match some ideal norm set by magazines, movies and TV; when she feels confused and ashamed of the menstrual blood that every month appears from some dark place in her body; when her internal body processes are a mystery to her and surface only to cause her trouble (an unplanned pregnancy, or cervical cancer); when she does not understand or enjoy sex and concentrates her sexual drives into aimless romantic fantasies, perverting and misusing a potential energy because she had been brought up to deny it. Learning to understand, accept, and be responsible for our physical selves, we are freed of some of these preoccupations and can start to use our untapped energies. Our image of ourselves is on a firmer base, we can be better friends and better lovers, better *people*, more self-confident, more autonomous, stronger and more whole.

109.

The Combahee River Collective Statement
(1977)

The "Combahee River Collective Statement" is an important articulation
of black feminist theory and practice. (The Collective gained its name from a
South Carolina river where abolitionist Harriet Tubman helped free 750
slaves during the Civil War.) It was formed in Boston in 1974 in an effort to
raise the consciousness of African-American women, especially around such
issues as sexual harassment, classism, and heterosexism. It lasted until 1980.
Although the following manifesto represented the collective thinking of
several leading black feminists, it was primarily written by Barbara Smith
(1946–) a pioneering literary critic and editor. According to one historian, it
was "crucial to building the [black feminist movement] in the 1970s," and it
continues to carry currency among black feminists today.

SOURCE: *The Combahee River Collective Statement: Black Feminist Organizing in
the Seventies and Eighties.* Foreword by Barbara Smith. Latham, NY: Kitchen
Table: Women of Color Press, 1986.

SELECTED READINGS: bell hooks, *Feminist Theory from Margin to Center* (1984).
Barbara Smith, ed., *Home Girls: A Black Feminist Anthology* (1983). Barbara
Smith, *Toward a Black Feminist Criticism* (1977).

. . . What We Believe

Above all else, our politics initially sprang from the shared belief that black
women are inherently valuable, that our liberation is a necessity not as an
adjunct to somebody else's but because of our need as human persons for
autonomy. This may seem so obvious as to sound simplistic, but it is apparent
that no other ostensibly progressive movement has ever considered our specific oppression a priority or worked seriously for the ending of that oppression. Merely naming the pejorative stereotypes attributed to black women

(e.g., mammy, matriarch, Sapphire, whore, bulldagger), let alone cataloguing the cruel, often murderous, treatment we receive, indicates how little value has been placed upon our lives during four centuries of bondage in the Western Hemisphere. We realize that the only people who care enough about us to work consistently for our liberation is us. Our politics evolve from a healthy love for ourselves, our sisters, and our community, which allows us to continue our struggle and work.

This focusing upon our own oppression is embodied in the concept of identity politics. We believe that the most profound and potentially the most radical politics come directly out of our own identity, as opposed to working to end somebody else's oppression. In the case of black women this is a particularly repugnant, dangerous, threatening, and therefore revolutionary concept because it is obvious from looking at all the political movements that have preceded us that anyone is more worthy of liberation than ourselves. We reject pedestals, queenhood, and walking ten paces behind. To be recognized as human, levelly human, is enough.

We believe that sexual politics under patriarchy is as pervasive in black women's lives as are the politics of class and race. We also often find it difficult to separate race from class from sex oppression because in our lives they are most often experienced simultaneously. We know that there is such a thing as racial-sexual oppression that is neither solely racial nor solely sexual, e.g., the history of rape of black women by white men as a weapon of political repression.

Although we are feminists and lesbians, we feel solidarity with progressive black men and do not advocate the fractionalization that white women who are separatists demand. Our situation as black people necessitates that we have solidarity around the fact of race, which white women of course do not need to have with white men, unless it is their negative solidarity as racial oppressors. We struggle together with black men against racism, while we also struggle with black men about sexism.

We realize that the liberation of all oppressed peoples necessitates the destruction of the political-economic systems of capitalism and imperialism as well as patriarchy. We are socialists because we believe the work must be organized for the collective benefit of those who do the work and create the products and not for the profit of the bosses. Material resources must be equally distributed among those who create these resources. We are not convinced, however, that a socialist revolution that is not also a feminist and antiracist revolution will guarantee our liberation. We have arrived at the necessity for developing an understanding of class relationships that takes into account the specific class position of black women who are generally marginal in the labor force, while at this particular time some of us are temporarily viewed as doubly desirable tokens at white-collar and professional levels. We need to articulate the real class situation of persons who are not merely raceless, sexless workers, but for whom racial and sexual oppression are significant determinants in their working/economic lives. Although we are in essential agreement with Marx's theory as it applied to the very specific economic relationships he analyzed, we know that this analysis must be extended further in order for us to understand our specific economic situation as black women.

A political contribution that we feel we have already made is the expansion of the feminist principle that the personal is political. In our consciousness-raising sessions, for example, we have in many ways gone beyond white women's revelations because we are dealing with the implications of race and class as well as sex. Even our black women's style of talking/testifying in black language about what we have experienced has a resonance that is both cultural and political. We have spent a great deal of energy delving into the cultural and experiential nature of our oppression out of necessity because none of these matters have ever been looked at before. No one before has ever examined the multilayered texture of black women's lives.

As we have already stated, we reject the stance of lesbian separatism because it is not a viable political analysis of strategy for us. It leaves out far too much and far too many people, particularly black men, women, and children. We have a great deal of criticism and loathing for what men have been socialized to be in this society: what they support, how they act, and how they oppress. But we do not have the misguided notion that it is their maleness, per se—i.e., their biological maleness—that makes them what they are. As black women we find any type of biological determinism a particularly dangerous and reactionary basis upon which to build a politic. We must also question whether lesbian separatism is an adequate and progressive political analysis and strategy, even for those who practice it, since it so completely denies any but the sexual sources of women's oppression, negating the facts of class and race. . . .

Black Feminist Issues and Practice

During our time together we have identified and worked on many issues of particular relevance to black women. The inclusiveness of our politics makes us concerned with any situation that impinges upon the lives of women, Third World, and working people. We are of course particularly committed to working on those struggles in which race, sex, and class are simultaneous factors in oppression. We might, for example, become involved in workplace organizing at a factory that employs Third-World women or picket a hospital that is cutting back on already inadequate health care to a Third World community, or set up a rape crisis center in a black neighborhood. Organizing around welfare or day-care concerns might also be a focus. The work to be done and the countless issues that this work represents merely reflect the pervasiveness of our oppression.

Issues and projects that collective members have actually worked on are sterilization abuse, abortion rights, battered women, rape, and health care. We have also done many workshops and educationals on black feminism on college campuses, at women's conferences, and most recently for high school women.

One issue that is of major concern to us and that we have begun to publicly address is racism in the white women's movement. As black feminists we are made constantly and painfully aware of how little effort white women have made to understand and combat their racism, which requires among other things that they have a more than superficial comprehension of race, color, and black history and culture. Eliminating racism in the white women's movement is by definition work for white women to do, but we will continue to speak to and demand accountability on this issue.

In the practice of our politics we do not believe that the end always justifies the means. Many reactionary and destructive acts have been done in the name of achieving "correct" political goals. As feminists we do not want to mess over people in the name of politics. We believe in collective process and a nonhierarchical distribution of power within our own group and in our vision of a revolutionary society. We are committed to a continual examination of our politics as they develop through criticism and self-criticism as an essential aspect of our practice. As black feminists and lesbians we know that we have a very definite revolutionary task to perform, and we are ready for the lifetime of work and struggle before us.

110. ANDREA DWORKIN

Pornography: Men Possessing Women
(1981)

In the controversial essay below, ANDREA DWORKIN (1946–) argued that pornography is one of the primary weapons used by men to control women. Born in Camden, New Jersey, Dworkin has been called "one of the most compelling voices" in the women's movement. She published two books by the time she was thirty, and in the early 1980s she teamed up with feminist lawyer Catharine A. MacKinnon to draft a controversial antipornography ordinance that asserted pornography is harmful to women and in violation of their civil rights. (The law was twice passed and vetoed in Minneapolis, and similar legislation was struck down by the U.S. Supreme Court in 1985 as a limitation on constitutionally protected free speech.) In *Pornography: Men Possessing Women,* Dworkin analyzed several types of pornography in support of her contention that it "demonstrates[s] the male lust for violence and power" and "creates hostility and aggression toward women, causing both bigotry and sexual abuse."

SOURCE: Andrea Dworkin. *Pornography: Men Possessing Women.* New York: Putnam, 1981.

SELECTED READINGS: Ronald J. Berger, Patricia Searles, and Charles E. Cottle, *Feminism and Pornography* (1991). Andrea Dworkin, *Life Against Death: Unapologetic Writings on the Continuing War against Women* (1997). Laura Lederer, *Take Back the Night: Women on Pornography* (1980).

The photograph is captioned "BEAVER HUNTERS." Two white men, dressed as hunters, sit in a black Jeep. The Jeep occupies almost the whole frame of the picture. The two men carry rifles. The rifles extend above the frame of the photograph into the white space surrounding it. The men and the Jeep face into the camera. Tied onto the hood of the black Jeep is a white woman.

She is tied with thick rope. She is spread-eagle. Her pubic hair and crotch are the dead center of the car hood and the photograph. Her head is turned to one side, tied down by rope that is pulled taut across her neck, extended to and wrapped several times around her wrists, tied around the rearview mirrors of the Jeep, brought back around her arms, crisscrossed under her breasts and over her thighs, drawn down and wrapped around the bumper of the Jeep, tied around her ankles. Between her feet on the car bumper, in orange with black print, is a sticker that reads: I brake for Billy Carter. The text under the photograph reads: "Western sportsmen report beaver hunting was particularly good throughout the Rocky Mountain region during the past season. These two hunters easily bagged their limit in the high country. They told HUSTLER that they stuffed and mounted their trophy as soon as they got her home."

The men in the photograph are self-possessed; that is, they possess the power of self. This power radiates from the photograph. They are armed: first, in the sense that they are fully clothed; second, because they carry rifles, which are made more prominent, suggesting erection, by extending outside the frame of the photograph; third, because they are shielded by being inside the vehicle, framed by the windshield; fourth, because only the top parts of their bodies are shown. The woman is possessed; that is, she has no self. A captured animal, she is naked, bound, exposed on the hood of the car outdoors, her features not distinguishable because of the way her head is twisted and tied down. The men sit, supremely still and confident, displaying the captured prey for the camera. The stillness of the woman is like the stillness of death, underlined by the evocation of taxidermy in the caption. He is, he takes; she is not, she is taken.

The photograph celebrates the physical power of men over women. They are hunters, use guns. They have captured and bound a woman. They will stuff and mount her. She is a trophy. While one could argue that the victory of two armed men over a woman is no evidence of physical superiority, the argument is impossible as one experiences (or remembers) the photograph. The superior strength of men is irrefutably established by the fact of the photograph and the knowledge that one brings to it: that it expresses an authentic and commonplace relationship of the male strong to the female weak, wherein the hunt—the targeting, tracking down, pursuing, the chase, the overpowering of, the immobilizing of, even the wounding of—is common practice, whether called sexual pursuit, seduction, or romance. The photograph exists in an immediate context that supports the assertion of this physical power; and in the society that is the larger context, there is no viable and meaningful reality to contradict the physical power of male over female expressed in the photograph.

In the photograph, the power of terror is basic. The men are hunters with guns. Their prey is women. They have caught a woman and tied her onto the hood of a car. The terror is implicit in the content of the photograph, but beyond that the photograph strikes the female viewer dumb with fear. One perceives that the bound woman must be in pain. The very power to make the photograph (to use the model, to tie her in that way) and the fact of the photograph (the fact that someone did use the model, did tie her in that way; that the photograph is published in a magazine and seen by millions of men who buy it specifically to see such photographs) evoke fear in the female observer unless she entirely dissociates herself from the photograph: refuses to believe or understand that real persons posed for it, refuses to see the bound person as a woman like herself. Terror is finally the content of the photograph, and it is also its effect on the female observer. That men have the power and desire to make, publish, and profit from the photograph engenders fear. That millions more men enjoy the photograph makes the fear palpable. That men who in general champion civil rights defend the photograph without experiencing it as an assault on women intensifies the fear, because if the horror of the photograph does not resonate with these men, that horror is not validated as horror in male culture, and women are left without apparent recourse. . . .

The threat in the language accompanying the photograph is also fierce and frightening. She is an animal, think of deer fleeing the hunter, think of seals clubbed to death, think of species nearly extinct. The men will stuff and mount her as a trophy: think of killing displayed proudly as triumph.

Here is the power of naming. Here she is named beaver. In the naming she is diminished to the point of annihilation; her humanity is canceled out. Instead of turning to the American Civil Liberties Union for help, she should perhaps turn to a group that tries to prevent cruelty to animals—beaver, bird, chick, bitch, dog, pussy, and so forth. The words that transform her into an animal have permanence: the male has done the naming. The power of naming includes the freedom to joke. The hunters will brake for Billy Carter. The ridicule is not deadly; they will let him live. The real target of the ridicule is the fool who brakes for animals, here equated with women. The language on the bumper sticker suggests the idea of the car in motion, which would otherwise be lacking. The car becomes a weapon, a source of death, its actual character as males use it. One is reminded of the animal run over on the road, a haunting image of blood and death. One visualizes the car, with the woman tied onto its hood, in motion crashing into something or someone.

Owning is expressed in every aspect of the photograph. These hunters are sportsmen, wealth suggested in hunting as a leisure-time pursuit of pleasure. They are equipped and outfitted. Their car shines. They have weapons: guns, a can They have a woman, bound and powerless, to do with as they like. They will stuff and mount hen Their possession of her extends over time, even into (her) death. She is owned as a thing, a trophy, or as something

dead, a dead bird, a dead deer; she is dead beaver. The camera and the photographer behind it also own the woman. The camera uses and keeps her.
The photographer uses her and keeps the image of her. The publisher of the
photograph can also claim her as a trophy. He has already mounted her and
put her on display. Hunting as a sport suggests that these hunters have hunted
before and will hunt again, that each captured woman will be used and
owned, stuffed and mounted, that this right to own inheres in man's relationship to nature, that this right to own is so natural and basic that it can be
taken entirely for granted, that is, expressed as play or sport.

Wealth is implicit in owning. The woman is likened to food (a dead animal), the hunter's most immediate form of wealth. As a trophy, she is wealth
displayed. She is a commodity, part of the measure of male wealth. Man as
hunter owns the earth, the things of it, its natural resources. She is part of
the wildlife to be plundered for profit and pleasure, collected, used. That they
"bagged their limit," then used what they had caught, is congruent with the
idea of economy as a sign of mature masculinity.

The fact of the photograph signifies the wealth of men as a class. One class
simply does not so use another class unless that usage is maintained in the
distribution of wealth. The female model's job is the job of one who is economically imperiled, a sign of economic degradation. The relationship of the
men to the woman in the photograph is not fantasy; it is symbol, meaningful
because it is rooted in reality. The photograph shows a relationship of rich to
poor that is actual in the larger society. The fact of the photograph in relation
to its context—an industry that generates wealth by producing images of
women abjectly used, a society in which women cannot adequately earn
money because women are valued precisely as the woman in the photograph
is valued—both proves and perpetuates the real connection between masculinity and wealth. The sexual-economic significance of the photograph is so
simple that it is easily overlooked: the photograph could not exist as a type
of photograph that produces wealth without the wealth of men to produce
and consume it.

Sex as power is the most explicit meaning of the photograph. The power
of sex unambiguously resides in the male, though the characterization of the
female as a wild animal suggests that the sexuality of the untamed female is
dangerous to men. But the triumph of the hunters is the nearly universal
triumph of men over women, a triumph ultimately expressed in the stuffing
and mounting. The hunters are figures of virility. Their penises are hidden but
their guns are emphasized. The car, beloved ally of men in the larger culture,
also indicates virility, especially when a woman is tied to it naked instead of
draped over it wearing an evening gown. The pornographic image explicates
the advertising image, and the advertising image echoes the pornographic
image.

The power of sex is ultimately defined as the power of conquest. They hunted her down, captured, tied, stuffed, and mounted her. The excitement is precisely in the nonconsensual character of the event. The hunt, the ropes, the guns, show that anything done to her was or will be done against her will. Here again, the valuation of conquest as being natural—of nature, of man in nature, of natural man—is implicit in the visual and linguistic imagery.

The power of sex, in male terms, is also funereal. Death permeates it. The male erotic trinity—sex, violence, and death—reigns supreme. She will be or is dead. They did or will kill her. Everything that they do to or with her is violence. Especially evocative is the phrase "stuffed and mounted her," suggesting as it does both sexual violation and embalming. . . .

We will know that we are free when the pornography no longer exists. As long as it does exist, we must understand that we are the women in it: used by the same power, subject to the same valuation, as the vile whores who beg for more.

The boys are betting on our compliance, our ignorance, our fear. We have always refused to face the worst that men have done to us. The boys count on it. The boys are betting that we cannot face the horror of their sexual system and survive. The boys are betting that their depictions of us as whores will beat us down and stop our hearts. The boys are betting that their penises and fists and knives and fucks and rapes will turn us into what they say we are—the compliant women of sex, the voracious cunts of pornography, the masochistic sluts who resist because we really want more. The boys are betting. The boys are wrong.

111. JENNIFER BAUMGARDNER AND AMY RICHARDS

ManifestA: Young Women, Feminism and the Future (2000)

JENNIFER BAUMGARDNER and AMY RICHARD'S book *ManifestA: Young Women, Feminism, and the Future* (2002) put forth a "third wave" feminist agenda for young women today. Baumgardner (1970–) and Richards (1970–) are both activists and journalists living in New York City. Richards is a contributing editor at *Ms.* magazine and co-founder of the Third Wave Foundation, an activist group for young feminists. Baumgardner is a former editor at *Ms.* and a frequent contributor to *The Nation, Jane, Nerve,* and *Out* magazines. In the following excerpt from *ManifestA,* the authors urge feminists to further the gains of the women's liberation movement of the 1960s and 1970s.

SOURCE: Jennifer Baumgardner and Amy Richards. *ManifestA: Young Women, Feminism, and the Future.* New York: Farrar, Straus, and Giroux, 2000.

SELECTED READINGS: Marcelle Karp and Debbie Stoller, eds., *Bust Guide to the New Girl Order* (1999). Natasha Walter, *The New Feminism* (1998). Barbara Findlen, *Listen Up: Voices from the Next Feminist Generation* (1995).

Third Wave Manifesta: A Thirteen-Point Agenda

1. To out unacknowledged feminists, specifically those who are younger, so that Generation X can become a visible movement and, further, a voting block of eighteen- to forty-year-olds.

2. To safeguard a woman's right to bear or not to bear a child, regardless of circumstances, including women who are younger than eighteen or impoverished. To preserve this right throughout her life and support the choice to be childless.

3. To make explicit that the fight for reproductive rights must include birth control; the right for poor women and lesbians to have children; partner adoption for gay couples; subsidized fertility treatments for all women who choose them; and freedom from sterilization abuse. Furthermore, to support the idea that sex can be—and usually is—for pleasure, not procreation.

4. To bring down the double standard in sex and sexual health, and foster male responsibility and assertiveness in the following areas: achieving freedom from STDs; more fairly dividing the burden of family planning as well as responsibilities such as child care; and eliminating violence against women.

5. To tap into and raise awareness of our revolutionary history, and the fact that almost all movements began as youth movements. To have access to our intellectual feminist legacy and women's history; for the classics of radical feminism, womanism, *mujeristas*, women's liberation, and all our roots to remain in print; and to have women's history taught to men as well as women as a part of all curricula.

6. To support and increase the visibility and power of lesbians and bisexual women in the feminist movement, in high schools, colleges, and the workplace. To recognize that queer women have always been at the forefront of the feminist movement, and that there is nothing to be gained—and much to be lost—by downplaying their history, whether inadvertently or actively.

7. To practice "autokeonony" ("self in community"): to see activism not as a choice between self and community but as a link between them that creates balance.

8. To have equal access to health care, regardless of income, which includes coverage equivalent to men's and keeping in mind that women use the system more often than men do because of our reproductive capacity.

9. For women who so desire to participate in all reaches of the military, including combat, and to enjoy all the benefits (loans, health care, pensions) offered to its members for as long as we continue to have an active military. The largest expenditure of our national budget goes toward maintaining this welfare system, and feminists have a duty to make sure women have access to every echelon.

10. To liberate adolescents from slut-bashing, listless educators, sexual harassment, and bullying at school, as well as violence in all walks of life, and the silence that hangs over adolescents' heads, often keeping them isolated, lonely, and indifferent to the world.

11. To make the workplace responsive to an individual's wants, needs, and talents. This includes valuing (monetarily) stay-at-home parents, aiding employees who want to spend more time with family and continue to work, equalizing pay for jobs of comparable worth, enacting a minimum wage that would bring a full-time worker with two children over the poverty line, and providing employee benefits for freelance and part-time workers.

12. To acknowledge that, although feminists may have disparate values, we share the same goal of equality, and of supporting one another in our efforts to gain the power to make our own choices.

13. To pass the Equal Rights Amendment so that we can have a constitutional foundation of righteousness and equality upon which future women's rights conventions will stand. . . .

CHAPTER

NINE

The New Left and Counterculture

112. ALLEN GINSBERG

Howl

(1956)

Originally printed as a chapbook for City Lights Press, **ALLEN GINSBERG**'s *Howl* has become one of the most widely read poems of all time. Ginsberg (1926–1997) was born in Newark, New Jersey, and attended Columbia University. In 1949, Ginsberg underwent psychiatric counseling at Rockland State Hospital, where he met Carl Solomon, to whom *Howl* is dedicated. The publication of *Howl* in 1956 is often used to signify the arrival of the Beat Generation, a group of alienated young people who expressed contempt for sterile mainstream society and bourgeois values. The poem's publication also led to a widely publicized "obscenity trial," and the eventual verdict that the book was not obscene. In the 1960s, Ginsberg identified with the antiwar movement. Although controversial, Ginsberg nevertheless received great acclaim from the literary world before his death, winning a Guggenheim Fellowship, a National Endowment for the Arts grant, and a National Arts Club Gold Medal.

SOURCE: Allen Ginsberg. *Howl and Other Poems.* San Francisco: City Lights Books, 1956.

SELECTED READINGS: Thomas F. Merrill, *Allen Ginsberg* (1988). Lewis Hyde, ed., *On the Poetry of Allen Ginsberg* (1984). John Tytell, *Naked Angels: The Lives and Literature of the Beat Generation* (1976).

For Carl Solomon

I

I saw the best minds of my generation destroyed by
    madness, starving hysterical naked,

dragging themselves through the negro streets at dawn
      looking for an angry fix,
angelheaded hipsters burning for the ancient heavenly
      connection to the starry dynamo in the machinery of night,
who poverty and tatters and hollow-eyed and high sat
      up smoking in the supernatural darkness of
      cold-water flats floating across the tops of cities
      contemplating jazz,
who bared their brains to Heaven under the El and
      saw Mohammedan angels staggering on tenement roofs
      illuminated,
who passed through universities with radiant cool eyes
      hallucinating Arkansas and Blake-light tragedy
      among the scholars of war,
who were expelled from the academies for crazy &
      publishing obscene odes on the windows of the
      skull,
who cowered in unshaven rooms in underwear, burn-
      ing their money in wastebaskets and listening
      to the Terror through the wall,
who got busted in their pubic beards returning through
      Laredo with a belt of marijuana for New York,
who ate fire in paint hotels or drank turpentine in
      Paradise Alley, death, or purgatoried their
      torsos night after night
with dreams, with drugs, with waking nightmares, al-
      cohol and cock and endless balls, . . .

II

What sphinx of cement and aluminum bashed open
      their skulls and ate up their brains and imagi-
      nation?
Moloch! Solitude! Filth! Ugliness! Ashcans and unob-
      tainable dollars! Children screaming under the
      stairways! Boys sobbing in armies! Old men
      weeping in the parks!
Moloch! Moloch! Nightmare of Moloch! Moloch the
      loveless! Mental Moloch! Moloch the heavy
      judger of men!
Moloch the incomprehensible prison! Moloch the
      crossbone soulless jailhouse and Congress of
      sorrows! Moloch whose buildings are judgment!

Moloch the vast stone of war! Moloch the stunned governments!

Moloch whose mind is pure machinery! Moloch whose
blood is running money! Moloch whose fingers
are ten armies! Moloch whose breast is a canni-
bal dynamo! Moloch whose ear is a smoking
tomb!

Moloch whose eyes are a thousand blind windows!
Moloch whose skyscrapers stand in the long
streets like endless Jehovahs! Moloch whose factories dream and croak in the fog! Moloch whose
smokestacks and antennae crown the cities!

Moloch whose love is endless oil and stone! Moloch
whose soul is electricity and banks! Moloch
whose poverty is the specter of genius! Moloch
whose fate is a cloud of sexless hydrogen!
Moloch whose name is the Mind!

Moloch in whom I sit lonely! Moloch in whom I dream
Angels! Crazy in Moloch! Cocksucker in
Moloch! Lacklove and manless in Moloch!

Moloch who entered my soul early! Moloch in whom
I am a consciousness without a body! Moloch
who frightened me out of my natural ecstasy!
Moloch whom I abandon! Wake up in Moloch!
Light streaming out of the sky!

Moloch! Moloch! Robot apartments! invisible suburbs!
skeleton treasuries! blind capitals! demonic
industries! spectral nations! invincible mad
houses! granite cocks! monstrous bombs!

They broke their backs lifting Moloch to Heaven! Pavements, trees, radios, tons! lifting the city to
Heaven which exists and is everywhere about
us!

Visions! omens! hallucinations! miracles! ecstasies!
gone down the American river!

Dreams! adorations! illuminations! religions! the whole
boatload of sensitive bullshit!

Breakthroughs! over the river! flips and crucifixions!
gone down the flood! Highs! Epiphanies! De-
spairs! Ten years' animal screams and suicides!
Minds! New loves! Mad generation! down on
the rocks of Time!

Real holy laughter in the river! They saw it all! the
      wild eyes! the holy yells! They bade farewell!
      They jumped off the roof! to solitude! waving!
      carrying flowers! Down to the river! into the street!

III

Carl Solomon! I'm with you in Rockland
      where you're madder than I am
I'm with you in Rockland
      where you must feel very strange
I'm with you in Rockland
      where you imitate the shade of my mother
I'm with you in Rockland
      where you've murdered your twelve secretaries
I'm with you in Rockland
      where you laugh at this invisible humor
I'm with you in Rockland
      where we are great writers on the same dreadful
      typewriter
I'm with you in Rockland
      where your condition has become serious and
      is reported on the radio
I'm with you in Rockland
      where the faculties of the skull no longer admit
      the worms of the senses
I'm with you in Rockland
      where you drink the tea of the breasts of the
      spinsters of Utica
I'm with you in Rockland
      where you pun on the bodies of your nurses the
      harpies of the Bronx
I'm with you in Rockland
      where you scream in a straightjacket that you're
      losing the game of the actual pingpong of the
      abyss
I'm with you in Rockland
      where you bang on the catatonic piano the soul
      is innocent and immortal it should never die
      ungodly in an armed madhouse
I'm with you in Rockland
      where fifty more shocks will never return your

soul to its body again from its pilgrimage to a
cross in the void

I'm with you in Rockland

where you accuse your doctors of insanity and
plot the Hebrew socialist revolution against the
fascist national Golgotha

I'm with you in Rockland

where you will split the heavens of Long Island
and resurrect your living human Jesus from the
superhuman tomb

I'm with you in Rockland

where there are twenty-five-thousand mad com
rades all together singing the final stanzas of
the Internationale

I'm with you in Rockland

where we hug and kiss the United States under
our bedsheets the United States that coughs all
night and won't let us sleep

I'm with you in Rockland

where we wake up electrified out of the coma
by our own souls' airplanes roaring over the
roof they've come to drop angelic bombs the
hospital illuminates itself imaginary walls collapse O skinny legions run outside O starry-
spangled shock of mercy the eternal war is
here O victory forget your underwear we're
free

I'm with you in Rockland

in my dreams you walk dripping from a sea
journey on the highway across America in tears
to the door of my cottage in the Western night

San Francisco 1955–56

113. STUDENTS FOR A DEMOCRATIC SOCIETY (SDS)

The Port Huron Statement

(1962)

The Port Huron Statement is the major political document of the New Left. Although it was written collectively by a group of nearly sixty radicals at a United Auto Workers retreat in Port Huron, Michigan, in June 1962, its primary author was Tom Hayden (1939–). Inspired by the critical sociology of C. Wright Mills and the African-American sit-in struggle, as well as less obviously political sources like French existentialism and Beat poetry, the Port Huron Statement greatly shaped the early intellectual development of **STUDENTS FOR A DEMOCRATIC SOCIETY (SDS)**, the premier New Left organization of the 1960s. Among other things, the document criticized American society for its conformity, militarism, and racism, and it endorsed the civil rights, labor, and peace movements. It also introduced the concept of "participatory democracy"—the notion that individuals should have a say in the decisions that affect their lives. Its opening salvo, "We are people of this generation, bred in at least modest comfort, housed now in universities, looking uncomfortably to the world we inherit," is probably the most oft-quoted line in the literature of the New Left.

SOURCE: James Miller. *"Democracy is in the Streets": From Port Huron to the Siege of Chicago.* New York: Simon and Schuster, 1987.

SELECTED READINGS: Tom Hayden, *Reunion: A Memoir* (1988). James Miller, *"Democracy is in the Streets": From Port Huron to the Siege of Chicago* (1987). Kirkpatrick Sale, *SDS* (1971).

Introduction: Agenda for a Generation

We are people of this generation, bred in at least modest comfort, housed now in universities, looking uncomfortably to the world we inherit.

When we were kids the United States was the wealthiest and strongest country in the world; the only one with the atom bomb, the least scarred by modern war, an initiator of the United Nations that we thought would distribute Western influence throughout the world. Freedom and equality for each individual, government of, by, and for the people—these American values we found good, principles by which we could live as men. Many of us began maturing in complacency.

As we grew, however, our comfort was penetrated by events too troubling to dismiss. First, the permeating and victimizing fact of human degradation, symbolized by the Southern struggle against racial bigotry, compelled most of us from silence to activism. Second, the enclosing fact of the Cold War, symbolized by the presence of the Bomb, brought awareness that we ourselves, and our friends, and millions of abstract "others" we knew more directly because of our common peril, might die at any time. We might deliberately ignore, or avoid, or fail to feel all other human problems, but not these two, for these were too immediate and crushing in their impact, too challenging in the demand that we as individuals take the responsibility for encounter and resolution.

While these and other problems either directly oppressed us or rankled our consciences and became our own subjective concerns, we began to see complicated and disturbing paradoxes in our surrounding America. The declaration "all men are created equal . . ." rang hollow before the facts of Negro life in the South and the big cities of the North. The proclaimed peaceful intentions of the United States contradicted its economic and military investments in the Cold War status quo.

We witnessed, and continue to witness, other paradoxes. With nuclear energy whole cities can easily be powered, yet the dominant nation-states seem more likely to unleash destruction greater than that incurred in all wars of human history. Although our own technology is destroying old and creating new forms of social organization, men still tolerate meaningless work and idleness. While two-thirds of mankind suffers undernourishment, our own upper classes revel amidst superfluous abundance. Although world population is expected to double in forty years, the nations still tolerate anarchy as a major principle of international conduct and uncontrolled exploitation governs the sapping of the earth's physical resources. Although mankind desperately needs revolutionary leadership, America rests in national stalemate, its goals ambiguous and tradition-bound instead of informed and clear, its democratic system apathetic and manipulated rather than "of, by, and for the people."

Not only did tarnish appear on our image of American virtue, not only did disillusion occur when the hypocrisy of American ideals was discovered, but we began to sense that what we had originally seen as the American Golden Age was actually the decline of an era. The worldwide outbreak of revolution against colonialism and imperialism, the entrenchment of totalitarian states, the menace of war, overpopulation, international disorder, supertechnology— these trends were testing the tenacity of our own commitment to democracy and freedom and our abilities to visualize their application to a world in upheaval.

Our work is guided by the sense that we may be the last generation in the experiment with living. But we are a minority—the vast majority of our people regard the temporary equilibriums of our society and world as eternally functional parts. In this is perhaps the outstanding paradox: we ourselves are imbued with urgency, yet the message of our society is that there is no viable alternative to the present. Beneath the reassuring tones of the politicians, beneath the common opinion that America will "muddle through," beneath the stagnation of those who have closed their minds to the future, is the pervading feeling that there simply are no alternatives, that our times have witnessed the exhaustion not only of Utopias, but of any new departures as well. Feeling the press of complexity upon the emptiness of life, people are fearful of the thought that at any moment things might be thrust out of control. They fear change itself, since change might smash whatever invisible framework seems to hold back chaos for them now. For most Americans, all crusades are suspect, threatening. The fact that each individual sees apathy in his fellows perpetuates the common reluctance to organize for change. The dominant institutions are complex enough to blunt the minds of their potential critics, and entrenched enough to swiftly dissipate or entirely repel the energies of protest and reform, thus limiting human expectancies. Then, too, we are a materially improved society, and by our own improvements we seem to have weakened the case for further change.

Some would have us believe that Americans feel contentment amidst prosperity—but might it not better be called a glaze above deeply felt anxieties about their role in the new world? And if these anxieties produce a developed indifference to human affairs, do they not as well produce a yearning to believe there *is* an alternative to the present, that something *can* be done to change circumstances in the school, the workplaces, the bureaucracies, the government? It is to this latter yearning, at once the spark and engine of change, that we direct our present appeal. The search for truly democratic alternatives to the present, and a commitment to social experimentation with them, is a worthy and fulfilling human enterprise, one which moves us and, we hope, others today. On such a basis do we offer this document of our convictions and analysis: as an effort in understanding and changing the conditions of humanity in the late twentieth century, an effort rooted in the ancient, still unfulfilled conception of man attaining determining influence over his circumstances of life. . . .

The Students

In the last few years, thousands of American students demonstrated that they at least felt the urgency of the times. They moved actively and directly against racial injustices, the threat of war, violations of individual rights of conscience, and, less frequently, against economic manipulation. They succeeded in restoring a small measure of controversy to the campuses after the stillness of the McCarthy period. They succeeded, too, in gaining some concessions from the people and institutions they opposed, especially in the fight against racial bigotry.

The significance of these scattered movements lies not in their success or failure in gaining objectives—at least, not yet. Nor does the significance lie in the intellectual "competence" or "maturity" of the students involved—as some pedantic elders allege. The significance is in the fact that students are breaking the crust of apathy and overcoming the inner alienation that remain the defining characteristics of American college life.

If student movements for change are still rarities on the campus scene, what is commonplace there? The real campus, the familiar campus, is a place of private people, engaged in their notorious "inner emigration." It is a place of commitment to business-as-usual, getting ahead, playing it cool. It is a place of mass affirmation of the Twist, but mass reluctance toward the controversial public stance. Rules are accepted as "inevitable," bureaucracy as "just circumstances," irrelevance as "scholarship," selflessness as "martyrdom," politics as "just another way to make people, and an unprofitable one, too."

Almost no students value activity as citizens. Passive in public, they are hardly more idealistic in arranging their private lives: Gallup concludes they will settle for "low success, and won't risk high failure." There is not much willingness to take risks (not even in business), no setting of dangerous goals, no real conception of personal identity except one manufactured in the image of others, no real urge for personal fulfillment except to be almost as successful as the very successful people. Attention is being paid to social status (the quality of shirt collars, meeting people, getting wives or husbands, making solid contacts for later on); much, too, is paid to academic status (grades, honors, the med school rat race). But neglected generally is real intellectual status, the personal cultivation of the mind.

"Students don't even give a damn about the apathy," one has said. Apathy toward apathy begets a privately constructed universe, a place of systematic study schedules, two nights each week for beer, a girl or two, and early marriage; a framework infused with personality, warmth, and under control, no matter how unsatisfying otherwise.

Under these conditions university life loses all relevance to some. Four hundred thousand of our classmates leave college every year.

But apathy is not simply an attitude; it is a product of social institutions, and of the structure and organization of higher education itself. The extracurricular life is ordered according to *in loco parentis* theory, which ratifies the Administration as the moral guardian of the young.

The accompanying "let's pretend" theory of student extracurricular affairs validates student government as a training center for those who want to spend their lives in political pretense, and discourages initiative from the more articulate, honest, and sensitive students. The bounds and style of controversy are delimited before controversy begins. The university "prepares" the student for "citizenship" through perpetual rehearsals and, usually, through emasculation of what creative spirit there is in the individual.

The academic life contains reinforcing counterparts to the way in which extracurricular life is organized. The academic world is founded on a teacher-student relation analogous to the parent-child relation which characterizes *in loco parentis*. Further, academia includes a radical separation of the student from the material of study. That which is studied, the social reality, is "objectified" to sterility, dividing the student from life—just as he is restrained in active involvement by the deans controlling student government. The specialization of function and knowledge, admittedly necessary to our complex technological and social structure, has produced an exaggerated compartmentalization of study and understanding. This has contributed to an overly parochial view, by faculty, of the role of its research and scholarship; to a discontinuous and truncated understanding, by students, of the surrounding social order; and to a loss of personal attachment, by nearly all, to the worth of study as a humanistic enterprise.

There is, finally, the cumbersome academic bureaucracy extending throughout the academic as well as the extracurricular structures, contributing to the sense of outer complexity and inner powerlessness that transforms the honest searching of many students to a ratification of convention and, worse, to a numbness to present and future catastrophes. The size and financing systems of the university enhance the permanent trusteeship of the administrative bureaucracy, their power leading to a shift within the university toward the value standards of business and the administrative mentality. Huge foundations and other private financial interests shape the under-financed colleges and universities, making them not only more commercial, but less disposed to diagnose society critically, less open to dissent. Many social and physical scientists, neglecting the liberating heritage of higher learning, develop "human relations" or "morale-producing" techniques for the corporate economy, while others exercise their intellectual skills to accelerate the arms race.

Tragically, the university could serve as a significant source of social criticism and an initiator of new modes and molders of attitudes. But the actual intellectual effect of the college experience is hardly distinguishable from that of any other communications channel—say, a television set—passing on the stock truths of the day. Students leave college somewhat more "tolerant" than when they arrived, but basically unchallenged in their values and political orientations. With administrators ordering the institution, and faculty the curriculum, the student learns by his isolation to accept elite rule within the university, which prepares him to accept later forms of minority control. The real function of the educational system—as opposed to its more rhetorical function of "searching for truth"—is to impart the key information and styles that will help the student get by, modestly but comfortably, in the big society beyond.

The Society Beyond

Look beyond the campus, to America itself. That student life is more intellectual, and perhaps more comfortable, does not obscure the fact that the fundamental qualities of life on the campus reflect the habits of society at large. The fraternity president is seen at the junior manager levels; the sorority queen has gone to Grosse Pointe; the serious poet burns for a place, any place, to work; the once-serious and never-serious poets work at the advertising agencies. The desperation of people threatened by forces about which they know little and of which they can say less; the cheerful emptiness of people "giving up" all hope of changing things; the faceless ones polled by Gallup who listed "international affairs" fourteenth on their list of "problems" but who also expected thermo-nuclear war in the next few years; in these and other forms, Americans are in withdrawal from public life, from any collective effort at directing their own affairs.

Some regard these national doldrums as a sign of healthy approval of the established order—but is it approval by consent or manipulated acquiescence? Others declare that the people are withdrawn because compelling issues are fast disappearing—perhaps there are fewer breadlines in America, but is Jim Crow gone, is there enough work and work more fulfilling, is world war a diminishing threat, and what of the revolutionary new peoples? Still others think the national quietude is a necessary consequence of the need for elites to resolve complex and specialized problems of modern industrial society—

but, then, why should *business* elites help decide foreign policy, and who controls the elites anyway, and are they solving mankind's problems? Others, finally, shrug knowingly and announce that full democracy never worked anywhere in the past—but why lump qualitatively different civilizations together, and how can a social order work well if its best thinkers are skeptics, and is man really doomed forever to the domination of today?

There are no convincing apologies for the contemporary malaise. While the world tumbles toward the final war, while men in other nations are trying desperately to alter events, while the very future qua future is uncertain—America is without community impulse, without the inner momentum necessary for an age when societies cannot successfully perpetuate themselves by their military weapons, when democracy must be viable because of its quality of life, not its quantity of rockets.

The apathy here is, first, *subjective*—the felt powerlessness of ordinary people, the resignation before the enormity of events. But subjective apathy is encouraged by the *objective* American situation—the actual structural separation of people from power, from relevant knowledge, from pinnacles of decision-making. Just as the university influences the student way of life, so do major social institutions create the circumstances in which the isolated citizen will try hopelessly to understand his world and himself.

The very isolation of the individual—from power and community and ability to aspire—means the rise of a democracy without publics. With the great mass of people structurally remote and psychologically hesitant with respect to democratic institutions, those institutions themselves attenuate and become, in the fashion of the vicious circle, progressively less accessible to those few who aspire to serious participation in social affairs. The vital democratic connection between community and leadership, between the mass and the several elites, has been so wrenched and perverted that disastrous policies go unchallenged time and again. . . .

University and Social Change

There is perhaps little reason to be optimistic about the above analysis. True, the Dixiecrat-GOP coalition is the weakest point in the dominating complex of corporate, military, and political power. But the civil rights, peace, and student movements are too poor and socially slighted, and the labor movement too quiescent, to be counted with enthusiasm. From where else can power and vision be summoned? We believe that the universities are an overlooked seat of influence.

First, the university is located in a permanent position of social influence. Its educational function makes it indispensable and automatically makes it a crucial institution in the formation of social attitudes. Second, in an unbeliev- ably complicated world, it is the central institution for organizing, evaluating, and transmitting knowledge. Third, the extent to which academic resources presently are used to buttress immoral social practice is revealed, first, by the extent to which defense contracts make the universities engineers of the arms race. Too, the use of modern social science as a manipulative tool reveals itself in the "human relations" consultants to the modern corporations, who intro- duce trivial sops to give laborers feelings of "participation" or "belonging," while actually deluding them in order to further exploit their labor. And, of course, the use of motivational research is already infamous as a manipulative aspect of American politics. But these social uses of the universities' resources also demonstrate the unchangeable reliance by men of power on the men and storehouses of knowledge: this makes the university functionally tied to so- ciety in new ways, revealing new potentialities, new levers for change. Fourth, the university is the only mainstream institution that is open to participation by individuals of nearly any viewpoint.

These, at least, are facts, no matter how dull the teaching, how paternalistic the rules, how irrelevant the research that goes on. Social relevance, the ac- cessibility to knowledge, and internal openness—these together make the uni- versity a potential base and agency in a movement of social change.

1. Any new left in America must be, in large measure, a left with real intellectual skills, committed to deliberativeness, honesy, reflection as working tools. The university permits the political life to be an adjunct to the academic one, and action to be informed by reason.

2. A new left must be distributed in significant social roles throughout the country. The universities are distributed in such a manner.

3. A new left must consist of younger people who matured in the post- war world, and partially be directed to the recruitment of younger people. The university is an obvious beginning point.

4. A new left must include liberals and socialists, the former for their rel- evance, the latter for their sense of thoroughgoing reforms in the system. The university is a more sensible place than a political party for these two traditions to begin to discuss their differences and look for political synthesis.

5. A new left must start controversy across the land, if national policies and national apathy are to be reversed. The ideal university is a community of controversy, within itself and in its effects on communities beyond.

6. A new left must transform modern complexity into issues that can be understood and felt close up by every human being. It must give form to the feelings of helplessness and indifference, so that people may see the political, social, and economic sources of their private troubles and organize to change society. In a time of supposed prosperity, moral complacency, and political manipulation, a new left cannot rely on only aching stomachs to be the engine

force of social reform. The case for change, for alternatives that will involve uncomfortable personal efforts, must be argued as never before. The university is a relevant place for all of these activities.

But we need not indulge in illusions: the university system cannot complete a movement of ordinary people making demands for a better life. From its schools and colleges across the nation, a militant left might awaken its allies, and by beginning the process towards peace, civil rights, and labor struggles, reinsert theory and idealism where too often reign confusion and political barter. The power of students and faculty united is not only potential; it has shown its actuality in the South, and in the reform movements of the North.

The bridge to political power, though, will be built through genuine cooperation, locally, nationally, and internationally, between a new left of young people and an awakening community of allies. In each community we must look within the university and act with confidence that we can be powerful, but we must look outwards to the less exotic but more lasting struggles for justice.

To turn these possibilities into realities will involve national efforts at university reform by an alliance of students and faculty. They must wrest control of the educational process from the administrative bureaucracy. They must make fraternal and functional contact with allies in labor, civil rights, and other liberal forces outside the campus. They must import major public issues into the curriculum—research and teaching on problems of war and peace is an outstanding example. They must make debate and controversy, not dull pedantic cant, the common style for educational life. They must consciously build a base for their assault upon the loci of power.

As students for a democratic society, we are committed to stimulating this kind of social movement, this kind of vision and program in campus and community across the country. If we appear to seek the unattainable, as it has been said, then let it be known that we do so to avoid the unimaginable.

114. HERBERT MARCUSE

One Dimensional Man
(1964)

HERBERT MARCUSE's *One Dimensional Man* is often credited with supplying a rationale for the youth revolt of the 1960s, and Marcuse was one of the New Left's foremost intellectual defenders. Born in Berlin, Marcuse (1898–1979) came to the United States in 1934 to escape Nazism. In 1940 he became a naturalized U.S. citizen. He taught at numerous American universities and made enduring contributions as a philosopher and social theorist of revolutionary change, drawing on the works of Marx and Freud in his effort to formulate a comprehensive critique of advanced industrial society. In his most famous work, *One Dimensional Man,* he argued that individuals were being sapped of their ability for critical thinking and oppositional behavior as they fell under the sway of existing patterns of production and consumption.

SOURCE: Herbert Marcuse. *One Dimensional Man: Studies in the Ideology of Advanced Industrial Society.* Boston: Beacon Press, 1964.

SELECTED READINGS: Barry Katz, *Herbert Marcuse and the Art of Liberation: An Intellectual Biography* (1982). Douglas Kellner, *Herbert Marcuse and the Crisis of Marxism* (1984). Morton Schoolman, *Imaginary Witness: The Critical Theory of Herbert Marcuse* (1984).

The Paralysis of Criticism:
Society Without Opposition

Does not the threat of an atomic catastrophe which could wipe out the human race also serve to protect the very forces which perpetuate this danger? The efforts to prevent such a catastrophe overshadow the search for its potential causes in contemporary industrial society. These causes remain unidentified, unexposed, unattacked by the public because they recede before the all too obvious threat from without—to the West from the East, to the East from the West. Equally obvious is the need for being prepared, for living on the brink, for facing the challenge. We submit to the peaceful production of the means of destruction, to the perfection of waste, to being educated for a defense which deforms the defenders and that which they defend.

If we attempt to relate the causes of the danger to the way in which society is organized and organizes its members, we are immediately confronted with the fact that advanced industrial society becomes richer, bigger, and better as it perpetuates the danger. The defense structure makes life easier for a greater number of people and extends man's mastery of nature. Under these circumstances, our mass media have little difficulty in selling particular interests as those of all sensible men. The political needs of society become individual needs and aspirations, their satisfaction promotes business and the commonweal, and the whole appears to be the very embodiment of Reason.

And yet this society is irrational as a whole. Its productivity is destructive of the free development of human needs and faculties, its peace maintained by the constant threat of war, its growth dependent on the repression of the real possibilities for pacifying the struggle for existence—individual, national, and international. This repression, so different from that which characterized the preceding, less developed stages of our society, operates today not from a position of natural and technical immaturity but rather from a position of strength. The capabilities (intellectual and material) of contemporary society are immeasurably greater than ever before—which means that the scope of society's domination over the individual is immeasurably greater than ever before. Our society distinguishes itself by conquering the centrifugal social forces with Technology rather than Terror, on the dual basis of an overwhelming efficiency and an increasing standard of living.

To investigate the roots of these developments and examine their historical alternatives is part of the aim of a critical theory of contemporary society, a theory which analyzes society in the light of its used and unused or abused capabilities for improving the human condition. But what are the standards for such a critique?

Certainly value judgments play a part. The established way of organizing society is measured against other possible ways, ways which are held to offer better chances for alleviating man's struggle for existence; a specific historical practice is measured against its own historical alternatives. From the beginning, any critical theory of society is thus confronted with the problem of historical objectivity, a problem which arises at the two points where the analysis implies value judgments:

1. the judgment that human life is worth living, or rather can be and ought to be made worth living. This judgment underlies all intellectual effort; it is

the *a priori* of social theory, and its rejection (which is perfectly logical) rejects theory itself;

2. the judgment that, in a given society, specific possibilities exist for the amelioration of human life and specific ways and means of realizing these possibilities. Critical analysis has to demonstrate the objective validity of these judgments, and the demonstration has to proceed on empirical grounds. The established society has available an ascertainable quantity and quality of intellectual and material resources. How can these resources be used for the optimal development and satisfaction of individual needs and faculties with a minimum of toil and misery? Social theory is historical theory, and history is the realm of chance in the realm of necessity. Therefore, among the various possible and actual modes of organizing and utilizing the available resources, which ones offer the greatest chance of an optimal development?

The attempt to answer these questions demands a series of initial abstractions. In order to identify and define the possibilities of an optimal development, the critical theory must abstract from the actual organization and utilization of society's resources, and from the results of this organization and utilization. Such abstraction which refuses to accept the given universe of facts as the final context of validation, such "transcending" analysis of the facts in the light of their arrested and denied possibilities, pertains to the very structure of social theory. It is opposed to all metaphysics by virtue of the rigorously historical character of the transcendence.* The "possibilities" must be within the reach of the respective society; they must be definable goals of practice. By the same token, the abstraction from the established institutions must be expressive of an actual tendency—that is, their transformation must be the real need of the underlying population. Social theory is concerned with the historical alternatives which haunt the established society as subversive tendencies and forces. The values attached to the alternatives do become facts when they are translated into reality by historical practice. The theoretical concepts terminate with social change.

But here, advanced industrial society confronts the critique with a situation which seems to deprive it of its very basis. Technical progress, extended to a whole system of domination and coordination, creates forms of life (and of power) which appear to reconcile the forces opposing the system and to defeat or refute all protest in the name of the historical prospects of freedom from toil and domination. Contemporary society seems to be capable of containing social change—qualitative change which would establish essentially different

---

*The terms "transcend" and "transcendence" are used throughout in the empirical, critical sense: they designate tendencies in theory and practice which, in a given society, "overshoot" the established universe or discourse and action toward its historical alternatives (real possibilities).

institutions, a new direction of the productive process, new modes of human existence. This containment of social change is perhaps the most singular achievement of advanced industrial industrial society; the general acceptance of the National Purpose, bipartisan policy, the decline of pluralism, the collusion of Business and Labor within the strong State testify to the integration of opposites which is the result as well as the prerequisite of this achievement.

A brief comparison between the formative stage of the theory of industrial society and its present situation may help to show how the basis of the critique has been altered. At its origins in the first half of the nineteenth century, when it elaborated the first concepts of the alternatives, the critique of industrial society attained concreteness in a historical mediation between theory and practice, values and facts, needs and goals. This historical mediation occurred in the consciousness and in the political action of the two great classes which faced each other in the society: the bourgeoisie and the proletariat. In the capitalist world, they are still the basic classes. However, the capitalist development has altered the structure and function of these two classes in such a way that they no longer appear to be agents of historical transformation. An overriding interest in the preservation and improvement of the institutional status quo unites the former antagonists in the most advanced areas of contemporary society. And to the degree to which technical progress assures the growth and cohesion of communist society, the very idea of qualitative change recedes before the realistic notions of a non-explosive evolution. In the absence of demonstrable agents and agencies of social change, the critique is thus thrown back to a high level of abstraction. There is no ground on which theory and practice, thought and action meet. Even the most empirical analysis of historical alternatives appears to be unrealistic speculation, and commitment to them a matter of personal (or group) preference.

And yet: does this absence refute the theory? In the face of apparently contradictory facts, the critical analysis continues to insist that the need for qualitative change is as pressing as ever before. Needed by whom? The answer continues to be the same: by the society as a whole, for every one of its members. The union of growing productivity and growing destruction; the brinkmanship of annihilation; the surrender of thought, hope, and fear to the decisions of the powers that be; the preservation of misery in the face of unprecedented wealth constitute the most impartial indictment—even if they are not the *raison d'être* of this society but only its by-product: its sweeping rationality, which propels efficiency and growth, is itself irrational.

The fact that the vast majority of the population accepts, and is made to accept, this society does not render it less irrational and less reprehensible. The distinction between true and false consciousness, real and immediate interest still is meaningful. But this distinction itself must be validated. Men must come to see it and to find their way from false to true consciousness, from their immediate to their real interest. They can do so only if they live in need of changing their way of life, of denying the positive, of refusing. It is precisely this need which the established society manages to repress to the degree to which it is capable of "delivering the goods" on an increasingly large scale, and using the scientific conquest of nature for the scientific conquest of man.

Confronted with the total character of the achievements of advanced industrial society, critical theory is left without the rationale for transcending this society. The vacuum empties the theoretical structure itself, because the categories of a critical social theory were developed during the period in which the need for refusal and subversion was embodied in the action of effective social forces. These categories were essentially negative and oppositional concepts, defining the actual contradictions in nineteenth century European society. The category "society" itself expressed the acute conflict between the social and political sphere—society as antagonistic to the state. Similarly, "individual," "class," "private," "family" denoted spheres and forces not yet integrated with the established conditions—spheres of tension and contradiction. With the growing integration of industrial society, these categories are losing their critical connotation, and tend to become descriptive, deceptive, or operational terms.

An attempt to recapture the critical intent of these categories, and to understand how the intent was cancelled by the social reality, appears from the outset to be regression from a theory joined with historical practice to abstract, speculative thought: from the critique of political economy to philosophy. This ideological character of the critique results from the fact that the analysis is forced to proceed from a position "outside" the positive as well as negative, the productive as well as destructive tendencies in society. Modern industrial society is the pervasive identity of these opposites—it is the whole that is in question. At the same time, the position of theory cannot be one of mere speculation. It must be a historical position in the sense that it must be grounded on the capabilities of the given society.

This ambiguous situation involves a still more fundamental ambiguity. *One-Dimensional Man* will vacillate throughout between two contradictory hypotheses: (1) that advanced industrial society is capable of containing qualitative change for the foreseeable future; (2) that forces and tendencies exist which may break this containment and explode the society. I do not think that a clear answer can be given. Both tendencies are there, side by side—and even the one in the other. The first tendency is dominant, and whatever preconditions for a reversal may exist are being used to prevent it. Perhaps an accident may alter the situation, but unless the recognition of what is being done and what is being prevented subverts the consciousness and the behavior of man, not even a catastrophe will bring about the change.

The analysis is focused on advanced industrial society, in which the technical apparatus of production and distribution (with an increasing sector of automation) functions, not as the sum-total of mere instruments which can be isolated from their social and political effects, but rather as a system which determines *a priori* the product of the apparatus as well as the operations of servicing and extending it. In this society, the productive apparatus tends to become totalitarian to the extent to which it determines not only the socially needed occupations, skills, and attitudes, but also individual needs and aspirations. It thus obliterates the opposition between the private and public existence, between individual and social needs. Technology serves to institute new, more effective, and more pleasant forms of social control and social cohesion. The totalitarian tendency of these controls seems to assert itself in still another sense—by spreading to the less developed and even to the pre-industrial areas of the world, and by creating similarities in the development of capitalism and communism.

In the face of the totalitarian features of this society, the traditional notion of the "neutrality" of technology can no longer be maintained. Technology as such cannot be isolated from the use to which it is put; the technological society is a system of domination which operates already in the concept and construction of techniques.

The way in which a society organizes the life of its members involves an initial *choice* between historical alternatives which are determined by the inherited level of the material and intellectual culture. The choice itself results from the play of the dominant interests. It *anticipates* specific modes of transforming and utilizing man and nature and rejects other modes. It is one "project" of realization among others.* But once the project has become operative in the basic institutions and relations, it tends to become exclusive and to determine the development of the society as a whole. As a technological universe, advanced industrial society is a political universe, the latest stage in the realization of a specific historical project—namely, the experience, transformation, and organization of nature as the mere stuff of domination.

As the project unfolds, it shapes the entire universe of discourse and action, intellectual and material culture. In the medium of technology, culture, politics, and the economy merge into an omnipresent system which swallows up or repulses all alternatives. The productivity and growth potential of this system stabilize the society and contain technical progress within the framework of domination. Technological rationality has become political rationality.

---

*The term "project" emphasizes the element of freedom and responsibility in historical determination: it links autonomy and contingency. In this sense, the term is used in the work of Jean-Paul Sartre.

115. MARIO SAVIO

Berkeley Fall: The Berkeley Student Rebellion of 1964 (1965)

The following essay by **MARIO SAVIO** explained the origins and rationale for Berkeley's Free Speech Movement (FSM), which was the first major student uprising of the 1960s. Savio (1942–1996) was born in New York and attended Manhattan College and Queens College before going to Berkeley in 1963, where he studied philosophy. In 1964, Savio volunteered to work on the storied "Freedom Summer" project, and soon thereafter he emerged as the most articulate and best known leader of the Free Speech Movement. Savio is often remembered for a speech he gave in front of Berkeley's Sproul Plaza on December 2, 1964: "There is a time," he said, "when the operation of the machine becomes so odious, makes you so sick at heart, that you can't take part; and you've got to put your bodies upon the gears and upon the wheels, upon the levers, upon all the apparatus, and you've got to make it stop. And you've got to indicate to the people who run it, to the people who own it, that unless you're free, the machine will be prevented from running at all." Savio's speech and the demonstrations he helped organize at Berkeley served as a model and inspiration for many other student actions during the 1960s.

SOURCE: Mario Savio, Eugene Walker, and Raya Dunayevskaya. *The Free Speech Movement and the Negro Revolution.* Detroit, MI: News and Letters, July 1965.

SELECTED READINGS: W. J. Rorabaugh, *Berkeley at War: The 1960s* (1989). Hal Draper, *Berkeley: The New Student Revolt* (1965). Seymour Martin Lipset and Sheldon S. Wolin, eds., *The Berkeley Student Revolt: Facts and Interpretations* (1965).

There are quite a few students who have attended school at Berkeley who went South to work with the Student Non-violent Co-ordinating Committee, and who have been active in the civil rights movement in the Bay Area. At the end of last summer, some of these students returned from Mississippi, having taken part in the COFO Summer Project. I was one of these returning students. We were greeted by an order from the Dean of Students' Office that the kind of on-campus political activity which had resulted in our taking part in the Summer Project was to be permitted no longer.

It is a lot easier to become angry at injustices done to other people than at injustices done to oneself. The former requires a lower degree of political consciousness, is compatible with a higher political boiling point. You become slowly, painfully aware of those things which disturb you in the ways society oppresses you by taking part in activities aimed at freeing and helping others. There is less guilt to suffer in opposing the arbitrary power exercised over someone else than in opposing the equally unjust authority exercised over yourself. Thus, the order banning student politics on campus was an ideal locus of fierce protest. It combined an act of bureaucratic violence against the students themselves with open attack on student participation in the Bay Area civil rights movement. The seemingly inexhaustible, energy which the Berkeley students had so long devoted to the struggle for Negro rights was now turned squarely on the vast, faceless University administration. This is what gave the Free Speech Movement its initial impetus.

But the new restrictions were not aimed so much at curtailing activity which would result in civil rights work in the South as at halting the very active participation of students in the civil rights movement in the Bay Area. The University was apparently under considerable pressure to "crackdown" on the student activists from the right-wing in California business and politics. William Knowland, who has become symbolic of this pressure, managed Goldwater's statewide campaign; the reactionary *Oakland Tribune*, which Knowland publishes, has played a major role in creating the myth of Berkeley, the "little red school house." Last March when about 160 demonstrators, including many University students, were arrested at the Sheraton-Palace Hotel while protesting a discriminatory hiring policy, Don Mulford, conservative Republican State Assemblyman from the University district, was severely critical of the Berkeley administration for not expelling the then arrested students. Student pressure on Bay Area business resulted in business pressure on the University; the University responded by trying to restrict student political activity.

The liberal University of California administration would have relished the opportunity to show off in the national academic community a public university enjoying complete political and academic freedom and academic excellence. And if student politics had been restricted either to precinct work for the Democrats and Republicans, or to advocacy (by public meetings and distribution of literature) of various forms of wholesale societal change, then I don't believe there would have been the crisis there was. In any case an accommodation between the bureaucrats and the students could more easily have been achieved. The corporations represented on the Board of Regents welcome Young Democrats and Young Republicans as eager apprentices, and sectarian "revolutionary" *talk* can be tolerated because it is harmless. The radical student activists, however, are a mean threat to privilege. Because the students were advocating consequential actions (because their advocacy was consequential): the changing of hiring practices of particular establishments, the ending of certain forms of discrimination by certain concrete acts—because of these radical acts, the administration's restrictive ruling was necessary.

Which is easy to understand. The First Amendment exists to protect consequential speech; First Amendment rights to advocacy come into question only when actions advocated are sufficiently limited in scope, and sufficiently threatening to the established powers. The action must be radical *and* possible: picket lines, boycotts, sit-ins, rent strikes. The Free Speech Movement demanded no more—nor less—than full First Amendment rights of advocacy on campus as well as off: that, therefore, only the courts have power to determine and punish abuses of freedom of speech. The Berkeley Division of the Academic Senate endorsed this position on December 8, 1964 by declaring against *all* University regulation of the content of speech or advocacy—by a vote of 824 to 115.

Probably the most meaningful opportunity for political involvement for students with any political awareness is in the civil rights movement. Indeed, there appears to be little else in American life today which can claim the allegiance of men. Therefore, the action of the administration, which seemed to the students to be directed at the civil rights movement, was felt as a form of emasculation, or attempted emasculation. The only part of the world which people could taste, that wasn't as flat and stale as the middleclass wasteland from which most of the University people have come, that part of the world was being cleanly eliminated by one relatively hygienic administrative act. The student response to this "routine directive" was outraged protest.

Student civil rights action in the Bay Area has been significant and will become increasingly so. I am sure we haven't seen the last of the administration's attempts either to limit, or, if possible, to eliminate activity of this kind. On the other side, I think last semester has shown that such attempts, if drastic enough to be effective, are bound to end in disaster. So, what we have to fear is not some extreme act, such as was attempted last September, but rather petty harrassments of various sorts, and the not-so-petty exclusion of "nonstudents" from the campus, toward which legislation recently passed by the State Legislature is directed. I believe it unlikely for the students to rally in opposition to such harassment; probably we shall have to be content with opposing decisively only gross provocation, which probably now the Administration has learned not to attempt.

But the civil rights movement is only one aspect of the dual motivation of FSM support. And this is so because people do find it easier to protest injustices done to *others*: even adverting to injustice done oneself is often too painful to be sustained for very long. When you oppose injustice done others, very often—symbolically sometimes, sometimes not so symbolically—you are really protesting injustice done to yourself. In the course of the events of the fall, students became aware, ever more clearly, of the monstrous injustices that were being done to them as students.

We found we were being denied the very possibility of "being a student"— unquestionably a *right*. We found we were severed from our proper roles: students denied the meaningful work one must do in order to be a student. Instead we were faced with a situation in which the pseudo-student role we were playing was tailor-made to further the interests of those who own the University, those vast corporations in whose interest the University is managed. Time past when the skills required of laborers were nowhere near so great as the ones required now, bosses built schools for their own children. Now the bosses build schools for the children of their workers. They build schools to further their own interests.

Accordingly, the schools have become training camps—and proving grounds—rather than places where people acquire education. They become factories to produce technicians rather than places to live student lives. And this perversion develops great resentment on the part of the students. Resentment against being subjected to standard production techniques of speedup and regimentation; against a tendency to quantify education—virtually a contradiction in terms. Education is measured in units, in numbers of lectures attended, in numbers of pages devoted to papers, number of pages read. This mirrors the gross and vulgar quantification in the society at large—the *real* world—where everything must be reduced to a lowest common denominator, the dollar bill. In our campus play-world we use play money, course units.

It is understandable that resentment should develop among the students. However, it was not always so easy for the students to understand the causes of their own resentment. It is not as easy to see what is oppressing the subject as to see what is oppressing the others. Nevertheless, we students did become more and more aware of the factory education which we were being provided.

It is significant that the President of the University of California should be the foremost ideologist of this "Brave New World" conception of education. President Clark Kerr dreamed up the frightening metaphors: "the knowledge industry," "the multiversity," which has as many faces as it has publics, be they industries of various kinds, or the Federal Government, especially the Pentagon and the AEC. He also invented the title "the captain of bureaucracy," which he is, by analogy with earlier captains of industry. He is the person directly charged with steering the mighty ship along the often perilous course of service to its many publics in government and industry. Not to *the* public, but to its many publics, the Kerrian whore is unlawfully joined.

Those disciplines with a ready market in industry and government are favored and fostered: the natural sciences, engineering, mathematics, and the social sciences when these serve the braintrusting propaganda purposes of "liberal" government. The humanities naturally suffer, so that what should be the substance of undergraduate education suffers. The emphasis is given to research instead of to teaching undergraduates. Teaching graduate students is less effected by this prostitution since such teaching is intimately bound to research. But the undergraduate has become the new dispossessed; the heart has been taken from his education—no less so for science students—for the humanities are no longer accorded the central role they deserve in the university.

And of course there are whole areas which never see the light in undergraduate instruction. Who takes undergraduate courses in the history of the labor movement, for example? Certainly no one at the University of California. Likewise, American Negro history is a rarity and is still more rarely taken seriously. To be taken at all seriously it would have to be seen as central to all American history.

In a healthy university an undergraduate would have time to do 'nothing.' To read what he wants to read, maybe to sit on a hill behind the campus all alone or with a friend, to 'waste time' alone, dreaming in the Eucalyptus Grove. But the university, after the manner of a pesky social director, sees to it the student's time is kept filled with anti-intellectual harassment: those three credits in each three unit course, those meaningless units themselves. The notion that one can somehow reduce Introductory Quantum Mechanics and Philosophy of Kant to some kind of lowest common denominator (three units apiece) is totally irrational, and reflects the irrationality of a society which tries to girdle the natural rhythms of growth and learning by reduction to quantitative terms, much as it attempts to market the natural impulses of sex.

From my experience, I should say the result is at best a kind of intellectual cacophony. There are little attractions in various places, philosophy in one corner, physics in another, maybe a bit of mathematics every now and again, some political science—nothing bearing any relationship to anything else. Everything requires too many papers, too much attendance at lectures, two-thirds of which should never have been given, and very few of which resulted from any serious thought later than several years or earlier than several minutes before the lecture period. It is easy to see that there should be real resentment on the part of the students. But it is resentment whose causes are, as we have seen, very difficult for the student to perceive readily. That is why what occurred last semester gained its initial impetus from the very different involvements of what are mostly middle-class students in the struggles of the Negro people. Thus, it was both the irrationality of society, that denies to Negroes the life of men, and the irrationality of the University, that denies to youth the life of students, which caused last semester's rebellion.

116. GREGORY CALVERT

In White America
(1967)

GREGORY CALVERT's speech, "In White America: Radical Consciousness and Social Change," represented one of the New Left's most important intellectual achievements. Born in poverty in southwest Washington, Calvert (1937–) attended the University of Oregon and did graduate work at Cornell University. He later served as editor of Students for a Democratic Society's (SDS) newspaper, *New Left Notes*, and as SDS national secretary. This speech was first delivered at a February 1967 conference at Princeton University, which was sponsored by SDS's Radical Education Project (REP). Whereas many white students looked to other oppressed peoples to serve as a "revolutionary vanguard," Calvert argued that white, middle-class students could be capable agents of revolutionary change so long as they understood the nature of their oppression.

SOURCE: Gregory Calvert. "SDS Official Analyzes Struggle for Freedom." *National Guardian*, March 25, 1967.

SELECT BIBLIOGRAPHY: Gregory Calvert. *Democracy from the Heart: Spiritual Values, Decentralism, and Democratic Idealism in the Movement of the 1960s* (1991). Gregory Calvert and Carol Neiman, *A Disrupted History* (1971). Kirkpatrick Sale, *SDS* (1973).

Let me begin by telling you a story which I recently heard. It is a story about the guerrilla forces in Guatemala and about how they work. I do not know what image you might have in your head about the mode of operation of Guatemalan guerrillas—I am not even certain about the accuracy of this story. But, in any case, it makes sense to me and it speaks to me about who we are—the new radicals.

It is said that when the Guatemalan guerrillas enter a new village, they do not talk about the "anti-imperialist struggle" nor do they give lessons on dialectical materialism—neither do they distribute copies of the "Communist Manifesto" or of Chairman Mao's "On Contradiction." What they do is gather together the people of the village in the center of the village and then, one by one, the guerrillas rise and talk to the villagers about their own lives: about how they see themselves and how they came to be who they are, about their deepest longings and the things they've striven for and hoped for, about the way in which their deepest longings were frustrated by the society in which they lived.

Then the guerrillas encourage the villagers to talk about their lives. And then a marvelous thing begins to happen. People who thought that their deepest problems and frustrations were their individual problems discover that their problems and longings are all the same—that no one man is any different than the others. That, in Sartre's phrase, "In each man there is all of man." And, finally, that out of the discovery of their common humanity comes the decision that men must unite together in the struggle to destroy the conditions of their common oppression.

That, it seems to me, is what we are about. . . .

I am going to speak today about the problem of consciousness in American society and about the possibility of developing radical or revolutionary consciousness. I approach the problem of organizing from this viewpoint because 1) the objective conditions of oppression in America seem to be manifest and 2) because those objective conditions are not perceived, and 3) because the major problem to which organizers must address themselves in this period is the problem of false consciousness.

Let me posit a first principle: All authentically revolutionary movements are struggles for human freedom.

Contrary to what was suggested here last evening, revolutionary mass movements are not built out of a drive for the acquisition of more material goods. That is a perversion and vulgarization of revolutionary thought and a misreading of history. Revolutionary movements are freedom struggles born out of the perception of the contradictions between human potentiality and oppressive actuality. Revolutionary consciousness interprets those social economic and political structures which maintain the existing gap between potentiality and actuality as the objective conditions of oppression which must be transformed. Revolutionary consciousness sees the transformation of those oppressive conditions as the act of liberation and sees the realization of the previously frustrated human potentiality as the achievement of freedom. The bonds of oppression are broken and the new reality is constructed.

What is fundamental to this process is the mass perception of the contradiction between potentiality and actuality. In a given historical situation that contradiction may take the concrete form of economic deprivation in the face of the possibility of material abundance and the struggle for liberation may take the form of a drive to eliminate the conditions which prevent the achievement of that abundance. In a situation of economic abundance, the drive for freedom will rest on different perceptions and will set different goals. But the struggle in either case is a struggle for freedom, the form of which depends on the given stage of historical development—that is, on the level of development of human potentiality.

There is only one impulse, one dynamic which can create and sustain an authentic revolutionary movement. The revolutionary struggle is always and always must be a struggle for freedom. No individual, no group, no class is genuinely engaged in a revolutionary movement unless their struggle is a struggle for their own liberation.

Radical or revolutionary consciousness perceives contradiction . . . not between oneself, what one is, and the underprivileged but as the gap between "what one could be" and the existing conditions for self-realization. It is the perception of oneself as unfree, as oppressed—and finally it is the discovery of oneself as *one of the oppressed* who must unite to transform the objective conditions of their existence in order to resolve the contradiction between potentiality and actuality. Revolutionary consciousness leads to the struggle for one's own freedom in unity with others who share the burden of oppression. It is, to speak in the classical vocabulary, class consciousness because it no longer sees the problem as someone else's, because it breaks through individualization and privatization, because the recognition of one's own unfreedom unites one in the struggle of the oppressed, because it posits a more universally human potentiality for all men in a liberated society.

The problem in white America is the failure to admit or recognize unfreedom. It is a problem of false consciousness, that is, the failure to perceive one's situation in terms of oppressive (class) relationships. Only when white America comes to terms with its own unfreedom can it participate in the creation of a revolutionary movement.

When we have talked about the "new radicalism," about the "freedom movement," with a passionate conviction, we have been talking about a movement which involves us, you and me, in a gut-level encounter with, disengagement from, and struggle against the America which keeps us in bondage. It may have begun in a very personalistic fashion, out of a private sense of our individual alienation from the U.S. corporate-liberal capitalist monster and from "the bomb" which was its logical but unthinkable conclusion. But, it has and must move beyond the level of our own bewilderment, confusion, and despair about America. It moves to the final realization of our common oppression.

We should realize that Marx was quite correct when he said the true revolutionary consciousness was class consciousness. What he meant by that was that in order to change society people must realize that they are united in common struggle for their own liberation from objective conditions of oppression. . . . [H]e was saying to people that their struggle was the struggle of unfree men—not for individual salvation—but a struggle for collective liberation of all unfree, oppressed men.

What has held the new radicalism together, what has given it its life and vitality, has been the conviction that the gut-level alienation from America-the-Obscene-and-the-Dehumanized was a sincere and realistic basis for challenging America. What has often left the new radicals impotent and romantic is their failure to understand the dynamics of the society which produced their gut-level alienation, that is their failure to understand that what seemed humanly and emotionally real could be understood in terms of a fundamental and critical analysis of American corporate-liberal capitalism. There was a crying out of their own being against America, but a failure to understand why that revolt was authentically related to the necessity and the possibility of revolutionizing America.

That situation has begun to change. The new radicals are beginning to produce an analysis of America which enables them to understand themselves and the greater reality of American society in a way which authenticates their own revolt as a realistic basis for understanding the way in which we can be freed. It begins to relate the anarchist demand, "I want freedom," to the revolutionary socialist analysis which points the way to collective liberation.

If the analysis is correct and if false consciousness is the major obstacle to organizing a revolutionary movement, then it would seem to follow that our primary task at this stage of development is the encouragement or building of revolutionary consciousness, of consciousness of the conditions of unfreedom. A question immediately arises however— . . . since the society can buy people off with goods, are there other sufficiently potent radicalizing experiences apart from economic deprivation which radicals can work with?

This is an important and complex question. It is perhaps the failure of the old left to arrive at a satisfactory answer to that question which was responsible for its fervent attachment to the concept of the inevitability of the collapse of capitalism—the catastrophic event which would reveal both the objective contradictions of the system and create the proper subjective response on the part of the exploited.

Without necessarily ruling out the possibility of such an economic cataclysm in the capitalist world, the new left is hardly notable for its faith in the inevitability of the event. Thus deprived of the *deus ex machina* which the old left was certain existed in the wings, we new leftists have been driven by a special urgency which gives rise to a variety of inventive activities designed to reveal to people their unfreedom and to offer them alternatives and hope. Certainly the organizing of the new radicals has been one of their most characteristic features. . . . The whole notion of the "new working class" provides a powerful tool for understanding the present structure of advanced industrial capitalism.

First, it breaks through the "myth of the great American middle class." Not only are millions of Americans held captive by that notion, but it has also been a major psychological obstacle for most radicals. If white America is mostly middle class, and if being middle class means not being oppressed, then there is no possibility for finding the resources upon which a radical movement can be built in white America. What we have come to understand is that the great American middle class is not middle class at all. . . . The vast majority of those whom we called the middle class must properly be understood as members of the "new working class": that is, as those workers who fill the jobs created by a new level of technological development within the same exploitive system.

Secondly, it enables us to understand the special role of students in relation to the present structure of industrial capitalism. Students are the "trainees" for the new working class and the factory-like multiversities are the institutions which prepare them for their slots in the bureaucratic machinery of corporate capitalism. We must stop apologizing for being students or for organizing students. Students are in fact a key group in the creation of the productive forces of this super-technological capitalism. We have organized them out of their own alienation from the multiversity and have raised the demand for "student control." That is important: because that is precisely the demand that the new working class must raise when it is functioning as the new working class in the economic system. It is that demand which the system cannot fulfill and survive as it is. That is why it is potentially a real revolutionary demand in a way that demands for higher wages can never be.

Thirdly, we can see that it was a mistake to assume that the only radical role which students could play would be as organizers of other classes. It is still important, vitally important that student organizers continue to involve themselves in ghetto organizing, in the organizing of the underclass. That work is a vital part of the movement and it is first from ghetto community organizing that the demand for control was clearly articulated. But it is now important to realize that we must organize the great majority of students as the trainees of the new working class. We must speak to them of the way in which the new working class is created—of the meaningless training which is passed off as education and of the special coercive devices like the Selective Service System with its student deferments designed to channel them into the multiversity.

Finally, we must be sensitive to those places in the social strata where false consciousness is being broken down, where the middle-class myth is crumbling, where groups are beginning to struggle for their own freedom. In terms of the concept of the new working class, certain groups have begun to respond: social workers; teachers, the medical profession. All of these are service groups, it is true, and, interestingly, there is in all these areas a characteristic contradiction between a high level of articulated aspiration and increasingly oppressive conditions. We need radicals in all those areas in order to articulate more clearly the political ramifications of the demands for control and meaningful work. . . .

We must be sensitive to the fact that a mass movement in America will take time to develop and that it requires the involvement of a broad range of social strata, old and new working class, students and underclass. What counts is that America is beginning to break up, that the myth of the great American middle class is crumbling, that white Americans as well as black Americans are beginning to recognize their common oppression and are raising their demands for freedom which can be the basis of a movement which could revolutionize America.

117. JERRY FARBER

The Student as Nigger
(1967)

JERRY FARBER's "The Student as Nigger" was hailed in *Esquire* magazine as "the underground [press's] first classic." Born in El Paso, Texas, Farber (1935–) earned his Ph.D. at Occidental College. He is currently a professor of English and Contemporary Literature at San Diego State University. He was a child actor and was active in the civil rights and antiwar movements. "The Student as Nigger" was first published in the *Los Angeles Free Press* in 1967 but it circulated widely as a pamphlet and has been reprinted in approximately five hundred underground newspapers, making it one of the most controversial and widely read essays to come out of the New Left. Farber used the provocative metaphor of students as "niggers" to illustrate the degraded condition of university students in the 1960s, and to persuade them to fight for their "educational liberation." Today he loathes professorial power-tripping and student slavishness as much as ever.

SOURCE: Jerry Farber. *The Student as Nigger: Essays and Stories.* North Holly-wood, CA: Contact Books, 1969.

SELECTED READINGS: Jerry Farber, *The Student as Nigger: Essays and Stories* (1969). Abe Peck, *Uncovering the Sixties: The Life and Times of the Underground Press* (1985).

Students are niggers. When you get that straight, our schools begin to make sense. It's more important, though, to understand why they're niggers. If we follow that question seriously enough, it will lead us past the zone of academic bullshit, where dedicated teachers pass their knowledge on to a new generation, and into the nitty-gritty of human needs and hang-ups. And from there we can go on to consider whether it might ever be possible for students to come up from slavery.

First let's see what's happening now. Let's look at the role students play in what we like to call education.

At Cal State L.A., where I teach, the students have separate and unequal dining facilities. If I take them into the faculty dining room, my colleagues get uncomfortable, as though there were a bad smell. If I eat in the student cafeteria, I become known as the educational equivalent of a niggerlover. In at least one building there are even rest rooms which students may not use. At Cal State, also, there is an unwritten law barring student-faculty lovemaking. Fortunately, this anti-miscegenation law, like its Southern counterpart, is not 100 percent effective.

Students at Cal State are politically disenfranchised. They are in an academic Lowndes County. Most of them can vote in national elections—their average age is about 26—but they have no voice in the decisions which affect their academic lives. The students are, it is true, allowed to have a toy government run for the most part by Uncle Toms and concerned principally with trivia. The faculty and administrators decide what courses will be offered; the students get to choose their own Homecoming Queen. Occasionally when student leaders get uppity and rebellious, they're either ignored, put off with trivial concessions, or manoeuvered expertly out of position.

A student at Cal State is expected to know his place. He calls a faculty member "Sir" or "Doctor" or "Professor"—and he smiles and shuffles some as he stands outside the professor's office waiting for permission to enter. The faculty tell him what courses to take (in my department, English, even electives have to be approved by a faculty member); they tell him what to read, what to write, and, frequently, where to set the margins on his typewriter. They tell him what's true and what isn't. Some teachers insist that they encourage dissent but they're almost always jiving and every student knows it. Tell the man what he wants to hear or he'll fail your ass out of the course. . . .

What school amounts to, then, for white and black kids alike, is a 12-year course in how to be slaves. What else could explain what I see in a freshman class? They've got that slave mentality: obliging and ingratiating on the surface but hostile and resistant underneath.

As do black slaves, students vary in their awareness of what's going on. Some recognize their own put-on for what it is and even let their rebellion break through to the surface now and then. Others—including most of the "good students"—have been more deeply brainwashed. They swallow the bullshit with greedy mouths. They honest-to-God believe in grades, in busy work, in General Education requirements. They're pathetically eager to be pushed around. They're like those old grey-headed house niggers you can still find in the South who don't see what all the fuss is about because Mr. Charlie "treats us real good."

College entrance requirements tend to favor the Toms and screen out the rebels. Not entirely, of course. Some students at Cal State L.A. are expert con artists who know perfectly well what's happening. They want the degree or the 2-S and spend their years on the old plantation alternately laughing and cursing as they play the game. If their egos are strong enough, they cheat a lot. And, of course, even the Toms are angry down deep somewhere. But it comes out in passive rather than active aggression. They're unexplainably thickwitted and subject to frequent spells of laziness. They misread simple questions. They spend their nights mechanically outlining history chapters while meticulously failing to comprehend a word of what's in front of them.

The saddest cases among both black slaves and student slaves are the ones who have so thoroughly introjected their masters' values that their anger is all turned inward. At Cal State these are the kids for whom every low grade is torture, who stammer and shake when they speak to a professor, who go through an emotional crisis every time they're called upon during class. You can recognize them easily at finals time. Their faces are festooned with fresh pimples; their bowels boil audibly across the room. If there really is a Last Judgment, then the parents and teachers who created these wrecks are going to burn in hell.

So students are niggers. It's time to find out why, and to do this we have to take a long look at Mr. Charlie.

The teachers I know best are college professors. Outside the classroom and taken as a group, their most striking characteristic is timidity. They're short on balls.

Just look at their working conditions. At a time when even migrant workers have begun to fight and win, college professors are still afraid to make more than a token effort to improve their pitiful economic status. In California state colleges the faculties are screwed regularly and vigorously by the Governor and Legislature and yet they still won't offer any solid resistance. They lie flat on their stomachs with their pants down, mumbling catch phrases like "professional dignity" and "meaningful dialogue."

Professors were no different when I was an undergraduate at UCLA during the McCarthy era; it was like a cattle stampede as they rushed to cop out. And in more recent years, I found that my being arrested in sit-ins brought from my colleagues not so much approval or condemnation as open-mouthed astonishment. "You could lose your job!"

Now, of course, there's the Vietnamese war. It gets some opposition from a few teachers. Some support it. But a vast number of professors who know perfectly well what's happening, are copping out again. And in the high schools, you can forget it. Stillness reigns.

I'm not sure why teachers are so chickenshit. It could be that academic training itself forces a split between thought and action. It might also be that the tenured security of a teaching job attracts timid persons and, furthermore, that teaching, like police work, pulls in persons who are unsure of themselves and need weapons and the other external trappings of authority.

At any rate teachers ARE short on balls. And, as Judy Eisenstein has eloquently pointed out, the classroom offers an artificial and protected environment in which they can exercise their will to power. Your neighbors may drive a better car; gas station attendants may intimidate you; your wife may dominate you; the State Legislature may shit on you; but in the classroom, by God, students do what you say—or else. The grade is a hell of a weapon. It may not rest on your hip, potent and rigid like a cop's gun, but in the long run it's more powerful. At your personal whim—any time you choose—you can keep 35 students up for nights and have the pleasure of seeing them walk into the classroom pasty-faced and red-eyed carrying a sheaf of typewritten pages, with title page, MLA footnotes and margins set at 15 and 91. . . .

Finally, there's the darkest reason of all for the master-slave approach to education. The less trained and the less socialized a person is, the more he constitutes a sexual threat and the more he will be subjugated by institutions, such as penitentiaries and schools. Many of us are aware by now of the sexual neurosis which makes white man so fearful of integrated schools and neighborhoods, and which makes the castration of Negroes a deeply entrenched Southern folkway. We should recognize a similar pattern in education. There is a kind of castration that goes on in schools. It begins before school years with parents' first encroachments on their children's free unashamed sexuality and continues right up to the day when they hand you your doctoral diploma with a bleeding, shriveled pair of testicles stapled to the parchment. It's not that sexuality has no place in the classroom. You'll find it there but only in certain perverted and vitiated forms.

How does sex show up in school? First of all, there's the sado masochistic relationship between teachers and students. That's plenty sexual, although the price of enjoying it is to be unaware of what's happening. In walks the teacher in his Ivy League equivalent of a motorcycle jacket. In walks the teacher—a kind of intellectual rough trade—and flogs his students with grades, tests, sarcasm and snotty superiority until their very brains are bleeding. In Swinburne's England, the whipped school boy frequently grew up to be a flagellant. With us the perversion is intellectual but it's no less perverse.

Sex also shows up in the classroom as academic subject matter—sanitized and abstracted, thoroughly divorced from feeling. You get "sex education" now in both high school and college classes: everyone determined not to be embarrassed, to be very up to date, very contempo. These are the classes for which sex, as Feiffer puts it, "can be a beautiful thing if properly administered." And then, of course, there's still another depressing manifestation of sex in the classroom: the "off-color" teacher who keeps his class awake with sniggering sexual allusions, obscene titters and academic inuendo. The sexuality he purveys. It must be admitted is at least What's missing, from kindergarten to graduate school, is honest recognition of what's actually happening—turned-on awareness of hairy goodies underneath the petti-pants, the chinos and the flannels. It's not that sex needs to be pushed in school; sex is push enough. But we should let it be, where it is and like it is. I don't insist that ladies in junior high school lovingly caress their students' cocks (someday maybe); however, it is reasonable to ask that the ladies don't, by example and stricture, teach their students to pretend that those cocks aren't there. As things stand now, students are psychically castrated or spayed—and for the very same reason that black men are castrated in Georgia; because they're a threat.

So you can add sexual repression to the list of causes, along with vanity, fear and will to power, that turn the teacher into Mr. Charlie. You might also want to keep in mind that he was a nigger once himself and has never really gotten over it. And there are more causes, some of which are better described in sociological than in psychological terms. Work them out, it's not hard. But in the meantime what we've got on our hands is a whole lot of niggers. And what makes this particularly grim is that the student has less chance than the black man of getting out of his bag. Because the student doesn't even know he's in it. That, more or less, is what's happening in higher education. And the results are staggering.

For one thing damn little education takes place in the schools. How could it? You can't educate slaves; you can only train them. Or, to use an even uglier and more timely word, you can only program them.

At my school we even grade people on how they read poetry. That's like grading people on how they fuck. But we do it. In fact, God help me, I do it. I'm the Adolph Eichmann of English 323. Simon Legree on the poetry plantation. "Tote that iamb! Lift that spondee!" Even to discuss a good poem in that environment is potentially dangerous because the very classroom is contaminated. As hard as I may try to turn students on to poetry, I know that the desks, the tests, the IBM cards, their own attitudes toward school, and my own residue of UCLA method are turning them off.

Another result of student slavery is equally serious. Students don't get emancipated when they graduate. As a matter of fact, we don't let them graduate until they've demonstrated their willingness—over 16 years—to remain slaves. And for important jobs, like teaching, we make them go through more years just to make sure. What I'm getting at is that we're all more or less niggers and slaves, teachers and students alike. This is a fact you want to start with in trying to understand wider school phenomena, say, politics, in our country and in other countries.

Educational oppression is trickier to fight than racial oppression. If you're a black rebel, they can't exile you; they either have to intimidate you or kill you. But in high school or college they can just bounce you out of the fold. And they do.

Rebel students and renegade faculty members get smothered or shot down with devastating accuracy. In high school, it's usually the student who gets it; in college it's more often the teacher. Others get tired of fighting and voluntarily leave the system. This may be a mistake though. Dropping out of college for a rebell is a little like going North for a Negro. You can't really get away from it so you might as well stay and raise hell.

How do you raise hell? That's a whole other article. But just for a start, why not stay with the analogy? What have black people done? They have, first of all, faced the fact of their slavery. They've stopped kidding themselves about an eventual reward in that Great Watermelon Patch in the sky. They've organized; they've decided to get freedom now, and they've started taking it.

Students, like black people, have immense unused power. They could, theoretically, insist on participating in their own education. They could make academic freedom bilateral. They could teach their teachers to thrive on love and admiration, rather than fear and respect, and to lay down their weapons. Students could discover community. And they could learn to dance by dancing on the IBM cards. They could make coloring books out of the catalogs and they could put the grading system in a museum. They could raze one set of walls and let life come blowing into the classroom. They could raze another set of walls and let education flow out and flood the streets. They could turn the classroom into where it's at—a "field of action" as Peter Marin describes it. And believe it or not, they could study eagerly and learn prodigiously for the best of all possible reasons—their own reasons.

They could. Theoretically. They have the power. But only in a very few places, like Berkeley, have they even begun to think about using it. For students, as for black people, the hardest battle isn't with Mr. Charlie. It's with what Mr. Charlie has done to your mind.

118. ED SANDERS

Predictions for Yippie Activities
(1968)

ED SANDERS's "Predictions for Yippie Activities" reflects the zaniness of the "Yippies," a group that blended the militant politics of the New Left with the creativity and humor of the emerging counterculture. Sanders (1939–) was born in Kansas City, Missouri. As a teenager, he was greatly influenced by Allen Ginsberg's poem "Howl," and after graduating high school he moved to New York City and established himself as a poet and countercultural icon, publishing a journal called *Fuck You: A Magazine of the Arts* and, with Tuli Kupferberg, founding the rock group the Fugs. Sanders's facetious list of "predictions" for what might occur at the 1968 Democratic National Convention at Chicago attempted to build a mystique around the Yippies, confuse "squares," and galvanize a large turnout of radical demonstrators at the convention.

SOURCE: Ed Sanders. "Predictions for Yippie Activities." *The Berkeley Barb.* August 2–8, 1968.

SELECTED READINGS: David Farber, *Chicago '68* (1994). Ed Sanders, *Tales of Beatnik Glory* (1975). Ed Sanders, *America, a History in Verse,* Volume 1 (1900–1939), Volume 2 (1940–1961), and Volume 3 (1962–1970) published in 2000 and 2003. Norman Mailer, *Miami and the Siege of Chicago: An Informal History of the Republican and Democratic National Conventions of 1968* (1968).

Predictions for Yippie Activities

1. Poetry readings, mass meditation, flycasting exhibitions, demagogic yippie political arousal speeches, rock music, and song concerts will be held on a precise timetable throughout the week August 25–30.

2. A dawn ass-washing ceremony with 10's of 1000's participating will

occur each morning at 5:00 AM as yippie revellers and protesters prepare for the 7:00 AM volleyball tournaments.

3. Several hundred Yippie friends with press passes will gorge themselves on 800 pounds of cocktail onions and puke in unison at the nomination of Hubert H. Pastry.

4. Psychedelic long haired mutant-jissomed peace leftists will consort with known dope fiends, spilling out onto the sidewalks in porn-ape disarray each afternoon.

5. The Chicago offices of the National Biscuit Company will be hijacked on principle to provide bread & cookies for 50,000 as a gesture of goodwill to the youth of America.

6. Universal Syrup Day will be held on Wednesday when a movie will be shown at Soldiers Field in which Hubert Humphrey confesses to Allen Ginsberg of his secret approval of anal intercourse.

7. Filth will be worshipped.

8. The Yippie Ecological Conference will spew out an angry report denouncing scheiss-poison in the lakes and streams industrial honky-fumes from white killer industrialists, and exhaust murder from a sick hamburger society of automobile freaks; with precise total assault solutions to these problems.

9. There will be public fornication whenever and wherever there is an aroused appendage and willing aperture.

10. Poets will re-write the bill of rights in precise language, detailing ten thousand areas of freedom in OUR OWN LANGUAGE, to replace the confusing and vague rhetoric of 200 years ago.

11. Reporters and media representatives will be provided free use of dope and consciousness altering thrill-chemicals for their education and refreshment.

12. Pissed off hordes of surly draft eligible poets will somehow confront conventioneers with 16 tons of donated fish eyes.

Note from author: This piece was written one morning in the summer of 1968 to be published in the underground newspapers after Allen Ginsberg had told me about a dream featuring Hubert Humphrey he'd had the night before.

119. THE COLUMBIA STRIKE COORDINATING COMMITTEE

Columbia Liberated

(1968)

In the spring of 1968 a major student rebellion erupted at Columbia University. Students there initially protested the scheduled construction of a gymnasium that was to be built in nearby Morningside Park in Harlem, thereby depriving local residents of already scarce land for recreation. Others protested the university's connections with the Department of Defense, and the lack of a student voice in academic governing. But as **THE COLUMBIA STRIKE COORDINATING COMMITTEE** indicated, students there were also concerns about the Vietnam War, racism, economic inequality, and social repression. Columbia students occupied five buildings for eight days, until they were brutally evicted by New York City Police. As a result, much of the campus community went on strike, and classes were not resumed that semester. As Tom Hayden later remarked, "Columbia students [took] an internationalist and revolutionary view of themselves in opposition to the imperialism of the very institution in which they have been groomed and educated."

SOURCE: Judith Clair Albert and Edward Albert Stewart. *The Sixties Papers: Documents of a Rebellious Decade.* New York: Praeger, 1984.

SELECTED READINGS: Jerry Avorn et al., *Up Against the Ivy Wall: A History of the Columbia Crisis* (1969). James S. Kunen, *The Strawberry Statement: Notes of a College Revolutionary* (1969). Columbia Spectator, *Crisis at Columbia: An Inside Report on the Rebellion at Columbia from the Pages of the* Columbia Daily Spectator (1968).

Something is happening here but you don't know what it is, do you, Mr. Jones?

B. DYLAN

"Up against the wall, motherfuckers!"
ENTIRE MATH COMMUNE TO SEVERAL HUNDRED MEMBERS OF THE
NEW YORK CITY POLICE DEPT'S TACTICAL PATROL FORCE,
APRIL 30, 1968.

The Strike in Context

The most important fact about the Columbia strike is that Columbia exists within American society. This statement may appear to be a truism, yet it is a fact too often forgotten by observers, reporters, administrators, faculty members, and even some students. These people attempt to explain the "disturbances" as reaction to an unresponsive and archaic administrative structure, youthful outbursts of unrest much like panty raids, the product of a conspiracy by communist agents in national SDS or a handful of hard-core nihilists ("destroyers") on the campus, or just general student unrest due to the war in Vietnam.

But in reality, striking students are responding to the totality of the conditions of our society, not just one small part of it, the university. We are disgusted with the war, with racism, with being a part of a system over which we have no control, a system which demands gross inequalities of wealth and power, a system which denies personal and social freedom and potential, a system which has to manipulate and repress us in order to exist. The university can only be seen as a cog in this machine; or, more accurately, a factory whose product is knowledge and personnel (us) useful to the functioning of the system. The specific problems of university life, its boredom and meaninglessness, help prepare us for boring and meaningless work in the "real" world. And the policies of the university—expansion into the community, exploitation of blacks and Puerto Ricans, support for imperialist wars—also serve the interests of banks, corporations, government, and military represented on the Columbia Board of Trustees and the ruling class of our society. In every way, the university is "society's child." Our attack upon the university is really an attack upon this society and its effects upon us. We have never said otherwise.

The development of the New Left at Columbia represents an organized political response to the society. We see our task, first as identifying for ourselves and for others the nature of our society—who controls it and for what ends—and secondly, developing ways in which to transform it. We understand that only through struggle can we create a free, human society, since the present one is dominated by a small ruling class which exploits, manipulates, and distorts for its own ends—and has shown in countless ways its determination to maintain its position. The Movement at Columbia began years ago agitating and organizing students around issues such as students' power in the university (Action), support of the civil rights movement (CORE), the war in Vietnam (the Independent Committee on Vietnam). Finally, Columbia chapter Students for a Democratic Society initiated actions against many of the above issues as they manifest themselves on campus. Politically speaking, SDS, from its inception on campus in November, 1966, sought to unite issues, "to draw connections," to view this society as a totality. SDS united the two main themes of the movement—opposition to racial oppression and to the imperialist war in Vietnam—with our own sense of frustration, disappointment, and oppression at the quality of our lives in capitalist society.

One of the most important questions raised by the strike was who controls Columbia, and for what ends? SDS pointed to the Board of Trustees as the intersection of various corporate, financial, real-estate, and government interests outside the university which need the products of the university—personnel and knowledge—in order to exist. It is this power which we are fighting when we fight particular policies of the university such as expansion at the expense of poor people or institutional ties to the war-machine. We can hope for and possibly win certain reforms within the university, but the ultimate reforms we need—the elimination of war and exploitation—can only be gained after we overthrow the control of our country by the class of people on Columbia's Board of Trustees. In a sense, Columbia is the place where we received our education—our revolutionary education.

President Emeritus Grayson Kirk, in his 5,000 word "Message to Alumni, Parents, and Other Friends of Columbia," concludes

> the leaders of the SDS—as distinct from an unknown number of their supporters—are concerned with local parochial university issues only as they serve as a means to a larger end.

Though Kirk perceives that we are interested in more than Columbia University, he ignores the fact that the issues we raise are not at all "local parochial university isues," but indeed transcend the physical and class boundary of the university to unite us, the students, with neighborhood people, blacks and Puerto Ricans, and even the Vietnamese, with all the people oppressed by this society.

But why do students, predominantly of the "middle-class," in effect, reject the university designed to integrate them into the system and instead identify with the most oppressed of this country and the world? Why did the gymnasium in Morningside Park become an issue over which Columbia was shut down for seven weeks? Why pictures of Che Guevara, Malcolm X, and red flags in the liberated buildings?

Basically, the sit-ins and strike of April and May gave us a chance to express the extreme dissatisfaction we feel at being *caught in this "system."* We rejected the gap between potential and realization in this society. We rejected our present lives in the university and our future lives in business, government or other universities like this one. In a word, we saw ourselves as oppressed, and began to understand the forces at work which make for our oppression. In turn, we saw those same forces responsible for the oppression and colonization of blacks and Puerto Ricans in ghettos, and Vietnamese and the people of the third world. By initiating a struggle in support of black and third world liberation, we create the conditions for our own freedom—by building a movement which will someday take power over our society, we will free ourselves.

120. STUDENTS FOR A DEMOCRATIC SOCIETY

Bring the War Home

(1969)

Faced with the intransigence of the Vietnam War and the persistence of racism and police repression against the Black Panthers and other militants, in 1969 an ultraradical faction of **STUDENTS FOR A DEMOCRATIC SOCIETY (SDS)** named Weatherman began calling for armed revolutionary struggle against the United States. (The group got its name from the Bob Dylan lyric, "You don't need a weatherman to know which way the wind blows.") Although they represented only a tiny minority of SDS's actual membership, they drew an enormous amount of media attention and bombed many symbolic targets. "Bring the War Home," was a popular Weatherman brochure (written under the auspices of SDS) that called for a "National Action" in Chicago in 1969, in response to the police riot at the 1968 Democratic National Convention. This protest, also dubbed the "Days of Rage," attracted only a few hundred demonstrators and involved property damage and violent confrontation with the police.

SOURCE: *New Left Notes*. August 1, 1969.

SELECTED READINGS: Jeremy Varon, *Utopia, Revolution, and Violence: The Weather Underground and the Red Army Faction* (2003). Bill Ayers, *Fugitive Days: A Memoir* (2001). Kirkpatrick Sale, *SDS* (1973).

Look at It: America, 1969

The war goes on, despite the jive double-talk about troop withdrawals and peace talks. Black people continue to be murdered by agents of the fat cats who run this country, if not in one way, then in another: by the pigs or the courts, by the boss or the welfare department.

Working people face higher taxes, inflation, speed-ups, and the sure knowledge—if it hasn't happened already—that their sons may be shipped off to Vietnam and shipped home in a box. And young people all over the country go to prisons that are called schools, are trained for jobs that don't exist or serve no one's real interest but the boss's, and, to top it all of, get told that Vietnam is the place to defend their "freedom."

None of this is very new. The cities have been falling apart, the schools have been bullshit, the jobs have been rotten and unfulfilling for a long time.

What's new is that today not quite so many people are confused, and a lot more people are angry: angry about the fact that the promises we have heard since first grade are all jive; angry that, when you get down to it, this system is nothing but the total economic and military put-down of the oppressed peoples of the world.

And more: it's a system that steals the goods, the resources, and the labor of poor and working people all over the world in order to fill the pockets and bank accounts of a tiny capitalist class. (Call it imperialism.) It's a system that divides white workers from blacks by offering whites crumbs off the table, and telling them that if they don't stay cool the blacks will move in on their jobs, their homes, and their schools. (Call it white supremacy.) It's a system that divides men from women, forcing women to be subservient to men from childhood, to be slave labor in the home and cheap labor in the factory. (Call it male supremacy.) And it's a system that has colonized whole nations within this country—the nation of black people, the nation of brown people—to enslave, oppress, and ultimately murder the people on whose backs this country was built. (Call it fascism.)

But the lies are catching up to America—and the slick rich people and their agents in the government bureaucracies, the courts, the schools, and the pig stations just can't cut it anymore.

Black and brown people know it.

Young people know it.

More and more white working people know it.

And you know it.

SDS Is Calling the Action This Year

But it will be a different action. An action not only against a single war or a "foreign policy," but against the whole imperialist system that made that war a necessity. An action not only for immediate withdrawal of all U.S. occupation troops, but in support of the heroic fight of the Vietnamese people and the National Liberation Front for freedom and independence. An action not only to bring "peace to Vietnam," but beginning to establish another front against imperialism right here in America—to "bring the war home."

We are demanding that all occupational troops get out of Vietnam and every other place they don't belong. This includes the black and brown communities, the workers' picket lines, the high schools, and the streets of Berkeley. No longer will we tolerate "law and order" backed up by soldiers in Vietnam and pigs in the communities and schools; a "law and order" that serves only the interests of those in power and tries to smash the people down whenever they rise up.

We are demanding the release of all political prisoners who have been victimized by the ever-growing attacks on the black liberation struggle and the people in general. Especially the leaders of the black liberation struggle like Huey P. Newton, Ahmed Evans, Fred Hampton, and Martin Sostre.

We are expressing total support for the National Liberation Front and the newly-formed Provisional Revolutionary Government of South Vietnam. Throughout the history of the war, the NLF has provided the political and military leadership to the people of South Vietnam. The Provisional Revolutionary Government, recently formed by the NLF and other groups, has pledged to "mobilize the South Vietnamese armed forces and people" in order to continue the struggle for independence. The PRG also has expressed solidarity with "the just struggle of the Afro-American people for their fundamental national rights," and has pledged to "actively support the national independence movements of Asia, Africa, and Latin America."

We are also expressing total support for the black liberation struggle, part of the same struggle that the Vietnamese are fighting, against the same enemy.

We are demanding independence for Puerto Rico, and an end to the colonial oppression that the Puerto Rican nation faces at the hands of U.S. imperialism.

We are demanding an end to the surtax, a tax taken from the working people of this country and used to kill working people in Vietnam and other places for fun and profit.

We are expressing solidarity with the Conspiracy 8 who led the struggle last summer in Chicago. Our action is planned to roughly coincide with the beginning of their trial.

And we are expressing support for GIs in Vietnam and throughout the world who are being made to fight the battles of the rich, like poor and working people have always been made to do. We support those GIs at Fort Hood, Fort Jackson, and many other army bases who have refused to be cannon fodder in a war against the people of Vietnam.

It's Almost Hard to Remember When the War Began

But, after years of peace marches, petitions, and the gradual realization that this war was no "mistake" at all, one critical fact remains: the war is not just happening in Vietnam.

It is happening in the jungles of Guatemala, Bolivia, Thailand, and all oppressed nations throughout the world.

And it is happening here. In black communities throughout the country. On college campuses. And in the high schools, in the shops, and on the streets.

It is a war in which there are only two sides; a war not for domination but for an end to domination, not for destruction, but for liberation and the unchaining of human freedom.

And it is a war in which we cannot "resist"; it is a war in which we must fight.

On October 11, tens of thousands of people will come to Chicago to bring the war home. Join us.

121. THE WEATHER UNDERGROUND

Communiqué #1
(1970)

This communiqué from **THE WEATHER UNDERGROUND** (formerly Weatherman) released on May 21, 1970, announced the group's plan to fight American imperialism sub rosa, through "strategic sabotage." It proclaimed that "Within the next fourteen days we will attack a symbol or institution of Amerikan injustice." On June 9, 1970, they took credit for bombing the New York City police headquarters. Although the group claimed responsibility for many bombings, no one was ever killed, save for three members of Weatherman who accidentally blew themselves up while making a bomb in a New York City townhouse in March 1970.

SOURCE: Harold Jacobs, ed. *Weatherman.* Berkeley, CA: Ramparts Press, Inc., 1970.

SELECTED READINGS: Ron Jacobs, *The Way the Wind Blew: A History of the Weather Underground* (1997). Jeremy Varon, *Utopia, Revolution and Violence: The Weather Underground and the Red Army Faction* (2003).

Hello. This is Bernardine Dohrn.
I'm going to read A DECLARATION OF A STATE OF WAR.
This is the first communication from the Weatherman underground.

All over the world, people fighting Amerikan imperialism look to Amerika's youth to use our strategic position behind enemy lines to join forces in the destruction of the empire.

Black people have been fighting almost alone for years. We've known that our job is to lead white kids into armed revolution. We never intended to spend the next five or twenty-five years of our lives in jail. Ever since SDS became revolutionary, we've been trying to show how it is possible to overcome the frustration and impotence that comes from trying to reform this system. Kids know the lines are drawn; revolution is touching all of our lives. Tens of thousands have learned that protest and marches don't do it. Revolutionary violence is the only way.

Now we are adapting the classic guerrilla strategy of the Viet Cong and the urban guerrilla strategy of the Tupamaros to our own situation here in the most technically advanced country in the world.

Che taught us that "revolutionaries move like fish in the sea." The alienation and contempt that young people have for this country has created the ocean for this revolution.

The hundreds and thousands of young people who demonstrated in the Sixties against the war and for civil rights grew to hundreds of thousands in the past few weeks actively fighting Nixon's invasion of Cambodia and the attempted genocide against black people. The insanity of Amerikan "justice" has added to its list of atrocities six blacks killed in Augusta, two in Jackson and four white Kent State students, making thousands more into revolutionaries.

The parents of "privileged" kids have been saying for years that the revolution was a game for us. But the war and the racism of this society show that it is too fucked-up. We will never live peaceably under this system.

This was totally true of those who died in the New York town-house explosion. The third person who was killed there was Terry Robbins, who led the first rebellion at Kent State less than two years ago.

The twelve Weathermen who were indicted for leading last October's riots in Chicago have never left the country. Terry is dead, Linda was captured by a pig informer, but the rest of us move freely in and out of every city and youth scene in this country. We're not hiding out but we're invisible.

There are several hundred members of the Weatherman underground and some of us face more years in jail than the fifty thousand deserters and draft dodgers now in Canada. Already many of them are coming back to join us in the underground or to return to the Man's army and tear it up from inside along with those who never left.

We fight in many ways. Dope is one of our weapons. The laws against marijuana mean that millions of us are outlaws long before we actually split. Guns and grass are united in the youth underground.

Freaks are revolutionaries and revolutionaries are freaks. If you want to find us, this is where we are. In every tribe, commune, dormitory, farmhouse, barracks and town-house where kids are making love, smoking dope and loading guns—fugitives from Amerikan justice are free to go.

For Diana Oughton, Ted Gold and Terry Robbins, and for all the revolutionaries who are still on the move here, there has been no question for a long time now—we will never go back.

Within the next fourteen days we will attack a symbol or institution of

Amerikan injustice. This is the way we celebrate the example of Eldridge
Cleaver and H. Rap Brown and all black revolutionaries who first inspired us
by their fight behind enemy lines for the liberation of their people.

Never again will they fight alone.

May 21, 1970

CHAPTER

TEN

Radical
Environmentalism

122. HENRY DAVID THOREAU

Walden

(1854)

HENRY DAVID THOREAU's *Walden; or Life in the Woods* is among the most influential works in American literature. Thoreau (1817–1862) was born in Concord, Massachusetts, and he attended Harvard University. In 1845 he built a cabin on the shore of Walden Pond, where he lived for two years and devoted his energies to nature and literature, and out of this experience came *Walden*, his masterpiece. Always an iconoclast, Thoreau critiqued materialism and social conformity, while idealizing individualism and nature. Accordingly, Thoreau was deeply influential to the conservation movement at the turn of the century as well as to the radical environmentalists of the 1960s and beyond.

SOURCE: Henry David Thoreau. *Walden*. London: Dent, 1854.

SELECTED READINGS: Daniel B Botkin, *No Man's Garden: Thoreau and a New Vision for Civilization* (2001). Wallace Kaufman, *Coming Out of the Woods: The Solitary Life of a Maverick Naturalist* (2000).

Every morning was a cheerful invitation to make my life of equal simplicity, and I may say innocence, with Nature herself. I have been as sincere a worshipper of Aurora as the Greeks. I got up early and bathed in the pond: that was a religious exercise, and one of the best things which I did. They say that characters were engraven on the bathing tub of king Tching-thang to this effect: 'Renew thyself completely each day; do it again, and again, and forever again.' I can understand that. Morning brings back the heroic ages. I was as much affected by the faint hum of a mosquito making its invisible and unimaginable tour through my apartment at earliest dawn, when I was sitting with door and windows open, as I could be by any trumpet that ever sang of fame. It was Homer's requiem; itself an Iliad and Odyssey in the air, singing its own wrath and wanderings. There was something cosmical about it; a standing advertisement, till forbidden, of the everlasting vigour and fertility of the world. The morning, which is the most memorable season of the day, is the awakening hour. Then there is least somnolence in us; and for an hour, at least, some part of us awakes which slumbers all the rest of the day and night. Little is to be expected of that day, if it can be called a day, to which we are not awakened by our Genius, but by the mechanical nudgings of some servitor, are not awakened by our newly acquired force and aspirations from within, accompanied by the undulations of celestial music, instead of factory bells, and a fragrance filling the air—to a higher life than we fell asleep from; and thus the darkness bear its fruit, and prove itself to be good, no less than the light. That man who does not believe that each day contains an earlier, more sacred, and auroral hour than he has yet profaned, has despaired of life, and is pursuing a descending and darkening way . . .

I went to the woods because I wished to live deliberately, to front only the essential facts of life, and see if I could not learn what it had to teach, and not, when I came to die, discover that I had not lived. I did not wish to live what was not life, living is so dear; nor did I wish to practise resignation, unless it was quite necessary. I wanted to live deep and suck out all the marrow of life. . . . Simplicity, simplicity, simplicity! I say, let your affairs be as two or three, and not a hundred or a thousand; instead of a million count half a dozen, and keep your accounts on your thumbnail. In the midst of this chopping sea of civilised life, such are the clouds and storms and quicksand and thousand-and-one items to be allowed for, that man has to live, if he would not founder and go to the bottom and not make his port at all, by dead reckoning, and he must be a great calculator indeed who succeeds. Simplify, simplify. . . .

I had long felt differently about fowling, and sold my gun before I went to the woods. Not that I am less humane than others, but I did not perceive that my feelings were much affected. I did not pity the fishes nor the worms. This was habit. As for fowling, during the last years that I carried a gun my excuse was that I was studying ornithology and sought only new or rare birds. But I confess that I am now inclined to think that there is a finer way of studying ornithology than this. . . .

Is it not a reproach that man is a carnivorous animal? True, he can and does live, in great measure, by preying on other animals; but this is a miserable way,—as any one who will go to snaring rabbits, or slaughtering lambs, may learn,—and he will be regarded as a benefactor of his race who shall teach man to confine himself to a more innocent and wholesome diet. Whatever my own practice may be, I have no doubt that it is a part of the destiny of the human race, in its gradual improvement, to leave off eating animals, as surely as the savage tribes have left off eating each other when they came into contact with the more civilised.

123. CHIEF SEATTLE

My People Are Ebbing Away Like a Fast-Receding Tide
(1855)

Although its authenticity has been questioned, **CHIEF SEATTLE**'s speech of 1855 "has become known worldwide as a treasure of indigenous American wisdom." Seattle (c. 1786–1866), also known as "Sealth," was chief of the Duwamish tribe of the Puget Sound region. He gave this speech in the 1850s while negotiating a treaty with U.S. Superintendent of Indian Affairs Isaac I. Stevens. A doctor named Henry A. Smith was present at the discussion, and he translated and took notes on the speech as it happened, although it's unclear just how proficient Smith's skills were as a translator. Smith's account of the speech was later printed in the *Seattle Sunday Star* in 1887; other versions of Chief Seattle's "ecology speech" have been revised and embellished. However, as Albert Furtwangler has remarked, in spite of lingering questions about their authenticity, these remarks are still often presented as "a symbolic encounter between indigenous America . . . and industrialized or imperialist America."

SOURCE: Chief Seattle. "Speech to Governor Isaac Stevens of the Washington Territory, 1855." As reprinted in the *Seattle Sunday Star*, October 29, 1887.

SELECTED READINGS: Albert Furtwangler, *Answering Chief Seattle* (1997). Kent Nerburn, ed., *The Wisdom of the Great Chiefs: The Classic Speeches of Chief Red Jacket, Chief Joseph, and Chief Seattle* (1994). Eva Greenslit Anderson, *Chief Seattle* (1943).

Yond[er] sky that has wep[t tears] of compassion on our fathers for centuries untold, and which, to us, looks et[erna]l, may change. Today it is fair [. tom]orrow it may be [overca]st with [clou]ds. My [words are like the] stars that never set. What Seattle says, the great chief, Washington, (The Indians in early times thought that Washington was still alive. They knew the name to be that of a president, and when they heard of the president at Washington they mistook the name of the city for the name of the reigning chief. They thought, also, that King George was still England's monarch, because the Hudson bay traders called themselves "King George men." This innocent deception the company was shrewd enough not to explain away for the Indians had more respect for them than they would have had, had they known England was ruled by a woman. Some of us have learned better.) can rely upon, with as much certainty as our pale-face brothers can rely upon the return of the seasons.

The son of the white chief says his father sends us greetings of friendship and good will. This is kind, for we know he has little need of our friendship in return, because his people are many. They are like the grass that covers the vast prairies, while my people are few, and resemble the scattering trees of a storm-swept plain.

The great, and I presume also good, white chief sends us word that he wants to buy our lands but is willing to allow us to reserve enough to to live on comfortably. This indeed appears generous, for the red man no longer has rights that he need respect, and the offer may be wise, also, for we are no longer in need of a great country.

There was a time when our people covered the whole land, as the waves of a wind-ruffled sea cover its shell-paved floor. But that time has long since passed away with the greatness of tribes now almost forgotten. I will not mourn over our untimely decay, nor reproach my pale-face brothers for hastening it, for we, too, may have been somewhat to blame.

When our young men grow angry at some real or imaginary wrong, and disfigure their faces with black paint, their hearts, also, are disfigured and turn black, and then their cruelty is relentless and knows no bounds, and our old men are not able to restrain them.

But let us hope that hostilities between the red-man and his pale-face brothers may never return. We would have everything to lose and nothing to gain.

True it is, that revenge, with our young braves, is considered gain, even at the cost of their own l[iv]es, but old men who stay at home [in] times of war, and old women, who have sons to lose, know better.

Our great father Washington, for I presume he is now our father, as well as yours, since George has moved his boundaries to the north; our great and good father, I say, sends us word by his son, who, no doubt, is a great chief among his people, that if we do as he desires, he will protect us. His brave armies will be to us a bristling wall of strength, and his great ships of war will fill our harbors so that our ancient enemies far to the northward, the Simsiams and Hydas, will no longer frighten our women and old men. Then he will be our father and we will be his children.

Your God loves your people and hates min[e]; he [folds his strong] arms [lovingly around the white man and] leads him as a father leads his infant son, but he has forsaken his red children; he makes your people wax strong every day, and soon they will fill the land; while my people are ebbing away like a fast-receding tide, that will never flow again. The white man's God cannot love his red children or he would protect them. They seem to be or-phans and can look nowhere for help. How then can we become brothers? How can your father become our father and bring us prosperity and awaken in us dreams of returning greatness?

Your God seems to us to be partial. He came to the white man. We never saw Him; never even heard His voice; He gave the white man laws but He had no word for His red children whose teeming millions filled this vast continent as the stars fill the firmament. No, we are two distinct races and must ever remain so. There is little in common between us. The ashes of our ancestors are sacred and their final resting place is hallowed ground, while you wander away from the tombs of your fathers seemingly without regret.

Your religion was written on tables of stone by the iron finger of an angry God, lest you might forget it. The red man could never remember nor com-prehend it.

Our religion is the traditions of our ancestors, the dreams of our old men, given them by the great Spirit, and the visions of our sachems, and is written in the hearts of our people.

Your dead cease to love you and the homes of their nativity as soon as they pass the portals of the tomb. They wander far off beyond the stars, are soon forgotten, and never return. Our dead never forget the beautiful world that gave them being. They still love its winding rivers, its great mountains and its sequestered vales, and they ever yearn in tenderest affection over the lonely hearted living and often return to visit and comfort them.

Day and night cannot dwell together. The red man has ever fled the ap-proach of the white man, as the changing mists on the mountain side flee before the blazing morning sun.

However, your proposition seems a just one, and I think my folks will accept it and will retire to the reservation you offer them, and we will dwell apart and in peace, for the words of the great white chief seem to be the voice of nature speaking to my people out of the thick darkness that is fast

THE RADICAL READER

gathering around them like a dense fog floating inward from a midnight sea.

It matters but little where we pass the remainder of our days.

The Indian's night promises to be dark. No bright star hovers about the horizon. Sad-voiced winds moan in the distance. Some grim Nemesis of our race is on the red man's trail, and wherever he goes he will still hear the sure approaching footsteps of the fell destroyer and prepare to meet his doom, as does the wounded doe that hears the approaching footsteps of the hunter. A few more moons, a few more winters, and not one of all the mighty hosts that once filled this broad land or that now roam in fragmentary bands through these vast solitudes will remain to weep over the tombs of a people once as powerful and hopeful as your own.

But why should we repine? Why should [I murmur at the] fate of my people? Tribes are made up of individuals and are no better than [th]ey. Men come and go like the waves of the sea. A tear, a tamanawus, a dirge, and they are gone from our longing eyes forever. Even the white man, whose God walked and talked with him, as friend to friend, is not exempt from the common destiny. We *may* be brothers after [all.] We shall see.

We will ponder your proposition, and when we have decided we will tell you. But should we accept it, I hear and now make this the first condition: That we will not be denied the privilege, without molestation, of visiting at will the graves of our ancestors and friends. Every part of this country is sacred to my people. Every hill-side, every valley, every plain and grove has been hallowed by some fond memory or some sad experience of my tribe.

Even the rocks that seem to lie dumb as they swelter in the sun along the silent seashore in solemn grandeur thrill with memories of past events connected with the fate of my people, and the very dust under your feet responds more lovingly to our footsteps than to yours, because it is the ashes of our ancestors, and our bare feet are conscious of the sympathetic touch, for the soil is rich with the life of our kindred.

The sable braves, and fond mothers, and glad-hearted maidens, and the little children who lived and rejoiced here, and whose very names are now forgotten, still love these solitudes, and their deep fastnesses at eventide grow shadowy with the presence of dusky spirits. And when the last red man shall have perished from the earth and his memory among white men shall have become a myth, these shores shall swarm with the invisible dead of my tribe, and when your children's children shall think themselves alone in the field, the store, the shop, upon the highway or in the silence of the woods they will not be alone. In all the earth there is no place dedicated to solitude. At night, when the streets of your cities and villages shall be silent, and you think them deserted, they will throng with the returning hosts that once filled and still love this beautiful land. The white man will never be alone. Let him be just and deal kindly with my people, for the dead are not altogether powerless.

124. GEORGE P. MARSH

Man and Nature

(1864)

GEORGE P. MARSH's classic book *Man and Nature* was influential to the development of organized conservationism. Marsh (1801–1882) grew up in Vermont, where he became acquainted with the natural world at a young age, and he was said to have mastered twenty languages. He was elected to Congress in 1843, where he helped found the Smithsonian Institution, and he later held several diplomatic positions. *Man and Nature* was a detailed, scientific book that drew attention to "the hostile influence of man" upon the environment and argued that proper management was needed to preserve nature's balance. As the excerpt below illustrates, Marsh built his arguments for conservation on moral as well as pragmatic grounds.

SOURCE: George P. Marsh. *Man and Nature; or Physical Geography as Modified by Human Action.* London: Sampson Low, Son and Marston, 1869.

SELECTED READINGS: David Lowenthal, *George Perkins Marsh: Prophet of Conservation* (2000). Roderick Nash, *Wilderness in the American Mind* (1967). Caroline Crane Marsh, comp., *Life and Letters of George Perkins Marsh* (1888).

Man has too long forgotten that the earth was given to him for usufruct alone, not for consumption, still less for profligate waste. Nature has provided against the absolute destruction of any of her elementary matter, the raw material of her works; the thunderbolt and the tornado, the most convulsive throes of even the volcano and the earthquake, being only phenomena of decomposition and recomposition. But she has left it within the power of man irreparably to derange the combinations of inorganic matter and of organic life, which through the night of aeons she had been proportioning and balancing, to prepare the earth for his habitation, when, in the fulness of time, his Creator should call him forth to enter into its possession.

Apart from the hostile influence of man, the organic and the inorganic world are, as I have remarked, bound together by such mutual relations and adaptations as secure, if not the absolute permanence and equilibrium of both, a long continuance of the established conditions of each at any given time and place, or at least, a very slow and gradual succession of changes in those conditions. But man is everywhere a disturbing agent. Wherever he plants his foot, the harmonies of nature are turned to discords. The proportions and accommodations which insured the stability of existing arrangements are overthrown. Indigenous vegetable and animal species are extirpated, and supplanted by others of foreign origin, spontaneous production is forbidden or restricted, and the face of the earth is either laid bare or covered with a new and reluctant growth of vegetable forms, and with alien tribes of animal life. These intentional changes and substitutions constitute, indeed, great revolutions; but vast as is their magnitude and importance, they are, as we shall see, insignificant in comparison with the contingent and unsought results which have flowed from them.

The fact that, of all organic beings, man alone is to be regarded as essentially a destructive power, and that he wields energies to resist which, nature—that nature whom all material life and all inorganic substance obey—is wholly impotent, tends to prove that, though living in physical nature, he is not of her, that he is of more exalted parentage, and belongs to a higher order of existences than those born of her womb and submissive to her dictates.

There are, indeed, brute destroyers, beasts and birds and insects of prey—all animal life feeds upon, and, of course, destroys other life,—but this destruction is balanced by compensations. It is, in fact, the very means by which the existence of one tribe of animals or of vegetables is secured against being smothered by the encroachments of another; and the reproductive powers of species, which serve as the food of others, are always proportioned to the demand they are destined to supply. Man pursues his victims with reckless destructiveness; and, while the sacrifice of life by the lower animals is limited by the cravings of appetite, he unsparingly persecutes, even to extirpation, thousands of organic forms which he cannot consume.

The earth was not, in its natural condition, completely adapted to the use of man, but only to the sustenance of wild animals and wild vegetation. These live, multiply their kind in just proportion, and attain their perfect measure of strength and beauty, without producing or requiring any change in the natural arrangements of surface, or in each other's spontaneous tendencies, except such mutual repression of excessive increase as may prevent the extirpation of one species by the encroachments of another. In short, without man, lower animal and spontaneous vegetable life would have been constant in type, distribution, and proportion, and the physical geography of the earth would have remained undisturbed for indefinite periods, and been subject to revolution only from possible, unknown cosmical causes, or from geological action.

But man, the domestic animals that serve him, the field and garden plants the products of which supply him with food and clothing, cannot subsist and rise to the full development of their higher properties, unless brute and unconscious nature be effectually combated, and, in a great degree, vanquished by human art. Hence, a certain measure of transformation of terrestrial surface, of suppression of natural, and stimulation of artificially modified productivity becomes necessary. This measure man has unfortunately exceeded. He has felled the forests whose network of fibrous roots bound the mould to the rocky skeleton of the earth; but had he allowed here and there a belt of woodland to reproduce itself by spontaneous propagation, most of the mischiefs which his reckless destruction of the natural protection of the soil has occasioned would have been averted. He has broken up the mountain reservoirs, the percolation of whose waters through unseen channels supplied the fountains that refreshed his cattle and fertilized his fields; but he has neglected to maintain the cisterns and the canals of irrigation which a wise antiquity had constructed to neutralize the consequences of its own imprudence. While he has torn the thin glebe which confined the light earth of extensive plains, and has destroyed the fringe of semi-aquatic plants which skirted the coast and checked the drifting of the sea sand, he has failed to prevent the spreading of the dunes by clothing them with artificially propagated vegetation. He has ruthlessly warred on all the tribes of animated nature whose spoil he could convert to his own uses, and he has not protected the birds which prey on the insects most destructive to his own harvests.

Purely untutored humanity, it is true, interferes comparatively little with the arrangements of nature, and the destructive agency of man becomes more and more energetic and unsparing as he advances in civilization, until the impoverishment, with which his exhaustion of the natural resources of the soil is threatening him, at last awakens him to the necessity of preserving what is left, if not of restoring what has been wantonly wasted. The wandering savage grows no cultivated vegetable, fells no forest, and extirpates no useful plant, no noxious weed. If his skill in the chase enables him to entrap numbers of the animals on which he feeds, he compensates this loss by destroying also the lion, the tiger, the wolf, the otter, the seal, and the eagle, thus indirectly protecting the feebler quadrupeds and fish and fowls, which would otherwise become the booty of beasts and birds of prey. But with stationary life, or rather with the pastoral state, man at once commences an almost indiscriminate warfare upon all the forms of animal and vegetable existence around him, and as he advances in civilization, he gradually eradicates or transforms every spontaneous product of the soil he occupies. . . .

125. JOHN MUIR

The Destruction of the Redwoods
(1901)

JOHN MUIR's essay on "The Destruction of the Redwoods" bolstered his reputation as the foremost founder of conservationism. Muir (1838–1914) was born in Scotland and he arrived in the United States in 1849. He attended the University of Wisconsin, but did not graduate; later, he spent much of his life in California. Thanks in large measure to his advocacy, the Yosemite Valley was declared a national park in 1889, earning Muir the sobriquet "Yosemite Prophet." In 1892, Muir helped found the Sierra Club, an organization that is dedicated to protecting the natural environment in the United States and throughout the world. Muir also wrote numerous popular books on nature. In this excerpt from his book *Our National Parks*, Muir rails against the commercial exploitation of forests by logging companies. (Privately, he referred to capitalism as the "gobble-gobble school of economics.") As a tribute to his activism, the Muir Woods National Monument—one of the last uncut stands of old-growth redwoods in the San Francisco Bay Area—was named in his honor.

SOURCE: John Muir. *Our National Parks*. Boston: Houghton Mifflin, 1901.

SELECTED READINGS: Thomas Wilkins, *John Muir: Apostle of Nature* (1995). Stephen R. Fox, *The American Conservation Movement: John Muir and His Legacy* (1985). Herbert F. Smith, *John Muir* (1965).

Under the timber and stone act of 1878, which might as well have been called the 'dust and ashes act', any citizen of the United States could take up one hundred and sixty acres of timber land, and by paying two dollars and a half an acre for it obtain title. There was some virtuous effort made with a view to limit the operations of the act by requiring that the purchaser should make affidavit that he was entering the land exclusively for his own use, and by

527

not allowing any association to enter more than one hundred and sixty acres. Nevertheless, under this act wealthy corporations have fraudulently obtained title to from ten thousand to twenty thousand acres or more. The plan was usually as follows. A mill company, desirous of getting title to a large body of redwood or sugar-pine land, first blurred the eyes and ears of the land agents, and then hired men to enter the land they wanted, and immediately deed it to the company after a nominal compliance with the law; false swearing in the wilderness against the government being held of no account. In one case which came under the observation of Mr. Bowers, it was the practice of a lumber company to hire the entire crew of every vessel which might happen to touch at any port in the redwood belt, to enter one hundred and sixty acres each and immediately deed the land to the company, in consideration of the company's paying all expenses and giving the jolly sailors fifty dollars apiece for their trouble.

By such methods have our magnificent redwoods and much of the sugar-pine forests of the Sierra Nevada been absorbed by foreign and resident capitalists. Uncle Sam is not often called a fool in business matters, yet he has sold millions of acres of timber land at two dollars and a half an acre on which a single tree was worth more than a hundred dollars. But this priceless land has been patented, and nothing can be done now about the crazy bargain. According to the everlasting law of righteousness, even the fraudulent buyers at less than one per cent of its value are making little or nothing, on account of fierce competition. The trees are felled, and about half of each giant is left on the ground to be converted into choice lumber and sold to citizens of the United States or to foreigners: thus robbing the country of its glory and impoverishing it without right benefit to anybody,—a bad, black business from beginning to end.

This redwood is one of the few conifers that sprout from the stump and roots, and it declares itself willing to begin immediately to repair the damage of the lumberman and also that of the forest-burner. As soon as a redwood is cut down or burned it sends up a crowd of eager, hopeful shoots, which, if allowed to grow, would in a few decades attain a height of a hundred feet, and the strongest of them would finally become giants as great as the original tree. Gigantic second and third growth trees are found in the redwoods, forming magnificent temple-like circles around charred ruins more than a thousand years old. But not one denuded acre in a hundred is allowed to raise a new forest growth. On the contrary, all the brains, religion, and superstition of the neighbourhood are brought into play to prevent a new growth. The sprouts from the roots and stumps are cut off again and again, with zealous concern as to the best time and method of making death sure. In the clearings of one of the largest mills on the coast we found thirty men at work, last summer, cutting off redwood shoots 'in the dark of the moon', claiming that all the stumps and roots cleared at this auspicious time would send up no more shoots. Anyhow, these vigorous, almost immortal trees are killed at last, and black stumps are not their only monuments over most of the chopped and burned areas.

The redwood is the glory of the Coast Range. It extends along the western slope, in a nearly continuous belt about ten miles wide, from beyond the Oregon boundary to the south of Santa Cruz, a distance of nearly four hundred miles, and in massive, substantial grandeur and closeness of growth surpasses all the other timber woods of the world. Trees from ten to fifteen feet in diameter and three hundred feet high are not uncommon, and a few attain a height of three hundred and fifty feet or even four hundred, with a diameter at the base of fifteen to twenty feet or more, while the ground beneath them is a garden of fresh, exuberant ferns, lilies, gaultheria, and rhododendron. This grand tree, Sequoia sempervirens, is surpassed in size only by its near relative, Sequoia gigantea, or Big Tree, of the Sierra Nevada, if, indeed, it is surpassed. The sempervirens is certainly the taller of the two. The gigantea attains a greater girth, and is heavier, more noble in port, and more sublimely beautiful. These two Sequoias are all that are known to exist in the world, though in former geological times the genus was common and had many species. The redwood is restricted to the Coast Range, and the Big Tree to the Sierra.

As timber the redwood is too good to live.

126. ALDO LEOPOLD

A Sand County Almanac
(1949)

ALDO LEOPOLD's *A Sand County Almanac* made him the most influential con-
servationist since John Muir. Leopold (1886–1948) was born in Burlington,
Iowa. He worked in the U.S. Forest Service, taught Wildlife Management at
the University of Wisconsin, and helped found the Wilderness Society, which
fused socialism with Muir's conservationism, proclaiming "the time has come,
with the brutalizing pressure of a spreading metropolitan civilization, to recognize the wilderness environment as a serious human need rather than a
luxury and a plaything." In 1935, Leopold bought a farm on the Wisconsin
River and built a small cabin there that he called "The Shack," where he
spent countless weekends, planting trees, hiking, and observing nature. This
helped generate material for *A Sand County Almanac*, in which he promoted
a "land ethic" that involved an understanding of humans as part of a natural
community and a greater reverence for the land and its ability to sustain all
forms of life.

SOURCE: Aldo Leopold. *A Sand County Almanac*. New York: Oxford University
Press, 1949.

SELECTED READINGS: J. Baird Callicott, ed., *In Defense of the Land Ethic: Essays
in Environmental Philosophy* (1989). J. Baird Callicott, ed., *Companion to* A Sand
County Almanac: *Interpretive and Critical Essays* (1987). Curt Meine, *Aldo Leopold: His Life and Work* (1988).

The Land Ethic

There are some who can live without wild things and some who cannot. These
essays are the delights and dilemmas of one who cannot.

Like winds and sunsets, wild things were taken for granted until progress began to do away with them. Now we face the question whether a still higher 'standard of living' is worth its cost in things natural, wild, and free. For us of the minority, the opportunity to see geese is more important than television, and the chance to find a pasque-flower is a right as inalienable as free speech.

These wild things, I admit, had little human value until mechanization assured us of a good breakfast, and until science disclosed the dram of where they come from and how they live. The whole conflict thus boils down to a question of degree. We of the minority see a law of diminishing returns in progress; our opponents do not. . . .

Conservation is getting nowhere because it is incompatible with our Abrahamic concept of land. We abuse land because we regard it as a commodity belonging to us. When we see land as a community to which we belong, we may begin to use it with love and respect. There is no other way for land to survive the impact of mechanized man, nor for us to reap from it the ethical harvest it is capable, under science, of contributing to culture. . . .

That land is a community is the basic concept of ecology, but that land is to be loved and respected is an extension of ethics. That land yields a cultural harvest is a fact long known, but latterly often forgotten. . . .

Such a view of land and people is, of course, subject to the lures and distortions of personal experience and personal bias. But wherever the truth may lie, this much is crystal-clear; our bigger-and-better society is now like a hypochondriac, so obsessed with its own economic health as to have lost the capacity to remain healthy. The whole world is so greedy for more bathtubs that it has lost the stability necessary to build them, or even to turn off the tap. Nothing could be more salutary at this stage than a little healthy contempt for a plethora of material blessings.

Perhaps such a shift of values can be achieved by reappraising things unnatural, tame, and confined in terms of things natural, wild, and free. . . .

It is inconceivable to me that an ethical relation to land can exist without love, respect, and admiration for land, and a high regard for its value. By value, I of course mean something far broader than mere economic value; I mean value in the philosophical sense.

Perhaps the most serious obstacle impeding the evolution of a land ethic is the fact that our educational and economic system is headed away from, rather than toward, an intense consciousness of land. Your true modern is separated from the land by many middlemen, and by innumerable physical gadgets. He has no vital relation to it; to him it is the space between cities on which crops grow. Turn him loose for a day on the land, and if the spot does not happen to be a golf link or 'scenic' area, he is bored stiff. If crops could be raised by hydroponics instead of farming, it would suit him very well.

Synthetic substitutes for wood, leather, wool, and other natural products suit him better than the originals. In short, land is something he has 'outgrown.'

Almost equally serious as an obstacle to a land ethic is the attitude of the farmer for whom the land is still an adversary, or a taskmaster that keeps him in slavery. Theoretically, the mechanisation of farming ought to cut the farmer's chains, but whether it really does is debatable.

One of the requisites for an ecological comprehension of land is an understanding of ecology, and this is by no means co-existensive with 'education'; in fact much higher education seems deliberately to avoid ecological concepts. An understanding of ecology does not necessarily originate in courses bearing ecological labels; it is quite as likely to be labelled geography, botany, agronomy, history, or economics. This is as it should be, but whatever the label, ecological training is scarce.

The case for a land ethic would appear hopeless but for the minority which is in obvious revolt against these 'modern' trends.

127. RACHEL CARSON

Silent Spring
(1962)

The beginning of the environmental movement of the 1960s is often dated to the publication of **RACHEL CARSON**'s *Silent Spring* in 1962. Carson (1907–1964) was born in Springfield, Pennsylvania, and she earned an M.A. in zoology from Johns Hopkins University in 1932. In 1935, she began working for the U.S. Bureau of Fisheries, and she wrote several books, including *The Sea Around Us* (1951) and *The Edge of the Sea* (1955). Carson began researching the lethal dangers of pesticides (especially DDT) after she learned that municipal aerial spraying near Boston had caused the death of neighborhood songbirds. Although *Silent Spring* provoked a fierce criticism from some industry spokesmen and government officials, the science that informed the book was later shown to be sound. *Silent Spring* became a worldwide best-seller, and it inspired further research on environmental pollution. Carson died of cancer in 1964.

SOURCE: Rachel Carson. *Silent Spring*. Boston: Houghton Mifflin Company, 1962.

The history of life on earth has been a history of interaction between living things and their surroundings. To a large extent, the physical form and the habits of the earth's vegetation and its animal life have been molded by the environment. Considering the whole span of earthly time, the opposite effect, in which life actually modifies its surroundings, has been relatively slight. Only within the moment of time represented by the present century has one species—man—acquired significant power to alter the nature of his world.

During the past quarter century this power has not only increased to one of disturbing magnitude but it has changed in character. The most alarming of all man's assaults upon the environment is the contamination of air, earth, rivers, and sea with dangerous and even lethal materials. This pollution is for the most part irrecoverable; the chain of evil it initiates not only in the world that must support life but in living tissues is for the most part irreversible. In this now universal contamination of the environment, chemicals are the sinister and little-recognized partners of radiation in changing the very nature of the world—the very nature of its life. Strontium 90, released through nuclear explosions into the air, comes to earth in rain or drifts down as fallout, lodges in soil, enters into the grass or corn or wheat grown there, and in time takes up its abode in the bones of a human being, there to remain until his death. Similarly, chemicals sprayed on croplands or forests or gardens lie long in soil, entering into living organisms, passing from one to another in a chain of poisoning and death. Or they pass mysteriously by underground streams until they emerge and, through the alchemy of air and sunlight, combine into new forms that kill vegetation, sicken cattle, and work unknown harm on those who drink from once pure wells. As Albert Schweitzer has said, "Man can hardly even recognize the devils of his own creation."

It took hundreds of millions of years to produce the life that now inhabits the earth—eons of time in which that developing and evolving and diversifying life reached a state of adjustment and balance with its surroundings. The environment, rigorously shaping and directing the life it supported, contained elements that were hostile as well as supporting. Certain rocks gave out dangerous radiation; even within the light of the sun, from which all life draws its energy, there were short-wave radiations with power to injure. Given time—time not in years but in millennia—life adjusts, and a balance has been reached. For time is the essential ingredient; but in the modern world there is no time.

The rapidity of change and the speed with which new situations are created follow the impetuous and heedless pace of man rather than the deliberate pace of nature. Radiation is no longer merely the background radiation of rocks, the bombardment of cosmic rays, the ultraviolet of the sun that have existed before there was any life on earth; radiation is now the unnatural creation of man's tampering with the atom. The chemicals to which life is asked to make its adjustment are no longer merely the calcium and silica and copper and all the rest of the minerals washed out of the rocks and carried in rivers to the sea; they are the synthetic creations of man's inventive mind, brewed in his laboratories, and having no counterparts in nature.

To adjust to these chemicals would require time on the scale that is nature's; it would require not merely the years of a man's life but the life of generations. And even this, were it by some miracle possible, would be futile, for the new chemicals come from our laboratories in an endless stream; almost five hundred annually find their way into actual use in the United States alone. The figure is staggering and its implications are not easily grasped—500 new chemicals to which the bodies of men and animals are required somehow to adapt each year, chemicals totally outside the limits of biologic experience.

Among them are many that are used in man's war against nature. Since the mid-1940's over 200 basic chemicals have been created for use in killing insects, weeds, rodents, and other organisms described in the modern vernacular as "pests"; and they are sold under several thousand different brand names.

These sprays, dusts, and aerosols are now applied almost universally to farms, gardens, forests, and homes—nonselective chemicals that have the power to kill every insect, the "good" and the "bad," to still the song of birds and the leaping of fish in the streams, to coat the leaves with a deadly film, and to linger on in soil—all this though the intended target may be only a few weeds or insects. Can anyone believe it is possible to lay down such a barrage of poisons on the surface of the earth without making it unfit for all life? They should not be called "insecticides," but "biocides."

The whole process of spraying seems caught up in an endless spiral. Since DDT was released for civilian use, a process of escalation has been going on in which ever more toxic materials must be found. This has happened because insects, in a triumphant vindication of Darwin's principle of the survival of the fittest, have evolved super races immune to the particular insecticide used, hence a deadlier one has always to be developed—and then a deadlier one than that. It has happened also because, for reasons to be described later, destructive insects often undergo a "flareback," or resurgence, after spraying, in numbers greater than before. Thus the chemical war is never won, and all life is caught in its violent crossfire.

Along with the possibility of the extinction of mankind by nuclear war, the central problem of our age has therefore become the contamination of man's total environment with such substances of incredible potential for harm—substances that accumulate in the tissues of plants and animals and even penetrate the germ cells to shatter or alter the very material of heredity upon which the shape of the future depends.

Some would-be architects of our future look toward a time when it will be possible to alter the human germ plasm by design. But we may easily be doing so now by inadvertence, for many chemicals, like radiation, bring about gene mutations. It is ironic to think that man might determine his own future by something so seemingly trivial as the choice of an insect spray.

All this has been risked—for what? Future historians may well be amazed by our distorted sense of proportion. How could intelligent beings seek to control a few unwanted species by a method that contaminated the entire environment and brought the threat of disease and death even to their own kind? Yet this is precisely what we have done. We have done it, moreover, for reasons that collapse the moment we examine them. We are told that the enormous and expanding use of pesticides is necessary to maintain farm production. Yet is our real problem not one of *overproduction?* Our farms, despite measures to remove acreages from production and to pay farmers *not* to produce, have yielded such a staggering excess of crops that the American taxpayer in 1962 is paying out more than one billion dollars a year as the total carrying cost of the *surplus-food* storage program. And is the situation helped when one branch of the Agriculture Department tries to reduce production while another states, as it did in 1958, "It is believed generally that reduction of crop acreages under provisions of the Soil Bank will stimulate interest in use of chemicals to obtain maximum production on the land retained in crops."

All this is not to say there is no insect problem and no need of control. I am saying, rather, that control must be geared to realities, not to mythical situations, and that the methods employed must be such that they do not destroy us along with the insects.

128. EDWARD ABBEY

Desert Solitaire
(1968)

EDWARD ABBEY has been called the "Thoreau of the American West." Born in the Appalachian area of Pennsylvania, Abbey (1927–1989) briefly served in the U.S. Army before attending the University of New Mexico, where he earned an M.A. in philosophy. A prodigious writer, Abbey's favorite themes were the Southwest deserts, anticapitalism, and radical environmentalism. His cult-classic novel *The Monkeywrench Gang* (1976) was about environmentalists who sabotaged developers who spoiled the landscape. Abbey also worked for many years as a part-time ranger and fire lookout for several national parks. His two seasons as a ranger at Arches National Monument (later a national park) in Utah provided the inspiration and raw material for the essay reprinted below, from his book *Desert Solitaire* (1968).

SOURCE: Edward Abbey. *Desert Solitaire: A Season in the Wilderness.* New York: McGraw-Hill, 1968.

SELECTED READINGS: James Bishop, Jr., *Epitaph for a Desert Anarchist: The Life and Legacy of Edward Abbey* (1994). Peter Quigley, *Coyote in the Maze: Tracking Edward Abbey in a World of Words* (1998). Ann Ronald, *The New West of Edward Abbey* (2000).

Industrial Tourism is a big business. It means money. It includes the motel and restaurant owners, the gasoline retailers, the oil corporations, the road-building contractors, the heavy equipment manufacturers, the state and federal engineering agencies and the sovereign, all powerful automotive industry. These various interests are well organized, command more wealth than most modern nations, and are represented in Congress with a strength far greater than is justified in any constitutional or democratic sense. (Modern politics is expensive—power follows money.) Through Congress the tourism industry can bring enormous pressure to bear upon such a slender reed in the executive branch as the poor old Park Service, a pressure which is also exerted on every other possible level—local, state, regional—and through advertising and the well-established habits of a wasteful nation.

When a new national park, national monument, national seashore, or whatever it may be called is set up, the various forces of Industrial Tourism, on all levels, immediately expect action—meaning specifically a road-building program. Where trails or primitive dirt roads already exist, the Industry expects—it hardly needs to ask—that these be developed into modern paved highways. On the local level, for example, the first thing that the superintendent of a new park can anticipate being asked, when he attends his first meeting of the area's Chamber of Commerce, is not "Will roads be built?" but rather "When does construction begin?" and "Why the delay?" . . .

Accustomed to this sort of relentless pressure since its founding, it is little wonder that the Park Service, through a process of natural selection, has tended to evolve a type of administration which, far from resisting such pressure, has usually been more than willing to accommodate it, even to encourage it. Not from any peculiar moral weakness but simply because such well-adapted administrators are themselves believers in a policy of economic development. "Resource management" is the current term. Old foot trails may be neglected, back-country ranger stations left unmanned, and interpretive and protective services inadequately staffed, but the administrators know from long experience that millions for asphalt can always be found; Congress is always willing to appropriate money for more and bigger paved roads, anywhere—particularly if they form loops. Loop drives are extremely popular with the petroleum industry—they bring the motorist right back to the same gas station from which he started.

Great though it is, however, the power of the tourist business would not in itself be sufficient to shape Park Service policy. To all accusations of excessive development the administrators can reply, as they will if pressed hard enough, that they are giving the public what it wants, that their primary duty is to serve the public not preserve the wilds. "Parks are for people" is the public-relations slogan, which decoded means that the parks are for people-in-automobiles. Behind the slogan is the assumption that the majority of Americans, exactly like the managers of the tourist industry, expect and demand to see their national parks from the comfort, security, and convenience of their automobiles.

Is this assumption correct? Perhaps. Does that justify the continued and increasing erosion of the parks? It does not. Which brings me to the final aspect of the problem of Industrial Tourism: the Industrial Tourists themselves.

They work hard, these people. They roll up incredible mileages on their odometers, rack up state after state in two-week transcontinental motor marathons, knock off one national park after another, take millions of square yards of photographs, and endure patiently the most prolonged discomforts: the tedious traffic jams, the awful food of park cafeterias and roadside eateries, the nocturnal search for a place to sleep or camp, the dreary routine of One-Stop Service, the endless lines of creeping traffic, the smell of exhaust fumes, the ever-proliferating Rules & Regulations, the fees and the bills and the service charges, the boiling radiator and the flat tire and the vapor lock, the surly retorts of room clerks and traffic cops, the incessant jostling of the anxious crowds, the irritation and restlessness of their children, the worry of their wives, and the long drive home at night in a stream of racing cars against the lights of another stream racing in the opposite direction, passing now and then the obscure tangle, the shattered glass, the patrolman's lurid blinker light, of one more wreck.

Hard work. And risky. Too much for some, who have given up the struggle on the highways in exchange for an entirely different kind of vacation—out in the open, on their own feet, following the quiet trail through forest and mountains, bedding down at evening under the stars, when and where they feel like it, at a time when the Industrial Tourists are still hunting for a place to park their automobiles.

Industrial Tourism is a threat to the national parks. But the chief victims of the system are the motorized tourists. They are being robbed and robbing themselves. So long as they are unwilling to crawl out of their cars they will not discover the treasures of the national parks and will never escape the stress and turmoil of those urban-suburban complexes which they had hoped, presumably, to leave behind for a while.

How to pry the tourists out of their automobiles, out of their back-breaking upholstered mechanized wheelchairs and onto their feet, onto the strange warmth and solidity of Mother Earth again? This is the problem which the Park Service should confront directly, not evasively, and which it cannot resolve by simply submitting and conforming to the automobile habit. The automobile, which began as a transportation convenience, has become a bloody tyrant (50,000 lives a year), and it is the responsibility of the Park Service, as well as that of everyone else concerned with preserving both wilderness and civilization, to begin a campaign of resistance. The automotive combine has almost succeeded in strangling our cities; we need not let it also destroy our national parks.

It will be objected that a constantly increasing population makes resistance and conservation a hopeless battle. This is true. Unless a way is found to stabilize the nation's population, the parks cannot be saved. Or anything else worth a damn. Wilderness preservation, like a hundred other good causes, will be forgotten under the overwhelming pressure of a struggle for mere survival and sanity in a completely urbanized, completely industrialized, ever more crowded environment. For my own part I would rather take my chances in a thermonuclear war than live in such a world.

Assuming, however, that population growth will be halted at a tolerable level before catastrophe does it for us, it remains permissible to talk about such things as the national parks. Having indulged myself in a number of harsh judgments upon the Park Service, the tourist industry, and the motoring public, I now feel entitled to make some constructive, practical, sensible proposals for the salvation of both parks and people.

(1) No more cars in national parks. Let the people walk. Or ride horses, bicycles, mules, wild pigs—anything—but keep the automobiles and the motorcycles and all their motorized relatives out. We have agreed not to drive our automobiles into cathedrals, concert halls, art museums, legislative assemblies, private bedrooms and the other sanctums of our culture; we should treat our national parks with the same deference, for they, too, are holy places. An increasingly pagan and hedonistic people (thank God!), we are learning finally that the forests and mountains and desert canyons are holier than our churches. Therefore let us behave accordingly. . . .

Excluding the automobile from the heart of the great cities has been seriously advocated by thoughtful observers of our urban problems. It seems to me an equally proper solution to the problems besetting our national parks. Of course it would be a serious blow to Industrial Tourism and would be bitterly resisted by those who profit from that industry. Exclusion of automobiles would also require a revolution in the thinking of Park Service officialdom and in the assumptions of most American tourists. But such a revolution, like it or not, is precisely what is needed. The only foreseeable alternative, given the current trend of things, is the gradual destruction of our national park system.

Let us therefore steal a slogan from the Development Fever Faction in the Park Service. The parks, they say, are for people. Very well. At the main entrance to each national park and national monument we shall erect a billboard one hundred feet high, two hundred feet wide, gorgeously filigreed in brilliant neon and outlined with blinker lights, exploding stars, flashing prayer wheels and great Byzantine phallic symbols that gush like geysers every thirty seconds. (You could set your watch by them.) Behind the fireworks will loom the figure of Smokey the Bear, taller than a pine tree, with eyes in his head that swivel back and forth, watching YOU, and ears that actually twitch. Push a button and Smokey will recite, for the benefit of children and government officials who might otherwise have trouble with some of the big words, in a voice ursine, loud and clear, the message spelled out on the face of the billboard. To wit:

HOWDY FOLKS, WELCOME. THIS IS **YOUR** NATIONAL PARK, ESTABLISHED FOR THE PLEASURE OF YOU AND ALL PEOPLE EVERYWHERE. PARK YOUR CAR, JEEP, TRUCK, TANK, MOTORBIKE, MOTORBOAT, JETBOAT, AIRBOAT, SUBMARINE, AIRPLANE, JET-PLANE, HELICOPTER, HOVERCRAFT, WINGED MOTORCYCLE, ROCKETSHIP, OR ANY OTHER CONCEIVABLE TYPE OF MOTORIZED VEHICLE IN THE WORLD'S BIGGEST PARKING LOT BEHIND THE COMFORT STATION IMMEDIATELY TO YOUR REAR. GET OUT OF YOUR MOTORIZED VEHICLE, GET ON YOUR HORSE, MULE, BICYCLE OR FEET, AND COME ON IN.

ENJOY YOURSELVES. THIS HERE PARK IS FOR <u>PEOPLE</u>.

129. CÉSAR CHÁVEZ

Letter From Delano
(1969)

In his famous "Letter From Delano," **CÉSAR CHÁVEZ** explained the United
Farm Workers' (UFW) grievances against the "agribusiness" system that kept
workers in poverty and forced them to toil amidst toxic poisons in vineyards.
Chávez (1927–1993) was born near Yuma, Arizona, and was a migrant
worker for many years before he became a full-time organizer. He served as
general director of the Community Service Organization (CSO) in California
from 1958 to 1962, and in 1966 he helped create the UFW. With a variety
of nonviolent tactics, including strikes, fasts, picketing, and marches, Chávez
won many labor victories, including an important one against American
table-grape growers in 1970. Modeled in part upon Martin Luther King, Jr.'s
"Letter From A Birmingham Jail," Chávez's "Letter from Delano" was originally published in *Christian Century* magazine, and it drew national attention
to the dreadful working conditions on many American farms.

SOURCE: César Chávez. "Letter from Delano." *Christian Century*. April 23,
1969.

SELECTED READINGS: Susan Ferriss, *The Fight in the Fields: César Chávez and the
Farmworkers Movement* (1997). Richard Griswold del Castillo, *César Chávez: A
Triumph of Spirit* (1995). John Gregory Dunne, *Delano: The Story of the Cali-
fornia Grape Strike* (1967).

"We are not Beasts of Burden . . . we are Men"

Dear Mr. Barr [President, California Grape and Tree Fruit League]:
I am sad to hear about your accusations in the press that our union movement and table grape boycott have been successful because we have used
violence and terror tactics. If what you say is true, I have been a failure and
should withdraw from the struggle; but you are left with the awesome moral

responsibility, before God and man, to come forward with whatever information you have so that corrective action can begin at once. If for any reason you fail to come forth to substantiate your charges, then you must be held responsible for committing violence against us, albeit violence of the tongue. I am convinced that you as a human being did not mean what you said but rather acted hastily under pressure from the public relations firm that has been hired to try to counteract the tremendous moral force of our movement. How many times we ourselves have felt the need to lash out in anger and bitterness.

Today on Good Friday 1969 we remember the life and the sacrifice of Martin Luther King, Jr., who gave himself totally to the nonviolent struggle for peace and justice. In his "Letter from Birmingham Jail" Dr. King describes better than I could our hopes for the strike and boycott: "Injustice must be exposed, with all the tension its exposure creates, to the light of human conscience and the air of national opinion before it can be cured." For our part I admit that we have seized upon every tactic and strategy consistent with the morality of our cause to expose that injustice and thus to heighten the sensitivity of the American conscience so that farm workers will have without bloodshed their own union and the dignity of bargaining with their agribusiness employers. By lying about the nature of our movement, Mr. Barr, you are working against nonviolent social change. Unwittingly perhaps, you may unleash that other force which our union by discipline and deed, censure and education has sought to avoid, that panacean shortcut: that senseless violence which honors no color, class or neighborhood.

You must understand—I must make you understand—that our membership and the hopes and aspirations of the hundreds of thousands of the poor and dispossessed that have been raised on our account are, above all, human beings, no better and no worse than any other cross-section of human society; we are not saints because we are poor, but by the same measure neither are we immoral. We are men and women who have suffered and endured much, and not only because of our object poverty but because we have been kept poor. The colors of our skins, the languages of our cultural and native origins, the lack of formal education, the exclusion from the democratic process, the numbers of our slain in recent wars—all these burdens generation after generation have sought to demoralize us, to break our human spirit. But God knows that we are not beasts of burden, agricultural implements or rented slaves; we are men. And mark this well, Mr. Barr, we are men locked in a death struggle against man's inhumanity to man in the industry that you represent. And this struggle itself gives meaning to our life and ennobles our dying.

As your industry has experienced, our strikers here in Delano and those who represent us throughout the world are well trained for this struggle. They have been under the gun, they have been kicked and beaten and herded by dogs, they have been cursed and ridiculed, they have been stripped and chained and jailed, they have been sprayed with the poisons used in the vineyards; but they have been taught not to lie down and die nor to flee in shame, but to resist with every ounce of human endurance and spirit. To resist not with retaliation in kind but to overcome with love and compassion, with ingenuity and creativity, with hard work and longer hours, with stamina and patient tenacity, with truth and public appeal, with friends and allies, with mobility and discipline, with politics and law, and with prayer and fasting. They were not trained in a month or even a year; after all, this new harvest season will mark our fourth full year of strike and even now we continue to plan and prepare for the years to come. Time accomplishes for the poor what money does for the rich.

This is not to pretend that we have everywhere been successful enough or that we have not made mistakes. And while we do not belittle or underestimate our adversaries—for they are the rich and the powerful and they possess the land—we are not afraid nor do we cringe from the confrontation. We welcome it! We have planned for it. We know that our cause is just, that history is a story of social revolution, and that the poor shall inherit the land.

Once again, I appeal to you as the representative of your industry and as a man. I ask you to recognize and bargain with our union before the economic pressure of the boycott and strike takes an irrevocable toll; but if not, I ask you to at least sit down with us to discuss the safeguards necessary to keep our historical struggle free of violence. I make this appeal because as one of the leaders of our nonviolent movement, I know and accept my responsibility for preventing, if possible, the destruction of human life and property. For these reasons and knowing of Gandhi's admonition that fasting is the last resort in place of the sword, during a most critical time in our movement last February 1968 I undertook a 25-day fast. I repeat to you the principle enunciated to the membership at the start of the fast: if to build our union required the deliberate taking of life, either the life of a grower or his child, or the life of a farm worker or his child, then I choose not to see the union built.

Mr. Barr, let me be painfully honest with you. You must understand these things. We advocate militant nonviolence as our means for social revolution and to achieve justice for our people, but we are not blind or deaf to the desperate and moody winds of human frustration, impatience and rage that blow among us. Gandhi himself admitted that if his only choice were cowardice or violence, he would choose violence. Men are not angels, and time and tide wait for no man. Precisely because of these powerful human emotions, we have tried to involve masses of people in their own struggle. Participation and self-determination remain the best experience of freedom, and free men instinctively prefer democratic change and even protect the rights guaranteed to seek it. Only the enslaved in despair have need of violent over-throw.

This letter does not express all that is in my heart, Mr. Barr. But if it says nothing else it says that we do not hate you or rejoice to see your industry destroyed; we hate the agribusiness system that seeks to keep us enslaved, and we shall overcome and change it not by retaliation or bloodshed but by a determined nonviolent struggle carried on by those masses of farm workers who intend to be free and human.

130. BARRY COMMONER

The Closing Circle
(1971)

BARRY COMMONER has been hailed in *Time* magazine as the "Paul Revere of Ecology." Commoner (1917–) earned his Ph.D. from Harvard and joined the faculty of the University of Washington in St. Louis in 1947. A scientific activist, Commoner has tried to reach a lay audience, and he has been involved in several environmentalist campaigns. In 1980 he ran for president as the Citizens Party candidate. His most famous work, the socialist-tinged *The Closing Circle* (1971), raised the alarm that different economic, social, and political forces in highly industrialized societies had broken "the circle," or ecosphere, which maintains a delicate balance of life on the planet.

SOURCE: Barry Commoner. *The Closing Circle: Nature, Man, and Technology.* Knopf: New York, 1971.

SELECTED READINGS: David Kriebel, ed., with the assistance of Mary Lee Dunn, *Barry Commoner's Contribution to the Environmental Movement: Science and Social Action* (2002). Barry Commoner, *Making Peace with the Planet* (1990). Barry Commoner, *The Closing Circle: Nature, Man, and Technology* (1971).

The environment has just been rediscovered by the people who live in it. In the United States the event was celebrated in April 1970, during Earth Week. It was a sudden, noisy awakening. School children cleaned up rubbish; college students organized huge demonstrations; determined citizens recaptured the streets from the automobile, at least for a day. Everyone seemed to be aroused to the environmental danger and eager to do something about it.

They were offered lots of advice. Almost every writer, almost every speaker, on the college campuses, in the streets and on television and radio broadcasts, was ready to fix the blame and pronounce a cure for the environmental crisis. . . .

We have met the enemy and he is us. —Pogo.

Earth Week and the accompanying outburst of publicity, preaching, and prognostication surprised most people, including those of us who had worked for years to generate public recognition of the environmental crisis. What surprised me most were the numerous, confident explanations of the cause and cure of the crisis. For having spent some years in the effort simply to detect and describe the growing list of environmental problems—radioactive fallout, air and water pollution, the deterioration of the soil—and in tracing some of their links to social and political processes, the identification of a single cause and cure seemed a rather bold step. During Earth Week, I discovered that such reticence was far behind the times.

After the excitement of Earth Week, I tried to find some meaning in the welter of contradictory advice that it produced. It seemed to me that the confusion of Earth Week was a sign that the situation was so complex and ambiguous that people could read into it whatever conclusion their own beliefs—about human nature, economics, and politics—suggested. Like a Rorschach ink blot, Earth Week mirrored personal convictions more than objective knowledge.

Earth Week convinced me of the urgency of a deeper public understanding of the origins of the environmental crisis and its possible cures. That is what this book is about. It is an effort to find out what the environmental crisis *means*.

Such an understanding must begin at the source of life itself: the earth's thin skin of air, water, and soil, and the radiant solar fire that bathes it. Here, several billion years ago, life appeared and was nourished by the earth's substance. As it grew, life evolved, its old forms transforming the earth's skin and new ones adapting to these changes. Living things multiplied in number, variety, and habitat until they formed a global network, becoming deftly enmeshed in the surroundings they had themselves created. This is the *ecosphere*, the home that life has built for itself on the planet's outer surface.

Any living thing that hopes to live on the earth must fit into the ecosphere or perish. The environmental crisis is a sign that the finely sculptured fit between life and its surroundings has begun to corrode. As the links between one living thing and another, and between all of them and their surroundings, begin to break down, the dynamic interactions that sustain the whole have begun to falter and, in some places, stop.

Why, after millions of years of harmonious co-existence, have the relationships between living things and their earthly surroundings begun to collapse? Where did the fabric of the ecosphere begin to unravel? How far will the process go? How can we stop it and restore the broken links?

Understanding the ecosphere comes hard because, to the modern mind, it is a curiously foreign place. We have become accustomed to think of separate, singular events, each dependent upon a unique, singular cause. But in the ecosphere every effect is also a cause: an animal's waste becomes food for soil bacteria; what bacteria excrete nourishes plants; animals eat the plants. Such ecological cycles are hard to fit into human experience in the age of technology, where machine A always yields product B, and product B, once used, is cast away, having no further meaning for the machine, the product, or the user.

Here is the first great fault in the life of man in the ecosphere. We have broken out of the circle of life, converting its endless cycles into man-made, linear events: oil is taken from the ground, distilled into fuel, burned in an engine, converted thereby into noxious fumes, which are emitted into the air. At the end of the line is smog. Other man-made breaks in the ecosphere's cycles spew out toxic chemicals, sewage, heaps of rubbish—testimony to our power to tear the ecological fabric that has, for millions of years, sustained the planet's life.

Suddenly we have discovered what we should have known long before: that the ecosphere sustains people and everything that they do; that anything that fails to fit into the ecosphere is a threat to its finely balanced cycles; that wastes are not only unpleasant, not only toxic, but, more meaningfully, evidence that the ecosphere is being driven towards collapse.

If we are to survive, we must understand *why* this collapse now threatens. Here, the issues become far more complex than even the ecosphere. Our assaults on the ecosystem are so powerful, so numerous, so finely interconnected, that although the damage they do is clear, it is very difficult to discover how it was done. By which weapon? In whose hand? Are we driving the ecosphere to destruction simply by our growing numbers? By our greedy accumulation of wealth? Or are the machines which we have built to gain this wealth—the magnificent technology that now feeds us out of neat packages, that clothes us in man-made fibers, that surrounds us with new chemical creations—at fault? . . .

In broad outline, these are the environmental cycles which govern the behavior of the three great global systems: the air, the water, and the soil. Within each of them live many thousands of different species of living things. Each species is suited to its particular environmental niche, and each, through its life processes, affects the physical and chemical properties of its immediate environment.

Each living species is also linked to many others. These links are bewildering in their variety and marvelous in their intricate detail. An animal, such as a deer, may depend on plants for food; the plants depend on the action of soil bacteria for their nutrients; the bacteria in turn live on the organic wastes dropped by the animals on the soil. At the same time, the deer is food for the mountain lion. Insects may live on the juices of plants or gather pollen from their flowers. Other insects suck blood from animals. Bacteria may live on the internal tissues of animals and plants. Fungi degrade the bodies of dead plants and animals. All this, many times multiplied and organized species by species in intricate, precise relationships, makes up the vast network of life on the earth.

The science that studies these relationships and the processes linking each living thing to the physical and chemical environment is *ecology*. It is the science of planetary housekeeping. For the environment is, so to speak, the house created on the earth *by* living things *for* living things. It is a young science and much of what it teaches has been learned from only small segments of the whole network of life on the earth. Ecology has not yet explicitly developed the kind of cohesive, simplifying generalizations exemplified by, say, the laws of physics. Nevertheless there are a number of generalizations that are already evident in what we now know about the ecosphere and that can be organized into a kind of informal set of "laws of ecology." These are described in what follows.

The First Law of Ecology: Everything Is Connected to Everything Else

Some of the evidence that leads to this generalization has already been discussed. It reflects the existence of the elaborate network of interconnections in the ecosphere: among different living organisms, and between populations, species, and individual organisms and their physico-chemical surroundings.

The single fact that an ecosystem consists of multiple interconnected parts, which act on one another, has some surprising consequences. Our ability to picture the behavior of such systems has been helped considerably by the development, even *more* recent than ecology, of the science of cybernetics. . . .

The Second Law of Ecology: Everything Must Go Somewhere

This is, of course, simply a somewhat informal restatement of a basic law of physics—that matter is indestructible. Applied to ecology, the law emphasizes that in nature there is no such thing as "waste." In every natural system, what is excreted by one organism as waste is taken up by another as food. Animals release carbon dioxide as a respiratory waste; this is an essential nutrient for green plants. Plants excrete oxygen, which is used by animals. Animal organic wastes nourish the bacteria of decay. Their wastes, inorganic materials such as nitrate, phosphate, and carbon dioxide, become algal nutrients. . . .

The Third Law of Ecology: Nature Knows Best

In my experience this principle is likely to encounter considerable resistance, for it appears to contradict a deeply held idea about the unique competence of human beings. One of the most pervasive features of modern technology is the notion that it is intended to "improve on nature"—to provide food, clothing, shelter, and means of communication and expression which are superior to those available to man in nature. Stated baldly, the third law of ecology holds that any major man-made change in a natural system is likely to be *detrimental* to that system. This is a rather extreme claim; nevertheless I believe it has a good deal of merit if understood in a properly defined context. . . .

The Fourth Law of Ecology: There Is No Such Thing as a Free Lunch

In my experience, this idea has proven so illuminating for environmental problems that I have borrowed it from its original source, economics. The "law" derives from a story that economists like to tell about an oil-rich potentate who decided that his new wealth needed the guidance of economic science. Accordingly he ordered his advisers, on pain of death, to produce a set of volumes containing all the wisdom of economics. When the tomes arrived, the potentate was impatient and again issued an order—to reduce all the knowledge of economics to a single volume. The story goes on in this vein, as such stories will, until the advisers are required, if they are to survive, to reduce the totality of economic science to a single sentence. This is the origin of the "free lunch" law.

In ecology, as in economics, the law is intended to warn that every gain is won at some cost. In a way, this ecological law embodies the previous three laws. Because the global ecosystem is a connected whole, in which nothing can be gained or lost and which is not subject to over-all improvement, anything extracted from it by human effort must be replaced. Payment of this price cannot be avoided; it can only be delayed. The present environmental crisis is a warning that we have delayed nearly too long.

131. PETER SINGER

Animal Liberation
(1975)

PETER SINGER's *Animal Liberation* (1975) has been called "the Bible of the Animal Liberation movement," and even today it continues to serve as this movement's intellectual bedrock. Singer (1946–) was born in Melbourne, Australia, and was educated at the University of Melbourne and Oxford. He has taught at Oxford, New York University, and Princeton University. Singer's work focuses on ethical issues, and has long been controversial. In *Animal Liberation*, Singer wrote about "speciesm," the practice whereby most humans "sacrifice the most important interests of members of other species in order to promote the most trivial interests of our own species." His work promoted vegetarianism and helped inspire a global movement against "factory farms," as well as unnecessarily cruel laboratory animal experimentation and product-testing procedures. Reprinted below is the preface to *Animal Liberation*.

SOURCE: Peter Singer, *Animal Liberation*. New York: Avon Books, 1975.

SELECTED READINGS: Gary L. Francione, *Rain Without Thunder: The Ideology of the Animal Rights Movement*, (1996). Dale Jamieson, ed., *Singer and His Critics* (1999). Tom Regan, *All That Dwell Therein: Animal Rights and Environmental Ethics* (1982).

A liberation movement demands an expansion of our moral horizons. Practices that were previously regarded as natural and inevitable come to be seen as the result of an unjustifiable prejudice. Who can say with any confidence that none of his or her attitudes and practices can legitimately be questioned? If we wish to avoid being numbered among the oppressors, we must be prepared to rethink all our attitudes to other groups, including the most fundamental of them. We need to consider our attitudes from the point of view of those who suffer by them, and by the practices that follow from them. If we can make this unaccustomed mental switch we may discover a pattern in our attitudes and practices that operates so as consistently to benefit the same group—usually the group to which we ourselves belong—at the expense of another group. So we come to see that there is a case for a new liberation movement.

The aim of this book is to lead you to make this mental switch in your attitudes and practices toward a very large group of beings: members of species other than our own. I believe that our present attitudes to these beings are based on a long history of prejudice and arbitrary discrimination. I argue that there can be no reason—except the selfish desire to preserve the privileges of the exploiting group—for refusing to extend the basic principle of equality of consideration to members of other species. I ask you to recognize that your attitudes to members of other species are a form of prejudice no less objectionable than prejudice about a person's race or sex.

In comparison with other liberation movements, Animal Liberation has a lot of handicaps. First and most obvious is the fact that members of the exploited group cannot themselves make an organized protest against the treatment they receive (though they can and do protest to the best of their abilities individually). We have to speak up on behalf of those who cannot speak for themselves. You can appreciate how serious this handicap is by asking yourself how long blacks would have had to wait for equal rights if they had not been able to stand up for themselves and demand it. The less able a group is to stand up and organize against oppression, the more easily it is oppressed.

More significant still for the prospects of the Animal Liberation movement is the fact that almost all of the oppressing group are directly involved in, and see themselves as benefiting from, the oppression. There are few humans indeed who can view the oppression of animals with the detachment possessed, say, by Northern whites debating the institution of slavery in the Southern states of the Union. People who eat pieces of slaughtered nonhumans every day find it hard to believe that they are doing wrong; and they also find it hard to imagine what else they could eat. On this issue, anyone who eats meat is an interested party. They benefit—or at least they think they benefit—from the present disregard of the interests of nonhuman animals. This makes persuasion more difficult. How many Southern slaveholders were persuaded by the arguments used by the Northern abolitionists, and accepted by nearly all of us today? Some, but not many. I can and do ask you to put aside your interest in eating meat when considering the arguments of this book; but I know from my own experience that with the best will in the world this is not an easy thing to do. For behind the mere momentary desire to eat meat on a particular occasion lie many years of habitual meat-eating which have conditioned our attitudes to animals.

Habit. That is the final barrier that the Animal Liberation movement faces.

Habits not only of diet but also of thought and language must be challenged and altered. Habits of thought lead us to brush aside descriptions of cruelty to animals as emotional, for "animal-lovers only"; or if not that, then anyway the problem is so trivial in comparison to the problems of human beings that no sensible person could give it time and attention. This too is a prejudice—for how can one know that a problem is trivial until one has taken the time to examine its extent? Although in order to allow a more thorough treatment this book deals with only two of the many areas in which humans cause other animals to suffer, I do not think anyone who reads it to the end will ever again think that the only problems that merit time and energy are problems concerning humans.

The habits of thought that lead us to disregard the interests of animals can be challenged, as they are challenged in the following pages. This challenge has to be expressed in a language, which in this case happens to be English. The English language, like other languages, reflects the prejudices of its users. So authors who wish to challenge these prejudices are in a well-known type of bind: either they use language that reinforces the very prejudices they wish to challenge, or else they fail to communicate with their audience. This book has already been forced along the former of these paths. We commonly use the word "animal" to mean "animals other than human beings." This usage sets humans apart from other animals, implying that we are not ourselves animals—an implication that everyone who has had elementary lessons in biology knows to be false.

In the popular mind the term "animal" lumps together beings as different as oysters and chimpanzees, while placing a gulf between chimpanzees and humans, although our relationship to those apes is much closer than the oyster's. Since there exists no other short term for the nonhuman animals, I have, in the title of this book and elsewhere in these pages, had to use "animal" as if it did not include the human animal. This is a regrettable lapse from the standards of revolutionary purity but it seems necessary for effective communication. Occasionally, however, to remind you that this is a matter of convenience only, I shall use longer, more accurate modes of referring to what was once called "the brute creation." In other cases, too, I have tried to avoid language which tends to degrade animals or disguise the nature of the food we eat.

The basic principles of Animal Liberation are very simple. I have tried to write a book that is clear and easy to understand, requiring no expertise of any kind. It is necessary, however, to begin with a discussion of the principles that underlie what I have to say. While there should be nothing here that is difficult, readers unused to this kind of discussion might find the first chapter rather abstract. Don't be put off. In the next chapters we get down to the little-known details of how our species oppresses others under our control.

There is nothing abstract about this oppression, or about the chapters that describe it.

If the recommendations made in the following chapters are accepted, millions of animals will be spared considerable pain. Moreover, millions of humans will benefit too. As I write, people are starving to death in many parts of the world; and many more are in imminent danger of starvation. The United States government has said that because of poor harvests and diminished stocks of grain it can provide only limited—and inadequate—assistance; but the heavy emphasis in affluent nations on rearing animals for food wastes several times as much food as it produces. By ceasing to rear and kill animals for food, we can make so much extra food available for humans that, properly distributed, it would eliminate starvation and malnutrition from this planet. Animal Liberation is Human Liberation too.

132. DAVE FOREMAN

Strategic Monkeywrenching

(1985)

DAVE FOREMAN was once a leading proponent of "monkeywrenching," defined as sabotage against machinery in defense of the environment. As a youngster, Foreman (1947–) was a national leader of Young Americans for Freedom (YAF), a conservative organization. However, he was later inspired by Edward Abbey's cult-classic *The Monkeywrench Gang* to form Earth First!, in 1980. Today, Earth First! is in the vanguard of the radical environmental movement. Earth First!'s motto is "No Compromise in Defense of Mother Earth!" Members put this motto into action with a variety of controversial tactics, including the "spiking" of trees so that they cannot be safely cut down. Foreman's 1985 book *Ecodefense* (coauthored with Bill Haywood) exemplified the militance, creativity, humor, and guerrilla tactics of Earth First! However, Foreman has since renounced the tactic of monkeywrenching.

SOURCE: Dave Foreman and Bill Haywood, eds. *Ecodefense: A Field Guide to Monkeywrenching.* Tucson: Ned Ludd Books, 1985.

SELECTED READINGS: Edward Abbey, *The Monkeywrench Gang* (1975). Dave Foreman, *Confessions of an Eco-Warrior* (1991). Derek Wall, *Earth First! and the Anti-Roads Movement: Radical Environmentalism and Comparative Social Movements* (1999).

Many of the projects that will destroy roadless areas are economically marginal. It is costly for the Forest Service, BLM, timber companies, oil companies, mining companies and others to scratch out the "resources" in these last wild areas. It is expensive to maintain the necessary infrastructure of roads for the exploitation of wild lands. The cost of repairs, the hassle, the delay, the downtime may just be too much for the bureaucrats and exploiters to accept if there is a widely-dispersed, unorganized, *strategic* movement of resistance across the land.

It is time for women and men, individually and in small groups, to act heroically and admittedly illegally in defense of the wild, to put a monkeywrench into the gears of the machine destroying natural diversity. This strategic monkeywrenching can be safe, it can be easy, it can be fun, and—most importantly—it can be effective in stopping timber cutting, road building, overgrazing, oil & gas exploration, mining, dam building, powerline construction, off-road-vehicle use, trapping, ski area development and other forms of destruction of the wilderness, as well as cancerous suburban sprawl.

But it must be strategic, it must be thoughtful, it must be deliberate in order to succeed. Such a campaign of resistance would follow these principles:

Monkeywrenching Is Non-Violent

Monkeywrenching is non-violent resistance to the destruction of natural diversity and wilderness. It Is Not directed toward harming human beings or other forms of life. It is aimed at inanimate machines and tools. Care is always taken to minimize any possible threat to other people (and to the monkeywrenchers themselves). . . .

Monkeywrenching Is Not Revolutionary

It does *not* aim to overthrow any social, political or economic system. It is merely non-violent self-defense of the wild. It is aimed at keeping industrial "civilization" out of natural areas and causing its retreat from areas that should be wild. It is not major industrial sabotage. Explosives, firearms and other dangerous tools are usually avoided. They invite greater scrutiny from law enforcement agencies, repression and loss of public support. (The Direct Action group in Canada is a good example of what monkeywrenching is *not*.) Even Republicans monkeywrench.

Monkeywrenching Is Simple

The simplest possible tool is used. The safest tactic is employed. Except when necessary, elaborate commando operations are avoided. The most effective means for stopping the destruction of the wild are generally the simplest: spiking trees and spiking roads. There are obviously times when more detailed and complicated operations are called for. But the monkeywrencher thinks: What is the simplest way to do this?

Monkeywrenching Is Deliberate and Ethical

Monkeywrenching is not something to do cavalierly. Monkeywrenchers are very conscious of the gravity of what they do. They are deliberate about taking such a serious step. They are thoughtful. Monkeywrenchers—although non-violent—are warriors. They are exposing themselves to possible arrest or injury. It is not a casual or flippant affair. They keep a pure heart and mind about it. They remember that they are engaged in the most moral of all actions: protecting life, defending the Earth.

A movement based on these principles could protect millions of acres of wilderness more stringently than any Congressional act, could insure the propagation of the grizzly and other threatened life forms better than an army of game wardens, and could lead to the retreat of industrial civilization from large areas of forest, mountain, desert, plain, seashore, swamp, tundra and woodland that are better suited to the maintenance of natural diversity than to the production of raw materials for overconsumptive technological human society.

If loggers know that a timber sale is spiked, they won't bid on the timber. If a Forest Supervisor knows that a road will be continually destroyed, he won't try to build it. If seismographers know that they will be constantly harassed in an area, they'll go elsewhere. If ORVers know that they'll get flat tires miles from nowhere, they won't drive in such areas.

John Muir said that if it ever came to a war between the races, he would side with the bears. That day has arrived.

133. ROBERT BULLARD

Environmental Racism and the
Environmental Justice Movement
(1993)

ROBERT BULLARD has been lauded for being "on the cutting edge of the environmental justice movement in America," which protests the fact that in the United States, less affluent minority groups are often put at greater health and environmental risks than the general population. Bullard (1946–) is Ware Professor of Sociology and head of the Environmental Justice Center at Clark Atlanta University. His book *Dumping in Dixie* (1991) has become a standard text on the topic of environmental racism. In the following excerpt, Bullard discusses the environmental hazards that poor communities face, and analyzes the failure of mainstream environmental organizations to address this problem.

SOURCE: Robert D. Bullard. *Confronting Environmental Racism: Voices from the Grassroots*. Boston: South End Press, 1993.

SELECTED READINGS: Luke W. Cole, *From the Ground Up: Environmental Racism and the Rise of the Environmental Justice Movement* (2001). Laura Westra and Bill E. Lawson, *Faces of Environmental Racism: Confronting Issues of Global Justice* (2001). Robert D. Bullard, *Dumping in Dixie: Race, Class, and Environmental Quality* (1990).

Racism plays a key factor in environmental planning and decisionmaking. Indeed, environmental racism is reinforced by government, legal, economic, political, and military institutions. It is a fact of life in the United States that the mainstream environmental movement is only beginning to wake up to. Yet, without a doubt, racism influences the likelihood of exposure to environmental and health risks and the accessibility to health care. Racism provides whites of all class levels with an "edge" in gaining access to a healthy physical environment. This has been documented again and again.

Whether by conscious design or institutional neglect, communities of color in urban ghettos, in rural "poverty pockets," or on economically impoverished Native-American reservations face some of the worst environmental devastation in the nation. Clearly, racial discrimination was not legislated out of existence in the 1960s. While some significant progress was made during this decade, people of color continue to struggle for equal treatment in many areas, including environmental justice. Agencies at all levels of government, including the federal EPA, have done a poor job protecting people of color from the ravages of pollution and industrial encroachment. It has thus been an up-hill battle convincing white judges, juries, government officials, and policymakers that racism exists in environmental protection, enforcement, and policy formulation.

The most polluted urban communities are those with crumbling infrastructure, ongoing economic disinvestment, deteriorating housing, inadequate schools, chronic unemployment, a high poverty rate, and an overloaded health-care system. Riot-torn South Central Los Angeles typifies this urban neglect. It is not surprising that the "dirtiest" zip code in California belongs to the mostly African-American and Latino neighborhood in that part of the city (Kay 1991a). In the Los Angeles basin, over 71 percent of the African Americans and 50 percent of the Latinos live in areas with the most polluted air, while only 34 percent of the white population does (Ong and Blumenberg 1990; Mann 1991). This pattern exists nationally as well. As researchers Wernette and Nieves note:

> In 1990, 437 of the 3,109 counties and independent cities failed to meet at least one of the EPA ambient air quality standards . . . 57 percent of whites, 65 percent of African Americans, and 80 percent of Hispanics live in 437 counties with substandard air quality. Out of the whole population, a total of 33 percent of whites, 50 percent of African Americans, and 60 percent of Hispanics live in the 136 counties in which two or more air pollutants exceed standards. The percentage living in the 29 counties designated as nonattainment areas for three or more pollutants are 12 percent of whites, 20 percent of African Americans, and 31 percent of Hispanics (pp. 16–17).

Income alone does not account for these above-average percentages. Housing segregation and development patterns play a key role in determining where people live. Moreover, urban development and the "spatial configuration" of communities flow from the forces and relationships of industrial production which, in turn, are influenced and subsidized by government policy (Feagin 1988; Gottdiener 1988). There is widespread agreement that vestiges of race-based decisionmaking still influence housing, education, employment, and criminal justice. The same is true for municipal services such as garbage pickup and disposal, neighborhood sanitation, fire and police protection, and library services. Institutional racism influences decisions on local land use, enforcement of environmental regulations, industrial facility siting, management of economic vulnerability, and the paths of freeways and highways.

People skeptical of the assertion that poor people and people of color are targeted for waste-disposal sites should consider the report the Cerrell Associates provided the California Waste Management Board. In their 1984 report, *Political Difficulties Facing Waste-to-Energy Conversion Plant Siting*, they offered a detailed profile of those neighborhoods most likely to organize effective resistance against incinerators. The policy conclusion based on this analysis is clear. As the report states:

> All socioeconomic groupings tend to resent the nearby siting of major facilities, but middle and upper socioeconomic strata possess better resources to effectuate their opposition. Middle and higher socioeconomic strata neighborhoods should not fall within the one-mile and five-mile radius of the proposed site (p. 43).

Where then will incinerators or other polluting facilities be sited? For Cerrell Associates, the answer is low-income, disempowered neighborhoods with a high concentration of nonvoters. The ideal site, according their report, has nothing to do with environmental soundness but everything to do with lack of social power. Communities of color in California are far more likely to fit this profile than are their white counterparts.

Those still skeptical of the existence of environmental racism should also consider the fact that zoning boards and planning commissions are typically stacked with white developers. Generally, the decisions of these bodies reflect the special interests of the individuals who sit on these boards. People of color have been systematically excluded from these decisionmaking boards, commissions, and governmental agencies (or allowed only token representation). Grassroots leaders are now demanding a shared role in all the decisions that shape their communities. They are challenging the intended or unintended racist assumptions underlying environmental and industrial policies. . . .

CHAPTER ELEVEN

Queer Liberation

134. LYN PEDERSON (JIM KEPNER)

The Importance of Being Different
(1954)

"The Importance of Being Different" appeared in *ONE,* the first widely distributed gay magazine, which was founded in Los Angeles in 1953, and took its name from a lyric by Victorian essayist Thomas Carlyle: "A mystic bond of brotherhood makes all men ONE." Of the three major U.S. homophile organizations of the 1950s (the others being the Mattachine Society and the Daughters of Bilitis), *ONE* was the most militant. **"LYN PEDERSON"** was a pseudonym for **JIM KEPNER** (1923–1997), who was believed to have been eight months old when he was found abandoned wrapped in newspaper in Galveston, Texas. He was a prolific writer for the gay underground press in the 1950s, and the founder and curator of the International Gay and Lesbian Archives, which remains the largest library of its kind. In this essay, Kepner argued that because of the repressive nature of society in the 1950s, homosexuals were by definition "rebels." This position was counter to the ideology of the Mattachine Society, which argued that gays could win tolerance in society by accommodating themselves as much as possible to heterosexual America.

SOURCE: *ONE Magazine* (1954); reprinted in Mark Blasius, and Shane Phelan, eds., *We Are Everywhere.* New York: Routledge, 1997.

SELECTED READINGS: Jim Kepner, *Rough News, Daring Views: 1950s Pioneer Gay Press Journalism* (1998). Eric Marcus, *Making History: The Struggle for Gay and Lesbian Equal Rights, 1945–1990* (1992). Rodger Streitmatter, *Unspeakable: The Rise of the Gay and Lesbian Press in America* (1995).

When in Rome, do as you damn please.
—JOHN ARNOLD.

Homosexuals have some problems heterosexuals don't have. Agreed?

That's as far as we go. Once we try to list or analyze the problems, or suggest remedies, and agreement vanishes. The Mattachine Society, nee Foundation, and ONE magazine hope to tackle said problems, but the means remain in dispute. And there is no little disagreement on the ends.

Are homosexuals in any important way different from other people? If so, ought that difference be cultivated, or hidden under a bushel, or extirpated altogether?

For myself, I must say with the French legislator, who had something quite different on his mind, "Vive la différence!"

While the magazine has been relatively clear in its policy, the Mattachine Society has become almost schizoid on the question of whether we're different, whether to admit it and what to do about it.

What can a Society accomplish if half of it feels its object is to convince the world we're just like everyone else and the other half feels homosexuals are variants in the full sense of the term and have every right to be? What can that Society do but tie itself in knots of protective coloration? What can it it do but publish statements one day contradicting those it published the day before, and seldom even knowing a contradiction is involved?

Are homosexuals different?

That is, does the one difference which we all know about, make any other difference in their attitudes, habits, etc.? Is it possible to make any generalizations about homosexuals except that they are drawn to their own sex? Recalling that generalizations need only apply directly to *most* members of a group, I think several valid ones could be made, the sum and substance of which would be that homosexuals are different in more ways than they often know. But I am concerned with one particular point.

Homosexuals are natural rebels.

In our society, only freak conditions or cowardice or total ignorance of his own nature would permit a homosexual any alternative. A rare homosexual is protected by a thoroughly sympathetic family, which performs for him the function that the family performs for members of most other minority groups, that of providing, early in life when it counts, the spirit of group solidarity. Unfortunately for the rest of us, that "mystic bond . . ." of wishful thinking ". . . that makes all men one," is less cohesive than the family bond, which for us, is likely to be the first thing shattered.

Leaving ignorance aside, for overt homosexuals, their chief problem is whether to do as society demands or whether to follow their own inclinations. For most, this is a moral crisis. The homosexuals find themselves impelled by wild and mysterious desires to cross the line which all the authorities have set between what they call Right and what they call Wrong.

In such crises, people react variously, and on different levels of consciousness. For many, the tabu will stifle the desire, and perhaps even disguise its nature. But for most, the rule must be broken, and the act must be given context. Either the sin must be repented, or the break somehow justified. The penitents need not concern us here, except to comment that repentance can only satisfy those who merely "go astray" occasionally.

Most homosexuals become inured to breaking the rules. They must somehow reject what they learned as children and still hear repeated about them. But when people break rules and know they have done so, and are not sorry, they usually are forced to decide that the rule is either irrelevant or wrong. Here, a new factor enters. They put their own judgement above the rules, which represent society's judgment, in short, they become rebels.

Therefore, homosexuals are natural rebels. Born or made, they are constitutionally incapable of being sincere conformists. They may try desperately, as many in fact do, to conform in little things, to put on the show of being just like everyone else; but in the basic "facts of life" they are inescapably different, and through all the veneer of normality with which they may seek to cover themselves, they must suspect that this one essential difference colors their outlook on all other matters.

Because he is clanless, set apart, a lone individual searching for others of his kind (if he even suspects their existence) he must come to judge the world, its morals, customs and beliefs by his own nature, or else, in contrition reject and despise his own nature.

Some make the judgments easily, unaware that they've done any such thing. They'll drop their religion or its practice, casually, say the-hell-with-the-law, and go blindly on thinking of themselves as conformists.

Some will limit their non-conformity to sex and its most inescapable consequences, such as telling a "white lie" now and then, or on the other hand, shocking an acquaintance with the sudden truth.

But most people require a certain consistency, superficial at least, in their attitudes. The rejection of some of the rules leaves gaping holes in the concept of orderly society. Anyone much motivated by consistency must begin examining other parts of the social picture with a jaundiced eye. And if one reads any of history, he is likely to come by the opinion that the world owes as much to the rule-breakers as to the rule-keepers. He will then become a rebel in principle. He will seek his own standards of good and true and beautiful and just, or may even reject standards entirely. Liberty will become his aim and cause: conformity his enemy.

This, I say, is the natural course for homosexuals. But few follow it. Some become merely anti-social, flaunting the laws, hating the cops, flagrantly trying to shock people for the fun it gives, and likely quite intolerant of any variant habits they don't happen to be personally addicted to. This is the homosexual society sees, the stereotype. It is an unnatural course because it is primarily unconscious.

The more common, and more unnatural course, is motivated by protective coloration. These become so enwrapped in the desire to make the world believe they are no different that they succeed at least in making themselves believe it. This attitude provides, as I see it, the greatest pitfall for any group that would seek to help homosexuals.

It is this sort that would turn a homosexual organization into a refuge for cowards. It is this sort that would so fear the specter of non-conformity, and the red tag that goes with it these days, that they would bend backwards with dishonest but popular slogans about "upholding the law," "sanctity of home, church and state," "loyalty to the American way of life," and such, even though they may admit in private that they don't mean a word of it.

It is this sort who will Puritanically attack the "swishes and fairies" insisting that they wouldn't think of associating with such trash, except *perhaps* for the very noble purpose of reforming them, teaching them to behave decently.

This sort will view the job of a Mattachine Society or a ONE Magazine as primarily a "public relations" job, the object being nothing more or less than to convince society at large that homosexuals are not different at all.

And finally, this sort will attempt to excommunicate any homosexual who belies their thesis that we aren't different. Neither rebels nor swishes, nor any others who fall short of their slightly personalized standards of respectability will be welcome in their society.

Which brings us back to the starting point.

We are all agreed that homosexuals have problems. And some seem now convinced that such agencies as ONE and the Mattachine can do something. But agreement stops there.

Will we be called pollyannas or paranoids? Is our aim to pacify or to fight? Will we concentrate on activities that ignore the variance and demonstrate that we're just like any other civic group, putting the best face on things, with covert attempts to sidle up to judges and police chiefs?

Or will we leave room for disagreement, but with the basic group energies attacking the present laws and customs as unjust, developing ourselves as free individuals and joining a broad defense of liberty against the dead hand of conformity?

There is room in one organization for both views, but at the sacrifice of coordinated purpose. Only by allowing the free action of individual groups within the structure of an elastic society can such diverse philosophies work together. But such schizophrenia is hard to handle. With other minorities, racial and religious, similar dichotomies have forced into existence a variety of opposing organizations, each with its own clearcut program. For homosexuals as well, this must probably come, in time.

It should barely be necessary to state that I am interested in defending my right to be as different as I damn please. And somewhere, I've picked up the notion that I can't protect my own rights in that quarter without fighting for everyone else's.

135. LUCIAN TRUSCOTT IV

Gay Power Comes to Sheridan Square
(1969)

First appearing in the *Village Voice,* **LUCIAN TRUSCOTT**'s "Gay Power Comes to Sheridan Square" heralded the birth of the modern gay liberation movement. Truscott (1947–) was born in Japan, the grandson of a four-star general and the son of an army colonel. He graduated from West Point in 1969, but after a short-lived military career that ended in a general discharge, he pursued a successful career as a journalist, novelist, and screenwriter. The Stonewall Rebellion of June 28, 1969, occurred after New York City police raided the Stonewall Inn, a gay bar in Greenwich Village. In response, patrons and onlookers gathered in the streets, chanting, starting small fires, and throwing stones and bottles in protest. Although written on a short deadline, Truscott was nevertheless prescient to note that the Stonewall Rebellion marked the beginning of a new phase of gay militancy.

SOURCE: Lucian Truscott IV. "Gay Power Comes to Sheridan Square." *The Village Voice*, June 31, 1969.

SELECTED READINGS: Dudley Clendinen, *Out for Good: The Struggle to Build a Gay Rights Movement in America* (1999). Martin Duberman, *Stonewall* (1993).

Sheridan Square this weekend looked like something from a William Burroughs novel as the sudden specter of "gay power" erected its brazen head and spat out a fairy tale the likes of which the area has never seen.

The forces of faggotry, spurred by a Friday night raid on one of the city's largest, most popular, and longest lived gay bars, the Stonewall Inn, rallied Saturday night in an unprecedented protest against the raid and continued Sunday night to assert presence, possibility, and pride until the early hours of Monday morning. "I'm a faggot, and I'm proud of it!" "Gay Power!" "I like boys!"—these and many other slogans were heard all three nights as the show of force by the city's finery met the force of the city's finest. The result was a kind of liberation, as the gay brigade emerged from the bars, back rooms, and bedrooms of the Village and became street people.

Cops entered the Stonewall for the second time in a week just before midnight on Friday. It began as a small raid—only two patrolmen, two detectives, and two policewomen were involved. But as the patrons trapped inside were released one by one, a crowd started to gather on the street. It was initially a festive gathering, composed mostly of Stonewall boys who were waiting around for friends still inside or to see what was going to happen. Cheers would go up as favorites would emerge from the door, strike a pose, and swish by the detective with a "Hello there, fella." The stars were in their element. Wrists were limp, hair was primped, and reactions to the applause were classic. "I gave them the gay power bit, and they loved it, girls." "Have you seen Maxine? Where is my wife—I told her not to go far."

Suddenly the paddywagon arrived and the mood of the crowd changed. Three of the more blatant queens—in full drag—were loaded inside, along with the bartender and doorman, to a chorus of catcalls and boos from the crowd. A cry went up to push the paddywagon over, but it drove away before anything could happen. With its exit, the action waned momentarily. The next person to come out was a dyke, and she put up a struggle—from car to door to car again. It was at that moment that the scene became explosive. Limp wrists were forgotten. Beer cans and bottles were heaved at the windows, and a rain of coins descended on the cops. At the height of the action, a bearded figure was plucked from the crowd and dragged inside. It was Dave Van Ronk, who had come from the Lion's Head to see what was going on. He was later charged with having thrown an object at the police.

Three cops were necessary to get Van Ronk away from the crowd and into the Stonewall. The exit left no cops on the street, and almost by signal the crowd erupted into cobblestone and bottle heaving. The reaction was solid they were pissed. The trashcan I was standing on was nearly yanked out from under me as a kid tried to grab it for use in the windowsmashing melee. From no where came an uprooted parking meter—used as a battering ram on the Stonewall door. I heard several cries of "Let's get some gas," but the blaze of flame which soon appeared in the window of the Stonewall was still a shock. As the wood barrier behind the glass was beaten open, the cops inside turned a firehose on the crowd. Several kids took the opportunity to cavort in the spray, and their momentary glee served to stave off what was rapidly becoming a full-scale attack. By the time the fags were able to regroup forces and come up with another assault, several carloads of police reinforcements had arrived, and in minutes the streets were clear.

A visit to the Sixth Precinct revealed the fact that 13 persons had been arrested on charges which ranged from Van Ronk's felonious assault of a police officer to the owners' illegal sale and storage of alcoholic beverages without a license. Two police officers had been injured in the battle with the crowd. By the time the last cop was off the street Saturday morning, a sign was going up announcing that the Stonewall would reopen that night. It did.

Protest set the tone for "gay power" activities on Saturday. The afternoon was spent boarding up the windows of the Stonewall and chalking them with signs of the new revolution: "We are Open," "There is all college boys and girls in here," "Support Gay Power—C'mon in, girls," "Insp. Smyth looted our: money, jukebox, cigarette mach, telephones, safe, cash register, and the boys tips." Among the slogans were two carefully clipped and bordered copies of the Daily News story about the previous night's events, which was anything but kind to the gay cause.

The real action Saturday was that night in the street. Friday night's crowd had returned and was being led in "gay power" cheers by a group of gay, cheerleaders. "We are the Stonewall girls/ We wear our hair in curls/ We have no underwear/ We show our pubic hairs!" The crowd was gathered across the street from the Stonewall and was growing with additions of on-lookers, Eastsiders, and rough street people who saw a chance for a little action. Though dress had changed from Friday night's gayery to Saturday night street clothes, the scene was a command performance for queers. If Friday night had been pick-up night, Saturday was date night. Hand-holding, kissing, and posing accented each of the cheers with a homosexual liberation that had appeared only fleetingly on the street before. One-liners were as practiced as if they had been used for years. "I just want you all to know," quipped a platinum blond with obvious glee, "that sometimes being homo-sexual is a big pain in the ass." Another allowed as how he had become a "left-deviationist." And on and on.

The quasi-political tone of the street scene was looked upon with disdain by some, for radio news announcements about the previous night's "gay power" chaos had brought half of Fire Island's Cherry Grove running back to home base to see what they had left behind. The generation gap existed even here. Older boys had strained looks on their faces and talked in concerned whispers as they watched the up-and-coming generation take being gay and flaunt it before the masses.

As the "gay power" chants on the street rose in frequency and volume, the crowd grew restless. The front of the Stonewall was losing its attraction, de-spite efforts by the owners to talk the crowd back into the club. "C'mon in and see what da pigs done to us," they growled. "We're honest businessmen here. We're American born boys. We run a legitimate joint here. There ain't nuttin bein' done wrong in dis place. Everybody come and see."

The people on the street were not to be coerced. "Let's go down the street and see what's happening, girls," someone yelled. And down the street went the crowd, smack into the Tactical Patrol Force, who had been called earlier to disperse the crowd and were walking west on Christopher from Sixth Avenue. Formed in a line, the TPF swept the crowd back to the corner of Waverly Place, where they stopped. A stagnant situation there brought on some gay tornfoolery in the form of a chorus line facing the line of helmeted and club-carrying cops. Just as the line got into a full kick routine, the TPF advanced again and cleared the crowd of screaming gay powerites down Christopher to Seventh Avenue. The street and park were then held from both ends, and no one was allowed to enter—naturally causing a fall-off in normal Saturday night business, even at the straight Lion's Head and 55. The TPF positions in and around the square were held with only minor incident—one busted head and a number of scattered arrest—while the cops amused themselves by arbitrarily breaking up small groups of people up and down the avenue. The crowd finally dispersed around 3.30 a.m. The TPF had come and they had conquered, but Sunday was already there, and it was to be another story.

Sunday night was a time for watching and rapping. Gone were the "gay power" chants of Saturday, but not the new and open brand of exhibitionism. Steps, curbs, and the park provided props for what amounted to the Sunday fag follies as returning stars from the previous night's performances stopped by to close the show for the weekend.

It was slow going. Around 1 a.m. a non-helmeted version of the TPF arrived and made a controlled and very cool sweep of the area, getting everyone moving and out of the park. That put a damper on posing and primping, and as the last buses were leaving Jerseyward, the crowd grew thin. Allen Ginsberg and Taylor Mead walked by to see what was happening and were filled in on the previous evenings' activities by some of the gay activities. "Gay power! Isn't that great!" Allen said. "We're one of the largest minorities in the country—10 per cent, you know. It's about time we did something to assert ourselves."

Ginsberg expressed a desire to visit the Stonewall—"You know, I've never been in there"—and ambled on down the street, flashing peace signs and helloing the TPF. It was a relief and a kind of joy to see him on the street. He lent an extra umbrella of serenity of the scene with his laughter and quiet commentary on consciousness, "gay power" as a new movement, and the various implications of what had happened. I followed him into the Stonewall, where rock music blared from speakers all around a room that might have come right from a Hollywood set of a gay bar. He was immediately bouncing and dancing wherever he moved.

He left, and I walked east with him. Along the way, he described how things used to be. "You know, the guys there were so beautiful—they've lost that wounded look that fags all had 10 years ago." It was the first time I had heard that crowd described as beautiful.

We reached Cooper Square, and as Ginsberg turned to head toward home, he waved and yelled, "Defend the fairies!" and bounced on across the square. He enjoyed the prospect of "gay power" and is probably working on a manifesto for the movement right now. Watch out. The liberation is under way.

136. MARTHA SHELLY

Notes of a Radical Lesbian
(1969)

Originally published in 1969 as "Step N' Fetchit Woman" in the obscure *Come Out* magazine, **MARTHA SHELLY**'s "Notes of a Radical Lesbian," was one of the earliest expressions of lesbian-feminism. Born Martha Altman, Shelly (1953–) grew up in Crown Heights, Brooklyn. She was president of the New York City chapter of the Daughters of Bilitis (DOB), which was the first lesbian organization in the United States, begun in San Francisco in 1955. Shelly was also a member of the New York City–based Radicalesbians, and she helped found the Gay Liberation Front, an organization that tried to link the struggle for gay liberation with other efforts that promoted radical social change. In the following essay, Shelly suggests that lesbian sexuality encouraged a feminist consciousness, and she challenges the pervasive heterosexism that existed in many late-60s activist movements.

SOURCE: Robin Morgan, ed. *Sisterhood Is Powerful: An Anthology of Writings from the Women's Liberation Movement.* New York: Vintage Books, 1970.

SELECTED READINGS: Barbara A. Crow, *Radical Feminism: A Documentary Reader* (2000). Margaret Cruikshank, *The Gay and Lesbian Liberation Movement* (1992). Eric Marcus, *Making History: The Struggle for Gay and Lesbian Equal Rights, 1945–1990* (1992).

Lesbianism is one road to freedom—freedom from oppression by men.

To see Lesbianism in this context—as a mode of living neither better nor worse than others, as one which offers its own opportunities—one must abandon the notion that deviance from the norm arises from personal illnesses.

It is generally accepted that America is a "sick society." There is an inevitable corollary to this statement, which has not been generally accepted: that people within our society are all crippled by virtue of being forced to conform to certain norms. (Those who conform most easily can be seen as either the most healthy, because adaptable, or most sick, because least spirited.) Black people are struggling to free themselves, not only from white oppression, but from the roles of self-contempt that they have been forced to play. Women are struggling to liberate their minds from sick sexual roles. It is clear that the suffering, supposedly self-abasing black is not someone with a personal neurosis, but society's victim; and someone who has been forced to learn certain techniques for survival. Few people understand that the same is true of the self-abnegating passive housewife. Fewer still understand this truth about the homosexual.

These techniques of survival help us meet certain needs, at the price of others.

For women, as for other groups, there are several American norms. All of them have their rewards, and their penalties. The nice girl next door, virginal until her marriage—the Miss America type—is rewarded with community respect and respectability. She loses her individuality and her freedom, to become a toothpaste smile and a chastity belt. The career woman gains independence and a large margin of freedom—if she is willing to work twice as hard as a man for less pay, and if she can cope with emotional strains similar to those that beset the black intellectual surrounded by white colleagues. The starlet, call girl, or bunny, whose source of income is directly related to her image as a sex object, gains some financial independence and freedom from housework. She doesn't have to work as hard as the career woman, but she pays through psychological degradation as a sex object, and through the insecurity of knowing that her career, based on youthful good looks, is short-lived.

The Lesbian, through her ability to obtain love and sexual satisfaction from other women, is freed of dependence on men for love, sex, and money. She does not have to do menial chores for them (at least at home), nor cater to their egos, nor submit to hasty and inept sexual encounters. She is freed from fear of unwanted pregnancy and the pains of childbirth, and from the drudgery of child raising.

On the other hand, she pays three penalties. The rewards of child raising are denied her. This is a great loss for some women, but not for others. Few women abandon their children, as compared with the multitudes of men who abandon both wives and children. Few men take much interest in the process of child raising. One suspects that it might not be much fun for the average person, and so the men leave it to the women.

The Lesbian still must compete with men in the job market, facing the same job and salary discrimination as her straight sister.

Finally, she faces the most severe contempt and ridicule that society can heap on a woman.

When members of the Women's Liberation Movement picketed the 1968 Miss America pageant, the most terrible epithet heaped on our straight sisters was "Lesbian." The sisters faced hostile audiences who called them "commies," and "tramps," but some of them broke into tears when they were called Lesbians. When a woman showed up at a feminist meeting and announced that she was a Lesbian, many women avoided her. Others told her to keep her mouth shut, for fear that she would endanger the cause. They felt that men could be persuaded to accept some measure of equality for women—as long as these women would parade their devotion to heterosexuality and motherhood.

A woman who is totally independent of men—who obtains love, sex, and self-esteem from other women—is a terrible threat to male supremacy. She doesn't need them, and therefore they have less power over her.

I have met many, many feminists who were not Lesbians—but I have never met a Lesbian who was not a feminist. "Straight" women by the millions have been sold the belief that they must subordinate themselves to men, accept less pay for equal work, and do all the shitwork around the house. I have met straight women who would die to preserve their chains. I have never met a Lesbian who believed that she was innately less rational or capable than a man; who swallowed one word of the "woman's role" horseshit.

Lesbians, because they are not afraid of being abandoned by men, are less reluctant to express hostility toward the male class—the oppressors of women. Hostility toward your oppressor is healthy, but the guardians of modern morality, the psychiatrists, have interpreted this hostility as an illness, and they say this illness causes and is Lesbianism.

If hostility to men causes Lesbiansim, then it seems to me that in a male-domintated society, Lesbiansim is a sign of mental health.

The psychiatrists have also forgotten that Lesbianism involves love between women. Isn't love between equals healthier than sucking up to an oppressor? And when they claim we aren't capable of loving men, even if we want to—I would ask a straight man, in turn: are you capable of loving another man so deeply that you aren't afraid of his body or afraid to put your body in his hands? Are you really capable of loving women, or is your sexuality just another expression of your hostility? Is it an act of love or an act of conquest?

I do not mean to condemn all males. I have found some beautiful, loving men among the revolutionaries, among the hippies, and the male homosexuals. But the average man, including the average student male radical, wants a passive sex-object *cum* domestic *cum* baby nurse to clean up after him while he does all the fun things and bosses her around—while he plays either big-shot executive or Che Guevara—and he is my oppressor and my enemy.

Society has taught most Lesbians to believe they are sick, and has taught most straight women to despise and fear the Lesbian as a perverted, diseased creature. It has fostered the myth that Lesbians are ugly and turn to each other because they can't get that prize, that prince, a male! In this age of the new "sexual revolution," another myth has been fostered: the beautiful Lesbians who play games with each other on the screen for the titillation of heterosexual males. They are not seen as serious people in love, but as performers in the "let's try a new perversion" game.

Freud founded the myth of penis envy, and men have asked me "But what can two women do together?" As though a penis were the *sine qua non* of sexual pleasure! Man, we can do without it, and keep it going longer, too!

Women are afraid to be without a man's protection—because other men will assault them on the streets. And this is no accident, no aberration performed by a few lunatics. Assaults on women are no more an accident than are lynchings of blacks in Mississippi. Men have oppressed us, and like most oppressors, they hate the oppressed and fear their wrath. Watch a white man walking in Harlem and you will see what I mean. Look at the face of a man who has accidentally wandered into a Lesbian bar.

Men fear Lesbians because they are less dependent, and because their hostility is less controlled.

Straight women fear Lesbians because of the Lesbian inside them, because we represent an alternative. They fear us for the same reason that uptight middle-class people fear hip people. They are angry at us because we have a way out that they are afraid to take.

And what happens to the Lesbian under all this pressure? Many of my sisters, confused by the barrage of anti-gay propaganda, have spent years begging to be allowed to live. They have come begging because they believed they were psychic cripples, and that other people were healthy and had the moral right to judge them. Many have lived in silence, burying themselves in their careers, like name-changing Jews or blacks who passed for white. Many have retreated into an apolitical domesticity, concerning themselves only with the attempt to maintain a love relationship in a society which attempts to destroy love and replace it with consumer goods, and which attempts to completely destroy any form of love outside the monogamous marriage.

Because *Lesbian* has become such a vile epithet, we have been afraid to fight openly. We can lose our jobs; we have fewer civil rights than any other minority group. Because we have few family ties and no children, for the most part, we have been active in many causes, but always in secret, because our name contaminates any cause that we work for.

To the radical Lesbian, I say that we can no longer afford to fight for everyone else's cause while ignoring our own. Ours is a life-style born out of a sick society; so is everyone else's. Our kind of love is as valid as anyone else's. The revolution must be fought for us, too, not only for blacks, Indians, welfare mothers, grape pickers, SDS people, Puerto Ricans, or mine workers. We must have a revolution for *human rights*. If we are in a bag, it's as good as anyone else's bag.

Maybe after the revolution, people will be able to love each other regardless of skin color, ethnic origin, occupation, or type of genitals. But if that's going to happen, it will only happen because we make it happen—starting right now.

137. CARL WITTMAN

Refugees from Amerika: A Gay Manifesto
(1970)

CARL WITTMAN's "A Gay Manifesto" was a flagship document in the gay liberation movement. Wittman (1943–1986) was born and raised in New Jersey, and was active in the Civil Rights Movement and Students for a Democratic Society (SDS) while he attended Swarthmore College. In 1967 he moved to San Francisco, where he worked as a labor organizer. Although published for the first time in December 1970, Wittman's "A Gay Manifesto" was actually written shortly before the Stonewall Rebellion, and it was well-received in the underground press because it drew together many of the early themes of gay liberation. Wittman called for a rejection of heterosexual standards and a politics of open confrontation that aimed to radically transform all of society.

SOURCE: Joseph A. McCaffrey. *The Homosexual Dialectic.* Englewood Cliffs, New Jersey: Prentice Hall, 1972.

SELECTED READINGS: Barry Adam, *The Rise of a Gay and Lesbian Movement* (1987). Donn Teal, *The Gay Militants: How Gay Liberation Began in America, 1969–1971* (1971). Karla Jay and Allen Young, *Out of the Closets: Voices of Gay Liberation* (1972).

San Francisco is a refugee camp for homosexuals. We have fled here from every part of the nation, and like refugees elsewhere, we came not because it is so great here, but because it was so bad there. By the tens of thousands, we fled small towns where to be ourselves would endanger our jobs and any hope of a decent life; we have fled from blackmailing cops, from families who disowned or "tolerated" us; we have been drummed out of the armed services, thrown out of schools, fired from jobs, beaten by punks and policemen.

And we have formed a ghetto, out of self-protection. It is a ghetto rather than a free territory because it is still theirs. Straight cops patrol us, straight legislators govern us, straight employers keep us in line, straight money exploits us. We have pretended everything is OK, because we haven't been able to see how to change it—we've been afraid.

In the past year there has been an awakening of gay liberation ideas and energy. How it began we don't know; maybe we were inspired by black people and their freedom movement; we learned how to stop pretending from the hip revolution. Amerika in all its ugliness has surfaced with the war and our national leaders. And we are revulsed by the quality of our ghetto life.

Where once there was frustration, alienation, and cynicism, there are new characteristics among us. We are full of love for each other and are showing it; we are full of anger at what has been done to us. And as we recall all the self-censorship and repression for so many years, a reservoir of tears pours out of our eyes. And we are euphoric, high, with the initial flourish of a movement.

We want to make ourselves clear: our first job is to free ourselves; that means clearing our heads of the garbage that's been poured into them. This article is an attempt at raising a number of issues, and presenting some ideas to replace the old ones. It is primarily for ourselves, a starting point of discussion. If straight people of good will find it useful in understanding what liberation is about, so much the better.

It should also be clear that these are the views of one person, and are determined not only by my homosexuality, but my being white, male, middle-class. It is my individual consciousness. Our group consciousness will evolve as we get ourselves together—we are only at the beginning.

I. On Orientation

1. *What homosexuality is:* Nature leaves undefined the object of sexual desire. The gender of that object is imposed socially. Humans originally made homosexuality taboo because they needed every bit of energy to produce and raise children: survival of species was a priority. With overpopulation and technological change, that taboo continued only to exploit us and enslave us.

As kids we refused to capitulate to demands that we ignore our feelings toward each other. Somewhere we found the strength to resist being indoctrinated, and we should count that among our assets. We have to realize that our loving each other is a good thing, not an unfortunate thing, and that we have a lot to teach straights about sex, love, strength, and resistance.

Homosexuality is *not* a lot of things. It is not a makeshift in the absence of the opposite sex; it is not hatred or rejection of the opposite sex; it is not genetic; it is not the result of broken homes except inasmuch as we could see the sham of American marriage. *Homosexuality is the capacity to love someone of the same sex.*

2. *Bisexuality:* Bisexuality is good; it is the capacity to love people of either sex. The reason so few of us are bisexual is because society made such a big stink about homosexuality that we got forced into seeing ourselves as either straight or non-straight. Also, many gays got turned off to the ways men are supposed to act with women and vice-versa, which is pretty fucked-up. Gays will begin to turn on to women when 1) it's something that we do because we want to, and not because we should, and 2) when women's liberation changes the nature of heterosexual relationships.

We continue to call ourselves homosexual, not bisexual, even if we do make it with the opposite sex also, because saying "Oh, I'm Bi" is a copout for a gay. We get told it's OK to sleep with guys as long as we sleep with women too, and that's still putting homosexuality down. We'll be gay until everyone has forgotten that it's an issue. Then we'll begin to be complete.

3. *Heterosexuality:* Exclusive heterosexuality is fucked up. It reflects a fear of people of the same sex, it's anti-homosexual, and it is fraught with frustration. Heterosexual sex is fucked up, too; ask women's liberation about what straight guys are like in bed. Sex is aggression for the male chauvinist; sex is obligation for the traditional woman. And among the young, the modern, the hip, it's only a subtle version of the same. For us to become heterosexual in the sense that our straight brothers and sisters are is not a cure, it is a disease. . . .

III. On Roles

1. *Mimicry of straight society:* We are children of straight society. We still think straight: that is part of our oppression. One of the worst of straight concepts is inequality. Straight (also white, English, male, capitalist) thinking views things in terms of order and comparison. A is before B, B is after A; one is below two is below three; there is no room for equality. This idea gets extended to male/female, on top/on bottom, spouse/not spouse, heterosexual/homosexual, boss/worker, white/black, and rich/poor. Our social institutions cause and reflect this verbal hierarchy. This is Amerika.

We've lived in these institutions all our lives. Naturally we mimic the roles. For too long we mimicked these roles to protect ourselves—a survival mechanism. Now we are becoming free enough to shed the roles which we've picked up from the institutions which have imprisoned us.

"Stop mimicking straights, stop censoring ourselves."

2. *Marriage:* Marriage is a prime example of a straight institution fraught with role playing. Traditional marriage is a rotten, oppressive institution.

Those of us who have been in heterosexual marriages too often have blamed our gayness on the breakup of the marriage. No. They broke up because marriage is a contract which smothers both people, denies needs, and places impossible demands on both people. And we had the strength, again, to refuse to capitulate to the roles which were demanded of us.

Gay people must stop gauging their self-respect by how well they mimic straight marriages. Gay marriages will have the same problems as straight ones except in burlesque. For the usual legitimacy and pressures which keep straight marriages together are absent, e.g. kids, what parents think, what neighbors say.

To accept that happiness comes through finding a groovy spouse and settling down, showing the world that "we're just the same as you" is avoiding the real issues, and is an expression of self-hatred.

3. *Alternatives to marriage:* People want to get married for lots of good reasons, although marriage won't often meet those needs or desires. We're all looking for security, a flow of love, and a feeling of belonging and being needed.

These needs can be met through a number of social relationships and living situations. Things we want to get away from are: 1) exclusiveness, propertied attitudes toward each other, a mutual pact against the rest of the world; 2) promise about the future, which we have no right to make and which prevent us from, or make us feel guilty about, growing; 3) inflexible roles, roles which do not reflect us at the moment but are inherited through mimicry and inability to define equalitarian relationships.

We have to define for ourselves a new pluralistic, role free social structure for ourselves. It must contain both the freedom and physical space for people to live alone, live together for a while, live together for a long time, either as couples or in larger numbers; and the ability to flow easily from one of these states to another as our needs change.

Liberation for gay people is defining for ourselves how and with whom we live, instead of measuring our relationship in comparison to straight ones, with straight values.

4. *Gay "stereotypes":* The straights' image of the gay world is defined largely by those of us who have violated straight roles. There is a tendency among "homophile" groups to deplore gays who play visible roles—the queens and the nellies. As liberated gays, we must take a clear stand. 1) Gays who stand out have become our first martyrs. They came out and withstood disapproval before the rest of us did. 2) If they have suffered from being open, it is straight society whom we must indict, not the queen.

5. *Closet queens:* This phrase is becoming analagous to "Uncle Tom." To pretend to be straight sexually, or to pretend to be straight socially, is probably the most harmful pattern of behavior in the ghetto. The married guy who

makes it on the side secretly; the guy who will go to bed once but who won't develop any gay relationships; the pretender at work or school who changes the gender of the friend he's talking about; the guy who'll suck cock in the bushes but who won't go to bed.

If we are liberated we are open with our sexuality. Closet queenery must end. *Come out.*

But in saying come out, we have to have our heads clear about a few things: 1) Closet queens are our brothers, and must be defended against attacks by straight people; 2) The fear of coming out is not paranoia; the stakes are high: loss of family ties, loss of job, loss of straight friends—these are all reminders that the oppression is not just in our heads. It's real. Each of us must make the steps toward openness at our own speed and on our own impulses. Being open is the foundation of freedom: it has to be built solidly; 3) "Closet queen" is a broad term covering a multitude of forms of defense, self-hatred, lack of strength, and habit. We are all closet queens in some ways, and all of us had to come out—very few of us were "flagrant" at the age of seven! We must afford our brothers and sisters the same patience we afforded ourselves. And while their closet queenery is part of our oppression, it's more a part of theirs. They alone can decide when and how.

IV. On Oppression

It is important to catalog and understand the different facets of our oppression. There is no future in arguing about degrees of oppression. A lot of "movement" types come on with a line of shit about homosexuals not being oppressed as much as blacks or Vietnamese or workers or women. We don't happen to fit into their ideas of class or caste. Bull! When people feel oppressed, they act on that feeling. We feel oppressed. Talk about the priority of black liberation or ending imperialism over and above gay liberation is just anti-gay propaganda.

1. *Physical attacks:* We are attacked, beaten, castrated and left dead time and time again. There are half a dozen known unsolved slayings in San Francisco parks in the last few years. "Punks," often of minority groups who look around for someone under them socially, feel encouraged to beat up on "queens," and cops look the other way. That used to be called lynching.

Cops in most cities have harassed our meeting places: bars and baths and parks. They set up entrapment squads. A Berkeley brother was slain by a cop in April when he tried to split after finding out that the trick who was making advances to him was a cop. Cities set up "pervert" registration, which if nothing else scares our brothers deeper into the closet.

One of the most vicious slurs on us is the blame for prison "gang rapes."

These rapes are invariably done by people who consider themselves straight. The victims of these rapes are us and straights who can't defend themselves. The press campaign to link prison rapes with homosexuality is an attempt to make straights fear and despise us, so they can oppress us more. It's typical of the fucked-up straight mind to think that homosexual sex involves tying a guy down and fucking him. That's aggression, not sex. If that's what sex is for a lot of straight people, that's a problem they have to solve, not us.

2. *Psychological warfare:* Right from the beginning we have been subjected to a barrage of straight propaganda. Since our parents don't know any homosexuals, we grow up thinking that we're alone and different and perverted. Our school friends identify "queer" with any non-conformist or bad behavior. Our elementary school teachers tell us not to talk to strangers or accept rides. Television, billboards and magazines put forth a false idealization of male/female relationships, and make us wish we were different, wish we were "in." In family living class we're taught how we're supposed to turn out. And all along the best we hear about homosexuality is that it's an unfortunate problem.

3. *Self-oppression:* As gay liberation grows, we will find our uptight brothers and sisters, particularly those who are making a buck off our ghetto, coming on strong to defend the status quo. This is self-oppression: "don't rock the boat"; "things in SF are OK"; "gay people just aren't together"; "I'm not oppressed." These lines are right out of the mouths of the straight establishment. A large part of our oppression would end if we would stop putting ourselves and our pride down.

4. *Institutional oppression:* Discrimination against gays is blatant, if we open our eyes. Homosexual relationships are illegal, and even if these laws are not regularly enforced, they encourage and enforce closet queenery. The bulk of the social work/psychiatric field looks upon homosexuality as a problem, and treats us as sick. Employers let it be known that our skills are acceptable only as long as our sexuality is hidden. Big business and government are particularly notorious offenders.

The discrimination in the draft and armed services is a pillar of the general attitude toward gays. If we are willing to label ourselves publicly not only as homosexual but as sick, then we qualify for deferment; and if we're not "discreet" (dishonest) we get drummed out of the service. Hell, no, we won't go, of course not, but we can't let the army fuck over us this way, either. . . .

VI. On Our Ghetto

We are refugees from Amerika. So we came to the ghetto—and as other ghettos, it has its negative and positive aspects. Refugee camps are better than what proceeded them, or people never would have come. But they are still enslaving, if only that we are limited to being ourselves there and only there.

Ghettos breed self-hatred. We stagnate here, accepting the status quo. The status quo is rotten. We are all warped by our oppression, and in the isolation of the ghetto we blame ourselves rather than our oppressors.

Ghettos breed exploitation. Landlords find they can charge exorbitant rents and get away with it, because of the limited area which is safe to live in openly. Mafia control of bars and baths in NYC is only one example of outside money controlling our institutions for their profit. In San Francisco the Tavern Guild favors maintaining the ghetto, for it is through ghetto culture that they make a buck. We crowd their bars not because of their merit but because of the absence of any other social institution. The Guild has refused to let us collect defense funds or pass out gay liberation literature in their bars—need we ask why?

Police or con men who shake down the straight gay in return for not revealing him; the bookstores and movie makers who keep raising prices because they are the only outlet for pornography; heads of "modeling" agencies and other pimps who exploit both the hustlers and the johns—these are the parasites who flourish in the ghetto.

San Francisco—ghetto or free territory: Our ghetto certainly is more beautiful and larger and more diverse than most ghettos, and is certainly freer than the rest of Amerika. That's why we're here. But it isn't ours. Capitalists make money off us, cops patrol us, government tolerates us as long as we shut up, and daily we work for and pay taxes to those who oppress us.

To be a free territory, we must govern ourselves, set up our own institutions, defend ourselves, and use our own energies to improve our lives. The emergence of gay liberation communes and our own paper is a good start. The talk about a gay liberation coffee shop/dance hall should be acted upon. Rural retreats, political action offices, food cooperatives, a free school, unalienating bars and after hours places—they must be developed if we are to have even the shadow of a free territory. . . .

Conclusion: An Outline of Imperatives for Gay Liberation

1. Free ourselves: come out everywhere; initiate self defense and political activity; initiate counter community institutions.

2. Turn other gay people on: talk all the time; understand, forgive, accept.

3. Free the homosexual in everyone: we'll be getting a good bit of shit from threatened latents: be gentle, and keep talking and acting free.

4. We've been playing an act for a long time, so we're consummate actors. Now we can begin to be, and it'll be a good show!

138. RADICALESBIANS

The Woman-Identified Woman
(1970)

"**The Woman-Identified Woman**" has been called "the definitive manifesto of lesbian-feminism." **RADICALESBIANS** was formed in New York in 1970 by activists who had been unable to persuade the National Organization for Women (NOW) to express public support for lesbian rights. Radicalesbians dissolved in 1971. "The Woman-Identified Woman" was first distributed at the Second Congress to Unite Women in New York City in May, 1970, and it had six primary authors. The paper argued that lesbianism is a sociopolitical choice, rather than an erotic one, and that by choosing lesbianism, women could resist having their love lives dominated by patriarchal power, and realize their goals of freedom, independence, and self-actualization.

SOURCE: Karla Jay and Allen Young. *Out of the Closets: Voices of Gay Liberation.* New York: Douglas Books, 1972.

SELECTED READINGS: Dan R. Shugar, *Separatism and Women's Community* (1995). Alice Echols, *Daring to Be Bad: Radical Feminism in America, 1967–1975* (1989). Sidney Abbott and Barbara Love, *Sappho Was a Right-On Woman* (1972).

What is a lesbian? A lesbian is the rage of all women condensed to the point of explosion. She is the woman who, often beginning at an extremely early age, acts in accordance with her inner compulsion to be a more complete and freer human being than her society—perhaps then, but certainly later—cares to allow her. These needs and actions, over a period of years, bring her into painful conflict with people, situations, the accepted ways of thinking, feeling and behaving, until she is in a state of continual war with everything around her, and usually with her self. She may not be fully conscious of the political implications of what for her began as personal necessity, but on some level she has not been able to accept the limitations and oppression laid on her by the most basic role of her society—the female role. The turmoil she experiences tends to induce guilt proportional to the degree to which she feels she is not meeting social expectations, and/or eventually drives her to question and analyse what the rest of her society, more or less accepts. She is forced to evolve her own life pattern, often living much of her life alone, learning usually much earlier than her "straight" (heterosexual) sisters about the essential aloneness of life (which the myth of marriage obscures) and about the reality of illusions. To the extent that she cannot expel the heavy socialization that goes with being female, she can never truly find peace with herself. For she is caught somewhere between accepting society's view of her—in which case she cannot accept herself—and coming to understand what this sexist society has done to her and why it is functional and necessary for it to do so. Those of us who work that through find ourselves on the other side of a tortuous journey through a night that may have been decades long. The perspective gained from that journey, the liberation of self, the inner peace, the real love of self and of all women, is something to be shared with all women—because we are all women.

It should first be understood that lesbianism, like male homosexuality, is a category of behavior possible only in a sexist society characterized by rigid sex roles and dominated by male supremacy. Those sex roles dehumanize women by defining us as a supportive/serving caste in *relation* to the master caste of men, and emotionally cripple men by demanding that they be alienated from their own bodies and emotions in order to perform their economic/political/military functions effectively. Homosexuality is a by-product of a particular way of setting up roles (or approved patterns of behavior) on the basis of sex; as such it is an inauthentic (not consonant with "reality") category. In a society in which men do not oppress women, and sexual expression is allowed to follow feelings, the categories of homosexuality and heterosexuality would disappear.

But lesbianism is also different from male homosexuality, and serves a different function in the society. "Dyke" is a different kind of put-down from "faggot," although both imply you are not playing your socially assigned sex role—are not therefore a "real woman" or a "real man." The grudging admiration felt for the tomboy and the queasiness felt around a sissy boy point to the same thing: the contempt in which women—or those who play a female role—are held. And the investment in keeping women in that contemptuous role is very great. Lesbian is the word, the label, the condition that holds women in line. When a woman hears this word tossed her way, she knows she is stepping out of line. She knows that she has crossed the terrible boundary of her sex role. She recoils, she protests, she reshapes her actions to gain approval. Lesbian is a label invented by the man to throw at any woman who dares to be his equal, who dares to challenge his prerogatives (including that of all women as part of the exchange medium among men), who dares to assert the primacy of her own needs. To have the label applied to people active in women's liberation is just the most recent instance of a long history; older women will recall that not so long ago, any woman who was successful, independent, not orienting her whole life about a man, would hear this word. For in this sexist society, for a woman to be independent means she can't be a woman—she must be a dyke. That in itself should tell us where women are at. It says as clearly as can be said: women and person are contradictory terms. For a lesbian is not considered a "real woman." And yet, in popular thinking, there is really only one essential difference between a lesbian and other women: that of sexual orientation—which is to say, when you strip off all the packaging, you must finally realize that the essence of being a "woman" is to get fucked by men.

"Lesbian" is one of the sexual categories by which men have divided up humanity. While all women are dehumanized as sex objects, as the objects of men, they are given certain compensations: identification with his power, his ego, his status, his protection (from other males), feeling like a "real woman," finding social acceptance by adhering to her role, etc. Should a woman confront herself by confronting another woman, there are fewer rationalizations, fewer buffers by which to avoid the stark horror of her dehumanized condition. Herein we find the overriding fear of many women towards exploring intimate relationships with other women: the fear of her being used as a sexual object by a woman, which not only will bring no male-connected compensations, but also will reveal the void which is woman's real situation. This dehumanization is expressed when a straight woman learns that a sister is a lesbian; she begins to relate to her lesbian sister as her potential sex object, laying a surrogate male role on the lesbian. This reveals her heterosexual conditioning to make herself into an object when sex is potentially involved in a relationship, and it denies the lesbian her full humanity. For women, especially those in the movement, to perceive their lesbian sisters through this male grid of role definitions is to accept this male cultural conditioning and to oppress their sisters much as they themselves have been oppressed by men. Are we going to continue the male classification system of defining all females in sexual relation to some *other* category of people? Affixing the label lesbian not only to a woman who aspires to be a person, but also to any situation of real love, real solidarity, real primacy among women is a primary form of divisiveness among women: it is the condition which keeps women within the confines of the feminine role, and it is the debunking/scare term that keeps women from forming any primary attachments, groups, or associations among ourselves. . . .

But why is it that women have related to and through men? By virtue of having been brought up in a male society, we have internalized the male culture's definition of ourselves. That definition views us as relative beings who exist not for ourselves, but for the servicing, maintenance and comfort of men. That definition consigns us to sexual and family functions, and excludes us from defining and shaping the terms of our lives. In exchange for our psychic servicing and for performing society's non-profit-making functions, the man confers on us just one thing: the slave status which makes us legitimate in the eyes of the society in which we live. This is called "femininity" or "being a real woman" in our cultural lingo. We are authentic, legitimate, real to the extent that we are the property of some man whose name we bear. To be a woman who belongs to no man is to be invisible, pathetic, inauthentic, unreal. He confirms his image of us—of what we have to be in order to be acceptable by him—but not our real selves; he confirms our womanhood—as he defines it, in relation to him—but cannot confirm our personhood, our own selves as absolutes. As long as we are dependent on the male culture for this definition, for this approval, we cannot be free.

The consequence of internalizing this role is an enormous reservoir of self-hate. This is not to say the self-hate is recognized or accepted as such; indeed most women would deny it. It may be experienced as discomfort with her role, as feeling empty, as numbness, as restlessness, a paralyzing anxiety at the center. Alternatively, it may be expressed in shrill defensiveness of the glory and destiny of her role. But it does exist, often beneath the edge of her consciousness, poisoning her existence, keeping her alienated from herself, her own needs, and rendering her a stranger to other women. Women hate both themselves and other women. They try to escape by identifying with the oppressor, living through him, gaining status and identity from his ego, his power, his accomplishments. And by not identifying with other "empty vessels" like themselves, women resist relating on all levels to other women who will reflect their own oppression, their own secondary status, their own self-hate. For to confront another woman is finally to confront one's self—the self we have gone to such lengths to avoid. And in that mirror we know we cannot really respect and love that which we have been made to be.

As the source of self-hate and the lack of real self are rooted in our male-given identity, we must create a new sense of self. As long as we cling to the idea of "being a woman," we will sense some conflict with that incipient self, that sense of I, that sense of a whole person. It is very difficult to realize and accept that being "feminine" and being a whole person are irreconcilable. Only women can give each other a new sense of self. That identity we have to develop with reference to ourselves, and not in relation to men. This consciousness is the revolutionary force from which all else will follow, for ours is an organic revolution. For this we must be available and supportive to one another, give our commitment and our love, give the emotional support necessary to sustain this movement. Our energies must flow toward our sisters, not backwards towards our oppressors. As long as women's liberation tries to free women without facing the basic heterosexual structure that binds us in one-to-one relationship with our own oppressors, tremendous energies will continue to flow into trying to straighten up each particular relationship with a man, how to get better sex, how to turn his head around—into trying to make the "new man" out of him, in the delusion that this will allow us to be the "new woman." This obviously splits our energies and commitments, leaving us unable to be committed to the construction of the new patterns which will liberate us.

It is the primacy of women relating to women, of women creating a new consciousness of and with each other which is at the heart of women's liberation, and the basis for the cultural revolution. Together we must find, reinforce and validate our authentic selves. As we do this, we confirm in each other that struggling incipient sense of pride and strength, the divisive barriers begin to melt, we feel this growing solidarity with our sisters. We see ourselves as prime, find our centers inside of ourselves. We find receding the sense of alienation, of being cut off, of being behind a locked window, of being unable to get out what we know is inside. We feel a realness, feel at last we are coinciding with ourselves. With that real self, with that consciousness, we begin a revolution to end the imposition of all coercive identifications, and to achieve maximum autonomy in human expression.

139. THIRD WORLD GAY LIBERATION

What We Want, What We Believe
(1971)

"What We Want, What We Believe" was a manifesto of the New York chapter of **THIRD WORLD GAY LIBERATION**, an organization of black and Latino gay revolutionaries. The statement was modeled on a platform put forth by the Black Panther Party in 1966, partly in response to heterosexism within the New Left. Along with the Gay Liberation Front (GLF), Third World Gay Liberation called for an alliance between gay activists and other groups committed to a "revolutionary socialist society . . . where the needs of the people come first."

SOURCE: Third World Gay Liberation. "What We Want, What We Believe." *Gay Flames* No. 11, March 1971.

SELECTED READINGS: Donn Teal, *The Gay Militants: How Gay Liberation Began in America, 1969–1971* (1971). Paul Mitchell, ed., *Pink Triangles: Radical Perspectives on Gay Liberation* (1980).

1. We want the right of self-determination for all Third World and gay people, as well as control of the destinies of our communities.

We believe that Third World and gay people cannot be free until we are able to determine our own destinies.

2. We want the right of self-determination over the use of our bodies: the right to be gay, anytime, anyplace; the right to free physiological change and modification of sex on demand; the right to free dress and adornment.

We believe that these are human rights which must be defended with our bodies being put on the line. The system as it now exists denies these basic human rights by implementing forced heterosexuality.

3. We want liberation for all women: We want free and safe birth control information and devices on demand. We want free 24-hour child care centers controlled by those who need and use them. We want a redefinition of ed-

ucation and motivation (especially for Third World women) towards broader educational opportunities without limitations because of sex. We want truthful teaching of women's history. We want an end to hiring practices which make women and national minorities 1) a readily available source of cheap labor; and 2) confined to mind-rotting jobs under the worst conditions.

We believe that the struggles of all oppressed groups under any form of government which does not meet the true needs of its people will eventually result in the overthrow of that government. The struggle for liberation of women is a struggle to be waged by all peoples. We must also struggle within ourselves and within our various movements to end this oldest form of oppression and its foundation—male chauvinism. We cannot develop a truly liberating form of socialism unless we fight these tendencies.

4. We want full protection of the law and social sanction for all human sexual self-expression and pleasure between consenting persons, including youth. We believe that present laws are oppressive to Third World people, gay people, and the masses. Such laws expose the inequalities of capitalism, which can only exist in a state where there are oppressed people or groups. This must end.

5. We want the abolition of the institution of the bourgeois nuclear family.

We believe that the bourgeois nuclear family perpetuates the false categories of homosexuality and heterosexuality by creating sex roles, sex definitions and sexual exploitation. The bourgeois nuclear family as the basic unit of capitalism creates oppressive roles of homosexuality and heterosexuality. All oppressions originate in the nuclear family structure. Homosexuality is a threat to this family structure and therefore to capitalism. The mother is an instrument of reproduction and teaches the necessary values of capitalist society, i.e., racism, sexism, etc., from infancy on. The father physically enforces (upon the mother and children) the behavior necessary in a capitalist system: intelligence and competitiveness in young boys and passivity in young girls. Further, it is every child's right to develop in a non-sexist, non-racist, non-possessive atmosphere which is the responsibility of all people, including gays, to create.

6. We want a free non-compulsory education system that teaches us our true identity and history, and presents the entire range of human sexuality without advocating any one form or style; that sex roles and determination of skills according to sex be eliminated from the school system; that language be modified so that no gender takes priority; and that gay people must share in the responsibilities of education.

We believe that we have been taught to compete with our sisters and brothers for power, and from that competitive attitude grows sexism, racism, male and national chauvinism and distrust of our sisters and brothers. As we

begin to understand these things within ourselves, we attempt to free ourselves of them and are moved toward a revolutionary consciousness.

7. We want guaranteed full equal employment for Third World and gay
people at all levels of production.

We believe that any system of government is responsible for giving every
woman and man a guaranteed income or employment, regardless of sex or
sexual preference. Being interested only in profits, capitalism cannot meet the
needs of the people.

8. We want decent and free housing, fit shelter for human beings.

We believe that free shelter is a basic need and right which must not be
denied on any grounds. Landlords are capitalists, and, like all capitalists, are
motivated only by the accumulation of profits, as opposed to the welfare of
the people.

9. We want to abolish the existing judicial system. We want all Third
World and gay people when brought to trial, to be tried by people's court with
a jury of their peers. A peer is a person from similar social, economic, geographical, racial, historical, environmental, and sexual background.

We believe that the function of the judicial system under capitalism is to
uphold the ruling class and keep the masses under control.

10. We want the reparation for and release of all Third World gay and all
political prisoners from jails and mental institutions.

We believe that these people should be released because they have not
received fair and impartial trials.

11. We want the abolition of capital punishment, all forms of institutional
punishment, and the penal system.

We want the establishment of psychiatric institutions for the humane treatment and rehabilitation of criminal persons as decided by the people's court.
We want the establishment of a sufficient number of free and non-compulsory
clinics for the treatment of sexual disturbances, as defined by the individual.

12. We want an immediate end to the fascist police force.

We believe that the only way this can be accomplished is by putting the
defense of the people in the hands of the people.

13. We want all Third World and gay men to be exempt from compulsory
military service in the imperialist army. We want an end to military oppression
both at home and abroad.

We believe that the only true army for oppressed people is the people's
army, and Third World, gay people, and women should have full participation
in the People's Revolutionary Army.

14. We want an end to all institutional religions because they aid in genocide by teaching superstition and hatred of Third World people, homosexuals
and women. We want a guarantee of freedom to express natural spirituality.

We believe that institutionalized religions are an instrument of capitalism, therefore an enemy of the People.

15. We demand immediate non-discriminatory open admission/membership for radical homosexuals into all left-wing revolutionary groups and organizations and the right to caucus.

We believe that so-called comrades who call themselves "revolutionaries" have failed to deal with their sexist attitudes. Instead they cling to male supremacy and therefore to the conditioned role of oppressors. Men still fight for the privileged position of man-on-the-top. Women quickly fall in line behind-their-men. By their counterrevolutionary struggle to maintain and to force heterosexuality and the nuclear family, they perpetuate decadent remnants of capitalism. To gain their anti-homosexual stance, they have used the weapons of the oppressor, thereby becoming the agent of the oppressor.

It is up to men to realistically define masculinity, because it is they, who, throughout their lives, have struggled to gain the unrealistic roles of "men." Men have always tried to reach this precarious position by climbing on the backs of women and homosexuals. "Masculinity" has been defined by capitalist society as the amount of possessions (including women) a man collects, and the amount of physical power gained over other men. Third World men have been denied even these false standards of "masculinity." Anti-homosexuality fosters sexual repressions, male-supremacy, weakness in revolutionary drive, and results in an inaccurate non-objective political perspective. Therefore, we believe that all left-wing revolutionary groups and organizations must immediately establish non-discriminatory, open admission/membership policies.

16. We want a new society—a revolutionary socialist society. We want liberation of humanity, free food, free shelter, free clothing, free transportation, free health care, free utilities, free education, free art for all. We want a society where the needs of the people come first.

We believe that all people should share the labor and products of society, according to each one's needs and abilities, regardless of race, sex, age, or sexual preferences. We believe the land, technology, and the means of production belong to the people, and must be shared by the people collectively for the liberation of all.

140. ARTHUR EVANS

How to Zap Straights
(1973)

"**How to Zap Straights**" was a primer on the confrontational, disruptive tactic of "zapping," which won adherents in the wake of the gay liberation movement. **ARTHUR EVANS (1942–)** was born in York, Pennsylvania, and he studied at Brown University, City College of New York, and Columbia University. Along with several other activists who were dissatisfied with the Gay Liberation Front (GLF), Evans helped found the influential Gay Activist Alliance (GAA) in December 1969. Unlike the GLF, the GAA devoted itself exclusively to gay rights issues. In "How to Zap Straights," Evans discusses some of the ways the GAA used "zapping" to raise consciousness, politicize homosexuals, and win concrete political victories.

SOURCE: Len Richmond and Gary Noguera. *The Gay Liberation Book.* San Francisco: Ramparts Press, 1973.

SELECTED READINGS: Dennis Altman, *Homosexual: Oppression and Liberation* (1993). Toby Marotta, *The Politics of Homosexuality* (1981).

Straight oppressors, watch out—gays are gonna zap you! And if you're zapped, it'll be a long time before you forget it. You're sure to be emotionally shaken. You'll get lots of bad publicity. And you may even get involved in a lengthy court suit.

The "zap" is specifically designed to do just these things. And more—to rouse closet gays from their apathy, direct gay anger toward oppressive straight institutions, and create a widespread feeling of gay identity.

Use of the zap was perfected by New York's Gay Activists' Alliance. It is a unique tactic of confrontation politics, combining the somber principles of *realpolitik* with the theatrics of high camp. . . .

Zapping works. The noise, abuse and general camping-up demoralize the oppressors. Sometimes even top pigs are not too proud of the work they do. Activists can capitalize on this weakness and degrade high-ranking bureaucrats in front of their employees. The oppressors are usually taken off guard and come out looking either ridiculous or violent. When the scene is replayed on TV news, they look foolish and vulnerable.

Zaps present the oppressor with a dilemma: either capitulate, or win by resorting to violence. In either case, the Gay Liberation Movement wins—for violence against gays, especially when well-publicized, always politicizes more gays.

The ensuing publicity helped make a success of a zap that took place against New York's "Inner Circle," an exclusive, elitist collection of political reporters, press agents, politicians, and union leaders who meet from time to time to lampoon current political events. Learning that the Inner Circle planned to stage a play ridiculing the gay community and Intro. 475 at its April 1972 meeting, GAA members slipped into the ornate room in the Hilton Hotel where the Inner Circle gathers. They distributed a leaflet aimed at the press agents, criticizing them for their usually jaundiced statements and reports concerning gay news. One gay activist took over a microphone and began to speak.

At this point, several men in tuxedos (later identified as members of the Inner Circle or employees of the Hilton) attacked the gays, punching them in the face and kicking them in the groin. One member of the Uniformed Firefighters Association (and a National Golden Gloves heavyweight champion) assaulted at least two gays, knocking one unconscious (the victim later had six stitches taken around his eye). New York City policemen on the scene refused to stop the mayhem, and would not allow the gays to press charges against the attackers.

Even though the gays were beaten and thrown out, the Gay Liberation Movement won: The event subsequently received enormous publicity, even from the straight press. Private contributions poured into GAA's treasury to fund a legal suit. Prominent civil rights lawyers offered to support GAA in legal action against the attackers. Most important of all, many closet gays learned of the assault and began to think about the nature of their oppression, and what they could do about it.

Zaps are thus a form of political theater for educating the gay masses. Gays who have as yet no sense of gay pride see a zap on television or read about it in the press. First they are vaguely disturbed at the demonstrators for "rocking the boat"; eventually, when they see how the straight establishment responds, they feel anger. This anger gradually focuses on the heterosexual oppressors, and the gays develop a sense of class-consciousness. And the no-longer-closeted gays realize that assimilation into the heterosexual main-stream is no answer: gays must unite among themselves, organize their common resources for collective action, and resist.

Gay people, unite! Organize! Resist!

141. ACT UP

Post-Action Position Statement on its *"Stop the Church"* Action

The following document is a defense of one of the most controversial direct actions of the AIDS era, when 111 members of the AIDS Coalition to Unleash Power (**ACT UP**) were arrested for civil disobedience inside New York City's St. Patrick's Cathedral on December 10, 1989, while over five thousand demonstrators gathered outside the church. The protest was against the Roman Catholic Church's homophobia and its opposition to safe sex education. Although ACT UP was widely criticized for conducting civil disobedience within a house of worship, the organization refused to apologize for its action. "As long as the [AIDS] epidemic rages," it concluded, "ACT UP will never be silent . . . not even in the Church itself."

SOURCE: Mark Blasisu and Shane Phelan, eds. *We Are Everywhere: A Historical Sourcebook of Gay and Lesbian Politics.* New York and London: Routledge, 1997.

SELECTED READINGS: Gilbert Elbaz, "The Sociology of AIDS Activism: The Case of ACT UP, New York, 1987–1992," Ph.D. dissertation, City College of New York (1992). Larry Kramer, *Reports from the Holocaust: The Making of an AIDS Activist* (1989).

Position Statement

In the days following the massive demonstration at St. Patrick's Cathedral, Cardinal O'Connor has portrayed himself as an innocent victim of the demonstrators who interrupted his sermon. ACT UP stresses that we do not apologize for the actions of the 5,000 people who came on Sunday to protest Church actions that limit the rights of all Americans to make personal decisions in their own lives.

We respect the Cardinal's right to believe what he chooses and to preach to any Catholics who choose to follow him. But we are alarmed at church leaders' oppressive public policies that infringe upon the rights of all Americans. The right of teenagers in public schools to have complete sex and AIDS education, and the right of women to decide about their own bodies.

We went to the church on Sunday to tell America that the Cardinal and Church leaders are using their immense political clout to push public policies that are dangerous for all Americans, not just for Catholics. For instance:

Cardinal O'Connor's knowledge of AIDS prevention or treatment methods is limited to the foolishly simplistic view "morality is good medicine," yet he sits on the Presidential AIDS Policy Panel, telling our President what to do about AIDS. AIDS is not a religious issue. The Cardinal's attempts to push Church moralizing as public health policy show a disrespect for those dead from AIDS and a profane lack of compassion for those who remain at grave risk of contracting this disease.

The Cardinal's representatives sit on the Board of Education's AIDS Curriculum Task Force and have prevented teenagers of all religious faiths from obtaining lifesaving AIDS information in their public schools. Americans did not elect the Cardinal. This kind of political bullying is a clear violation of the constitutional separation of church and state—in fact, this issue is currently on trial in the courts.

Homeless teenagers who turn to prostitution or drug use are at greatest AIDS risk. But the Church's policy at Covenant House, which is touted as New York's best hope for runaway kids, is to prohibit distribution of any AIDS prevention literature. Worse, when some young residents brought in such flyers given by ACT UP and WHAM!, the kids were promptly expelled—thrown out in the street. Is this what the Cardinal means when he boasts about merciful, charitable response to the AIDS crisis?

Individual ACT UP and WHAM members who chose to enter the church—a number of them Catholics and People With AIDS—were not trying to deny parishioners' right to worship. Instead, these demonstrators felt so strongly about the issues that they needed to make this peaceful, non-violent political statement—some silently, some vocally—in the place where Cardinal O'Connor himself has made so many dangerous and misguided political statements. They entered peacefully, as members of the congregation, and were greeted by a sea of uniformed police officers.

The real victims today are not the Cardinal and his followers whose service was interrupted for a half hour on Sunday. The real victims are the hundreds of thousands of people in New York City and across the USA with HIV and AIDS, who might have been spared from this terrible disease if it weren't for the Church's ongoing distortion of the AIDS crisis to further its own moralistic and political goals.

As long as the epidemic rages and the Church fights in direct opposition to the policies recommended by responsible doctors, scientists and public health officials, ACT UP will never be silent—not in the streets, not in the capital, and not even in the Church itself.

142. MICHELANGELO SIGNORILE

A Queer Manifesto
(1993)

MICHELANGELO SIGNORILE's advocacy of "outing"—the practice of publicizing a closeted person's homosexuality—has made him a controversial figure in contemporary gay journalism. Signorile (1960–) grew up in Brooklyn and Staten Island, and attended Syracuse University. Upon graduating, he moved to Manhattan, where he joined the militant activist group ACT UP and helped cofound *OutWeek* magazine. Writing a regular column there (Signorile joked that his trademark was the "upper-case invective"), he argued that "if the media are going to report heterosexual love affairs—whether that is right or not—it is simply homophobic for them to refuse to report homosexual ones. By not reporting about famous gays, the message the media send is clear: Homosexuality is so utterly grotesque that it should never be discussed." In his "Queer Manifesto," Signorile put forth a militant agenda for queer activism.

SOURCE: Michelangelo Signorile. *Sex, the Media, and the Closets of Power*. New York: Random House, 1993.

SELECTED READINGS: Larry Gross, *Contested Closets: The Politics and Ethics of Outing* (1993). Michelangelo Signorile, *Sex, the Media, and the Closets of Power* (1993). Richard D. Mohr, *Gay Ideas: Outing and Other Controversies* (1992).

To All Queers

There is no "right" to the closet.

If you are in it, it is not by your choice. You were forced into it as a child, and you are being held captive by a hypocritical, homophobic society.

Now is the time to plan your escape. The power to do so is inside of you, and only you can unleash it.

Stop sitting around blaming your parents, your school, the government, the media.

Stop whining about your existence and wallowing in self-pity.

Stop wishing yourself dead.

If you are already out of the closet, it is your obligation to help all those who are still being held prisoner.

If you are not yet out of the closet—if you are a teenager dependent on your parents, if you are trapped in a homophobic town or a rough city neighborhood where they beat up queers, if you are in any way in danger—hold on and plan for the day when you are older, when you have saved some money, when you can leave that place, when you can stand up on your own two feet and take charge of your life. No one can keep you where you are—except yourself. But you must come out wisely.

Everyone must come out of the closet, no matter how difficult, no matter how painful.

We must all tell our parents.

We must all tell our families.

We must all tell our friends.

We must all tell our coworkers.

These people vote. If they don't know that we're queer—if they think only the most horrible people are queer—they will vote against us.

What was done to us when we were children was nothing less than child abuse: Our psyches were tampered with, our personalities stunted.

Now we have a responsibility to speak out when we witness such crimes. If a child being viciously beaten by his parents confided in another child, would we expect the second child to respect the "privacy" of the other child's pain? Or would we praise him or her for speaking out?

Liberate yourself and all others who are locked in the closet. Don't be codependent with those whose dysfunction enables the bigots who bash us.

Badger everyone you know who is closeted—your friends, your family members, your coworkers—to come out. Put pressure on those in power whom you know to be queer. Send them letters. Call them on the phone. Fax them. Confront them in the streets.

Tell them they have a responsibility: to themselves, to you, to humanity.

Tell them they have to face the truth. And tell the truth yourself.

Tell them that you will not stop until they are out—until their closets no longer affect your life.

Remember that all those in the closet, blinded by their own trauma, hurt themselves and all other queers. The invisibility they perpetuate harms us more than any of their good deeds might benefit us.

As the demagogues of the religious right push ahead with their campaign of hatred against homosexuals, the moment of truth is upon us.

Now is the time for all queers to come out and be counted.

To the Closeted in Power

Get yourself some professional help.

The walls are caving in around you, and there's nothing you can do. Your future is going to be painful and difficult, and you would be wise to seek counseling rather than continue to live in denial. While it is hard for you to think rationally about coming out, try just for a moment:

An army of lovers is marching forth: women and women, men and men, arm in arm, hand in hand. Our numbers keep growing every day as we become more and more impatient with the likes of you. All of the hell you've lived through—the hiding, the sweating, the crying, the lying—is only going to become more unbearable. Unless you come out, you'll eventually be revealed as just another cowering, sad, self-loathing homosexual. You'll be remembered as just another Roy Cohn, just another Terry Dolan, just another J. Edgar Hoover.

Deep down, you know you have no "right" to be where you are, that you were shoved in your closet a long time ago. Deep down, you know why you must now come out and why it is wrong for you not to. It's better if you do it yourself. It's liberating and invigorating and empowering.

And it's time.

Just think: You'll be one of the people who have decided to be honest and make the world a better place for all queers. You'll be another Barney Frank, another Martina Navratilova, another k. d. lang, another David Geffen. You'll be a hero.

Now is the time for those who occupy the closets of power to come out and be counted.

To the Sympathetic Straights

From now on, discount the opinions of the closeted gays around you. Everything they have to say is colored by the closet, tinged by the repressed and fearful existence they lead.

Talk to the out-of-the-closet people you know, talk to several who represent a spectrum of opinions and experiences.

Admit it: All of you have some discomfort with homosexuality. Your minds have been as polluted as ours by the homophobic society in which we live.

You must now be part of changing that society, beginning in your own home. Your children must be brought up without the hatred, without the slurs, without the closet. They must be taught not only that they should have respect for lesbians and gay men but also that it's okay if they are gay themselves. And this honest, compassionate teaching must come not only from you but from their schools and from their churches.

Your queer children must not be forced into the closet.

If your children are being closeted—by you, by their teachers, or by their churches—you are engaging in child abuse, brutal psychological terror, the kind that may lead them to consider or even commit suicide. Stop the terror. Stop other parents from engaging in such abuse. Start thinking about the future, about constructing legislation that will punish people who abuse their children in this way.

Teach your straight children that it's okay if their brothers, their sisters, their cousins, their friends, their uncles, their aunts—even their moms or dads—are gay. Understand this: If your children are straight they cannot be made gay, but they *can* be made into gay bashers.

Those of you in positions of power, stop rewarding the closeted around you for being "discreet." Be there for your closeted friends and colleagues, help them and comfort them. Let them know how much you care. But do not aid in their self-destructive behavior. If a heroin addict were looking for a fix, wouldn't you help him through the withdrawal, no matter how painful it was?

If you really and truly love your closeted friends—as well as all humanity—you will not be party to maintaining their closets.

Now is the time for sympathetic straights to help their queer friends come out and be counted.

To the Religious Right

You say we're coming for your children, and you're right.

We're coming for your *queer* children. We *are* your queer children.

God—your God, our God—made us that way. And there's nothing you can do about it.

So now we have to be saved—from you—because you do nothing but warp innocent minds.

We will not allow you to force future generations into the closet.

We will not allow you to abuse them in that way.

We will not allow you to poison all of American life.

We will not allow you to breed hatred in our schools.

We will not allow you to create queer bashers and murderers.

We will not allow you to push us all back into the closet—in the military, on Capitol Hill, in Hollywood, or on Main Street.

We are never going back into the closet.

Your most articulate and ardent spokespeople and politicians still claim that homosexuality is a "choice."

This we find curious.

Sexuality is not a choice—it is a natural, immutable orientation. It's those who speak of "choice" who made a choice—a choice to fight their own queer urges. Many of them are repressed bisexuals and homosexuals, obsessed with routing out of society what is coming from deep inside them. Quite a few of them—we know for a fact—are even active but deeply closeted homosexuals who preach the gospel of homophobia.

But the army of lovers will no longer be silent; the greatest casualty in this war you've declared will be the closet.

To All Queer Activists

We have come to an exciting, critical juncture, one for which we have all worked hard.

But we are fractured, split into a million opposing factions. It is essential that we put our differences aside, at least for this crucial moment in history.

We must focus not on that which divides us—our genders, races, classes, ages, political ideologies—but on the one powerful enemy that we all have in common: the closet.

Our diversity is in fact our greatest weapon.

Now is the time for the gay Republicans and the black lesbian mothers and the computer nerds and the congressional staffers and the queer radicals and the gossip columnists and the AIDS activists and the television executives and the gay lobbyists and the record moguls and the outing proponents and the businesspeople and the drag queens to come together.

Our brainpower, resources, talent, and experiences will break down the closets of power forever.

And future generations will be able to be out, proud, and queer in America.

143. TONY KUSHNER

Matthew's Passion
(1998)

TONY KUSHNER's essay "Matthew's Passion" was a stirring and indignant commentary on the October 1998 murder of Matthew Shepard, a Laramie, Wyoming, teen who was brutally killed by two homophobes. Kushner (1956–) was born in Louisiana, and attended Columbia University. He won worldwide acclaim for his epic play *Angels in America*, which appeared on Broadway in two parts in 1992 and 1993. In "Matthew's Passion," Kushner drew a connection between Shepard's murder and the intolerance and bigotry of the religious right, and demanded that gay rights activists lobby strategically for a federal bill that would mandate stiff sentences for "hate crimes" against people who are targeted because of their sexual orientation. As of the publication of this book, no such law exists.

SOURCE: Tony Kushner. "Matthew's Passion." *The Nation.* November 11, 1998.

SELECTED READINGS: Beth Luffreda, *Losing Matt Shepard: Life and Politics in the Aftermath of Anti-Gay Murder* (2000). Tony Kushner, *Angels in America: A Gay Fantasia on National Themes* (1993).

When Trent Lott heard the news about the murder of Matthew Shepard, the first thoughts that flashed through his mind were all about spin. Trent Lott worried about how to keep his promise to the religious right, to speak out against the homosexual agenda, without seeming to endorse murder. Trent Lott endorses murder, of course; his party endorses murder, his party endorses discrimination against homosexuals and in doing so it endorses the ritual slaughter of homosexuals.

Democracy is a bloody business, demanding blood sacrifice. Every advance American democracy has made toward fulfilling the social contract, toward justice and equality and true liberty, every step forward has required offerings of pain and death. The American people demand this, we need to see the burnt bodies of the four little black girls, or their sad small coffins; we need to see the battered, disfigured face of the beaten housewife; we need to see the gay man literally crucified on a fence. We see the carnage and think, Oh, I guess things are still tough out there, for those people. We daydream a little: What does that feel like, to burn? To have your face smashed by your husband's fist? To be raped? To be dragged behind a truck till your body falls to pieces? To freeze, tied to a fence on the Wyoming prairie, for eighteen hours, with the back of your head staved in? Americans perfected the horror film, let's not kid ourselves: These acts of butchery titillate, we glean the news to savor the unsavory details.

And then, after we've drawn a few skin-prickling breaths of the aromas of torture and agony and madness, we shift a little in our comfortable chairs, a little embarrassed to have caught ourselves in the act of prurient sadism, a little worried that God has seen us also, a little worried that we have lazily misplaced our humanity, a little sad for the victims: Oh, gee, I guess I sort of think that shouldn't happen out there to those people, and something should be done. As long as I don't have to do it.

And having thought as much, having, in fact, been edified, changed a very little bit by the suffering we have seen, our humanity as well as our skin having been pricked, we turn our back on Matthew Shepard's crucifixion and return to our legitimate entertainments. When next the enfranchisement of homosexuals is discussed, Matthew Shepard's name will probably be invoked, and the murder of gay people will be deplored by decent people, straight and gay; and when the religious right shrills viciously about how the murder doesn't matter, as it has been doing since his death, decent people everywhere will find the religious right lacking human kindness, will find these Gary Bauers and Paul Weyrichs and Pat Robertsons un-Christian, repulsive, in fact. And a very minute increment toward decency will have been secured. But poor Matthew Shepard. Jesus, what a price!

Trent Lott endorses murder. He knows that discrimination kills. Pope John Paul II endorses murder. He, too, knows the price of discrimination, having declared anti-Semitism a sin, having just canonized a Jewish-born nun who died in Auschwitz. He knows that discrimination kills. But when the Pope heard the news about Matthew Shepard, he too worried about spin. And so, on the subject of gay-bashing, the Pope and his cardinals and his bishops and priests maintain their cynical political silence. Rigorously denouncing the abuse and murder of homosexuals would be a big sin against spin; denouncing the murder of homosexuals in such a way that it received even one-thousandth of the coverage his and his church's attacks on homosexuals routinely receive, this would be an act of decency the Pope can't afford, for the

Pope knows: Behind this one murdered kid stand legions of kids whose lives are scarred by the bigotry this Pope defends as sanctioned by God. None of these kids will ever be allowed to marry the person she or he loves, not while the Pope and his church can prevent it; all of these kids are told, by the Holy Catholic Church, and by the Episcopalians and Lutherans and Baptists and Orthodox Jews: Your love is cursed by God. To speak out against murdering those who are discriminated against is to speak out against discrimination. To remain silent is to endorse murder.

A lot of people worry these days about the death of civil discourse. The Pope, in his new encyclical, *Fides et Ratio* (Faith and Reason), laments the death of civil discourse and cites "ancient philosophers who proposed friendship as one of the most appropriate contexts for sound philosophical inquiry." It's more than faintly ludicrous, this plea for friendship coming from the self-same Pope who has tried so relentlessly to stamp out dissent in churches and Catholic universities, but let's follow the lead of the crazies who killed Matthew Shepard and take the Pope at his word.

Friendship is the proper context for discussion. Fine and good. Take the gun away from the head, Your Holiness, and we can discuss the merits of homosexual sex, of homosexual marriage, of homosexual love, of monogamy versus promiscuity, of lesbian or gay couples raising kids, of condom distribution in the schools, of confidential counseling for teenagers, of sex education that addresses more than abstinence. We can discuss abortion, we can discuss anything you like. Just promise me two things, *friend*: First, you won't beat my brains out with a pistol butt and leave me to die by the side of the road. Second, if someone else, someone a little less sane than you, feeling entitled to commit these terrible things against me because they understood you a little too literally, or were more willing than you to take your distaste for me and what I do to its most full-blooded conclusion, if someone else does violence against me, *friend*, won't you *please* make it your business to make a big public fuss about how badly I was treated? Won't you please make a point, *friend*, you who call yourself, and who are called, by millions of people, the Vicar on Earth of the very gentle Jesus, won't you please in the name of friendship announce that no one who deliberately inflicts suffering, whether by violence or by prejudice, on another human being, can be said to be acting in God's name? And announce it so that it is very clear that you include homosexuals when you refer to "human beings," and announce it so that the world hears you, really hears you, so that your announcement makes the news, as you are capable of doing when it suits your purposes? Won't you make this your purpose too? And if you won't, if you won't take responsibility for the consequences of your militant promotion of discrimination, won't you excuse me if I think you are not a friend at all but rather a homicidal liar whose claim to spiritual and moral leadership is fatally compromised, is worth nothing more than . . . well, worth nothing more than the disgusting, opportunistic leadership of Trent Lott.

A lot of people worry these days about the death of civil discourse, and would say that I ought not call the Pope a homicidal liar, nor (to be ecumenical about it) the orthodox rabbinate homicidal liars, nor Trent Lott a disgusting opportunistic hatemonger. But I worry a lot less about the death of civil discourse than I worry about being killed if, visiting the wrong town with my boyfriend, we forget ourselves so much as to betray, at the wrong moment in front of the wrong people, that we love one another. I worry much more about the recent death of the Maine antidiscrimination bill, and about the death of the New York hate crimes bill, which will not pass because it includes sexual orientation. I worry more about the death of civil rights than civil discourse. I worry much more about the irreversible soul-deaths of lesbian, gay, bisexual, transgendered children growing up deliberately, malevolently isolated by the likes of Trent Lott and Newt Gingrich than I worry about the death of civil discourse. I mourn Matthew Shepard's actual death, caused by the unimpeachably civil "we hate the sin, not the sinner" hypocrisy of the religious right, endorsed by the political right, much more than I mourn the lost chance to be civil with someone who does not consider me fully a citizen, nor fully human. I mourn that cruel death more than the chance to be civil with those who sit idly by while theocrats, bullies, panderers and hatemongers, and their crazed murderous children, destroy democracy and our civic life. Civic, not civil, discourse is what matters, and civic discourse mandates the assigning of blame.

If you are lesbian, gay, transgendered, bi, reading this, here's one good place to assign blame: The Human Rights Campaign's appalling, post-Shepard endorsement of Al D'Amato dedicates our resources to the perpetuation of a Republican majority in Congress. The HRC, ostensibly our voice in Washington, is in cahoots with fag-bashers and worse. If you are a heterosexual person, and you are reading this: Yeah yeah yeah, you've heard it all before, but *if* you have not called your Congressperson to demand passage of a hate crimes bill that includes sexual orientation, and e-mailed every Congressperson, if you have not gotten up out of your comfortable chair to campaign for homosexual and all civil rights—*campaign*, not just passively support—may you think about this crucified man, and may you mourn, and may you burn with a moral citizen's shame. As one civilized person to another: *Matthew Shepard shouldn't have died. We should all burn with shame.*

EPILOGUE

New Directions

144. THOMAS FRANK

Why Johnny Can't Dissent
(1995)

In the following essay, author and editor **THOMAS FRANK** argues that countercultural ideals of rebellion and creative independence have also become business ideals. Johnny can't dissent, Frank suggests, because dissent has become an official ideology of capitalists and entrepreneurs. This article first appeared in *The Baffler,* a journal of cultural criticism that Frank founded when he was an undergraduate at the University of Virginia. In 1994 he received his Ph.D. in history from the University of Chicago. He has published in *Harper's, The Nation, In These Times,* and many other venues, and he has written two well-received books, *The Conquest of Cool* and *One Market Under God.*

SOURCE: Thomas Frank and Matt Weiland, eds. *Commodify Your Dissent: Salvos from* The Baffler. New York: W. W. Norton, 1997.

SELECTED READINGS: Thomas Frank, *The Conquest of Cool: Business Culture, Counterculture, and the Rise of Hip Consumerism* (1997).

Capitalism is changing, obviously and drastically. From the moneyed pages of the *Wall Street Journal* to TV commercials for airlines and photocopiers we hear every day about the new order's globe-spanning, cyber-accumulating ways. But our notion about what's wrong with American life and how the figures responsible are to be confronted haven't changed much in thirty years. Call it, for convenience, the "countercultural idea." It holds that the paramount ailment of our society is conformity, a malady that has variously been described as over-organization, bureaucracy, homogeneity, hierarchy, logocentrism, technocracy, the Combine, the Apollonian. We all know what it is and what it does. It transforms humanity into "organization man," into "the man in the gray flannel suit." It is "Moloch whose mind is pure machinery," the "incomprehensible prison" that consumes "brains and imagination." It is artifice, starched shirts, tailfins, carefully mowed lawns, and always, always, the consciousness of impending nuclear destruction. It is a stiff, militaristic order that seeks to suppress instinct, to forbid sex and pleasure, to deny basic human impulses and individuality, to enforce through a rigid uniformity a meaningless plastic consumerism.

As this half of the countercultural idea originated during the 1950s, it is appropriate that the evils of conformity are most conveniently summarized with images of 1950s suburban correctness. You know, that land of sedate music, sexual repression, deference to authority, Red Scares, and smiling white people standing politely in line to go to church. Constantly appearing as a symbol of arch-backwardness in advertising and movies, it is an image we find easy to evoke.

The ways in which this system are to be resisted are equally well understood and agreed-upon. The Establishment demands homogeneity; we revolt by embracing diverse, individual lifestyles. It demands self-denial and rigid adherence to convention; we revolt through immediate gratification, instinct uninhibited, and liberation of the libido and the appetites. Few have put it more bluntly than Jerry Rubin did in 1970: "Amerika says: Don't! The yippies say: Do It!" The countercultural idea is hostile to any law and every establishment. "Whenever we see a rule, we must break it," Rubin continued. "Only by breaking rules do we discover who we are." Above all, rebellion consists of a sort of Nietzschean antinomianism, an automatic questioning of rules, a rejection of whatever social prescriptions we've happened to inherit. Just Do It is the whole of the law.

The patron saints of the countercultural idea are, of course, the Beats, whose frenzied style and merry alienation still maintain a powerful grip on the American imagination. Even forty years after the publication of *On the Road*, the works of Kerouac, Ginsberg, and Burroughs remain the *sine qua non* of dissidence, the model for aspiring poets, rock stars, or indeed anyone who feels vaguely artistic or alienated. That frenzied sensibility of pure experience, life on the edge, immediate gratification, and total freedom from moral restraint, which the Beats first propounded back in those heady days when suddenly everyone could have their own TV and powerful V-8, has stuck with us through all the intervening years and become something of a permanent American style. Go to any poetry reading and you can see a string of junior Kerouacs go through the routine, upsetting cultural hierarchies by pushing themselves to the limit, straining for that gorgeous moment of original vice when Allen Ginsberg first read "Howl" in 1955 and the patriarchs of our fantasies recoiled in shock. The Gap may have since claimed Ginsberg and *USA Today* may run feature stories about the brilliance of the beloved Kerouac, but the rebel race continues today regardless, with ever-heightening shit-references calculated to scare. Jesse Helms, talk about sex and smack that is supposed to bring the electricity of real life, and ever-more determined defiance of the repressive rules and mores of the American 1950s—rules and mores that by now we know only from movies.

But one hardly has to go to a poetry reading to see the countercultrual idea acted out. Its frenzied ecstasies have long since become an official aesthetic of consumer society, a monotheme of mass as well as adversarial culture. Turn on the TV and there it is instantly: the unending drama of consumer unbound and in search of an ever-heightened good time, the inescapable rock 'n' roll soundtrack, dreadlocks and ponytails bounding into Taco Bells, a drunken, swinging-camera epiphany of tennis shoes, outlaw soda pops, and mind-bending dandruff shampoos. Corporate America, it turns out, no longer speaks in the voice of oppressive order that it did when Ginsberg moaned in 1956 that *Time* magazine was

> always telling me about responsibility. Business-
> men are serious. Movie producers are serious.
> Everybody's serious but me.

Nobody wants you to think they're serious today, least of all Time Warner. On the contrary: the Culture Trust is now our leader in the Ginsbergian search for kicks upon kicks. Corporate America is not an oppressor but a sponsor of fun, provider of lifestyle accoutrements, facilitator of carnival, our slang-speaking partner in the quest for that ever-more apocalyptic orgasm. The countercultural idea has become capitalist orthodoxy, its hunger for transgression upon transgression now perfectly suited to an economic-cultural regime that runs on ever-faster cyclings of the new; its taste for self-fulfillment and its intolerance for the confines of tradition now permitting vast latitude in consuming practices and lifestyle experimentation.

Consumerism is no longer about "conformity" but about "difference." Advertising teaches us not in the ways of puritanical self-denial (a bizarre notion on the face of it), but in orgiastic, never-ending self-fulfillment. It counsels not rigid adherence to the tastes of the herd but vigilant and constantly updated individualism. We consume not to fit in, but to prove, on the surface at least, that we are rock 'n' roll rebels, each one of us as rule-breaking and hierarchy-defying as our heroes of the 60s, who now pitch cars, shoes, and beer. This imperative of endless difference is today the genius at the heart of American capitalism, an eternal fleeing from "sameness" that satiates our thirst for the New with such achievements of civilization as the infinite brands of identical cola, the myriad colors and irrepressible variety of the cigarette rack at 7-Eleven.

As existential rebellion has become a more or less official style of Information Age capitalism, so has the countercultural notion of a static, repressive Establishment grown hopelessly obsolete. However the basic impulses of the countercultural idea may have disturbed a nation lost in Cold War darkness, they are today in fundamental agreement with the basic tenets of Information Age business theory. So close are they, in fact, that it has become difficult to understand the countercultural idea as anything more than the self-justifying ideology of the new bourgeoisie that has arisen since the 1960s, the cultural means by which this group has proven itself ever so much better skilled than its slow-moving, security-minded forebears at adapting to the accelerated, always-changing consumerism of today. The anointed cultural opponents of capitalism are now capitalism's ideologues. . . .

For with the assumption of power by Drucker's and Reich's new class has come an entirely new ideology of business, a way of justifying and exercising power that has little to do with the "conformity" and the "establishment" so vilified by the countercultural idea. The management theorists and "leader-ship" charlatans of the Information Age don't waste their time prattling about hierarchy and regulation, but about disorder, chaos, and the meaninglessness of convention. With its reorganization around information, capitalism has de-veloped a new mythology, a sort of corporate antinomianism according to which the breaking of rules and the elimination of rigid corporate structure have become the central article of faith for millions of aspiring executives.

Dropping *Naked Lunch* and picking up *Thriving on Chaos*, the groundbreak-ing 1987 management text by Tom Peters, the most popular business writer of the past decade, one finds more philosophical similarities than one would expect from two manifestos of, respectively, dissident culture and business culture. If anything, Peters' celebration of disorder is, by virtue of its hard statistics, bleaker and more nightmarish than Burroughs'. For this popular lecturer on such once-blithe topics as competitiveness and pop psychology there is nothing, absolutely nothing, that is certain. His world is one in which the corporate wisdom of the past is meaningless, established customs are ri-diculous, and "rules" are some sort of curse, a remnant of the foolish fifties that exist to be defied, not obeyed. We live in what Peters calls "A World Turned Upside Down," in which whirl is king and, in order to survive, busi-nesses must eventually embrace Peters' universal solution: "Revolution!" "To meet the demands of the fast-changing competitive scene," he counsels, "we must simply learn to love change as much as we have hated it in the past." He advises businessmen to become Robespierres of routine, to demand of their underlings, " 'What have you changed lately?' 'How fast are you changing?' and 'Are you pursuing bold enough change goals?' " "Revolution," of course, means for Peters the same thing it did to Burroughs and Ginsberg, Presley and the Stones in their heyday: breaking rules, pissing off the suits, shocking the bean-counters: "Actively and publicly hail defiance of the rules, many of which you doubtless labored mightily to construct in the first place." Peters even suggests that his readers implement this hostility to logocentrism in a carnivalesque celebration, drinking beer out in "the woods" and destroying "all the forms and rules and discontinued reports" and, "if you've got real nerve," a photocopier as well.

Today corporate antinomianism is the emphatic message of nearly every new business text, continually escalating the corporate insurrection begun by Peters. Capitalism, at least as it is envisioned by the best-selling management handbooks, is no longer about enforcing Order, but destroying it. "Revolution," once the totemic catchphrase of the counterculture, has become the totemic catchphrase of boomer-as-capitalist. The Information Age business-man holds inherited ideas and traditional practices not in reverence, but in high suspicion. Even reason itself is now found to be an enemy of true competitiveness, an out-of-date faculty to be scrupulously avoided by conscientious managers. A 1990 book by Charles Handy entitled *The Age of Unreason* agrees with Peters that we inhabit a time in which "there can be no certainty" and suggests that readers engage in full-fledged epistemological revolution: "Thinking Upside Down," using new ways of "learning which can . . . be seen as disrespectful if not downright rebellious," methods of approaching problems that have "never been popular with the upholders of continuity and of the status quo." Three years later the authors of *Reengineering the Corporation* ("A Manifesto for Business Revolution," as its subtitle declares) are ready to push this doctrine even farther. Not only should we be suspicious of traditional practices, but we should cast out virtually everything learned over the past two centuries!

> Business reengineering means putting aside much of the received wisdom of two hundred years of industrial management. It means forgetting how work was done in the age of the mass market and deciding how it can best be done now. In business reengineering, old job titles and old organizational arrangements—departments, divisions, groups, and so on—cease to matter. They are artifacts of another age.

As countercultural rebellion becomes corporate ideology, even the beloved Buddhism of the Beats wins a place on the executive bookshelf. In *The Leader as Martial Artist* (1993), Arnold Mindell advises men of commerce in the ways of the Tao, mastery of which he likens, of course, to surfing. For Mindell's Zen businessman, as for the followers of Tom Peters, the world is a wildly chaotic place of opportunity, navigable only to an enlightened "leader" who can discern the "timespirits" at work behind the scenes. In terms Peters himself might use were he a more meditative sort of inspiration professional, Mindell explains that "the wise facilitator" doesn't seek to prevent the inevitable and random clashes between "conflicting field spirits," but to anticipate such bouts of disorder and profit thereby.

Contemporary corporate fantasy imagines a world of ceaseless, turbulent change, of centers that ecstatically fail to hold, of joyous extinction for the craven gray-flannel creature of the past. Businessmen today decorate the walls of their offices not with portraits of President Eisenhower and emblems of suburban order, but with images of extreme athletic daring, with sayings about "diversity" and "empowerment" and "thinking outside the box." They theorize their world not in the bar car of the commuter train, but in weepy corporate retreats at which they beat their tom-toms and envision themselves as part of the great avant-garde tradition of edge-livers, risk-takers, and ass-kickers. Their world is a place not of sublimation and conformity, but of "leadership" and bold talk about defying the herd. And there is nothing this new enlightened species of businessman despises more than "rules" and "reason." The prominent culture-warriors of the right may believe that the counterculture was capitalism's undoing, but the antinomian businessmen know better. "One of the t-shirt slogans of the sixties read, 'Question authority,' " the authors of *Reengineering the Corporation* write. "Process owners might buy their reengineering team members the nineties version: 'Question assumptions.' "

The new businessman quite naturally gravitates to the slogans and sensibility of the rebel sixties to express his understanding of the new Information World. He is led in what one magazine calls "the business revolution" by the office-park subversives it hails as "business activists," "change agents," and "corporate radicals." He speaks to his comrades through commercials like the one for "Warp," a type of IBM computer operating system, in which an electric guitar soundtrack and psychedelic video effects surround hip executives with earrings and hairdos who are visibly stunned by the product's gnarly 'tude (It's a "totally cool way to run your computer," read the product's print ads). He understands the world through *Fast Company*, a successful new magazine whose editors take their inspiration from Hunter S. Thompson and whose stories describe such things as a "dis-organization" that inhabits an "anti-office" where "all vestiges of hierarchy have disappeared" or a computer scientist who is also "a rabble rouser, an agent provocateur, a product of the 1960s who never lost his activist fire or democratic values." He is what sociologists Paul Leinberger and Bruce Tucker have called "The New Individualist," the new and improved manager whose arty worldview and creative hip derive directly from his formative sixties days. The one thing this new executive is definitely *not* is Organization Man, the hyper-rational counter of beans, attender of church, and wearer of stiff hats.

In television commercials, through which the new American businessman presents his visions and self-understanding to the public, perpetual revolution and the gospel of rule-breaking are the orthodoxy of the day. You only need to watch for a few minutes before you see one of these slogans and understand the grip of antinomianism over the corporate mind:

Sometimes You Gotta Break the Rules	*—Burger King*
If You Don't Like the Rules, Change Them	*—WXRT-FM*
The Rules Have Changed	*—Dodge*
The Art of Changing	*—Swatch*
There's no one way to do it.	*—Levi's*
This is different. Different is good.	*—Arby's*
Just Different From the Rest	*—Special Export beer*
The Line Has Been Crossed: The Revolutionary New Supra	*—Toyota*
Resist the Usual *—the slogan of both Clash Clear Malt and Young & Rubicam*	
Innovate Don't Imitate	*—Hugo Boss*
Chart Your Own Course	*—Navigator Cologne*
It separates you from the crowd	*—Vision Cologne*

In most, the commercial message is driven home with the vanguard iconography of the rebel: screaming guitars, whirling cameras, and startled old timers who, we predict, will become an increasingly indispensable prop as consumers require ever-greater assurances that, Yes! You *are* a rebel! Just look at how offended they are! . . .

The structure and thinking of American business have changed enormously in the years since our popular conceptions of its problems and abuses were formulated. In the meantime the mad frothings and jolly apolitical revolt of Beat, despite their vast popularity and insurgent air, have become powerless against a new regime that, one suspects, few of Beat's present-day admirers and practitioners feel any need to study or understand. Today that beautiful countercultural idea, endorsed now by everyone from the surviving Beats to shampoo manufacturers, is more the official doctrine of corporate America than it is a program of resistance. What we understand as "dissent" does not subvert, does not challenge, does not even question the cultural faiths of Western business. What David Rieff wrote of the revolutionary pretensions of multiculturalism is equally true of the countercultural idea: "The more one reads in academic multiculturalist journals and in business publications, and the more one contrasts the speeches of CEOs and the speeches of noted multiculturalist academics, the more one is struck by the similarities in the way they view the world." What's happened is not co-optation or appropriation, but a simple and direct confluence of interest.

The problem with cultural dissent in America isn't that it's been co-opted, absorbed, or ripped-off. Of course it's been all of these things. But it has proven so hopelessly susceptible to such assaults for the same reason it has become so harmless in the first place, so toothless even before Mr. Geffen's boys discover it angsting away in some bar in Lawrence, Kansas: It is no longer any different from the official culture it's supposed to be subverting. The basic impulses of the countercultural idea, as descended from the holy Beats, are about as threatening to the new breed of antinomian businessmen as Anthony Robbins, selling success & how to achieve it on a late-night infomercial.

The people who staff the Combine aren't like Nurse Ratched. They aren't Frank Burns, they aren't the Church Lady, they aren't Dean Wormer from *Animal House*, they aren't those repressed old folks in the commercials who want to ban Tropicana Fruit Twisters. They're hipper than you can ever hope to be because *hip is their official ideology,* and they're always going to be there at the poetry reading to encourage your "rebellion" with a hearty "right on, man!" before you even know they're in the auditorium. You can't outrun them, or even stay ahead of them for very long: it's their racetrack, and that's them waiting at the finish line to congratulate you on how *outrageous* your new style is, on how you *shocked* those stuffy prudes out in the heartland.

145. ASHA BANDELE

Habeus Corpus is a Legal Entitlement
(1996)

The popularity of spoken word—poetry that is performed aloud without music—exploded during the 1990s. Inspired by the 1950s Beat generation, the protest aesthetic of the Black Arts Movement, and contemporary Hip Hop culture, spoken word is a multicultural medium through which poetry and performance combine to produce improvisational rhythms and rhymes in public settings. At once personal and political, spoken word has spread from its original venue in cafes and clubs in New York City and Los Angeles to other cities across the United States and abroad. Increasingly popular in high schools and on college campuses, "poetry slams," wherein spoken word poets compete against one another at an "open-mic" for audience approval, are dominated by young people, members of the so-called "Hip Hop Generation." One of the major poets of the spoken word movement, **ASHA BANDELE**, editor-at-large for *Essence* magazine, published the following poem in her acclaimed first volume of poetry, *Absence in the Palms of My Hands* (1996). In "Habeus Corpus is a Legal Entitlement," bandele confronts head on the brutal realities of contemporary America—poverty and racism, as well as the legal assault on black men by the prison–industrial system—with the frank, liberated voice of a black woman poet.

SOURCE: asha bandele. *Absence in the Palms of My Hands & Other Poems.* New York and London: Harlem River Press, 1996.

SELECTED READINGS: Mark Eleveld, *The Spoken Word Revolution: Slam, Hip Hop, and the Poetry of the Underground.* (2003). Gil Scott-Heron, *Now and Then: The Poems of Gil Scott-Heron* (2001). Zoe Anglesey, ed., *Listen Up!: Spoken Word Poetry* (1999). Jessica Care Moore, *The Words Don't Fit in My Mouth* (1997). Jill Battson and Ken Norris, eds., *Word Up: Spoken Word Poetry in Print* (1995).

habeus corpus is a legal entitlement

for the men at eastern correctional facility who felt
i should not include curses in my poetry
1.
this poem is a writ of habeus corpus meaning
get yo/hands off me
b4 i kill you

2.
in america
1 in 21 blkmen will be shot 2 death/being shot
is the leading cause of death
4 blkmen aged 15 to 24
u wanna hear more?
had u been in vietnam during the war
u were more likely to survive than u are today
if you're blk / male / & btwn 15 & 25
&
u
ask
me

why i curse & rage & sound obscene
explain whatchu mean
what is more offensive than the way we live
except perhaps
the way we die
    & this poem is a call out

where are the warriors
where are the truth tellers
where are the fearless dragons
where are the life creators/the life sustainers
the singers of songs of liberation
where are the builders of the nation
where are the war dancers & blkpanthers
the righteous & the mighty

where are the race men
the proud people
the Holy Spirits
the tireless foot soldiers carrying the word
(carry the word soldier)
use the spear & shield & lite
let it shine in the underground tunnels taking us back
way way on back blkpeople   we been gone so long
did we forget
there was life b4 the brandings the auction blocks   the rapes
(our mommies shredded on the inside/torn by more violations than even
she could count/noooo don't touch my mommy don't hurt my
mommy/daddy please . . . yet he too was silenced/his mouth stuffed with his
   own genitalia)

but b4 this
there was life
came back 2 that
came back blk 2 that
come way on back   *we had been a peaceful people*
                      original east african languages had no
                      words 2 denote possession

                      we had been a correct people
                      known 2 welcome strangers
                      & 2 honor the land
                      & 2 the honor the magic produced by the land
come back blk/magic people
allow no one to replace
the pyramids
with those crack houses & prisons
allow no one
2
replace the pyramids

3.
yo/baby
fuck dat
!!!BANG BANG BLAU BLAU!!!
dats how we livin now

minute 2 minute
& bullet 2 bullet
> *(now the only shorts i takes are the one's that i wear   ain't takin' no shorts
> no mo)**

BLAU BLAU!!!
harder than rock 17 rounds in my glock
is my best friend 2 the muthafuckin end
BLAU BLAU!!!
so
tell
me
how
?
how do i write a poem about life in my city
about racism hatred & the resulting tribal wars
that leave in their wake bloody open sores
swelling prison doors
locking down the daily promise
the 360 degrees
of life / strengh
& knowledge

&
someone asked me
why i curse
?
!
u tell me what words sound worse than
starvation
homelessness
oppression
prison
murder
&
greed
what sounds worse than children in need
of safety love clothing
housing & healthcare
of education & food

*sung by A Tribe Called Quest

or simply put

> *justice*
> *a*
> *one*
> *word*
> *prayer***

4.

& i wanna write poems that make beauty appear
but 2 do that i gotta write poems that create anger & fear
poems that make us so afraid 4 our lives
we'll finally fight 4 lives
we need poems that straight up
terrorize
all those among us
who worship not children
but gold
we need poetry that breaks the american mold
that tears open at the core all the lies & more
poetry that makes blk/lions roar
freedom
while building a world safe to live in
a world where blk/dead & 16
is no longer a given
we need poetry that screams
this cracka's a deadly muthafucka & there ain't no reason we got 2 go out
& go out like suckers
& 4 my people on the inside
what can be said that sounds nice or pretty
about any so-called correctional facility
the path travelled that brought each one of us here
is a long train of abuses & a trail of tears***
& this poet feels war-torn with blood in my eyes
my throat is scratched raw with desperate cries
> retribution! 4 john kelly killed the last day of '91
> (he was blk they was wite that's the only reason)
> retribution! 4 more people than i ever could mention
> including prisoners & the long years of detention

**sung by Ziggy Marley
***from the American Declaration of Independence

if we want liberation
we gotta stand firm & show it
& never again tell any blk/poet
to play words games
& put harsh language on ice
& somehow make our genocide
sound nice.

146. Transgender Movement

International Bill of Gender Rights (1995) and
Read My Lips
(1997)

The struggle of transgendered people for visibility and equal rights poses a fundamental challenge to contemporary notions of gender and sexuality. Speaking at once to their marginalization within the Feminist and Queer Liberation movements, as well as their almost total exclusion from mainstream discussions of the rights of citizenship, members of the transgender (or trans-identified) movement seek to alter the unequal relations of power that perpetuate forms of sex- and gender-based discrimination. A cornerstone of this movement is the International Bill of Gender Rights (IBGR), drafted at the International Conference on Transgender Law and Employment Policy, Inc., in August 1993, which outlines ten fundamental human and civil rights from a gender perspective. Among the movement's leading voices is Riki Anne Wichins, an activist/writer who co-founded Transsexual Menace and now serves as executive director of GenderPAC, a coalition of advocacy groups that fight for the rights of "transpeople." Wilchins's pathbreaking book, *Read My Lips* (1997)—part theory, part autobiography, part performance art—radically challenges the way we think about bodies, sex, gender, and power.

SOURCES: Riki Anne Wilchins. *Read My Lips: Sexual Subversion and the End of Gender*. Ithaca: New York, 1997; Leslie Feinberg. *Transgender Warriors: Making History from Joan of Arc to Rupaul*. Boston: Beacon Press, 1996

SELECTED READINGS: Viviane K. Namaste, *Invisible Lives: The Erasure of Transsexual and Transgendered People* (2000). Bonnie Bullough, Vern L. Bullough, and James Elias, eds., *Gender Blending* (1997). Zachary I. Nataf, *Lesbians Talk*

Transgender (1996). Gordene Olga MacKenzie, *Transgender Nation* (1994). Judith Butler, *Gender Trouble* (1990).

International Bill of Gender Rights
As Adopted June 17, 1995

The Restatement Of

the International Bill of Gender Rights (IBGR) was first drafted in committee and adopted by the International Conference on Transgender Law and Employment Policy, Inc. (ICTLEP) at that organization's second annual meeting, held in Houston, Texas, August 26–29, 1993.

The IBGR combines and expands from two earlier documents authored separately by Jo Ann Roberts of Pennsylvania and Sharon Stuart of New York.

The IBGR strives to express fundamental human and civil rights from a gender perspective. However, the ten rights enunciated below are not to be viewed as special rights applicable to a particular interest group. Nor are these rights limited in application to persons for whom gender identity and role issues are of paramount concern. All ten parts of the IBGR are universal rights which can be claimed and exercised by every human being.

The IBGR is a theoretical expression which has no force of law absent its adoption by legislative bodies and recognition of its principles by courts of law, administrative agencies and international bodies such as the United Nations.

However, individuals are free to adopt the truths and principles expressed in the IBGR, and to lead their lives accordingly. In this fashion, the truths expressed in the IBGR will liberate and empower humankind in ways and to an extent beyond the reach of legislators, judges, officials and diplomats.

When the truths expressed in the IBGR are embraced and given expression by humankind, the acts of legislatures and pronouncements of courts and other governing structures will necessarily follow. Thus, the paths of free expression trodden by millions of human beings seeking to define and express themselves, and give meaning to their lives, will ultimately determine the course of governing bodies.

The IBGR is a transformative and revolutionary document, but it is grounded in the bedrock of individual liberty and free expression. As our lives unfold, these kernels of truth are here for all who would claim and exercise them.

This document, though copyrighted, may be reproduced by any means and freely distributed by anyone supporting the principles and statements contained in the International Bill of Gender Rights.

The IBGR remains subject to review and revision by ICTLEP. Proposed revisions to the IBGR and comments should be forwarded to Sharon Stuart, International Bill of Gender Rights Project, P.O. Box 930, Cooperstown, NY 13326, U.S.A. Telephone: (607) 547–4118. E-mail: StuComOne@aol.com

The Right to Define Gender Identity

All human beings carry within themselves an ever-unfolding idea of who they are and what they are capable of achieving. The individual's sense of self is not determined by chromosomal sex, genitalia, assigned birth sex, or initial gender role. Thus, the individual's identity and capabilities cannot be circumscribed by what society deems to be masculine or feminine behavior. It is fundamental that individuals have the right to define, and to redefine as their lives unfold, their own gender identities, without regard to chromosomal sex, genitalia, assigned birth sex, or initial gender role.

Therefore, all human beings have the right to define their own gender identity regardless of chromosomal sex, genitalia, assigned birth sex, or initial gender role; and further, no individual shall be denied Human or Civil Rights by virtue of a self-defined gender identity which is not in accord with chromosomal sex, genitalia, assigned birth sex, or initial gender role.

The Right to Free Expression of Gender Identity

Given the right to define one's own gender identity, all human beings have the corresponding right to free expression of their self-defined gender identity.

Therefore, all human beings have the right to free expression of their self-defined gender identity; and further, no individual shall be denied Human or Civil Rights by virtue of the expression of a self-defined gender identity.

The Right to Secure and Retain Employment and to Receive Just Compensation

Given the economic structure of modern society, all human beings have a right to train for and to pursue an occupation or profession as a means of providing shelter, sustenance, and the necessities and bounty of life, for themselves and for those dependent upon them, to secure and retain employment, and to receive just compensation for their labor regardless of gender identity, chromosomal sex, genitalia, assigned birth sex, or initial gender role.

Therefore, individuals shall not be denied the right to train for and to pursue an occupation or profession, nor be denied the right to secure and retain employment, nor he denied just compensation for their labor, by virtue of their chromosomal sex, genitalia, assigned birth sex, or initial gender role, or on the basis of a self-defined gender identity or the expression thereof.

The Right of Access to Gendered Space and Participation in Gendered Activity

Given the right to define one's own gender identity and the corresponding right to free expression of a self-defined gender identity, no individual should be denied access to a space or denied participation in an activity by virtue of a self-defined gender identity which is not in accord with chromosomal sex, genitalia, assigned birth sex, or initial gender role.

Therefore, no individual shall be denied access to a space or denied participation in an activity by virtue of a self-defined gender identity which is not in accord with chromosomal sex, genitalia, assigned birth sex, or initial gender role.

The Right to Control and Change One's Own Body

All human beings have the right to control their bodies, which includes the right to change their bodies cosmetically, chemically, or surgically, so as to express a self-defined gender identity.

Therefore, individuals shall not be denied the right to change their bodies as a means of expressing a self-defined gender identity; and further, individuals shall not be denied Human or Civil Rights on the basis that they have changed their bodies cosmetically, chemically, or surgically, or desire to do so as a means of expressing a self-defined gender identity.

The Right to Competent Medical and Professional Care

Given the individual's right to one's own gender identity, and the right to change one's own body as a means of expressing a self-defined gender identity, no individual should be denied access to competent medical or other professional care on the basis of the individual's chromosomal sex, genitalia, assigned birth sex, or initial gender role.

Therefore, individuals shall not be denied the right to competent medical or other professional care when changing their bodies cosmetically, chemically, or surgically, on the basis of chromosomal sex, genitalia, assigned birth sex, or initial gender role.

The Right to Freedom From Psychiatric Diagnosis or Treatment

Given the right to define one's own gender identity, individuals should not be subject to psychiatric diagnosis or treatment solely on the basis of their gender identity or role.

Therefore, individuals shall not be subject to psychiatric diagnosis or treatment as mentally disordered or diseased solely on the basis of a self-defined gender identity or the expression thereof.

The Right to Sexual Expression

Given the right to a self-defined gender identity, every consenting adult has a corresponding right to free sexual expression.

Therefore, no individual's Human or Civil Rights shall be denied on the basis of sexual orientation; and further, no individual shall be denied Human or Civil Rights for expression of a self-defined gender identity through sexual acts between consenting adults.

The Right to Form Committed, Loving Relationships and Enter into Marital Contracts

Given that all human beings have the right to free expression of self-defined gender identities, and the right to sexual expression as a form of gender expression, all human beings have a corresponding right to form committed, loving relationships with one another, and to enter into marital contracts, regardless of their own or their partner's chromosomal sex, genitalia, assigned birth sex, or initial gender role.

Therefore, individuals shall not be denied the right to form committed, loving relationships with one another or to enter into marital contracts by virtue of their own or their partner's chromosomal sex, genitalia, assigned birth sex, or initial gender role, or on the basis of their expression of a self-defined gender identity.

The Right to Conceive, Bear, or Adopt Children
The Right to Nurture and Have Custody of Children and to Exercise Parental Capacity

Given the right to form a committed, loving relationship with another, and to enter into marital contracts, together with the right to express a self-defined gender identity and the right to sexual expression, individuals have a corresponding right to conceive and bear children, to adopt children, to nurture children, to have custody of children, and to exercise parental capacity with respect to children, natural or adopted, without regard to chromosomal sex, genitalia, assigned birth sex, or initial gender role, or by virtue of a self-defined gender identity or the expression thereof.

Therefore, individuals shall not be denied the right to conceive, bear, or adopt children, nor to nurture and have custody of children, nor to exercise parental capacity with respect to children, natural or adopted, on the basis of their own, their partner's, or their children's chromosomal sex, genitalia, assigned birth sex, or initial gender role, or by virtue of a self-defined gender identity or the expression thereof. . . .

Foreword, *Read My Lips*

The First time I'd seen white cuffs like these was in my women's incest group. It happened that two of us were trans-identified. We'd kept fairly quiet out of fear, although, in truth, I was pretty much "out."

Our fears were not misplaced: after a year of unremarkable participation, the casual mention that one of us was "pre-op" blossomed quickly into into weeks of acrimonious exchange. We looked on in silence, gripped by a kind of dazed fascination, as people we thought we knew discussed us animatedly in the third person, as if we weren't there. In a sense, we weren't.

While part of me listened to the argument over whether we were "women enough" to stay, another part quietly wondered how it was that only my identity and body were suddenly "in play." Who had made these rules so others got to vote on me in a way that I was not symmetrically empowered to vote on them? Why were their bodies a priori legitimate while mine was somehow the product of group resolution? And how was it that I knew, even if the vote went in our favor, we would have already been disempowered?

I did not know. I lacked the conceptual tools to understand anything about my situation except that it hurt. I wouldn't have any answers until years later.

It was during this time, in the lull of an inexplicably calm Thanksgiving meeting, that a woman blew like a winter breeze through the crack in our door, folded herself onto the edge of the gunmetal gray chair nearest the exit, and, perching there, began quietly examining the linoleum floor as if it contained the key to the scriptures. By unspoken agreement, we shared in a "go-around" that night so she wouldn't have to raise her hand to speak.

We needn't have bothered. She bolted the room without a backward glance when her turn came, leaving a wraithlike hole where she'd sat. Then it was the rest of us carefully examining the floor, until someone quietly mentioned the whitetape on her wrists.

There had been two others after that. One was my friend Hannah, a sculptor. She'd nearly severed her hand in a radial arm saw when she was eighteen. She swears she was lucid and calm at the time; yet she was also so desperate, lonely, and disconnected, she hoped it would kill her, or bring someone running—anyone—who'd finally listen to the pain inside her.

The other was Christine, a guitarist, writer, and sometime working-girl. Trying to escape from her life for one night, she stoned out on a mix of booze and PCP. Then, using the sharp blade of a sword, she severed the fingers of her guitar-picking hand right above the top knuckle, one-two-three-four, and didn't feel a thing until the next morning. The cops had seen this particular tranny in the tank so many times they didn't even try to have her fingers sewn back on.

And then, of course, there's Susan here. Her hands on the steering wheel look strong and capable in the bright Georgia sunlight. I have just come from addressing an indifferent Atlanta Pride parade audience on this hot June afternoon. She is winding her car along the endless freeways, expertly negotiating each turn and on-ramp, hauling me back to the air-conditioned Delta lounge and my plane to New York.

The baking heat must have made me more brain-dead than usual, because only now do I notice her wrists. Around each, barely above the coffee tan of her hands, are two bands of surgical cotton gauze so immaculate and neatly taped they look for all the world like a matching pair of white shirt cuffs.

There is something peculiarly incestuous about trans-experience. It robs us of our bodies, our intimate moments, our sexuality, our childhood. It robs us of honesty, of open friendship, of the luxury of looking into a mirror without pain staring back at us.

It means hiding from friends and family, from spouses and children, as surely as it means hiding from the police car during an evening stroll, or from that knot of laughing boys down at the corner when we go out for a Coke. In the end, it is as tiring as a constant pain and as barren as the bottom of an empty well at high noon.

So why, with the surge of trans and gender theory flooding from the presses, does so little address or assuage our pain? Why is it mostly irrelevant to translives? Why have all the observations and theories been so utterly useless for transpeople themselves?

The earliest works were usually about people in rehab somewhere. The psychiatrists who wrote them inspected our fetishes, fixations, and gender confusions, producing carefully distanced narratives which were couched in the obscure, analytic language of dysfunction and derangement. We were patients.

Then came the feminist theorists who—while erasing our own voices, and without soiling their pages with the messy complexities of our lived experience—appropriated us as illustrations for their latest telling theories or perceptive insights. We had become examples.

Upon us now is the "transgender studies" anthology, a ticket to an academic grant and a book. These come from earnest anthropologists and sociologists who study us as if we were some isolated and inexplicable distant tribe. Their gaze is firmly fixed on such pressing issues as our native dress, social organization, kinship structures, and relationship with the local gender witch doctors. They employ the objective and nuanced language of ethnography. We have become "natives."

Is there not something deeply immoral in the way these writers fail to help those whose lives they blithely mine for new insights and incantations? Do they never feel a twinge of guilt as their "studies" merely escalate the politicalizatian of our bodies, choices, and desires, so that, with each new book, while their audience enjoys the illusion of knowing more about us, we find ourselves more disempowered, dislocated, and exploited than before?

Aren't you still a male? Do transpeople reinforce gender stereotypes? Are you a "third sex"? Why do transpeople divide themselves up into men and women—shouldn't you be "gender-free"? Is sex-change surgery voluntary mutilation? Is transgenderism a pathology or mental disorder, and is it learned or genetic?

Academics, shrinks, and feminist theorists have traveled through our lives and problems like tourists on a junket. Picnicking on our identities like flies at a free lunch, they have selected the tastiest tidbits with which to illustrate a theory or push a book. The fact that we are a community under fire, a people at risk, is irrelevant to them. They pursue Science and Theory, and what they produce by mining our lives is neither addressed to us nor recycled within our community. It is not intended to help, but rather to explicate us as Today's Special: trans under glass, or perhaps only gender à la mode.

Our performance of gender is invariably a site of contest, a problem which—if we could but bring enough hi-octane academic brainpower to bear—might be "solved." The academician's own gender performance is never at issue, nor that of the "real" men and women who form the standard to which ours is compared. Through the neat device of "othering" us, *their* identities are quietly, invisibly naturalized. How nice to be normal, to know that the gender-trash is safely locked in the Binary Zoo when they turn off the word processor at night. . . .

Trans-identity is not a natural fact. Rather, it is the political category we are forced to occupy when we do certain things with our bodies. That so many of us try to take our own lives, mutilate ourselves, or just succeed in dying quietly of shame, depression, or loneliness is not an accident. We are supposed to feel isolated and desperate. Outcast. That is the whole point of the system. Our feelings are not causes but effects.

The regime of gender is an intentional, systemic oppression. As such, it cannot be fought through personal action, but only through an organized, systemic response. It is high time we stopped writing our hard-luck stories, spreading open our legs and our yearbooks for those awful before-and-after pictures, and began thinking clearly about how to fight back. It is time we began producing our own theory, our own narrative. No one volume can hope to achieve all this. At best, this is a rough set of beginnings.

I intend to wage a struggle for my life. I intend to fight for my political survival. And until other authors wade down into the deep end of the pool and confront the challenges we face every day, until their gender is seen as just as queer as mine, then they are simply another part of the system I seek to overturn.

147. KALLE LASN

Culture Jamming
(1999)

In the following essay, media analyst **KALLE LASN** (1942–) rages against mindless American consumerism and corporate branding, and argues in favor of "culture jamming," the practice of parodying and subverting corporate messages. Lasn was born in Estonia, educated in Australia, and he has lived in Tokyo, Japan and Vancouver, Canada, where he has won numerous awards as a film producer. In 1989 he founded *Adbusters* magazine and the Culture Jammers Network, "a loose global network of artists, activists, writers, students, educators and entrepreneurs who want to launch a new social activist movement of the information age."

SOURCE: Kalle Lasn. *Culture Jam: How to Reverse America's Suicidal Consumer Binge—And Why We Must.* New York: HarperCollins, 1999.

SELECTED READINGS: Naomi Klein, *No Logo: Taking Aim at the Brand Bullies* (1999). Mark Dery, *Culture Jamming: Hacking, Slashing and Sniping in the Empire of Signs* (1993).

The [essay] you're [reading] carries a message that your first instinct will be to distrust. That message is, *We can change the world*. It's risky these days to make such a promise because it sounds like one of those meaningless "awaken the inner giant"-type bromides: "If you can dream it, you can do it," "The journey of a thousand miles begins with a single step," and so on.

But it's true. We're serious. We call ourselves culture jammers. We're a loose global network of media activists who see ourselves as the advance shock troops of the most significant social movement of the next twenty years. Our aim is to topple existing power structures and forge major adjustments to the way we will live in the twenty-first century. We believe culture jamming will become to our era what civil rights was to the '60s, what feminism was to the '70s, what environmental activism was to the '80s. It will alter the way we live and think. It will change the way information flows, the way institutions wield power, the way TV stations are run, the way the food, fashion, automobile, sports, music and culture industries set their agendas. Above all, it will change the way we interact with the mass media and the way in which meaning is produced in our society.

We are a very diverse tribe. Our people range from born-again Lefties to Green entrepreneurs to fundamentalist Christians who don't like what television is doing to their kids; from punk anarchists to communications professors to advertising executives searching for a new role in life. Many of us are longtime activists who in the midst of our best efforts suddenly felt spiritually winded. For us feminism had run out of steam, the environmental movement no longer excited, the fire no longer burned in the belly of the Left, and youth rebellion was looking more and more like an empty gesture inspired by Nike. We were losing.

Then we had an idea. Maybe if we banged together the heads of all these activists and reconfigured the fragmented forces of identity politics into a new; empowered movement, we could start winning again.

We weren't looking for it necessarily, but each one of us in our own way has had a political awakening; a series of very personal "moments of truth" about ourselves and how the world works. For some, these insights have come on like powerful, secular epiphanies. Sometimes they have been triggered by things we overheard or read or stumbled upon. Sometimes they have involved things we thought we knew but now, suddenly, *felt.* These truths have left us shaken; it's no exaggeration to say they have changed our lives. I'd like to share with you some of the insights that have occurred to me over the last decade or so.

America is no longer a country. It's a multitrillion-dollar brand. America™ is essentially no different from McDonald's, Marlboro or General Motors. It's an image "sold" not only to the citizens of the U.S.A., but to consumers worldwide. The American brand is associated with catchwords such as "democracy," "opportunity" and "freedom." But like cigarettes that are sold as symbols of vitality and youthful rebellion, the American reality is very different from its brand image. America™ has been subverted by corporate agendas. Its elected officials bow before corporate power as a condition of their survival in office. A collective sense of powerlessness and disillusionment has set in. A deeply felt sense of betrayal is brewing.

American culture is no longer created by the people. Our stories, once passed from one generation to the next by parents, neighbors and teachers, are now told by distant corporations with "something to sell as well as to tell." Brands, products, fashions, celebrities, entertainments—the spectacles that surround the production of culture—*are* our culture now. Our role is mostly to listen and watch—and then, based on what we have heard and seen, to buy.

A free, authentic life is no longer possible in America™ today. We are being manipulated in the most insidious way. Our emotions, personalities and core values are under siege from media and cultural forces too complex to decode. A continuous product message has woven itself into the very fabric of our existence. Most North Americans now live designer lives—sleep, eat, sit in car, work, shop, watch TV, sleep again. I doubt there's more than a handful of free, spontaneous minutes anywhere in that cycle. *We ourselves have been branded.* The human spirit of prideful contrariness and fierce independence has been oddly tamed. We have evolved into a smile-button culture. We wear the trendiest fashions, drive the best cars industry can produce and project an image of incredible affluence—cool people living life to the hilt. But behind that happy mask is a face so ugly it invariably shocks the hell out of my friends from developing countries who come to visit, expecting the giddy Americana depicted on TV and finding instead a horror show of disconnection and anomie.

Our mass media dispense a kind of Huxleyan "soma." The most powerful narcotic in the world is the promise of belonging. And belonging is best achieved by conforming to the prescriptions of America™. In this way a perverted sense of cool takes hold of the imaginations of our children. And thus a heavily manipulative corporate ethos drives our culture. Cool is indispensable—and readily, endlessly dispensed. You can get it on every corner (for the right price), though it's highly addictive and its effects are short-lived. If you're here for cool today, you'll almost certainly be back for more tomorrow.

American cool is a global pandemic. Communities, traditions, cultural heritages, sovereignties, whole histories are being replaced by a barren American monoculture.

Living in Japan during its period of sharpest transition to a western way of life, I was astonished by the speed and force with which the American brand took hold. I saw a culture with thousands of years of tradition behind it vanquished in two generations. Suddenly, high school girls were selling themselves after class for $150 a trick so they'd have cash to buy American jeans and handbags.

The Earth can no longer support the lifestyle of the coolhunting American-style consumer. We have sought, bought, spewed and devoured too much, too fast, too brazenly, and now we're about to pay. Economic "progress" is killing the planet.

This did not fully hit home for me until 1989, when a spate of nightmarish environmental stories suddenly appeared on the news: acid rain, dying seals in the North Sea, medical waste washing up on New York beaches, garbage barges turned away from port after port, a growing hole in the ozone layer, and the discovery that the milk in American mothers' breasts had four times the amount of DDT permitted in cow's milk. In that year a critical mass of people saw the light and became "environmentalists." We were witnessing the specter of a whole planet heading for ruin. To people like me for whom time had always seemed like a constant, eternally moving train which people got on and, seventy years later, got off, it was the end of innocence. The premonition of ecocide—planetary death—became real for the first time, and it terrified me. It still does.

Once you experience even a few of these "moments of truth," things can never be the same again. Your life veers off in strange new directions. It's very exciting and a little scary. Ideas blossom into obsessions. The imperative to live life differently keeps building until the day it breaks through the surface.

When it happened to me I was in my neighborhood supermarket parking lot. I was plugging a coin into a shopping cart when it suddenly occurred to me just what a dope I was. Here I was putting in my quarter for the privilege of spending money in a store I come to every week but hate, a sterile chain store that rarely carries any locally grown produce and always makes me stand in line to pay. And when I was finished shopping I'd have to take this cart back to the exact place their efficiency experts have decreed, and slide it back in with all the other carts, rehook it and push the red button to get my damn quarter back.

A little internal fuse blew. I stopped moving. I glanced around to make sure no one was watching. Then I reached for that big bent coin I'd been carrying in my pocket and I rammed it as hard as I could into the coin slot. And then with the lucky Buddha charm on my keyring I banged that coin in tight until it jammed. I didn't stop to analyze whether this was ethical or not—I just let my anger flow. And then I walked away from that supermarket and headed for the little fruit and vegetable store down the road. I felt more alive than I had in months.

Much later I realized I had stumbled on one of the great secrets of modern urban existence: Honor your instincts. Let your anger out. When it wells up suddenly from deep in your gut, don't suppress it—channel it, trust it, use it. Don't be so unthinkingly civil all the time. When the system is grinding you down, unplug the grinding wheel.

Once you start thinking and acting this way, once you realize that consumer capitalism is by its very nature unethical, and therefore it's *not* unethical to jam it; once you understand that civil disobedience has a long and honorable history that goes back to Gandhi, Martin Luther King, Jr., and Henry David Thoreau; once you start trusting yourself and relating to the world as an empowered human being instead of a hapless consumer drone, something remarkable happens. Your cynicism dissolves.

If cool is the Huxleyan "soma" of our time, then cynicism is its poisonous, paralytic side effect. It is the dark side of cool. It's part of the reason we watch too much TV and don't bother to vote. It's why we get stuck year after year in tedious, meaningless jobs. It's why we're bored so much of the time and become compulsive shoppers.

To find a way out of cynicism is to find a way out of the postmodern malaise. On the far side of cynicism lies freedom. And the pursuit of freedom is what revolutions—and this book—are all about.

The Situationists saw this revolution coming long ago. The French philosophical movement that inspired the 1968 Paris riots predicted what might happen to a society driven by consumer capitalism. The Situationists intuited how hard it would be to hang on to one's core self in a "society of spectacle," a world of manufactured desires and manipulated emotions. Guy Debord, the leader of the Situationist movement, said: *"Revolution is not showing life to people, but making them live."* This instinct to be free and unfettered is hard-wired into each one of us. It's a drive as strong as sex or hunger, an irresistible force that, once harnessed, is almost impossible to stop.

With that irresistible force on our side, we will strike.

We will strike by smashing the postmodern hall of mirrors and redefining what it means to be alive. We will reframe the battle in the grandest terms. The old political battles that have consumed humankind during most of the twentieth century—black versus white, Left versus Right, male versus female—will fade into the background. The only battle still worth fighting and winning, the only one that can set us free, is The People versus The Corporate Cool Machine.

We will strike by unswooshing America™, by organizing resistance against the power trust that owns and manages that brand. Like Marlboro and Nike, America™ has splashed its logo everywhere. And now resistance to that brand is about to begin on an unprecedented scale. We will uncool its fashions and celebrities, its icons, signs and spectacles. We will jam its image factory until the day it comes to a sudden, shuddering halt. And then on the ruins of the old consumer culture, we will build a new one with a noncommercial heart and soul.

It will be an enormous culture jam, a protracted war of ideas, ideologies and visions of the future. It may take a generation or even more. But it will be done.

148. RONI KROUZMAN

WTO: The Battle in Seattle (An Eyewitness Account) (1999)

Taking most pundits and analysts by surprise, protestors rocked the 1999 meeting of the World Trade Organization (WTO) in Seattle, Washington, shutting down the opening ceremony, preventing President Clinton from addressing WTO delegates, and forcing the delegates to confront tough questions about global inequality and world trade. In the following essay, **RONI KROUZMAN** (1977–)—a young journalist and organizer who has published articles in *Extra!*, *Middle East Report*, the *San Francisco Bay Guardian* and elsewhere—delivers a firsthand account of the "Battle in Seattle." While there was much discussion in the media about the "mindless anarchy" of fringe radicals and the righteous behavior of the Seattle police who tried to bring order to the city, Krouzman highlights the optimism and responsibility of the protestors, and the violent and reactionary behavior of Seattle's police.

SOURCE: Roni Krouzman, http://www.tompaine.com, December 6, 1999.

SELECTED READINGS: Janet Thomas, *The Battle in Seattle: The Story Behind the WTO Demonstrations* (2000). Alexander Cockburn, Jeffrey St. Clair, and Allan Sekula, *5 Days That Shook the World: Seattle and Beyond* (2000).

As I looked upon the sea of people occupying Fourth Street in downtown Seattle last Tuesday, I could not help but feel energized and proud. We were occupying the city and dancing in its streets. We were nonviolently stopping the WTO and corporate globalization. We were making history.

But when I left the demonstrations and turned on the local news, I heard talk of rioters and chaos, not singing and dancing. I heard talk of police restraint in the face of "anarchist" violence, not police brutality against nonviolent direct action. I heard talk of a city driven to the brink of collapse by "angry protesters," and not an unjust system of exploitation creatively and beautifully stopped in its tracks.

They say that truth is the first casualty of war. Unfortunately, it is also the first casualty of popular rebellion. Now it's time to set the record straight about what happened and is still happening in Seattle.

I witnessed and took part in an incredible week of action and thought, one that united diverse interests to creatively challenge a global order that places profits over people. On Friday night and all day Saturday, 2,500 of us attended a series of lectures and were motivated and informed by intelligent, inspiring people from across the U.S. and around the world. But the media wasn't there.

Teach-ins and workshops continued on Sunday, when the first sign of protests emerged. Several hundred people, including French farmer and anti-globalization activist Jose Bove, demonstrated in front of a downtown McDonald's, creatively and energetically. Toward the end of the rally, someone broke a window, and that's what the media concentrated on.

That night I stumbled upon the Convergence Center, Seattle's grassroots direct action headquarters, and could not believe what I saw. Hundreds of young people filled this commercial space on Capitol Hill, milling about three massive rooms cluttered with flyers, banners and props. They all seemed so engaged, holding discussions in intimate circles, creating signs and teaching each other about civil disobedience and legal aid, and occasionally studying a giant 200-square-foot map of the city that hung from a wall.

Suddenly, an activist barged in on a bustling meeting and announced that people had seized a vacant building downtown, and they needed our help to protect it from police. We walked those ten blocks briskly, and arrived just in time to see people in masks on top of the building unfurl a banner that read, "Housing is a right, not a privilege."

I returned to the Convergence Center the next day and participated in the general spokescouncil meeting, a five-hour affair during which delegates, representing one of thirteen clusters of three to four affinity groups each, each themselves composed of five to twenty members, finalized plans for Tuesday's actions. The meeting felt frustrating at times, but it was the essence of grassroots democracy, with each representative speaking his or her mind, and conferring with fellow affinity group representatives that sat beside them to plan a coherent, well-organized strategy.

After that meeting, I understood the giant map. Each cluster would occupy one of thirteen intersections surrounding the Washington Convention and Trade Center, and nonviolently shut it down. Incredible that such a well-organized effort could be planned so creatively and democratically.

That evening, I attended the Peoples' Gala, an anti-corporate festival featuring music, comedy, and inspiring words. And seeing steelworkers sitting beside vegans, old lefties beside new, I was inspired indeed.

I could hardly relax enough to close my eyes that night, and awoke to my radio alarm at 5 A.M., one hour after I'd finally managed to fall asleep. I left my ID on the night table, donned a sweater, coat and poncho, packed my bag, and began my trek through the cold, wet, predawn hours, confident that today, I would make history.

Our rain-soaked rally began shortly before 7 A.M., long after dozens of affinity groups had slipped into the night to occupy the city. We sang and we huddled, and cheered when the head of the longshoreman union announced that there would be no business in West Coast ports that day. And over and over again, we heard the code of nonviolence repeated: no alcohol, no drugs, no physical or verbal assault, no property damage.

As the sun began to filter through the morning clouds, we began our march through a waking city, a contingent of steelworkers leading the way. We hit the first police barricade of many shortly thereafter, thousands of us facing down a few dozen cops, who stood guarding one of the many streets that led to the convention center. And so the march continued around the city, with groups of ten and twenty and fifty at a time leaving the procession to join the activists who had seized those thirteen intersections. We cheered, and we chanted, and we felt in control. Everywhere I looked, I saw rivers of demonstrators milling excitedly through the streets.

And then the tear gas and the rubber bullets came. At midmorning, the police went on the offensive, demanding a mass of at least one thousand nonviolent demonstrators positioned at the intersection of Sixth and Union disperse to make way for WTO delegates. We did not, and as dozens of demonstrators sat down in front of the police line, a squadron of ten officers carrying what appeared to be automatic or semiautomatic machine guns charged over them from behind, trampling several.

The crowd booed and jeered, refusing to disperse, and chanting, "We're nonviolent, how about you?" Riot-gear-clad police responded with a barrage of tear gas, overcoming dozens with noxious fumes and causing hundreds of us to flee the intersection. Some protesters quickly donned gas masks, refusing to give up their ground, and were met with a hail of rubber bullets. At least two were struck, one in the leg and one in the mouth. Legal observers reported that neither was seriously injured.

Demonstrators were shocked and confused, but did not panic, as direct action medics and other activists rushed to the aid of the injured. Thousands chanted, "Shame!" and "The world is watching!" amidst an eerie cloud of white gas and the steady hum of helicopters flying overhead.

By late morning, Seattle's coffee shops were buzzing with talk of the actions, which had now drawn over 5,000 demonstrators and hundreds of police, and diverted car and bus traffic from half the downtown area. As the day progressed and tensions mounted, some protesters adopted more aggressive tactics. Several young activists rolled van-sized garbage dumps into alleyways and intersections, including the intersection of Fourth and University. At noon, police ordered the raucous crowd there to disperse, and fired tear-gas canisters when it refused. Hundreds of us fled yet again as some demonstrators threw the canisters back at the officers.

On the northern side of the Convention Center, along Pike Street, several small groups of youths dressed in black and donning ski masks or bandanas damaged property at stores including Nike Town, Old Navy, and Planet Hollywood. To the chagrin of activists who had attempted to enforce a code of nonviolence, they scrawled anticorporate graffiti on walls and displays, and smashed corporate store windows with hammers, crowbars, and street signs, destroying a Starbucks storefront.

The overwhelming majority of activists did not engage in such activities, successfully blocking access to the Convention Center for 2,500 to 3,000 delegates through well-coordinated, nonviolent civil disobedience. In an effort to break the protesters' grip, police moved to take more intersections, shooting streams of pepper spray at nonviolent protesters who were sitting around the intersection of Sixth and Union, and attempting to break through their lines with an armored personnel carrier. The police did not succeed, drawing chants of "Protect and Serve!" from an outraged crowd. Similar clashes erupted throughout downtown, with floods of protestors weaving in and out of key intersections—and securing them with barricades—visible in every direction. Police moved to take the intersections back one by one, and were often surrounded on both sides by thousands of demonstrators. I could not believe what I was seeing.

At 2 P.M. an estimated 25,000 activists, mainly union rank and file, marched into downtown from a rally at Memorial Stadium, joining the ten thousand or so direct-action activists who had seized control of the city. The demonstrations displayed a level of diversity rare in American movements, as anarchists, environmentalists, and vegan hippies marched side by side with teamsters, steelworkers, and social-justice activists. Though television media is concentrating overwhelmingly on protest violence and the restraint shown by officers, most of the protesters did not engage in violence, despite being assaulted by police. The day was marked by many events large and small that were overlooked by the media, like the several dozen students who held Sixth and University all day, or the protestors who joked with police at Pike and Seventh, offering the officers food and engaging in lively debate.

Across the city, thousands of activists learned about democracy and direct action, discussing plans, supporting one another, and using their collective people power to force the hand of one of the world's most powerful institutions. That power was made evident throughout the day, for example, when activists stationed at Pike and Boren, who had held their intersection for nine hours, where asked by a police sergeant to let his men cross the activists' line in order to relive exhausted coworkers.

That night, Seattle's mayor declared a Civil Emergency, and placed downtown under nighttime curfew. The National Guard was mobilized, and police teargassed protesters out of downtown and into Seattle's progressive Capitol Hill neighborhood, where the clashes continued.

After successfully using mass civil disobedience to prevent the WTO from carrying on its business Tuesday, several thousand people returned to the streets on Wednesday in an attempt to do the same. By noon, nearly 300 nonviolent protesters had been arrested and taken to the former Sand Point naval station for booking. Police and national guardsmen maintained a heavy presence throughout much of downtown, especially in a twenty-block area around the Washington Convention and Trade Center, where WTO talks had convened earlier during the day. Dozens of police and guardsmen also surrounded the Westin Hotel, where President Clinton was staying, barricading the hotel's front entrance with eight Seattle metro buses.

At 1 P.M. a crowd of protesters assembled around a line of police clad in riot gear stationed in front of Old Navy, whose boarded up windows, like those of many other downtown corporate retailers, displayed anticorporate graffiti. The small group of demonstrators chanted antiglobalization and antipolice slogans, but violence did not ensue.

Shortly there after, close to one thousand protesters, including steelworkers, environmentalists, students, and social-justice activists gathered in the northern section of downtown for an anti-WTO rally. We joined them, and began a march toward the convention center, where WTO negotiations were well under way. As the lively, nonviolent crowd approached the part of downtown where protests had been banned, police opened fire with tear gas, causing the demonstrators to flee and chant, "Shame!"

Stunned and angry that police had used violence to quell a nonviolent march, we regrouped and continued our procession. Hundreds of police, some riding in armored personnel carriers and carrying pepper spray and rubber-bullet launchers, swarmed around the area, intermittently firing tear gas and forcing us from one intersection to the next. For the first time that week, I was frightened. The police seemed bent on hurting people.

Chanting "Peaceful Protest!" and "No Violence!" we grew more and more disoriented and were eventually cornered. Police, some on horseback, surrounded us, and opened fire with more tear gas and possibly rubber bullets and percussion grenades, causing us to flee down alleyways and disperse.

About half an hour later, hundreds of protesters regrouped and began to march again, occupying an intersection after being stopped by police. Night was falling, and a police helicopter flew overhead, shining a spotlight down on us. Suddenly, people began to shout, "They're surrounding us!" as a squad of twenty police marched in goose-step from behind. Just as I managed to get out of the intersection, a group of officers on horseback quickly rode in, and about one hundred protesters were surrounded on three sides.

The intersection was engulfed by an eerie silence, as trapped demonstrators contemplated their fate and hundreds of us on the outside watched in disbelief. Within minutes, dozens of police cars began arriving on the scene, several riding in an SUV whose back was full of weapons. The officers distributed percussion grenades and donned gas masks, drawing chants of "Fascists!" and "Police State!" from angry onlookers. Suddenly, chaos ensued, as police threw at least a dozen grenades at protesters. Deafening, smoky explosions went off in the middle of the demonstration, forcing protesters to flee up the street. Stunned onlookers yelled angry slogans at police, who marched methodically up the street after the fleeing demonstrators.

One enraged officer returned to the scene, and began pepper spraying a line of onlookers at will, yelling "Yeah!" before being pulled away by a fellow officer. I saw all of this with my own eyes.

The crowd regrouped, and suddenly downtown Seattle resembled a war zone, with police sirens blaring and hundreds of police marching and jogging through swarms of angry people. The clashes continued throughout evening, with police attempting to force people off the streets by the 7 P.M. curfew.

Activists worried the police might raid their organizing headquarters, which had been used by thousands of direct-action protesters to coordinate their efforts before the WTO conference began. Members of the Independent Media Center, which had housed a slew of independent journalists throughout the week, were worried as well, tensely guarding the entrance of their downtown headquarters.

Sizeable protests continued throughout the night. At 8 P.M. demonstrators marched through the streets of Capitol Hill, a progressive Seattle neighborhood one mile east of downtown and not subject to marshal law. Still, police ordered the peaceful crowd to disperse, and angry local residents joined protesters in demanding the police "go home!" Eyewitnesses report that a police riot ensued, with police indiscriminately firing tear gas, pepper spray, and rubber bullets, and making 600 arrests. Reports of police brutality filtered in throughout the night, with witnesses stating that police were using physical violence against protesters, including twisting arms and pulling hair. Police reportedly placed a sack over the head of one detainee, filling it with pepper spray until the man was knocked unconscious. Witnesses also reported that some detainees were denied food and placed in solitary confinement, and that most have been denied legal assistance.

My week in Seattle was unlike anything I had ever seen, or ever thought I would see. Unlike many protests I had attended, the participants in Seattle were overwhelmingly young—people in their twenties, people in college, people in high school. The scope of the demonstrations was incredible as well; the Seattle protests were marked by a level of diversity, organization, and nonviolent direct action not witnessed in the United States in years, perhaps since Chicago, 1968, with activists of all stripes sharing thoughts and experiences with one another. Finally, we actually succeeded. We shut down the WTO, and prevented it from reaching a world trade agreement.

Our success had a lot to do with grassroots organizing processes and structures, made evident by a week of teach-ins, human chains, and grassroots mobilizations. It also had a lot to do with the issue. The WTO has managed to bring so many different, and in the past conflicting, interests together because corporate globalization affects everyone and everything on the planet. This movement is not just about protecting labor rights or sea turtles. It's about demanding a say, and taking power back from the institutions, corporations, and governments that rule our lives and our communities.

The mainstream media have painted the story as one of police attempting to restore order, instead of police using police-state tactics to create chaos and trample on the constitutional rights of thousands of nonviolent demonstrators and bystanders. I know what really happened. I saw it with my own eyes. I took part in the meetings. I marched through the streets. I smelled the tear gas and ducked to avoid the rubber bullets. Seattle marked a real watershed, with people of diverse beliefs coming together to demand a just, democratic world. Now we can only hope they return to their communities and begin the difficult work of making that world a reality. The Battle of Seattle may very well have been the first "shot across the bow" of a global peoples' movement grassroots organizers had hoped for.

149. BLACK RADICAL CONGRESS

Freedom Agenda
(1999)

The **BLACK RADICAL CONGRESS (BRC)** was formed in an effort to renew the Black radical movement through increased unified action. To that end, the organization sponsors conferences, seminars, and forums in order to promote dialogue among African-American activists and scholars on the Left. They have launched several activist campaigns, the latest being "Education Not Incarceration! Fight the Police State." Made up of university professors, former Black Power activists, and college students, the BRC recognizes the diverse tendencies within Black radicalism and opposes all forms of oppression, including class exploitation, racism, patriarchy, homophobia, anti-immigration prejudice, and imperialism.

SOURCE: The "Freedom Agenda" of the Black Radical Congress (BRC) was ratified by the BRC National Council on April 17, 1999, in Baltimore, Maryland. http://www.blackradicalcongress.org/aboutus/freedomagenda.html

SELECTED READINGS: Mumia-Abu Jamal, *Death Blossoms: Reflections from a Prisoner of Conscience* (1997). Manning Marable, *Dispatches from the Ebony Tower: Intellectuals Confront the African-American Experience* (2000).

Preamble

During the last 500 years, humanity has displayed on a colossal scale its capacity for creative genius and ruthless destruction, for brutal oppression and indomitable survival, for rigid tradition and rapid change. The Americas evolved to their present state of development at great cost to their original, indigenous peoples, and at great cost to those whose labor enabled modernization under the yoke of that protracted crime against humanity, slavery.

Even so, a good idea is implicit in the Declaration of Independence of the United States: that all people are "endowed with certain inalienable rights, and among these are life, liberty, and the pursuit of happiness." That the idea of a just society, contained in those words, remains unrealized is what compels this declaration.

Not only has the idea not been realized, but we are moving further away from its realization by the hour. Global capitalism, both the cause and effect of neo-liberal and Reaganist policies, has facilitated the transfer of enormous wealth from the bottom to the top of society in recent years, concentrating the control of abundant resources in ever fewer hands. As a result, the working people who constitute the vast majority of people have confronted a steady decline in their prospects for earning a decent living and controlling their lives. In the U.S., the threat of sudden unemployment hangs over most households. We pay unfair taxes and receive fewer services, while multibillion-dollar fortunes accumulate in the private sector. Prisons proliferate as budgets are slashed for public schools, day care, healthcare and welfare. The grip of big money on the two-party electoral process has robbed us of control over the political institutions that are mandated to serve us. We are losing ground, and democracy is more and more elusive.

As for people of African descent, most of whose ancestors were among the shackled millions who helped build the edifices and culture of the Americas, we carry an enormously disproportionate burden. In the U.S., the living legacy of slavery, and the pervasiveness of institutional white supremacy, have placed us on all-too-familiar terms with poverty, urban and rural; exploitative conditions of employment; disproportionately high rates of unemployment and underemployment; inferior health care; substandard education; the corrosive drug trade, with its accompanying gun violence; police brutality and its partner, excessive incarceration; hate-inspired terrorism; a biased legal system, and discrimination of every kind—persistent even after the end of legal segregation.

Resistance is in our marrow as Black people, given our history in this place. From the Haitian revolution, to the U.S. abolitionist movement against slavery, to the 20th Century movement for civil rights and empowerment, we have struggled and died for justice. We believe that struggle must continue, and with renewed vigor. Our historical experiences suggest to us, by negative example, what a truly just and democratic society should look like: It should be democratic, not just in myth but in practice, a society in which all people— regardless of color, ethnicity, religion, nationality, national origin, sex, sexual orientation, age, family structure, or mental or physical capability—enjoy full human rights, the fruits of their labor, and the freedom to realize their full human potential. If you agree, and if you are committed to helping achieve justice and democracy in the 21st Century, please sign your name and/or the name of your organization to this 15-point Freedom Agenda.

The Freedom Agenda

I. We will fight for the human rights of Black people and all people.

We will struggle for a society and world in which every individual enjoys full human rights, full protection of the United Nations Declaration of Human Rights, and in the United States equal protection of the Constitution and of all the laws. We seek a society in which every individual—regardless of color, nationality, national origin, ethnicity, religion, sex, sexual orientation, age, family structure, or mental or physical capability—is free to experience "life, liberty, and the pursuit of happiness." We affirm that all people are entitled to:

a. a safe and secure home;

b. employment at a living wage—that is, compensation for the full value of their labor;

c. free, quality health care, including full reproductive freedom with the right to choose when or whether to bear children, and free, quality child care;

d. free, quality public education.

We oppose the Human Genome Project in its current form and with its current leadership, and we oppose all sociobiological or genetic experiments that are spurred by, and help perpetuate, scientific racism.

We will fight for a society and world in which every individual and all social groups can live secure, dignified lives.

II. We will fight for political democracy.

We will struggle to expand political democracy to ensure the people's greater participation in decision-making. In the U.S., we will work to replace the current two-party, winner-take-all electoral system with a more democratic multiparty system based on proportional representation, and we will fight to abolish all registration procedures that restrict the number of eligible voters. We oppose private financing of electoral campaigns, especially corporate contributions; we will work to replace the present corrupt system with public financing.

*III. We will fight to advance beyond capitalism, which has
demonstrated its structural incapacity to address basic human needs
worldwide and, in particular, the needs of Black people.*

Guided by our belief that people should come before profits, we will fight
to maximize economic democracy and economic justice:

a. We seek full employment at livable wages, public control of private-
sector financial operations, worker control of production decisions, and a
guaranteed annual income for the needy;

b. we will fight to end racial discrimination by capitalist enterprises, especially banks, insurance companies and other financial institutions;

c. we seek a society in which working people enjoy safe working conditions
and flexible hours to accommodate family responsibilities, leisure and vaca-
tions;

d. we seek laws mandating public ownership of utilities, and mandating
federal and local budgetary emphases on programs for the general welfare—
health care, education, public transportation, recreation and infrastructure;

e. we will struggle for laws that regulate private-sector business practices,
especially regarding prices, fees, plant shutdowns and job relocations—where
shutdowns are permitted, adequate compensation to workers shall be required;

f. we support the historical mission of trade unions to represent workers'
interests and to negotiate on their behalf;

g. we seek a fair, equitable, highly progressive tax system that places the
heaviest taxes on the wealthiest sector, and we seek expansion of the earned-
income tax credit.

IV. We will fight to end the super-exploitation of Southern workers.

More than 50 percent of people of African descent residing in the U.S. live
in the South, where workers' earnings and general welfare are besieged by
corporate practices, and where "right to work" laws undermine union organizing. Thus, we seek relief for Southern workers from corporate oppression,
and we will struggle to repeal anti-union laws. We will also fight for aid to
Black farmers, and for the restoration of farm land seized from them by agribusiness, speculators and real estate developers.

*V. We will struggle to ensure that all people in society receive free
public education.*

We affirm that all are entitled to free, quality public education throughout
their lifetime. Free education should include adult education and retraining
for occupational and career changes. We will fight to ensure that curricula in
U.S. schools, colleges and universities are antiracist, antisexist and antihomo-

phobic, and for curricula that adequately accommodate students' needs to express and develop their artistic, musical or other creative potential.

VI. *We will struggle against state terrorism.*

We will fight for a society in which every person and every community is free from state repression, including freedom from state-sponsored surveillance. We seek amnesty for, and the release of, all political prisoners. We will struggle to repeal all legislation that expands the police power of the state and undermines the U.S. Constitution's First and Fourth Amendments. We will fight to eliminate the deliberate trafficking in drugs and weapons in our communities by organized crime, and by institutions of the state such as the Central Intelligence Agency.

VII. *We will struggle for a clean and healthy environment.*

We will fight for a society in which the welfare of people and the natural environment takes precedence over commercial profits and political expediency. We will work to protect, preserve and enhance society's and the planet's natural heritage—forests, lakes, rivers, oceans, mountain ranges, animal life, flora and fauna. In the U.S., we will struggle against environmental racism by fighting for laws that strictly regulate the disposal of hazardous industrial waste, and that forbid both the discriminatory targeting of poor and nonwhite communities for dumping and despoilment of the natural environment.

VIII. *We will fight to abolish police brutality, unwarranted incarceration and the death penalty.*

We are determined to end police brutality and murder:

a. We will fight for strong civilian oversight of police work by elected civilian review boards that are empowered to discipline police misconduct and enforce residency requirements for police officers;

b. we seek fundamental changes in police training and education to emphasize public service over social control as the context in which law enforcement occurs, and to stress respect for the histories and cultures of the U.S.–born and immigrant communities served;

c. we seek to limit incarceration to the most violent criminals, only those who have clearly demonstrated their danger to the lives and limbs of others;

d. regarding nonviolent offenders, we demand that they be released and provided with appropriate medical, rehabilitative and educative assistance without incarceration;

e. we will struggle for abolition of the death penalty, which has been abolished in the majority of developed nations. In the U.S., the history of the death penalty's application is inextricable from the nation's origins as a slave state. Since Emancipation, it has been a white supremacist tool intended to maintain control over a population perceived as an alien, ongoing threat to the social order. Application of the death penalty, which is highly discriminatory on the basis of color and class, violates international human rights law and must be eliminated.

IX. We will fight for gender equality, for women's liberation, and for women's rights to be recognized as human rights in all areas of personal, social, economic and political life.

We will work to create a society and world in which women of African descent, along with their sisters of other colors, nationalities and backgrounds, shall enjoy nondiscriminatory access to the education, training and occupations of their choice. We will struggle to ensure that all women enjoy equal access to quality health care and full reproductive rights, including the right to determine when or whether they will bear children and the right to a safe, legal abortion. We will fight to end domestic abuse and sexual harassment in the workplace.

X. We recognize lesbian, gay, bisexual and transgender people as full and equal members of society, and of our communities.

We affirm the right of all people to love whom they choose, to openly express their sexuality, and to live in the family units that meet their needs. We will fight against homophobia, and we support antihomophobic instruction in public schools. We will fight for effective legal protections for the civil rights and civil liberties of lesbian, gay, bisexual and transgender people, and we demand that violence and murder committed against such people be prosecuted as hate crimes. We will also fight to end discrimination against this sector in employment, health care, social welfare and other areas.

XI. We support affirmative action.

We will fight to retain and expand affirmative action policies in education, employment, the awarding of government contracts and all other areas affected by historical and contemporary injustices. Affirmative action, with goals and timetables, is indispensable for achieving equal opportunity, justice and fairness for the members of all historically oppressed groups.

XII. We will fight for reparations.

Reparations is a well-established principle of international law that should be applied in the U.S. Historically, the U.S. has been both the recipient and disburser of reparations. As the descendants of enslaved Africans, we have the legal and moral right to receive just compensation for the oppression, systematic brutality and economic exploitation Black people have suffered historically and continue to experience today. Thus, we seek reparations from the U.S. for

    a. its illegal assault on African peoples during the slave trade;

    b. its exploitation of Black labor during slavery; and

    c. its systematic and totalitarian physical, economic and cultural violence against people of African descent over the last four centuries.

XIII. We will struggle to build multicultural solidarity and alliances among all people of color.

We will fight against white supremacist tactics aimed at dividing people of color. We seek alliances with other people of color to develop unified strategies for achieving multicultural democracy, and for overcoming the divisions that exist around such issues as immigration, bilingual education, political representation and allocation of resources.

XIV. We will uphold the right of the African American people to self-determination.

The formation of the Black Radical Congress in June 1998 was an act of African American self-determination, a principle which is codified in the United Nations Declaration of Human Rights. The African American people are entitled to define the direction, priorities, allies and goals of our struggle against national and racial oppression. Building the power to exercise these prerogatives is central to our struggle against all the systems of oppression confronting our people.

Therefore, we will fight for both a national program of liberation and for a mass base of power in the social sectors, institutions, all levels of government, communities and territories of society that affect the lives of our people.

XV. We support the liberation struggles of all oppressed people.

We affirm our solidarity with peoples of African descent throughout the African diaspora. We support their struggles against imperialism and neocolonialism from without, as well as against governmental corruption, exploitation and human rights abuses from within. We especially support struggles against transnational corporations, whose global market practices gravely exploit all workers, abuse workers' rights and threaten all workers' welfare. We affirm our solidarity with all oppressed people around the world, whatever their color, nation or religion—none of us is free unless all are free. We believe that all people everywhere should enjoy the right to self-determination and the right to pursue their dreams, unfettered by exploitation and discrimination.

150. KEVIN MATTSON

The Academic Labor Movement: Understanding Its Origins and Current Challenges
(2000)

In the following essay, KEVIN MATTSON analyzes the growing academic labor movement. Mattson (1966–) is currently associate professor of history at Ohio University. He is author of several books, including *Intellectuals in Action: The Origins of the New Left and Radical Liberalism, 1945–1970* and is co-editor (with Benjamin Herbert Johnson and Patrick Kavanaugh) of *Steal This University*, which explores the rise of the corporate university and the academic labor movement. Mattson has also written for numerous academic and popular publications. Before entering academia, he was a political activist in the Washington, D.C. area.

SOURCE: Kevin Mattson. "The Academic Labor Movement." *Social Policy*, Summer 2000.

SELECTED READINGS: Benjamin Herber Johnson, Kevin Mattson, and Patrick Cavanaugh, eds., *Steal This University* (2003). Randy Martin, ed., *Chalk Lines: The Politics of Work in the Managed University* (1998). Carl Nelson, ed., *Will Teach For Food: Academic Labor in Crisis* (1997).

There is one fact that helps explain why an academic labor movement has emerged today: More than fifty percent of the teaching in higher education is being done by people who are not tenure-track, full-time professors. In community colleges, that number is much higher. This means that most of the teaching at America's colleges is done by graduate students and what are known as "adjunct" professors (translation: part-time instructors).

If you think the complaints of adjuncts and graduate students are just the whining of the privilegentsia—white-collar types who have never lifted a brick or cleaned a toilet in their lives—consider this: "Good" pay for an adjunct professor is, before taxes, $2,500 for a full-semester course (four months of teaching). And this is without health benefits or job security. It often includes no office support and, more often than not, *no office*. The current economic prosperity has not reached this part of the ivory tower.

Recently, some academics have decided that they have had enough and are demanding a say in their work lives. At the University of California, graduate students have organized with the United Auto Workers (UAW) to win recognition for their union, as well as national media attention. New York University students have followed suit and, presently, students at the University of Washington and University of Maryland are organizing. Much of this was inspired by struggles at Yale University that began years ago. Adjuncts have also successfully organized, sometimes alongside full-time professors as they did at Miami-Dade Community College, sometimes on their own like at state colleges throughout New Jersey. There is a movement developing here.

The Historical Context

Historically, social movements have raised pressing questions about the society in which they emerge. The civil rights movement forced Americans to examine how racism threatened democratic equality. Martin Luther King, Jr.'s call to a "beloved community" helped spark important debates about the role of citizens in changing public policy. The women's movement encouraged people to analyze gender privilege and ask why certain forms of work such as those that sustained the family went unrecognized. Recent protests against the WTO and the IMF have prompted serious debate about the inequities of global capitalism.

So it follows that the academic labor movement raises significant questions about the future of higher education and the broader labor movement in America. If education is so central to the "new economy," why don't we reward its workers? What is the meaning of "work" in our new economy and within academia more specifically? Should we think of work solely in terms of manual labor? And, if the labor movement wants to renew itself—as recent discussions at the AFL-CIO seem to suggest—then could this new movement deliver on the promise by confronting "labor issues" where people least expect them? The essays that follow provide some answers to these questions; these introductory remarks will try to bring some overview to the possibilities and impediments that face this movement. To understand it, we must examine its peculiar context—the world of higher education.

Though academia has become increasingly corporate, it also preserves elements of medieval thinking. Many tenured professors, for example, believe academic labor follows a "guild" model of employment. Graduate students serve as "apprentices" under their "masters" (tenured professors), eventually becoming "journeymen" (assistant professors) and then masters themselves. This conception of work, of course, goes against academic unionization, since unions would simply muck up academia's otherwise paternalistic and personal training.

As a historian, it is remarkable for me to hear such arguments still used with seriousness today. Once, there *was* a guild system in America that had integrity, dating back to the 18th century. Those who have taken the time to study it recognize that it broke down and that the modern labor movement followed immediately in the wake of its failure. By the 1820s, journeymen and apprentices in America found it increasingly difficult to make the transition to master craftsmen. The small shopowner was quickly being displaced by what was called a "putting-out system," which itself was a forerunner of the modern factory. No longer did workers own their tools or raw materials; these were controlled by merchants and factory owners.

During this critical juncture in American history, journeymen started to question the underpinning philosophy of the guild system. As Sean Wilentz, a labor historian, points out, the "notion of independence," embodied in the master craftsperson ideal, and "the artisan system" propelled the journeyman's "critique of proletarianization." Master craftsmen themselves became increasingly defensive of their privileged positions while clinging to the rhetoric of the guild system. At the same time, they started operating more and more like modern capitalists and factory owners. Wilentz calls their arguments against journeymen a form of "republican anti-unionism." By the 1840s—after a tumultuous and difficult period—most journeymen decided they needed to unionize against the wishes of master craftsmen. And so the modern labor movement was born.

Why the Movement Matters

The analogy seems appropriate for the current academic labor system, one that is marked by guild-system rhetoric, degraded labor conditions, and a burgeoning labor movement. There is something quite appealing—indeed, humane—about the idea that people could be trained for employment and then placed in their positions. And yet today, adjunct professors (journeymen) are no longer finding permanent employment, but only what many other workers face, namely, the "tempting" of America. Graduate students who are teaching more and more courses look at this gloomy scenario and ask serious questions about their own prospects and the meaning of their "training," which, they are starting to realize, is just underpaid work. The modern university is no medieval institution; not only does it sit squarely within a modern if not postmodern and flexible set of capitalist institutions, it is increasingly acting like one itself.

Institutions, of course, can change while the consciousness of those who work within them stays the same. In his classic work, *White Collar* (1951), the social critic C. Wright Mills argued that while white-collar workers were being increasingly proletarianized (their "salaries" being the equivalent of wages), they did not necessarily act as if they were. Status intervened. For the sake of this discussion, call this "white-collar exceptionalism." Many academics fall prey to it today, thinking of themselves as far from union material. They believe that unions are for autoworkers on the assembly line.

The problem with the guild argument is that it fails to hold. After all, two of the most visible recent union efforts have involved white-collar employees. In April 2000, engineers at Boeing walked off the job and got much of what they demanded. Before that, doctors tried to get the National Labor Relations Board (NLRB) to recognize them as union employees in order to press their complaints against HMOs that act increasingly like cold-blooded institutions obsessed with the "bottom line." Though this initiative failed, these doctors made clear that many white-collar employees believe the integrity of their work is threatened by business-minded principles. "Professional" concerns often lend themselves to the ideas of collective bargaining and democratic governance at work. Faculty at Miami-Dade Community College, for example, concluded in 1998, "Concern for our students and the future of the college and our community have led us to realize that collective bargaining is the best solution." These developments make clear that white-collar exceptionalism need not lead to anti-unionism.

The white-collar argument also forces us to question what we mean by *work*. In the American lexicon, work has often been associated with manual labor, something abhorred by professional types. As Christopher Lasch once wrote, "The thinking classes are fatally removed from the physical side of life" and thus take a derisive attitude toward manual labor. Though this may be true, one of the things discovered by adjuncts and graduate students is that academic labor is precisely that—labor. A famous poster from the Yale University struggles depicted a harried graduate student, huddled over a stack of exams that she needs to grade. As she sweats, she repeats a mantra to herself: "This isn't work, this isn't work, this isn't . . . ."

The point is well taken: the art of teaching, with its physical and mental demands, *is* work. Further, the formation of a democratic culture—the making and self-making of cultivated, thoughtful citizens—requires concerted effort, no matter if it takes place in academia or in the making of books or the production of cultural events. The labor involved in the making of a democratic culture is worthy of dignity, as is labor in general. That is why academic unions must try their best to reach out and form alliances with other employees within academia, especially those who historically have been undervalued like custodial and administrative employees. When Yale students chose the Hotel Employees Restaurant Employees (HERE) union and NYU students the UAW as their representatives, they made one thing clear: academic labor is labor.

151. ALEXANDER COCKBURN AND JEFFREY ST. CLAIR

5 Days That Shook the World
(2000)

In the following essay, muckraking journalists **ALEXANDER COCKBURN** and **JEFFREY ST. CLAIR** hail some of the recent accomplishments of antiglobalization protestors even as they suggest how much more needs to be done to reform world trade. Cockburn (1941–) is a regular columnist for *The Nation* and *New York Press*. St. Clair (1959–) is a contributing editor to *In These Times*. Together, they edit the biweekly newsletter *Counterpunch*, and they have collaborated on several books.

SOURCE: Alexander Cockburn, Jeffrey St. Clair, and Allan Sekula, *5 Days That Shook the World: Seattle and Beyond*. New York and London: Verso, 2000.

SELECTED READINGS: Jeffrey J. Schott, ed., *The WTO After Seattle* (2000). Jane Thomas, *The Battle in Seattle: The Story Behind the WTO Demonstrations (2000).*

What we saw in Seattle across those tumultuous days stretching from November 28 through December 3, 1999, and then in Davos, Switzerland, Washington DC, Philadelphia, Los Angeles and Prague was the flowering of a new radical movement in America and across the world, rambunctious, anarchic, internationalist, well informed and in some ways more imaginative and supple than kindred popular eruptions in recent decades.

After the initial rout of the WTO in Seattle many in this new movement didn't always comprehend the extent of their victory. Five months later, some demonstrators in Washington DC across the weekend April 15–17, 2000 grumbled about press coverage of "A16" suggesting that they had "failed" in their efforts to close down the World Bank talks in the nation's capital and that therefore the Seattle momentum was sputtering to a halt. These protesters were missing the full depth of their triumph: namely that they had managed to place their issues squarely on the national and indeed global political agenda.

A decade, even five years ago, officials of the World Bank and International Monetary Fund were florid with righteous self satisfaction at the good works their institutions were performing round the world. By the spring of 2000 these same officials were apologizing for the sins of their past and nervously contending that they are re-engineering themselves as forces for good. It was the same on the sweatshop issue. Hardly a month goes by, without a firm like Nike edgily advertising its efforts to be responsive to the charges of critics about pay scales and labor practices in the Third World. . . .

Beyond the wildest hopes of the street warriors, five days in Seattle brought one victory after another. Protesters initially shunned and denounced by the respectable "inside strategists", scorned by the press, gassed and bloodied by the cops and national guard: shut down the opening ceremony; prevented Clinton from addressing the WTO delegates at a Wednesday night gala; turned the corporate press from prim denunciations of "mindless anarchy" to bitter criticisms of police brutality; forced the WTO to cancel its closing ceremonies and to adjourn in disorder and confusion, without an agenda for the next round.

In the annals of popular protest in America, these were shining hours, achieved entirely outside the conventional arena of orderly protest, white paper activism and the timid bleats of the professional leadership of big labor and establishment greens. This truly was an insurgency from below in which all those who strove to moderate and deflect the turbulent flood of popular outrage managed to humiliate themselves.

The contradiction between the demure agenda of the genteel element and the robust, tear it all down approach of the street legions was already apparent by Tuesday.

Here's a might-have-been. All day long, Tuesday, November 30, the street warriors in downtown Seattle, hopefully awaited reinforcement from the big labor rally taking place around the space needle, some fifteen or twenty blocks from downtown.

But the absent legions of labor never showed. Suppose they had. Suppose there had been 30,000 to 40,000 protesters around the convention center, vowing to keep it shut down all week. Would the cops have charged such a force? Downtown could have been held all night, and perhaps President Bill would have been forced to make his welcoming address from SeaTac or from the sanctuary of his ardent campaign funder, the Boeing Company. That would have been a humiliation for imperial power of historic proportions, like the famous greeting the Wobblies organized to greet president Woodrow Wilson after the breaking of the Seattle general strike in 1919. Workers and their families lined the streets, block after block, standing in furious silence as the President's motorcade passed by Wilson had his stroke not long thereafter.

This might-have-been is not posed out of churlishness, but to encourage a sense of realism about what is possible in the struggle against the trading arrangements now operative in the WTO.

Take organized labor, as embodied in the high command of the AFL-CIO. Are these people truly committed to the destruction of the WTO? Of course they aren't. Labor might huff and labor might puff, but when it comes to the WTO what labor wants, in James Hoffa's phrase, is a seat at the table. In Seattle Big Labor called for a "working group"—a bit of face-saving, actually— which, on the WTO's schedule at that time, wouldn't be up and running till at least 2014AD.

There are unions—the Autoworkers, Steelworkers, Teamsters, Machinists, UNITE—which have rank and file members passionately concerned about "free trade". But how many of these unions are truly ready to break ranks and holler Death to the WTO? For that matter, how many of them are prepared to think in world terms, as the capitalists do? Take the Steelworkers, the only labor group which, in the form of the Alliance for Sustainable Jobs and the Environment, took up position in downtown that Tuesday morning (and later fought with the cops and endured tear gas themselves). But on that same day, November 30, the *Moscow Tribune* ran a story reporting that the Clinton administration had effectively stopped all cold-rolled steel imports from Russia by imposing penalty duties of 178 per cent. Going into winter those Russian working families at Severstal, Novolipetsk and Magnitogorsk were facing tougher times than ever. The *Moscow Tribune*'s report, John Helmer, wasn't in doubt why: "Gore must try to preserve steel company and steel worker support."

Labor came out of Seattle and headed into a Bash China campaign, hoping to keep China out of the WTO. Some greens also opposed China's entry, fearing that an expanding Chinese economy would fuel CO_2 emissions which (a very debatable scientific proposition) would increase any trend to global warming. In other words, deny China economic development.

As internationalists, we shouldn't be caught in a debate whose terms we don't set, and whose premises are forced on us. James O'Connor put this very well in an editorial in his journal *Capitalism, Nature, Socialism*, written right after Seattle. "Boeing workers might say, 'we're not against industrialization in China or anywhere else but we're the ones who suffer the bad consequences of technology transfer, and we refuse to.' The internationalist rejoinder: 'you don't have to absorb the entire loss yourselves; join us and we can spread the loss over society as a whole via higher unemployment benefits, better job retraining programs, and government-assisted green investment.' . . . If labor sides with Boeing et al., it's against a redistribution of technology and capital to China; if internationalists side against Boeing and friends, they side with Southern elites against Northern labor."

So we have to stake out our own ground, which is not always that of organized labor in North America which as a matter of self-interest seeks limits to the internationalist effort to redistribute wealth, and also limits to the struggle to redefine wealth in human and natural ecological terms. As O'Connor puts it, "The internationalist struggle to redistribute wealth from capital to labor, rich to poor, North to South, and so on is a 'red moment' of internationalist practice; the internationalist 'green moment' is the struggle to subordinate exchange value to use value and to create ecological societies. The red moment is the quantitative side of things, the green moment the qualitative side."

There's no such thing as "free trade". The present argument is not about trade, for which (except for maybe a few bioregionialists in Ecotopia) all are in favor in some measure. One can denounce General Electric and still be in favor of electricity. The argument is about how trade is to be controlled, how wealth is to be made and distributed. The function of the WTO is to express in trade rules the present balance of economic power on the world held by the big corporations, which see the present WTO round as an opportunity to lock in their gains, to enlist its formal backing in their ceaseless quest for cheap labor and places to dump their poisons.

So ours is a worldwide guerrilla war, of publicity, harassment, obstructionism. It's nothing simple, like the "Stop the War" slogan of the 1960s. Capitalism could stop that war and move on. American capitalism can't stop trade and survive on any terms it cares for.

We truly don't want a seat at the table to "reform" trade rules, because capitalism only plays by the rules if it wrote those rules in the first place. The day the WTO stipulates the phase-in of a world minimum wage of $3 an hour is the day the corporations destroy it and move on. Anyone remember those heady days in the 1970s of the New World Economic Order when third world countries were going to get a fair shake for their commodities? We were at a far more favorable juncture back then, but it wasn't long before the debt crisis had struck, the NWEO was dead and the mildly progressive UN Commission on Trade and Development forever sidelined.

Publicity, harassment, obstructionism . . . Think always in terms of international solidarity. Find targets of opportunity. South Africa forces domestic licensing at cheaper rates of AIDS drugs. Solidarity. The Europeans don't want bio-engineered crops. Fight on that front. Challenge the system at the level of its pretensions. Make demands in favor of real free trade. Get rid of copyright and patent restrictions and fees imposed on developing nations. Take Mexico, Dean Baker, of the Center for Economic and Policy Research reckons that Mexico paid the industrial nations in 1999 $4.2 billion in direct royalties, fees and indirect costs. And okay, let's have real free trade in professional services, with standardization in courses and tests so that kids from Mexico and elsewhere can compete with our lawyers, accountants and doctors.

The truth about capitalism, as O'Connor remarks, "is that trade and market competition are the ways that property owners overcome society's taboo against theft." Our anti-WTO movement opposes the very definition of capitalism as a 'market economy', which destroys human culture and community, exploits labor and degrades nature. The WTO is the mouthpiece of neoliberalism, an outlook and an economic philosophy that finds radical democracy equality intolerable. So, justice in world trade is by definition a revolutionary and utopian aim. Let's get on with it.

152. RALPH NADER

A Crisis of Democracy
(2000)

The following speech by **RALPH NADER** announced his candidacy for the Green Party's nomination for president in the 2000 campaign. Nader (1934–) was born in Winsted, Connecticut, and he was educated at Princeton University and Harvard Law School. Nader practiced law in Connecticut and taught history and government at the University of Hartford. In 1965 he published *Unsafe at Any Speed,* a best-selling exposé of the poor safety standards of the auto industry. He later founded or helped start dozens of citizens' organizations, including the Center for the Study of Responsive Law, and Public Citizen, and became one of America's most trenchant social critics. Nader's run for president in 2000 sought to return power to ordinary citizens by building a democratic, grassroots movement in opposition to the malfeasance of corporations and the arrogance and hypocrisy of the Democrats and Republicans. Although Nader received dismissive treatment from the media and was prohibited from participating in the presidential debates, his campaign helped to energize the Green Party, attracted tens of thousands of activists to his rallies, and earned nearly 3 million votes.

SOURCE: Ralph Nader, "Speech Announcing Ralph Nader's Candidacy for the Green Party's Nomination for President, Washington, D.C., February 21, 2000," reprinted in Ralph Nader, *Crashing the Party: How to Tell the Truth and Still Run for President.* New York: St. Martin's Books, 2002.

SELECTED READINGS: Stephen Gaskin, *An Outlaw in My Heart: A Political Activist's User's Manual* (2000). Ralph Nader, *The Ralph Nader Reader* (2000).

Today I wish to explain why, after working for years as a citizen advocate for consumers, workers, taxpayers, and the environment, I am seeking the Green Party's nomination for president. A crisis of democracy in our country convinces me to take this action. Over the past twenty years, big business has increasingly dominated our political economy. This control by the corporate government over our political government is creating a widening "democracy gap." Active citizens are left shouting their concerns over a deep chasm between them and their government. This state of affairs is a world away from the legislative milestones in civil rights, the environment, and health and safety of workers and consumers seen in the sixties and seventies. At that time, informed and dedicated citizens powered their concerns through the channels of government to produce laws that bettered the lives of millions of Americans.

Today we face grave and growing societal problems in health care, education, labor, energy, and the environment. These are problems for which active citizens have solutions, yet their voices are not carrying across the democracy gap. Citizen groups and individual thinkers have generated a tremendous capital of ideas, information, and solutions to the point of surplus, while our government has been drawn away from us by a corporate government. Our political leadership has been hijacked.

Citizen advocates have no other choice but to close the democracy gap by direct political means. Only effective national political leadership will restore the responsiveness of government to its citizenry. Truly progressive political movements do not just produce more good results, they enable a flowering of progressive citizen movements to effectively advance the quality of our neighborhoods and communities outside of politics.

I have a personal distaste for the trappings of modern politics, in which incumbents and candidates daily extol their own inflated virtues, paint complex issues with trivial brushstrokes, and propose plans quickly generated by campaign consultants. But I can no longer stomach the systemic political decay that has weakened our democracy. I can no longer watch people dedicate themselves to improving their country while their government leaders turn their backs, or worse, actively block fair treatment for citizens. It is necessary to launch a sustained effort to wrest control of our democracy from the corporate government and restore it to the political government under the control of citizens.

This campaign will challenge all Americans who are concerned with systemic imbalances of power and the undermining of our democracy, whether they consider themselves progressives, liberals, conservatives, or others. Presidential elections should be a time for deep discussions among the citizenry regarding the down-to-earth problems and injustices that are not addressed because of the gross power mismatch between the narrow vested interests and the public or common good.

The unconstrained behavior of big business is subordinating our democracy to the control of a corporate plutocracy that knows few self-imposed limits to the spread of its power to all sectors of our society. Moving on all fronts to advance narrow profit motives at the expense of civic values, large corporate lobbies and their law firms have produced a commanding, multifaceted, and powerful juggernaut. They flood public elections with cash, and they use their media conglomerates to exclude, divert, or propagandize. They brandish their willingness to close factories here and open them abroad if workers do not bend to their demands. By their control in Congress, they keep the federal cops off the corporate crime, fraud, and abuse beats. They imperiously demand and get a wide array of privileges and immunities: tax escapes, enormous corporate welfare subsidies, federal giveaways, and bailouts. They weaken the common law of torts in order to avoid their responsibility for injurious wrongdoing to innocent children, women, and men.

Abuses of economic power are nothing new. Every major religion in the world has warned about societies allowing excessive influences of mercantile or commercial values. The profiteering motive is driven and single-minded. When unconstrained, it can override or erode community, health, safety, parental nurturing, due process, clean politics, and many other basic social values that hold together a society. Abraham Lincoln, Theodore Roosevelt, Franklin Roosevelt, Supreme Court Justices Louis Brandeis and William Douglas, among others, eloquently warned about what Thomas Jefferson called "the excesses of the monied interests" dominating people and their governments. The struggle between the forces of democracy and plutocracy has ebbed and flowed throughout our history. Each time the cycle of power has favored more democracy, our country has prospered ("a rising tide lifts all boats"). Each time the cycle of corporate plutocracy has lengthened, injustices and shortcomings proliferate.

In the sixties and seventies, for example, when the civil rights, consumer, environmental, and women's rights movements were in their ascendancy, there finally was a constructive responsiveness by government. Corporations, such as auto manufacturers, had to share more decision making with affected constituencies, both directly and through their public representatives and civil servants. Overall, our country has come out better, more tolerant, safer, and with greater opportunities. The earlier nineteenth-century democratic struggles by abolitionists against slavery, by farmers against large oppressive railroads and banks, and later by new trade unionists against the brutal workplace conditions of the early industrial and mining era helped mightily to make America and its middle class what they are today. They demanded that economic power subside or be shared.

Democracy works, and a stronger democracy works better for reputable, competitive markets, equal opportunity, and higher standards of living and justice. Generally, it brings out the best performances from people and from businesses.

A plutocracy—rule by the rich and powerful—on the other hand, obscures our historical quests for justice. Harnessing political power to corporate greed leaves us with a country that has far more problems than it deserves, while blocking ready solutions or improvements from being applied.

It is truly remarkable that for almost every widespread need or injustice in our country, there are citizens, civic groups, small and medium-size businesses, and farms that have shown how to meet these needs or end these injustices. However, all the innovative solutions in the world will accomplish little if the injustices they address or the problems they solve have been shoved aside because plutocracy reigns and democracy wanes. For all optimistic Americans, when their issues are thus swept from the table, it becomes civic mobilization time. . . .

The "democracy gap" in our politics and elections spells a deep sense of powerlessness by people who drop out, do not vote, or listlessly vote for the "least worst" every four years and then wonder why after another cycle the "least worst" gets worse. It is time to redress fundamentally these imbalances of power. We need a deep initiatory democracy in the embrace of its citizens, a usable brace of democratic tools that brings the best out of people, highlights the humane ideas and practical ways to raise and meet our expectations and resolve our society's deficiencies and injustices.

A few illustrative questions can begin to raise our expectations and suggest what can be lost when the few and powerful hijack our democracy:

• Why can't the wealthiest nation in the world abolish the chronic poverty of millions of working and nonworking Americans, including our children?

• Are we reversing the disinvestment in our distressed inner cities and rural areas and using creatively some of the huge capital pools in the economy to make these areas more livable, productive, and safe?

• Are we able to end homelessness and wretched housing conditions with modern materials, designs, and financing mechanisms, without bank and insurance company redlining, to meet the affordable housing needs of millions of Americans?

• Are we getting the best out of known ways to spread renewable, efficient energy throughout the land to save consumers money and to head off global warming and other land-based environmental damage from fossil fuels and atomic energy?

• Are we getting the best out of the many bright and public-spirited civil servants who know how to improve governments but are rarely asked by their politically appointed superiors or members of Congress?

• Are we able to provide wide access to justice for all aggrieved people so that we apply rigorously the admonition of Judge Learned Hand, "If we are to keep our democracy, there must be one commandment: Thou Shall Not Ration Justice"?

• Can we extend overseas the best examples of our country's democratic processes and achievements instead of annually using billions in tax dollars to subsidize corporate munitions exports, as Republican Senator Mark Hatfield always used to decry?

• Can we stop the giveaways of our vast commonwealth assets and become better stewards of the public lands, better investors of trillions of dollars in worker pension monies, and allow broader access to the public airwaves and other assets now owned by the people but controlled by corporations?

• Can we counter the coarse and brazen commercial culture, including television that daily highlights depravity and ignores the quiet civic heroisms in its communities, a commercialism that insidiously exploits childhood and plasters its logos everywhere?

• Can we plan ahead as a society so we know our priorities and where we wish to go? Or do we continue to let global corporations remain astride the planet, corporatizing everything, from genes to education to the Internet to public institutions, in short, planning our futures in their image? If a robust civic culture does not shape the future, corporatism surely will.

To address these and other compelling challenges, we must build a powerful, self-renewing civil society that focuses on ample justice so we do not have to desperately bestow limited charity. Such a culture strengthens existing civic associations and facilitates the creation of others to watch the complexities and technologies of a new century. Building the future also means providing the youngest of citizens with citizen skills that they can use to improve their communities.

This is the foundation of our campaign, to focus on active citizenship, to create fresh political movements that will displace the control of the Democratic and Republican parties, two apparently distinct political entities that feed at the same corporate trough. They are in fact simply the two heads of one political duopoly, the DemRep Party. This duopoly does everything it can to obstruct the beginnings of new parties, including raising ballot access barriers, entrenching winner-take-all voting systems, and thwarting participation in debates at election times.

As befits its name, the Green Party, whose nomination I seek, stands for the regeneration of American politics. The new populism that the Green Party represents involves motivated, informed voters who comprehend that "freedom is participation in power," to quote the ancient Roman orator Cicero. When citizen participation flourishes, as this campaign will encourage it to do, human values can tame runaway commercial imperatives. The myopia of the short-term bottom line so often debases our democratic processes and our public and private domains. Putting human values first helps to make business responsible and to put government on the right track.

It is easy and true to say that this deep democracy campaign will be an uphill one. However, it is also true that widespread reform will not flourish without a fairer distribution of power for the key roles of voter, citizen, worker, taxpayer, and consumer. Comprehensive reform proposals from the corporate suites to the nation's streets, from the schools to the hospitals, from the preservation of small farm economies to the protection of privacies, from livable wages to sustainable environments, from more time for children to less time for commercialism, from waging peace and health to averting war and violence, from foreseeing and forestalling future troubles to journeying toward brighter horizons, will wither while power inequalities loom over us. . . .

Our political campaign will highlight active and productive citizens who practice democracy often in the most difficult of situations. I intend to do this in the District of Columbia, whose citizens have no full-voting representation in Congress or other rights accorded to states. The scope of this campaign is also to engage as many volunteers as possible to help overcome ballot barriers and to get the vote out. In addition it is designed to leave a momentum after Election Day for the various causes that committed people have worked so hard to further. For the Greens know that political parties need also to work between elections to make elections meaningful. The focus on fundamentals of broader distribution of power is the touchstone of this campaign. As Supreme Court Justice Louis Brandeis declared for the ages, "We can have a democratic society or we can have great concentrated wealth in the hands of a few. We cannot have both."

Thank you.

153. VINCENT BUGLIOSI

None Dare Call It Treason
(2000)

The following essay by **VINCENT BUGLIOSI** generated more letters and inquiries than any other article that has ever been published in *The Nation*
magazine. In it, Bugliosi (1934–) denounced as criminals the five Supreme
Court Justices who settled the dispute over the 2000 election in George
Bush's favor. Bugliosi received his law degree from UCLA Law School in
1964, and during his tenure in the L.A. District Attorney's Office he won
convictions in 105 of 106 felony cases, including the prosecution of Charles
Manson. Although many who disagreed with the Court's decision argued that
Americans must nevertheless rally behind it, Bugliosi suggested that Justices
Scalia, Thomas, Rehnquist, O'Connor, and Kennedy "have forfeited their
right to be respected."

SOURCE: Vincent Bugliosi. "None Dare Call It Treason." *The Nation*, February
5, 2001.

SELECTED READINGS: Vincent Bugliosi, *The Betrayal of America: How the Supreme
Court Undermined the Constitution and Chose Our President* (2001). John Nichols,
*Jews for Buchanan: Did You Hear the One About the Theft of the American Presi-
dency* (2001). Jeffrey Toobin, *Too Close to Call: The Thirty-Six Day Battle to Decide
the 2000 Election* (2001).

In the December 12 ruling by the US Supreme Court handing the election to
George Bush, the Court committed the unpardonable sin of being a knowing
surrogate for the Republican Party instead of being an impartial arbiter of the
law. If you doubt this, try to imagine Al Gore's and George Bush's roles being
reversed and ask yourself if you can conceive of Justice Antonin Scalia and
his four conservative brethren issuing an emergency order on December 9
stopping the counting of ballots (at a time when Gore's lead had shrunk to
154 votes) on the grounds that if it continued, Gore could suffer "irreparable

harm," and then subsequently, on December 12, bequeathing the election to Gore on equal protection grounds. If you can, then I suppose you can also imagine seeing a man jumping away from his own shadow, Frenchmen no longer drinking wine.

From the beginning, Bush desperately sought, as it were, to prevent the opening of the door, the looking into the box—unmistakable signs that he feared the truth. In a nation that prides itself on openness, instead of the Supreme Court doing everything within its power to find a legal way to open the door and box, they did the precise opposite in grasping, stretching and searching mightily for a way, any way at all, to aid their choice for President, Bush, in the suppression of the truth, finally settling, in their judicial coup d'état, on the untenable argument that there was a violation of the Fourteenth Amendment's equal protection clause—the Court asserting that because of the various standards of determining the voter's intent in the Florida counties, voters were treated unequally, since a vote disqualified in one county (the so-called undervotes, which the voting machines did not pick up) may have been counted in another county, and vice versa. Accordingly, the Court reversed the Florida Supreme Court's order that the undervotes be counted, effectively delivering the presidency to Bush.

Now, in the equal protection cases I've seen, the aggrieved party, the one who is being harmed and discriminated against, almost invariably brings the action. But no Florida voter I'm aware of brought any action under the equal protection clause claiming he was disenfranchised because of the different standards being employed. What happened here is that Bush leaped in and tried to profit from a hypothetical wrong inflicted on someone else. Even assuming Bush had this right, the very core of his petition to the Court was that he himself would be harmed by these different standards. But would he have? If we're to be governed by common sense, the answer is no. The reason is that just as with flipping a coin you end up in rather short order with as many heads as tails, there would be a "wash" here for both sides, i.e., there would be just as many Bush as Gore votes that would be counted in one county yet disqualified in the next. (Even if we were to assume, for the sake of argument, that the wash wouldn't end up exactly, 100 percent even, we'd still be dealing with the rule of *de minimis non curat lex*—the law does not concern itself with trifling matters.) So what harm to Bush was the Court so passionately trying to prevent by its ruling other than the real one: that he would be harmed by the truth as elicited from a full counting of the undervotes?

And if the Court's five-member majority was concerned not about Bush but the voters themselves, as they fervently claimed to be, then under what conceivable theory would they, *in effect,* tell these voters, "We're so concerned that *some* of you undervoters may lose your vote under the different Florida county standards that we're going to solve the problem by making sure that *none* of you undervoters have your votes counted"? Isn't this exactly what the Court did? . . .

Other than the unprecedented and outrageous nature of what the Court did, nothing surprises me more than how it is being viewed by the legal scholars and pundits who have criticized the opinion. As far as I can determine, most *have* correctly assailed the Court for issuing a ruling that was clearly political. As the December 25 *Time* capsulized it, "A sizable number of critics, from law professors to some of the Court's own members, have attacked the ruling as . . . politically motivated." A sampling from a few law professors: Vanderbilt professor Suzanna Sherry said, "There is really very little way to reconcile this opinion other than that they wanted Bush to win." Yale's Amar lamented that "for Supreme Court watchers this case will be like BC and AD. For many of my colleagues, this was like the day President Kennedy was assassinated. Many of us [had] thought that courts do not act in an openly political fashion." Harvard law professor Randall Kennedy called the decision "outrageous."

The only problem I have with these critics is that they have merely lost respect for and confidence in the Court. "I have less respect for the Court than before," Amar wrote. The *New York Times* said the ruling appeared "openly political" and that it "eroded public confidence in the Court." Indeed, the always accommodating and obsequious (in all matters pertaining to the High Court, in front of which he regularly appears) Harvard law professor Laurence Tribe, who was Gore's chief appellate lawyer, went even further in the weakness of his disenchantment with the Court. "Even if we disagree" with the Court's ruling, he said, Americans should "rally around the decision."

Sometimes the body politic is lulled into thinking along unreasoned lines. The "conventional wisdom" emerging immediately after the Court's ruling seemed to be that the Court, by its political ruling, had only lost a lot of credibility and altitude in the minds of many people. But these critics of the ruling, even those who flat-out say the Court "stole" the election, apparently have not stopped to realize the inappropriateness of their tepid position vis-à-vis what the Court did. You mean you can steal a presidential election and your only retribution is that some people don't have as much respect for you, as much confidence in you? That's all? If, indeed, the Court, as the critics say, made a politically motivated ruling (which it unquestionably did), this is tantamount to saying, and can *only* mean, that the Court did not base its ruling on the law. And if this is so (which again, it unquestionably is), this means that these five Justices *deliberately and knowingly* decided to nullify the votes of the 50 million Americans who voted for Al Gore and to steal the election for Bush. Of course, nothing could possibly be more serious in its enormous ramifications. The stark reality, and I say this with every fiber of my being, is that the institution Americans trust the most to protect its freedoms and principles committed one of the biggest and most serious crimes this nation has ever seen—pure and simple, the theft of the presidency. And by definition, the perpetrators of this crime *have* to be denominated criminals. . . .

Though the five Justices clearly are criminals, no one is treating them this way. As I say, even those who were outraged by the Court's ruling have only lost respect for them. And for the most part the nation's press seems to have already forgotten and/or forgiven. Within days, the Court's ruling was no longer the subject of Op-Ed pieces. Indeed, just five days after its high crime, the caption of an article by Jean Guccione in the *Los Angeles Times* read, "The Supreme Court Should Weather This Storm." The following day an AP story noted that Justice Sandra Day O'Connor, on vacation in Arizona, had fired a hole-in-one on the golf course.

The lack of any valid legal basis for their decision and, most important, the fact that it is inconceivable they would have ruled the way they did for Gore, proves, *on its face,* that the five conservative Republican Justices were up to no good. Therefore, not one stitch of circumstantial evidence beyond this is really necessary to demonstrate their felonious conduct and state of mind. (The fact that O'Connor, per the *Wall Street Journal,* said before the election that she wanted to retire but did not want to do so if a Democrat would be selecting her successor, that Thomas's wife is working for the conservative Heritage Foundation to help handle the Bush transition and that Scalia's two sons work for law firms representing Bush is all unneeded trivia. We already know, without this, exactly what happened.) But for those who want more, let me point out that there is no surer way to find out what parties meant than to see what they have done. And like typical criminals, the felonious five left their incriminating fingerprints everywhere, showing an unmistakable consciousness of guilt on their part.

1. Under Florida statutory law, when the Florida Supreme Court finds that a challenge to the certified result of an election is justified, it has the power to "provide *any* relief appropriate under the circumstances" (§ 102.168(8) of the Florida Election Code). On Friday, December 8, the Florida court, so finding, ordered a manual recount (authorized under § 102.166(4)(c) of the Florida Election Code) of all disputed ballots (around 60,000) throughout the entire state. As a *New York Times* editorial reported, "The manual recount was progressing smoothly and swiftly Saturday . . . with new votes being recorded for both Vice President Al Gore and Governor George W. Bush . . . serving the core democratic principle that every legal vote should be counted" when, in midafternoon, the US Supreme Court "did a disservice to the nation's tradition of fair elections by calling a halt" to the recount. The stay (requested by Bush), the *Times* said, appeared "highly political."

Under Supreme Court rules, a stay is supposed to be granted to an applicant (here, Bush) only if he makes a substantial showing that in the absence of a stay, there is a likelihood of "irreparable harm" to him. With the haste of a criminal, Justice Scalia, in trying to justify the Court's shutting down of the vote counting, wrote, unbelievably, that counting these votes would "threaten irreparable harm to petitioner [Bush] . . . by casting a cloud upon what *he* claims to be the legitimacy of *his* election." [Emphasis added.] In other words, although the election had not yet been decided, the absolutely incredible Scalia was presupposing that Bush had won the election—indeed, had a *right* to win it—and any recount that showed Gore got more votes in Florida than Bush could "cloud" Bush's presidency. Only a criminal on the run, rushed for time and acting in desperation, could possibly write the embarrassing words Scalia did, language showing that he knew he had no legal basis for what he was doing, but that getting something down in writing, even as intellectually flabby and fatuous as it was, was better than nothing at all. (Rehnquist, Thomas, O'Connor and Kennedy, naturally, joined Scalia in the stay order.) . . .

In yet another piece of incriminating circumstantial evidence, Scalia, in granting Bush's application for the stay, wrote that "the issuance of the stay suggests that a majority of the Court, while not deciding the issues presented, believe that the petitioner [Bush] has a substantial probability of success." But Antonin, why would you believe this when neither side had submitted written briefs yet (they were due the following day, Sunday, by 4 pm), nor had there even been oral arguments (set for 11 am on Monday)? It wouldn't be because you had already made up your mind on what you were determined to do, come hell or high water, would it? Antonin, take it from an experienced prosecutor—you're as guilty as sin. In my prosecutorial days, I've had some worthy opponents. You wouldn't be one of them. Your guilt is so obvious that if I thought more of you I'd feel constrained to blush *for* you.

2. When prosecutors present their circumstantial case against a defendant, they put one speck of evidence upon another until ultimately there is a strong mosaic of guilt. One such small speck is that in its 5-to-4 decision handing the election to Bush, the Court's ruling was set forth in a thirteen-page "per curiam" (Latin for "by the court") opinion (followed by concurring and dissenting opinions). Students of the Supreme Court know that per curiam opinions are almost always issued for unanimous (9-to-0) opinions in relatively unimportant and uncontroversial cases, or where Justices wish to be very brief. But as *USA Today* pointed out, "Neither was the case here." Again, on the run and in a guilty state of mind, none of the five Justices, even the brazenly shameless Scalia, wanted to sign their name to a majority opinion of the Court reversing the Florida Supreme Court's order to recount the undervotes. A per curiam opinion, which is always unsigned, was the answer. It is not even known who wrote the per curiam opinion, though it is believed to be O'Connor and/or Kennedy, neither of whose names is mentioned anywhere in the Court's sixty-two-page document. After they did their dirty work by casting their two

votes on the case for their favorite—two votes that overruled and rendered worthless the votes of 50 million Americans in fifty states—O'Connor and Kennedy wanted to stay away from their decision the way the devil stays away from holy water. Indeed, by their per curiam opinion, it was almost as if the felonious five felt that since their names would not be on the legally sacrilegious opinion, maybe, just maybe, the guilt they knew they bore would be mitigated, at least somewhat, in posterity.

3. The proof that the Court itself knew its equal protection argument had no merit whatsoever is that when Bush first asked the Court, on November 22, to consider three objections of his to the earlier, more limited Florida recount then taking place, the Court only denied review on his third objection— yeah, you guessed it, that the lack of a uniform standard to determine the voter's intent violated the equal protection clause of the Fourteenth Amendment. Since the Court, on November 22, felt that this objection was so devoid of merit that it was unworthy of even being considered by it, what did these learned Justices subsequently learn about the equal protection clause they apparently did not know in November that caused them just three weeks later, on December 12, to embrace and endorse it so enthusiastically? The election was finally on the line on December 12 and they knew they had to come up with something, anything, to save the day for their man.

The bottom line is that nothing is more important in a democracy than the right to vote. Without it there cannot be a democracy. And implicit in the right to vote, obviously, is that the vote be counted. Yet with the election hanging in the balance, the highest court in the land ordered that the valid votes of thousands of Americans *not* be counted. That decision gave the election to Bush. When Justice Thomas was asked by a skeptical high school student the day after the Court's ruling whether the Court's decision had anything to do with politics, he answered, "Zero." And when a reporter thereafter asked Rehnquist whether he agreed with Thomas, he said, "Absolutely, absolutely." Well, at least we know they can lie as well as they can steal.

4. The Court anchored its knowingly fraudulent decision on the equal protection clause of the Fourteenth Amendment. But wait. Since the electors in the fifty states weren't scheduled to meet and vote until December 18, and the Court's ruling was on December 12, if the Court was really serious about its decision that the various standards in the counties to determine the voter's intent violated the equal protection clause, why not, as Justices Stevens, Souter, Ginsburg and Breyer each noted in separate dissents, simply remand the case back to the Florida Supreme Court with instructions to establish a uniform, statewide standard and continue the recount until December 18? The shameless and shameful felonious five had an answer, which, in a sense, went to the heart of their decision even more than the bogus equal protection

argument. The unsigned and anonymously written per curiam opinion noted that under Title 3 of the United States Code, Section 5 (3 USC § 5), any controversy or contest to determine the selection of electors should be resolved "six days prior to the meeting of the Electoral College," that is, December 12, and inasmuch as the Court issued its ruling at 10 pm on December 12, with just two hours remaining in the day, the Court said, "That date [December 12] is upon us," and hence there obviously was no time left to set uniform standards and continue the recount. But there are a multiplicity of problems with the Court's oh-so-convenient escape hatch. Writing in the *Wall Street Journal,* University of Utah law professor Michael McConnell, a legal conservative, pointed out that the December 12 "deadline" is only a deadline "for receiving 'safe harbor' protection for the state's electors" (i.e., if a state certifies its electors by that date, Congress can't question them), not a federal deadline that must be met. New York University law professor Larry Kramer observed that if a state does not make that deadline, "nothing happens. The counting could continue." . . .

But even if December 12 were some kind of actual deadline, nothing was sillier during this whole election debate than the talking heads on television, many of whom were lawyers who should have known better, treating the date as if it were sacrosanct and set in stone (exactly what the Supreme Court majority, on the run and trying to defend their indefensible position, said). In the real world, mandatory dates always have an elliptical clause attached to them, "unless there is just cause for extending the date." I cannot be accused of hyperbole when I say that perhaps no less than thousands of times a day in courthouses throughout the country, mandatory ("shall") dates to do this or that (file a brief, a motion, commence a trial, etc.) are waived by the court on the representation of one party alone that he needs more time. If extending the December 12 (or the December 18 date, for that matter) deadline for a few days for the counting of votes to determine who the rightful winner of a presidential election is does not constitute a sufficient cause for a short extension of time, then what in the world does? No one has said it better than columnist Thomas Friedman: "The five conservative Justices essentially ruled that the sanctity of dates, even meaningless ones, mattered more than the sanctity of votes, even meaningful ones. The Rehnquist Court now has its legacy: In calendars we trust." In other words, to Scalia and his friends, speed was more important than justice. More important than accuracy. Being the strong-armed enforcer of deadlines, even inconsequential ones, was more important to these five Justices than being the nation's protector and guardian of the right to vote. . . .

5. If there are two sacred canons of the right-wing in America and ultra-conservative Justices like Scalia, Thomas and Rehnquist, it's their ardent federalism, i.e., promotion of states' rights (Rehnquist, in fact, wrote in his

concurring opinion about wanting, wherever possible, to "defer to the decisions of state courts on issues of state law"), and their antipathy for Warren Court activist judges. So if it weren't for their decision to find a way, any way imaginable, to appoint Bush President, their automatic predilection would have been to stay the hell out of Florida's business. The fact that they completely departed from what they would almost reflexively do in ninety-nine out of a hundred other cases is again persuasive circumstantial evidence of their criminal state of mind.

6. Perhaps nothing Scalia et al. did revealed their consciousness of guilt more than the total lack of legal stature they reposed in their decision. Appellate court decisions, particularly those of the highest court in the land, *all* enunciate and stand for legal principles. Not just litigants but the courts themselves cite prior holdings as support for a legal proposition they are espousing. But the Court knew that its ruling (that differing standards for counting votes violate the equal protection clause) could not possibly be a constitutional principle cited in the future by themselves, other courts or litigants. Since different methods of counting votes exist throughout the fifty states (e.g., Texas counts dimpled chads, California does not), forty-four out of the fifty states do not have uniform voting methods, and voting equipment and mechanisms in all states necessarily vary in design, upkeep and performance, to apply the equal protection ruling of *Bush v. Gore* would necessarily invalidate virtually all elections throughout the country.

This, obviously, was an extremely serious problem for the felonious five to deal with. What to do? Not to worry. Are you ready for this one? By that I mean, are you sitting down, since if you're standing, this is the type of thing that could affect your physical equilibrium. Unbelievably, the Court wrote that its ruling was *"limited to the present circumstances,* for the problem of equal protection in election processes generally presents many complexities." (That's pure, unadulterated moonshine. The ruling sets forth a very simple, noncomplex proposition—that if there are varying standards to count votes, this violates the equal protection clause of the Fourteenth Amendment.) In other words, the Court, in effect, was saying its ruling "only applied to those future cases captioned *Bush v. Gore*. In all other equal protection voting cases, litigants should refer to prior decisions of this court." Of the thousands of potential equal protection voting cases, the Court was only interested in, and eager to grant relief to, one person and one person only, George W. Bush. Is there any limit to the effrontery and shamelessness of these five right-wing Justices? Answer: No. This point number six here, all alone and by itself, clearly and unequivocally shows that the Court knew its decision was not based on the merits or the law, and was solely a decision to appoint George Bush President.

Conservatives, the very ones who wanted to impeach Earl Warren, have now predictably taken to arguing that one shouldn't attack the Supreme Court as I am because it can only harm the image of the Court, which we have to respect as the national repository for, and protector of, the rule of law, the latter being a sine qua non to a structured, nonanarchistic society. This is just so much drivel. Under what convoluted theory do we honor the rule of law by ignoring the violation of it, (here, the sacred, inalienable right to vote of all Americans) by the Supreme Court? With this unquestioning subservience-to-authority theory, I suppose the laws of the Third Reich—such as requiring Jews to wear a yellow Star of David on their clothing—should have been respected and followed by the Jews. Blacks should have respected Jim Crow laws in the first half of the twentieth century. Naturally, these conservative exponents of not harming the Supreme Court, even though the Court stole a federal election disfranchising 50 million American citizens, are the same people who felt no similar hesitancy savaging the President of the United States not just day after day, but week after week, month after month, yes, even year after year for having a private and consensual sexual affair and then lying about it. And this was so even though the vitriolic and never-ending attacks crippled the executive branch of government for months on end, causing incalculable damage to the office of the presidency and to this nation, both internally and in the eyes of the world. Indeed, many of them are delighted to hound and go after the President even after he leaves office.

These five Justices, by their conduct, have forfeited the right to be respected, and only by treating them the way they deserve to be treated can we demonstrate our respect for the rule of law they defiled, and insure that their successors will not engage in similarly criminal conduct.

Why, one may ask, have I written this article? I'll tell you why. I'd like to think, like most people, that I have a sense of justice. In my mind's eye, these five Justices have gotten away with murder, and I want to do whatever I can to make sure that they pay dearly for their crime. Though they can't be prosecuted, I want them to know that there's at least one American out there (and hopefully many more because of this article) who knows (not thinks, but knows) precisely who they are. I want these five Justices to know that because of this article, which I intend to send to each one of them by registered mail, there's the exponential possibility that when many Americans look at them in the future, they'll be saying, "Why are these people in robes seated above me? They all belong behind bars." I want these five Justices to know that this is America, not a banana republic, and in the United States of America, you simply cannot get away with things like this.

At a minimum, I believe that the Court's inexcusable ruling will severely stain its reputation for years to come, perhaps decades. This is very unfortunate. As Justice Stevens wrote in his dissent: "Although we may never know with complete certainty the identity of the winner of this year's presidential election, the identity of the loser is perfectly clear. It is the nation's confidence in [this Court] as an impartial guardian of the rule of law." Considering the criminal intention behind the decision, legal scholars and historians should place this ruling above the Dred Scott case (*Scott v. Sandford*) and *Plessy v. Ferguson* in egregious sins of the Court. The right of every American citizen to have his or her vote counted, and for Americans (not five unelected Justices) to choose their President was callously and I say criminally jettisoned by the Court's majority to further its own political ideology. If there is such a thing as a judicial hell, these five Justices won't have to worry about heating bills in their future. Scalia and Thomas in particular are not only a disgrace to the judiciary but to the legal profession, for years being nothing more than transparent shills for the right wing of the Republican Party. If the softest pillow is a clear conscience, these five Justices are in for some hard nights. But if they aren't troubled by what they did, then we're dealing with judicial sociopaths, people even more frightening than they already appear to be.

The Republican Party had a good candidate for President, John McCain. Instead, it nominated perhaps the most unqualified person ever to become President, and with the muscular, thuggish help of the Court, forced Bush down the throats of more than half the nation's voters. As Linda Greenhouse wrote in the *New York Times,* when Rehnquist administers the presidential oath of office to Bush on January 20, for the first time in our nation's history the Chief Justice will not just be a prop in the majestic ceremony but a player. Rehnquist will be swearing in someone he made sure would be President. Obscenity has its place in a free and open society, but it's in the seedy, neon-light part of town, not on the steps of the nation's Capitol being viewed by millions of Americans on television screens throughout the land.

That an election for an American President can be stolen by the highest court in the land under the deliberate pretext of an inapplicable constitutional provision has got to be one of the most frightening and dangerous events ever to have occurred in this country. Until this act—which is treasonous, though again not technically, in its sweeping implications—is somehow rectified (and I do not know how this can be done), can we be serene about continuing to place the adjective "great" before the name of this country?

154. HARVARD LIVING WAGE CAMPAIGN

Why We Are Sitting In

(2001)

On April 18, 2001, forty-six students from the **HARVARD LIVING WAGE CAM-PAIGN** entered Massachusetts Hall, the administrative building that houses Harvard's Office of the President, to demand that Harvard pay all of its employees a "living wage." For the next three weeks, Harvard Yard witnessed the largest campus protests in recent years. In addition to the sit-in, hundreds of protestors and sympathizers marched outside, built an expansive "tent city," held panel discussions and daily rallies, and launched an impressive outreach and petition campaign to raise consciousness, both on campus and across the country, about the issues at stake in this labor battle at the United States' wealthiest university. As a result of these protests, Harvard has begun addressing the problems of low-wage poverty. "Why We Are Sitting In" was distributed around campus as a poster on the first evening of the sit-in. It both enumerates the principal demands of the students involved, and justifies the act of civil disobedience.

SOURCE: Harvard Living Wage Campaign, http://www.livingwagenow.com, 2002.

SELECTED READINGS: Barbara Ehrenreich, *Nickel and Dimed: On (Not) Getting By in America* (2001). John Hoerr, *We Can't Eat Prestige: The Women Who Organized Harvard* (1997). Robert N. Pollin and Stephanie Luce, *The Living Wage: Building a Fair Economy* (1998).

During the last two years, poverty-level wages and benefits have emerged as a pressing problem at our university. From directly-hired janitors in our dorms to outsourced dining hall workers in our graduate school cafeterias, over 1,000 Harvard employees face a daily struggle to support themselves and their families as Harvard pays them wages as low as $6.50 per hour without benefits.

They face 90-hour work weeks, they face days and months without seeing their children or spouses, they face medical emergencies without health care, and they face evictions and homelessness. As thousands of students, workers, faculty members, unions, alumni/ae, and community members have agreed, no one should face these circumstances, and we can not permit them in our community.

The Living Wage Campaign has worked since 1998 to ensure that all Harvard employees can afford to decently live and raise their families in the Cambridge community. Today, after more than two years of meetings, coalition-building, and public demonstrations, we have begun an indefinite sit-in in Harvard's administrative offices. This move represents an escalation of our pressure on the administration, and we believe that such escalation is justified.

We are sitting in because we have exhausted every avenue of dialogue with the administration that could lead to a living wage. Since March 1999, we have met repeatedly with administrators including the President, Provost, Vice President for Administration, Associate Vice President for Human Resources, Director of Labor Relations, Dean of Students, and Associate Dean of the College. We have asked to meet with the Corporation and have been refused: President Rudenstine explained that "they usually deliberate on their own," and the Secretary to the Corporation falsely claimed that wage and benefit policies fall outside the jurisdiction of the Corporation. The meetings we did have uniformly consisted of administrative refusals to adopt or even consider a living wage policy. Before the release of the findings of the Presidents appointed Ad Hoc Committee on Employment Policies in May 2000, administrators claimed that the committee's ongoing deliberations prevented them from approving any changes. And since the committee released its recommendations—rejecting the implementation of any wage standard whatsoever for Harvard workers—administrators have told us that the issue is closed: they will consider no further changes, or even investigations into possible changes.

We are sitting in because we have exhausted every other strategy when dialogue with the administration has failed. We have written op-eds, we have sponsored teach-ins, we have collected student, faculty, and parent petitions, and we have organized alumni/ae to refuse to donate money to Harvard. We have spoken on both local and national television and radio, and we have spoken at conferences on labor and economic affairs. Since February 1999, we have sponsored dozens of public demonstrations, attracting crowds of 150 to 1,000 people. And we have tried less imposing forms of direct action: in April 2000, we occupied Harvard's admissions office for one day during Pre-Frosh Weekend, distributing literature and holding teach-ins to educate prospective students about poverty at Harvard.

We are sitting in because administrators have not only failed to improve wages and benefits, but have aggressively worked to slash them as support for a living wage policy has grown. In the face of opposition from unions, workers, faculty, and students, the university has outsourced hundreds of jobs to firms which pay poverty-level wages and benefits. An egregious case is that of Harvard's security guards, whose ranks have been cut from roughly 120 to 18 by outsourcing, and whose union has been decimated in the process. Outsourcing meant that guards' wages fell overnight from roughly $12 to $8 per hour, benefits were similarly slashed, the guards' union was effectively busted, and the subcontracted workers have no union through which to contest their inadequate conditions. Moreover, just this semester, Harvard has subcontracted and reclassified hundreds more jobs—janitors at the Medical School and dining workers at the Business School—with similarly destructive results for workers.

We are sitting in because Harvard's wage and benefit policies threaten the economic survival and violate the dignity of university workers, and our community overwhelmingly recognizes this fact. Every campus union has endorsed our campaign, and the hundreds of workers with whom we have spoken—unionized and not—have made clear that they need a living wage. Over 150 Harvard faculty members have endorsed our campaign. Two thousand students have signed our petition, and according to a Crimson poll, more than three-quarters of students support the implementation of a living wage policy. Over 100 alumni/ae have gone so far as to refuse to donate money to Harvard until it implements a living wage. Dozens of community, religious, and labor organizations have endorsed the Campaign or taken part in demonstrations. The Cambridge City Council has twice passed resolutions or orders calling on Harvard to implement a living wage policy, and City Councillors have been joined by other local and national politicians in endorsing the Campaign, demonstrating with us, and personally communicating their concerns to the administration. Finally, a wide array of public figures have endorsed our campaign and spoken for it: these people include actors Ben Affleck, Warren Beatty, and Matt Damon; NAACP Chairman Julian Bond; linguist Noam Chomsky; writers Barbara Ehrenreich, Leslie Feinberg, and Jim Hightower; Rev. Jesse Jackson; Senators Edward Kennedy and Paul Wellstone; and historian Howard Zinn.

Finally, we are sitting in because poverty on our campus is brutal and cannot wait any longer for remedy. Today, over 1,000 Harvard workers are paid wages as low as $6.50 per hour without benefits. This is a wage that puts a parent with one child below the federal poverty line. The people who clean our buildings, cook our meals, and guard our dorms routinely work two and even three jobs—as many as 90 hours per week—and still struggle to support themselves and their families. They are regularly forced to make impossible and unfair sacrifices—sacrificing their health, their interests, and their responsibilities to

their families—simply to make ends meet. And some ultimately find themselves unable even to do that: today, there are Harvard janitors who regularly
eat in soup kitchens and sleep in shelters because they can not pay for food
and rent. These people, and the rest of us who are forced to be complicit in
their exploitation, cannot wait for the remote possibility that administrators
will decide to reopen what they have called a "closed issue." The human and
social costs of Harvard's policies are immense, and require remedy now.

With these considerations in mind, we are sitting in for the following demand:
*All Harvard workers, whether directly employed or hired through outside firms, must
be paid a living wage of at least $10.25 per hour, adjusted annually to inflation, and
with basic health benefits.* Complete implementation of such a living wage policy
requires three other simple steps:

1. To ensure that the university does not use subcontracting and reclassi-
fication to cut wages and benefits—as the Harvard Corporation has agreed it
should not—Harvard must adopt a policy of maintaining wage and benefit
levels when jobs are outsourced or reclassified. Our Implementation Report
contains methods for assuring this which should be adopted.
2. A board must be created, not appointed by the administration, to over-
see implementation of the living wage policy. The board should have binding
policy-making power to enforce the policy, and should consist of workers,
union representatives, faculty, members of PSLM, and an administrator.
3. Harvard relies on the labor of workers both on campus and off, and both
must be covered by the university's living wage policy. Workers in factories
that produce Harvard goods must therefore be assured a living wage for their
community; indeed, Harvard has already agreed to a Code of Conduct which
contains a commitment to this very idea. In order to determine whether factories are complying with Harvard's Code, however, the university must join
the Worker Rights Consortium, the only independent factory monitoring
group which satisfies the Codes guidelines.

We believe that participants in and supporters of this sit-in should face no
academic or disciplinary repercussions within the university, and those employed by the university should be assured job security. Participants and supporters should additionally face no civil or criminal charges brought at the
request of the university or its members. These immunity guidelines have
routinely been demanded and met in the dozens of student sit-ins that have
taken place nationally during the last three years.
All of us who have entered Massachusetts Hall have done so with our eyes
open, and are prepared for any repercussions that we may face. We do not

think that punishment is justified, however, because we do not believe that what we are doing is criminal. Harvard is falling short of basic standards of economic fairness and human dignity, and in acting to make it meet those standards, we are acting to make our community what it ought to be. We are acting to make it the kind of place that thousands of students, workers, faculty members, unions, alumni/ae and community members have said it should be. We are acting to make it a better university. This is not a criminal act.

155. Antiwar Documents

The Boondocks (2002) and We Oppose Both Saddam Hussein and the U.S. War on Iraq: A call for a new democratic U.S. foreign policy (2003)

Following the deadly attacks on the World Trade Center and the Pentagon on September 11, 2001, Americans have been divided over whether and how the United States should respond. In the wake of the Bush Administration's exceedingly hawkish approach to military intervention in both Afghanistan and Iraq—its unilateralism abroad and its assault on civil liberties at home—Americans from every walk of life have reinvigorated the peace movement. The following documents are just two examples of growing antiwar sentiment in the United States. Aaron McGruder's cartoon series, "The Boondocks," is one of the country's sharpest political commentaries. First published in 1996, when McGruder was still a student at the University of Maryland, the cartoon exposes the "silliness and hypocrisy of our world" through the experiences of its main character, Huey Freeman, a highly intelligent, revolutionary black youth who has moved with his family from South Chicago to the suburbs. The second document, "We Oppose Both Saddam Hussein and the U.S. War on Iraq," was written by Joanne Landy, Thomas Harrison, and Jennifer Scarlott, co-directors of the Campaign for Peace and Democracy, and as of March 2003, it has been signed by four thousand activists and intellectuals (including the editors of this book). Opposing at once a reckless war and the oppressive Iraqi regime, this petition, which began circulation in December 2002, represents the important role the Internet will play in the formation of a new kind of "imagined community" among radicals—a role that will be even more crucial as political crises and coalitions become increasingly global.

SOURCES: *The Progressive*, August 2002; *The Nation*, January 6, 2003.

SELECTED READINGS: Aaron McGruder, *The Boondocks: Because I Know You Don't Read the Newspaper* (2000). Aaron McGruder, *Fresh for '01 . . . You Suckas: A Boondocks Collection (2001)*. Lewis Lapham, *Theater of War* (2002). <www.com mondreams.org>, www.endthewar.org, www.zmag.org, www.cpdweb.org, www.noattackiraq.org, www.unitedforpeace.org, www.globalexchange.org

We Oppose Both Saddam Hussein and the U.S. War on Iraq:

A call for a new, democratic U.S. foreign policy

The Bush administration has already exploited its "War on Terrorism" to intimidate critics, undermine civil liberties and push through a blatantly pro-corporate agenda. Now we are on the verge of an illegitimate and dangerous war on Iraq. With each day, preparations for this onslaught take on more and more alarming dimensions, including the threat to use nuclear weapons; around the world, the United States is perceived as the leading "rogue state." We must do all we can to stop this war, including, crucially, challenging the Administration's claim that U.S. military action would bring freedom to Iraqis and strengthen global security. The following statement makes this challenge, and offers an alternative policy for dealing with dictatorships, terrorism and weapons of mass destruction. We invite you to join this effort.

JOANNE LANDY, THOMAS HARRISON, JENNIFER SCARLOTT,

CO-DIRECTORS, CAMPAIGN FOR PEACE AND DEMOCRACY

We oppose the impending U.S.-led war on Iraq, which threatens to inflict vast suffering and destruction, while exacerbating rather than resolving threats to regional and global peace. Saddam Hussein is a tyrant who should be removed from power, both for the good of the Iraqi people and for the security of neighboring countries. However, it is up to the Iraqi people themselves to oust Saddam Hussein, dismantle his police state regime, and democratize their country. People in the United States can be of immense help in this effort—not by supporting military intervention, but by building a strong peace movement and working to ensure that our government pursues a consistently democratic and just foreign policy.

We do not believe that the goal of the approaching war against Iraq is to bring democracy to the Iraqis, nor that it will produce this result. Instead, the Bush administration's aim is to expand and solidify U.S. predominance in the Middle East, at the cost of tens of thousands of civilian lives if necessary. This war is about U.S. political, military and economic power, about seizing control of oilfields and about strengthening the United States as the enforcer of an inhumane global status quo. *That is why we are opposed to war against Iraq, whether waged unilaterally by Washington or by the UN Security Council, unaccountable to the UN General Assembly and bullied and bribed into endorsing the war.*

The U.S. military may have the ability to destroy Saddam Hussein, but the United States cannot promote democracy in the Muslim world and peace in the Middle East, nor can it deal with the threat posed to all of us by terrorist networks such as Al Qaeda, and by weapons of mass destruction, by pursuing its current policies. Indeed, the U.S. could address these problems only by doing the *opposite* of what it is doing today—that is, by:

• Renouncing the use of military intervention to extend and consolidate U.S. imperial power, and withdrawing U.S. troops from the Middle East.

• Ending its support for corrupt and authoritarian regimes, e.g. Saudi Arabia, the Gulf states and Egypt.

• Opposing, and ending U.S. complicity in, all forms of terrorism worldwide—not just by Al Qaeda, Palestinian suicide bombers and Chechen hostage takers, but also by Colombian paramilitaries, the Israeli military in the Occupied Territories and Russian counterinsurgency forces in Chechnya.

• Ending the cruel sanctions on Iraq, which inflict massive harm on the civilian population.

• Supporting the right of national self-determination for all peoples in the Middle East, including the Kurds, Palestinians and Israeli Jews. Ending one-sided support for Israel in the Palestinian-Israeli conflict.

• Taking unilateral steps toward renouncing weapons of mass destruction, including nuclear weapons, and vigorously promoting international disarmament treaties.

• Abandoning IMF/World Bank economic policies that bring mass misery to people in large parts of the world. Initiating a major foreign aid program directed at popular rather than corporate needs.

These initiatives, taken together, would constitute a truly *democratic* foreign policy. Only such a policy could begin to reverse the mistrust and

outright hatred felt by so much of the world's population toward the
U.S. . . .

The Administration's frantic and flagrantly dishonest efforts to portray Saddam Hussein as an imminent military threat to people in this country and to
the inhabitants of other Middle Eastern countries lack credibility. Saddam
Hussein is a killer and serial aggressor who would doubtless like nothing better
than to wreak vengeance on the U.S. and to dominate the Gulf Region. But
there is no reason to believe he is suicidal or insane. . . .

Weapons of mass destruction endanger us all and must be eliminated.
But a war against Iraq is not the answer. War threatens massive harm to Iraqi
civilians, will add to the ranks of terrorists throughout the Muslim world, and
will encourage international bullies to pursue further acts of aggression.
Everyone is legitimately concerned about terrorism; however, the path to genuine security involves promoting democracy, social justice and respect for the
right of self-determination along with disarmament, weapons-free-zones and
inspections. Of all the countries in the world, the United States possesses by
far the most powerful arsenal of weapons of mass destruction. If the U.S. were
to initiate a democratic foreign policy and take serious steps toward disarmament, it would be able to encourage global disarmament as well as regional
demilitarization in the Middle East.

The Bush administration has used the alleged Iraqi military danger to justify
an alarming new doctrine of preemptive war. In the National Security Strategy, publicly released on September 20, 2002, the Bush administration asserted that the U.S. has the right to attack any country that might be a *potential*
threat, not merely in response to an act of military aggression. Much of the
world sees this doctrine for what it is: the proclamation of an undisguised U.S.
global imperium.

Ordinary Iraqis, and people everywhere, need to know that there is *another*
America, made up of those who both recognize the urgent need for democratic
change in the Middle East and reject our government's militaristic and imperial foreign policy. By signing this statement we declare our intention to
work for a new democratic U.S. foreign policy. That means helping to rein in
the war-makers and building the most powerful antiwar movement possible,
and at the same time forging links of solidarity and concrete support for democratic forces in Iraq and throughout the Middle East.

We refuse to accept the inevitability of war on Iraq despite the enormous
military juggernaut that has been put in place, and we declare our commitment to work with others in this country and abroad to avert it. And if war
should start, we will do all in our power to end it immediately.

Permissions

ton Women's Health Book Collective. Copyright © 1984 by Our Bodies Ourselves. Reprinted with permission of Our Bodies Ourselves.

Excerpt from "The Enemy Within" by Susan Brownmiller. Copyright © 1970 Susan Brownmiller. Reprinted by permission of the author.

Excerpt from "None Dare Call It Treason" by Vincent Bugliosi, from *The Nation*, February 5, 2001. Copyright © 2001 Vincent Bugliosi. Reprinted by permission of the author.

Excerpt from *Environmental Racism and the Environmental Justice Movement* by Robert Bullard. Copyright © 1993 by Robert Bullard. Reprinted by permission of the author.

Excerpt from "In White America" by Gregory Calvert. Copyright © 1967 by Gregory Calvert. Reprinted by permission of the author.

"We Oppose Both Saddam Hussein and the U.S. War on Iraq: A Call for a New Democratic U.S. Foreign Policy" by The Campaign for Peace and Democracy, Copyright © 2003 by The Campaign for Peace and Democracy. Reprinted with permission of The Campaign for Peace and Democracy.

Excerpt from "An Obligation to Endure" from *Silent Spring* by Rachel Carson. Copyright © 1962 by Rachel L. Carson, renewed 1990 by Roger Christie. Reprinted by permission of Houghton Mifflin Company. All rights reserved.

"Letter from Delano" by César Chávez, from the April 23, 1969 issue of *The Christian Century*. Reprinted by permission of The César Chávez Foundation.

Excerpt from *5 Days That Shook the World* by Alexander Cockburn and Jeffrey St. Clair. Copyright © 2000 by Verso. Reprinted by permission of Verso.

Excerpt from *The Closing Circle* by Barry Commoner, copyright © 1971 by Barry Commoner. Used by permission of Alfred A. Knopf, a division of Random House, Inc.

Excerpt from "Political Prisoners, Prisons, and Black Liberation" by Angela Y. Davis from Angela Y. Davis, ed., *If They Come in the Morning: Voices of Resistance* (New York: Third Press, 1971). Copyright © 1971 by Angela Y. Davis. Reprinted by permission of the author.

Excerpt from *Pornography: Men Possessing Women* by Andrea Dworkin. Copyright © 1981 by Andrea Dworkin. Reprinted by permission of The Elaine Markson Literary Agency, Inc.

Excerpt from "The Student as Nigger" by Jerry Farber. Copyright © 1967 by Jerry Farber. Reprinted by permission of the author.

Excerpt from "Strategic Monkeywrenching" by Dave Foreman. Copyright © 1985 by EarthFirst! Reprinted by permission of EarthFirst!

Excerpt from "Why Johnny Can't Dissent" by Thomas Frank. Copyright © 1995 by Thomas Frank. Reprinted with permission of the author.